August 9-13, 2015
Omaha, Nebraska, USA

I0028730

Association for Computing Machinery

Advancing Computing as a Science & Profession

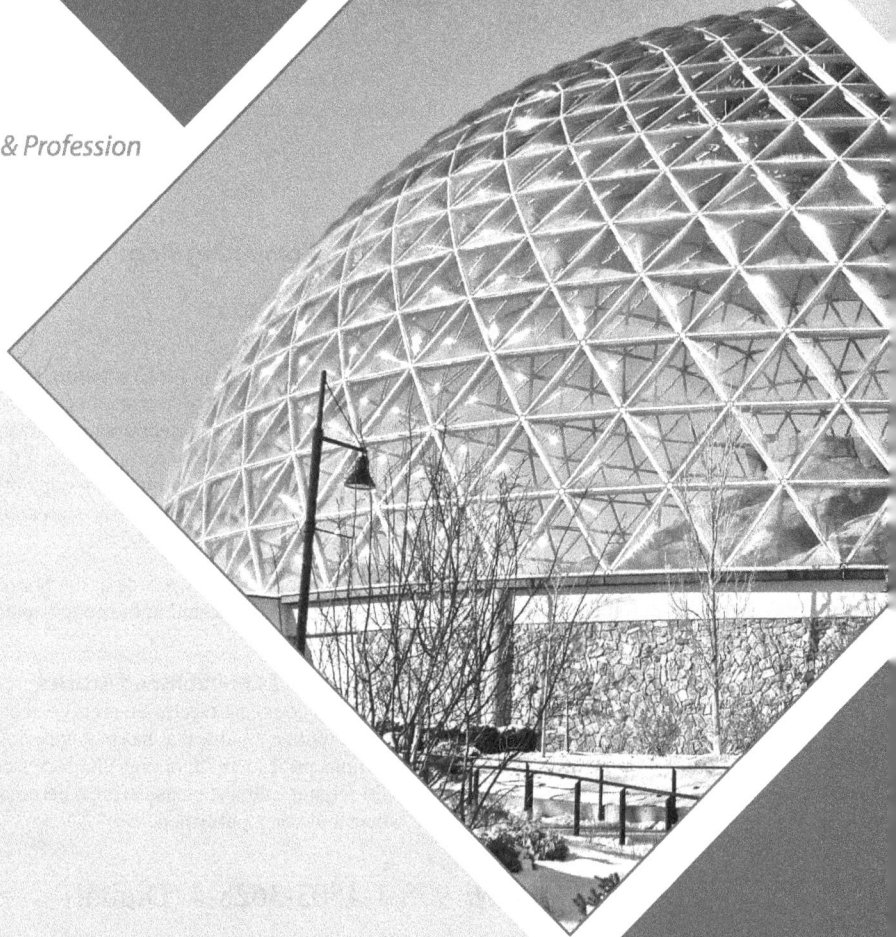

ICER'15

Proceedings of the 2015 ACM Conference on
International Computing Education Research

Sponsored by:
ACM SIGCSE

Supported by:
**University of Nebraska at Omaha,
Omaha Convention and Vistors Bureau, & Interpublic Group**

Association for Computing Machinery

Advancing Computing as a Science & Profession

The Association for Computing Machinery
2 Penn Plaza, Suite 701
New York, New York 10121-0701

Notice to Past Authors of ACM-Published Articles
ACM intends to create a complete electronic archive of all articles and/or other material previously published by ACM. If you have written a work that has been previously published by ACM in any journal or conference proceedings prior to 1978, or any SIG Newsletter at any time, and you do NOT want this work to appear in the ACM Digital Library, please inform permissions@acm.org, stating the title of the work, the author(s), and where and when published.

ISBN: 978-1-4503-3628-4 (Digital)

ISBN: 978-1-4503-3887-5 (Print)

Additional copies may be ordered prepaid from:

ACM Order Department
PO Box 30777
New York, NY 10087-0777, USA

Phone: 1-800-342-6626 (USA and Canada)
+1-212-626-0500 (Global)
Fax: +1-212-944-1318
E-mail: acmhelp@acm.org
Hours of Operation: 8:30 am – 4:30 pm ET

Printed in the USA

ICER 2015 Chairs' Welcome

We are delighted to welcome you to the eleventh annual International Computing Education Research Conference, ICER'15, sponsored by the ACM Special Interest Group on Computer Science Education (SIGCSE). Omaha, Nebraska, USA, is the host city for this year's conference, with sessions taking place on the campus of the University of Nebraska at Omaha.

Now entering its second decade, ICER proudly continues its tradition as the premier ACM forum for dissemination and lively discussion of the latest findings in computing education research. ICER papers represent significant, rigorous contributions to the field, and the conference provides avenues for discussion of preliminary work by continuing the lightning talks track and adding a new poster track for 2015. The conference also serves a vital mentoring and advising role for upcoming CS discipline-based education researchers through the doctoral consortium. For the second year, the work in progress workshop (formerly called the critical research review) provides an opportunity for other researchers to receive extensive feedback on draft manuscripts or proposals related to a new computing education research project.

ICER'15 has seen dramatic growth across all categories, and we saw 40% more paper submissions than in 2014. The call for papers attracted 96 full research papers. These papers were double-blind peer-reviewed by members of our international program committee, with the three conference co-chairs and two associate chairs serving as meta-reviewers. Ultimately, 25 papers (26%) were accepted for publication and presentation. We also had a record 27 students apply for the doctoral consortium, and 20 were selected for participation this year. Papers and student abstracts are included in these proceedings. In addition, the conference program includes 10 lightning talks and 23 poster presentations. A further 10 researchers will take part in the work in progress workshop. Authors and presenters represent 9 countries: Australia, Canada, Chile, China, Finland, Germany, Jamaica, the United Kingdom, and the United States.

This year's program highlights a wide range of research topics, including block-based programming languages, cognitive and social aspects of learning computing, computing education policy matters, e-books, and novice compilation behaviors—just to name a few. We are thrilled to welcome Dr. Jim Spohrer from IBM for the ICER'15 keynote address. Spohrer's early work on novice programmers is widely recognized as foundational for much of today's computer science education research. His keynote, *Empowering Makers in the Cognitive Era*, will examine how past and present research findings can be leveraged to foster a true generation of independent, creative, and responsible technology creators.

ICER's exciting program is the result of the program committee and conference organizing team's combined effort. We thank all of our volunteers for their hard work in making this year a success, and we are especially grateful for the help of our two associate chairs, Lauri Malmi and Tony Clear. As always, Simon's technical and organizational prowess kept the submission system running smoothly, even during power outages. Lastly, we thank our supporters for their generous contributions, which help ensure ICER 2015 will be both successful and memorable for all.

Brian Dorn	**Quintin Cutts**	**Judy Sheard**
ICER 2015 Chair	*ICER 2015 Co-Chair*	*ICER 2015 Co-Chair*
University of Nebraska at Omaha	*University of Glasgow*	*Monash University*
Omaha, NE, USA	*Glasgow, Scotland*	*Caulfield East, VIC, Australia*

Table of Contents

Keynote Address
Session Chair: Brian Dorn *(University of Nebraska at Omaha)*

Papers: Cognition and Procrastination
Session Chair: Quintin Cutts *(University of Glasgow)*

Papers: Social and Cultural Dynamics
Session Chair: Sally Fincher *(University of Kent)*

Papers: Understanding and Informing Policy
Session Chair: William Doane *(STPI)*

Papers: Blocks vs. Text
Session Chair: Philip East *(University of Northern Iowa)*

Papers: Compilation Behavior Metrics

Session Chair: Leigh Ann Delyser *(NYC Foundation for CS Education)*

Papers: Identity and Affect

Session Chair: Sarah Heckman *(North Carolina State University)*

Papers: E-Books

Session Chair: Leen-Kiat Soh *(University of Nebraska-Lincoln)*

Papers: Designing and Evaluating Curricula

Session Chair: Elizabeth Patitsas *(University of Toronto)*

Papers: Alternative Approaches

Session Chair: Judy Sheard *(Monash University)*

Doctoral Consortium

Session Chair: Mark Guzdial *(Georgia Institute of Technology)*

ICER 2015 Conference Organization

General and Program Chairs: Brian Dorn *(University of Nebraska at Omaha, USA)*
Judy Sheard *(Monash University, Australia)*
Quintin Cutts *(University of Glasgow, UK)*

Associate Program Chairs: Tony Clear *(Auckland University of Technology, New Zealand)*
Lauri Malmi *(Aalto University, Helsinki, Finland)*

Lightning Talk and Poster Chair: Leo Porter *(University of California San Diego, USA)*

Work in Progress Workshop Chair: Colleen Lewis *(Harvey Mudd College, USA)*

Doctoral Consortium Chairs: Mark Guzdial *(Georgia Institute of Technology, USA)*
Anthony Robins *(University of Otago, New Zealand)*

Local Arrangements Committee: Harvey Siy *(University of Nebraska at Omaha, USA)*
LeenKiat Soh *(University of Nebraska at Lincoln, USA)*

Submissions Chair: Simon *(University of Newcastle, Australia)*

Website and Social Media Chairs: Jan Erik Moström *(Umeå University, Sweden)*
Briana Morrison *(Georgia Institute of Technology, USA)*

Program Committee: Christine Alvarado *(University of California San Diego, USA)*
Michal Armoni *(Weizmann Institute of Science, Rehovot, Israel)*
Owen Astrachan *(Duke University, USA)*
Cynthia Bailey Lee *(Stanford University, USA)*
Andrew Begel *(Microsoft Research, USA)*
Moti Ben-Ari *(Weizmann Institute of Science, Israel)*
Yifat Ben-David Kolikant *(The Hebrew University of Jerusalem, Israel)*
Matthew Berland *(University of Wisconsin Madison, USA)*
Jonas Boustedt *(Hogskolan i Gavle, Sweden)*
Kristy Boyer *(North Carolina State University, USA)*
Niel Brown *(University of Kent, UK)*
Kevin Buffardi *(California State University Chico, USA)*
Tzu-Yi Chen *(Pomona College, USA)*
Donald Chinn *(University of Washington Tacoma, USA)*
Michael Clancy *(University of California Berkeley, USA)*
Steve Cooper *(Stanford University, USA)*
Betsy DiSalvo *(Georgia Institute of Technology, USA)*
Anna Eckerdal *(Uppsala University, Sweden)*
Stephen Edwards *(Virginia Tech, USA)*
Allison Elliott Tew *(AET Consulting, USA)*
Katrina Falkner *(University of Adelaide, Australia)*

ICER 2015 Sponsor & Supporters

Sponsor:

Supporters:

UNIVERSITY OF NEBRASKA AT OMAHA
COLLEGE OF INFORMATION SCIENCE
& TECHNOLOGY

CONVENTION AND VISITORS BUREAU

VISITOMAHA.COM

Interpublic Group

Empowering Makers in the Cognitive Era

Jim Spohrer
IBM
San Jose, CA, USA
sphorer@us.ibm.com

Abstract

After briefly surveying the history of knowledge, computing, programming, and software engineering, computing education will be reframed as empowering makers in the cognitive era. The makers' movement is about the democratization of the tools of self-expression and production. From global cloud-based deployment of apps on smart phones to nano-manipulation of advanced materials in custom jewelry and clothing with open designs downloadable for 3D printers, software empowers makers to co-create value in smart service systems. Smart service systems are based on provider platforms that enable customer to interact and co-create value together. In addition, cognitive assistants for all business occupations and societal roles are beginning to appear democratizing access to knowledge and expertise in smart service systems.

Teaching about the elegance, not just correctness, of solutions and how they serve customers wants, needs, and aspiration will be of increasing importance. The implications for a next generation of students who "make a job, not just take a job" even before graduation will be explored. Also, issues of sustainability and resilience of smart service systems with empowered makers in the cognitive era will be explored. Rethinking the rights and responsibilities of empowered makers at all ages will require an especially close examination of the way teamwork is encouraged and rewarded in families, neighborhoods, and educational institutions.

Categories and Subject Descriptors

K.3.0 [Computers and Education]: General

Keywords

Makers; Cognitive Systems; T-shaped Adaptive Innovators; Smart Service Systems

BIO

Jim Spohrer is Director IBM Global University Programs (GUP) and leads IBM's Cognitive Systems Institute. Group (CSIG) The Cognitive Systems Institute Group works to align cognitive systems researchers in academics, government, and industry globally to boost the creativity and productivity of people in smart service systems. IBM University Programs works to align IBM and universities globally to empower makers (T-shaped adaptive innovators). Jim co-founded IBM's first Service Research group, ISSIP Service Science community, and was founding CTO of IBM's Venture Capital Relations Group in Silicon Valley. He was awarded Apple Computers' Distinguished Engineer Scientist and Technology title for his work on next generation learning platforms.

Jim has a Yale PhD in Computer Science/Artificial Intelligence and MIT BS in Physics. His research priorities include service science, cognitive systems for smart holistic service systems, especially universities and cities. With over ninety publications and nine patents, he is also a PICMET Fellow and a winner of the S-D Logic award.

ICER '15, August 9-13, 2015, Omaha, Nebraska, USA.
ACM 978-1-4503-3630-7/15/08.
http://dx.doi.org/10.1145/2787622.2787623

The Effects of Procrastination Interventions on Programming Project Success

Joshua Martin, Stephen H. Edwards, and Clifford A. Shaffer
Virginia Tech
2202 Kraft Drive
Blacksburg, VA 24060
+1 540-231-5723
jdm522@vt.edu, edwards@cs.vt.edu, shaffer@vt.edu

ABSTRACT

In computer science, procrastination and related problems with managing programming projects are viewed as primary causes of student attrition. Unfortunately, the most successful techniques for reducing procrastination (such as courses in study skills) are resource-intensive and do not scale to large classrooms. In this paper, we describe three course interventions that are designed to be scalable for large classrooms and require few resources to implement. *Reflective writing assignments* require students to consciously consider how their time management choices impact their classroom performance. *Schedule sheets* force students to actively plan out the time required to solve a programming project. *Email alerts* inform students of their progress relative to their peers as they work on an assignment, and suggest ways to improve behavior if their progress is found to be unsatisfactory. We implemented these interventions in a junior-level data structures course and analyzed data from 330 students over two semesters. Separate analyses of reflective writing responses, schedule sheet contents, and e-mail alert contents are discussed, along with student opinions about the value and effectiveness of each treatment. We found a statistically significant relationship between the time when work is completed and its quality, with late work being of lower quality. We found that one of the three interventions had a statistically significant effect on reducing late work: e-mail alerts sent to students to make them more aware of how they were doing with respect to expectations were associated with both a reduction in assignments completed late, and an increase in assignments completed at least one day early. This result was found despite the fact that students reported subjectively that e-mail alerts were of marginal utility.

General Terms

Education

Keywords

programming, procrastination, self-regulation, self-efficacy, scheduling, schedule sheets, e-mail alerts, reflective writing

1. INTRODUCTION

It is a common problem in programming-intensive courses that students fail to complete their programming projects in a timely manner. A common hypothesis among CS educators is that such students may have the necessary skills, but lack the time management skills or the commitment needed to complete individual project assignments. Procrastination and poor choices are often used as excuses. 70-95% of undergraduates procrastinate on coursework to some degree, while 20-30% exhibit chronic or severe procrastination [10]. By procrastination, we mean "to voluntarily delay an intended course of action despite expecting to be worse off for the delay" [10]. "Negative procrastinators" are those who procrastinate to the extent that they actually do experience negative consequences from their delays.

In STEM disciplines that involve project-based learning activities, students may be at greater risk when they procrastinate. When a student has two or more weeks to complete a project or paper—one that presumably will take more than a single afternoon to finish—it is certainly easier to procrastinate, because the deadline is farther in the future. However, it is also more dangerous, since putting off the work both reduces the available time, should the project take more effort than the student expects, and also reduces the opportunities available to seek assistance or ask questions, should unexpected difficulties arise. In our own courses, we see that typically a quarter to a third of students are unable to satisfactorily complete any given multi-week programming project.

In a previous study of 1,101 CS students over a period of five years [4], we looked at students who sometimes performed well on work and sometimes performed poorly, and used a within-subjects comparison to look at the differences in when they started their work. We found a statistically significant correlation between when students start working on a project and the quality of their work: when a student starts earlier, he or she is significantly more likely to earn an A or B on work than if the work is started later.

Many techniques have been proposed to combat procrastination. The most successful techniques seem to be supplementary courses or workshops on time management strategies [12]. While this has been shown to be effective, they are costly in terms of time and manpower. An ideal mechanism to reduce procrastination must be feasible at a larger scale and applicable to courses with hundreds of students.

In this paper, we examine three classroom interventions to reduce procrastination. These interventions are designed to require little additional manpower or class time, and so can be used in large courses. These interventions included active reflection writing tasks, schedule sheets, and situational awareness alerts that describe student performance relative to expectations. We examined how these treatments affected the times at which students started submitting work to an automated grading system, as well as when students finished their assignments. While two of the interventions did not provide evidence of significant impact, the e-mail alert intervention did show a significant increase in the number of assignments submitted early and a significant decrease in the number of assignments submitted late, in comparison to the control condition. Further, by examining relationships between on-time vs. late work and quality of student work, this study re-confirms that late assignments score lower and typically contain more bugs, as measured by instructor reference tests. In addition, work completed early, ahead of the deadline, scores significantly higher.

This work extends a preliminary examination of this same experiment presented at ITiCSE 2015 [3], where only the main treatment effect was examined. The contributions of this paper include a more thorough examination of the impact of the treatments after filtering out students who dropped or failed to complete the course, along with an examination of the times when students start submitting work for assessment, rather than only their finish times. Also, separate analyses of the data collected on each individual treatment are provided, along with the results of student opinion surveys indicating student perceptions of the value, effectiveness, and time required for each of the interventions. While the Tuckman procrastination scale [11] was used to measure procrastination tendency among subjects in this study, no significant relationship between procrastination scale scores and assignment submission times was found. Finally, this paper compares the quality of student work with its time of completion to assess whether late work was of measurably lower quality in this study.

2. BACKGROUND

While procrastination is a pervasive problem throughout education, there is still a lack of understanding about the phenomenon. Perhaps the best summary of procrastination research so far comes from Steel, who published a meta-analysis of procrastination research in 2007 [10]. Steel defined procrastination as a "prevalent and pernicious form of self-regulatory failure." Some research indicates that procrastination may be an individual personality trait, and several instruments have been developed to measure this tendency [10, 6, 11]. We used Tuckman's procrastination scale instrument [11] to measure the procrastination tendency of students in our study, described in Section 5.

Several potential causes of procrastination have been proposed. However, procrastination is primarily a failure of self-regulation. In a study of 456 undergraduates, Klassen et al. [5] found that a person's view of their own ability to self-regulate was a strong predictor of procrastination. Tuckman theorized that an inability to overcome procrastination tendencies might be related to the gradual transfer of responsibility from teachers and parents to individual students that occurs throughout the school years. Because this transfer of responsibility reaches its peak during the college years, he theorized that researchers should examine techniques that can assist students in the regulation of their own learning [11]. Such techniques should include providing information to students so that they are aware of the appropriate progress needed to successfully complete a task.

Steel [10] has proposed temporal motivation theory (TMT) for modeling procrastination. TMT incorporates four factors to account for the desirability of a task: expectancy of success (E), value of the task to the individual (V), the delay before one is rewarded for the task (D), and the individual's sensitivity towards that delay (Γ). Utility is defined as $(E \times V)/(\Gamma \times D)$. This theory influences the interventions we designed.

3. INTERVENTIONS

The focus of our study is three interventions that we made, with the goal of reducing procrastination or otherwise improving the performance of students on projects in a junior-level Data Structures and Algorithms course. This course is taken typically one year after a traditional CS2 course, and is typically about the fourth programming course that a student encounters. Each of the interventions studied is relatively easy to administer (assuming availability of the infrastructure that we built to support some of these), and can scale to large courses. In total, there were four course sections involved, over two years. One section was the control (no explicit interventions targeted toward procrastination were administered, and this course was taught in a manner similar to prior years), and each of the interventions was administered to one section of the course. We first describe the three interventions, and then we discuss our experiences and analyze the results. See [3] for details on the specific instruments used in each intervention.

The key activity studied was the semester programming projects. Students in all sections had a similar experience in that they were required to implement four projects during the semester. Each project had a life cycle of approximately one month, from the time when the initial specification for the project was made available (and discussion of the project was initiated in class) until the assignment due date. In total, the projects accounted for 45% of the semester grade. However, the projects are even more important than this figure would indicate, as scores on projects explain about 95% of the variance on total semester score. Thus, good performance on the projects is crucial to a successful grade. The projects are generally considered by the students to be quite challenging, involving interactions between typically two to four major classes (in the object-oriented sense), requirements for student-generated unit tests, meaningful design choices by the students (that affect project scoring), and complex programming skills such as advanced recursion and dynamic memory allocation. Success on the projects requires project management skills such as time management along with skills in software design, testing, and debugging. A typical project might require 30–80 hours, resulting in approximately 500-2,000 lines of code, including software tests but excluding comments.

3.1 Active Reflection

The first intervention we examined is *reflective writing assignments*. These assignments were inspired by active learning techniques, specifically the technique called the "minute paper" [9][2]. The goal of these writing assignments was to engage students in reflection about their own time management behavior and how it affects their individual performance on the programming projects. The initial concept of writing a single response was expanded to four responses after consulting with the course instructors. In our study, these responses were completed using an on-line form near the beginning of each project, asking the student to reflect on the impact of their time management choices on their previous project experience. The activity was designed so that students could complete it in under 15–20 minutes. Students in the targeted section were required to do the reflections, with each one being worth approximately 1% of the semester grade.

3.2 Schedule Sheets

The second intervention examined is the use of *schedule sheets*. In prior years, instructors for thise course have used "painless" schedule sheets [8]. Student survey data indicate a mixed response to the schedule sheets, with some students finding them useful while others find them unhelpful. The goal behind the schedules is to encourage students to break a large project assignment into smaller, more manageable pieces. The sheets are also designed to have students consider their progress on an assignment periodically. This intervention aims to reduce procrastination by helping students form, express, manage, and track smaller-scale deadlines.

To effectively manage the schedule sheets for students, we designed and implemented an electronic system to handle the submission and grading of these sheets. Students entered or changed their work breakdown structure as a series of tasks. Often these tasks consisted of specific classes, program behavior, or modules a particular assignment required. Each task had subfields for the estimated design time, coding time, and testing time, as well as a personal target deadline for when the student anticipated completing the entire task.

Students were required to fill out or edit a schedule sheet three times during a project. Collectively, the three schedule sheets for a given project constituted about 1% of the semester grade (for a total of 4% for schedule sheets over the four projects). For each project, the first sheet was an initial schedule that was due within a week of receiving the assignment. The second sheet was an intermediate schedule due one week before the assignment was due, allowing students to update their progress and modify their own task deadlines as necessary. A final schedule was due after the project was completed, with students reporting the actual amount of time spent on each project task.

To ensure student schedules were reasonable, the system provided automatic feedback as schedule information was entered by the students. A "check my work" button allowed students to get immediate feedback at any point while editing their schedule. The work check mechanism included multiple diagnostics used to verify that a schedule was appropriate for the particular project based on the number of anticipated components, the time estimates made by the student, and the personal task deadlines set by the student. Additionally, the system allowed an instructor to manually review the submitted schedules for any additional discrepancies, to provide their own feedback comments, or to adjust scores where necessary.

3.3 E-mail Alerts

The third intervention examined is the use of automated e-mail *situational awareness alerts*. We developed a mechanism to send periodic e-mail alerts to students throughout the time allotted to work on a project. These alerts were designed to raise awareness of a student's level of effort compared to his or her peers, and compared to expectations.

Instructors will often inform students that working early and often on a particular assignment will yield a higher score, but this information often may be ignored. This intervention is designed to take a different approach by providing individualized information that is more relevant to a student. In particular, the system is integrated into Web-CAT, an automated grading tool used at our institution. Because students were required to submit their work to Web-CAT for evaluation, we could provide feedback on a student as they worked towards a project solution, and include data extracted from their current work to produce more informative messages.

The e-mails sent by this intervention began roughly one week before the project was due. Second and third e-mails were sent at 4 days and 2 days before the assignment due date, respectively. The content of each alert was customized to reflect the work submitted so far to Web-CAT. The student's work was classified along 4 dimensions: the amount of code written (relative to an approximate target size for the given assignment), the proportion of instructor written reference tests passed (an approximation of functional correctness), the degree of testing performed (if the assignment requires students to write their own software tests), and the number of static analysis checks failed (measuring adherence to coding style guidelines, if required by the assignment). Based on the scores for each of the dimensions, each student's work would be given an internal grade: Good (indicating advanced progress compared to the ideal rate of progression), Neutral (indicating average progress compared to the ideal rate), Bad (indicating poor progress compared to the ideal rate), and Undefined (indicating no work has yet been submitted).

Based on these internal ratings, a customized e-mail was constructed and sent to students. The subject line of the e-mail was phrased as "CS 3114: Your progress on Project 2". However, if the student's work indicated insufficient progress in one or more dimensions, the subject line would instead be "CS 3114: You may be at risk on Project 2", or even "CS 3114: You are at risk on Project 2". The body of the e-mail message contained a separate paragraph corresponding to each of the 4 dimensions on which the student's work was rated. Messages were phrased in an attempt to recognize progress and reinforce good practices without being judgmental or negative.

4. EXPERIENCES WITH THE INTERVENTIONS

The three interventions were employed in four sections of CS 3114: Data Structures and Algorithms, a junior-level data structures course at our university. Two of the sections were taught in Fall 2013, with the other two in Fall 2014, all by the same instructor (an author on this paper and Co-PI on the project). Three of the sections each received one of the three interventions, and one section acted as a control. The course involved four separate programming assignments, with students being given approximately one month for each assignment. Each section received the same intervention across all four assignments.

The following subsections describe our experiences employing these interventions. In addition, we gave an opinion survey at the end of each semester asking students for their reactions to the intervention they experienced, in terms of how useful they felt it was, whether they felt it took too much time, and whether they believe it affected the way they managed their time on projects. The assignment consisted of writing one-paragraph responses to four prompts: describing the key elements of the plan they used to manage their time on their most recent project, describing how that affected the quality of their work, describing the plan they intend to use on the new project, and describing their development strategy and how it impacted their results.

4.1 Active Reflection

4.1.1 Response Themes

Many students emphasized starting early as a way to avoid stress and turn in quality work. In fact, on the first reflective writing assignment, 85% of respondents indicated they would use a strategy of submitting earlier than previously. However, analyzing the responses from the next sheet, we found the number of students who reported starting earlier on the project reduced to 68%. This trend did not improve with Project 3, were students who reported working early dropped to around 46%. This indicates students underestimated their own ability to start a project early (as self defined), and while the reflective writing assignments forced students to consider their time management choices, it did little to improve their self-reported performance.

Besides starting early, many students emphasized a lack of team work as a key element to finishing on-time. One student wrote: "After deciding to work with a friend, we broke up sections of the project to focus on. By partially splitting up the project, we were able to maximize our development over time." Another student lamented a lack of planning, writing "I began working on my last project way too late. The key elements was that my partner and I waited for a mutually agreeable time to work on the project. We waited too long for a perfect time and ended up starting very late."

Reasons for starting late varied. Some students complained about a lack of knowledge, while others blamed the amount of additional coursework they had. A few students had difficulties working with teammates, which led to a later start than they assumed was ideal.

Overall, the responses reveal that most students know the correct way to avoid procrastination, but fail to follow through—reconfirming a failure of self-regulation. A variety of reasons could be to blame for this, including some that are not the fault of the student. The reflective writing assignments made students consider how to schedule their time, but did not seem to change their actual behavior.

4.1.2 Survey Results

At the end of the semester, students were given a brief on-line opinion survey on their experiences with the intervention consisting of nine Likert-style questions that were answered on a five-point scale. Questions covered whether the intervention helped the student manage projects better, made them think critically about time management, made

them more aware of how much they procrastinate, or caused them to change the way they managed their time. Questions also covered whether students felt the intervention was a waste of time, or took too much time to complete.

Overall, student responses to the reflective writing treatment were more positive than for the other interventions. 50% of respondents indicated that the intervention helped them manage their projects better, giving a response of 4 or 5. Only 23% agreed that the reflective writing assignments were a waste of time, although 64% agreed that they took too much time to complete (the highest of any intervention). Finally, when students were asked if the intervention caused them to start at least one assignment sooner, 68% of students either agreed or strongly agreed, the highest of any intervention. This seems to indicate that students valued the experience of reflective writing.

4.2 Schedule Sheet Data

4.2.1 Schedule Data

While individual projects differed in complexity, the average across all students for the student-reported estimates of total project time on the first schedule sheet ranged from 33–54 hours (33 hours for Project 1, s.d. 15.0, 53.6 hours for Project 2, s.d. 17.7, 41 hours for Project 3, s.d. 16.6, and 39.5 hours for Project 4, s.d. 10.8). These initial estimates were usually underestimates, however, with the final reported time spent by students averaging 43–79 hours (66.4 hours for Project 1, s.d. 34.9, 79 hours for Project 2, s.d. 33.0, 43.9 hours for Project 3, s.d. 15.5, and 47.7 hours for Project 4, s.d. 21.3). Individual students underestimated the effort required 72% of the time. Figure 1 summarizes the distribution of initial time estimates made by students, their revised estimates on their intermediate schedule sheets, and the final self-reported time spent (all values are student-reported on their own schedule sheets).

On the intermediate time sheets due one week before the project was due, students reported having spent an average of about one third of the total time they would report by the end of the project. One would expect that estimates of time remaining at this point would be more accurate than

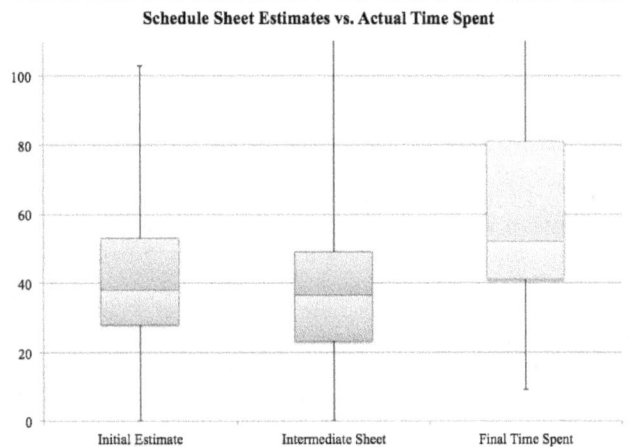

Figure 1: Schedule sheet estimates on the initial schedule and intermediate schedule, compared to total time reported across all sheets.

the initial estimates. However, the opposite appeared to be the case, with most students underestimating the time remaining–in fact, on average, students estimated it would take less total time by the intermediate time sheet than their original (under-)estimate before work began. Figure 1 shows the distribution of estimates across all three sheets, illustrating this underestimation trend.

We examined the accuracy of the final schedule sheet and its potential impact on the time students submitted their final work to Web-CAT using a two-way analysis of variance. We found a significant relationship between these factors ($F = 17.79$, $p < 0.001$). Students who underestimated the amount of work required for a project submitted their final solutions later, while students who overestimated the amount of work required submitted their final solutions earlier.

We hoped that schedule accuracy would improve as the semester went on, indicating that students were improving their own time management skills. We did find that the assignment itself had a significant relationship with schedule accuracy ($F = 10.41$, $p < 0.001$), where students had the largest average underestimates for Project 1, followed by Project 2, with the smallest underestimates for the two later projects. Because the assignments differed in level of effort and complexity, one would expect differences in the ability of students to estimate the level of effort required, however.

4.2.2 Survey Results

From the survey of student opinions, student responses to the schedule sheet intervention were less positive. Only 21% of respondents agreed or strongly agreed that schedule sheets helped them manage their projects better, with 56% disagreeing or strongly disagreeing. Additionally, 62% of respondents agreed or strongly agreed that the intervention was a waste of time (the highest of any intervention), although only 29% agreed that they took too much time to complete. Finally, only 44% of respondents agreed or strongly agreed that schedule sheets caused them to start their next assignment earlier.

4.3 E-mail Alert Data

4.3.1 Email Analysis

For the students who received e-mail alerts, students usually received three alerts, seven days before the assignment was due, then again four days before the due date, and finally one last alert two days before the due date. For two of the assignments, we added a fourth alert ten days ahead of the due date as well.

For each e-mail alert, the student's work so far, as characterized by their most recent submission to Web-CAT, was analyzed, and rated on four different aspects. If students had not made any submission to Web-CAT yet at the time of the alert, they received a message specifically addressing that fact, and including encouraging language about the benefit of starting early.

When alerts were sent ten days ahead of the due date, only 2–7% of students had made a submission to the electronic grading system. Thus, the bulk of the students received a "form letter" alert because there was no data available to use for a more personalized message. For alerts one week ahead of the due date, 6–18% of students had made a submission. Four days ahead, 17–33% of students had made at least one

submission, and two days ahead, the number had grown to 43–54%.

Because of the low percentages of students who had submitted work, in almost all cases, the majority–sometimes the vast majority–of students simply received an alert indicating they had not yet submitted any work, and reminding them that starting earlier is associated with better success on project assignments.

We examined more closely the alert status of students 4 days ahead of the due date, roughly in the middle of the series of alerts. A two-way analysis of variance indicated a significant difference ($F = 12.9$, $p < 0.001$) between the project grades earned by students who had made at least one submission to Web-CAT at that point (mean of 80.7%, s.d. 24.6%, not including any extra credit incentives for early completion) and those who had not yet made any submission (mean of 69.2%, s.d. 29.3%).

4.3.2 Survey Results

In the survey of student opinions, student responses to the e-mail alert intervention were somewhat negative. Only 14% of respondents agreed that the e-mail alerts helped them manage their own projects better, with no students at all strongly agreeing. Additionally, 55% of respondents agreed or strongly agreed the e-mail alerts were a waste of time, and 37% agreed or strongly agreed they took too much time. Finally, only 24% of respondents agreed or strongly agreed that the e-mail alerts caused them to start their next assignment earlier, the lowest of any of the interventions.

5. EVALUATION

The primary purpose of this study was to determine if any of the interventions positively affected the timeliness of student work. In particular, we hypothesized that treatment groups would be less likely to turn work in late, and correspondingly more likely to turn work in on time, or even early. Because prior research indicates that work completed late often earns lower scores in multiple dimensions [4], secondarily we also wanted to confirm this link was also present for this study.

Our study involved a total of 330 students in four sections over a two-semester period who agreed to allow access to their assignment data, all enrolled in our university's junior-level data structures course. Of these students, 82 (24.8%) either dropped the course, withdrew from the course, or did not complete all programming assignments. We excluded these students from our analysis, so the data reported in this section are based on students who completed all programming assignments and received a grade for the course. Among the remaining students, the size of each treatment group were similar (control N = 60, reflective writing N = 64, schedule sheets N = 59, and e-mail alerts N = 65).

All four groups completed four programming projects of varying difficulty, with Projects 1 and 3 being somewhat easier or smaller, and Projects 2 and 4 being more involved. All projects focused on implementing complete programs built on data structures implemented as part of that assignment. Sections offered at the same time—the control and reflective writing sections in Fall 2013, and the e-mail alert and schedule sheet sections in Fall 2014—used identical assignments. However, between the two semesters the assignments were changed, although both semesters used assignments that were intended to be comparable in terms of level of effort. The same instructor taught all four sections.

In all programming projects for all sections, students were offered a 10% extra credit bonus for completing their assignment at least one day ahead of the due date. Students did not receive any grade penalty for turning in work late, however. Instead, a "time bank" of individual 1-day extensions was permitted, similar to the model described in [1]. Each student had a small, fixed number of these no-penalty grace days they could use, but late submissions were no longer accepted once a student had expended all of their late days. Students in Fall 2013 were allotted five late days, but this number was reduced to three in Fall 2014.

5.1 Procrastination Tendency

We used Tuckman's procrastination scale [11] to measure the individual procrastination tendency for students in all groups at the start of the course. This instrument has been independently validated as a procrastination measure. The instrument consists of 16 questions answered on a 4-point Likert scale regarding one's perceptions about putting off required tasks versus starting them when necessary. Aggregating answers across all questions produces scores ranging from 16-64, with higher scores indicating a greater tendency to procrastinate. After giving the instrument questions to students using an electronic survey, aggregate scores were compiled and then normalized to a 0–1 scale.

We compared scores across groups to determine whether course sections were of similar procrastination tendencies. A one-way analysis of variance did not indicate any significant differences between the groups (F = 1.6, p = 0.20), with average scores of 60% for the control group, 58% for the reflective writing group, 64% for the schedule sheet group, and 59% for the e-mail alert group. Also, we did not find any significant relationship between scores on the procrastination scale and the times when students finished work (F = 0.77, p = 0.38).

5.2 Treatment Impact on Submission Time

Because we wished to determine if any of the interventions positively affected the timeliness of student work, we classified each final submission for each assignment as being either early (finished at least one day before the deadline to earn extra credit), on time (finished on the due date), or late (finished after the due date). Figure 2 shows the relative proportion of student work falling into each category for each treatment group.

Of the groups, the e-mail treatment group had the lowest number of late submissions and also the highest number of early submissions, making that group's on-time performance significantly different than the control group ($\chi^2 = 10.05$, p = 0.0015). The other two treatments did not differ from the control group in a statistically significant way (reflective writing: $\chi^2 = 0.03$, p = 0.87; schedule sheets: $\chi^2 = 0.52$, p = 0.47).

In addition, we also looked at the finish times as a continuous variable, in terms of the difference between the deadline and the time when students completed their projects. The results of a two-way analysis of variance (F = 3.81, p <0.01) followed by Tukey's HSD, the students in the e-mail alert group turned in their assignments significantly earlier than those in both the control and reflective writing groups (but not significantly earlier than the schedule sheets

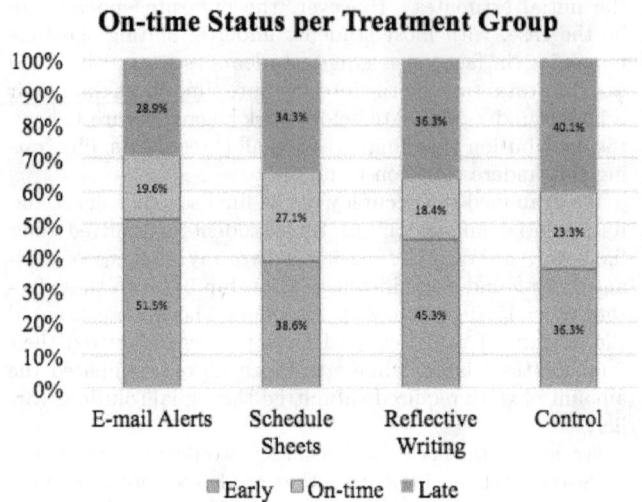

Figure 2: The percentage of early, on time, and late assignments turned in per treatment group.

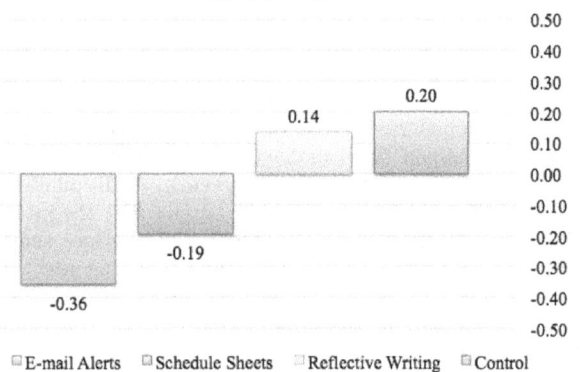

Figure 3: The average project submission time relative to the due date per treatment group. A negative value indicates the mean submission time was before the deadline, while a positive value indicates the mean submission time was late.

group), while other groups were not significantly different from each other. Figure 3 shows the mean finish times for each group. The pooled standard deviation across all groups was 2.2 days, so the difference between the finish times of the e-mail alert group and the control group represents an effect size of 0.25 (schedule sheets: 0.18 (not significant), and reflective writing: 0.03).

We also wanted to check whether students *started* any earlier. Because we only had data from students once they began submitting their work electronically to Web-CAT, we do not have direct access to their start times. However, previous work suggests that student behaviors for starting work [7] and for beginning to submit to an electronic grading system follow similar patterns [4]. As a result, we examined the time of each student's first submission to Web-CAT.

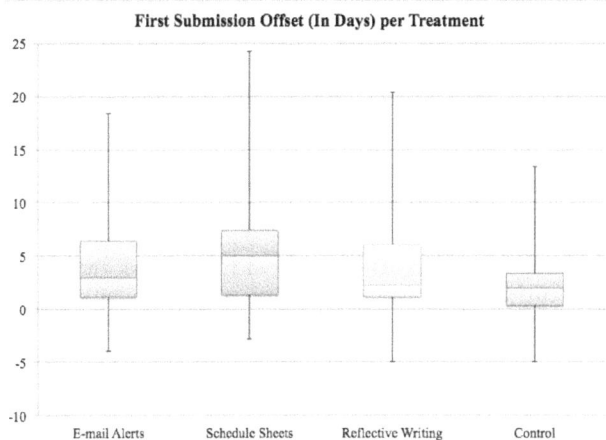

Figure 4: The first submission timestamp offset per treatment group. Note that a larger value indicates an earlier mean first submission time, while a negative value indicates a late first submission.

Figure 4 shows the relationship of first submission times among the groups. An analysis of variance (F = 24.7, p <0.001) followed by Tukey's HSD indicated that the schedule sheet group has significantly earlier first submission times on average (mean 5.3 days, s.d. 4.3) than all other groups. Both the e-mail alerts group (mean 4.0 days, s.d. 3.9) and the reflective writing group (mean 3.4 days, s.d. 3.7) were also significantly earlier than the control (mean 2.4 days, s.d. 3.1). Similarly, students in the schedule sheet group had a larger spread of time between their first submission and final submission (mean 5.1 days, s.d. 3.8) compared to the other groups (e-mail alerts: mean 3.6 days, s.d. 3.4; reflective writing: mean 3.6 days, s.d. 4.1; control: mean 2.6 days, s.d. 3.1). Again the schedule sheets group was significantly different than the other three (F = 19.9, p <0.001), with both e-mail alerts and reflective writing being significantly different than the control, but not each other.

One possible explanation for the earlier start times by the schedule sheets group is that students in that group were required to make an initial submission to Web-CAT before or with their intermediate schedule sheet, which was due one week before the deadline. This may have artificially altered the time of the first submission. One possibility is that students in the schedule sheet group simply turned in their work to meet the requirement, without it being "authentic" in the sense of having reached the point where they believed checking their work with the automated grader was needed. To explore this possibility, we also looked at the sizes of student programs on their first submissions, ignoring comments and blank lines, relative to their final product. Students in the schedule sheet group were the only group to submit significantly different amounts of code in their first submissions compared to the control group (F = 3.83, p <0.01). Students in the schedule sheet group made initial submissions containing an average of 78.6% of their final amount of code (s.d. 28.1%), which was less than the control group (89.2%, s.d. 35.6%). Neither the e-mail alerts group (mean 85.6%, s.d. 30.6%) nor the reflective writing group (mean 84.3%, s.d. 35.0%) were statistically different from any other groups. Based on this, it is plausible that

the earlier times of first submission for the schedule sheets group do not consistently represent "starting earlier" in this study, since this group's first submissions were smaller, and were not significantly associated with finishing earlier than other groups.

Finally, we also analyzed the use of time bank days by students—the individual 1-day extensions allowed, as described at the start of Section 5. Analyzing the number of bank days used across all four projects (normalized to account for the different number of available bank days across semesters), there was no significant relationship between treatment and the proportion of bank days used (F = 1.4, p = 0.25, mean proportion of days used, control: 55%, reflective writing: 42%, schedule sheets: 57%, e-mail alerts: 52%). This seems to indicate that no treatment had an impact on a student's tendency to use these days. There also was no significant difference in proportion of bank days used between semesters. That might indicate that the number of actual bank days available is was not important in this study.

5.3 Impact of Lateness on Quality

Previous work indicates that a student's programs tend to score lower and behave less correctly when that student finishes work late, after the due date, compared to when that same student finishes earlier [4]. To analyze the impact of lateness on project quality, we examined two key indicators. First, we considered the grade (total score) received by students on each project, without including any extra credit bonus received for early completion. In addition to the automated score produced by Web-CAT, this score also includes the manual grading performed by course teaching assistants. Second, we also considered the percentage of reference tests passed by each final submission, which is a measure of the functional correctness achieved, independent of other aspects of the grade.

Figure 5 shows the relationship between early, on time, or late submission and project grade. Completing projects early was significantly associated with earning higher scores (t = 4.28, p <0.001), although there was no significant difference between on time and late submissions (t = 1.21, p = 0.23). When considering functional correctness, however, the differences are even more apparent. Figure 6 shows

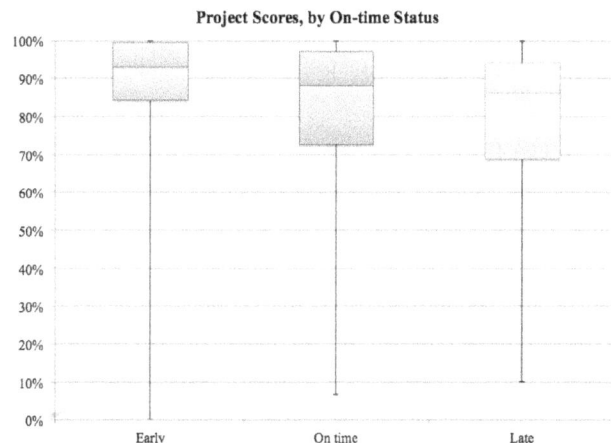

Figure 5: Project score distributions for early, on time, and late submissions.

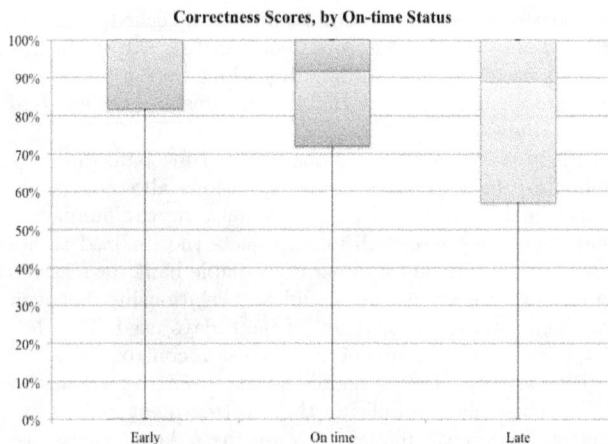

Figure 6: Correctness percentages for early, on time, and late submissions, in terms of instructor reference tests passed.

the relationship between the correctness scores for programs completed at different times, in terms of the percentage of instructor-provided reference tests passed by the program. Here, on-time work was significantly more correct (t = 2.43, p = 0.015) than late work, and early work was significantly more correct than on-time work (t = 3.87, p <0.001).

While these results support the notion that late work is of lower quality, one possibility is that "stronger students" simply finish their work earlier, and that weaker students, who are less able to complete an assignment, finish later. To account for this, we examined our data set to identify students who turned in at least one of the four projects late, and at least one of the four projects on time or early. We then performed a within-subjects comparison of both project scores and of reference test pass rates, comparing each student's late work against that same student's non-late work. In this within-subjects comparison, the on-time status of the student's final submission was a significant factor in his or her overall project grade (F = 7.5, p <0.001), with earlier work scoring higher. Similarly, the on-time status of the student's final submission was also a significant factor in the percentage of reference tests passed by his or her program–that is, its functional correctness (F = 13.7, p <0.001). As in [4], this within-subjects comparison suggests that finishing on time or early is related to project success independent of any individual-specific traits.

6. CONCLUSION AND FUTURE WORK

This paper summarizes experiences with three new classroom interventions designed to reduce student procrastination. While two of the interventions did not provide significant evidence of impact, the e-mail alert intervention showed some promise in reducing the frequency of late submissions and increasing the frequency of early submissions. At the same time, however, students subjectively reported that they did not feel the e-mail alert intervention affected how they managed their time, and generally reported that they believed these alerts were a waste of time. Nevertheless, from the point of view of our interventions, our results indicate the e-mail alert intervention was somewhat effective in the most obvious measures of earlier start times and

earlier finish times, and may potentially be more effective if we improve them and base them on more accurate data, perhaps by directly collecting student data from their IDE instead of only from their grading system submissions.

At the same time, this study confirmed earlier findings that late submissions have lower quality, receiving lower scores on functional correctness, while early submissions earn higher scores overall. Further, a within-subjects comparison indicates that individual students see higher scores on the work they complete early, compared to the work they complete late. Clearly, finishing earlier is associated with higher scores.

Based on these results, we plan to continue exploring the e-mail alert intervention described here, with the aim of providing more accurate and directed feedback that students may find more useful. It is possible that by collecting activity data directly from the student's development environment as they work on assignments, it will be possible to gain fine-grained insights into the entire period of development rather than simply the snapshots when the student turns in work for checking. This additional information could lead to more valuable information in e-mail alerts, aimed at increasing awareness of progress against the rest of the group and against expectations.

Ultimately, all of these interventions will only be effective if they can be used in a large scale classroom. While we have demonstrated such scalability in this paper, our implementations definitely are still prototypes. Ideally, we will eventually create a system that can accurately monitor student progress based on years of previous student effort on similar assignments, and provide feedback to instructors based on at-risk students as needed.

7. ACKNOWLEDGMENTS

This work is supported in part by the National Science Foundation under grant DUE-1245334. Any opinions, findings, conclusions, or recommendations expressed in this material are those of the authors and do not necessarily reflect the views of the National Science Foundation.

8. REFERENCES

[1] J. Aycock and J. Uhl. Choice in the classroom. *SIGCSE Bull.*, 37(4):84–88, Dec. 2005.

[2] C. C. Bonwell and J. A. Eison. *Active Learning: Creating Excitement in the Classroom. 1991 ASHE-ERIC Higher Education Reports.* ERIC, 1991.

[3] S. H. Edwards, J. Martin, and C. A. Shaffer. Examining classroom interventions to reduce procrastination. In *Proceedings of the 2015 ACM Conference on Innovation and Technology in Computer Science Education*, ITiCSE '15, pages 254–259, New York, NY, USA, 2015. ACM.

[4] S. H. Edwards, J. Snyder, M. A. Pérez-Quiñones, A. Allevato, D. Kim, and B. Tretola. Comparing effective and ineffective behaviors of student programmers. In *Proceedings of the fifth International Workshop on Computing Education Research*, pages 3–14. ACM, 2009.

[5] R. M. Klassen, L. L. Krawchuk, and S. Rajani. Academic procrastination of undergraduates: Low self-efficacy to self-regulate predicts higher levels of

procrastination. *Contemporary Educational Psychology*, 33(4):915–931, 2008.

[6] C. H. Lay. At last, my research article on procrastination. *Journal of Research in Personality*, 20(4):474–495, 1986.

[7] C. Norris, F. Barry, J. B. Fenwick Jr., K. Reid, and J. Rountree. Clockit: collecting quantitative data on how beginning software developers really work. In *Proceedings of the 13th Annual Conference on Innovation and Technology in Computer Science Education*, ITiCSE '08, pages 37–41, New York, NY, USA, 2008. ACM.

[8] J. Spolsky. Painless software schedules. `www.joelonsoftware.com/articles/fog0000000245.html`, 2000.

[9] D. R. Stead. A review of the one-minute paper. *Active Learning in Higher Education*, 6(2):118–131, 2005.

[10] P. Steel. The nature of procrastination: a meta-analytic and theoretical review of quintessential self-regulatory failure. *Psychological bulletin*, 133(1):65, 2007.

[11] B. W. Tuckman. The development and concurrent validity of the procrastination scale. *Educational and Psychological Measurement*, 51(2):473–480, 1991.

[12] B. W. Tuckman. Relations of academic procrastination, rationalizations, and performance in a web course with deadlines 1. *Psychological Reports*, 96(3c):1015–1021, 2005.

Spatial Skills Training in Introductory Computing

Stephen Cooper
Stanford University
353 Serra Mall
Stanford, CA 94305
1.650.723.9798
coopers@stanford.edu

Karen Wang, Maya Israni
Stanford University
353 Serra Mall
Stanford, CA 94305
kywang, mayai@stanford.edu

Sheryl Sorby
The Ohio State University
2070 Neil Avenue
Columbus, OH 43210
sorby.1@osu.edu

ABSTRACT

This paper explores the question as to whether there is a relationship between a student's spatial abilities and her achievement in learning to program. After noting that there does seem to be a correlation, the paper explores the impact of trying to improve a student's spatial abilities. The paper reports on a preliminary study involving high school students. The study results suggest a correlation exists between receiving training in spatial skills and improved student performance in introductory computing. While the sample size in the study is small, this improvement appears to occur for students of different races/ethnicities and across different socio-economic statuses.

Categories and Subject Descriptors

K.3.2 [**Computer and Information Science Education**]: Computer Science Education

General Terms

Measurement, Human Factors.

Keywords

Introductory computer science; spatial skills; training.

1. INTRODUCTION

Strong spatial skills are a predictor of success in many engineering disciplines [38, 29]. Spatial abilities have been linked to higher-level thinking, reasoning, and the creative process [1, 5, 34, 38]. But it is not clear exactly why and how spatial abilities lead to success. In conversations with many leading engineering educators, we have heard that the engineers think that spatial abilities may be linked to students' abilities to think at different levels of abstraction, an essential skill for engineers (and computer scientists) to develop.

Within engineering, studies have shown that women and those from low socio-economic status (SES) backgrounds have lower spatial abilities [4, 25], and, not surprisingly, are under-represented in many engineering disciplines. Fortunately, a good deal of work has been done, and students can be taught how to improve their spatial skills, which has been linked to improved retention within many engineering majors.

ICER '15, August 9--13, 2015, Omaha, Nebraska, USA.
© 2015 ACM. ISBN 978-1-4503-3630-7/15/08…$15.00.
DOI: http://dx.doi.org/10.1145/2787622.2787728

There have been several studies within computer science classrooms suggesting that there is a link between a student's spatial abilities and the student's ability to learn to program [11, 21, 22, 46]. We designed an experiment to see if we could replicate the results from these other studies. Beyond that, if we could replicate the correlation between spatial and programming abilities, we wanted to see what would happen if we tried to improve students' spatial abilities: Would the students have greater programming success?

We ran a pair of two-week summer workshops for rising twelfth grade students, targeting women and under-represented minorities. **Would we see any cognitive or affective differences if we exposed one group to spatial skills training while not teaching spatial skills to the other group?**

2. RELATED WORK

2.1 Spatial Skills Differences Between Sexes

Hyde [20] performed a meta-analysis on studies of males and females that occurred prior to 1974. In identifying 30 studies, she notes small but statistically significant differences between the visual-spatial abilities of males and females. Linn and Peterson [27] performed a meta-analysis of studies occurring from 1974-1982. They found large gender differences (with males scoring much higher) on measures of mental rotation. Many other studies note spatial abilities differences between males and females, with females having lower spatial abilities. While there is a difference of opinion between whether these differences appear prior to or after puberty (for example, Maccoby and Jacklin [28] provide evidence of differences appearing in adolescence while Newcombe et. al. [33] suggest male-female differences exist prior to adolescence), all of these studies do confirm these differences by the time students are adolescents.

2.2 Spatial Skills in Different Disciplines

Many researchers have tried to understand the extent to which differences in spatial abilities impact students across a range of STEM disciplines. Smith [38] conducted research in spatial visualization, identifying numerous careers for which spatial skills play an important role. Norman [34] found that a person's spatial skill level was the most significant predictor of success in his/her ability to interact with and take advantage of the computer interface in performing database manipulations. Barke [1] found that well developed spatial skills are essential for understanding basic and structural chemistry. Sorby [41] found that a person's spatial skills are related to his/her ability to effectively learn to use computer aided design software.

Some people might argue that with the multitude of data visualizations available today, the need for well-developed spatial skills has diminished, letting the computer do the visualizing. However, Cohen and Hegarty [5] found an individual's ability to manipulate/understand computer-based visualization of complex phenomena is correlated with her spatial skill level. In other words, students with poorly developed spatial skills do not understand the visualizations and do not really learn from them.

Gender and SES Differences in Spatial Skills: There is evidence to suggest that the 3-D spatial visualization skills of women lag significantly behind those of males. Theories for the cause of these differences include the belief that spatial ability is related to a male sex hormone [18], or that environmental factors are the primary reasons for male-female differences in spatial skill levels [8]. There are conflicting opinions as to whether differences on spatial performance between genders are linked to differences in mathematics performance. Tartre suggests that this may be the case [45], while Fennema and Sherman found that while there were few sex-related cognitive differences in mathematical abilities between males and females, there were differences in spatial visualization abilities between male and female students [9]. Fennema and Sherman's observations were echoed by Lindberg et al. [26], who did a meta-analysis of studies involving a much larger student population. Gender differences in 3-D spatial skills are likely due to a combination of several factors.

There has been little research on the differences in spatial abilities by race, but what has been done seems to confirm that there is a difference. Study [44] studied minority students at a historically black college. As part of her study on the impact of spatial skills training to improve retention, she noted that minority students' spatial skills were initially significantly behind those of students from a non-minority school.

Levine et al [25] found that the spatial skills for students from low SES groups were significantly lower than the skills for students from middle or high SES groups. Furthermore, there were no gender differences for students in low-SES groups, but there were significant gender differences for students from middle and high SES groups. However, spatial skills for the low SES group males were significantly lower than those for the females from the middle and high SES groups. Casey et al [4] also found significant differences in spatial skills, favoring students from middle or high SES groups. In the US, as under-represented minorities make up a significant portion of the students from the low SES groups, poorly developed spatial skills for these students could have serious implications for broadening participation in STEM.

There is a good deal of evidence to suggest that sketching 3-D objects is a significant factor in the development of these skills [2, 10, 31, 39, 40]. Gimmestad (now Baartmans) [13] conducted a study at Michigan Technological University and found significant gender differences in spatial abilities as measured by the Purdue Spatial Visualization Test: Rotations (PSVT:R) [14]. She also found a person's score on the PSVT:R was the most significant predictor of success in an engineering graphics course, of eleven variables tested. Design graphics courses are often among the first courses in which many first-year engineering students enroll. Students who have poorly developed spatial skills, particularly women, may become discouraged and drop out of engineering altogether if they struggle in their very first "engineering" course. In 1991, Baartmans [39] conducted a pilot study course for improving spatial skills. The results from her pilot study were promising and led to what has turned out to be a sustained journey in improving 3-D spatial skills for engineering students. In a longitudinal study conducted in 2000 [42], Sorby found that for students who initially demonstrated poorly developed spatial skills, enrollment in a spatial skills course improved student success in graphics courses by a half-letter grade (approximately 5 points in a 100 point system), and improved retention in their engineering majors.

2.3 Spatial Skills in Computing

Several researchers have explored the relationship between spatial skills and student programming ability/success. Fincher et al. [11] ran a study with 177 participants from eleven post-secondary educational institutions in Australia, New Zealand, and Scotland. They found a "small positive correlation" between scores in a spatial visualization task and programming marks, though attributed programming success to higher IQ components rather than to spatial skills. Jones and Burnett [21] conducted a study with 24 participants from a Masters course in the UK. They found participants with high spatial abilities completed code comprehension exercises faster than those with lower spatial abilities, along with a strong relation "between spatial ability and results in programming modules." A later study of 49 students [22] found a correlation between mental rotation skills and programming success. Mayer et al. [30] found, running a study with 57 college students in a course in Basic, "success in learning Basic was related to general intellectual ability, especially logical reasoning and spatial ability." Fisher, Cox, and Zhao [12], in a study with 30 undergraduate and graduate students with experience in Java, found "programmers use equivalently risky strategies for program comprehension and spatial cognition." Furthermore, they argued that "similar cognitive skills are used for spatial cognition and program comprehension/development." Webb [46] ran a study with 35 students aged 11 and 14, and found "spatial ability was the best predictor of knowledge of basic commands; and a combination of spatial ability and field independence best predicted scores on generated graphics programs" after learning Logo for one week.

It is important to note that while we were able to find several studies exploring the relationship between spatial and programming abilities (and providing evidence that a correlation exists), we were unable to find any studies where the researchers attempted to improve student spatial abilities as part of the study, as a means to hopefully improve programming ability.

3. METHODOLOGY

3.1 Procedure

In this study, the target students were rising high school seniors who had minimal previous experience in computer science. (Rising high school seniors are those students about to enter 12th grade, the last year of secondary school. Most are 17 years old.) We have been working with several high schools in Oakland and San Jose, as well as throughout the San Francisco Bay Area. High school math and science teachers from select schools were invited to ask their strong math and science students to apply to spend two weeks in an introductory computing workshop at Stanford University. We ran two workshops consecutively in summer 2014. The first workshop was the control group, and the second was the treatment group.

Both groups met from 9 to 5 each day for two weeks. We covered approximately half of Stanford's introductory computing class (for majors). The first two days introduced programming using Alice, while the remaining days covered programming using Java. In addition to computing lectures and labs, each group had 3-4 invited speakers from industry and academia visit (who spoke about different aspects of computing). Each day at lunch, 3-5 college interns, recent alumni working in Silicon Valley, and/or graduate students joined the high school students to discuss different computing career options. Each group had a field trip to a local technology company.

To mitigate covariant factors, both groups were given a 45 minute activity that was separate from the daily planned lecture schedule. For the control group, each day began with a review of the previous day's material led by one of the student teaching assistants for 45 minutes. These sessions consisted of group problem-solving exercises where the teaching assistant guided students through coding tasks targeting specific concepts. This is similar to what is done by Stanford's undergraduate teaching assistants in weekly sessions as part of Stanford's CS1 course.

Similarly, for the treatment group, one of the student teaching assistants led a 45 minute presentation/activity on developing spatial skills. While the content presented was different for each group (computer science material vs. spatial skills material), the activity flow for both was the same. In particular, rather than working on computers, the activities, for both the control and treatment groups, involved presentations on a white board followed by pencil and paper exercises. The rest of the day for both groups was spent with short lectures and longer laboratory periods where the students worked individually and in pairs on various programming activities.

Spatial skills: The spatial skills development sessions were held immediately after breakfast and before starting the day's computer science lesson. During each session, the topic was presented with a slideshow. The 5-7 minute slideshow demonstration introduced the topic by defining terms and showing examples related to the topic. After the demonstration, students completed worksheets that included sketching, matching, and measuring. Students typically completed the exercises individually and confirmed answers with one another upon completion; a few students also assisted their tablemates (students were arranged in pairs, with a table holding three student pairs) in answering the more difficult worksheet questions. Students completed the majority of the exercises on the worksheets. Students used building blocks to assist in completing the worksheets. Often, students built physical models of the worksheets' exercises using the blocks to sketch and measure from. These blocks were simple Lego-like cubes. At the end of each session, the workshop assistants collected all worksheets, pencils, and blocks. A researcher graded all worksheets immediately after the workshop ended. Graded worksheets were not returned to the participants. Students also completed Alice world exercises that taught double rotations and revolutions of objects. These exercises used animations of objects to further reinforce these more difficult topics.

Spatial Skills Curriculum: The curriculum of the daily spatial skills training workshops was adapted from Sorby's workbook [43] and curriculum. It focused on the teaching of mental rotations. Topics covered included:

• Isometric drawings (2 days): These drawings depict a 3-D object on a 2-D sheet of paper. An isometric view is the view looking down a diagonal of a cube that is part of the object.
• Orthographic drawings (1 day): These drawings depict "the faces of the object straight on or parallel to the viewing plane," including top, side, and front views [43].
• Single and double rotations of objects (3 days): This transformation includes turning an object about a straight line, or axis of rotation.
• Reflections and symmetry of objects (1 day): The reflection transformation happens when an object is reflected across an entire plane. An object is symmetrical if a plane can cut the object into two halves that are mirror images of each other.
• Surfaces and solids of revolution (1 day): These shapes are "created by revolving a set of 2-D curves about a coordinate axis" [43].

Other topics included in this workbook but excluded from our curriculum include combining solid objects, inclined and curved surfaces, paper folding, cutting planes, and cross sections. These topics were excluded due primarily to time limitations.

3.2 Data Measures

3.2.1 Assessment Instruments
Four instruments were used. The first instrument was a collection of demographic information about the students. The second instrument included eight Likert scale questions we created concerning student confidence towards learning computing as well as gender roles concerning computing. The Revised Purdue Spatial Visualization Test (Revised PSVT:R) [49] was used to assess the spatial skills ability of participants. This test measures the ability to complete mental rotations, a crucial indicator of spatial ability. The fourth instrument was an adapted version of the AP Computer Science Test administered in 2009 [6]. The AP tests are administered by the College Board, and most colleges in the US give college credit for high performance by high school students who are subsequently admitted to their college. It drew sixteen multiple choice questions from the official AP test.

3.2.2 Data Collection
All appropriate human subject procedures were followed in this study. Both the treatment and control groups completed the demographic instrument (as a pre-test), the attitudes instrument (as both a pre-test and as a post-test), the spatial skills instrument (as a pre- and post-test), and the AP CS test (as a pre- and post-test). The pre-tests were given on the first day of the workshop. The post-tests were given on the last (tenth) day of the workshop. For the control group, we erroneously did not provide a time limit for the Revised PSVT:R exam. (Students should have been given 20 minutes to complete the exam.) To be consistent, we did not provide a time limit for the treatment group. Most students took 20-25 minutes to complete the spatial skills test. Likewise, we did not provide a time limit for completing the 16 AP CS multiple choice questions. Most students completed this exam within 20 minutes. Students completed all instruments online.

3.2.3 Data Analysis
One of the challenges of this project was working with a small sample size (19 students per workshop, 38 students in total) due to the limitations imposed on our resources. A small sample size would be skewed by the presence of outliers, and could invalidate the assumption of a t-test that the variables are normally distributed. Thus, small sample sizes bring up the need for non-parametric tests, which make no assumptions about the probability distributions of variables.

Student's t-tests were used to analyze the aggregate CS, spatial, and attitude data for each session, and non-parametric Mann-Whitney and Kruskal-Wallis tests were used to analyze the categorical data, divided by socio-economic status (SES) and race/ethnicity. We did not divide students by gender; since the workshop was geared towards females, each session only had two males. While our sample size for each session (n=17 to 19) was relatively small, the Shapiro-Wilk normality test [37] showed that the aggregate datasets followed normal distributions at an alpha level of 0.01. When each session was further divided into SES and race/ethnicity categories, however, some categories had sample sizes too small to apply reasonable analyses of normality, and thus warranted non-parametric testing. Non-parametric tests such as Mann-Whitney and Kruskal-Wallis are useful for comparing two and three populations, respectively, where the sample sizes are small and the population distributions are unknown.

3.3 Student Population

The targeted students were those under-represented rising seniors who had a strong background in mathematics and/or science, with little to no previous programming experience. For both the control and the treatment groups, twenty students were selected. From partner high schools, we invited math and science teachers to have 2-4 of their students apply. Each workshop had two males, both of whom were of minority groups. Nineteen students completed each workshop. We allowed students to request one workshop (students did not know which was the control session and which was the treatment session), and tried to honor their preferences. This did lead to the situation where the two workshops were not perfectly balanced in terms of demographics or SES.

Table 1. Student demographics

	Hispanic	African American	Asian + Caucasian
Control	9	3	7
Treatment	5	4	10

We decided not to separate by sex, as each group (control and treatment) had only two males. This was somewhat disappointing given that much of the existing spatial skills literature has focused on differences between male and female spatial abilities.

We decided to not separate race from ethnicity. Many of the Hispanic students struggled to identify what their race was, as they identified as being Latina/o. Other studies have also shown that Hispanics are often unsure of what race they are [23]. We grouped Asian and Caucasian together because there was only one non-Hispanic Caucasian student in the control group.

Table 2 shows the socio-economic breakdown of the students. For the treatment group, we collected data on students' mothers' highest level of education, as a person's mother's educational level is a strong predictor of SES [24, 7, 36]. However, this SES data was not directly collected for the control group. We did know what high schools the students attended. The school status level was calculated based on each school's Academic Performance Index (API) score [3]. The API score is a value between 200-1000, with a target of 800 for every high school. We divided high school groups into 200-750 (lower SES schools students attended had APIs ranging from 450-700), 750-850 (middle SES schools students attended had APIs ranging from 780-820), and 850-1000 (upper SES schools students attended had APIs ranging from 880-910). Using this division, we had a close match (all but two students for the treatment group) with the students' self-reported mother's highest level of education. We were thus confident in using the school attended as a proxy for SES level. In our analyses, we combined the middle and upper SES groups, as the treatment group only had two middle class students.

Table 2. Student Socio-Economic Status

	Lower	Middle	Upper
Control	10	4	5
Treatment	8	2	9
Mother's Education Level	High school, or lower	Some college	College graduate or Graduate school
Treatment	6	3	10

4. RESULTS AND DISCUSSIONS
4.1 Spatial Skills/Programming Correlation

Our first step was to verify or refute the previous research on the correlation between spatial and programming skills [12, 21, 22, 30, 11, 46]. Is there a relationship between students having high spatial abilities and better performance in programming?

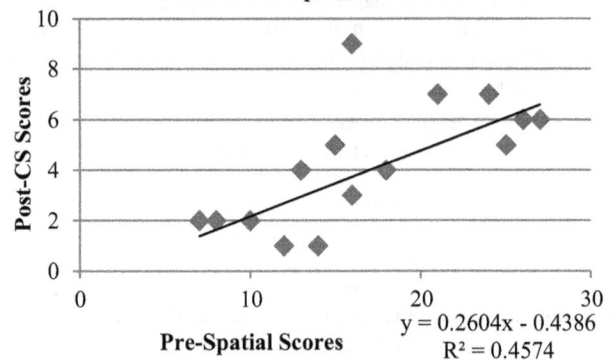

Control: Pre-Spatial vs. Post-CS

$y = 0.2604x - 0.4386$
$R^2 = 0.4574$

Figure 1. Control group pre-spatial versus post-CS scores

Figure 1 shows the graph of student scores on the spatial exam given at the start of the workshop versus their scores of the AP CS exam given at the end of the workshop. The control group scores confirm a positive correlation ($R^2=0.46$, $R^2=0.65$ upon removal of the one outlier who scored high on the post-CS exam, but low on the pre-spatial exam) between pre-spatial and post-CS scores. We can infer the relationship between spatial and programming abilities accounts for sixty-five percent (upon removing the outlier) of the variability in the data set. In the control group, it seems we could have predicted a student's CS performance at the end of the workshop from her original spatial score.

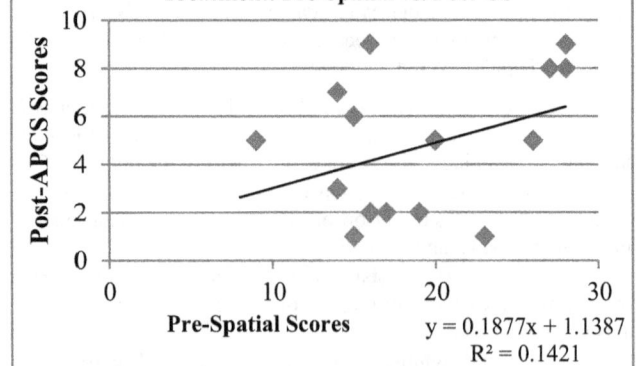

Treatment: Pre-Spatial vs. Post-CS

$y = 0.1877x + 1.1387$
$R^2 = 0.1421$

Figure 2. Treatment group pre-spatial versus post-CS scores

We also plotted results from the control group post-spatial versus post-CS scores and the treatment group pre-spatial versus post-CS and post-spatial versus post-CS. The graph of the control group's post-spatial versus post-CS scores was similar to Figure 1 (which is not surprising as we did not teach the control group spatial skills, and their post-spatial scores were similar to their pre-spatial scores). For the treatment group, as shown in Figure 2, the correlation between the pre-spatial and post-CS scores was low. This could suggest that the treatment group's spatial skills training impacted students' programming abilities.

When we graphed the treatment group's post-CS versus post-spatial scores (as shown in Figure 3), the correlation was again low. We are not sure why there was not a stronger correlation, as we had expected a stronger correlation between the students in the treatment group who scored well on the spatial skills exam as well as on the CS exam. One possible reason for this seeming anomaly is stereotype threat and/or testing bias. All six of the students who scored a 1 or a 2 on the CS test (all of whom scored at least a 16 on the spatial exam) were low-income and/or minority (African American or Hispanic). As part of the AP exam, the CS test looked and felt more like a standardized exam than did the spatial skills test. Students with less exposure to and experience with such AP exams might not have developed as efficient test-taking strategies.

Another possible reason has to do with the CS exam itself. The focus of the workshop was on code writing, whereas the multiple choice portion of the AP CS exam was on code reading. The AP CS multiple choice exam thus required a greater amount of inference ability for the students. As this code reading ability was not practiced at all during the workshop, students likely felt less confident concerning the taking of this exam. Certainly, we could have chosen to use a sample free-response question from the AP CS exam instead – this would more directly have measured a student's code writing abilities. However, one of the authors of this paper has previously worked at grading the AP CS exam. (College and high school instructors are hired each summer by the College Board to grade the free-response questions.) Even with a detailed grading rubric, much of the first day of AP CS grading involves calibrating and agreeing upon the correct interpretation of the rubric by the graders. This works well when the graders are able to use the first few hundred exams to agree upon how to equitably grade the remaining 20-30,000 exams. This may well have worked less well for us, when we had fewer than 40 exams to grade, and a lack of inter-grader reliability would likely have left us with an inability to interpret the results of our study. Section 5.2 explores this decision further.

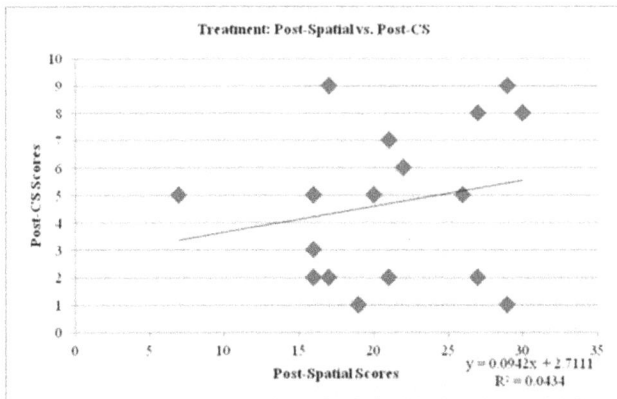

Figure 3. Treatment group post-spatial versus post-CS scores

4.2 Student Performance
We were interested to see how much, on average, students improved in each group, and whether or not this improvement was significant. We looked at student performance in the pre and post-tests for spatial skills and in CS (as measured by the AP exam). We considered the mean CS and spatial deltas of each group, where a delta is the difference between the pre and post-score.

Using paired t-tests (comparing mean pre-test to mean post-test scores), the gains in CS scores were not significant for the control group, but neared significance for the treatment group (p=0.07). Table 3 can be read noting that the treatment group improved by an average score of 1.06, and that this was significant at the p=0.07 level. Moreover, when the scores for the subset of CS questions with high item discrimination were considered, the gains in CS were significant for the treatment group (p<0.05). The gains in spatial scores were significant for the treatment group (p<0.005).

Item Discrimination (ID): In order to factor out random guessing, we looked at student CS performance on the subset of six questions that had high item discrimination. Because the AP CS multiple choice exam included questions from the year-long AP class (of which we covered about half), there were questions on the exam on material which the students had either not seen or only covered slightly. ID is an index of a test item's effectiveness at discriminating those who know the content from those who do not. ID values ≥ 0.2 are desired [35]. The label CS ID* denotes this subset of questions on the CS test that had an ID of equal to or greater than 0.3. We chose a value of 0.3 rather than 0.2 as the questions that had a value above 0.2 also had a value above 0.3.

Table 3. Mean deltas (p-values in parentheses)

	Control Δ	Treatment Δ
CS	0.50 (0.23)	1.06 (0.07)
CS ID*	0.72 (0.11)	0.82 (p<0.05)
Spatial	0.89 (0.11)	2.63 (p<0.005)

4.3 Relationships between Categories
Next we divided each session into categories based on SES and race/ethnicity, and considered the difference in CS and spatial deltas between these categories. Mann-Whitney U-tests were used for the two SES categories (low and middle/high), and Kruskal-Wallis tests were used for the three race/ethnicity categories (African American, Hispanic and Asian/Caucasian). Generally speaking, Mann-Whitney U-tests are used to compare two populations, and Kruskal-Wallis tests are used to compare three or more populations. Ordinal tests such as Mann-Whitney and Kruskal-Wallis take raw scores and rank them from lowest to highest (in our case from 1 to 19, where 19 is the highest), and are particularly useful when analyzing smaller sample sizes, where there may or may not be a normal distribution of the data. A mean rank is simply the mean of the all the ranks in a group. In Table 4, we report the mean scores for consistency, and include the mean ranks in parentheses.

4.3.1 SES
In the control group there was a significant difference in CS deltas (the student's score on the CS post exam minus her score on the CS pre exam) by SES (p<0.001). Lower SES students in the control group had a significantly lower CS delta than their middle and upper SES counterparts. This meant that on average, lower

SES students in the control group did not improve in their CS content knowledge as much as their higher SES counterparts by the end of the workshop; in fact, the lower SES students' raw scores decreased slightly, which we attribute to random guessing. For the treatment group, however, low-SES students' CS deltas were positive and large enough to create a non-significant difference in CS deltas between them and their higher SES peers. This meant that on average, there were not significant differences between the learning gains from lower SES students in the treatment group and their higher SES counterparts. For spatial deltas, there were no significant differences within either the control or treatment group. In the table below, we show the results of performing a Mann-Whitney U-test between the two categories. The mean scores are shown, and the mean ranks are shown in parentheses. The U-statistics, also shown, are used to compute the p-values.

Table 4. Differences by SES

Control	Lower	Middle + Upper	U	p
CS Δ	-1.56 (5.5)	2.56 (13.5)	4.5	p<0.001
CS ID* Δ	-0.78 (5.3)	3.00 (13.7)	3.0	p<0.001
Spatial Δ	1.20 (10.7)	0.56 (9.2)	38.0	0.28
Treatment	Lower	Middle + Upper	U	p
CS Δ	0.57 (8.4)	1.40 (9.5)	30.5	0.33
CS ID* Δ	0.57 (8.1)	1.09 (9.60)	29.0	0.28
Spatial Δ	2.38 (9.6)	2.82 (10.3)	41.0	0.40

This data analysis suggests that the spatial skills training helped the low-SES students, so that their CS knowledge gain was not distinguishable from the middle/high-SES students. In other words, in the group given spatial skills training, the lower SES students improved just as much as the higher SES students did in CS. This was not true in the control group, where there was a statistically significant distinction between the high-SES and low-SES students in terms of improvement in CS. Coupled with the results in Table 3, which shows that there was a statistically significant CS learning gain for the treatment group, this suggests that spatial skills training benefitted students from all SES levels.

4.3.2 Race/Ethnicity
In the control group we found a significant difference in CS deltas, with Hispanic students having the lowest CS delta (p<0.01). Since a Kruskal-Wallis test does not say anything about where the difference occurs, in order to determine which pairs of groups differ, we performed a Mann-Whitney U-test and then used a Bonferroni correction. Running a Mann-Whitney U-test and then using a Bonferroni correction showed that the significant differences were between Hispanic and Asian/Caucasian students.

But, in the treatment group, there was no significant difference. For spatial deltas, there was no significant difference within either the control or treatment group. We show the results of performing a Kruskal-Wallis test between the three categories, showing the mean scores, mean ranks in parentheses, and p-values.

One interpretation of this data analysis suggests that the spatial skills training especially helped the Hispanic students, so that their CS knowledge gain was not distinguishable from the other students. An alternate interpretation is that Hispanic students did better at the same time that Asian and Caucasian students did

comparatively (as compared to the control group) less well. At a minimum, a larger study seems warranted.

Table 5. Deltas by race/ethnicity

Control	Hispanic	African American	Asian + Caucasian	p
CS Δ	-1.63 (5.3)	0.33 (9.8)	3.00 (14.2)	p<0.01
CS ID* Δ	-0.88 (5.8)	0.00 (8.2)	2.86 (14.4)	p<0.01
Spatial Δ	1.00 (10.2)	1.67 (11.7)	0.43 (9.0)	0.78
Treatment	Hispanic	African American	Asian + Caucasian	p
CS Δ	1.20 (9.1)	-0.67 (6.5)	1.56 (9.5)	0.62
CS ID* Δ	0.80 (8.7)	0.00 (7.0)	0.80 (9.2)	0.69
Spatial Δ	1.80 (8.9)	4.00 (12.5)	2.50 (8.7)	0.59

4.4 Attitudes
Students rated their attitudes before and after the workshop on three categories: perceived programming experience, confidence in their ability to learn programming, and notions about gender performance in CS. Gains in perceived programming experience and confidence in their ability to learn programming were significant for both groups (p<0.05), which is not often the case for students receiving their first programming course [32]. In both control and treatment groups, students scored high (24.1 and 23.2 out of 25, respectively) on notions about gender performance to begin with, so there was no significant change in gender scores.

Lower SES students reported lower confidence before and after the workshop than middle and upper SES students in the treatment group. In the control group, lower SES students reported higher perceived programming skills at the end of the workshop (p<0.05). African American and Hispanic students reported higher perceived programming skills than Asian/Caucasian students at the end of the workshop in the treatment group (p<0.05).

5. ANALYSIS AND CONCLUSION
5.1 Student Learning
Despite the fact that the treatment workshop contained less CS content (replacing the first 45 minutes of CS review with spatial skills training for eight of the ten days of the workshop), students in the treatment section did better on the CS instrument as well as performing better on the spatial skills instrument at the end of the workshop. The students also had greater gains with respect to their confidence and their perceived programming experience. Note that we are not claiming causation, but rather an interesting correlation.

5.2 Covariant Factors/Issues
Several other factors may have accounted for the changes that we saw. The first was that the instructors for the two workshops were different. It may be the case that the treatment instructor explained the material more clearly to the students. That said, the lead author of this paper taught the control section. He has nearly 20 years teaching experience at the college level, and has taught more than 1000 high and middle school students as part of more than 20 previous outreach efforts. The instructor for the treatment group has been teaching undergraduates for two years. This was his first time teaching a high school student group. It would have been better to have the same instructor teach both groups, but there is a non-trivial physical toll taken teaching a summer workshop for two weeks, eight hours a day.

Another possible factor was that the demographics of the student groups varied across the two workshops. The control group consisted of more students from lower SES backgrounds, and had more African American and Hispanic students.

Additional concerns lie in only using standardized tests as instruments of measure. Standardized tests may favor certain income or race/ethnicity groups while negatively impacting others due to a variety of factors including stereotype threat, difference in standardized testing experience and coaching, among others.

We did not use a validated (or even a well-established) attitudes instrument, such as Hoegh [19] or Wiebe [48] or McKlin [16]. This was done because the validated instruments are longer, and we were worried about "survey overload." Using a validated instrument would have given us greater confidence regarding the student attitude results.

We did not set a time limit on the PSVT:R exam. It is not clear to us what the impact of a 20 minute time limit would have had.

Using the multiple choice section of the AP CS exam tested student ability to interpret and trace code, rather than the ability to write code. The focus of the workshop was on having the students learn to write code. As noted above (in section 4.1), we could have chosen one or two of the free response questions from the AP CS exam. Asking students to write a method or program would have more closely matched what we were asking them to do during the workshop. However, it would have been harder to fairly grade those students whose responses were not perfectly correct, as the sample AP CS rubrics (or any rubric we could have developed to grade the free response questions) would have been dependent on having multiple graders agree upon interpretations. And we were concerned about this given our small sample size.

Hattie [17] conducted a meta-analysis of more than 800 studies. He found several factors that influenced student achievement in schools. These included the home (and in particular, the role parents play), the school environment including the classroom climate and peer influences, the teacher, the curriculum, and the pedagogy used. Any of these factors could be at play in our setting.

There has been a good deal of study as to how student attitudes are related to their successes and lack of successes in STEM. For example, in her meta-analysis, Weinburgh [47] found significant differences in attitudes towards science, with males having a significantly more positive view of science than females. And Gunderson et al. [15] explored the role that adults play in trying to understand why females have more negative attitudes towards math than males. We did not see particularly interesting attitudes differences (as noted above in section 4.4). However, we did not study this possible covariant factor at depth.

Finally, we administered all exams online. Due to our error, students were not provided with scratch paper. This would likely have been useful for the AP CS exam, to allow students to trace on paper the sample code they were reading.

5.3 Concluding Remarks

We have much to learn about how best to teach students to improve spatial skills, and how best to incorporate spatial skills training into existing curricula/courses. The results from our pilot study are positive. Our results indicate that it may be possible to improve spatial skills in a short amount of time, which can be promising for students with low spatial skills. We recommend further exploring the relationship between spatial skills and programming, and how best to teach spatial skills to improve student programming abilities. If results of our pilot study can be replicated and expanded upon by

others, it would seem worthwhile to investigate why this relationship seems to exist, to better understand the nature of students learning to program and to develop their spatial abilities.

One of the most important areas for improvement would be to acquire a larger sample size of students, which would allow for more robust statistical analyses and avoid some of the roadblocks that we encountered. We also intend, in future interventions, to use a free response question from a previous AP CS exam to measure student CS content knowledge. We believe a free response question will better reflect the content covered during the workshop, where the focus is more on code writing than code reading.

6. ACKNOWLEDGMENTS
Thanks to S-Y Yoon who allowed us to use the Revised PSVT. Thanks to M. Sahami for his insightful comments on an earlier draft of this paper.

7. REFERENCES
[1] Barke, H.-D. & Engida, T. 2001. *Structural Chemistry and Spatial Ability in Different Cultures*. Chemistry Education: Research and Practice in Europe, 2(3): p. 227-239.

[2] Bowers, D. & Evans, D. 1990. The role of visualization in engineering design. *Proceedings of the NSF Symposium on Modernization of the Engineering Design Graphics Curriculum*, Austin, TX, 89-94.

[3] California Department of Education. Academic performance index. http://www.cde.ca.goc/ta/ac/ap/ Accessed 8/28/2014

[4] Casey, B. M., Dearing, E., Vasilyeva, M., Ganley, C. and Tine, M. 2011. Spatial and numerical predictors of measurement performance: The moderating effects of community poverty and gender. *Journal of Educational Psychology*, 103: 296–311.

[5] Cohen, C. & Hegarty, M. 2007. Individual differences in use of external visualization to perform an internal visualization task. *Applied Cognitive Psychology*, 21, 701-711.

[6] College Board. (2010). *2009 ap computer science a released exam*. New York: The College Board.

[7] Fahey, T., Keilthy, P. & Polek, E. 2012. *Family relationships and family well-being: A study of the families of nine year-olds in ireland*. Dublin: University College Dublin.

[8] Fennema, E. & Sherman, J. 1977. Sexual stereo-typing and mathematics learning. *Arithmetic Teacher*, 24(5), 369-372.

[9] Fennema, E., & Sherman, J. 1977. Sex-related differences in mathematics achievement, spatial visualization and affective factors. *American educational research journal*, 14(1), 51-71.

[10] Field, B. W. 1994. A course in spatial visualization. *Proceedings of the 6th International Conference on Engineering Design Graphics and Descriptive Geometry*, Tokyo, Japan, 257-261.

[11] Fincher, S., Baker, B., Box, I., Cutts, Q., de Raadt, M., Haden, P., Hamer, J., Hamilton, M., Lister, R. & Petre, M. 2005. *Programmed to succeed? A multi-national, multi-institutional study of introductory programming courses* (University of Kent, Computing Laboratory Technical Report 1-05). http://www.cs.kent.ac.uk/pubs/2005/2157/ Accessed 8/25/2014

[12] Fisher, M., Cox, A. & Zhao, L. 2006. Using sex differences to link spatial cognition and program comprehension. In *Proceedings of the 22nd IEEE International Conference on Software Maintenance (ICSM)*, 289 - 298.

[13] Gimmestad, B. J. 1989. Gender differences in spatial visualization and predictors of success in an engineering design course. *Proceedings of the National Conference on Women in Mathematics and the Sciences*, St. Cloud, MN, 133-136.

[14] Guay, R. B. 1976. *Purdue spatial visualization test: Rotations.* West Lafayette, IN, Purdue Research Foundation.

[15] Gunderson, E. A., Ramirez, G., Levine, S. C., & Beilock, S. L. 2012. The role of parents and teachers in the development of gender-related math attitudes. *Sex Roles*, 66(3-4), 153-166.

[16] Guzdial, M., Ericson, B., McKlin, T. & Engelman, S. 2012. A statewide survey on computing education pathways and influences: factors in broadening participation in computing. In *Proceedings of the ninth annual international conference on International computing education research (ICER '12)*, 143-150.

[17] Hattie, J. 2013. *Visible learning: A synthesis of over 800 meta-analyses relating to achievement*. Routledge.

[18] Hier, D.B. & Crowley, Jr., W.F. 1982. Spatial ability in androgen-deficient men. *New England Journal of Medicine*, 306(20), 1202-1205.

[19] Hoegh, A. & Moskal, B. 2009. Examining science and engineering students' attitudes toward computer science. In *Proceedings of the Frontiers in Education Conference*, San Antonio, Texas (6 pages).

[20] Hyde, J. S. 1981. How large are cognitive gender differences? A meta-analysis using ω^2 and d. *American Psychologist*, 36(8), 892-901.

[21] Jones, S. & Burnett, G. 2007. Spatial skills and navigation of source code. In *Proceedings of ITiCSE 2007*, 231-235.

[22] Jones, S. & Burnett, G. 2008. Spatial ability and learning to program. *Human Technology*, 4(1), 47-61.

[23] Krogstad, J. & Cohn, D. 2014. U.S. census looking at big changes in how it asks about race and ethnicity. Available from: http://www.pewresearch.org/fact-tank/2014/03/14/u-s-census-looking-at-big-changes-in-how-it-asks-about-race-and-ethnicity/ Accessed 8/29/2014

[24] Liberatos, P., Link, B. & Kelsey, J. 1988. The measurement of social class in epidemiology. *Epidemiologic Reviews*, 10, 87-121.

[25] Levine, S. C., Vasilyeva, M., Lourenco, S. F., Newcombe, N. S. & Huttenlocher, J. 2005. Socioeconomic status modifies the sex difference in spatial skill. *Psychological Science. American Psychological Society*, 16(11) 841-845.

[26] Lindberg, S. M., Hyde, J. S., Petersen, J. L., & Linn, M. C. 2010. New trends in gender and mathematics performance: a meta-analysis. *Psychological Bulletin*, 136(6), 1123-1135.

[27] Linn, M. C. & Petersen, A. C. 1985. Emergence and characterization of sex differences in spatial ability: A meta-analysis. *Child Development*, 56, 1479-1498.

[28] Maccoby, E. E. & Jacklin, C. N. (Eds.). 1974. *The psychology of sex differences (Vol. 1)*. Stanford, CA: Stanford University Press.

[29] Maier, P. H. (1994). *Raeumliches vorstellungsvermoegen*. Frankfurt a.M., Berlin, Bern, New York, Paris, Wien: Lang.

[30] Mayer, R. E., Dyck, J. L. & Vilberg, W. 1986. Learning to program and learning to think: What's the connection? *Communications of the ACM*, 29, 605–610.

[31] McKim, R. H. 1980. *Experiences in visual thinking*. Boston, MA: PWS Publishers.

[32] Moskal, B., Lurie, D. & Cooper, S. 2004. Evaluating the effectiveness of a new instructional approach. *SIGCSE Bull.* 36, 1 (March 2004), 75-79.

[33] Newcombe, N., Bandura, M. M., & Taylor, D. G. 1983. Sex differences in spatial ability and spatial activities. *Sex Roles*, 9(3), 377-386.

[34] Norman, K.L. 1994. Spatial visualization-A gateway to computer-based technology. *Journal of Special Educational Technology*, XII(3), 195-206.

[35] Office of Measurement and Evaluation of Teaching, University of Pittsburgh. Item difficulty item discrimination. http://www.omet.pitt.edu/docs/OMET%20Test%20and%20Item%20Analysis.pdf Accessed 8/29/2014

[36] Ou, S-R. & Reynolds, A. 2008. Predictors of educational attainment in the chicago longitudinal study. *School Psychology Quarterly*, 23(2), 199–229.

[37] Shapiro, S. S., & Wilk, M. B. 1965. An analysis of variance test for normality (complete samples). *Biometrika*, 591-611.

[38] Smith, I. M. 1964. *Spatial ability-Its educational and social significance*. London: University of London.

[39] Sorby, S. A. & Baartmans, B. J. 1996. A course for the development of 3-D spatial visualization skills. *Engineering Design Graphics Journal*, 60(1), 13-20.

[40] Sorby, S. A. & Gorska, R. A. 1998. The effect of various courses and teaching methods on the improvement of spatial ability. *Proceedings of the 8th International Conference on Engineering Design Graphics and Descriptive Geometry*, Austin, TX, 252-256.

[41] Sorby, S. A. 2000. Spatial abilities and their relationship to effective learning of 3-d modeling software. *Engineering Design Graphics Journal*, 64(3), 30-35.

[42] Sorby, S. A. 2001. A course in spatial visualization and its impact on the retention of women engineering students. *Journal of Women and Minorities in Science and Engineering*, 7(2), 153-172.

[43] Sorby, S. A. 2011. *Developing Spatial Thinking Workbook*. Boston, MA: Cengage Learning.

[44] Study, N. E. 2006. Assessing and improving the below average visualization abilities of a group of minority engineering and technology students. *Journal of Women and Minorities in Science and Engineering*, 12 (4) 363-374.

[45] Tartre, L. 1990. Spatial skills, gender, and mathematics. In E. H. Fennema & G. C. Leder (Eds.), *Mathematics and Gender*, (pp. 27-59). New York, NY: Teachers College Press.

[46] Webb, N. 1984. Microcomputer learning in small groups: Cognitive requirements and group processes. *Journal of Educational Psychology*, 76, 1076–1088.

[47] Weinburgh, M. 1995. Gender differences in student attitudes toward science: A meta-analysis of the literature from 1970 to 1991. *Journal of Research in Science Teaching*, 32(4), 387-398.

[48] Wiebe, E. N., Williams, L., Yang, K. & Miller, C. 2003. Computer Science Attitude Survey. (Report No.: NCSU CSC TR-2003-1) NC State University, Raleigh, NC.

[49] Yoon, S. Y. (2011). *Revised purdue spatial visualization test: Visualization of rotations (Revised PSVT:R)* [Psychometric Instrument]

Subgoals, Context, and Worked Examples in Learning Computing Problem Solving

Briana B. Morrison
School of Interactive Computing
Georgia Institute of Technology
85 5th Street NW
Atlanta, GA, 30332-0760
bmorrison@gatech.edu

Lauren E. Margulieux
School of Psychology
Georgia Institute of Technology
654 Cherry Street
Atlanta, GA, 30332-0170
l.marg@gatech.edu

Mark Guzdial
School of Interactive Computing
Georgia Institute of Technology
85 5th Street NW
Atlanta, GA, 30332-0760
guzdial@cc.gatech.edu

ABSTRACT

Recent empirical results suggest that the instructional material used to teach computing may actually overload students' cognitive abilities. Better designed materials may enhance learning by reducing unnecessary load. Subgoal labels have been shown to be effective at reducing the cognitive load during problem solving in both mathematics and science. Until now, subgoal labels have been given to students to learn passively. We report on a study to determine if giving learners subgoal labels is more or less effective than asking learners to generate subgoal labels within an introductory CS programming task. The answers are mixed and depend on other features of the instructional materials. We found that student performance gains did not replicate as expected in the introductory CS task for those who were given subgoal labels. Computer science may require different kinds of problem-solving or may generate different cognitive demands than mathematics or science.

Categories and Subject Descriptors

K.3.2 [**Computers and Education**]: Computer and Information Science Education: computer science education, information systems education

General Terms

Measurement, Design, Experimentation

Keywords

Subgoal labels; Cognitive Load; Contextual Transfer

1. INTRODUCTION

As educators, we want to simplify the learning process to provide the maximum results. As researchers, we want find empirical evidence for what *exactly* it means to simplify the learning process. One proven method for enhancing learning is to reduce unnecessary cognitive load on the student while they are trying to learn to solve problems [22]. There are several ways to reduce cognitive load, including using worked examples [14].

Worked examples typically include a problem statement along with a step-by-step procedure for how to solve the problem. Worked examples are most effective when used in worked example-practice pairs [2]. In these pairs, students study a worked example solution and immediately practice by solving a similar problem.

Segmenting worked examples and including subgoal labels have also been shown to be effective in improving learning [2]. Segmenting includes separating portions of the worked example to isolate each step in the process [23]. Subgoal labels are names given to a set of steps in the solution process allowing the user to "chunk" the information to ease learning [10].

While these cognitive load reducing techniques have been empirically tested in math and science disciplines, we have been the first to test these with computer science learning [15]. Margulieux et al. [15] demonstrated learning benefits for subgoal labels with a drag-and-drop programming language. This paper reports on a study undertaken to empirically determine the effectiveness of worked examples and subgoal labels within introductory computer science using a more traditional textual language. Some of the findings confirm the results from other disciplines while some were unexpected.

Specifically, instructional material was created to teach introductory programming students about the process of using and writing a `while` loop to solve programming problems. There were three treatment conditions: (1) *no* subgoal labels provided, (2) subgoal labels *given*, and (3) subgoal labels *generated*, in which students were asked to generate their own labels for groups of solution statements. Within each treatment group, participants were randomly assigned to either an *isomorphic* or *contextual transfer* group. In the isomorphic transfer group, the problem to be solved in the worked example-practice problem pair was identical to the worked example in both procedural steps and cover story (i.e., context). The only thing changed was the actual values of the numbers to be calculated. In the contextual transfer group, the problem to be solved in the worked example-practice problem pair involved the same procedural steps but the cover story and numeric values changed. Participants' learning was measured with performance on novel problem solving tasks and a post-test. Problem solving tasks during the assessment were different from practice problems solved as part of the instructions.

The research questions to be addressed through this study were: How do students who generate their own subgoal labels perform compared to those who were given subgoal labels and those who learned without subgoal-oriented instructions? Does changing the context or "cover story" between the worked example and practice problem have an effect on learning?

2. BACKGROUND

In this section we review the current literature for cognitive load, worked examples, and subgoal labeling.

ICER '15, August 09-13, 2015, Omaha, NE, USA
ACM 978-1-4503-3630-7/15/08.
http://dx.doi.org/10.1145/2787622.2787744

2.1 Cognitive Load

Cognitive load can be defined as "the load imposed on an individual's working memory by a particular (learning) task" [28]. The cognitive load required to comprehend materials directly affects how much students learn, and affects their performance scores on assessments related to that task. If students have to keep too many things in working memory in order to understand a concept, learning suffers. As designers of instructional material, it is our responsibility to ensure that we do not overload the learner's working memory where possible when presenting new material. That is, we should help ensure that students' <u>attention is directed at what's important</u> for learning, rather than extraneous aspects of the material.

The central problem identified by Cognitive Load Theory (<u>CLT</u>) is that learning is impaired when the total amount of processing requirements exceeds the limited capacity of working memory [20]. Currently CLT [17, 24, 26] defines two different types of cognitive load on a student's working memory: intrinsic load and extraneous load.

Intrinsic load is a combination of the innate difficulty of the material being learned as well as the learner's characteristics [13]. Extraneous load is the load placed on working memory that does not contribute directly toward the learning of the material---for example, the resources consumed while understanding poorly written text or diagrams without sufficient clarity [13]. Working memory resources that are devoted to information that is relevant or germane to learning are referred to as 'germane resources' [25].

The intrinsic and extraneous loads can be controlled through instructional design. When designing instructional material care should be given to eliminate any possible extraneous load while attempting to minimize the intrinsic load. It is believed that worked examples, when carefully designed, can accomplish both of these goals [24].

2.2 Worked Examples

Worked examples are one type of instruction used to teach procedural process to students for problem solving activities. Worked examples give learners concrete examples of the procedure being used to solve a problem.

Eiriksdottir and Catrambone argue that learning primarily from worked examples does not inherently promote deep processing of concepts [12]. While it may result in better initial performance because examples are more easily mapped to problems, it is less likely result in the retention and transfer [12]. When studying examples, learners tend to focus on incidental features rather than the fundamental features because incidental features are easier to grasp and novices do not have the necessary domain knowledge to recognize fundamental features of examples [11]. For example, when studying physics worked examples, learners are more likely to remember that the example has a ramp than that the example uses Newton's second law [11]. A focus on incidental features leads to ineffective organization and storage of information that, in turn, leads to ineffective recall and transfer [6].

2.3 Subgoal Labels

To promote deeper processing of worked examples and, thus, improve retention and transfer, worked examples have been manipulated to promote subgoal learning. Subgoal learning refers to a strategy used predominantly in STEM fields that helps students deconstruct problem solving procedures into subgoals, functional parts of the overall procedure, to better recognize the fundamental components of the problem solving process [1].

Subgoals are the building blocks of procedural problem solving and they are inherent in all procedures except the most basic.

Subgoal labeling is a technique used to promote subgoal learning that has been used to help learners recognize the fundamental structure of the procedure being exemplified in worked examples [8–10]. Subgoal labels are function-based instructional explanations that describe the purpose of a subgoal to the learner. For example, in the problem in Figure 1 for the first two lines of code the subgoal label might read "Initialize Variables." This label provides information about the purpose of that subgoal and the function behind the steps within it. Studies [3, 4, 8–10, 15, 16] have consistently found that subgoal-oriented instructions improved problem solving performance across a variety of STEM domains, such as programming (e.g., [15]) and statistics (e.g., [10]).

Studies have found that giving subgoal labels in worked examples improves performance while solving novel problems without increasing the amount of time learners spend studying instructions or working on problems (e.g., [15]). Subgoal labels are believed to be effective because they visually group the steps of worked examples into subgoals and meaningfully label those groups [1]. This format highlights the structure of examples, helping students focus on structural features and more effectively organize information [2].

By helping learners organize information and focus on structural features of worked examples, subgoal labels are believed to reduce the extraneous cognitive load that can hinder learning but is inherent in worked examples [21]. Worked examples introduce extraneous cognitive load because they are necessarily specific to a context, and students must process the incidental information about the context even though it is not relevant to the underlying procedure [26]. Subgoal labels can reduce focus on these incidental features by highlighting the fundamental features of the procedure [21]. Subgoal labels further improve learning by reducing the intrinsic load by providing a mental organization (i.e., subgoals) for storing information.

Subgoal labels that are independent from a specific context have been the most effective type of subgoal labels in the past [7, 10]. Catrambone found that learners who were given labels that were abstract (e.g., Ω) and had sufficient prior knowledge performed better than those who were given labels that were context-specific (e.g., isolate x) on problem solving tasks done after a week long delay or in problems that required using the procedure differently than demonstrated in the examples [10]. Catrambone explained this exception by arguing that learners with sufficient prior knowledge were able to correctly explain to themselves the purpose of the subgoal and that by self-explaining the function of the subgoal--the self-explaining presumably due to the abstract label--was more effective than providing labels.

3. METHOD OF STUDY
3.1 Purpose

Participants in introductory programming classes were given instructional material designed to teach them to solve programming problems using `while` loops. This common introductory programming task requires only minimal prior programming knowledge (arithmetic operations and Boolean expressions) to complete at a basic level. The study was conducted before students had formally learned about `while` loops in their courses. Participants were recruited from 4 different introductory programming courses at a technical university in the southeast United States and the study was conducted over a two week period. Because the courses teach different programming languages (see Table 1), pseudo-code was used in the task to make it independent from any one programming language.

Table 1. Classes Participating in Study

Programming Language	Majors
C++	Engineering
C#	Game Development
Java	Computer Science, Information Technology, Software Engineering, Non-Majors (mostly physics and math)

Pseudo-code is relatively easy for programmers to understand regardless of the programming languages that they know [27].The study was conducted in a closed lab setting with up to 30 computers in a single room. Students received an introduction to the study explaining that the material in the study was designed to help them learn how to write loops. Students were then given a URL to the first page of the study, which was housed in SurveyMonkey. Participants worked independently, but each session included between 15 and 30 people. The sessions typically lasted between 1 and 2 hours, depending on the rate at which participants completed the tasks.

3.2 Instructional Materials

To learn the procedure for using `while` loops to solve programming problems, participants were given three worked examples and three practice problems. The worked examples and practice problems were interleaved so that after studying the first worked example, participants solved the first practice problem before moving on to the second worked example. The worked examples came in three formats, which varied between participants. The first format was not subgoal oriented, meaning that steps of the examples did not provide any information about the underlying subgoals of the procedure. The second format grouped steps of the example by subgoal and provided meaningful subgoal labels for each group as is typical in subgoal label research (e.g.,[15]). The third format grouped steps of the example by subgoal and provided a spot for participants to write generated subgoal labels for each group. Each of the groups was numbered as "label 1," "label 2," etc., and groups that represented the same subgoal had the same number; therefore, groups that represented subgoal 1 were numbered as "label 1" regardless of where in the example they appeared (see Figure 1). Participants were told that each of the worked examples would have the same subgoals, and they were encouraged to update and improve upon their generated labels as they learned more.

Participant groups also received different practice problems to test how contextual transfer may affect learning. In the isomorphic transfer condition, the procedure and context used to solve the worked example and practice problem were exactly the same but the exact values in the problem changed. For example, if a worked example asked participants to find the average of quiz scores with values 70, 80, and 90, then the practice problem asked participants to find the average of quiz scores with values 75, 85, and 95. In the contextual transfer condition, the procedure used to solve the worked example and practice problem were the same except the context of the problem changed. For example, if a worked example asked participants to find the average of quiz scores, then the practice problem asked participants to find the average of money amounts. The contextual transfer was intended to be harder for participants to map concepts from the worked example to the practice problem. More difficult mapping can improve learning by

No labels	Given Labels (Passive)	Placeholder for Label (Constructive)

sum = 0
lcv = 1
 	
WHILE lcv <= 100 DO
 	
sum = sum + lcv
 	
lcv = lcv + 1
 	
ENDWHILE
	Initialize Variables
	sum = 0
	lcv = 1
	
	Determine Loop Condition
	WHILE lcv <= 100 DO
	
	Update Loop Var
	lcv = lcv + 1
	ENDWHILE
		Label 1:_____
		sum = 0
		lcv = 1
		Label 2:_____
		WHILE lcv <= 100 DO
		
		Label 3:_____
		lcv = lcv + 1
		ENDWHILE

Figure 1. Partial worked example formatted with no labels, given labels, or placeholders for generated labels.

reducing illusions of understanding caused by shallow processing thus inducing deeper processing of information [5, 12, 19]. However it can also increase cognitive load and potentially hinder learning [26].

After completing the instructions, participants completed novel programming tasks to measure their problem solving performance. We hypothesized that students who generated subgoal labels would learn better than those who were given the subgoal labels, and both groups would do better than those who had no subgoals at all. We also hypothesized that learners whose practice problems required contextual transfer would perform better than learners whose practice problems were the same context, unless the contextual transfer required too much cognitive load during the learning process.

3.3 Design

The experiment was a 3-by-2, between-subjects, factorial design: the format of worked examples (unlabeled, subgoal labels given, or subgoal labels generated) was crossed with the transfer distance between worked examples and practice problems (isomorphic or contextual transfer). The dependent variables were performance on the pre- and post-test, problem solving tasks, and time on task.

3.4 Participants

Participants were 66 students from a technical university in the Southeast United States (Table 2). Students were offered credit for completing a lab activity as compensation for participation. All students from these courses were allowed to participate, regardless of prior experience with programming or using while loops. To account for prior experience, participants were asked about their prior programming experience in high school (either regular or advanced placement courses) and college and whether they had experience using while loops. Other demographic information collected included gender, age, academic major, high school grade point average (GPA), college GPA, number of years in college, reported comfort with computer, expected difficulty of the programming task, and primary language. There were no statistical differences between the groups for demographic data, which is expected because participants were randomly assigned to treatment groups. Participants also took a multiple-choice pre-test to measure problem solving performance for using `while` loops. Average scores on the pre-test were low, 24% (1.2 out of 5 points), with 32% (21 out of 66) of participants earning no points.

Table 2. Participant Demographics

Age	Gender	GPA	Major
M = 21	89% male	M = 3.1/4	50% CS major

Many participants did not complete all tasks of the experiment. Participants received compensation regardless of the amount of time or effort that they devoted to the experiment, which might have caused low motivation in some participants. Participants who did not attempt all tasks were excluded from analysis. Participants who answered more than two questions correctly out of the five on the pre-test were excluded from analysis because the instructions were designed for novices. To make the group size equal across conditions, an assumption of general linear model analysis, randomly chosen participants from some groups were excluded from analysis. Based on these exclusion criteria, we analyzed data from 66 of the 96 participants in the experiment.

3.5 Procedure

An outline of the entire study is given in Table 3. After granting consent (Step 1), the participants completed a demographic questionnaire (Step 2) and pre-test (Step 3). The pre-test was comprised of multiple choice questions about `while` loops from previous Advanced Placement Computer Science exams. Because the questions were multiple-choice, participants needed to only recognize correct answers rather than create correct answers.

When participants finished the demographic questionnaire and pre-test, they began the instructional period (Steps 4-6). The instructional period started with training. Participants who generated their own subgoal labels received training on how to create subgoal labels. The training included expository instructions about generating subgoal labels and an example of a subgoal labeled worked example similar to that in Figure 1. Then the training asked participants to complete activities to practice generating subgoal labels.

The first activity asked participants to apply the subgoal labels from the example to a new worked example. The second activity asked participants to generate their own subgoal labels for an

order of operations math problem. After participants generated their own subgoal labels, they were given labels created by an instructional designer for comparison.

Participants who did not generate their own subgoal labels received training to complete verbal analogies. Verbal analogies (e.g., water : thirst :: food : hunger) were considered a comparable task to subgoal label training because they both require analyzing text to determine an underlying structure. Participants who were not asked to generate their own labels were not given subgoal label training because it might have prompted them to process the instructions more similarly than would be expected to participants who were asked to generate their own labels, which might confound the results. Like the subgoal label training, the analogy training included expository instructions, worked examples, and activities to carry out.

Following the training, the instructional period provided worked examples and practice problem pairs (Step 6) to help participants learn to use `while` loops to solve problems. The worked example format differed between subjects among three levels: unlabeled, subgoal labels given, and subgoal labels generated. Furthermore, the transfer distance between worked example and practice problem differed between subjects between two levels: isomorphic or contextual transfer. For a summary of the procedure during the instructional period, please refer to Table 3.

Having completed the instructional period, participants were then asked to complete a 10 item survey designed to measure cognitive load [18]. The placement of the cognitive load survey at this point is to ensure measurement of the actual learning process and not the assessment elements.

Table 3. Study Outline

Step	No Subgoal Labels		Subgoal Labels Given		Subgoal Labels Generated	
1	Consent					
2	Demographics					
3	Pre test					
4	Training Problem – summing					
5	Analogy Training & Activity				Subgoal Training & Activity	
Groups	None-Isomorphic	None-Context Transfer	Given-Isomorphic	Given-Context Transfer	Generate-Isomorphic	Generate-Context Transfer
6	Worked Example 1 (no subgoal labels)		Worked Example 1 (subgoal labels given)		Worked Example 1 (space to generate subgoal labels)	
	Problem 1 (no subgoal labels)	Problem 1A (no subgoal labels)	Problem 1 (subgoal labels given)	Problem 1A (subgoal labels given)	Problem 1 (space to generate subgoal labels)	Problem 1A (space to generate subgoal labels)
	Worked Example 2 (no subgoal labels)		Worked Example 2 (subgoal labels given)		Worked Example 2 (space to generate subgoal labels)	
	Problem 2 (no subgoal labels)	Problem 2A (no subgoal labels)	Problem 2 (subgoal labels given)	Problem 2A (subgoal labels given)	Problem 2 (space to generate subgoal labels)	Problem 2A (space to generate subgoal labels)
	Worked Example 3 (no subgoal labels)		Worked Example 3 (subgoal labels given)		Worked Example 3 (space to generate subgoal labels)	
	Problem 3 (no subgoal labels)	Problem 3A (no subgoal labels)	Problem 3 (subgoal labels given)	Problem 3A (subgoal labels given)	Problem 3 (space to generate subgoal labels)	Problem 3A (space to generate subgoal labels)
7	Cognitive Load Measurement					
8	Problem Solving Assessment (4 problems; 2 near transfer, 2 far transfer)					
9	Assessment Task 2					
10	Assessment Task 3					
11	Post Test					

Once participants completed the cognitive load survey, they started the assessment period (Steps 8-11). The assessment period included three types of tasks, but only the problem solving tasks (Step 8) will be discussed here because they are the only measure of novel problem solving performance. The problem solving tasks asked participants to use the problem-solving structure that they had learned during the worked example-practice problem pairs to solve four novel problems. Two of these problems required contextual transfer, meaning that they followed the same steps found in the instructions but in a different context, or cover story. The other two problems required both contextual and structural transfer. In these problems the context was new to the participants and the solution to the problem required a different structure than the problems found in the instructional material (e.g., the practice problem is summing values, the assessment is counting matching values). These tasks were intended to measure participants' problem solving performance as a 'far' transfer. After the assessment period, participants completed a post-test that had the same questions as the pre-test to measure their learning (Step 11).

Throughout the procedure, we recorded the time taken to complete each task. We also collected process data throughout the instructional period. We collected performance on the training activities and practice problems to ensure that participants were completing tasks. We also collected the labels that participants created.

We entered into the study with the following hypotheses:

H1. Participants who learn with subgoal labels (given or generated) will perform better on programming assessments and a post-test.

H1A. Those who generate their own subgoal labels and receive multiple variations of the problems (contextual transfer condition) will perform the best on the assessments, unless dealing with transfer overloads their mental resources.

H2. Participants who generate subgoal labels will perform better on problem solving tasks that require farther transfer. Those groups exposed to contextual transfer practice problems will perform better on transfer tasks than the isomorphic transfer groups.

H3. Participants who are given subgoal labels will complete the worked example-practice problem pairs in less time than others.

H3A. Those who generate subgoal labels and are exposed to contextual transfer practice problems will take the most time to complete the worked example-practice problem pairs.

H4. Participants with the deepest learning, those required to generate subgoal labels, should spend the least time on the programming assessments than other groups.

H4A. Participants with the most shallow learning, those with no subgoal labels and not exposed to contextual transfer problems, should spend the most time on the programming assessments.

4. ANALYSIS AND RESULTS
4.1 Accuracy
We scored participants' solutions for accuracy to generate a problem solving score. Participants earned one point for each correct line of code that they wrote. This scoring scheme allowed for more sensitivity than scoring solutions as wholly right or wrong. If participants wrote lines that were conceptually correct but contained typos or syntax errors (e.g., missing a parenthesis), they received points. We scored logic errors (having < rather an

<=) as incorrect. We considered scoring for conceptual and logical accuracy more valuable than scoring for absolute syntactical accuracy because participants were still early in the learning process. Participants could earn a maximum score of 44.

The effect of the interventions on problem solving performance depended on the interaction of the worked example manipulation and transfer distance manipulation. We found no main effect of worked example format, $F (2, 60) = 2.16$, $MSE = 123.5$, $p = .13$, est. $\omega^2 = .07$. In addition, we found no main effect of transfer distance, $F (2, 60) = 0.04$, $MSE = 123.5$, $p = .83$, est. $\omega^2 = .001$. There was, however, a statistically significant interaction between worked example format and transfer distance, $F (2, 60) = 6.5$, $MSE = 123.5$, $p = .003$, est. $\omega^2 = .18$, $f = .31$ (see Figure 2).

In this interaction the difference between the group that was given subgoal labels with isomorphic transfer ($M = 12.1$, $SD = 13.5$) and the group that was given subgoal labels with contextual transfer ($M = 25.5$, $SD = 11.4$) was statistically significant with a large effect size, $t (20) = -2.51$, $p = .021$, $d = 1.07$. Furthermore, the difference between the group that generated subgoal labels with isomorphic problems ($M = 25.5$, $SD = 8.7$) and the group that generated subgoal labels with contextual transfer ($M = 17.5$, $SD = 11.5$) was not statistically significant but had a medium effect size, $t (20) = 1.86$, $p = .077$, $d = .78$. These results mean that participants who were given subgoal labels performed better when they had contextual transfer, and participants who generated subgoal labels performed better with isomorphic problems.

We found three levels of performance, as can be seen in Figure 2. The best performing groups were those that were given subgoal labels with contextual transfer (M = 25.46) and generated subgoal labels with isomorphic problems (M = 25.55). The middle groups were those that received no labels with isomorphic problems (M = 18.09) and generated subgoal labels with contextual transfer (M = 17.46). The worst performing groups were those that received no labels with contextual transfer (M = 11.09) and were given subgoal labels with isomorphic problems (M = 12.09). The difference between the middle and best level of performance was not statistically significant but had a medium effect size, as shown by the t-test comparing groups that generated subgoal labels, t (20) = 1.86, p = .077, d = .78. Similarly, the difference between the middle and worst level of performance was not statistically significant but had a medium effect size, as shown by the t-test comparing groups that did not receive any subgoal labels, t (20) = 1.56, p = .13, d = .67. Given these effect sizes, we would expect these differences to be statistically different with a larger sample size.

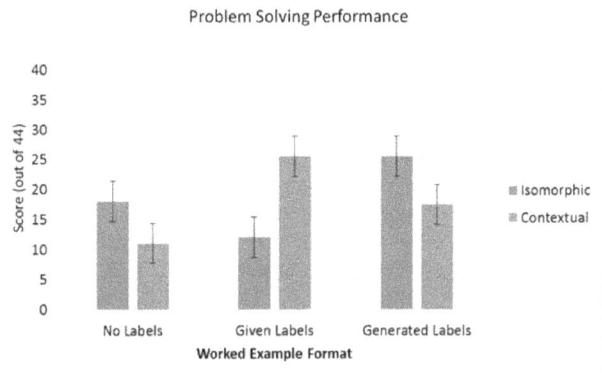

Figure 2. Problem solving performance graphed with worked example format on the x-axis, transfer distance as separate colors, and score on the y-axis.

Performance on the post-test was similar to that on the pre-test. Average scores on the post-test were low, 31% (1.5 out of 5 points). We found no statistical differences for main effect of worked example format, $F(2, 60) = .39$, $MSE = 1.29$, $p = .68$, est. $\omega^2 = .02$, main effect of transfer distance, $F(2, 60) = .83$, $MSE = 1.29$, $p = .37$, est. $\omega^2 = .02$, or interaction, $F(2, 60) = 1.63$, $MSE = 1.29$, $p = .21$, est. $\omega^2 = .06$.

Some demographic characteristics correlated with performance on the problem solving tasks. Self-reported comfort with solving programming problems, collected on a Likert-type scale from "1 – Not at all comfortable" to "7 – Very comfortable," correlated positively with performance, $r = .47$, $p < .001$. Prior experience using while loops to solve programming problems, collected as a "yes" or "no" question, correlated positively with performance, $r = .29$, $p = .018$. Higher scores on these characteristics correlated with higher scores on performance. We found no differences among groups on these characteristics; thus, these correlations are not expected to confound the results.

4.2 Time Efficiency

4.2.1 Time on Worked Example-Practice Pairs
For time spent studying worked examples and solving practice problems, we found a main effect of worked example format, $F(2, 60) = 6.55$, $MSE = 155.1$, $p = .003$, est. $\omega2 = .18$, $f = .32$. We also found a main effect of transfer distance, $F(2, 60) = 6.24$, $MSE = 155.1$, $p = .015$, est. $\omega2 = .09$, $f = .31$. In addition, we found an interaction, $F(2, 60) = 4.48$, $MSE = 155.1$, $p = .015$, est. $\omega2 = .13$, $f = .26$ (see Figure 3). Based on this pattern of results, the interaction is likely causing the main effect of transfer distance because there is little difference between transfer groups except when participants generated subgoal labels (see Figure 3).

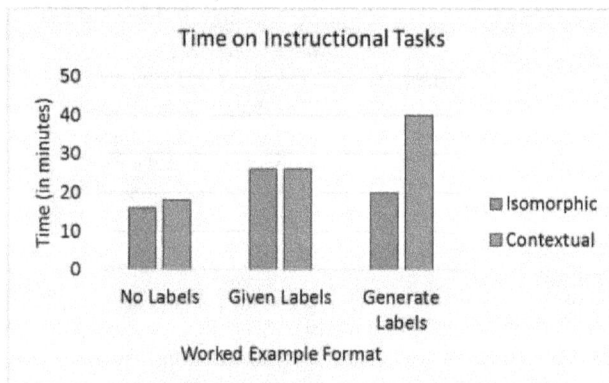

Figure 3. Time on instructional tasks graphed with worked example format on the x-axis, transfer distance as separate colors, and score on the y-axis.

4.2.2 Time on Programming Assessments
As in the results of the problem solving tasks, we found an interaction for time spent on the problem solving tasks, $F(2, 60) = 3.97$, $MSE = 71.63$, $p = .024$, est. $\omega2 = .12$, $f = .25$ (see Figure 4). The main effect of worked example format was not statistically significant, $F(2, 60) = .57$, $MSE = 71.63$, $p = .57$, est. $\omega2 = .02$, and we found no main effect of transfer distance, $F(2, 60) = 1.34$, $MSE = 71.63$, $p = .25$, est. $\omega2 = .02$. This interaction is interesting because it almost exactly matches the pattern of problem solving performance so that more time on task maps to better performance. The exception is that the group that received no subgoal labels with isomorphic problems took the longest to complete the tasks but performed in the middle.

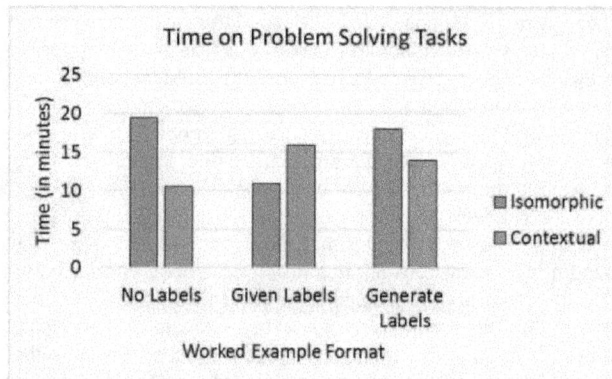

Figure 4. Time on problem solving tasks graphed with worked example format on the x-axis, transfer distance as separate colors, and score on the y-axis.

5. DISCUSSION
In this section we summarize our findings related to our original hypotheses. Table 4 contains a synopsis of all findings.

Table 4. Summary of Findings

Hypothesis	Finding
H1. Those with subgoal labels (given or generated) will perform better on programming assessments and a post-test.	Partially supported - Given-Isomorphic performed poorly
H1A. Those who generate subgoal labels and have contextual transfer in practice problems will perform the best on the assessments, unless transfer overloads their mental resources.	Generate-Context Transfer did better on the assessment, but not on the programming
H2. Participants who generate subgoal labels and those exposed to contextual transfer will perform better than other groups on problem solving tasks that require farther transfer.	Refuted
H3. Participants who are given subgoal labels will complete the worked example-practice problem pairs in less time than others.	Supported
H3A. Those who generate subgoal labels and have contextual transfer in practice problems will take the most time to complete the worked example-practice problem pairs.	Supported
H4. Participants required to generate subgoal labels, should spend the least time on the programming assessments.	Refuted
H4A. Participants with the most shallow learning, those with no subgoal labels and isomorphic practice problems should spend the most time on the programming assessments.	Supported - No subgoal labels and isomorphic transfer took the most time.

5.1 Accuracy

5.1.1 Assessments
Three groups performed the best on the assessments—combining the programming assessment and post test: those that were given subgoal labels with contextual transfer (Given-Context Transfer), and both groups that generated subgoal labels (Generate-Isomorphic and Generate-Context Transfer) (Figure 5).

Interestingly, the Generate-Context Transfer group did better on the post-test while the Generate-Isomorphic group performed better on the programming assessments. However the group that was given subgoal labels with no contextual transfer performed poorly on both the programming assessment and the post-test.

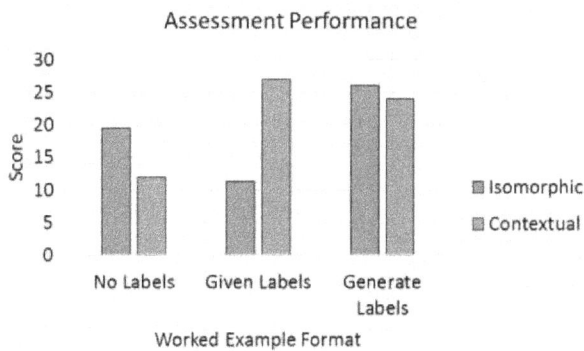

Figure 5. Assessment Performance by Treatment Groups

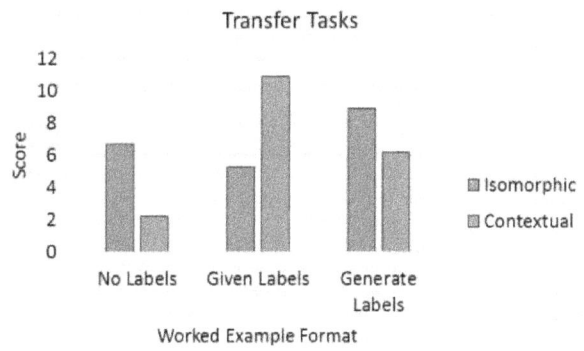

Figure 6. Transfer Task Performance

Thus we have partial support for H1. For the related hypothesis H1A, it was the case that the Generate-Context Transfer group performed statistically significantly better on the post-test assessment; they did not outperform the other groups on the programming assessment tasks. This may be because the generation of subgoal labels while also considering the contextual transfer overloaded the participants during the programming assessments when they were required to retrieve information from memory. However, performance on the post-test indicates that this group had the deepest learning when only considering conceptual recall and not problem solving issues.

When the commonalities between worked examples and practice problems were evident, as in the isomorphic transfer conditions, generating subgoal labels might have encouraged deep processing of information without overloading the participants. Similarly, when subgoal labels are given to participants, finding commonalities between contextually different examples and problems might have encouraged deep processing of information without overloading the participants. Participants who both generated subgoal labels and had contextual transfer did not perform as well as these groups. It is possible that both generating subgoal labels and finding commonalities between contextually different worked examples and practice problems was too cognitively demanding for many of the participants, which hindered performance.

5.1.2 Transfer Tasks

The best performing group on the transfer tasks (programming assessments 3 and 4) was the group that was given subgoal labels and contextually different practice problems (Given-Context Transfer) (see Figure 6). However the other two groups receiving contextual transfer practice problems did not perform particularly well on the transfer programming tasks and nothing was statistically different.

So we must refute H2. Those groups who were exposed to contextual transfer problems did not perform better than their isomorphic problem counterparts and this included the group that generated their own subgoal labels. However it should be noted that it was a contextual transfer group that did perform the best on the far transfer tasks – those that were *given* the subgoal labels.

5.2 Time

5.2.1 Worked Examples – Practice Problem Pairs

As expected, the group that took the most time on the instructional material of the worked examples and practice problem pairs was the group that had to generate their subgoal labels and contend with contextual transfer in the practice problems (Figure 3). This

result was statistically significant and supports H3A. However we must refute H3. The given subgoal label groups did not complete the worked example-practice problem pairs in the least amount of time. In fact, it was the non-subgoal label groups who took the least time in completing the worked-example practice problem pairs. This may indicate that they were simply reading the material for shallow understanding. Notice also that the group with no subgoal labels and contextual transfer (None-Context Transfer) did take slightly longer than the None-Isomorphic group indicating that some time is likely spent translating the worked example solution into a new context.

5.2.2 Assessments

We have no support for H4 (see Figure 4). Indeed, the groups that spent the least amount of time on the programming assessments were the ones that received no subgoal labels with contextual transfer (None-Context Transfer) and the group that was given subgoal labels with no contextual transfer (Given-Isomorphic).

However, we have support for H4A. It was the group that did not receive any subgoal labels and no contextual transfer that took the most time on the programming assessment tasks.

5.3 Implications

Groups that generated subgoal labels performed overall better than those that did not have subgoal labels. The pattern of results for these groups is similar, though. In both cases, the condition that had isomorphic problems performed better than the condition that had contextual transfer, quite possibly because solving the isomorphic problems required less cognitive load. This pattern is reversed for groups that were given subgoal labels. It might be the case that learners who contend with contextual transfer problems need help identifying the analogous subgoals of the worked examples and practice problems. Participants who were given subgoal labels with contextual transfer might have been one of the highest performing groups because they received a framework of meaningful subgoal labels that guided their transfer between worked examples and practice problems. Though participants who generated subgoals labels received placeholders that indicated analogous subgoals between examples and problems, some of their generated labels were context-specific to the problem, which would not likely promote transfer to a contextually-different problem. In addition, if participants were unsure of the labels that they generated, they might rely less on them to guide future problem solving.

The most surprising result from this experiment was the group that was given subgoal labels and isomorphic problems was one of the worst performing groups. It could be that being given the labels in addition to being able to more easily recognize commonalities between worked examples and practice problems led to superficial processing of information. Because participants could solve practice problems by using the worked example as an isomorphic guide and because the subgoal labels explained the function of programming steps, participants might have been overconfident about their understanding of the procedure and devoted less effort to learning.

We believe that there is an interesting interaction between the time spent during the instructional period and on the programming assessments that is related to performance. We now examine each group separately.

The None-Isomorphic group spent the least amount of time on the worked-example practice problem pairs which likely resulted in them spending the most amount of time on the programming assessment tasks. Their learning was most likely superficial learning which resulted in more thrashing when trying to solve the programming assessment tasks. And this group performed neither well nor poorly on the performance of the assessment tasks.

The None-Context Transfer group also spent the least amount of time on the worked example-practice problem pairs. However, they also spent the least amount of time statistically on the programming assessment tasks. This may be because these participants gave up and quit trying. For many of our participants it became obvious that if they felt they did not know the answer, they simply skipped attempting the task or put some form of "I don't know" for the result. While some did attempt the beginning of a solution-perhaps the first one or two lines of the solution, it was clear that they did not learn much overall.

The Given-Isomorphic group provides us the most puzzling results. We predicted that the Given-Isomorphic group would do well on the assessment tasks, based on previous research. However, this group performed the worst on the programming assessment tasks. Initially we thought it might be because this group was simply copying and pasting the results (the worked example problem and practice problem were on the same survey page). However, examination of their submissions show that the responses were not copied as the spacing is very different in their responses, some only entered the specific line related to the subgoal, and some wrote solutions in their "native" programming language rather than the pseudo-code. In addition, this group spent a fair amount of time during the instructional material period indicating that they were actually attempting to work through the solutions.

The Given-Context Transfer group is equally puzzling as they were among the best performing for the assessment tasks yet spent among the least amount of time on those assessments. These results are more in line with previous research – those that study worked examples can perform as well as those who solve problems in less time. It appears that this group internalized the most of the problem solving process allowing them to perform well on the assessments while not taking much time.

The Generate-Isomorphic group performed as expected on the assessment tasks – being among the best. However this group also took among the most time on the programming assessment. This may mean that they did not learn the material as deeply as the Generate-Context Transfer group or the Given-Context Transfer group.

The final group, the Generate-Context Transfer group behaved as expected related to previous research findings. They took the most amount of time while learning but also had among the best performance on the assessment tasks. It should be noted, however, that this group also had the most attrition amongst the groups (from an original number of 11 down to only 6 who completed the post-test). It may be that those who persisted until the end of the study are characteristically different than those who did not, so these results should be interpreted cautiously.

We collected and analyzed cognitive load component measurements using [18], however the differences were not statistically significant. No group reported significantly higher cognitive load, even though we know that generating subgoal labels requires more thought and mental effort than just reading and understanding given subgoal labels. Likewise, contextual transfer had no effect on the cognitive load component measures. This may be explained because all conditions had the same amount of intrinsic load, or because the measurement tool is not sensitive enough to capture the differences in this instance. This is definitely an area that needs further exploration.

6. CONCLUSION

The conclusion of these experiments is the colloquial expression, "There ain't no such thing as a free lunch." There are trade-offs in the design of learning opportunities. More time spent in learning does result in better performance later: Time on task matters for learning. If you spend less time on learning, students can still perform well on assessments. They will have to spend more time on the assessments to do as well.

Our findings continue to support the belief that subgoal labeling does improve learning. Generating those labels takes more time, and more time does result in more learning. However, being given labels may result in about the same amount of learning. In terms of efficiency (the most learning for the least amount of resources, including time), being given the subgoal labels may be the best option.

Having a context shift, from the example to the practice problem, has an interaction with subgoal labels in a way that is hard to explain. The best performance on the assessments comes from giving students the subgoal labels and requiring contextual transfer, or having students generate the subgoal labels but using only isomorphic transfer from example to practice.

The problem is that cognitive load in computer science is high due to the intrinsic nature of the material. Students have to keep in mind variables, their roles, their own process in problem-solving, and the process of the computer that they are attempting to model and control. While generating subgoal labels intuitively should lead to greater learning, there comes a point (e.g., if we add in contextual transfer) when the cognitive load of tracking everything makes learning difficult.

The intrinsic cognitive load of computer science is related to the languages we use (e.g., the fact that textual languages require *naming* of data and process, and we must remember and use those names) and the challenge of understanding and controlling a computational agent other than ourselves. That kind of problem does not occur frequently in science, mathematics, and engineering – but occurs from the very first classes in computer science. Because of this intrinsic load and the differences from other disciplines, we need to conduct replication studies. We cannot simply assume that findings from these other disciplines will predict learning in computer science.

The interventions for this study are strongly grounded in instructional design theory, and they were also applied in an authentic educational setting with an authentic educational task. Therefore, we expect that the internal and external validity of this work is high. However, because this study is the first experiment to use this type of task and because the results were different than previous work with subgoal labels, research to replicate these results is needed to ensure the validity of this work.

7. ACKNOWLEDGMENTS

We would like to thank the students who participated in the study and their instructors who graciously gave us the time. We also thank the anonymous reviewers who supplied comments which improved this paper.

This work is funded in part by the National Science Foundation under grant 1138378. Any opinions, findings, and conclusions or recommendations expressed in this material are those of the authors and do not necessarily reflect the views of the NSF.

8. REFERENCES

[1] Atkinson, R.K., Catrambone, R., and Merrill, M.M., 2003. Aiding Transfer in Statistics: Examining the Use of Conceptually Oriented Equations and Elaborations During Subgoal Learning. *Journal of Educational Psychology*. 95, 4 (2003), 762.

[2] Atkinson, R.K., Derry, S., Renkl, A., and Wortham, D., 2000. Learning from examples: Instructional principles from the worked examples research. *Review of educational research*. 70, 2 (2000), 181–214.

[3] Atkinson, R.K. 2002. Optimizing learning from examples using animated pedagogical agents. *Journal of Educational Psychology*. 94, 2 (2002), 416.

[4] Atkinson, R.K. and Derry, S.J. 2000. Computer-based examples designed to encourage optimal example processing: A study examining the impact of sequentially presented, subgoal-oriented worked examples. (2000).

[5] Bjork, R.A. 1994. Memory and metamemory considerations in the training of human beings. *Metacognition: Knowing about Knowing*. MIT Press.

[6] Bransford, J.D., Brown, A., and Cocking, R.R., 2000. *How People Learn: Brain, Mind, Experience, and School*. National Academy Press.

[7] Catrambone, R. 1995. Aiding subgoal learning: Effects on transfer. *Journal of educational psychology*. 87, 1 (1995), 5.

[8] Catrambone, R. 1996. Generalizing solution procedures learned from examples. *Journal of Experimental Psychology: Learning, Memory, and Cognition; Journal of Experimental Psychology: Learning, Memory, and Cognition*. 22, 4 (1996), 1020.

[9] Catrambone, R. 1994. Improving examples to improve transfer to novel problems. *Memory & Cognition*. 22, 5 (1994), 606–615.

[10] Catrambone, R. 1998. The subgoal learning model: Creating better examples so that students can solve novel problems. *Journal of Experimental Psychology: General*. 127, 4 (1998), 355.

[11] Chi, M.T., Bassok, M., Lewis, M.W., Reimann, P., and Glaser, R., 1989. Self-explanations: How students study and use examples in learning to solve problems. *Cognitive science*. 13, 2 (1989), 145–182.

[12] Eiriksdottir, E. and Catrambone, R. 2011. Procedural instructions, principles, and examples how to structure instructions for procedural tasks to enhance performance, learning, and transfer. *Human Factors: The Journal of the Human Factors and Ergonomics Society*. 53, 6 (2011), 749–770.

[13] Leppink, J, Paas, F., van der Vleuten, C., van Gog, T., and van Merriënboer, J., 2013. Development of an instrument for measuring different types of cognitive load. *Behavior research methods*. 45, 4 (2013), 1058–1072.

[14] Leppink, J., Paas, F., van Gog, T., van der Vleuten, C., and van Merriënboer, J., 2014. Effects of pairs of problems and examples on task performance and different types of cognitive load. *Learning and Instruction*. 30, (2014), 32–42.

[15] Margulieux, L.E., Guzdial, M., and Catrambone, R., 2012. Subgoal-labeled instructional material improves performance and transfer in learning to develop mobile applications. *Proceedings of the ninth annual international conference on International computing education research* (2012), 71–78.

[16] Margulieux, L.E. and Catrambone, R. 2014. Improving problem solving performance in computer-based learning environments through subgoal labels. *Proceedings of the first ACM conference on Learning@ scale conference* (2014), 149–150.

[17] Van Merriënboer, J.J. and Sweller, J. 2005. Cognitive load theory and complex learning: Recent developments and future directions. *Educational psychology review*. 17, 2 (2005), 147–177.

[18] Morrison, B.B., Dorn, B., and Guzdial, M., 2014. Measuring cognitive load in introductory CS: adaptation of an instrument. *Proceedings of the tenth annual conference on International computing education research* (2014), 131–138.

[19] Palmiter, S. and Elkerton, J. 1993. Animated demonstrations for learning procedural computer-based tasks. *Human-Computer Interaction*. 8, 3 (1993), 193–216.

[20] Plass, J.L., Moreno, R., and Brünken, R., 2010. *Cognitive load theory*. Cambridge University Press.

[21] Renkl, A. and Atkinson, R.K. 2002. Learning from examples: Fostering self-explanations in computer-based learning environments. *Interactive learning environments*. 10, 2 (2002), 105–119.

[22] Renkl, A. and Atkinson, R.K. 2003. Structuring the transition from example study to problem solving in cognitive skill acquisition: A cognitive load perspective. *Educational psychologist*. 38, 1 (2003), 15–22.

[23] Spanjers, I.A., van Gog, T., van Merriënboer, J., 2012. Segmentation of worked examples: Effects on cognitive load and learning. *Applied Cognitive Psychology*. 26, 3 (2012), 352–358.

[24] Sweller, J., van Marriënboer, J., Paas, F., 1998. Cognitive architecture and instructional design. *Educational psychology review*. 10, 3 (1998), 251–296.

[25] Sweller, J., Ayres, P., and Kalyuga, S., 2011. *Cognitive load theory*. Springer.

[26] Sweller, J. 2010. Element interactivity and intrinsic, extraneous, and germane cognitive load. *Educational psychology review*. 22, 2 (2010), 123–138.

[27] Tew, A.E. and Guzdial, M., 2011. The FCS1: a language independent assessment of CS1 knowledge. *Proceedings of the 42nd ACM technical symposium on Computer science education* (2011), 111–116.

[28] van Gog, T. and Paas, F., 2012. Cognitive Load Measurement. *Encyclopedia of the Sciences of Learning*. Springer.

Boys' Needlework: Understanding Gendered and Indigenous Perspectives on Computing and Crafting with Electronic Textiles

Kristin A. Searle
University of Pennsylvania
3700 Walnut St.
Philadelphia, PA 19104
searle@gse.upenn.edu

Yasmin B. Kafai
University of Pennsylvania
3700 Walnut St.
Philadelphia, PA 19104
kafai@upenn.edu

ABSTRACT

We draw attention to the intersection of race/ethnicity and gender in computing education by examining the experiences of ten American Indian boys (12-14 years old) who participated in introductory computing activities with electronic textiles. To date, the use of electronic textiles (e-textiles) materials in introductory computing activities have been shown to be particularly appealing to girls and women because they combine craft, circuitry, and computing. We hypothesized that e-textiles would be appealing to American Indian boys because of a strong community-based craft tradition linked to heritage cultural practices. In order to understand boys' perspectives on learning computing through making culturally-relevant e-textiles artifacts, we analyzed boys' completed artifacts as documented in photographs and code screenshots, their design practices as documented in daily field notes and video logs of classroom sessions, and their reflections from interviews guided by the following research questions: (1) How did American Indian boys initially engage with e-textiles materials? (2) How did boys' computational perspectives develop through the process of making and programming their own e-textiles artifacts? Our findings highlight the importance of connecting to larger community value systems as a context for doing computing, the importance of allowing space for youth to make decisions within the constraints of the design task, and the value of tangible e-textiles artifacts in providing linkages between home and school spaces. We connect our work to other efforts to engage racial and ethnic minority students in computing and discuss the implications of our work for computer science educators designing computing curricula for increasingly diverse groups of students, especially as pertains to the emerging field of culturally responsive computing.

Categories and Subject Descriptors

K.3.0 [Computers and Education]: General

General Terms

Human Factors

Keywords

Electronic textiles; Indigenous peoples; American Indian/Alaska Native; gender; K-12; broadening participation in computing

1. INTRODUCTION

Most of the conversations about broadening participation in computing have focused on gendered differences in participation [11, 40]. Much less attention has been paid to the equally important but far more complicated intersections of gender with race and ethnicity [41]. Discussions around broadening participation often assume that boys and men are dominant in computing circles, effectively erasing the experiences of males from non-dominant racial and ethnic groups within a given context. In the United States, for instance, African American and Latino men each represent just 6% of the computing workforce and American Indian/Alaska Native men represent less that 2% of the computing workforce [46]. The situation is equally troubling when we examine the participation of minorities in computing activities in K-12 settings [16, 34]. In this paper, we want to draw attention to the intersection of race/ethnicity and gender by examining the experiences of a middle school class of American Indian boys who participated in an introductory computing activity with electronic textiles. While American Indian boys represent a small subset of the U.S. population, we believe their experiences provide insight into engaging non-dominant racial and ethnic groups in computing across a multiplicity of contexts. In particular, this paper has implications for engaging Indigenous populations throughout the world [17], especially those with strong heritage craft traditions [29].

The use of electronic textiles (e-textiles) materials in introductory computing activities has been shown to be particularly appealing to girls and women because of their hybrid nature and the strong connection to craft [7]. E-textiles construction kits like the LilyPad Arduino kit [8], consist of a small, sewable microcontroller and a variety of sensors and actuators. These sewable, electronic components are affixed to fabric and connected to one another using conductive thread. The completed circuit is then hooked up to a computer via a USB cable and programmed, resulting in a small, wearable computer. We hypothesized that, in spite of gendered cultural histories surrounding craft practices as "women's work" [48], e-textiles would appeal to American Indian boys because of a strong community-based craft tradition linked to heritage cultural practices and Indigenous Knowledge Systems [5, 13, 27]. The community where the research took place is known for its pottery and basketry. Though few individuals in the community still practice these crafts, the designs are finding new homes in graffiti art and in apparel, such as the desert collection designed for Nike by community-member Dwayne Manuel [37]. These shifts are an important reminder that culture has a fixed, enduring quality but is also adaptable over time. It is this adaptable nature of cultural craft practices that we drew upon in designing a culturally responsive, introductory computing activity employing e-textiles.

We focus on the intersections of gender, craft, computing, and culture from boys' (rather than girls') perspectives. We examine the experiences of ten American Indian boys (12-14 years) engaged in a three-week, culturally responsive e-textiles unit as part of their Native Studies class. In order to understand boys' perspectives on learning computing through making culturally-relevant e-textiles artifacts, we analyzed their completed artifacts as documented in photographs and code screenshots, their design practices as documented in daily field notes and video logs of classroom sessions, and their reflections from interviews guided by the following research questions: (1) How did boys initially engage with e-textiles materials? (2) How did boys' computational perspectives develop through the process of making and programming their own e-textiles artifacts? Drawing upon three case studies from the larger data set, our findings highlight the importance of connecting to larger community value systems as a context for doing computing, the importance of allowing space for youth to make decisions within the constraints of the design task, and the value of tangible e-textiles artifacts in providing linkages between home and school spaces. In our discussion, we highlight the broader implications of our work for computer science educators who are designing computing curricula for increasingly diverse groups of students, especially as pertains to the emerging field of culturally responsive computing.

2. BACKGROUND

Our focus on American Indian boys' perspectives on computing contributes to larger efforts to broaden participation. Recent research suggests that, more significant than a "participation gap" may be actually be the "identity gap" where young men of color struggle to reconcile their ethnic and academic identities [45] and are unable to see themselves taking on the identity of a "scientist" [52]. One potential solution is to develop computing activities with a strong connection to boys' multiple identities, including their ethnic identities [16, 28] Here culturally responsive approaches have been known to successfully bridge the "identity gap" by connecting the cultural practices of particular groups to mathematical and computational principles [20].

One of the best-known examples of culturally responsive computing is the Culturally Situated Design Tool, designed by Eglash and his colleagues [19] where, for instance, Shoshone beadwork is mapped onto a Cartesian coordinate system and learners design on a Virtual Bead Loom. Another example is the game design curriculum created by Lameman and her colleagues [39] for use with First Nations students in Canada that was based on traditional storytelling practices. Within each of these approaches, there is some level of cultural affirmation and/or critique built into either the tools themselves or the curricula [21]. This means that when youth engage in culturally responsive computing activities, they are engaging in identity work and develop what Eglash & Bennett [18] have called "design agency," the practice of working out one's identity within the technical constraints of the design tool and the environmental constraints of the space and place where the activity is situated.

In our work, we are building on these important ideas around culture and identity for making computing accessible and extending them into culturally responsive open design [34]. Culturally responsive open design connects community cultural practices with more open-ended design tools whose reach extends beyond the screen. Culturally responsive open design with e-textiles materials also creates a rich space for exploring the intersections of gender and race/ethnicity in computing by incorporating the distinct, gendered cultural histories associated with craft and engineering practices [47]. Rather than attempting to "unlock" the existing clubhouse of computing [39] with its focus on games and robotics, learning with e-textiles introduces computing through arts, crafting, and textiles. By design, e-textiles materials draw upon a hybrid foundation in crafting, engineering, and computing. Through this purposeful mashup of old and new materials and high and low technologies, e-textiles challenge and critique distinct cultural and epistemological foundations, including the strongly gendered (and often racialized and colonized) histories of crafting [48] circuitry design [44] computing [22], and technology writ-large [2, 47].

Like many other introductory computing curricula that provide a context for computing [3, 4, 15, 24, 36, 42, 49, 54] engaging learners with e-textiles materials develops computational thinking skills [53]. Specifically, we draw upon Brennan and Resnick's [6] framework for studying and assessing computational thinking, which encompasses learning computational concepts (sequences, loops, etc.), engaging with computational practices (remixing, for instance), and developing computational perspectives. Computational perspectives, or worldviews that designers develop as they engage in digital media [33], connect to a core concern in broadening CS participation that focuses on learners' perceptions of computing, where they see applications for computing, and how they see themselves within the field and future careers. When researchers ask about students' perceptions of computing [14, 55], they often hear an assortment of statements such as "being boring or tedious," "only for smart students," "antisocial," or "lacking creativity." The classroom implementation we conducted affords us the opportunity to re-examine these perceptions because of the particular positioning of e-textiles within a larger computing culture.

Brennan and Resnick [6] identified three types of common computational perspectives that learners developed through programming interactive digital media: (1) expressing, (2) connecting, and (3) questioning. Expressing refers to the ability to create something that allows for self-expression through computation. Connecting emphasizes the value of making something computationally in collaboration with others and for an authentic audience (as opposed to just a teacher who will evaluate the assignment). Questioning highlights learners' abilities to ask questions of and with technology. The development of these perspectives about computation is important because it marks a shift from viewing technology as something to be consumed to something one can harness as a tool for self-expression, relationship building, and democratic participation [30]. In Indigenous communities where electronic technologies are often seen as a threat to the persistence of heritage craft practices, Native languages, and other aspects of culture, the development of computational perspectives is an especially rich, but contentious, space for exploration.

3. METHODS

3.1 Participants

The participants in our study were ten eighth grade American Indian boys (12-14 years) who attended a charter school on tribal lands located just outside of Phoenix, Arizona. We call the school Eagle High School (a pseudonym). The boys participated in a three-week e-textiles unit as the culminating project in an elective, gender- segregated Native Studies class. The students reflected the demographic of the school, which was almost entirely American Indian (99%), with slightly less than half of students (46%) eligible for free or reduced lunch. Prior exposure to computing was limited to general technology use. Most of the participants had cell phones or tablets and played video games for entertainment but, like youth elsewhere, they had little sense of what computing entailed and who could or could not do it.

3.2 E-Textile Design

The e-textile design activity described here focused on making "human sensor" sweatshirts [32] using the LilyPad Arduino construction kit (see Figure 1) [8]. This kit enables novice makers to embed electronic components into textiles and consists of a sewable, programmable microcontroller and a variety of sewable sensors (e.g., temperature sensor, accelerometer) and actuators (e.g., LED lights, sound buzzers). Sensors and actuators are sewn to ports (holes that can be sewn through) on the LilyPad using conductive thread, which acts like the wire in more traditional electronics projects, and is knotted to secure a particular connection. When these components are sewn together using conductive thread and then programmed, they become a small, wearable, student-built computer. In order to program the LilyPad Arduino, either the Arduino or Modkit [43] development environments were used.

Figure 1: LilyPad Arduino kit

The activity was designed in consultation with the Native Studies classroom teacher and the community's Cultural Resources Department. After a quarter spent talking about community stories and their connections to place, students made e-textile designs connected to the elements (fire, water, earth, etc.) and to places that were of significance to local Indigenous communities. One goal was that making a light up, wearable versions of natural phenomena and significant local places would reinforce what students had already learned about living in the desert environment through the telling of community stories and perhaps spark larger community-level conversations when students took their projects home. Another goal was that students would learn something about computation and its connections to culture through the process of designing and making e-textiles. Students were asked to design and make e-textile patches comprised of a culturally-relevant aesthetic design, a LilyPad Arduino, at least two LED lights, and two metal snaps attached to the negative ground and an analog port respectively. These snaps connected to snaps on hooded sweatshirts that were pre-"wired" with conductive fabric patches on the cuffs that connected to metal snaps on the front of the sweatshirt. When a student's e-textile patch was connected to the snaps on the sweatshirt, it created a "human sensor" e-textile project (see Figure 2). In a "human sensor" project, the two conductive fabric patches on the cuffs of the sweatshirt function as a sensor to measure resistance from the human body when touched simultaneously. This adds a dimension of computational complexity to students' e-textile projects. In a longer workshop, students would have "wired" the hoodies themselves but, given the time constraints, the conductive fabric patches and conductive fabric "wiring" that connected the cuffs to the snaps and, by extension, to the LilyPad Arduino were pre-ironed. In addition to the added degree of computational complexity, if the human sensing components of the hoodies are wired identically, the sweatshirt wearers can then be united in a circle and all of the e-textile designs should light up, highlighting the importance of relationships between individuals and between elements within an ecosystem.

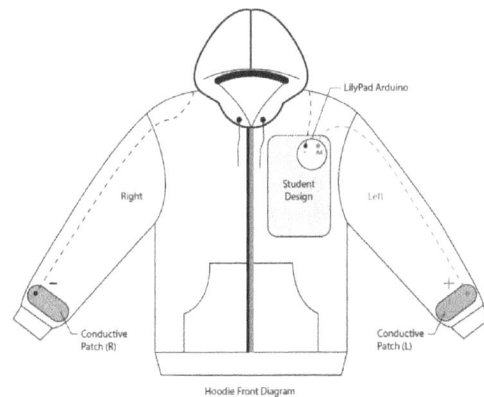

Figure 2: Human Sensor Hoodie

3.3 Native Studies E-Textile Unit

The class took place over three weeks, meeting daily for about an hour. In addition to daily classroom sessions during the three-week unit, course instructors also held lunchtime sessions where students could bring their lunch and work on their projects. These sessions were not mandatory but provided an important space for students to engage in making without some of the physical and behavioral constraints of the classroom, opening up spaces for peer-to-peer mentoring and relationship building. The first week provided students with the necessary background knowledge in crafting, circuits and coding to enable them to design and make their own "human sensing" hoodies, including the sewing of simple circuits on scrap felt. Sample projects were shown to help students conceptualize their own e-textiles projects. In the second week, each student chose a design from one of ten templates based on a list we received from the classroom teacher. Designs included several forms of water (raindrops, river, snowflake), fire, wind, lightning, sun, moon, stars, and earth in the form of several locally significant mountains. Students then drew a circuitry blueprint to determine where to place the LilyPad, how to orient the LED lights, and how to create the circuitry in such a way as to minimize potential short circuits created by crossing wires. They then moved on to crafting their designs out of felt and affixing the electronic components. Because students' sewing abilities varied greatly, instructors provided instruction on an as-needed basis and focused primarily on the ways in which sewing with conductive thread differs from sewing with regular, non-conductive thread. In the third week, students turned to coding their e-textiles projects. Due to limited computer access and project completion, students learned to setup up their boards and write simple code in Modkit while working with one of the course instructors on an individual basis or in small groups of two to three students. In the third week, students also explored multiple definitions of technology, with a goal of developing counter-narratives about technology in Indigenous communities.

To give you a sense of what the boys made, we have included a table with samples of some of the boys' e-textiles projects (see Table 1). Included in the table is a circuitry diagram, completed design, and an explanation of the project's code for each featured design. With one exception, boys' designs stuck closely to the templates they were provided with, though creative license was taken with the colors of the designs and the lights. Designs ranged in complexity from having two to nine LED lights connected to the LilyPad microcontroller, with most boys choosing to connect either two (4/10) or three (4/10) lights.

Table 1: Boys' E-Textile Designs

Pedro	Sammy	Lance	Harry
If 2 conductive patches are touched, both LEDs blink simultaneously. Else, each LED blink individually in an alternating sequence.	If 2 conductive patches are touched, 3 LEDs blink simultaneously. Else, each LED blinks individually in an alternating sequence.	If 2 conductive patches are touched, 3 LEDs stay on. Else, all 3 LEDs blink in rapid sequence.	If 2 conductive patches are touched. 3 LEDs blink in rapid sequence. Else, all 3 LEDs stay on.

3.4 Data Collection and Analysis

Daily field notes documented what happened in the class each day, focusing on what students were learning and what they were struggling with in designing and crafting with e-textiles. We also collected students' circuitry blueprints, daily photographs of students' design progress, and code screenshots. Most classroom sessions were video recorded (depending on the permission of the classroom teacher and students) and then logged, meaning that the actions seen in the video were reduced to a minute-by-minute written log of classroom activities. Sections of interest were returned to and fully transcribed as a later stage of analysis. Six students also participated in final reflective interviews, which were video recorded and lasted around twenty minutes. Topics included where students saw connections between the cultural content of Native Studies and the e-textiles unit, what aspects of their projects they were most proud of, what aspects of their projects were the most challenging, and how other individuals (family and friends) responded to their projects. Interviews were then transcribed.

We used a multi-faceted identity lens [23, 52] to understand how the heritage craft element of e-textiles might be leveraged to attract boys from non-dominant backgrounds to learn computing and to address the identity gap. Analysis of boys' e-textiles artifacts and field notes allowed us to better understand their practices and participation in the classroom community. A portfolio was created for each student that combined his initial circuitry blueprint, photographs of his in-process and completed project, and any available iterations of the code for his project. Field notes and interview transcripts were initially coded using a two-step open coding process [10] allowing themes to emerge from the data and then be refined. Salient codes included the gendered nature of craft and boys' uncertainty about participating in craft practices, design agency, and the importance of a culturally-connected assignment. This analysis of field notes helped us to better understand boys' practices during the Native Studies e-textiles unit and analysis of interviews allowed us to better understand boys' perspectives on learning computing through e-textiles activities. Because the codes that emerged from the open coding closely mirrored Brennan and Resnick's [6] conceptualization of computational frameworks, we chose to draw upon their framework because of its familiarity to a larger computing audience.

4. FINDINGS

Like other youth we have worked with in many different contexts, the American Indian boys whose experiences and perspectives are the focus of this paper initially had vague or non-existent ideas about what computing involved. Over the course of the e-textiles unit, however, we saw students' perspectives on computing change as they realized that computing could be used as a medium for self-expression and creativity, as a way to connect with others, and as a way of critically engaging in the world by asking questions of technology and using technology to ask questions. Each of the case studies that follows highlights one of the computational perspectives outlined by Brennan and Resnick [6] as they played out in an e-textiles unit within a gender segregated Native Studies class.

4.1 Computational Perspectives: *Expressing*

Though a member of the community, Sammy had previously attended a non-reservation public school and was new to Eagle High School. When the e-textiles unit began, Sammy was nervous about crafting, especially using the iron (FN, 9/24/13, p.5). He had some previous experience doing beadwork in his Native Arts class at school but reported that, "it's not the same" (int., 10/22/13, p.8). Sammy also returned to school after learning about the project and reported that his mom had said sewing was for ladies. When asked what he thought in response, he replied, "I think it doesn't matter" (FN, 9/19/13, p.2). Indeed, Sammy would later reflect that "the threading" was one of the most challenging aspects of the project.

Judging by the pace at which he worked and his dedication to the project, Sammy embraced the hybrid dimensions of the project. While he initially wanted to work on a design based on one of the community's sacred mountains, another student beat him to it and Sammy instead chose to create an e-textile design around lightning "because I wanted to be like Shazam or Captain Marvel, Captain Marvel from DC Comics" (int., 10/22/13, p.5). As Sammy delved into the crafting process, he continued to add elements to the project that married his initial attraction to the design because of a particular superhero with the cultural context of the assignment and the Native Studies class more broadly. The lightning design Sammy received only had one lightning bolt, to which Sammy decided to add a gray-blue thunder cloud, after very carefully considering the available colors (FN, 9/24/13, p.5). Initially, the addition of the cloud was meant to illustrate an important relationship in the natural world (lightning and thunder clouds "just go together," in Sammy's words), but also to cover up the LilyPad so it wouldn't be visible or, as Sammy put it, "the LilyPad wasn't going to just sit there on the sweatshirt" (int., 10/22/13, p.6). As his design evolved, however, Sammy decided to sew lights along the length of the lightning bolt and use the cloud as an anchor for his LilyPad because it made the sewing easier. Sammy asked questions at every step of the project as to avoid mistakes, so he managed to sew a functional project with relative ease.

When it came time to program his project, Sammy was very clear about the aesthetic he wanted to achieve through programming his lightning bolt. During an extended classroom session, Sammy sat with one of the instructors (Searle) and another student who was waiting to program his project at the back of the room:

> Instructor: Okay, so, what do you want it to do when your patches are touched?
>
> Sammy: I want, because, you know, you know how lightning, it goes chung, chung, chung [uses hands to show how lightning flashes once and then spreads out across the sky].
>
> Instructor: Okay, that's what I thought.
>
> Sammy: You know, how lightning flashes once together and then flashes twice.
>
> Instructor: [using right hand to demonstrate a blinking pattern] Okay, so, you want them all to blink together once or you want it to be, like, really quick down the line? So, it's like, ch-chung [uses right hand to demonstrate lightning spreading out].
>
> Sammy: [Repeats motion with his own hand, seemingly testing it out for fit] Yeah. Or...
>
> Instructor: Let's try that.
>
> Sammy: And see how it looks (video log, 10/04/13, p. 2).

Working together, Sammy and the instructor created two different programming scenarios for the lights to flash, one in which all three lights flashed at once and another where they flashed one at a time. For Sammy, like many other novice e-textile designers, there was an added degree of personalization to be found in altering the delay function, which controls how long lights stay on and off, creating a blinking or flashing effect. As the proposed codes got closer to Sammy's desired aesthetic, he started exclaiming, "Oh! That's cool! Yeah, that's how I want them all to go," and repeatedly touched the cuffs of his sweatshirt together to see the desired effect play out with subtle changes. Ultimately, Sammy preferred having all of the lights flash at once, with one added flourish. He added an extra long delay after the lights flashed to emphasize the idea of lightning striking. Then he decided to use the other code that had been developed, with each light blinking individually in rapid sequence, to meet the second condition of his project, when the conductive fabric patches were not touching. In his experiences making an e-textile project and

programming it, Sammy found a new venue for creativity and self-expression at school while also being challenged academically. Asked to reflect on what he had learned at the end of the unit, Sammy replied, "Negative and positive stuff. You know, electronic stuff. The good stuff" (int., 10/22/13, p.5). Through this process, Sammy not only learned key computational concepts and practices but also developed a sense of computing as something that can be used for personal expression. Indeed, the idea of using one's e-textiles project as a means of personal expression was a theme in all of the interviews we conducted, with each boy choosing to highlight particular aspects of his identity through the design he chose to make, the colors used, and how the lights blinked when the patches were and were not touched.

4.2 Computational Perspectives: *Connecting*

Harry was a quiet but thoughtful student who participated in one of the e-textiles pilot projects but initially struggled with sewing and circuitry concepts. For his Native Studies project, Harry chose to make a fire design because of multiple personal connections. Fire reminded him of "sitting by a fire or camping" (int., 11/18/13, p.3) and also helping his grandmother to cook outside, a practice still observed by many community elders. Harry decided to craft his design out of multiple colors of felt because "that's how I really see flames, like, red, yellow, orange, dark red. That's what I think of flames" (int., 11/18/13, p.2). For Harry, this design phase of the project was especially important. Not only was he interested in creating a realistic representation of fire, the process also provided another way to connect with his grandmother. In a final reflective interview, Harry reported that his grandmother "always sews," making handkerchiefs, quilts, and shirts for sale. He reported that he often helped her with the designs and enjoyed this aspect of the project. Asked what his grandmother would think of his completed project, Harry replied sheepishly, "She's probably gonna say you can help me now with sewing. I'd just rather do the designs, but I'll help her sometimes" (int., 11/18/13, p.7).

It was probably the opportunity to strengthen his connection with his grandmother, combined with a desire to wear a light up hoodie when attending the Phoenix Light Zoo event with one of his classmates and his young nephew, that propelled Harry through a design process filled with moments of what we might term "productive failure" [35]. When it came to the circuitry for his project, Harry's initial circuitry blueprint showed three lights located about midway up the flame, all connected to a single port on the LilyPad, meaning that they all would have been programmed together. Harry also envisioned the LilyPad and lights being sewn into the back of the design so that the lights could glow through the felt. Because Harry often continued to work through questions rather than asking for help, his circuitry design process was iterative, involving lots of resewing and debugging as the design evolved through a trial and error process. Ultimately, after receiving some sewing help from one of the instructors, Harry ended up with a completed fire e-textile artifact with three LEDs, each wired to its own port. He programmed it so that, when the patches on his hoodie were touched, they blinked in rapid sequence and, when the patches were not touched, the lights stayed on. Asked about how his completed e-textile artifact connected to other things he had been learning in Native Studies, Harry explained, "[My hoodie] kind of does the same thing. Like, stories, they're always connected to something else, so that's how

I know" (int., 11/18/13, p.8). In other words, his human sensor hoodie, which could be linked with other hoodies made by his classmates, provided a computational perspective of connecting with others, much like community stories connected members to one another and to their surroundings.

Like Harry, other boys we interviewed emphasized two ways in which computation allowed them to connect with others. First, the cultural significance of their designs created a point of connection with other community members, especially around conceptions of time as cyclical and the significance of water. As Brian said about his e-textile design, "I chose a river because it flows like energy and whatever's around it can feed off of it and grow" (int., 11/18/13, p.2). Second, students saw points of connection to their immediate family members, with their light up hoodies serving as a marker of academic accomplishment and a source of pride.

4.3 Computational Perspectives: *Questioning*

Jason entered the e-textiles assignment with some trepidation even though his mom was an avid crafter and Jason had watched her sew traditional dresses for his sister and use a glue gun to create holiday decorations. Initially, Jason was concerned that he would be unable to finish his project, saying things like, "I never thought I could do this" or "I didn't think I'd get this far" (Int., 10/18/13, p.5). However, with concentrated help from one of the instructors during a study hall period, Jason was able to make significant progress on his design, a white crescent moon with two red LEDs sewn into it (see figure 3). Jason then programmed his moon, deciding on a blinking pattern where the top and bottom LEDs blinked in rapid succession when the conductive fabric patches were touched and otherwise stayed lit (see figure 4).

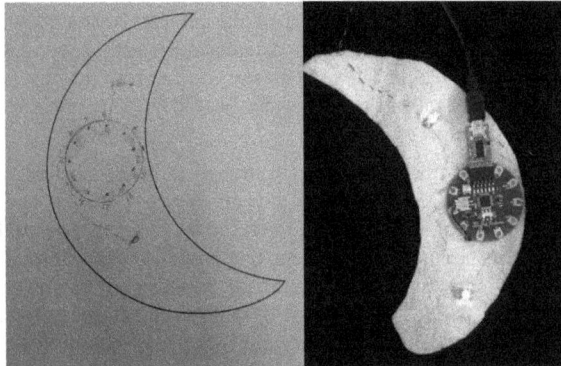

Figure 3: Jason's circuitry blueprint showing the placement of two LEDs and his LilyPad within a moon design and his completed design.

Later, asked to reflect back on the process of making, Jason emphasized his own power to make decisions about and with technology. For instance, he said, "I got excited because we get [sic] to design our own lights and, like, go on the computer and [choose] what speed we liked and I thought that was pretty cool. Honest" (Interview, 2/3/14, p.3). While Jason brought a sense of excitement and empowerment to the conversation when he talked about being able to program the lights in his project to blink, he still hesitated when asked if his project was a Native technology. He replied, "Not really because native technology is, well, we didn't really have technology. I would say ours would be like art, it would be like our technology, and how to tell time and stuff so, yeah, I don't know" (int., 10/21/13, p.9). What's remarkable

about this statement is that Jason's examples are actually powerful examples of technologies, period. But dominant discourses of Western science have created a master narrative about what is and what isn't a technology. As a result, we view Jason's experiences with learning to take a questioning stance towards technology as an important first step that requires further practice and exploration.

By the end of the e-textiles unit, most students could recognize that their e-textiles projects functioned like the circuit boards inside their phones, but they had also developed a more critical stance towards technology. In some cases, students embraced their e-textiles projects as examples of "Native technologies" because they had largely designed the projects themselves. In other cases, students persisted in locating Indigenous technologies in the past and electronic technologies in the present and future. Rather than view these students' experiences as deficient or anti-technological in any way, we wish to use their experiences with questioning technology to highlight the persistence of colonial narratives and the importance of projects like this one in helping students to think about alternative narratives where their own and their communities' experiences 'count' as technological.

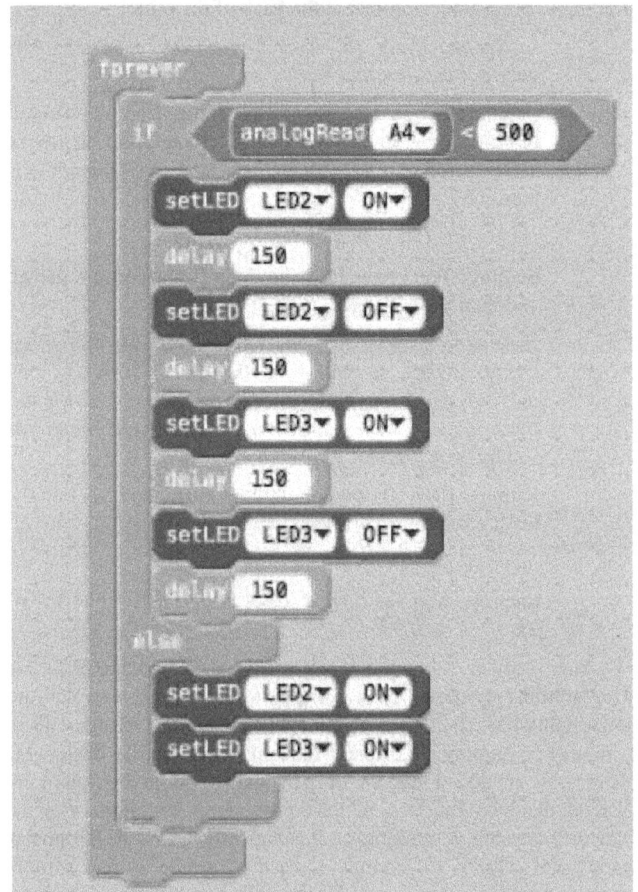

Figure 4: Code for Jason's completed project showing rapid blinking when patches are touched.

5. DISCUSSION

Although there is certainly evidence of American Indian boys learning of computational concepts and practices in our findings, we have chosen to focus more on their developing computational perspectives. Understanding how boys from non-dominant communities think about and connect with computing activities is an important step towards lessening the participation and identity gaps in computing, especially in the space of e-textiles research, which has primarily examined girls' connections to computing. What did it mean for boys to engage with e-textiles materials? How did connections to culture and community come into play? What does it mean for the design of culturally-responsive computing activities?

5.1. Challenges to Gender in Crafting and Computing

The hybrid nature of e-textiles materials [9, 25] has the potential to both reify and challenge existing gendered and cultural norms around who can engage in craft practices and who can engage in computing [1, 31]. We found examples of both in our data, though, as our findings highlight, the culturally responsive aspect of the assignment rapidly pushed boys beyond thinking about craft, circuitry, and computing as gendered and helped them to instead think about how to employ them as tools in service of the particular message they wanted to convey through their designs. Although some boys had initial preconceptions about craft as "women's work," they were also nervous about engaging in craft practices because the skills required were new and often challenging. Of the six boys we interviewed, four of them reported that sewing was the most challenging part of the project. However, as Sammy's experiences with making and programming his lightning bolt e-textile project illustrated, the hybrid nature of e-textiles materials ultimately facilitated boys' engagement with computation as a space for personal expression. Rather than merely working with code on a screen, boys were able to see their code enacted in a tangible way as the lights on their project lit up, such as when Sammy carefully tested multiple codes to achieve the desired effect of lightning flashing.

5.2. Reflections on Computation and Community Connections

In addition to viewing e-textiles materials as tools to be used in the service of expressing themselves computationally, boys also leveraged the hybrid and culturally-connected nature of their e-textiles artifacts to connect with others through e-textiles. For instance, our findings show how Harry's connection to his grandmother and her sewing practices not only strengthened his engagement in the assignment but also reinforced familial ties. In other work [42], we have shown how the tangibility of e-textiles artifacts allowed them to serve as boundary objects [50], which facilitated students' abilities to make connections through computation. More than just extending beyond the screen, students' e-textiles artifacts extended across home and school spaces. Though the boys who we focused on here didn't often tell us about seeking advice from others, we do know that finished projects were often shown off in the lunchroom at school and worn to other classes. Harry's English teacher reported that he had worn his fire-themed design to English class, where they happened to be reading one of the books from *The Hunger Games* trilogy. As researchers think about developing introductory computing activities to engage students from non-dominant backgrounds, we believe that having an artifact-based, tangible element that connects to community practices and can travel across spaces where computers may not be found is key.

Our findings also highlight boys' developing abilities to question with and through computation. While this may seem irrelevant to many computer science educators, we view critique and questioning of our taken-for-granted understandings of technology as an important element of addressing the "identity gap" for American Indian youth and others from non-dominant racial and ethnic backgrounds. Technologies in Indigenous communities have often been defined exclusively by Western science and have been used for colonization [12]. We sought to push back against these dominant narratives by engaging students in thinking about their community's long history of adapting useful technologies and also by exploring some of the ways in which Indigenous communities throughout the world are reclaiming technologies in the service of linguistic and cultural revitalization efforts [2, 26]. However, as Jason's experiences with deciding whether to call his e-textiles project an Indigenous technology or not highlight, narratives about technology as defined by Western science are incredibly powerful and will take repeated efforts to develop strong counter-narratives in which American Indian students (and others from non-dominant communities) recognize the rich technological histories of their own communities.

5.3 Considerations for Culturally-Relevant Computing

Though most computer science educators will likely encounter few American Indian students in their careers, we want to suggest that our work has implications for why we might want to develop computational perspectives amongst a wide range of student populations in the United States and beyond and provides one pathway for doing so through the incorporation of novel, hybrid materials and heritage craft practices. As more and more youth worldwide experience computing not just in schools but also in after school clubs and community makerspaces [38], it is important that educators not only engage the variety of perspectives, experiences, and cultural backgrounds that students bring with them but also recognize that computing must make a contribution back to the community to be valued, whether through developing language learning software or encouraging youth to take up heritage cultural practices. In addition, computing education needs to explicitly address legacies of colonization, racism, and gender disparities. While we drew upon community stories around the elements in crafting the computing activity described here, there is a wide range of heritage and vernacular cultural practices that educators might take up, depending on the student population and the comfort level of community partners.

6. ACKNOWLEDGEMENTS

This work was supported by a collaborative grant (#1150150 and #1150604) from the National Science Foundation to Yasmin Kafai and Bryan Brayboy. Any opinions, findings, and conclusions or recommendations expressed in this paper are those of the authors and do not necessarily reflect the views of the National Science Foundation, the University of Pennsylvania or Arizona State University.

7. REFERENCES

[1] Aal, K., von Rekpwski, T., Yerousis, G., Wulf, V., & Weibert, A. (2015). Bridging (gender-rleated) barriers: A comparative study of intercultural computer clubs. *Proceedings of Gender and Information Technology (Gender IT)*. Philadelphia, PA: USA: ACM.

[2] Bang, M., Marin, A., Faber, L., & Suzokovich, E., III. (2013). Repatriating Indigenous technologies is an urban Indian community. *Urban Education, 48*(5), 705-733.

[3] Baretto, F. & Benitti, V. 2012. Exploring the educational potential of robotics in schools: A systematic review. *Computers & Education, 58*, 978–988.

[4] Biju, S.M. (2013). Taking advantage of Alice to teach programming concepts. *E-Learning and Digital Media, 10*(1), 22-29.

[5] Brayboy, B.M.J. & Maughan, E. (2009). Indigenous knowledges and the story of the bean. *Harvard Educational Review, 79*(1), 1-21.

[6] Brennan, K. & Resnick, M. 2012, April. New frameworks for studying and assessing the development of computational thinking. Paper presented at the annual meeting of the American Educational Research Association, Vancouver, BC, Canada.

[7] Buechley, L. & Hill, B. (2010). LilyPad in the Wild: How hardware's long tail issupporting new engineering and design communities. *Proceedings of Designing Interactive systems (DIS)* (pp. 199-207). Aarhus: Denmark: ACM.

[8] Buechley, L. & Eisenberg, M. (2008). The LilyPad Arduino: Toward wearable engineering for everyone. *IEEE Pervasive Computing, 7*(2), 12-15.

[9] Buechley, L. & Perner-Wilson, H. (2012). Crafting technology: Reimagining the processes, materials, and cultures of electronics. *ACM Transactions on Computer-Human Interaction, 19*(3), 21:1-21:21.

[10] Charmaz, C. (2000). Grounded theory: objectivist and constructivist methods. In N.K. Denzin and Y.S. Lincoln (Eds.), *Handbook of qualitative research* (pp. 509-535). Thousand Oaks, CA: Sage.

[11] Cohoon, J., & Aspray, W. (Eds.). (2006). *Women and information technology*. Cambridge, MA: Massachusetts Institute of Technology Press.

[12] Deloria, V., Deloria, B., Foehner, K., & Scinta, S. (1999). *Spirit & Reason: The Vine Deloria, Jr., Reader*. Fulcrum Publishing.

[13] Dewhurst, M., Keawe, L., MacDowell, M., Okada-Carlson, C.N.K., & Wong, A.K. (2013). Ka ulana 'ana i ka piko (In weaving you begin at the center): Perspectives from a culturally specific approach to arts education. *Harvard Educational Review, 83*(1), 136-146.

[14] Dimond, J. & Guzdial, M. 2008. More than paradoxes to Offer: Exploring motivations to attract women to computing. Georgia Institute of Technology Technical Report. Retrieved on August 27, 2012 from: http://gacomputes.cc.gatech.edu/Members/jpdimond/dimond Paradoxes.pdf

[15] DiSalvo, B. & Bruckman, A. (2011). From interests to values: Computer science is not that difficult but wanting to learn it is. *Communications of the ACM 54*, 8, 27-29.

[16] DiSalvo, B., Guzdial, M., Bruckman, A., & McKlin, T. (2014). Saving face while geeking out: Video game testing as a justification for learning computer science. *Journal of the Learning Sciences, 23*(3), 272-315.

[17] Dyson, L.E., Hendriks, M., & Grant, S. (Eds.). (2007). *Information technology and indigenous people*. Hershey, PA: Information Science Publishing.

[18] Eglash, R. & Bennett, A. (2009). Teaching with hidden capital: Agency in children's explorations of cornrow hairstyles. *Children, Youth, and Environments, 19*(1), 58-73.

[19] Eglash, R., Bennett, A., O'Donnell, C., Jennings, S., & Cintorino, M. (2006). Culturally situated design tools: Ethnocomputing from field site to classroom. *American Anthropologist, 108*(2), 347-362.

[20] Eglash, R., Gilbert, J., & Foster, E. (2013). Broadening participation: Toward culturally responsive computing education. *Communications of the ACM, 56*(7), 33-36.

[21] Eglash, R., Gilbert, J., Taylor, V., & Geier, S.R. (2013). Culturally responsive computing in two urban, after-school contexts: Two approaches. *Urban Education, 48*(5), 629-656.

[22] Ensmenger, N. (2010). *The computer boys take over.* Cambridge, MA: Massachusetts Institute of Technology Press.

[23] Fields, D. & Enyedy, N. (2013). Picking up the mantle of "expert": Assigned roles, assertion of identity, and peer recognition within a programming class. *Mind, Culture, and Activity, 20*(2), 113-131.

[24] Forte, A. & Guzdial, M. 2004. Motivation and nonmajors in computer science: Identifying discrete audiences from introductory courses. *IEEE Transactions on Education, 48* (2), 248-253.

[25] Golsteijn, C., van den Hoven, E., Frolich, D., & Sellen, A. (2014). Hybrid crafting: Towards an integrated practice of crafting with physical and digital components. *Personal and Ubiquitous Computing, (18)*, 593-611.

[26] Hermes, M., Bang, M. and Marin, A. (2012). Designing Indigenous Language Revitalization. *Harvard Educational Review, 82*(3), 381-402.

[27] Hill, S.H. (1997). *Weaving new worlds: Southeastern Cherokee women and their basketry*. Chapel Hill: University of North Carolina Press.

[28] Hull, G. A., Kenney, N. L., Marple, S., & Forsman-Schneider, A. (2006, Spring). Many versions of masculine: An exploration of boys' identity formation through digital storytelling in an afterschool program. *Afterschool Matters, 6*, 1–42.

[29] Jacobs, J. & Zoran, A. (2015). Hybrid practices in the Kalahari: Design collaboration through digital tools and hunter-gatherer craft. *Proceedings of CHI 2015* (pp. 619-628). Seoul, Republic of Korea: ACM.

[30] Kafai, Y. B., & Burke, W. Q. (2014). *Connected code.* Cambridge, MA: Massachusetts Institute of Technology Press.

[31] Kafai, Y. B. Fields, D. A., & Searle, K. A. (2014). Electronic textiles as disruptive designs in schools: Supporting and challenging maker activities for learning. *Harvard Educational Review, 84*(4), 532-556.

[32] Kafai, Y., Lee, E., Searle, K., Kaplan, E., Fields, D., & Lui, D. (2014). A Crafts-Oriented Approach to Computing in High School: Introducing Computational Concepts,

Practices, and Perspectives with Electronic Textiles. *ACM Transactions on Computing Education, 14*(1), 1-20.

[33] Kafai, Y.B. & Peppler, K.A. (2011). Youth, technology, and DIY: Developing participatory competencies in creative media production. *Review of Research in Education, 35*, 89-119.

[34] Kafai, Y.B., Searle, K.A., Martinez, C., & Brayboy, B. (2014). Ethnocomputing with Electronic Textiles: Culturally Responsive Open Design to Broaden Participation in Computing in American Indian Youth and Communities. *SIGCSE '14: Proceedings of the 45th SIGCSE technical symposium on computer science education* (pp. 241-246). Atlanta, GA: Association of Computing Machinery.

[35] Kapur, M. (2014). Comparing learning from productive failure and vicarious failure. *The Journal of the Learning Sciences, 23*(4), 651-677.

[36] Kelleher, C., Pausch, R., and Kiesler, S. (2007). Storytelling Alice Motivates Middle School Girls to Learn Computer Programming. In Proceedings of the SIGCHI Conference on Human Factors in Computing Systems (pp. 1455-1464). San Jose, CA.

[37] Keene, A. (2015, Feb. 4). Nike gets it right; Brand collaborates with O'odham designer. *Indian Country Today.* Retrieved on April 19, 2015 from: http://indiancountrytodaymedianetwork.com/2015/02/04/kee ne-nike-gets-it-right-brand-collaborates-oodham-designer-159028

[38] Kulkarni, Y.R. (2013). Small ideas, big opportunities: FabLab at Vigyan Ahram Oabal, India. In, Walter-Hermann, J. & Büching, C. (Eds.), *FabLab: Of machines, makers and inventors* (pp. 231-237). Bielefeld: Transcript Verlag.

[39] Lameman, B.A., Lewis, J.E., & Fragnito, S. (2010). Skins 1.0: A curriculum for designing games with First Nations youth. In *Proceedings of FuturePlay 2010* (pp. 105-112). Vancouver BC: ACM.

[40] Margolis, J. & Fisher, A. 2002. *Unlocking the clubhouse.* Cambridge, MA: The MIT Press.

[41] Margolis, J.. Estella, R., Goode, J., Holme, J., & Nao, K. 2008. *Stuck in the shallow end: Education, race, and computing.* Cambridge, MA: MIT Press.

[42] Meerbaum-Salant, O., Armoni, M., &Ben-Ari, M. (2010). Learning computer science concepts with Scratch. *Proceedings of ICER 2010* (pp. 69-76). Aarhus, Denmark: ACM.

[43] Millner, A. & Baafi, E. (2011). Modkit: Blending and extending approachable platforms for creating computer programs and interactive objects. In *Proceedings of the 10th*

International Conference on Interaction Design and Children (IDC '11) (pp. 250-253). ACM: Ann Arbor, MI.

[44] Nakamura, L. (2014). Indigenous circuits: Navajo women and the racialization of early electronics manufacture. *American Quartery, 66*(4), 919-941.

[45] Nasir, N.S. (2012). *Racialized Identities.* Stanford, CA: Stanford University Press.

[46] National Science Foundation (2014). Science and Engineering Indicators 2014. Retrieved on February 19, 2015 from http://www.nsf.gov/statistics/seind14/content/etc/nsb1401.pd f.

[47] Oldenziel, R. (1999). Making technology masculine: Men, women, and modern machines in America. Amsterdam: Amsterdam University Press.

[48] Parker, R. (1986/2011). *The subversive stitch.* New York: I. B. Tauris.

[49] Porter, L., Guzdial, M., McDowell, C., & Simon, B. (2013). Success in introductory programming: What works? *Communications of the ACM, 56*(8), 34-36.

[50] Searle, K.A. & Kafai, Y.B. (2015). Culturally responsive making with American Indian girls: Bridging the identity gap in crafting and computing with electronic textiles. To appear in *Proceedings of Gender IT.*

[51] Star, S.L. & Griessemer, J.R. (1989). Institutional ecology, 'translations' and boundary objects: Amateurs and professionals in Berkeley's Museum of Vertebrate Zoology, 1907-39. *Social Studies of Science, 19*(3), 387-420.

[52] Tan, E., Calabrese-Barton, A., Kang, H., & O'Neill, T. (2013). Desiring a career in STEM-related fields: How middle school girls articulate and negotiate identities-in-practice in science. *Journal of Research in Science Teaching, 50*(10), 1143-1179.

[53] Wing, J. (2006). Computational thinking. *Communications of the ACM, 49*, 33-35.

[54] Wolber, D., Abelson, H., Spertus, E. & Looney, L. 2011. *App Inventor: Create your own Android apps.* Sebastopol, CA: O'Reilly Media, Inc.

[55] Yardi, S. & Bruckman, A. 2007. What is computing? Bridging the gap between teenagers' perceptions and graduate students' experiences. *Proceedings of the 3rd International Workshop on Computing Education Research* (pp. 39-50), Atlanta, GA.

How Equity and Inequity Can Emerge in Pair Programming

Colleen M. Lewis
Harvey Mudd College
301 Platt Blvd
Claremont, CA 91711
001-909-607-0443
lewis@cs.hmc.edu

Niral Shah
Michigan State University
116P Erickson Hall
East Lansing, MI 48824
001-517-432-9991
niral@msu.edu

ABSTRACT

Research suggests that pair programming increases student performance and decreases student attrition. However, less is known about the ways in which pair programming can unintentionally lead to inequitable relationships between students. Audio data were collected from pair programming interactions in a sixth-grade computer science enrichment program designed to promote equity. However, even in this context, there were surprising instances of inequity. We measured inequity by documenting the distribution of students' questions, commands, and total talk within four pairs. Analysis revealed that less equitable pairs sought to complete tasks quickly and this may have led to patterns of marginalization and domination. Notably, this focus on speed was not evident in the more equitable pairs. These findings are important for understanding mechanisms of inequity and designing equitable collaboration practices in computer science.

Categories and Subject Descriptors

K.3.2 [Computers and Education]: Computer and Information Science Education—computer science education

General Terms

Human Factors.

Keywords

Equity; diversity; pair programming; collaborative learning

1. INTRODUCTION

Research has shown that pair programming (i.e., having two students share a computer while programming) can increase students' learning, retention in a CS major, and sense of belonging (see [31] for a review of pair programming benefits). While in aggregate these results appear overwhelmingly positive, students and educators have noted instances where pair programming appears to limit one or both of the partners' opportunities to learn. We found that while the pair-programming structures were designed to promote equitable participation [34], in some cases gross inequity emerged within a partnership. In the examples presented here, we attribute the students' goals for completing work as quickly as possible (i.e., speed) as facilitating inequitable interactions.

With student and parent consent, data were collected in a 2012 summer computer science (CS) course taken by academically advanced students entering the sixth grade (i.e., 11-12 years old). Our main data source was audio recordings of pairs of students working together to solve computer-programming problems on a single computer. To triangulate this data source and guide the research focus, we considered additional data including: students' written and electronic work, videos of the class, and ethnographic fieldnotes focused on students' interactions and whole class discussion.

We chose to focus on a single student, "Jason" (pseudonym), and the interactions with his partners because the research and teaching teams perceived Jason's interactions to span from more equitable to less equitable. This variety offered an opportunity to understand the ways in which a single student may engage in very different interactions. Our prior work developed a coding scheme to measure the approximate level of equity within a pair [35]. This coding scheme allowed us to quantify features of collaboration that we argue are indicative of equity or inequity (e.g., the distribution of students' questions, commands, and total talk). Additionally, this coding scheme allowed us to compare across interactions.

Our current analysis focused on four 90-minute audio recordings of Jason. In each of these he is working with a different partner. Our analysis began by applying the coding scheme from our prior work to gauge the relative equity within each of the four dyads. Based upon this coding we were left with the following open question: Why were two of the dyads (Aaron-Jason and Peter-Jason) far less equitable than the other two dyads (Samantha-Jason and Kim-Jason)? We attempted to catalogue differences between the more and less equitable dyads to try to explain the differences.

We identified three central patterns in the less equitable collaborations: sequences of commands interspersed with Jason asking clarifying questions (*command-clarify sequences*); the use of shortcuts (*shortcuts*); and frequent comparison of progress or accomplishment with peers (*peer comparison*).

Across these patterns, we observed a central focus on completing tasks quickly (i.e., speed), which may have produced the patterns of inequity within the Aaron-Jason and Peter-Jason dyads. Upon evaluating a number of alternate hypotheses, we argue that a focus on speed best explains the patterns of inequity that developed. This insight is relevant for understanding how inequity can emerge within pair programming, which was designed to improve students' learning opportunities.

2. THEORETICAL FRAMEWORK

In educational research, the term "equity" has been used to refer to the degree of students' access to the resources needed for learning [10, 29]. Defined in this way, equity can be analyzed at a structural level, in terms of students' access to qualified teachers, material resources like textbooks, and opportunities to take advanced coursework at their school (see [17]). Research in CS education is increasingly focused on ensuring that all students have equitable access to the resources needed for learning [35, 24]. This scholarship recognizes that large segments of the population—particularly women and people of color—remain excluded from opportunities to learn CS [14, 24, 47]. Not only can such inequities have implications for these groups' access to future economic opportunities, but they also raise basic moral concerns about fairness.

Complementary to this structural view of equity, our equity research emphasizes whether all students have opportunities to participate in the everyday social interactions central to learning environments [15, 21]. This approach is grounded in situated [22] and sociocultural perspectives [38, 32, 45] on learning, which illuminate the impact of student participation on student learning. Participation, from a situated and sociocultural perspective, draws attention to the particular ways in which students participate in particular classroom activities, such as working with peers or explaining their ideas. This use of "participation" differs from how the term is often used in conversations about equity (e.g., representation of different groups in CS).

Using participation as a measure of equity, researchers have focused on different dimensions of the collaborative learning setting [7, 8, 15, 21]. Research shows that, while promising, collaborative learning is complex and insufficient to guarantee equity [13, 33].

Ideally, an equitable collaboration would mean that no student disproportionately dominates the conversational floor. For example, when students are brought together in a collaborative learning situation, the teacher's intention is that all of the students will contribute ideas that influence the ultimate outcome of the joint problem solving process. Further, all of the students would feel they have license to critique and build on their group mates' ideas.

Our research is important because it expands considerations of equity beyond issues related to the K-16 "pipeline." That is, while it is important that we continue to strive for equitable representation of all demographic groups in CS, it is also important that we consider how inequities can arise in classroom interactions as students engage in the learning process. In that sense, the present study complements much of the existing literature on equity in CS education—which tends to focus on structural inequities—by considering how equity and inequity operate at the level of everyday activity in learning environments.

3. PREVIOUS RESEARCH

A significant body of research shows that collaborative learning is beneficial for students' learning (see [15]). Researchers have identified a number of conditions and interactional forms conducive to learning in collaborative contexts (for comprehensive reviews, see [6, 40, 15]). The literature has primarily focused on the impact of particular discursive moves, such as asking questions [20], explaining one's thinking [16, 28, 41], and taking up a peer's ideas [2].

Building upon the success of collaborative learning, research has demonstrated the value of a CS-specific form of collaboration: pair programming [19, 23, 25, 26, 31, 46, 18]. Pair programming involves two students sharing a single computer as they work on solving programming problems [46]. Pair programming has demonstrated improved performance outcomes in introductory CS courses [25, 27] and software engineering courses [5, 46]. It has been used to improve student performance [25, 27] and increase retention among students who are underrepresented in CS [26].

Pair programming research has focused on the compatibility of pairs [18]. Researchers frequently recommend pairing students of similar ability to increase compatibility. This pairing strategy has been correlated with increased student satisfaction [11, 36, 37], decreased reports of compatibility problems [39], and increased performance for students in the lowest quartile of performance [4]. Students in our class were not paired with similar ability students. In fact, the current work explores the interactions among four higher performing students (Aaron, Kim, Peter, & Samantha) when paired with a lower performing student (Jason). Our analysis may add complexity to the field's understanding of the nature of interactions between higher and lower performing partners.

The majority of pair programming research has taken place in industry and at the college level; the generalizability of these results to middle school students remains an open question [18]. While less common, researchers focusing on middle-school students have sought to explore the conditions under which pair programming is most effective [23, 12], as well as the dynamics within pair interactions [43, 44]. While it is unclear if research focused on adults generalizes to younger students, the current and prior qualitative research focused on middle-school students [12, 43, 44] illuminates patterns of interaction that are likely applicable to adults.

4. METHODS

4.1 Research Context

Data were collected in a twelve-day summer CS course for students entering the sixth grade. This 36-hour course was offered through a university-sponsored program for academically high-achieving students. The course was taught by the co-authors with assistance from two adult teaching assistants.

In the course, students learned the basics of computer programming using the programming languages Scratch and Logo. Although the course required no prior programming experience, the course was designed to be challenging and to offer significant practice with iteration, and other CS topics. Each of the twelve instructional days typically included lecture, programming tasks sequenced within an online curriculum, and a 15-minute, paper-based assessment. On alternating days students completed programming tasks in pairs using pair programming. The course instructors assigned students to pairs. Every five minutes, students in the course alternated roles of "driver," who operated the keyboard and mouse, and "navigator," who provided verbal direction without touching the keyboard and mouse. These roles were intended to promote equitable collaboration (cf. [30]). Details regarding the goals, structure, and design of the class have been documented in a previous publication [34].

All data presented here are from one of two offerings of the course in the summer of 2012. In that offering, there were 45 students, 23 (51%) of whom were identified as female on course enrollment paperwork.

4.2 Data Collection

With student and parent consent, we collected all of students' hand-written and electronic work as well as audio recordings of students working, video recordings of the class, teachers' notes, and ethnographic fieldnotes. All class time was video recorded and observed by at least one of three ethnographic researchers. After the first class, six students from each course offering were selected as focal students; these students were selected to attempt to maximize the variation between focal students with respect to gender, race, and personality. For each of the remaining eleven class days, a researcher observed each focal student for at least forty-five minutes and audio recorded for approximately 90 minutes.

4.3 Selection of Analytic Focus

Analysis of the data began with a review of the collection of fieldnotes. Three researchers read, discussed, and summarized each of the 98 total fieldnotes. Based upon these preliminary analyses, our analysis narrowed in on one of the 12 focal students, Jason (all names pseudonyms), and his interactions with four partners: Aaron, Peter, Samantha, and Kim. Jason was selected as the primary focus because his interactions varied considerably across each of his pair programming collaborations. Across these pairs, we perceived Jason as both engaged and unengaged and to be positioned as both competent and incompetent. Our analysis sought insight about supporting equitable collaborations through exploring what may have produced this dramatic variety in participation by one student across four dyads.

The goal of our analysis, and the focus of this paper, is to gain insight into what could explain Jason's varied behavior. Since Jason's collaborations appeared to span from equitable to inequitable, understanding these interactions can help illuminate the dynamics of equitable and inequitable collaboration. In our previous work, we developed methods to document equitable and inequitable collaborations [35]. In the current paper, we build upon these methods for describing and documenting equity, or lack of equity, within a pair programming dyad.

4.4 Quantitative Methods for Classifying Equity in Pair Programming

While a goal of the paper was to explain Jason's varied behavior, a prerequisite for this analytical work was verifying that Jason's behavior or, more accurately, his interactions varied. In previous work [35], we used an iterative process of open coding [9] to develop a coding scheme to capture the degree of equity within a pair programming dyad. This coding scheme was applied to transcripts of audio recordings of individual pairs. The coding scheme was designed to provide multiple levels of granularity. In prior work [35], we showed how additional granularity provided insights into the nature of two of Jason's collaborations. In the current paper, we apply the same coding scheme across transcripts of four of Jason's collaborations. The coding scheme served to document the variation in Jason's interactions, which then allowed for further qualitative analysis of differences.

Our coding scheme privileged quantity and content of talk within the dyads and was customized to capture characteristics of pair programming. We developed metrics for measuring equity within a pair programming dyad. Four of these metrics are featured in the current paper and for each, we describe what we measured, our rationale and any tradeoffs we made.

4.4.1 Distribution of Total Talk
Our first of four metrics for a collaboration was the distribution of talk between the pair. Transcripts of students' interactions were divided into turns. Turns indicate a new sentence or topic by one speaker or a new speaker. We assumed that an equitable collaboration would provide both students access to the conversational floor. Prior research has found that participation in social practices is a core element of the learning process [22, 44]. We used a 50-50 split of students' total talk to evaluate a coarse measurement of the equity within the collaboration. Although equal amounts of talk does not guarantee equity, an expectation of a 50-50 split within an equitable collaboration provided a helpful, coarse evaluation of the pairs.

4.4.2 Distribution of Talk within Pair Programming Roles
Our second metric for a collaboration was the distribution of talk when partners were in each pair-programming role. The roles of navigator and driver lend themselves to different interactional patterns. For example, students might expect the navigator to do the majority of the talking. We calculated the percentage of turns each student took when they were acting as driver and when they were acting as navigator. We anticipated that an equitable collaboration would demonstrate mirroring in the distribution of talk. For example, if the distribution of talk was 70-30 when the first partner was navigating, we hope that the distribution of talk with the second partner was navigating would mirror that distribution (i.e., 30-70). While we expect mirroring to be an indication of equity, we could still observe mirroring if the navigator is consistently unengaged (e.g., 5-95 and 95-5) or if the driver has few opportunities to talk (e.g., 95-5 and 5-95).

4.4.3 Distribution of Commands
Our third metric for a collaboration was the distribution of commands within the dyad. We tagged all lines of transcript that included a command. We classified a command as any statement that included a request to perform an action. Indirect requests (e.g., requests starting with "we should") were not classified as commands. The tag of "command" was one of two high-frequency tags that we selected from a large collection of tags that we developed through an open coding of the transcripts (see [35] for additional details).

While the navigator is expected to help direct the actions of the driver, a prevalence of commands may position a partner as incapable of contributing to the collective task. We expect that an equitable collaboration will have a 50-50 distribution of commands. However, it is unlikely that a collaboration is equitable if it is dominated by commands, even if the partners equally issue commands. Therefore, it may be important to identify if a collaboration has minimal commands, which may be additional evidence of an equitable collaboration.

We expect that the tone of commands shapes the impact the command has on equity. A command issued with an urgent tone or dismissive tone may communicate a lack of respect to the partner. Given that tone would be difficult to consistently document and we cannot know the impact on the participant of a particular command, we aggregate all commands and examine commands that appear particularly impactful using qualitative methods. We accept that not all commands will have the same impact to the equity within the collaboration.

4.4.4 Distribution of Questions
Our fourth metric for a collaboration was the distribution of questions within the dyad. We tagged all lines of transcript that included a question. This was the second, high-frequency tag that we decided to highlight from our original, open coding [35]. We assume that questions are an important mechanism for shaping the relative status of the partners. It appears that being asked a question provides that individual with additional status. Therefore by asking a question a student might give their partner status and by being asked a question a student might receive status. We

expect that within an equitable collaboration partners will ask each other questions at similar rates (i.e., a 50-50 distribution). Like commands, not all questions are likely to have the same impact. A student could ask a question with the tone or content indicative of an insult. We accept that including tone could improve our understanding of the impact of these questions, but have chosen to not do so because of difficulty achieving consistency.

4.5 Qualitative Methods

The quantitative methods described above are novel contributions from our prior work [35] and identified gross inequities within the Aaron-Jason and Peter-Jason dyads when compared to the Samantha-Jason and Kim-Jason dyads. However, these quantitative methods provide a relatively narrow lens on the four audio recordings. Their primary contribution in analyzing these data is in identifying a pattern of inequity, which we can then seek to explore and explain using qualitative methods. After completing the quantitative analysis, we employed the following three modes of qualitative analysis for the purpose of exploring and explaining the pattern of inequity in the Aaron-Jason and Peter-Jason dyads.

First, we read, discussed, and re-read transcripts of the four audio recordings. From these readings and discussions we sought to build upon our existing familiarity with the transcripts to identify the salient patterns of interaction within the Aaron-Jason and Peter-Jason dyads that contrasted with patterns within the Samantha-Jason and Kim-Jason dyads. From these reviews, we identified patterns in the Aaron-Jason and Peter-Jason dyads that we referred to as *command-clarify sequences*, *shortcuts*, and *peer-comparison*. Based upon these patterns we attempted to identify representative cases of the patterns.

Second, we looked for commonality across these three patterns of interaction to see larger themes that distinguished the Aaron-Jason and Peter-Jason dyads from the Samantha-Jason and Kim-Jason dyads and from each other. Through this process we identified an overarching focus on speed within the Aaron-Jason and Peter-Jason dyads, which appeared to be absent from the Samantha-Jason and Kim-Jason dyads.

In parallel with other research tasks, we attempted to develop a comprehensive list of plausible alternative hypotheses that could explain the differences between the Aaron-Jason and Peter-Jason dyads and the Samantha-Jason and Kim-Jason dyads. For each of these alternative hypotheses we enumerated what data we would need to confirm or deny the hypothesis and when possible we reviewed these data.

5. QUANTITATIVE RESULTS

Tables 1 and 2 show how talk was distributed between Jason and his four partners measuring the distribution of: total talk, talk within pair programming roles, commands, and questions. The quantitative data suggest patterns of domination and marginalization in Jason's collaborations with Aaron and Peter, and patterns of equity in his collaborations with Samantha and Kim.

Within the Aaron-Jason and Peter-Jason dyads, Jason only contributed roughly one-third of the total turns in both collaborations. Analysis of the distribution of talk within pair programming roles also suggests an inequitable dynamic. Neither dyad exhibited a mirroring pattern when they switch roles. When Jason was the navigator in his partnerships with Aaron and Peter, he contributed only 50% and 45% of turns, respectively. When Aaron or Peter was the navigator, Jason contributed fewer turns

than his partners, 33% and 31%, respectively. That Jason did not contribute more than half of the turns when he was navigating further suggests that he may not have had an opportunity to take up a leadership role. Additionally, Jason asked the majority of the questions and Aaron and Peter issued the majority of commands.

Like the Aaron-Jason and Peter-Jason dyads, the data from the Samantha-Jason and Kim-Jason dyads were nearly identical, but in the opposite direction along most metrics. Unlike the Aaron-Jason and Peter-Jason dyads, overall talk was equally distributed and exhibited a mirroring pattern within pair programming roles. The one area where the Samantha-Jason and Kim-Jason dyads were similar to the Aaron-Jason and Peter-Jason dyads was discursive moves: Samantha and Kim asked fewer questions than Jason. Additionally, Samantha issued disproportionately more commands than Jason.

Overall, the quantitative findings in Tables 1 and 2 reveal a stark contrast with respect to equity across the dyads. What might explain this pattern? In the next section, we consider several hypotheses before discussing our conclusion that a focus on speed produced the inequitable patterns present with the Aaron-Jason and Peter-Jason dyads.

Table 1. In each of the four dyads, the percentage of talk Jason contributed in total (row 1) and when serving as navigator (row 2) and driver (row 3). N indicates the combined turns taken by Jason and his partner.

	Aaron	Samantha	Kim	Peter
Total Talk	37% (N=772)	49% (N=526)	50% (N=419)	35% (N=311)
Jason as Navigator	50% (N=282)	55% (N=274)	55% (N=197)	45% (N=82)
Jason as Driver	33% (N=490)	47% (N=252)	46% (N=222)	31% (N=229)

Table 2. In each of the four dyads, the percentage of commands issued (row 1) and questions asked (row 2) by Jason. N indicates the combined count of commands issued and questions asked by Jason and his partner.

	Aaron	Samantha	Kim	Peter
Commands Issued	7% (N=116)	35% (N=68)	47% (N=44)	18% (N=37)
Questions Asked	63% (N=82)	59% (N=52)	75% (N=66)	65% (N=74)

6. QUALITATIVE RESULTS

6.1 Alternative Hypotheses

The quantitative data presented above suggests a stark difference in interactions when Jason was partnered with Aaron or Peter versus when Jason was partnered with Samantha or Kim. This aligned with our fieldnotes and researchers' initial instincts about the quality of these collaborations. We claim that the focus on speed within the Aaron-Jason and Peter-Jason dyads best explains these differences, but we originally explored many plausible explanations. Below we describe hypotheses that we considered and either evaluated to be less likely or determined that the necessary data was not available.

6.1.1 Hypothesis: Friendship

Jason's more equitable collaborations with Samantha and Kim could be caused by Jason's friendship with them. We expect that friends would be more cordial with each other, which could produce a more equitable interaction. Reviewing the fieldnotes, teacher notes, and research recollection, we have no evidence that Jason was friends with Samantha or Kim outside of class (i.e., spent time together during recess). Based upon this we rejected this hypothesis. In fact, we have evidence that Jason and Peter were friends because they both requested to work together on their final project. However, we have no evidence that Aaron and Jason were friends outside of class, so the opposite hypothesis that friendship produces inequitable interactions is unlikely.

6.1.2 Hypothesis: Task Content

Jason's less equitable collaborations with Aaron and Peter could be caused by the more difficult, and possibly more frustrating, nature of their task. We expect that difficult tasks are more likely to be perceived as high-status and are more likely to result in more active positioning. Additionally, we expect that students engaged in frustrating tasks may engage less equitably because their frustration distracts from the interpersonal demands of collaboration. In contrast, Jason's more equitable collaborations with Samantha and Kim could be caused by the more playful tasks that they were engaged in. We expect that when engaged in cooperative play students would engage more equitably because the task is not high-status and the playful tasks require a partner (e.g., playing tag). Reviewing the curriculum from the day, Samantha and Kim both worked with Jason on making and testing games while Aaron and Peter worked with Jason on non-game tasks that involved creating drawings in Scratch and Logo, respectively. After first inspection, this is a strong hypothesis. Additionally, this aligns with the work of Chizhik [8] and Ames [1]. Chizhik argues that open-ended tasks (e.g., designing a game) produce more equal collaborative participation rates, and Ames [1] argues that "personal relevance and meaningfulness of the content" (p. 263) is associated with students' productive engagement. We expect that the nature of the task plays an important role in shaping students' interaction and equity. We expect that this effect was secondary to the focus on speed because those data present a clear connection between the focus on speed and particular inequitable interactions.

6.1.3 Hypothesis: Difference is Content Knowledge

Jason's less equitable collaborations with Aaron and Peter could be caused by gaps in Jason's content knowledge. We expect that collaborations between students with drastically different content knowledge would tend to be less equitable because the students are unequally prepared to contribute to the collaboration. Reviewing students' performance on daily, paper-based assessments, we found that Aaron, Samantha, Kim, and Peter all had scores among the highest scores in the class and Jason had scores among the lowest in the class. This gap in content knowledge could explain the less equitable collaborations with Aaron and Peter, but does not explain the relatively equitable collaborations with Samantha and Kim.

6.1.4 Hypothesis: Preferences for Collaboration

We expect that students who prefer to work alone, rather than in pairs, might engage in less equitable interaction. Before the class began, students were asked to complete a survey about their prior experience with programming, which included the question: "Do you prefer to work alone or with a partner" Jason indicated that he preferred to work alone, as did Peter. This is surprising given that they chose to work together for the final project when working alone was an option. Additionally, Aaron indicated that he preferred to work with a partner, but did not chose to work with a partner on the final project. We have incomplete information for Samantha and Kim. Samantha wrote in "it depends" and Kim did

not answer the question or any of the other questions on the back page of this survey.

On the 10th day of class, students turned in a homework assignment on which they answered a similar question of whether they prefer to work alone or in a partner. Jason replied "I think I work well with either because I've had experience in both areas." In contrast, Aaron, Samantha, Peter, and Kim reported a preference for working alone. Aaron's and Peter's responses suggested a lack of investment in collaboration. Aaron wrote "Solo. Pair is too slow and drivers switch rapidly." and Peter wrote "Solo because you don't have to explain anything." Both of these responses seem to focus on speed, either directly in Aaron's frustration with going "too slow" or indirectly in Peter's desire to avoid explaining things to his partner. Aaron's and Peter's responses hint at experiences with partners who were not as competent because Aaron described it as "slow" and Peter seemed to want to avoid having to explain concepts to his partner. In contrast, Samantha and Kim preferred to work alone, but their responses hinted at experiences working with a more competent partner. For example, Samantha wrote, "I like solo programming better because I just like doing things on my own, and not having someone constantly interrupting/bossing me around. I just like to keep up with my own pace and have some quiet." Similarly, Kim wrote, "Solo programming, because I feel that I am never confused, and I feel more confident alone."

These survey data provide more questions than answers. However, the written explanations provided by Aaron and Peter strengthens our hypothesis that they were focused on speed, while those provided by Samantha and Kim do not indicate a speed focus.

6.1.5 Hypothesis: Beliefs about Collaboration

Jason's more equitable collaboration with Samantha and Kim could have been caused by Samantha and Kim's prosocial beliefs about how to treat a low-performing partner. There is strong support for this from Samantha and Kim's written responses to questions on the homework assignment that was collected on the 10th day of class. Kim demonstrated a number of prosocial attitudes on this homework. When explaining whether she preferred to be the driver or the navigator she wrote "Driver, because then I can be sure that my partner and I are both contributing the same [amount] to the project." Additionally, when identifying things you should do during pair programming she wrote "Pay attention, answer your partner's question." When identifying what you should not do, she wrote, "Don't do too much. Don't get side tracked." Samantha when identifying things you should not do during pair programming she wrote that you should not "Go ahead of your partner, even if they don't understand, and do all the quizzes yourself. They won't learn anything." Aaron and Peter also replied to these questions, but their responses demonstrate less evidence of a commitment to equal partnership. Aaron wrote that partners should "try to work together" and should not "touch mouse and keyboard as navigator." Peter wrote that partners should "check in with each other" and not "boss each other around."

While Kim and Samantha's answers restated classroom policies, they also included explanations that mention the classroom goals of partners. For example, they echoed the classroom policies by stating that it is important to "pay attention" (Kim), "don't get side tracked" (Kim), and don't "go ahead of your partner" (Samantha). However, they both seemed to provide an explanation for these policies, for example, Kim explains the goal of "both contributing" and Samantha seems focused on her partner's learning opportunities, "they won't learn anything."

These prosocial beliefs may be inseparable from students' maturity or personality. Women are frequently stereotyped as more collaborative, but this stereotype alone provides insufficient explanation for why Jason's collaborations with Samantha and Kim were more equitable.

6.1.6 Summary of Alternative Hypotheses

While there were a number of hypotheses that could not be eliminated, none of the hypotheses described above explained the differences we observed to our satisfaction. Most promising was the hypothesis that Samantha and Kim both held beliefs about engaging equally with a partner. While neither Aaron nor Peter demonstrated these beliefs, the absence of these beliefs seemed to be an insufficient explanation for the similarly inequitable Aaron-Jason and Peter-Jason dyads.

6.2 Qualitative Evidence of a Speed Focus

6.2.1 Command-Clarify Sequences

In our quantitative analysis of the transcripts, we focused on the distribution of commands within the dyad. This was based upon our assumption that commands shape the equity of the collaboration because frequent commands may communicate a lack of respect for the partner being commanded. Below we present examples from the Aaron-Jason and Peter-Jason dyads to demonstrate one of the prevalent patterns, *command-clarify sequences*. We interpret these interactions as evidence of a focus on speed. These interactions additionally suggest a focus on accurately completing the tasks, but in examining the use of shortcuts we see counterexamples showing that the dyads were not focused on accurately completing the tasks.

6.2.1.1 Aaron-Jason: Command-Clarify Sequences

There is ample evidence that Jason and Aaron's interaction was dominated by Aaron issuing Jason commands [35]. Throughout the ninety minute episode Aaron issued 108 commands, which accounted for 23% of all of Aaron's statements during the interaction. We described the dominant pattern as *command-clarify sequences*, in which Aaron issued commands and Jason occasionally clarified content from the commands.

The following transcript shows a prototypical example of the *command-clarify sequence*. Immediately before the following transcript, Jason and Aaron acknowledged that the code did not work as intended. The example below begins with Jason making a suggestion of how they can change the picture they drew to achieve the goal.

105 Jason: Just gotta move - this - over.
106 Aaron: Oh! I got an idea.
107 Aaron: So completely take that second script off.
108 Aaron: From the "Go to y 55 x 55" (referring to a block)
109 Aaron: No.
110 Aaron: No. Yeah - And take - and take that block off the blue block at the bottom.
111 Aaron: Run that script.
112 Jason: This script?
113 Aaron: That - uh - the C. C. (referring to a script that starts when you press the C key)
114 Jason: C?
115 Aaron: Yeah
116 Jason: Okay.
117 Aaron: Okay - then.
118 Aaron: Now, now move the cat away. (pause)

119 Aaron: So now. Select image.

This excerpt serves as an example of the dominant interaction pattern within the Jason-Aaron dyad, which we refer to as command-clarify sequences. In the interaction above, we identified seven of Aaron's statements as commands where he appears to be directly telling Jason what to do (Lines 105, 107, 110, 111, 113, 118, 119). We classified Jason's two questions ("This script?" and "C?" Lines 112 and 114) as clarifications of Aaron's commands. Of Aaron's remaining three statements, two were responses to Jason's questions ("No" and "Yeah" Lines 109 and 115) and the third "Okay - then." appears to be an incomplete command. Although we have not classified these statements as commands, they contribute to the command-clarify pattern.

Most notably these statements (i.e., "No" and "Yeah" Lines 109 and 115) are noteworthy in that Jason's clarifying questions did not elicit explanations from Aaron. Similarly, Aaron did not respond to Jason's suggestion "Just gotta move - this - over." (Line 105). Instead, Aaron said "Oh! I got an idea." (Line 106), but did not explain the idea and only provided commands to execute the idea. This lack of an explanation happened at other times within the interaction. Most notably, in the following excerpt, Aaron ignored Jason's request for more information.

069 Aaron: I've got an idea that is gonna make it faster. (pause)
070 Jason: How do you know?
071 Aaron: Trust me, it's gonna make it exactly two times as fast.

Aaron's statement "Trust me" (Line 071) is blatant in not providing an explanation. This highlights a central feature of the command-clarify pattern: the lack of an explanation. Due to space constraints, we have not included contrasting examples from the Samantha-Jason and Kim-Jason dyads where Jason's clarifying questions elicited explanations.

Overall, the pattern appears to provide minimal collaboration. The dominant pattern of command-clarify appears to be optimized for having Jason quickly construct and test programs. Although Aaron and Jason made distinct contributions to this pattern, the pattern was one that prioritized completing tasks and appears to compromise intellectual engagement.

6.2.1.2 Peter-Jason: Command-Clarify Sequences

Similarly, the Peter-Jason dyad included examples of the command-clarify pattern. In the following exchange, Peter was giving Jason, the driver, instructions. Peter's instructions include references to Logo commands "Forward" and "RT," which move the character forward and right, respectively.

326 Peter: Not at the end!
327 Peter: Forward 1, RT 1.
328 Peter: Down there.
329 Peter: You're doing it wrong, there's another (unclear speech).
330 Jason: Here?
331 Peter: No, not that.
332 Jason: Here?
333 Peter: Yeah, basically.

When Jason was driving, command-clarify sequences were less common than command sequences that had no clarifying questions. These command sequences sometimes resulted in a dispute between Peter and Jason. For example, in the following exchange, Peter issued commands with increasing intensity and then Peter and Jason both raised their voices and appeared agitated with each other. In the excerpt below, Peter and Jason were trying to run their "square" function in Logo. Peter appears to realize (Line 218) that to run the function Logo "square" you type "square" even though when you are defining the function in Logo you type "to square."

216 Peter: Now you type "to square."
217 Peter: You have to press enter
218 Peter: Oh it's just "square."
219 Peter: It's JUST SQUARE. (sounds exasperated)
220 Peter: Just "SQUARE," not "to square."
221 Peter: It's "square" dude. (30 second pause)
222 Peter: Told you.
223 Jason: Told me what?
224 Peter: You're not supposed to use "to"!
225 Jason: You never said that.
226 Peter: Yes they did.
227 Peter: Go to that - go to the curriculum.
228 Peter: You're supposed to have a "to square"! (raised voice)
229 Jason: That's what I did! (raised voice)
230 Peter: I'm just saying, you don't type "To square" up there.
231 Jason: Stop yelling.

In the exchange above, Peter's insight about the difference between running and defining functions was correct. He attempted to explain that it is "just 'SQUARE,' not 'to square.'" (Line 220). However, from this interaction it does not appear that Jason understood Peter's point. Near the end of the exchange, Jason retorted, "That's what I did!" (Line 229) and there is no evidence from the audio that Jason understood Peter's point.

Throughout the interaction, Peter seemed focused on quickly completing the task of running the function square. It is noteworthy, that here Peter attempted to explain his command (Line 230). However, Jason's response of "stop yelling" (Line 231) suggests that Peter's tone may have been consistent with a pattern of marginalization.

6.2.2 Shortcuts

A second pattern that we observed within the Aaron-Jason and Peter-Jason dyads was taking shortcuts. These shortcuts served to speed the dyad's progress through the curriculum by leaving required steps incomplete or subverting the intended challenge of the task. Shortcuts are clearly consistent with a goal for speed. However, they are also consistent with a disregard for accurately completing the tasks. Therefore this seems to reinforce our claim that command-clarify sequences are a result of a focus on speed and not, as our recent alternative hypothesis suggests, a focus on accurately completing the tasks. The examples below demonstrate the nature of the shortcuts the dyads pursued and some of the interactions that accompanied these shortcuts.

6.2.2.1 Aaron-Jason: Shortcuts

There were four clear examples where Aaron was taking, or was directing Jason to take, a shortcut.

While Aaron was driving and Jason was navigating, the pair was trying to draw a five-sided star (Lines 199-229). In determining the amount to turn between each side, the students tried multiple values, most of which were just a little off the correct value of 144. After a particular modification to the angle, Aaron said, "Yes!" (Line 217), but Jason realizes it was not correct and seemed to suggest trying 146. Jason interjects "Eh - you're off just a tiny bit - you should put 6. Try 6," (Line 218-220). While Jason said this, Aaron interjected "I don't care" (Line 219), which we interpret as expressing an intention to move on even though the

angle of the star was not correct. However, Aaron appeared to concede, next saying, "Fine" (Line 221).

A second shortcut took place when Aaron was driving. When Aaron went to upload the Scratch project, Jason objected by saying, "Hey, it didn't finish" (Line 260) Aaron responded by saying, "I don't care" (Line 261). From this interaction, we infer that Aaron did not wait for the Scratch project to complete the drawing (i.e., finish executing the code) before he began uploading the file. Within this interchange, Aaron's behavior appears consistent with a goal for speed.

In two other instances, Jason described Aaron's behavior as "cheating" (Lines 145 & 378) and these appear to mark instances when Aaron was taking a shortcut in lieu of completing the assigned task as intended. In one case (Lines 106-145), Aaron avoided creating a complex script to draw a picture by superimposing screenshots from a previous problem. In a second case (Line 378), Aaron used the paint editor to avoid creating a script to draw a football. This second case is noteworthy because Jason had two different responses to Aaron's actions. When this happened, Jason accused Aaron of "cheating" (Line 378), but when questioned about it by a teacher, Jason claimed with faux ignorance, "He drew it." (Line 382) These cases generally support the hypothesis that Aaron had a goal of working through the activities as quickly as possible.

These shortcuts appear to be a clear indication of Aaron's focus on speed. Jason does not appear to condone these shortcuts except when he defends one of Aaron's shortcuts to a teacher.

6.2.2.2 Peter-Jason: Shortcuts

There were fewer instances in the Peter-Jason dyad in which they pursued shortcuts. Of two clear examples, Jason challenged one and Jason initiated one.

In the first example of a shortcut, Peter and Jason had just successfully drawn a pentagon in Logo and Peter was the driver. After it completed drawing, Peter said "Yay!" (Line 279). Jason responded by noting "It's sideways." (Line 280), presumably because the pentagon had a different orientation than the pentagon shown in the assignment. Peter dismissed Jason concern by saying "Whatever." (Line 281). In response, Jason mocked, "Everything is 'whatever, whatever, whatever.'" (Line 282). Peter did not respond to this verbally and continued saving the file and then moved on to the next step in the curriculum and exclaimed "Circle!" (Line 284).

In the second example of a shortcut, Jason suggested moving on to the next activity before completing the current activity. Jason said, "Do you just want to save and keep going?" (Line 511). Peter rejected the proposed shortcut and responded "No! I know what's wrong." (Line 512). They proceeded to discuss the issue and eventually received assistance from one of the course instructors.

6.2.3 Peer Comparison

Overall, though, the primary way that a focus on speed manifested in the Peter-Jason dyad highlights a different theme: peer-comparison. This played out in two ways: competitiveness with other classmates, and competitiveness with each other. These peer comparisons were unique to the Peter-Jason dyad. In the following transcript. Jason compared Peter's and his progress on that day's curriculum against that of a nearby pair of classmates. By noting several times that these classmates were further along than Peter and him, Jason's comments indicate a focus on speed.

556	Jason:	Wait, you guys finished already?! (directed at classmates nearby)
557	Jason:	They finished!
558	Teacher:	Okay, we're getting back to work (attempting to get Jason to re-focus)
559	Jason:	You guys finished? (directed at the same classmates nearby)
560	Classmate:	Yeah.

Immediately following this, Jason asked the same group how much progress they had made on the next part of the curriculum, programming the computer to make different letters.

His first comment, "Wait, you guys finished already?!" (Line 556), suggests that Jason was initially surprised and perhaps envious that another team was moving faster than his team. Even after the teacher attempted to re-focus Jason (Line 558), Jason persisted in asking these students whether they had finished, which is followed by a third, more specific inquiry into his classmates' progress, "What letters did you finish" (Line 563). The frequency and nature of Jason's inquiries suggests that he is anxious that he is falling behind, and that being the first to complete a task is desirable. Although this was the only exchange of this kind in the data from this pair, it does indicate that speed was something Jason valued. There was no evidence that Peter was also attending to his classmates' progress, but we saw evidence of Peter's focus on speed as he competed with Jason.

There was considerable evidence that Jason and Peter were competitive with each other, and typically this manifested in the form of the students comparing their progress on class assignments. For example, each class period began with a daily written warm-up. After a few minutes of working on it, Jason and Peter discussed how many of the problems each of them was able to complete. Later, Jason and Peter discuss and compare the progress they have made on their final projects, as well as the sophistication of their projects. Students' progress on the final projects could have been a source of anxiety, especially for a lower-performing student like Jason. Overall, these exchanges indicate a speed-orientation that was embraced at different times by both Jason and Peter. Similar kinds of interactions took place during the previous week on Day 5 when Jason and Peter were also sitting next to each other, but were not pair programming.

7. DISCUSSION
We investigated a number of hypotheses to see what could explain the patterns of equity and inequity we observed. Our primary hypothesis was that a focus on speed contributed to inequity within the Aaron-Jason and Peter-Jason dyads. This appeared to be the common thread among the dominant patterns of: command-clarify sequences, shortcuts, and peer comparison. The command-clarify sequences could also be an indication of a focus on accurately completing the assignments, but the prevalence of shortcuts, which involve not accurately completing the assignments, weakens this alternative hypothesis.

The Samantha-Jason and Kim-Jason dyads did not appear to pursue speed, which may explain their more equitable interactions. However, it is likely that the more equitable relationships observed in the Samantha-Jason and Kim-Jason dyads were influenced by the more playful tasks and Samantha and Kim's pro-social attitudes toward collaboration.

Our finding that there were gross inequities in the Aaron-Jason and Peter-Jason dyads is surprising because the classroom practices were designed to support equity [34]. For example, the

pair-programming structures were carefully designed to ensure that both students had equal time as driver and navigator, and that students reliably switched roles of driver and navigator.

Using a self-paced curriculum was also designed to promote equity, but may have inadvertently contributed to the students' focus on speed and the resulting inequitable interactions. The self-paced curriculum was intended to provide students the opportunity to progress at their own pace, while offering daily synchronization points so that all students were exposed to the same material [34].

The students were allowed to progress through the curriculum at their own pace. We intended to promote mastery of the material rather than a prescriptive pace for all students. By design, the self-paced curriculum meant that students were often working on a range of different steps within the curriculum. Unfortunately, these differences in progress were visible to the students, by observing the computer monitor of their surrounding peers. The public dimension of this self-paced curriculum may have further focused students on the goal of speed.

These synchronization points took the form of open-ended projects at the end of each three-hour session. The curriculum was designed so that these open-ended projects would reinforce, but not introduce, content. Although students were exposed to all of the content even if they spent little time on these open-ended projects, students in the class valued getting time on these open-ended projects. This use of open-ended projects and the resulting value system may have promoted the students' focus on speed. In future work we plan to examine how classroom practices shape students' goals, and how these goals relate to patterns of equity and inequity. The attempt to use a self-paced curriculum may have provided more challenges than it addressed.

8. CONCLUSION
This paper builds primarily upon two lines of prior work: research on equity and research on collaborative learning. Our findings complement research focused on issues of structural equity/inequity within CS [35, 14, 24, 47] by focusing on equity at the level of interactions. Additionally, this work connects research on equity to research focused on collaborative learning, which includes research on pair programming.

Beyond the impact of equity and inequity on students' opportunities to learn, there are broader moral and political reasons to care about equity in the collaborative context. Boaler [2] has argued that how students treat each other in classrooms relates to how they end up treating people in society, as they become adults. To the extent that students can learn to respect their classmates and value their diversity of perspectives and strengths—as is necessary in collaborative learning situations—students put themselves in a better position to be good citizens later in life. In this sense, equity in collaborative learning contexts is about more than students' access to opportunities to learn content, but it is also related to the kinds of societies we hope for outside the classroom walls.

9. ACKNOWLEDGMENTS
We would like to thank the students and staff of the summer enrichment program. The research reported here was supported in part by grants from the National Science Foundation (#1044106 & #1339404), and the Institute of Education Sciences pre-doctoral training grant R305B090026 to the University of California, Berkeley. The opinions expressed are those of the authors and do

not represent views of the National Science Foundation or the Institute of Education Sciences.

10. REFERENCES

[1] Ames, C. (1992). Classrooms: Goals, structures, and student motivation. *Journal of educational psychology, 84(3),* 261.

[2] Barron, B. (2003). When smart groups fail. *Journal of the Learning Sciences, 12*(3), 307-359.

[3] Boaler, J. (2008). Promoting 'relational equity' and high mathematics achievement through an innovative mixed-ability approach. *British Educational Research Journal,* 34(2), 167-194.

[4] Braught, G., MacCormick, J., & Wahls, T. (2010, March). The benefits of pairing by ability. In*Proceedings of the 41st ACM technical symposium on Computer science education* (pp. 249-253). ACM.

[5] Cockburn, A., & Williams, L. (2000). The costs and benefits of pair programming. Extreme programming examined, 223-247.

[6] Cohen, E. G. (1994). *Designing groupwork.* New York, NY: Teachers College Press.

[7] Cohen, E. G., & Lotan, R. A. (1995). Producing equal-status interaction in the heterogeneous classroom. American Educational Research Journal, 32(1), 99-120.

[8] Chizhik, A. W. (2001). Equity and status in group collaboration: Learning through explanations depends on task characteristics. Social Psychology of Education, 5(2), 179-200.

[9] Corbin, J., & Strauss, A. (2014). Basics of qualitative research: Techniques and procedures for developing grounded theory. Sage publications.

[10] Darling-Hammond, L. (2010). The flat world and education: How America's commitment to equity will determine our future. New York, NY: Teachers College Press.

[11] DeClue, T. H. (2003). Pair programming and pair trading: effects on learning and motivation in a CS2 course. *Journal of Computing Sciences in Colleges,18(5),* 49-56.

[12] Denner, J., Werner, L., Campe, S., & Ortiz, E. (2014). Pair Programming: Under What Conditions Is It Advantageous for Middle School Students?. *Journal of Research on Technology in Education, 46*(3), 277-296.

[13] Engle, R. A., Langer-Osuna, J. M., & McKinney de Royston, M. (2014). Toward a model of influence in persuasive discussions: Negotiating quality, authority, privilege, and access within a student-led argument. Journal of the Learning Sciences, 23(2), 245-268.

[14] Ericson, B., & Guzdial, M. (2014, March). Measuring demographics and performance in computer science education at a nationwide scale using AP CS data. In Proceedings of the 45th ACM technical symposium on Computer science education (pp. 217-222). ACM.

[15] Esmonde, I. (2009). Mathematics learning in groups: Analyzing equity in two cooperative activity structures. *Journal of the Learning Sciences, 18*(2), 247-284.

[16] Fawcett, L. M., & Garton, A. F. (2005). The effect of peer collaboration on children's problem-solving ability. British Journal of Educational Psychology, 75(2), 157-169.

[17] Flores, A. (2007). Examining disparities in mathematics education: Achievement gap or opportunity gap? The High School Journal, 91(1), 29–42.

[18] Hanks, B., Fitzgerald, S., McCauley, R., Murphy, L., & Zander, C. (2011). Pair programming in education: a literature review. *Computer Science Education, 21(2),* 135-173.

[19] Jermann, P., & Nüssli, M. A. (2012, February). Effects of sharing text selections on gaze cross-recurrence and interaction quality in a pair programming task. In Proceedings of the ACM 2012 conference on Computer Supported Cooperative Work (pp. 1125-1134). ACM.

[20] King, A. (1991). Effects of training in strategic questioning on children's problem solving performance. *Journal of Educational Psychology, 83*(3), 307-317.

[21] Langer-Osuna, J. M. (2011). How Brianna became bossy and Kofi came out smart: Understanding the trajectories of identity and engagement for two group leaders in a project-based mathematics classroom. *Canadian Journal of Science, Mathematics and Technology Education*, 11(3), 207-225.

[22] Lave, J., & Wenger, E. (1991). Situated learning: Legitimate peripheral participation. Cambridge university press.

[23] Lewis, C. M. (2011). Is pair programming more effective than other forms of collaboration for young students?. *Computer Science Education,* 21(2), 105-134.

[24] Margolis, J., Estrella, R., Goode, J., Holme, J. J. and Nao, K. 2008. Stuck in the shallow end: Education, race, and computing. MIT Press, Cambridge, MA.

[25] McDowell, C., Werner, L., Bullock, H., & Fernald, J. (2002, February). The effects of pair-programming on performance in an introductory programming course. In ACM SIGCSE Bulletin (Vol. 34, No. 1, pp. 38-42). ACM.

[26] McDowell, C., Werner, L., Bullock, H. E., & Fernald, J. (2006). Pair programming improves student retention, confidence, and program quality. Communications of the ACM, 49(8), 90-95.

[27] Nagappan, N., Williams, L., Ferzli, M., Wiebe, E., Yang, K., Miller, C., & Balik, S. (2003, February). Improving the CS1 experience with pair programming. In ACM SIGCSE Bulletin (Vol. 35, No. 1, pp. 359-362). ACM.

[28] Nattiv, A. (1994). Helping behaviors and math achievement gain of students using cooperative learning. The Elementary School Journal, 285-297.

[29] Oakes, J. (2005). Keeping track: How schools structure inequality. New Haven, CT: Yale University Press.

[30] Palinscar, A. S., & Brown, A. L. (1984). Reciprocal teaching of comprehension-fostering and comprehension-monitoring activities. Cognition and instruction, 1(2), 117-175.

[31] Salleh, N., Mendes, E., & Grundy, J. (2011). Empirical studies of pair programming for CS/SE teaching in higher education: A systematic literature review. Software Engineering, IEEE Transactions on, 37(4), 509-525.

[32] Saxe, G. B. (1988). Candy selling and math learning. Educational Researcher, 17(6), 14-21.

[33] Sfard, A., & Kieran, C. (2001). Cognition as communication: Rethinking learning-by-talking through multi-faceted analysis of students' mathematical interactions. Mind, Culture, and Activity, 8(1), 42-76.

[34] Shah, N., Lewis, C. M., Caires, R., Khan, N., Qureshi, A., Ehsanipour, D., & Gupta, N. (2013). Building equitable computer science classrooms: elements of a teaching approach. In ACM SIGCSE Bulletin. 263-268.

[35] Shah, N., Lewis, C. M., & Caires, R. (2014) Analyzing Equity in Collaborative Learning Situations: A Comparative Case Study in Elementary Computer Science. *Proceedings for the 11th International Conferences of the Learning Sciences (ICLS)*. 495-502.

[36] Thomas, L., Ratcliffe, M., & Robertson, A. (2003, February). Code warriors and code-a-phobes: a study in attitude and pair programming. In ACM SIGCSE Bulletin (Vol. 35, No. 1, pp. 363-367). ACM.

[37] Vivekanandan, K., & Kuppuswami, S. (2004). The effects of pair programming on learning efficiency in short programming assignments. Informatics in Education-An International Journal, (Vol 3_2), 251-266.

[38] Vygotsky, L. S. (1978). Mind in society: The development of higher psychological processes. Cambridge: Harvard University Press.

[39] Watkins, K. Z., & Watkins, M. J. (2009). Towards minimizing pair incompatibilities to help retain under-represented groups in beginning programming courses using pair programming. *Journal of Computing Sciences in Colleges, 25*(2), 221-227.

[40] Webb, N. M. (1991). Task-related verbal interaction and mathematics learning in small groups. *Journal for Research in Mathematics Education*, 22(5), 366-389.

[41] Webb, N. M., Farivar, S. H., & Mastergeorge, A. M. (2002). Productive helping in cooperative groups. Theory into practice, 41(1), 13-20.

[42] Wenger, E. (1998). Communities of practice: Learning as a social system. Systems thinker, 9(5), 2-3.

[43] Werner, L., McDowell, C., & Denner, J. (2013, March). Middle school students using Alice: what can we learn from logging data?. *In Proceeding of the 44th ACM technical symposium on Computer science education* (pp. 507-512). ACM.

[44] Werner, L., & Denner, J. (2009). Pair programming in middle school: What does it look like?. *Journal of Research on Technology in Education, 42(1),* 29-49.

[45] Wertsch, J. V. (1998). Mind as action. New York, NY: Oxford University Press.

[46] Williams, L., Kessler, R. R., Cunningham, W., & Jeffries, R. (2000). Strengthening the case for pair programming. IEEE software, 17(4), 19-25.

[47] Wilson, C., Sudol, L. A., Stephenson, C., & Stehlik, M. (2010). Running on empty: The failure to teach K-12 computer science in the digital age. Association for Computing Machinery. Computer Science Teachers Association.

Using Distributed Cognition Theory to Analyze Collaborative Computer Science Learning

Elise Deitrick♡, R. Benjamin Shapiro†♡, Matthew P. Ahrens♡,
Rebecca Fiebrink♣, Paul D. Lehrman♡, & Saad Farooq♡
♡ Tufts University   ♣ Goldsmiths, University of London
† r@benshapi.ro

ABSTRACT

Research on students' learning in computing typically investigates how to enable individuals to develop concepts and skills, yet many forms of computing education, from peer instruction to robotics competitions, involve group work in which understanding may not be entirely locatable within individuals' minds. We need theories and methods that allow us to understand learning in cognitive systems: culturally and historically situated groups of students, teachers, and tools. Accordingly, we draw on Hutchins' Distributed Cognition [16] theory to present a qualitative case study analysis of interaction and learning within a small group of middle school students programming computer music. Our analysis shows how a system of students, teachers, and tools, working in a music classroom, is able to accomplish conceptually demanding computer music programming. We show how the system does this by 1) collectively drawing on individuals' knowledge, 2) using the physical and virtual affordances of different tools to organize work, externalize knowledge, and create new demands for problem solving, and 3) reconfiguring relationships between individuals and tools over time as the focus of problem solving changes. We discuss the implications of this perspective for research on teaching, learning and assessment in computing.

Keywords

Learning, Research Methods, Music

1. INTRODUCTION

Nearly thirty years ago, Pea, Soloway, and Spohrer [24] argued that becoming a programmer requires developing new kinds of knowledge. They wrote: "For programming, as in other domains from mathematics to the physical and engineering sciences, students are engaged through their learning activities in actively building a knowledge system of concepts and procedural skills." This perspective suggests a need to develop "characterization[s] of a student's current understanding in terms of the knowledge he or she is utilizing to make sense of the problem solving activities in computer programming" (ibid.). But all of these years later, we still know relatively little about *how* learners develop knowledge in computing, especially in group work.

Researchers have developed numerous approaches to studying computer science learning. One overarching approach has been to mine student code, including logs of changes in students' code over time. Such work includes charting changes in students' use of language constructs and practices of recycling code from their own or others' projects [7]. Others have used students' code to investigate how students transfer program design patterns from game programming to making science simulations [3]. And still others have used time-series records of students' code to find "sink states" where students seem to be stuck [5]. Analysis of massive amounts of BlueJ data permitted researchers to identify mismatches between teachers' perceptions of common student needs and students' actual needs [9].

But investigators have not limited themselves to analyses of code alone, applying interview and think-aloud methods wherein students explain their code to researchers or to peers as they author, debug, use, or retrospectively discuss it [20, 10, 19]. Analysts of students' computational thinking have looked at discourse in small groups and within whole classroom conversations [30]. In most of this work, the unit of analysis has been the individual student or the individual student's idea: how a student's utterances (verbal or textual) represent particular disciplinary (e.g., computational, biological, or physical) ideas.

But shifts in how CS is learned make this individual frame problematic. Computer science education is increasingly collaborative, employing approaches like pair programming [22], peer teaching [25], and decomposition of projects into pieces to be done by individuals and then stitched together [13]. These structures mirror those found in industrial software development, and they can be quite effective at improving learning and retention [26]. However, there is little published work describing *how* these small groups solve problems and the *processes through which* participants develop computational thinking and programming skills over time. Moreover, assessing what students can do individually does not necessarily predict all that a team made up of those same individuals can accomplish, or what they can learn from one another. Teams may be able to accomplish more than the sum of their individual members' skills would suggest, but they may also get bogged down in group dynamics that hamper their capabilities. Further, we should not take for granted that groups of youth learning together will all emerge from their groupwork with identical understandings [28]; different group members may participate in projects in different ways, work on different pieces of overall problems, and have different goals for their own skill development. As we as a field continue to adopt collaborative learning, we need theories and methods that the richness of what happens in student groups. Specifically: We need research on the ways in which groups work together so that we can get to the process of learning: the micro-genesis of students' computer science thinking, at both the individual and the collective levels.

2. DEVELOPING AND APPLYING RELEVANT THEORY

Much Computing Education Research (CER) links pedagogies (or pedagogical interventions) to outcomes, but does not sufficiently explain why — i.e., through what mechanisms, and with what potential limitation — those outcomes are achieved. *Why* questions raise all manner of theoretical and methodological questions for CER researchers, who currently operate from a wide variety of perspectives [21, 32].

Studying group interactions in CS learning environments is a potent opportunity to adapt, apply, and refine theories of learning from the other fields into CER. There are many possible ways to do this: Some theoretical perspectives on group work give primacy to questions about cognition, such as about how disciplinary ideas are conceptualized. For example, discourse analysis of student group talk can reveal subtle discursive (e.g., metaphorical) processes through which members of groups can converge on shared understandings [28]. But conceptual development is not the only possible focus for research. Questioning power and equity within groups orients us to look at which group members hold disproportionate sway over joint activity, and the mechanisms through which this power is constructed, wielded, and perpetuated. For example, one inquiry into the distribution, content, and positioning of talk within groups of elementary students learning computer science found that even when a group looked equitable in terms of how much different group members were talking, they were quite inequitable at the level of peer perceptions of computing competence [29]. These dynamics can replicate existing societal inequalities [1] and may be difficult to intervene in, even given explicit role assignments [34]. Finally, social network analyses, drawing on the evolution of code similarity across the classroom, can enable insights into how social dynamics enable knowledge flow and co-construction in collaboration and competition [4].

2.1 Theories of Cognition

Most research on cognition in computing (and STEM generally), even research that attends to social dynamics in learning, ultimately focuses on how *individuals* develop computational ideas. As we shall now explain, this stance is deeply problematic, and new theories that adopt distributed, social, and material definitions for cognition are necessary to account for the richness of how learning actually happens. The current ubiquity of mentalist (i.e., focused on individual minds) approaches to understanding learning is unsurprising, as thinking and learning have historically been understood as things that individuals do. But social [33], situated [2, 12, 18], and cultural [11, 27] understandings of cognition and learning challenge this tradition. They suggest that human activities can best be understood as culturally- and historically-situated, technologically-mediated, socially-enacted processes. Knowledge development, in this view, is intrinsically linked to social context, and research on learning that strips away the contextuality of activity is incompatible with socio-cultural theories of learning [8]. This is not merely a theoretical concern: a century of research on learning has shown that it is extremely difficult for learners to transfer knowledge from one context to another [23, 6].

One reason for this is that different conditions (settings, problems, partnerships) can activate different knowledge in learners' minds; learners frequently develop and demonstrate different, even contradictory, ideas about the world, and which ideas are operational at any moment is highly context dependent [31]. Attempts to generalize from data borne from collaborative interaction to claims about students' decontextualized and individualized knowledge are, therefore, neither valid nor practical. Instead, the CER community must adapt and develop theories and methods for studying students' groupwork as activities within which functional roles and conceptual development may be distributed across the group, and in which we may not be able to locate knowing in individuals alone, but in the group (and its setting) as a whole system.

The term *cognition* traditionally refers to the brain's mechanisms for information processing, error correction, memory, perception, and communication. However, research on situated, embodied, and social cognition challenges this model, highlighting ways in which real-world cognition cannot be easily located solely within the skull. Consider Lave's classic example of The Cottage Cheese Problem [18]: "Dieters were asked to prepare their lunch to meet specifications laid out by the observer. In this case, they were to fix a serving of cottage cheese, supposing that the amount allotted for the meal was three-quarters of the two-thirds cup the program allowed. The problem solver began the task muttering that he had taken a calculus course in college. Then after a pause he suddenly announced that he had 'got it!' He filled a measuring cup two-thirds full of cottage cheese, dumped it out on a cutting board, patted it into a circle, marked a cross on it, scooped away one quadrant, and served the rest."

An alternative method to solving this problem is to multiply $^2/_3$ by $^3/_4$ to find that the answer is $^1/_2$, and then to locate a suitable measuring cup. Were the dieter doing this work in a mathematics classroom where there is no cottage cheese, measuring cup, or cutting board, this would likely have been the preferred problem solving approach. But the physicality of the materials makes another solution approach ready-to-hand [14], one in which the cognition happens in the interaction between the dieter and the physical materials. The mathematical result is the same but the means — distributed across dieter, cheese, cup, and board, and no longer purely symbolic — is quite different. Theories of embodied and social cognition provide a framework within which we can analyze the multi-facetedness of the dieter's actual work. It isn't mental work alone, and any definition of cognition that ignores the situated, material, embodied character of the work is, therefore, necessarily ill-fitting to actual everyday cognition. Instead, to better "carve nature at its joints," (as Plato put it) we must bring setting, body, tools, and culture into our definition — and our empirical study — of cognition, treating all of these constituents of activity as just as crucial to cognitive accomplishment as what happens inside the head.

Distributed Cognition [16] (DCOG) theory generalizes this perspective on real-world cognition, arguing that all of the cognitive functions (e.g., memory) that have historically been analytically located in the head can also be seen in the emergent properties of interactions between people and tools in culturally- and historically-produced settings. In proposing a framework for studying "Cognition in the Wild," Distributed Cognition theorists highlight several key aspects of cognitive systems that researchers should attend to [15]:

- The distribution of cognitive processes across social groups, including ongoing redistribution of activity to balance cognitive load.
- That culture intimately shapes cognition by offering tools, settings, and social norms through which to work or through which work can break down.
- Effortful coordination between internal (to the head) and external (tools and environment) structure, including through the use of the body of the problem-solver.
- The event-driven path dependence of cognition, where "the products of earlier events can transform the nature of later events."

DCOG has many strengths over traditional approaches to understanding cognition. Perhaps most powerful is its ability to account how a diversity of tools and representations are key elements in socio-technical systems of problem-solving; specifically, that external tools and representations are not just objects used by people, but can do cognitive or social work, such as transforming one kind of information into another or prompting a group to talk about their knowledge in particular ways. DCOG challenges researchers to take careful account of how individuals interact with one another, tools, and setting, and to observe the ways in which those interactions produce the cognitive functions of information processing, memory, sensing, error correction, etc.

In this view, *learning* is no longer just change in individuals' conceptual models (a constructivist take on what learning is) or behavior (a behaviorist take), but also includes changes in the relationships between individuals and in their individual and joint relations to tools and settings, which can also be modified over time. For example, introducing a new tool (say, a slide rule or a computer) to an engineering team that previously had been required to do mental or paper-based calculations is a form of learning: the team becomes able to do existing work faster and possibly also becomes able to take on newer, harder problems. The group has learned, but that learning cannot be fully located in any of the individuals alone, nor in the individuals without their tools (who possibly might only be able demonstrate knowledge through the use of the tools). Rather, the learning consists in how their emergent system of interaction reconfigures itself to solve problems in new ways, such as by re-distributing cognitive load onto tools. Using DCOG in the analysis of learning can offer insights into how activity (including learning) happens that are not possible within the traditional cognition-is-inside-the-head paradigm. To study learning through the paradigm of classical cognition is necessarily to devalue the many nuanced ways in which real-world knowledge and real-world learning is intimately bound to social and material context. Instead,

DCOG offers access to the social, material, cultural, embodied, and mental richness of activity and learning.

3. CASE STUDY

In order to illustrate the affordances of DCOG for analyzing collaborative CS learning, we now present a qualitative case study analysis of one group of youth programming a computer music system. As we shall show, DCOG theory enables us to richly analyze how that group works and learns, including understanding the specific student knowledge and tool design weaknesses that cause a breakdown within the group work to occur, and to carefully understand the influence of a teacher's intervention when the breakdown occurs.

3.1 Context

The example presented here is a few brief minutes of student group work that occurred within a computer music summer camp that we conducted in Summer 2014. We chose this example because of its richness as a case of students' prior knowledge and tool design decisions shaping learning, though many other comparably rich examples exist within our data set (described below). We present it here not so much as a characterization of what all students' participation in the summer camp was like, but, rather, to show how DCOG offers a framework to understand learning in collaborative CS group work.

The summer camp was a research vehicle for us to investigate how computer music can be a productive medium for engaging under-represented populations of students in parallel and distributed computing through designing, building, programming, and performing with tangible computer music instruments. We hosted the camp at a community center in a lower/mixed socio-economic area of a large Northeast U.S. city. The camp was two weeks (9 days) long, and met for 3 hours in the morning each day. Fourteen rising sixth- and seventh-grade students participated, of whom 3 were girls. Only 12 youth consented to participate in data collection. All students were African-American and/or Latino. All camp activities occurred in the music room of the community center, which was well-appointed with musical instruments (a piano, guitars, drums, and DJ equipment). At least four members of our research team were always present in the room and available to students for help on their projects.

Students in the camp used a prototype computer music tool called *BlockyTalky*. BlockyTalky runs on small physical computing devices, called BlockyTalky Units or BTUs. BTUs can be hooked up to various sensors, and they have holes to mate with LEGO bricks. This enables users to create their own prototype tangible computer music input devices. Each BTU runs a web server that hosts a graphical blocks-based programming interface for musical programming. The BlockyTalky language has music-specific blocks, such as a block to create rhythmic phrases and another to define melodic phrases. Melodic phrases are specified by stringing together blocks that take two parameters each: the first parameter is how long a note should play (e.g., a quarter note) and the second is what the pitch should be, specified as a note letter and the octave to play it in. For example, C4 is the note middle-C, while C5 is the C one octave above.

3.2 Data set

All camp sessions were recorded using video cameras placed

across the space, creating about 215 hours of video data; to maximize audio quality every participant wore a wireless microphone. The cameras were positioned to capture maximum group activity around the table the group was working on. However, students sometimes knocked these cameras out of alignment. The audio/video data presented in this paper were collected early in the second day of the camp.

3.3 Prelude

Our camp curriculum dedicated the first week of the camp to enabling youth to learn their way around BlockyTalky by modifying and creating instruments. This was intended to prepare students for the second week's goal: musical performances using instruments of the students' own making.

During Day 1 of the camp, students clapped out and drew their own representations of rhythms before inputting their patterns into a web-based drum machine. The data we present here were collected early in Day 2 and revolve around a pair of participants.

Due to the novelty of our system and the students' limited computational and musical backgrounds, we began Day 2 by offering students an assortment of pre-made BlockyTalky instruments to play with and then modify. We expected students to begin creating their own instruments on Day 3, though some students had modified the pre-built projects beyond recognition by the end of Day 2! On Day 2 in particular, we hoped to see students begin to understand the idea of sequencing [17] as it cut across music and computation. In music, sequencing refers to defining a pattern of specific sounds to occur at specific times (e.g., defining a sequence of notes to create a melody). Computationally, we can understand this as a program that executes an ordered sequence of instructions, each separated by a specific length of time. In BlockyTalky, these two ideas of sequencing are complementary and both are needed to program a melody or rhythm.

Chris and Nathan began Day 2 by programming and playing music on a pre-built drum instrument for about 30 minutes before switching to a different pre-built unit that used a light sensor's detection of changing color values to trigger a melody. Soon after, the boys shifted focus to building a device to play a melody of their own choosing. The process through which they worked toward this goal is the focus of our case study. As we will show, the boys worked together with each other, BlockyTalky, a guitar, and a teacher's help as part of a continually adapting distributed cognition system.

3.4 Phase 1: Choosing what to program

In the first phase of the episode, a pair of students, Nathan and Chris, are the central actors in a distributed cognition system which makes a collective decision about what song to program. The system not only includes the pair of students, but also elements of the setting (guitars within easy reach), and a shared history of the boys' prior participation in a music camp at the community center together (including a repertoire of songs both boys know how to play on guitar). At the end of this phase, the system will have reached a decision about what to program.

This episode starts with Jake, an undergraduate facilitator from Tufts University, encouraging Chris and Nathan to modify the pre-built project. Jake then explains briefly how the existing code works.

[0:16] **Jake** Do you guys want to make your own song to play?
[0:19] **Nathan** Yeah
[0:19] **Jake** Alright, so have you guys played with these blocks at all yet?
[0:22] **Nathan** Not yet
[0:24] **Jake** Alright, let's stop. So basically what this does is ummm it basically just plays all these notes in order
[0:38] **Nathan** In order, okay
[0:40] **Jake** And then this block says on the next beat start looping so basically it just plays this string of notes over and over and over and you can choose

Jake then explains that every note in BlockyTalky needs a pitch and a duration. This will become relevant later when the system's demands for this information lead the boys to recognize a gap between their own knowledge and the system's requirements.

[0:54] **Jake** But basically you choose the length of how long you want the note to play here
[1:08] **Nathan** Ok
[1:08] **Jake** And then you choose the note itself right here

With this information in mind, the boys discuss how they want to modify the pre-built unit.

[1:24] **Nathan** Ok. I have an idea. Maybe if we look up the—
[1:28] **Chris** I know what we can do!
[1:29] **Nathan** We could look up the notes for a song
[1:31] **Jake** Right
[1:32] **Nathan** Yeah, let's look up the notes for a song
[1:32] **Chris** No no no no we could do one of the songs we learned on guitar
[1:37] **Nathan** Smoke on the Water, yeah!
[1:44] **Nathan** *typing* smoke
[1:49] **Chris** We already know the notes for that
[1:52] **Nathan** We don't know how long to play them for

Nathan initially proposes ([1:24] and [1:29]) to look up the notes for a song. Chris makes a counter proposal—that they program a song they already know on the guitar ([1:32]). These seem like two mutually exclusive proposals but the boys do not see them that way. Nathan proposes a song that fits Chris's criteria of a song they know how to play on the guitar, *Smoke on the Water*, but then immediately proceeds to search for the notes on the computer. Chris protests this action by stating that they already know the notes for the song. Nathan follows up with the fact that they know the pitches of the notes, but they don't know the durations, essential details of programming notes in BlockyTalky that Jake mentioned earlier ([0:54]). This nuance reflects a difference in the kind of information that can be produced and processed by the different kinds of actors in the distributed cognition system at work here. While a beginning musician can know how to play a song in a rough sense (first put your fingers here, then put your fingers there...), these kinds of performances tend to get the sequence of pitches right but not the timing. It takes more guitar practice than these boys have had to be able to fluidly move between finger and hand positions at the proper tempo. In contrast, BlockyTalky demands more precise information, both pitch and timing. The boys have a way to produce the pitches but do not know the timing. As we see next, Nathan seems to view the mismatch between what they know and what BlockyTalky requires as problematic, while Chris does not. A negotiation now ensues about whether they need to know note durations or not. As this begins, Nathan retrieves a second computer to look up sheet music.

[3:23] **Chris** Nathan, we don't know how ... we don't have to know how long to play to — play it for

[3:28] **Nathan** I know, that's why we have to look it up though

[3:29] **Chris** No, we already know how long to play it

[3:35] **Nathan** We don't know exactly one sixth or one fourth of a note. Like, do you know that? Do you know how long — like do you see right here? how long to play it for. Like one sixteenth note of note C5, we don't know how long to play it for. We know the notes, yeah

[3:50] **Chris** We just play one note. We don't have to play part of the note. We can play the whole thing.

Chris still disbelieves that they need to know how long to play each note, but Nathan insists that they do. We interpret Chris's remark at [3:50] as a proposal that they not worry about duration of the notes and that they should just set them all to whole notes. Nathan does not acknowledge this proposal and continues searching on the computer for sheet music with Jake's help. He finds guitar tablature.

[4:24] **Jake** Alright, so that's a tab. That's for guitar. Do you want to play Smoke on the Water?

[4:33] **Nathan** Yeah

[4:35] **Jake** Umm, this one probably isn't going to help you much because it's like — it's guitar music so it doesn't really — this one is probably your best bet. So, it looks like — so they're chords

[4:51] **Nathan** This is — this is supposed to start at zero

[4:53] **Jake** What?

[4:55] **Nathan** It's supposed to start at zero. That's how you play it. I know how you play it on guitar but this is not how you play it.

[5:02] **Jake** Interesting

[5:03] **Nathan** You're supposed to start at zero.

[5:08] **Jake** It might just be in a different key.

[5:10] **Nathan** Like this one would help us. Oh, this is a trumpet's. This one would help us the most. Yeah, this one, 0033553.

[5:24] **Jake** So looks like it's going to be a D and an F and a G. Is this actually Smoke on the Water?

[5:37] **Nathan** Yeah. I can play it for you on the guitar.

[5:40] **Jake** But I mean — the rhythm of it

[5:43] **Nathan** Do you want me to play it for you?

This exchange began with Jake pointing out that what Nathan found is tablature, which specifies sequences of chords and so will not help much with the boys' quest for timing information. In response Nathan provides a piece of knowledge from his experience playing the song on the guitar, that it's supposed to start at zero (an open string), as a proposed criterion for judging their search results. When Nathan seems to find a result he is happy with, he points it out, saying and repeating "this one would help us." To make his point that it fits his criterion, he says a string of numbers starting with zero. Jake looks at the pitches indicated by the actual notes and wonders out loud if these notes actually correspond to the song they are trying to play. Nathan makes his

first ([5:37]) and second ([5:43]) offer to play *Smoke on the Water* for Jake on one of the acoustic guitars in the music room. Jake seems skeptical this sheet music is accurate as he continues analyzing it, this time noting that the rhythm seems wrong. Jake then gets pulled away from this problem by a question from Chris.

[5:44] **Chris** Like, when it's putting the numbers next to the letter on the program, does that mean that it's putting the like what the note it would be on and the position it would be on?

[5:56] **Nathan** I could actually show you

[5:57] **Jake** What do you mean? Looking at this?

[5:59] **Chris** Yeah

[6:01] **Jake** Okay, so what was your question again?

[6:05] **Chris** so if — when it has the note and the number together

[6:13] **Jake** yes

[6:10] **Chris** Is that like the umm the note and the position it's going to be played in?

[6:17] **Jake** So it's going to be — it plays a .... it plays a

[6:26] **Nathan** I can actually play it if you want me to

[6:26] **Jake** Alright, one sec, I need to answer this question first

[6:28] **Nathan** Want to play Chris?

[6:31] **Jake** Umm, it plays the note B4 one sixteenth of a beat. And it's the first note that's played. And the next note that's played is a B flat 4 for one sixteenth of a beat. Does that make sense?

[6:57] **Nathan** [inaudible]

[6:58] **Chris** Yeah

Jake clarifies for Chris that one enters notes into Blocky-Talky by specifying a pitch (denoted by a letter between A and G) and octave. Jake also reiterates his earlier description of the system's execution of musical programs as "it basically just plays all these notes in order" by walking through the example of a couple of notes in the pre-made code. Right after Chris says "Yeah" at the end of the episode ([6:58]), Nathan plays the intro to *Smoke on the Water* on the guitar he has retrieved from the wall.

Notably, from this point forward, the question of whether the boys need to know precise timings is dropped. Blocky-Talky supplies default timing of a $1/4$ note. However, because each note has two formal parameters (timing and pitch), Nathan may have felt a premature need (relative to guitar-learning) to supply this information. This in turn led to a back and forth exchange between the boys and a search for information online. Ultimately, this formal, but optional, parameter does not impact the rest of the boys' interactions in the episode. This is probably because the exchange just described ends with a guitar in Nathan's hands and Chris in control of the laptop. Chris, who earlier ([3:50]) suggested assigning a uniform note duration to all notes, is in a position to use the system's default uniform timing while Nathan produces a sequence of pitches on the guitar.

3.5 Phase 2: Representational Transformation

Our narrative continues with Jake asking if Nathan knows the notes he just played, referring to the standard musical notation they need to input the notes into BlockyTalky. This event triggers a shift in cognitive system's function from memory recall to information transformation. The transformation process will eventually map each note of *Smoke on the Water* from Nathan's knowledge of how to play the song to a symbolic, formal representation that BlockyTalky can execute.

Crucially, Nathan's knowledge of the notes in the song is only externally visible in the moments that he is putting his fingers into position on the fretboard and plucking the strings. Outside of those moments, the knowledge is internal to him, but it is an embodied understanding that he might have a very hard time mentally reasoning about without use of his body and an instrument. So the moments that it is most accessible to him are also the moments that it is most accessible to others. That is, he does not know the names for these fingers positions and can only communicate his partial and non-symbolic knowledge of the notes by playing them with his hands around a guitar. In contrast, BlockyTalky requires a symbolic (note letter) description of what notes to play (e.g., C4); its interface does not allow input in the form of finger positions (i.e. there is no virtual instrument or way to hook in a real guitar as input into the program). Thus, as we shall see, there is a breakdown between the representation of knowledge that the boys can produce with a guitar and the representation that BlockyTalky needs; the boys and tools alone cannot create mappings between these two representational systems (see Figure 1).

[7:36] **Jake** Alright so, do you know what notes those are?
[7:45] **Nathan** [unclear] This is an E
[7:47] **Jake** An E? So this would be what — a D#?
[7:56] **Nathan** I don't know. I know —
[7:59] **Jake** This is an E and that's an F and that's an F# and that's a G. So it's an E, then a G and then an A.
[8:13] **Nathan** I don't know. Do you know someone that knows guitar?
[8:14] **Jake** I mean I — so each of these is a half note. So this would be — the lowest string is an E so then this would be a G so then this would be an A.
[8:27] **Nathan** Awesome. Okay.
[8:32] **Jake** So, we're going to want to do —

As we see above, even though Nathan can play the song and has an embodied knowledge of the notes of *Smoke on the Water*, and even though Chris knows how to put notes into the BlockyTalky system, they cannot proceed. Jake steps in to fill the gap between these two representational forms. This is a notable shift in the structure (see Figure 2) of the system; it was only directly preceding this phase of the episode that Chris started interacting with Jake at all (first interaction at [5:44]). Prior to this, Nathan had been talking to any adults that addressed the group, and no adults had been a part of the boys' problem solving.

As we now show, this new distributed cognition structure (see Figure 3) allows the system to accomplish its function of information transformation in the following way: Each note of the song is retrieved from Nathan's memory, and is externalized using a finger position on the guitar that Nathan holds. Jake then employs his musical knowledge to transform the finger position supplied by Nathan (expressed using his body and the guitar) into a letter note. Jake also fills in a duration and octave he deems an appropriate approximation of the song based on his musical background. Chris hears Jake say these details aloud, then enters 3 pieces of information for each note — duration, letter and octave — as formal parameters in his program code. This emergent distribution is due to the individuals' background knowledge (from prior

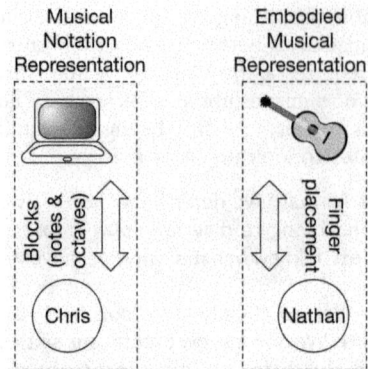

Figure 1: Representational Breakdown

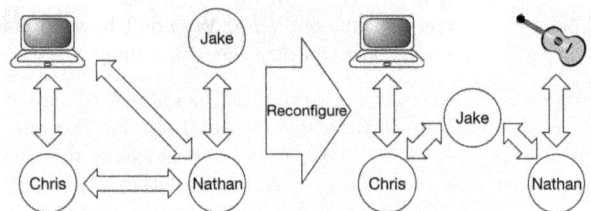

Figure 2: System Reconfiguration

to our camp), as well as the requirements of the BlockyTalky language. Of the three, only Nathan and Chris know how to play the song on the guitar, meaning that the students supplied the starting representation. The instructor, Jake, then had the task of helping them transform this representation to a more standard one, because of the three he was the only one with enough musical background to figure out the letter notes, octaves and approximate note duration. The new arrangement enables the distributed cognition work of recall from memory, information processing (transformation), and memory storage (as program code) for later playback by the program that Chris and Nathan are writing.

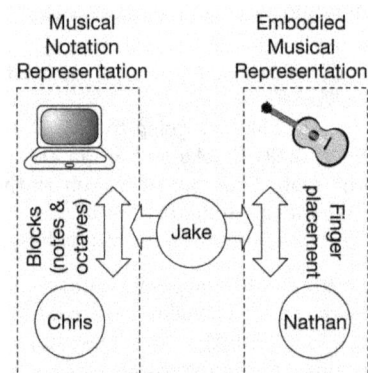

Figure 3: Representational Bridge

[8:43] **Nathan** It's E, it starts out with an E. Chris do you want to start writing it down? It starts out with an E as a - and these are half notes, right?
[9:07] **Jake** Yeah
[9:07] **Nathan** Half notes.

[9:07] **Jake** They're probably half notes.

[9:10] **Nathan** And it starts out with an E

[9:11] **Jake** So do an E4. And then we're going to have another half note.

[9:19] **Nathan** Oh, I could ask him, he probably knows. Oh-okay okay okay.

[10:00] **Chris** So what would ummm, this one be? Would it be G#?

[10:13] **Jake** So that's going to be A#

[10:14] **Chris** A#

[10:17] **Jake** B flat

[10:21] **Jake** Yeah, the important thing to remember on a guitar is that every fret is a half note.

[10:27] **Nathan** Okay

[10:29] **Jake** So if you know that the bottom string you can just count up

Nathan, despite his prior claims that they should know the duration of each note ([3:35]), proposes that they set all the notes to have the duration of a half note ([8:43]). Chris starts trying to figure out how the transformation works by asking for confirmation on the next note ([10:00]). In response, Jake supplies the correct answer and a key piece of knowledge he is using for the transformation process ([10:21]). This could have been an opening for another reconfiguration, Jake stepping out of the system and Chris taking over his role. However, as we show, Chris does not attempt the transformation process on his own. The conversation begins to shift to Chris's part of the process — programming the notes into the BlockyTalky. Jake continues to help Nathan transform notes from his embodied representation to a more standard representation so Chris can program them, as well as intermittently providing support when Chris asks for it.

[10:31] **Chris** Would it be A#4 or A#3?

[10:35] **Jake** A#4. So the numbers start on C so like CDE-FGAB are all the same number then the number goes up.

[11:07] **Jake** So right here *pointing to screen* what do you want this to sound like? So do you want to play Smoke on the Water for us again?

[11:13] **Nathan** Okay. Wait. Wait...

[11:22] **Jake** You're missing one

[11:24] **Nathan** Oh yeah

[11:29] **Jake** So we go an E, we go a G. We go an E, we go an G -

[11:38] **Nathan** Then we go up: zero, this one, this one and then we go here. Yeah, 0, 3 5, 0, 3 6 5

[11:41] **Jake** E G A and then .....

[11:46] **Jake** Right, okay, so right now, there we go.

[11:53] **Chris** Ummm, where do you enter [inaudible]

[11:54] **Jake** Where do you- oh, so you want to add more notes you have to drag new notes in there. So you drag a note slot and you just drag it into the bottom there and then that adds a new note slot. And if you want to delete a note slot, you just go there and you pull it out.

[12:46] **Chris** What happened?

[13:10] **Jake** Alright, so where is our new thing?

[13:12] **Chris** I don't know where the other ones went. I put the notes in there but they disappeared.

[13:19] **Jake** What happened?

[13:19] **Chris** They disappeared

[13:23] **Jake** Hmmmm. So what were you.. Oh oh oh, so

okay. Were you trying to- are you trying to add more these into those?

[13:35] **Chris** Yeah

[13:37] **Jake** Alright, so the easiest way to do it is to just - you can just go into music and the thing is right here

[13:45] **Chris** Oh, okay

[13:48] **Jake** So it's just right there in the music

[13:48] **Chris** Wait, umm, how do I take away one?

[13:51] **Jake** Take away one?

[13:53] **Chris** Can I just pull out one?

[13:54] **Jake** Yes but you have to pull out the correct one. So you want to go down to the bottom and pull out the last one.

[14:00] **Nathan** Oh, did you get it? Do you need help?

[15:57] **Nathan** We gotta stop, we gotta stop for a minute. Wait wait. Put it on blue now

[16:06] **Jake** So you know that putting it on blue color will make your new song play.

[16:24] **Nathan** Shouldn't it go a little faster?

[16:24] **Jake** Alright, so we have the right notes but they aren't all the right lengths, you know.

The episode's end is marked by the boys expressing their next goal: fixing the timing. Nathan expresses dissatisfaction ([16:24]) with the speed of the song overall, and then Jake points out that the duration of the notes are not all half notes so they need to be changed. It is important to note at this point that the students' familiarity with the song gives them a resource for constructing a feedback loop with BlockyTalky as they proceed to address this weakness. When running the program or testing their code, the students can hear whether the song sounds correct — in the above case they are noting that the timing is not the same in their code as compared to the actual song that they remember. This feedback loop enables students to critique their own projects, enabling them to capture the sound of the original song by iterating over their code.

4. DISCUSSION AND CONCLUSIONS

Nathan and Chris used their musical and computational knowledge to customize a pre-built computer music project to meet their own goals. Through a DCOG process of recall, representation, and data transformation, they programmed a melody with BlockyTalky. At the beginning of the episode, it was clear that Nathan could play the song and had an embodied, non-symbolic representation of it. Chris demonstrated he was capable of putting standard music notation into computer code. However, they were only successful because the group reconfigured social structure to include the impromptu support provided by Jake and his extensive musical background. Despite the representation transformation roadblock they encountered, the students successfully programmed a sequence of notes that played one after another by programming a sequence of blocks that was based upon a sequence of notes plucked on a guitar.

This episode illustrates how the DCOG offers insights into how thinking and learning are happening that are not possible with a traditional theory of cognition. Cognition in this episode was distributed across the group. Nathan retrieved from his long-term memory a representation of what the notes in the song were. The format of this representation was not usable within the BlockyTalky software, which led Nathan and Chris to detect that they were at an impasse and then to initiate a reconfiguration of the group. They roped in Jake, who assisted with crucial information processing work, which Chris then encoded in the computer's memory (in the form of program code). The work was deeply shaped by cultural resources: the students and Jake all knew what *Smoke on the Water* should sound like because it is a mainstay of classic rock. This provided a common ground in which to problem solve, as well as motivation to the boys. The cultural artifact of the guitar, available because of the setting of the camp in a music room, was instrumental in Nathan's ability to articulate what the notes of the song should be; together with his body (his fingers, in particular) it became the mechanism through which Nathan's knowledge went from an internal (to the head) resource to a shared resource for problem solving. The event of Nathan's retrieval of a guitar sent the group down a particular problem solving path; had they continued searching online they may have found other ways to find the notes of the song, such as by finding ways to transform guitar tablature to standard musical note names or by simply finding a list of notes to directly input into the computer. Finally, the events that took place after the episode detailed here, tweaking the note durations to comport with the boy's memories of the song, reflects the computer's instrumentality to the boys' cognition: they are not skilled enough musicians to reverse-engineer timing from their own intuitive senses of the song, and so the artifact of the computer becomes a cognitive resource that enables problem solving through easy trial-end-error experimentation with note lengths. With more musical practice this system could be rebalanced to not need this technological affordance, but until then, the computer is a vital part of the boys' musical cognition.

The DCOG analysis also enables us to ask nuanced questions about assessment: Was the boys' dependence upon help from Jake problematic? Was their getting stuck a reflection of difficulties with understanding programming, or something else? They could not have achieved their goal without Jake doing a key aspect of the representation transformation with them, but the help he provided was not primarily about computing. This suggests that if we want students to be able to explore computer science and engineering through media like music, then our learning environment designs (including tools, curriculum, and teaching) need to allow students to succeed even if they do not yet possess virtuosity in the media that they are computing with. To wit: Music is a very powerful cultural resource, and one that could be quite useful for supporting learning in computing. But students should not need to know how to read someone else's hands on a guitar in order to learn to program a computer. This suggests a design problem: how should we provide support for computer music that facilitates progress without requiring such extensive music disciplinary knowledge? For example, should we change our system to support plugging a guitar into the computer so that simply playing it creates a program? That would certainly circumvent the need to know standard music notation, but it would also obviate most of the project's programming in the process. In our current design, even with Jake's help, Chris still modified the existing program, first changing existing note blocks and then adding new ones as the sequence of instructions lengthened to match Nathan's guitar plucking. Going directly from a guitar to program code would skip this programming work, a prospect that we find undesirable. In future work we will explore intermediate representations that are within students' zones of proximal development [33].

Jake's preservation of students' agency raises exciting questions for curriculum design: He was able to scaffold the activity for the boys, becoming part of the system while letting the boys do the computer programming entirely themselves. Agency in the group remained with the students. In our experiences, it is often the case that when a teacher assists a group with a hard problem, agency over the group's problem solving shifts to the teacher. That was not so here. This may mean that the interdisciplinary nature of the project, combined with the teacher demonstrating authority in the musical content but not overtly so in the computer programming aspects of the project, enabled a less agency-stripping enactment of the role of expert. This leads us to the question: Can future media computation curricula deliberately include productive participatory roles for teachers where they can play an expert role in a non-computing domain (like music) to afford them close observation of students' emerging computation without interfering with the computing agency and skill that students are developing?

New programmers sometimes treat computers as if they were intelligent partners, as machines that can ask for clarification [24]. This conceptual bug is a source of errors in learning. Yet computer interfaces, including programming languages, frequently demand information from their users. BlockyTalky's prompting for note durations led the boys to argue about the amount of information about each note that they would need to know to be productive. This set of discursive events was spurred by students' differing interpretations of what clarification the system needed in order to be programmed. In a sense, the computer's interface imbued it with agency to guide the group's discussion. Though the timing discussion in this case was ultimately inconsequential, computing education researchers might investigate ways that future tools could use this potential for agency to guide group problem solving discussion.

We have shown how DCOG can be a powerful theoretical framework for analyzing collaborative CS learning. But its utility is not limited to studying multi-student groupings, as most of the properties of cognitive systems that DCOG highlights also inhere in single-student learning (which is also culturally- and historically-situated, involves external and internal representations, tools, etc.). A limitation of this approach is that detailed discourse analysis of the sort we performed here is time consuming and therefore difficult to scale. However, as DCOG opens up possibilities for understanding student learning in CS that other perspectives and methodologies lack, it could become a powerful tool for improving research on computing education.

5. ACKNOWLEDGMENTS

We thank the National Science Foundation for funding this work (Award 1418463), and especially appreciate Jeff Forbes's advocacy within NSF for this EAGER project. We also thank Theresa Perry for her advice and assistance, and Nick Benson, Ben Helm, Case Jemison, Michael Ferdico, & Anthony Ambroso for their help in collecting these data.

6. REFERENCES

[1] D. Abrahamson and U. Wilensky. The stratified learning zone: Examining collaborative-learning

design in demographically-diverse mathematics classrooms. In *Annual Meeting of the American Educational Research Association*, 2005.

[2] J. R. Anderson, L. M. Reder, and H. A. Simon. Situated learning and education. *Educational Researcher*, 25(4):5–11, 1996.

[3] A. Basawapatna, K. H. Koh, A. Repenning, D. C. Webb, and K. S. Marshall. Recognizing computational thinking patterns. In *Proceedings of the 42nd ACM Technical Symposium on Computer Science Education*, pages 245–250, 2011.

[4] M. Berland, C. Smith, and D. Davis. Visualizing live collaboration in the classroom with AMOEBA. In *Proceedings of the Tenth International Conference on Computer-Supported Collaborative Learning*, 2013.

[5] P. Blikstein, M. Worsley, C. Piech, M. Sahami, S. Cooper, and D. Koller. Programming pluralism: Using learning analytics to detect patterns in the learning of computer programming. *Journal of the Learning Sciences*, 23(4):561–599, 2014.

[6] J. D. Bransford, A. L. Brown, and R. R. Cocking. *How people learn: Brain, mind, experience, and school*. National Academy Press, 1999.

[7] K. Brennan and M. Resnick. New frameworks for studying and assessing the development of computational thinking. In *Proceedings of the 2012 Annual Meeting of the American Educational Research Association*, 2012.

[8] A. L. Brown. Design experiments: Theoretical and methodological challenges in creating complex interventions in classroom settings. *The Journal of the Learning Sciences*, 2(2):141–178, 1992.

[9] N. C. Brown and A. Altadmri. Investigating novice programming mistakes: Educator beliefs vs. student data. In *Proceedings of the Tenth Annual Conference on International Computing Education Research*, pages 43–50, 2014.

[10] A. S. Bruckman. *MOOSE Crossing: Construction, community, and learning in a networked virtual world for kids*. PhD thesis, Massachusetts Institute of Technology, 1997.

[11] M. Cole. *Cultural psychology: A once and future discipline*. Harvard University Press, 1998.

[12] A. Collins, J. Brown, and S. Newinan. Cognitive apprenticeship: Teaching the craft of reading, writing, and mathematics. In *Knowing, learning, and instruction: Essays in honor of Robert Glaser*, pages 453–494. Lawrence Erlbaum Associates, Inc., 1989.

[13] D. A. Fields, V. Vasudevan, and Y. B. Kafai. The programmers' collective: Connecting collaboration and computation in a high school scratch mashup coding workshop. In *Learning and Becoming in Practice: ICLS 2014 Conference Proceedings*, 2014.

[14] M. Heidegger. *Being and time: A translation of Sein und Zeit*. SUNY Press, 1996.

[15] J. Hollan, E. Hutchins, and D. Kirsh. Distributed cognition: Toward a new foundation for human-computer interaction research. *ACM Transactions on Computer-Human Interaction (TOCHI)*, 7(2):174–196, 2000.

[16] E. Hutchins. *Cognition in the Wild*. MIT press, 1995.

[17] E. R. Kazakoff, A. Sullivan, and M. U. Bers. The effect of a classroom-based intensive robotics and programming workshop on sequencing ability in early childhood. *Early Childhood Education Journal*, 41(4):245–255, 2013.

[18] J. Lave. *Cognition in practice: Mind, mathematics and culture in everyday life*. Cambridge University Press, 1988.

[19] S. T. Levy and U. Wilensky. Inventing a "mid level" to make ends meet: Reasoning between the levels of complexity. *Cognition and Instruction*, 26(1):1–47, 2008.

[20] C. M. Lewis. *Applications of Out-of-domain Knowledge in Students' Reasoning About Computer Program State*. PhD thesis, Berkeley, CA, USA, 2012. AAI3555787.

[21] L. Malmi, J. Sheard, R. Bednarik, J. Helminen, P. Kinnunen, A. Korhonen, N. Myller, J. Sorva, A. Taherkhani, et al. Theoretical underpinnings of computing education research: What is the evidence? In *Proceedings of the Tenth Annual Conference on International Computing Education Research*, pages 27–34, 2014.

[22] C. McDowell, L. Werner, H. E. Bullock, and J. Fernald. Pair programming improves student retention, confidence, and program quality. *Communications of the ACM*, 49(8):90–95, 2006.

[23] M. Packer. The problem of transfer, and the sociocultural critique of schooling. *The Journal of the Learning Sciences*, 10(4):493–514, 2001.

[24] R. D. Pea, E. Soloway, and J. C. Spohrer. The buggy path to the development of programming expertise. *Focus on Learning Problems in Mathematics*, 9:5–30, 1987.

[25] L. Porter, C. Bailey Lee, and B. Simon. Halving fail rates using peer instruction: A study of four computer science courses. In *Proceeding of the 44th ACM Technical Symposium on Computer Science Education*, pages 177–182, 2013.

[26] L. Porter, C. Bailey Lee, B. Simon, and D. Zingaro. Peer instruction: Do students really learn from peer discussion in computing? In *Proceedings of the Seventh International Workshop on Computing Education Research*, pages 45–52, 2011.

[27] B. Rogoff. *The cultural nature of human development*. Oxford University Press, 2003.

[28] J. Roschelle. Learning by collaborating: Convergent conceptual change. *The Journal of the Learning Sciences*, 2(3):235–276, 1992.

[29] N. Shah, C. M. Lewis, and R. Caires. Analyzing equity in collaborative learning situations: A comparative case study in elementary computer science. In *Proceedings of the 11th International Conference of the Learning Sciences*, 2014.

[30] B. Sherin, A. A. diSessa, and D. Hammer. Dynaturtle revisited: Learning physics through collaborative design of a computer model. *Interactive Learning Environments*, 3(2):91–118, 1993.

[31] J. P. Smith III, A. A. Disessa, and J. Roschelle. Misconceptions reconceived: A constructivist analysis of knowledge in transition. *The Journal of the Learning Sciences*, 3(2):115–163, 1994.

[32] J. Tenenberg and Y. B.-D. Kolikant. Computer programs, dialogicality, and intentionality. In *Proceedings of the Tenth Annual Conference on International Computing Education Research*, pages 99–106. ACM, 2014.

[33] L. S. Vygotsky. *Mind in society: The development of higher psychological processes*. Harvard University Press, 1980.

[34] T. White. Code talk: Student discourse and participation with networked handhelds. *International Journal of Computer-Supported Collaborative Learning*, 1(3):359–382, 2006.

Scaling up Women in Computing Initiatives:
What Can We Learn from a Public Policy Perspective?

Elizabeth Patitsas, Michelle Craig, and Steve Easterbrook
Department of Computer Science
University of Toronto
Toronto, Ontario, Canada
patitsas, mcraig, sme@cs.toronto.edu

ABSTRACT

How to increase diversity in computer science is an important open question in CS education. A number of best practices have been suggested based on case studies; however, for scaling these efforts up in a sustainable fashion, it remains unclear which types of initiatives are most effective in which contexts. We examine gender diversity initiatives in CS education from a policy analysis perspective, adapting McDonnell and Elmore's 1987 notion of policy instruments, wherein the initiative is the unit of analysis. We present a conceptual framework for categorizing the different policy instruments by a cross of 'leverage' and 'targetedness', and discuss how different types of initiatives will scale. We argue that universally-targeted, high-leverage initiatives are most important for scaling up diversity initiatives in CS education, with medium-leverage change being a stepping stone to high leverage change.

1. INTRODUCTION

In the past three decades, a great deal of effort has been put into trying to improve female participation in computer science. Yet, the numbers in North America haven't budged: women continue to make up only 18% of CS majors [21].

Some efforts have had tremendous, sustained results. For example, Carnegie Mellon and Harvey Mudd have both increased the percentage of women studying CS from around 15% to around 40% in the span of a few years [1, 38].

These initiatives remain unusual, however. While they provide proof that change can happen, they do not provide a roadmap on how to bring that change to scale.

Scale has become a new focus for CS education [28, 20]: as CS is increasingly taught to a wider audience – especially in k-12 school systems – how can we handle the scale? To look at the issue of scale, we adopt the lens of public policy analysis: we consider women-in-computing initiatives as acts of policy.

Researchers who study education at scale – particularly education policy – often work with units of analysis such as initiatives, policies, schools, or regions. In comparison, in the CS education community we tend to work with individuals as our units of analysis. Even when we evaluate initiatives, we tend to evaluate one initiative at a time, using the beneficiaries of the initiative as the unit of analysis.

In this paper we will be considering initiatives as the unit of analysis, rather than individuals. We present a conceptual framework for classifying diversity initiatives, providing a first step toward a policy analysis approach to computer science education.

2. POLICY INSTRUMENTS

In this paper we treat women-in-computing initiatives as acts of department or classroom policy. This framing of diversity initiatives allows us to draw on literature from public policy analysis. To simplify the scope of this paper, when we talk about 'diversity' we will focus on gender diversity specifically. We will return to the broader diversity issues in subsection 7.1.

We use a broad definition of 'initiative': any formal effort to increase female engagement in computing. Some examples of what we mean by initiative, or policy, include:

Admissions criteria change: changing admissions criteria to focus on 'non-numerics' like at CMU [38]

Degree requirement change: having multiple CS1s separated by experience level / applications [1]

Curriculum change: using MediaComputation to teach CS1 in a context-focused fashion [26]

Pedagogy change: randomly calling on students to ensure that all students speak equally in the classroom and overcome a 'defensive climate' [24]

Sending students to the Grace Hopper Celebration: to foster community amongst female students and expose them to the 'real world' of computer science [1]

Research opportunities for first-years: to foster early interest in CS [1]

K-12 outreach: bringing k-12 students to the university to expose them to computer science activities, such as via a summer camp or day-camp [14]

The education policy literature provides us a notion of 'policy instrument': thinking about qualities of policies themselves, using the policies as units of analysis. The approach comes from McDonnell and Elmore's 1987 classification of macro-level policies as being mandates, initiatives, system change, or capacity-building [40].

Other policy researchers have classified policies differently (e.g. [18]); the insight here is that policies themselves can be classified and their classifications theorized upon.

As our focus here is on department-level policies – rather than nation/state-level – with a focus on scaling up women-in-computing initiatives, we have constructed our own conceptual framework of policy instruments. We classify women-in-computing initiatives by two axes: 'targetedness' (how broad the audience is) and 'leverage' (how deeply the system is changed).

3. TARGETEDNESS

In public health, the Universal/Selective/Indicated (USI) model has proven to be an effective conceptual tool for forming public health initiatives [51]. In this model, initiatives are categorized by the intended audience: universal strategies are aimed at whole populations; selective strategies are aimed toward at-risk groups; and indicated strategies are aimed toward individuals displaying signs of the condition in question.

To give some more concrete examples from suicide prevention:

Universal initiatives: restricting exposure to suicide content in mass media, adding barriers on bridges, and restrictions on pharmaceutical dispensing [17]

Selective initiatives: selective initiatives here include suicide prevention centres and hot-lines, community or school suicide prevention programmes, and programmes for veterans and military personnel [17]

Indicated initiatives: training general practitioners to spot warning signs in patients and how to talk to patients about suicide, postvention, and crisis hot-lines [17]

Here we'll extend the USI model from public health to an education setting. We will refer to the spectrum it represents as 'targetedness': with universal initiatives being less 'targeted' and indicated ones being most 'targeted'. 'Targetedness' refers to how *wide* the audience is, not which audience is being targeted.

3.1 Universal initiatives

In an education context, our idea of "population" differs. A "population" can be a whole classroom of students, a whole CS department or school – or even the general population of a country. The key notion is that universal initiatives are carried out without regard to population target groups or risk factors. Examples of diversity initiatives in CS education which are universal include:

- A CS department makes a mentorship programme available to all students
- Pair-programming and peer instruction for a whole classroom
- A university mandates that all students need to take CS, and its CS department provides multiple, engaging, versions of CS1 that are tailored to different students' interests – like at HMC
- A department changes their admission process that affects all CS students – like at CMU
- A conference switches to using blind review of its submissions.
- A CS professor implements a 'social-psychological intervention' in their classroom (e.g. values-affirming essay), to improve the self-efficacy of all students [53]

Each of these initiatives affects a differently sized population, but the initiative affects all members of its population. It is worth noting that all of the above practices are known (or thought to) to improve female representation in CS. They disproportionately benefit women and other minorities, but also aid majority-members. The same is true of the universal initiatives for suicide prevention: restricting suicide content in the mass media affects all mass media consumers, but disproportionately helps those with suicidal ideations.

While it may seem quite costly to run a universal initiative, given that it has to reach the whole population, recent meta-reviews in public health have found universal initiatives are actually the most cost-effective: "a large number of people at small risk may give rise to more cases of disease than a small number who are at high risk" [17]. And as many diseases are contagious, universal initiatives can improve the resilience of the whole population.

Furthermore, as universal initiatives target the whole population, they provide a means of reaching at-risk individuals who are not in contact with institutional services [17].

3.2 Selective initiatives

In comparison, selective initiatives target a population known to be underrepresented in CS; they specifically and explicitly benefit that group, and provide them with targeted support to 'level the playing field' with dominant groups in CS. Examples include:

- A CS department makes a mentorship programme available to all female students
- Departmental women-in-CS clubs
- Giving the opportunity for female students to go to the Grace Hopper Celebration
- Outreach initiatives for school-age girls
- Scholarships for women in CS

Many selective initiatives in public health – suicide-related or otherwise – have been found effective. Meta-reviews have noted that long-term selective initiatives tend to be more successful than short-term ones. Selective initiatives need to be culturally and contextually appropriate to the audience(s) in order to be effective [17].

Certain selective initiatives have been noted as having potential harm – for example, being seen associated with a group for a stigmatized disease/condition. Like in public health, stigmatization has the potential to be an issue in education. Audit studies have found that job candidates associated with affirmative action (which targets specific groups) are perceived as less competent than identical job candidates without those associations [31]. This effect is strongest when the job candidate's competence is ambiguous [31]. Some qualitative studies of women in science have also noted that beneficiaries of research grants for women in physics feel they are perceived as less competent for receiving the "women's award" rather than a traditional research grant [48].

3.3 Indicated initiatives

Finally, some examples of indicated initiatives in CS education would include:

- A CS department makes a mentorship programme available to students who have been flagged as struggling in their studies
- A teacher takes the time to encourage a student to study more CS
- An academic adviser notices a student is lacking motivation to study CS, and takes the student to Grace Hopper with them
- A supervisor notices a student is facing sexual harassment in their research lab, and makes appropriate steps to protect the student

The effect of indicated initiatives can be quite strong for the individuals it affects: one-on-one encouragement is a strong indicator of whether black students will take CS [42, 55, 28]; it is strongly beneficial to women also [42].

Indicated initiatives, however, rely on educators to be able to recognize students who need help, and be able to effectively help them. For us to rely on indicated initiatives requires all (or nearly all) CS educators to take part – and as a result scales poorly.

4. LEVERAGE

In contemplating scaling up changes, it is also worth considering whether the changes are system-changing or are relatively superficial. Systems thinking offers the notion of *leverage points*: places and ways one can change a system. Donella Meadows constructed a categorization scheme of types of leverage points, and organized them by how much leverage they have in a system. The list in this section goes from least leverage to most – in other words, how deeply (and effectively) the system is changed.

Jay Forrester, a pioneer of systems thinking, noted that although people in a system often know intuitively where to find leverage points, "more often than not they push the change in the wrong direction" [41]. For example, in one of Forrester's studies of urban dynamics from the 1960s, he found that subsidized low-income housing is a leverage point. However, Forrester's model counterintuitively found that the *less* low-income housing there was in a city, the better off the city was – including the low-income citizens [22]. Many more examples of unintuitive leverage-points can be found in [41].

Thinking about leverage points gives us a tool for identifying when changes could be superficial – so that we can focus resources on deeper changes. It also allows to better understand and describe system changes.

It's worth noting upfront that high-leverage changes are often the hardest to make. Systems are resilient and can resist the change; too much change too suddenly can quickly be undone. On the other end, the categories with least leverage – "constants, parameters, numbers" and "the sizes of buffers" – are often superficial. While easier to alter, they rarely lead to systemic change.

4.1 Meadows' Leverage Points

Constants, parameters, numbers: In systems thinking, systems are thought of as having *stocks* (quantities of things) and *flows* (the altering of stocks). A simple example is a bathtub: there is a flow of water from the faucet into the bathtub, a stock of water in the bathtub, and a flow of water out the drain. Changing the rate of flow in and out of the bathtub has an effect on the system – but does not change the fundamental structure of the system.

Meadows notes that much of politics focuses on this leverage point: how much we spent on x, the value of the minimum wage, the value of a tax rate, etc. However, changing the parameter rarely changes the behaviour of the entire system [41]. At the same time, humans tend to focus on parameters [41]; they are concrete and easy to identify.

Sizes of buffers: Some systems have *buffers*: stabilizing stocks that are large relative to their flows. Buffers play an important role in many systems – for example, stores keep inventory rather than ordering new stock every time a customer buys something new. The inventory gives the store a buffer from any delays in deliveries or sudden increases in sales.

The structure of stocks and flows: The structure of how stocks and flows can have an enormous impact on a system [41]. Redesigning a plumbing system, or refactoring a code base, can have large effects.

The delays in the system: Delays in a system affect feedback loops, and can cause unpredictable behaviour in a system. Reducing or increasing delays in the system can have large effects. Often, delays cannot be changed: it takes a fixed amount of time for a baby to mature or for electrons to travel a given distance.

The strength of negative feedback loops: A thermostat is a classic example of a system controlled by a negative feedback loop: if it gets too cold, the furnace turns on. If it gets too hot, the furnace turns off. The result is a room with a temperature which varies slightly around a set equilibrium; any disturbance in the equilibrium and it is programmed to return to that state.

The strength of a negative feedback loop is important relative to the impact it is designed to correct [41]. A thermostat may work well on a cold winter day – until somebody opens a window, decreasing the strength of the negative feedback loop.

The gain of positive feedback loops: Positive feedback loops are self-reinforcing – such as how the more people catch the flu, the more it spreads; or how the more money you have in the bonk, the more interest you earn. Positive feedback loops can also be known as 'success to the successful': for example, the more research grants a professor receives, the easier it is for them to receive subsequent grants.

The structure of information flows: A famous case in energy usage behaviour comes from the Netherlands in the 70s: in a particular suburb of Amsterdam, some otherwise identical houses were built with their electric meters in the basement, and some in the front hall. The houses with the meter in the front hall used one third the electricity as the houses with the meter in the basement, where people rarely saw it. Those who saw their meter every day were hence more conscious of their electricity usage – and used less [41].

Adding a flow of information to the system adds a new loop to the system: it is not increasing the strength of an existing one or its parameters [41]. Removing an information flow is a similarly high leverage change: censorship can have drastic impacts on social systems.

The rules of the system: Even more fundamental than the stocks and flows in a system are the rules which govern it: incentives, punishments, constraints, laws, etc. The rules of a system determine its scope and boundaries. Changing a constitution of a country or an organization is an example of this leverage point.

The power of self-organization: The system's ability to change its own rules and structures is known as *self-organization*. In a biological context, evolution is an example of self-organization. In a political context, social movements provide a different example.

The goals of the system: One of the most fundamental things about a system is its purpose: a school has a goal of teaching students, a hospital of healing patients, a corporation of making profits. If a university changes its purpose from teaching students to producing research – or to making profits – then lower leverage points will be influenced towards that goal.

The paradigm of the system: The shared ideas of those in a system – the great unstated assumptions – make up that system's paradigm[1]. Goals are articulated and made within paradigms. People involved in self-organization act in ways affected by their paradigms. And so, the deepest way to change a system is to change the paradigms affecting or defining it.

---

[1]Meadows lists a final leverage point, 'transcending paradigms', which contradicts the notion of a paradigm, and has been omitted as a result. Her argument that we should 'transcend paradigms' in favour of systems thinking is in itself a reflection of her own paradigm.

4.2 Simplifying Meadows: 4 Leverage Groups

To simplify Meadows' leverage-point continuum we group her leverage points into four categories, intentionally borrowing the names from Structure-Behaviour-Function Theory [32]:

Structural change: the constants and parameters, the sizes of the buffers, the structure of the stocks and flows.

System behaviour change: changing the gains and delays of the feedback loops.

Function change: changing how a system is controlled (information flows, rules, self-organization, goals)

Paradigm change: changing the very paradigms (in a Kuhnian sense) upon which the system's control is based.

For women-in-computing initiatives, structural changes would include:

- Having CS1 taught by a woman [5] (a parameter change)
- Using female pronouns in assignment instructions [25] (parameter change)
- The size of the departmental Women in CS support group [38] (buffers)
- Assigning groups based on gender [19] (buffers)
- Provide multiple entry points into a CS major [14] (structure of stocks/flows)
- Build "breaks" into the CS1 curriculum as reported in [1] (structure of stocks/flows)

While all these structural changes surely help, they *on their own* do not make for systemic change in CS programmes and classrooms.

System behaviour changes have higher leverage. When it comes to improving diversity in CS, reducing the effects of "success to the successful" makes a major difference. Some system behaviour changes would include:

- Change when students have access to research opportunities [1] (changing delays)
- In CS1, have students write meaningful programs from day one [1] (changing delays)
- Use blind review for scholarship applications [10] (strength of negative feedback loops)
- Reduce and remove potential triggers of stereotype threat, such as posters of Star Trek [13] (strength of negative feedback loops)
- Provide community service learning and co-op opportunities to undergraduates [14] (gain of positive feedback loops)
- Provide more individual encouragement and mentorship to students [14] (gain of positive feedback loops)

Changing how the system is controlled ("function") goes even further in terms of leverage; some examples include:

- Outreach efforts designed to increase/add information flows [14] (information flows)
- More feedback for students (information flows)
- Change entry requirements to the CS major to focus more on 'non-numerics' rather than prior experience [38] (rules)
- Establish a new classroom rule to call on all students randomly, to overcome a 'defensive climate' [24] (rules)
- Perform action research with women and underrepresented minorities in your department [38] (self-organization)
- Empower students to direct some or all of the course content, or use open-ended projects [8] (self-organization)
- Change the goal of the programme to provide an inclusive, positive learning environment for all students [8] (goals)
- Change the learning goals of the class to focus on problem-solving and applications (e.g. MediaComputation [26]) (goals)

And the final leverage point would be paradigm change – some relevant ones would be:

- Shift in thinking: it's the institution that has the problems, not the minority groups [48] (paradigm)
- Shift to an approach to teaching which empowers students, rather than the 'banking model' of education when we deposit 'coins' of knowledge into our students 'bank accounts' [23] (paradigm)
- Shift in thinking: seeing the excellence in computing as something which can be taught/learnt rather than seeing excellence in computing as tied to innate ability (or 'geek genes') [27, 35] (paradigm)

Paradigm changes are difficult to carry out, given the broad change needed to accompany them. When it comes to making change in a system, jumping straight to a paradigm change is usually impractical.

5. TARGETEDNESS AND LEVERAGE

The 'targetedness' and 'leverage' qualities of a diversity initiative are independent; in Table 1 we show some examples of initiatives with varying levels of targetedness/leverage.

For example, the table shows different ways an instructor can provide an indicated intervention with a student: giving a student a buffer from a hostile culture is lower leverage (structure); encouragement affects feedback loops and hence provides more leverage (behaviour); providing information on different study and career goals has more leverage (function); and changing their mindset (paradigm) would be a high leverage change.

A particular leverage point can also vary by targetedness: a CS department launching a mentorship programme could open it to all students (universal), open it only to female students (selective), or have it private to students who have been flagged by faculty as needing extra help (indicated).

On the ground, educators spend a great deal of time on indicated initiatives: working with individual students, wondering what to say to them and how to nurture positive growth. Psychology papers often enjoy a lot of attention amongst educators: they focus on these individual changes. As CS educators, when it comes to diversity, we like to talk about issues such as mindset [47], identity [44], stereotype threat [13] and self-efficacy [7]. When we talk about groups, we still talk about the individuals; e.g. "women are more likely to have low-self efficacy". Although these discuss groups, the unit of analysis remains the individual.

While indicated initiatives call for a background in psychology, universal initiatives more often call for a background in sociology. Effective universal initiatives call for thinking about the 'population' in question as a whole, rather than a collection of individuals.

The CS education literature has an understandable tendency to draw upon more disciplinary approaches from psychology than sociology. In Malmi et al's recent survey of theoretical bases of CS education literature, sociology was not even common enough to warrant a category in their data [36]. Often when we talk about universal/selective initiatives we still do so in the language of psychology – increases to self-efficacy of the individuals in a population [7], reducing stereotype threat of the individuals in a group [13], etc.

	Universal	Selective	Indicated
Structure	Whether to use female pronouns in assignment instructions	The size of a women-in-CS club	Add a female student you know is struggling to the women-in-CS club's mailing list
Behaviour	A CS department provides a mentorship programme for all CS undergraduates	A women-in-CS club provides a mentorship programme	Provide specific encouragement to a student you know has been discouraged by their peers
Function	Change the learning goals of introductory CS to focus on problem-solving and applications	Change your department's decision making process so a women-in-CS committee provides input on department policies	Counsel a student you know is not engaged with CS about new career goals they can have within the field
Paradigm	Change the goal of your CS major to promote a collaborative, participatory learning environment	Change the paradigm of a Women in CS club to be intersectional and trans-inclusive	Change a struggling student's mindset from a fixed one to a growth mindset

Table 1: Examples of how different initiatives can vary by both targetedness and leverage.

When we look at cases like HMC [1] and CMU [38], they describe their successes as a series of smaller initiatives, typically with medium or low leverage. To a systems thinker, those smaller initiatives are secondary to the high-leverage changes in organizational goals/paradigms. HMC and CMU both made holistic changes to their CS programmes with the goal of increasing diversity, and making this part of how they teach CS. While not acknowledged in their work, the interaction effects of all their changes is likely greater than the sum of each individual initiative: the changes reinforce each other and change the cultures at those institutions.

6. SCALING UP

6.1 Targetedness and Scale

When it comes to scaling up, indicated initiatives do poorly: they require nearly every educator to be ready to help a struggling student one-on-one. This requires both buy-in from educators *and* a time commitment from them: some educators may want to help struggling students but not feel they have the resources to do so. Indicated initiatives also suffer from variability: different educators will vary in their ability to diagnose and help different students.

Selective initiatives at first glance look promising for scaling up. Selective initiatives often seem like an obvious choice and follow a clear logic: a group (such as women) is not studying CS, so we should help them. There is a directness to selective initiatives, and it looks good (optics) to those running it.

6.1.1 Optics

Selective initiatives win when it comes to optics: a CS department can tout their 'commitment to diversity' by showing off their selective initiatives. Selective initiatives often *look* more like an intended group is being helped than universal initiatives – and meanwhile indicated initiatives are usually invisible to the public.

The optics of selective initiatives can be both a blessing and a curse. The upside is that it can be easier to rally resources and political support to help a disadvantaged group directly – indeed, it's often easier to do so than to change the whole system around their needs. 'Band-aid' solutions are common in policy for good reason: everybody wants to help, but only so much. The downside is that ineffective selective initiatives can act as "pink-washing": superficial efforts used to make people/organizations look good, in turn draining resources from other initiatives and impeding higher leverage change.

6.1.2 Illusion of Fairness

Companies which are described as having selective and indicated initiatives are perceived by the public as being fairer companies and better places to work [33].

Problematically, these initiatives can cause an 'illusion of fairness'. In six studies by Kaiser et al [33], participants were grouped in a 2x2 design. Half of the participants were shown information on a fictional company described as having some selective initiative; the other half were given information on a company without any mention of diversity. Then half of the participants in each group were shown evidence that the company they had seen was discriminating against some group (women, blacks); the other half were shown evidence that the company was not discriminating. And then all participants were shown an article about a woman or black man who was suing the company for discrimination.

All participants were then asked to evaluate the company with regard to qualities such as procedural fairness. Troublingly, participants who saw that the company had some diversity initiative thought the company was more procedurally fair, regardless of whether they saw a report showing evidence of discrimination at the company.

Participants were less likely to believe the credibility of the discrimination lawsuit if they saw that the company had some selective initiative. And supporting the paper's findings are a number of legal cases that Kaiser et al reported upon: judges in the US deferring to companies in discrimination cases because the company had enacted selective initiatives – *regardless of how effective they were!* [33].

This phenomenon seems most problematic when the selective initiative is low-leverage. In that case, the lack of real change to the system means that women (or other groups) are still going to be discriminated against — but now they may encounter even more bias *because* of the presence of the selective initiative.

6.1.3 Stigma and Stereotypes

Like in public health, there is potential for selective initiatives in CS education to have counter-productive effects for the beneficiaries. Stigma has been reported surrounding receiving women-in-CS 'help': Margolis and Fisher noted a "you're only here because you're a girl" phenomenon [38]. This has been observed in other fields of science: female physics professors who received research grants intended for women found they were taken less seriously as a result and felt a loss of self-efficacy for "needing to get the women's award" rather than a "normal" research grant [48].

Audit studies have found that resumes of women who benefited from initiatives specifically for women are ranked as less competent than identical resumes without the selective initiatives mentioned [31].

Informing women that they have been selective for special positions to do mathematical work *because* they were women was in one psychology study found to trigger stereotype threat [9] – however, if women were told they were selective based on *both* ability and gender, stereotype threat was not triggered [9].

Yet another social psychological phenomenon associated with selective initiatives is 'subtyping'. When women in CS (or another field) are consistently subtyped as "female computer scientists" rather than "computer scientists", rather than change peoples' ideations of what a computer scientist is, it instead creates a new type in peoples' minds: the *female* computer scientist [45, 6]. This subtype, the *female computer scientist*, is not only separate from the notion of a *computer scientist*, but reinforces that a regular *computer scientist* is not female – effectively further masculinizing the stereotype of computer scientists.

The subtyping effect becomes stronger with repeated exposure. The more effort we put into "women-in-CS" efforts, the more we highlight female computer scientists as *female computer scientists* (rather than computer scientists like any other), the stronger the effect. In short: this effect becomes *worse* with scale.

This is not to say that selective initiatives do not have merit. Instead, organizers of these initiatives need to be cautious of their implementation and wary of the potential side-effects. If selective initiatives are to be scaled up, then even more organizers must be counted on to navigate the potential side-effects.

Universal initiatives do much better with regard to the social psychology around them. If *everybody* receives the same initiative, then you're not making one particular minority group's status salient. Issues of stereotype threat, subtyping and stigma disappear.

6.1.4 Who is Selective?

By helping everybody, universal initiatives also avoid the issue of defining who and who does not fall into a selective group. Feminist theorists such as Judith Butler have well established that gender and sex are both social constructs [11]. If you only offer a programme for 'women', then you need to consider who is a 'woman'. Do you include male-to-female transgender individuals? Female-to-male? When in a trans person's transition do they count (or not count) as a 'woman'? What about intersex individuals (those born with biological aspects of both sexes) or individuals who do not have XX or XY chromosomes?

Other underrepresented minorities in CS suffer from similarly ambiguous boundary lines: race is another social construct with poorly defined boundaries [29]. If you offer a programme for black youth, are half-black youth allowed to attend? One quarter? One sixteenth? What about youth who are black but are adopted by white parents? White youth adopted by black parents?

Selective initiatives essentialize the groups they intend to help. Considering the issue of scale, helping only one group (or a set of groups) can be inefficient, given that people hold multiple identities at any given time.

A computer science department which only provides selective initiatives to women will wind up neglecting other underrepresented groups – who may need the help more than some (but not necessarily all) of the women. It is easy for departments to focus resources on visible minorities such as women and racial groups; invisible minorities tend to lose out on the selective initiative identity politics.

Universal diversity initiatives as a result have the potential to save resources. For example, rather than create a women-in-CS mentorship programme, an aboriginal-in-CS mentorship programme, a deaf-in-CS mentorship programme, and a trans-in-CS mentorship programme, a CS department can implement a mentorship programme for all students. Minority-member students can be stealthily matched with minority-member mentors. Not only are the visible minority groups aided, but the invisible minorities – especially those without faculty advocating on their behalf in department decision-making – are aided as well.

6.1.5 Resources Needed

On the note of resources, fiscal slack can be a necessary (but not sufficient) condition for policy innovation [40]. While universal initiatives are typically cheaper than selective initiatives, they often require a greater upfront cost: this can be politically difficult.

Indicated initiatives require low levels of 'governmental capacity'. This is defined as the ability of the initiating level to implement a policy, and the target to meet its requirements [40]. As professors have a great deal of autonomy over their teaching they have high governmental capacity in their own classrooms. On the other side, universal and selective initiatives suffer from the need for greater governmental capacity.

6.2 Leverage and Scale

Unlike targetedness, the amount of leverage an initiative has does not have a direct relationship with scalability. Leverage doesn't directly relate to who or how many people are affected/involved.

Leverage is about having *lasting* change: higher leverage changes are more likely to be sustained over time. The relevant scale here is not scaling over a population, but scaling over time.

Systems are notoriously difficult to change. Policymakers have long noted that enacting a policy doesn't mean it will be implemented as desired ('fidelity') or be sustained as future policies are brought forward [52, 18]. Higher leverage changes are more difficult to enact but they are more likely to stick once made.

Many selective and indicated initiatives are based on the assumption that a group needs special help. This is part of a paradigm that the *problem is the group itself, rather than what the greater system is doing to that group* [8]. This reflects a paradigm well-documented in the women-in-science literature: whether to change the women or to change the system [30].

Low-leverage changes are easy to understand and explain. They're easier from an optics point of view to work on; they provide a concrete change that one can focus on or take credit for. High-leverage changes are harder to pinpoint, especially when the changes are happening. The path to changing a curriculum is more evident than the path to changing a paradigm, and as a result is easier to rally resources around.

Low-leverage changes are also more easily co-opted by agents with other agendas. Sociologists have repeatedly documented cases of "false change": low-leverage change with little effect used to give a false sense that progress is being made, to stave off more radical change [2].

6.2.1 The Goldilocks Zone

Trying to change just a paradigm of a system is a difficult, if not impossible, task. Instead, queer theorists have referred to the need to start by making change by a *Goldilocks process* [16]. This involves starting with medium-leverage changes, then eventually switching to high-leverage changes.

This process is reminiscent of Vygotsky's notion of *Zone of Proximal Development* [50] but on a system-wide scale. You challenge the system with changes which are at the periphery of what is possible[2], and once you have your 'foot in the door' you continue shifting the system towards your goal.

Psychologists have documented that behaviour affects attitudes [43]. If a department starts making some medium-leverage changes, then people may engage more with the need for these changes, and become more inclined towards high-leverage changes.

6.2.2 Resources Needed

Making high- and medium- leverage changes to a system requires an understanding of the system. Information can be one of the most vital resources needed for high/medium leverage changes.

Counterintuitively, high-leverage changes can be the cheapest to implement: it costs very little *money* to change a paradigm, but to change your TA-to-student ratio is likely quite expensive. But while high-leverage changes may need fewer fiscal resources, they need much more political capital and governmental capacity. Changing the goals of an organization requires a great deal of political support – and lack of organized opposition.

Institutional context hence becomes vital here: how is formal/informal authority allocated amongst policy actors, and how are decisions made [40]? For example, one CS department could make decisions through committees; another through consensus-building. Consensus-focused departments are vulnerable to having policies blocked by professors who oppose the changes. This makes it harder to pass policies that have opponents – meaning that high-leverage changes are harder to make. But a consensus-focused department where everybody is brought on-board for a high-leverage change means the change is more likely to last.

6.3 Policy Space

The concept of *policy space* refers to the cumulative effects of previous policies, and how they shape the creation and implementation of new policies [4, 40]. Policies do not live independently, and cannot be thought of independently. Policymakers considering new diversity initiatives in their jurisdictions need to consider how new initiatives would fit into existing systems and interact with existing policies.

If a department or a professor has been used to making changes with a certain level of leverage/targetedness, they are more likely to stick to that level of leverage/targetedness [40]; alternative approaches may be too unfamiliar to them.

Research on how education policies are scaled up has documented multiple stages to the process: first demonstrating a proof of concept that the initiative can be implemented at all, then evaluating that it works, then showing it works in several other contexts, *then* scaling it up and refining it [39]. Frequently, context is the most important factor: many well-intentioned policies have 'failed' for neglecting the impact of context [52].

7. DISCUSSION

A couple papers ([15, 12]) have been written asking the question: why are there more women in other STEM fields than CS? Cohoon attributed the difference between biology and CS to the following: biology faculty have more favourable attitudes towards female students, spend more time mentoring students, and feel more of a shared responsibility for student success [15].

Selective initiatives in biology are relatively rare compared to computer science. Instead the biology faculty have goals more focused towards undergraduate teaching, and the

greater buy-in toward teaching has resulted in faculty doing more indicated work.

Other work looking at the differences between STEM fields also points to the paradigms in CS teaching as problematic – the collective belief held by CS educators that ability to perform in CS is fixed [27] is attributed to lower diversity [35].

7.1 Diversity

Our paper has focused on gender diversity in CS. It must be noted that many other facets of diversity exist: race, class, disability, sexual orientation, gender expression, etc. Different underrepresented groups in computer science have differing reasons for their underrepresentation – and individuals belonging to multiple minority-groups face interaction-effects from the multiple biases they encounter.

At the same time, many of the reasons non-gender minority groups are underrepresented in CS are the same as women: lack of encouragement [28], lack of prior exposure [37], stereotypes [49], hostile attitudes and biases [42], lack of role models [42], not knowing the 'hidden curriculum' [38], and not being part of the 'old boys' network' [54].

In many ways, the culture in computing discriminates against those who do not fit the stereotype of the white/Asian male 'nerd': even white male 'jocks' have reported feeling out of place in the CS classroom [38].

Gender has received the lion's share of the diversity research in CS education, and as a result we found it most appropriate to focus on it for this paper. Given the large number of women-in-CS initiatives to draw upon in creating our framework. Since we adapted very general frameworks to do so, we believe our framework will appropriately transfer to other diversity initiatives.

7.2 Limitations

Our conceptual framework provides some insights to the properties of different diversity initiatives, but the work we used to put it together has not been without critique. Meadows' approach to systems thinking ignores issues of historicity and power. While we included the concepts of political support/opposition and policy space in our discussion of resources and constraints, these still leave historicity and power in the background of our analysis.

Both the USI model and the leverage points fall into the structuralist approach to sociology, which traditionally ignores or backgrounds issues of historicity and power. Given the importance of power in diversity issues, future work in examining CS education policy may find it useful to foreground historicity/power – some alternate approaches could have been to use the concept of co-construction [18].

We chose a structuralist approach in this paper because it gives directions forward. While poststructural approaches are useful for exposing the reproduction of inequalities in organizations, they can give very little in terms of ideas for what to do about them. Structuralism gives concrete ideas for educators: *let's try a higher-leverage change; how about something selective?* etc.

7.3 Future work

Policy research, especially at scale, has a difficult time of comparing two policies: you can't necessarily scale up both, and you can't scale them both up on the same population. Experimental research becomes infeasible: policies hence need theoretical backing for scaling up, and research on relevant contexts.

Having developed a conceptual framework for classifying diversity initiatives, and presented some preliminary evidence of the importance of high-leverage changes, our next step is to conduct a mapping study of the CS education literature. It appears that much of the literature focuses on

---

[2]Political theorists refer to the scale of what is possible as the 'Overton window' [46].

the indicated and selective initiatives; universal initiatives appear underrepresented.

Future work is needed to look at the *micropolitics* of how CS departments make decisions on diversity initiatives. Micropolitics refers to the study of politics in organizations [3], and provides valuable insight for why schools and universities favour particular policies over others.

Existing papers on large-scale efforts, such as at HMC [1] and CMU [38], focus on describing the medium- and low-leverage changes that were enacted – rather than the high-leverage points or the context of their institutions. Furthermore, both works fail to describe the micropolitics of their organizations, only providing short and vague messages like "have a champion" for proposed policy changes.

Within the CS education literature, a paradigm of positivism can easily be spotted in papers on diversity. In Maria Klawe's account of the changes at HMC [34] she boasts that "other institutions can easily replicate" HMC's successes in attracting women into CS. We find this overly optimistic, as it ignores the cultural factors at HMC which made these changes possible – factors which include a president like Maria Klawe!

Klawe gives CMU and UBC as other examples of success, but again ignores cultural factors there. Most CS departments feature professors who care about diversity – but their resources and constraints may not favour the changes that worked at HMC. Context is a vital part of understanding what made a diversity initiative 'work', particularly the relevant existing resources and constraints.

In order for other institutions to understand *how* to make changes like at HMC and CMU, we need research on how policy actors navigate the political waters to enact change. This political knowledge is vital for scaling up.

As CS educators strive to make widespread changes to the demographics of their classrooms, we need to think about how to transfer and scale up the findings from the existing CS education literature – much more can be done to use the tools from education policy analysis in this research area.

7.4 Take-homes

The purpose of McDonnell and Elmore's paper was not only to reconceptualize policy, but to give conceptual tools to policymakers. They observed that policymakers are often unaware of the range of policy tools available to them, and stick to instruments that have worked for them in the past. McDonnell and Elmore's paper gives a structured way for policymakers to brainstorm policy approaches that would be in their blind spots [40].

Similar to McDonnell and Elmore, this paper gives CS educators a conceptual framework for thinking through what policy alternatives are available to them. When educators find themselves seeking to improve diversity, they have an activity available to them now: to brainstorm a change for each leverage point, and for each level of targetedness. The activity may uncover ideas that educators would not have otherwise considered.

8. CONCLUSIONS

While low-leverage, indicated initiatives may be the easiest for a CS educator to start with if they want to make a difference, these initiatives are likely the least effective – and least likely to scale well. Selective initiatives, while popular, present numerous challenges for scaling up; universal initiatives provide greater promise for effective policy at scale.

High leverage changes are most effective long-term, but are difficult to make on their own; medium leverage changes (system behaviour and function) fall into a 'Goldilocks zone': they provide an effective place to start, to start shifting the system toward high-leverage change. CS educators may

want to consider what feedback loops, goals and rules privilege majority-group members in their classrooms and CS programmes – and how their undergraduate programmes can be changed to level the playing field for all students.

9. ACKNOWLEDGMENTS

A thank you to Greg Wilson for providing a pointer to the USI model, to Nina Bascia for introducing us to the literature on micropolitics, and to Aditya Bhargava for proofreading. The first author has received funding from the Social Sciences and Humanities Research Council of Canada; the third author from the Natural Sciences and Engineering Research Council of Canada.

10. REFERENCES

[1] C. Alvarado, Z. Dodds, and R. Libeskind-Hadas. Increasing women's participation in computing at Harvey Mudd College. *ACM Inroads*, 3(4):55–64, Dec. 2012.

[2] N. Aschoff. *The New Prophets of Capital*. Verso Books, 2015.

[3] S. J. Ball. *The micro-politics of the school: Towards a theory of school organization*. Routledge, 2012.

[4] N. Bascia and B. Faubert. Primary class size reduction: How policy space, physical space, and spatiality shape what happens in real schools. *Leadership and Policy in Schools*, 11(3):344–364, 2012.

[5] E. P. Bettinger and B. T. Long. Do faculty serve as role models? the impact of instructor gender on female students. *American Economic Review*, pages 152–157, 2005.

[6] D. E. Betz and D. Sekaquaptewa. My fair physicist? Feminine math and science role models demotivate young girls. *Social Psychological and Personality Science*, 2012.

[7] S. Beyer. Why are women underrepresented in computer science? gender differences in stereotypes, self-efficacy, values, and interests and predictors of future cs course-taking and grades. *Computer Science Education*, 24(2-3):153–192, 2014.

[8] J. S. Brotman and F. M. Moore. Girls and science: A review of four themes in the science education literature. *Journal of research in science teaching*, 45(9):971–1002, 2008.

[9] R. P. Brown, T. Charnsangavej, K. A. Keough, M. L. Newman, and P. J. Rentfrow. Putting the "affirm" into affirmative action: preferential selection and academic performance. *Journal of personality and social psychology*, 79(5):736, 2000.

[10] A. E. Budden, T. Tregenza, L. W. Aarssen, J. Koricheva, R. Leimu, and C. J. Lortie. Double-blind review favours increased representation of female authors. *Trends in eco. & evo.*, 23(1):4–6, 2008.

[11] J. Butler et al. *Gender trouble*. routledge, 2002.

[12] S. Cheryan. Understanding the paradox in math-related fields: Why do some gender gaps remain while others do not? *Sex Roles*, 66:184–190, 2012. 10.1007/s11199-011-0060-z.

[13] S. Cheryan, V. C. Plaut, P. G. Davies, and C. M. Steele. Ambient belonging: How stereotypical cues impact gender participation in computer science. *Journal of Personality and Social Psychology*, 97(6):1045–1060, 2009.

[14] J. M. Cohoon. Recruiting and retaining women in undergraduate computing majors. *SIGCSE Bull.*, 34(2):48–52, June 2002.

[15] J. M. Cohoon. Women in CS and biology. *SIGCSE Bull.*, 34(1):82–86, Feb. 2002.

[16] D. K. Cortese. *Are We Thinking Straight?: The Politics of Straightness in a Lesbian and Gay Social Movement Organization.* Taylor & Francis, 2006.

[17] A. Dalton, J. Patterson, A. Stover, and H. Rilkoff. Suicide prevention in Toronto, 2014.

[18] A. Datnow and V. Park. Conceptualizing policy implementation: Large-scale reform in an era of complexity. *Handbook of education policy research*, pages 348–361, 2009.

[19] N. Ding and E. Harskamp. How partner gender influences female students' problem solving in physics education. *Journal of Science Education and Technology*, 15(5-6):331–343, 2006.

[20] S. Fincher. What are we doing when we teach computing in schools? *Communications of the ACM*, 58(5):24–26, 2015.

[21] N. C. for Women and I. Technology. By the numbers, 2013.

[22] J. W. Forrester. Urban dynamics. *IMR; Industrial Management Review (pre-1986)*, 11(3):67, 1970.

[23] P. Freire. *Pedagogy of the oppressed.* Bloomsbury Publishing, 2000.

[24] K. Garvin-Doxas and L. J. Barker. Communication in computer science classrooms: Understanding defensive climates as a means of creating supportive behaviors. *J. Educ. Resour. Comput.*, 4(1), Mar. 2004.

[25] J. Gastil. Generic pronouns and sexist language: The oxymoronic character of masculine generics. *Sex roles*, 23(11-12):629–643, 1990.

[26] M. Guzdial. Exploring hypotheses about media computation. In *Proceedings of the Ninth Annual International ACM Conference on International Computing Education Research*, ICER '13, pages 19–26, New York, NY, USA, 2013. ACM.

[27] M. Guzdial. Anyone can learn programming: Teaching > genetics, 2014.

[28] M. Guzdial, B. J. Ericson, T. McKlin, and S. Engelman. A statewide survey on computing education pathways and influences: Factors in broadening participation in computing. In *Proceedings of the Ninth Annual International Conference on International Computing Education Research*, ICER '12, pages 143–150, New York, NY, USA, 2012. ACM.

[29] S. Hall. New ethnicities. *Stuart Hall: Critical dialogues in cultural studies*, pages 441–49, 1996.

[30] S. G. Harding. *The science question in feminism.* Cornell University Press, 1986.

[31] M. E. Heilman, C. J. Block, and P. Stathatos. The affirmative action stigma of incompetence: Effects of performance information ambiguity. *Acad. of Mgmnt. J.*, 40(3):603–625, 1997.

[32] C. E. Hmelo-Silver and M. G. Pfeffer. Comparing expert and novice understanding of a complex system from the perspective of structures, behaviors, and functions. *Cognitive Science*, 28(1):127 – 138, 2004.

[33] C. R. Kaiser, B. Major, I. Jurcevic, T. L. Dover, L. M. Brady, and J. R. Shapiro. Presumed fair: Ironic effects of organizational diversity structures. 2012.

[34] M. Klawe. Increasing female participation in computing: The Harvey Mudd College story. *Computer*, 46(3):56–58, 2013.

[35] S.-J. Leslie, A. Cimpian, M. Meyer, and E. Freeland. Expectations of brilliance underlie gender distributions across academic disciplines. *Science*, 347(6219):262–265, 2015.

[36] L. Malmi, J. Sheard, Simon, R. Bednarik, J. Helminen, P. Kinnunen, A. Korhonen, N. Myller, J. Sorva, and A. Taherkhani. Theoretical underpinnings of

computing education research: What is the evidence? In *Proceedings of the Tenth Annual Conference on International Computing Education Research*, ICER '14, pages 27–34, New York, NY, USA, 2014. ACM.

[37] J. Margolis. *Stuck in the shallow end: Education, race, and computing.* MIT Press, 2008.

[38] J. Margolis and A. Fisher. *Unlocking the clubhouse: Women in computing.* MIT press, 2003.

[39] S.-K. McDonald. Scale-up as a framework for intervention, program, and policy evaluation research. *Handbook of education policy research*, pages 191–208, 2009.

[40] L. M. McDonnell and R. F. Elmore. Getting the job done: Alternative policy instruments. *Educational evaluation and policy analysis*, 9(2):133–152, 1987.

[41] D. H. Meadows. *Thinking in systems: A primer.* Chelsea Green Publishing, 2008.

[42] K. Modi, J. Schoenberg, and K. Salmond. Generation STEM: What girls say about science, technology, engineering, and math. *A Report from the Girl Scout Research Institute. New York, NY: Girl Scouts of the USA*, 2012.

[43] S. Owens and L. Driffill. How to change attitudes and behaviours in the context of energy. *Energy Policy*, 36(12):4412–4418, 2008.

[44] E. Pronin, C. M. Steele, and L. Ross. Identity bifurcation in response to stereotype threat: Women and mathematics. *Journal of Experimental Social Psychology*, 40(2):152–168, 2004.

[45] Z. Richards and M. Hewstone. Subtyping and subgrouping: Processes for the prevention and promotion of stereotype change. *Personality and Social Psychology Review*, 5(1):52–73, 2001.

[46] N. Russell. An introduction to the overton window of political possibilities. *published online at Mackinac Center web site*, 2006.

[47] B. Simon, B. Hanks, L. Murphy, S. Fitzgerald, R. McCauley, L. Thomas, and C. Zander. Saying isn't necessarily believing: influencing self-theories in computing. In *Proceedings of the Fourth international Workshop on Computing Education Research*, pages 173–184. ACM, 2008.

[48] M. Van den Brink and L. Stobbe. The support paradox: Overcoming dilemmas in gender equality programs. *Scand. J. of Mgmnt.*, 2013.

[49] R. Varma. Women in computing: The role of geek culture. *Science as culture*, 16(4):359–376, 2007.

[50] L. L. S. Vygotsky. *Mind in society: The development of higher psychological processes.* Harvard university press, 1978.

[51] D. Wasserman, T. Durkee, C. Wasserman, and C. Wasserman. Strategies in suicide prevention, 2009.

[52] W. Werner. Curriculum and uncertainty. *Social change and education in Canada*, 2:105–115, 1991.

[53] D. S. Yeager and G. M. Walton. Social-psychological interventions in education. *Rev. of Ed. Research*, 81(2):267–301, 2011.

[54] N. Zarrett, O. Malanchuk, P. E. Davis-Kean, and J. Eccles. Examining the gender gap in it by race: Young adults' decisions to pursue an it career, 2006.

[55] N. R. Zarrett and O. Malanchuk. Who's computing? Gender and race differences in young adults decisions to pursue an information technology career. *New directions for child and adolescent development*, 2005(110):65–84, 2005.

Does Outreach Impact Choices of Major for Underrepresented Undergraduate Students?

Monica M. McGill
Bradley University
1501 W. Bradley Ave.
Peoria, IL 61625 USA
01-309-677-4148
mmcgill@bradley.edu

Adrienne Decker
Rochester Institute of Technology
2145 Golisano Hall, 2nd Floor
Rochester, NY 14623 USA
01-585-475-4653
adrienne.decker@rit.edu

Amber Settle
DePaul University
243 S. Wabash Ave.
Chicago, IL 60604 USA
01-312-362-5324
asettle@cdm.depaul.edu

ABSTRACT

Over the last decade, there has been a concerted effort to bring more diverse voices to the technology field, with much of this being done through outreach activities to girls and boys. Unfortunately, data demonstrating the long-term impact of outreach activities remains rare. To contribute to knowledge on the longitudinal effect of outreach programs, we used a quantitative methodology that followed a descriptive design approach to explore the impact of participation in outreach activities on the choice of undergraduate major. Of those surveyed, 45.3% of the 770 respondents recalled participating in these activities. The results indicate that these activities had a more positive impact on Asians and more negative impact on Hispanics. Blacks/African Americans were more likely to voluntarily participate in outreach activities than Hispanics, and whites were more likely to feel that they were a welcome part of the group than non-whites. The results also may indicate that when outreach programs are available in earlier grades, they are not reaching non-white participants to the same extent as white participants.

Categories and Subject Descriptors

K.3.2 [**Computers and Education**]: Computer and Information Science Education – *computer science education*

General Terms

Measurement, Experimentation, Human Factors, Verification

Keywords

Computing outreach, Underrepresented groups in computing, Impact, Effectiveness, Minorities, Choice of Major

1. INTRODUCTION

A lack of diversity has existed in the field of computer science for decades, although the issue has taken on new urgency in recent years as the popular press has drawn attention to the low numbers of ethnic minorities earning degrees in computer science in the U.S. For example, the 2013 Taulbee Survey shows that while

41.3% of computer science Ph.D.s granted by U.S. institutions are earned by American citizens, only 12.9% are granted to ethnic minorities with 9.5% to Asians and 3.4% to all other minorities combined [85].

The situation is similar for computer science Masters students, since 35% of Masters degrees are awarded to American citizens, but only 11.7% are awarded to non-white[1] students with 8.5% to Asian students and 3.2% to all other minorities combined [85]. The situation is slightly better at the undergraduate level since 91.7% of all computer science bachelor's degrees awarded at U.S. institutions are given to American citizens, and 30.5% are awarded to minorities with 18.4% to Asians and 12.1% to all other minorities combined [85].

Data from previous Taulbee Surveys shows the persistence of the problem. In 2003, 20.6% of Ph.D.s, 19.4% of Masters, and 34.6% of bachelors in computer science were awarded to American citizens belonging to an ethnic minority [84]. Of the 20.6% of Ph.D.s awarded to minorities, 14% were to Asians and 6.6% were to all other minorities combined. Of the 19.4% of Masters awarded to minorities, 15% were awarded to Asians and 4.4% to all other minorities combined. Of the 34.6% of bachelor's degrees awarded to minorities, 24.5% were to Asians and 10.1% to all other minorities combined.

Moving back another decade, 21% of PhDs, 23% of Masters, and 25% of bachelors in computer science were awarded to U.S. citizens who are ethnic minorities in 1993 [4]. Of the 21% of Ph.D.s, 15% were awarded to Asians and 6% to all other minorities combined. Of the 23% of Masters, 18% were awarded to Asians and 5% to all other minorities combined. Of the 25% of bachelors, 16% were awarded to Asians and 9% to all other minorities combined.

As this data shows, lack of ethnic diversity is not only a long-standing problem in computing, it is one that has become worse among advanced-degree holders. Computer science educators have been cognizant of this far longer than the popular press, and outreach programs for ethnic minorities have existed for decades. Many U.S. institutions of higher education have some form of outreach program for K-12 students, although finding centralized directories of the programs is difficult. Centralized efforts at outreach do exist, and the Association for Computing Machinery (ACM) has played a role in several of them. For example, the Computer Science Teachers Association was formed by the ACM

ICER '15, August 9–13, 2015, Omaha, Nebraska, USA.
© 2015 ACM. ISBN 978-1-4503-3630-7/15/08…$15.00.
DOI: http://dx.doi.org/10.1145/2787622.2787711

---

[1] The terms *whites*, *non-whites*, and *blacks* are used in this paper to align with the U.S. Census Bureau, the Computing Research Association, and previous studies of this nature, all of which informed the study and survey.

in part to address the need for diversifying the computer science pipeline. The National Science Foundation has also actively encouraged outreach programs in the U.S. through the funding of various broadening participation initiatives.

In this work we consider the following question: is there a long-term impact of computing outreach activities for underrepresented minority students? To answer this, we first conducted a systematic literature review of previous studies with a long-term evaluative component. Based on these results, we then conducted a study of undergraduate students' past experiences with such outreach activities to understand the long-term impact of outreach programs, comparing white students and minority students. This paper presents the results of both.

2. BACKGROUND

In order to determine what others have found with regards to longitudinal results for outreach initiatives, we undertook a systematic literature review framed by Khan, Kunz, Kleijnen, and Antes [44]. The systematic review framework includes framing the question, identifying relevant work, assessing quality of the studies, summarizing evidence, and interpreting findings.

The free-form question we sought to answer was "Is there a long-term impact on under-represented minorities who have participated in computing outreach activities?" To answer this question, we looked for studies with the following characteristics:

- *The populations studied*—Students enrolled in computing outreach programs as defined by the researchers
- *The interventions*—Programs that exposed students to computing concepts that were outside of their normal required school work
- *The outcomes analyzed*—Interest in pursuing a degree in a computing field and/or actual enrollment and completion of a degree in a computing field
- *The study designs*—Quantitative, qualitative, or mixed methods studies that tracked the participants in computing outreach programs over a period of time that extended beyond the length of the intervention itself

We then identified relevant work of quality by considering ACM and IEEE journal and conference publications, which have a long history of publishing quality papers. We further refined that to venues within these organizations that emphasize education, including the following peer-reviewed journals and conference proceedings in electronic form: ACM SIGCSE Technical Symposium on Computer Science Education, Computer Science Education, IEEE Frontiers in Education, Innovation and Technology in Computer Science Education, International Computing Education Research Workshop, and Transactions on Computing Education from the years 2009 to 2014 inclusive. This effort resulted in 3,672 citations from which relevant studies were selected for the review. Their potential relevance was examined, and 3571 citations were excluded as irrelevant, leaving 101 articles.

To determine relevance, we started with an analysis of the title of each article. An article was determined to have a title associated with outreach by using keywords: outreach, K-12, elementary school, high school, secondary school, after school clubs, summer camp. Once a title was determined to be related, further examination was given to the article's abstract. If the abstract also included the keywords and indicated that an intervention that introduced computing to students outside of their required classroom setting and curricula took place, the articles were left

for the review. These articles were then examined in detail. Each article was read and the following information was recorded:

- Target audience of the outreach
- Country in which the target audience lived
- Whether or not the intervention was designed to increase gender diversity
- Whether or not the intervention was designed to increase ethnic diversity
- If data was collected from participants
- Whether the study was quantitative or qualitative
- The number of participants in the study
- The gender of the participants in the study
- The ethnicity of the participants in the study
- What variables were assessed by the study
- Whether there was a longitudinal component to the study
- The number of years for the study (if longitudinal)
- The summary of the findings (if longitudinal)

Of the 101 articles considered, 28 were removed from further analysis because during this careful read stage, it was discovered that they did not fit the model for a discussion about the impact of a computing outreach activity. Many of these simply described an activity, gave advice for running an activity, gave example curriculum for activities, or were work in progress papers that did not include any reporting of results.

The remaining 73 papers [1, 2, 3, 5, 7, 8, 9, 10, 11, 12, 13, 14, 15, 17, 18, 19 20, 21, 22, 23, 24, 25, 27, 28, 29, 30, 31, 32, 33, 34, 35, 36, 37, 38, 39, 40, 41, 42, 43, 45, 46, 47, 48, 49, 50, 51, 52, 53, 54, 55, 56, 57, 58, 59, 60, 62, 63, 64, 65, 66, 67, 68, 69, 70, 71, 72, 73, 74, 77, 78, 79, 80, 82, 83] were dominated by results from interventions in the U.S. (75%). We therefore converted results of non-US interventions to the U.S. education system. We found that a majority of the interventions (82%) were outreach efforts aimed at high school and/or middle school students.

Within our analyzed sample, 46 (63%) were quantitative studies, 13 (18%) were qualitative studies, 13 (18%) were mixed methods, and 1 (1%) was not characterized as either. The number of study participants was reported in 62 of the articles (85%), with the number of participants ranging from 2 to 9956. Of the 73 interventions discussed in the articles, 25 (34%) indicated that they were designed to increase ethnic diversity, 41 (56%) indicated that they were not created to address ethnic imbalance, and seven (10%) did not provide enough evidence to categorize the intervention.

Participant ethnicity was reported by 27 (37%) of the articles. Of the studies conducted on interventions designed to increase ethnic diversity, 18 (72% of that group) indicated the ethnicity of the participants in and subsequent study of the intervention.

Many of the articles undertook some form of data collection about the participants of the programs. Of the 73 articles analyzed, only three (< 1%) did not report on any systematic data collection and analysis. Since we are most interested in longitudinal studies as it relates to our work, we identified that only seven (9.5%) of the 73 articles that presented information about longitudinal studies. Of those seven, four articles discussed interventions designed to increase ethnic diversity.

Two of the four papers examined outreach programs provided to K-12 students. The Berkeley Foundation for Opportunities in Information Technology (BFOIT), a project of the International Computer Science Institute (ICSI), has two full-scale programs, one for middle school students: Science for Youth (SCI-FY), and one for high school students: Information Technology Leadership Program (ITLP), and a third fledgling program for elementary students, Early Techies (ET) [17]. The longitudinal aspect of this study was the tracking of BFOIT students' mental rotation ability and perspective-taking ability through the use of standardized tests. They found a modest correlation between the number of years that students have been in BFOIT and their mental rotation score. Of the 153 participants of BFOIT, 65 have matriculated high school and have gone onto college/university.

One article summarized findings from Georgia Computes!, a six year effort (2006-2012) designed to improve computing education in Georgia through summer camps for students and professional development for teachers [35]. The study investigated the impact computing outreach activities had on the number of schools offering computer science courses and the number of students taking Advanced Placement (AP) Computer Science exams over the course of the project and in the two years after the project. Findings indicate that early interventions appear to have an impact on whether or not students choose computing as a major.

The two remaining papers analyzed outreach activities' impact on undergraduate students, examining engagement, retention, self-efficacy, and several other related factors [19, 21]. One study, the INSPIRED (Increasing Student Participation in Research Development) Program, collected and analyzed two years of data [21], while the other, Students and Technology in Academia, Research, and Service (STARS) Alliance, covered three years [19]. Due to the limited span of time that the studies covered as well as their on undergraduate students rather than K-12 students, details of the studies are not included here.

Once summarized, we considered the evidence from these studies holistically with respect to our free-form question. Within the four studies that presented evidence of longer-term impact, none answered the question about the long-term impact on the participants after the outreach activities concluded. Therefore, we concluded that more systematic study of the long-term effects of outreach programs is needed. In the following sections we describe the methodology and the results of our study of the long-term impact on underrepresented minorities of computing outreach activities.

3. METHODOLOGY

In this study, we used a quantitative methodology that followed a descriptive design approach to investigate whether or not undergraduate students believed that their participation in computing activities prior to college contributed to their decision to major in a computing field. [16].

We created the Effectiveness of Technology Outreach Survey. In addition to basic demographic data, the survey required respondents to recall activities, thoughts, and feelings about their participation in these activities. In order to gauge validity and to limit recall bias, two additional steps were taken. First, respondents were asked to participate in retaking the survey to determine the recall bias and to establish validity of the results [16]. Second, we integrated recall prompts (aided recall) within the survey to serve as memory aids to respondents [76].

Respondents were recruited using three different methods. We recruited undergraduate students at three institutions, Bradley University, DePaul University, and Rochester Institute of Technology. Second, we asked colleagues and peers at a variety of other universities to send requests for participation to their undergraduate students. These universities were carefully chosen to be diverse in their geographic location as well as their institution type (size, private versus public, etc.) to help ensure a more representative sample of students. These institutions included University of California Santa Cruz, Ball State University, and University of Buffalo. Lastly, we used findparticipants.com to recruit additional undergraduate students.

Upon approval by our institutions' Institutional Review Board (IRB), the request to participate was sent to faculty and to students at the identified institutions. To gather the data, an electronic form of the survey instrument was created using the Qualtrics online survey tool. Only respondents who agreed to the letter of consent that appeared on the first page of the survey were able to complete the survey. The letter of consent required them to indicate that they were at least 18 years of age.

As an incentive, respondents at universities were offered entry for a prize drawing of a $50 Amazon gift card upon completion of the survey. To enter, respondents followed a link to a second survey thereby keeping the survey responses separate from the drawing survey that required respondents to enter contact information, thus removing the potential of linking personally identifiable data with survey responses. At the end of the survey, respondents were asked if they were interested in retaking the survey in approximately 2-4 weeks. As an incentive, respondents who retook the survey were offered entry for a prize drawing of a second $50 Amazon gift card.

To analyze the data, a test of equivalence among the initial and retake survey results was performed. A total of 770 respondents completed the initial survey indicating gender and ethnicity and 411 completed the retake. Only three respondents were from findparticipants.com, while the remaining were from the educational institutions previously noted.

A Kurskal-Wallis Test was performed on non-parametric data to determine equivalence between the results of the initial and retake surveys [81]. The results of the test indicated that for all non-parametric data, there were no differences found, with p values in the range of 0.75 and 1.00.

To determine equivalence between the two samples for the Likert-like items, an unpaired t-test was performed with a confidence interval setting of 90% using GraphPad Prism [75, 81]. The entire range of the 90% confidence interval was between the zone of indifference (0.35) for all but two items, "The majority of students participating in the activities were boys" (0.36) and "The majority of students participating in the activities were girls" (0.42). For this test of equivalence, since the entire range of the 90% confidence interval lies within the zone of indifference, then we can conclude that all other items are equivalent across the two groups with 95% confidence [75].

However, the recall for whether or not the majority of the participants were boys or girls was higher than for the other items, indicating that these values may not be as reliable. For example, the confidence interval range for "I enjoyed many of the activities" was 0.28, well below the 0.36 and 0.42 values for the items related to gender of the participants. Respondents recalled this item more consistently between the first and second survey. Therefore, extra caution should be taken when interpreting results related to the two items related to gender (see 4.4.2).

4. RESULTS

Using SPSS, we analyzed the data to evaluate similarities and differences among white and non-white respondents.

4.1 Respondent Demographics

The ethnicity survey item was modeled from the U.S. Census Bureau's list of ethnicities. We asked respondents to select the group(s) with which they most closely identify (Table 1). Guamanian or Chamorro, Other Asian (not previously mentioned), and Samoan are not included in the list, since each had 0 responses.

Table 1. Ethnicity demographics

	#	Percent
White	614	79.7
Hispanic/Latino/Latina	53	6.9
Asian	52	6.8
Black or African American	38	4.9
Multi-racial	26	3.4
Chinese	17	2.2
Filipino	12	1.6
Middle Eastern	12	1.6
Japanese	8	1.0
Asian Indian	7	0.9
Korean	7	0.9
Some other race	4	0.5
American Indian or Alaska Native	3	0.4
Native American	2	0.3
Vietnamese	2	0.3
Native Hawaiian	1	0.1
Other Pacific Islander	1	0.1
Decline to Answer	23	3.0

For the remainder of this analysis, "whites" refer to all participants who only selected White as their ethnicity. Non-whites are participants who selected at least one ethnicity other than White.

4.2 Mandated versus voluntary participation

Respondents were asked to recall if they had participated in a computing activity prior to entering college. Though we loosely defined computing, we left the question open for interpretation by the respondent. Our loose definition prompted the respondent to recall clubs and activities in and out of school that included "…activities for learning about computers, such as programming, games, hardware, robotics, and more."

Results show that 45.3% of all respondents had participated in the activities, with 43.6% of white respondents and 50% of non-whites indicating that they had participated (Figure 1, Table 2).

Of those that participated in a computing outreach activity, 18.9% indicating that they were required to and 26.1% indicating that they participated voluntarily. With respect to white respondents, 18.1% indicated that they were required to participate and 25.5% voluntarily chose to participate. 50.4% of white respondents did not participate in any computing activity prior to college.

With respect to non-white respondents, 21.4% indicated that they were required to participate and 28.0% indicated that they voluntarily participated. 44.5% of non-whites did not participate in any computing activity prior to college. This data, along with the data from the three largest segments of non-white ethnicity, are shown in Table 2.

Table 2. Type of participation by subgroups

	White	Asian	Black or African American	Hispanic/ Latino/ Latina	All Non-white
Yes, required	18.1%	26.9%	21.1%	22.6%	21.4%
Yes, voluntary	25.5%	26.9%	39.5%	15.1%	28.0%
No	50.4%	40.4%	31.6%	58.5%	44.5%
Don't recall	4.6%	3.8%	2.6%	3.8%	3.8%
Unsure	1.4%	1.9%	5.3%	0.0%	2.2%

4.3 Timeline of Participation

Respondents who indicated that they had participated in a computing activity (336 or 45%) were asked to recall at what point in their education they had participated: elementary school, junior high/middle school, high school, or other.

Overall, 54.5% of respondents who participated in a computing activity did so while in high school, 30.2% in junior high or middle school, and 13.3% in elementary school. For whites the breakdown was 51.9%, 32.1%, and 14.1% respectively, while for all non-whites it was 60.8%, 25.7%, and 10.1% respectively. Table 3 provides the values for white, nonwhite, and the three largest segments of the non-white population. Figure 2 displays this data visually.

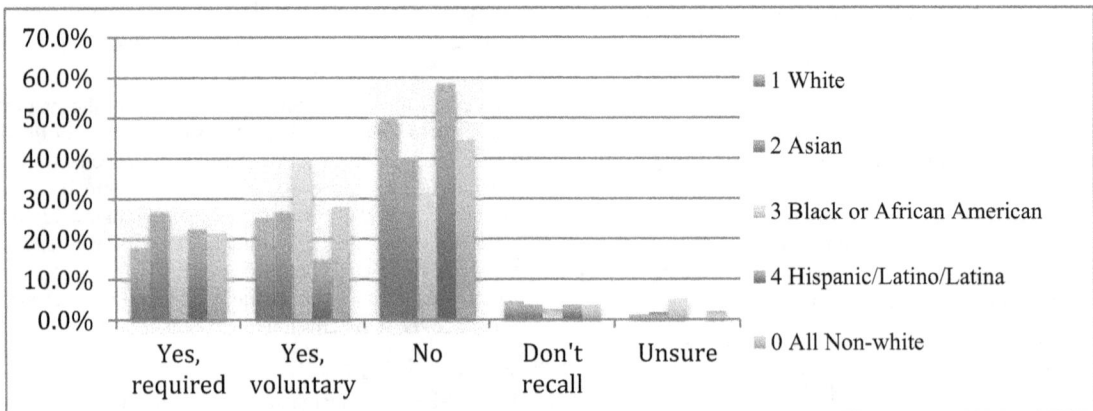

Figure 1. Participation in a computing activity prior to college

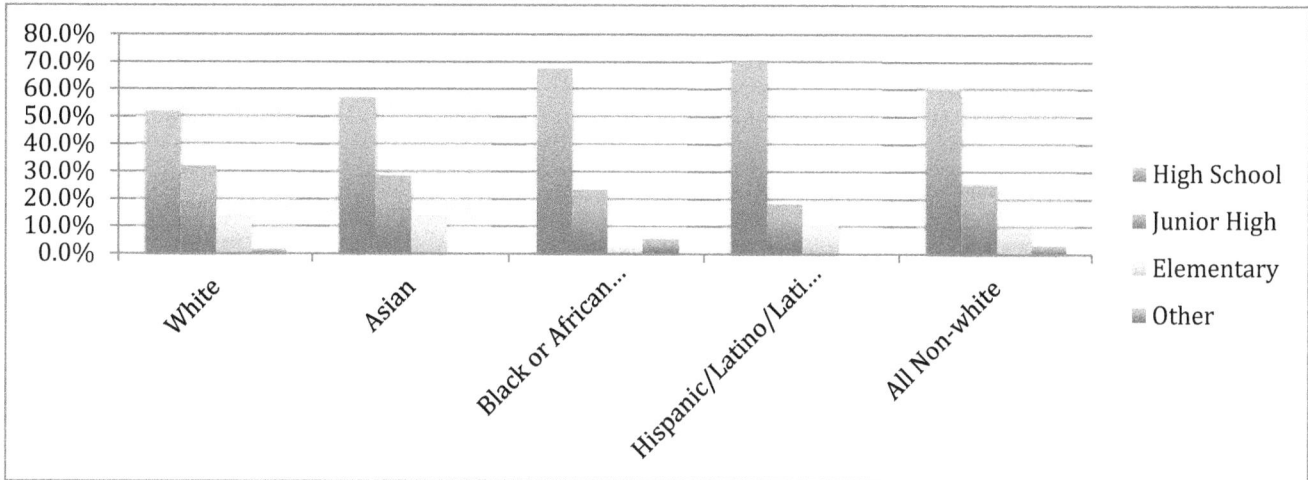

Figure 2. Period of activity participation

Table 3. Period of participation

	High School	Junior High	Elementary	Other
White	51.9%	32.1%	14.1%	1.8%
Asian	57.1%	28.6%	14.3%	0.0%
Black/African American	67.6%	23.5%	2.9%	5.9%
Hispanic/Latino/Latina	70.4%	18.5%	11.1%	0.0%
All nonwhite	60.8%	25.7%	10.1%	3.4%

4.4 Perceived Impact on Major

Respondents were asked how participating in these activities affected their choice of major. Of the respondents who answered this question (n=336), 22.3% indicated that it affected their decision to choose a computer science or related major and an additional 7.1% indicated it affected their decision to choose game design or development as a major.

With respect to impact of participation in these activities on willingness to choose to take a computing course in college for those who did not major in a computing related field, 30.1% said it had a positive effect, and that they chose to take a course in computing because of the activities. 5.4% said it had a negative effect, and they choose not to take a course in computing in college because of the activities.

Drilling down into the data more, we found that there wide variances in the answers from the major subgroups. We provide the data both in table format (Tables 4 and 5) as well as graphically (Figures 3 and 4).

4.4.1 Computing and activity participation

A Chi-Square test was conducted to determine if there was a correlation between participation in an activity before college and whether or not the respondent was majoring in a computing field.

Table 4. Perceived effects of activities on choice of major

	White	Asian	Black or African American	Hispanic /Latino/ Latina	All Non-white
Affected my decision to choose a game design or development major	2.7%	10.7%	17.4%	5.0%	4.4%
Affected my decision to choose a computer science or related major	9.3%	35.7%	21.7%	10.0%	13.1%
Affected my decision to choose a major that does not require me to study computers or programming	2.8%	0.0%	17.4%	30.0%	5.3%
Did not affect my decision when choosing my major	24.0%	35.7%	30.4%	50.0%	20.9%
I am unsure what affect, if any, the activity had on me choosing my major.	4.8%	17.9%	13.0%	5.0%	6.3%

We discovered a weak relationship (ϕ = -0.12) between respondents who participated in an activity prior to entering college and are majoring in a computing field ($\chi(1)$ = 10.83, p = .001). However, for nonwhite respondents, the relationship was not significant (ϕ = 0.104, X(4) = 2.24, p = 0.69). Breaking this down further, we find the following relationships between those studying computing and attending an activity:

- For Asians (N=49), we found no significant relationship (ϕ = -0.169), X(1) = 1.41, p = 0.24).
- For African Americans (N=35), we found no significant relationship (ϕ = -0.12, X(1) = 0.54, p = 0.46).
- For Hispanics (N=51), we found no significant relationship (ϕ = -0.17, X(1) = 1.41, p = 0.24).

- For whites (N=576), we discovered a weak relationship, with $\Phi = -0.12$, $X(1) = 8.24$, $p = 0.004$.

4.4.2 Respondent Perceptions of the Activities

We collected responses on perspectives of the computing activities and evaluated them using an independent t-test. The Likert-like items consisted of the following:

- The majority of students participating in the activities were boys.
- I enjoyed many of the activities.
- I enjoyed learning about computers.
- I was interested in computers before I participated in the activities.
- I felt like I was a welcome part of the group participating in the activities.
- The majority of students participating in the activities were girls.
- Participating in the activities increased my interest in computers.

No significant differences between whites and non-whites for those presently majoring in computing were found. However, one significant difference was found in the responses of those who chose not to major in a computing field. "I felt like I was a welcome part of the group participating in the activities" yielded $t(130.53) = -2.18$, $p = 0.046$. Whites (M=4.04, SD=0.95) were more likely to choose this option over non-whites (M=3.76, SD=1.14).

We also compared the same five major groups against each of the perspectives with an analysis of variance (ANOVA). When comparing all five, the only item found to have a significant difference was the first, "The majority of participants were boys.", $t(3)=2.85$, $p = 0.04$. When examining the high and low means, we find that Blacks/ African Americans had M=4.68, SD = 0.99 while Asians had an M=3.68, SD = 1.19. For whites and Hispanics, the means were nearly similar, with M=4.14, SD=1.23 for whites and M=4.11, SD=1.05 for Hispanics.

Table 5. Perceived effects on computing outreach activities on choice of taking computing classes (Non-majors)

	White	Asian	Black/African American	Hispanic/ Latina/Latino	Non-white
Affected my decision to choose to take a computer related class in college	13.9%	56.0%	40.9%	29.4%	20.4%
Affected my decision to choose NOT to take a computer related class in college	2.3%	0.0%	4.5%	23.5%	3.4%
Did not affect my decision to take or not take a computer related class in college	32.9%	40.0%	27.3%	29.4%	29.6%
I am unsure what affect, if any, the activity had on my decision to take or not take a computer related class in college	9.1%	4.0%	27.3%	17.6%	11.2%

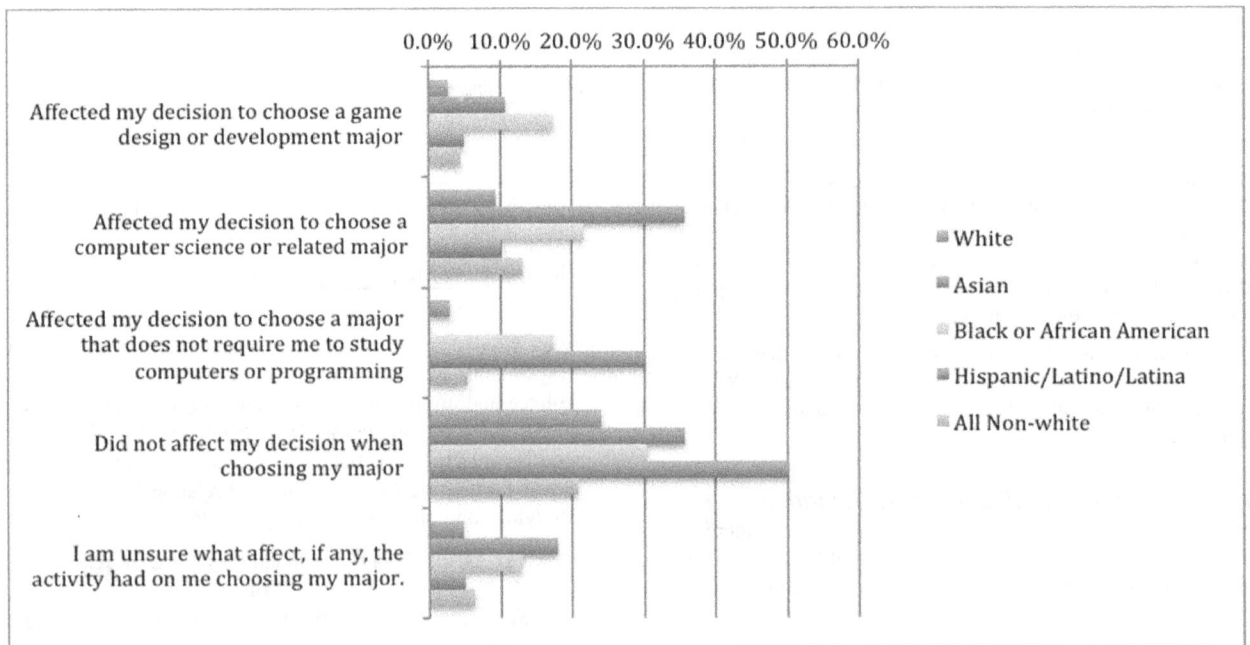

Figure 3. Effect of participation on choice of major (self-reported)

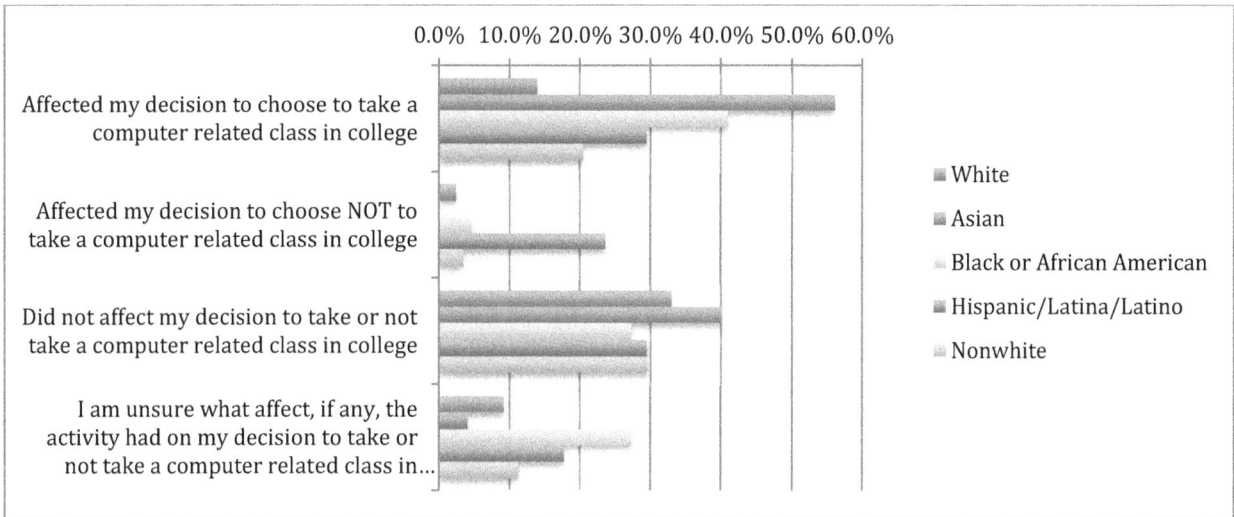

Figure 4. Effect of participation on choice of computing courses (non-majors) as self-reported by respondents

5. DISCUSSION

Despite constructing a sample group from both private and public institution in geographically diverse locations, we found that whites (79.7%) are overrepresented in our survey respondents and non-whites are underrepresented compared to enrollment data from all U.S. educational institutions (60.2%) [61]. Likewise, subgroups evaluated in this study (Hispanic, Asian and Black or African American) were underrepresented (Table 6). Respondents are also less diverse than the population of students in the U.S. earning computer science bachelor degrees [85].

Table 6. Survey response rates comparison

	Study	US Enrollment	2013 Taulbee
Whites	79.7%	60.2%	60.6%
Non-whites (major groups)	18.6%	36.3%	29.8%
Hispanic/Latino/Latina	6.9%	15.2%	6.5%
Asian	6.8%	5.8%	18.8%
Black/African American	4.9%	15.3%	4.5%

This may be partially explained by the distribution of the survey. At some institutions, email addresses from a sample of all students at the university were obtained and those students were contacted about survey participation. At other institutions, the survey was distributed only to students majoring in particular colleges or majors, which may explain the breakdown of the population receiving the survey, although we rely only on self-reports and we are unable to confirm this hypothesis. We also note that the response rate of different subgroups may also have influenced the number of responses.

This should be noted as a limitation of the study, and care should be taken in interpreting the results. We also note that there may be self-selection bias, since survey participation was voluntary, and the consideration of accurately recalling activities that took place over ten years ago, despite constructing to the survey with recall prompts. Though this study cannot replace a properly constructed longitudinal study, we present the following for consideration based on these results.

5.1 Activity Participation

Just under half (45.3%) of the responses indicated that they had participated in an outreach activity prior to entering college.

Slightly fewer whites (43.6%) than non-whites (50%) indicated that they participated. Given that many outreach programs focus on underrepresented populations, this result is not surprising.

More respondents (26.1%) indicated that they voluntarily participated in the activities than that they were required to participate in the activities (18.9%). The difference in type of participation was nearly equal for white respondents (25.5% voluntary versus 18.1% required) than for non-white respondents (28.0% voluntary versus 21.4% required).

In a U.S. study, Guzdial, et al, provide the results of a survey administered to undergraduate students enrolled in an introductory computer science class in Georgia [34]. Though not strictly longitudinal in nature, the results of this recollective study found that 28% of the undergraduate respondents (N=1,434) had participated in computing activities in middle school and 14% had participated in out-of-school activities. In high school, 32% of the respondents indicated participation with computing activities, with 16% participating in out-of-school activities.

Our study found that a majority of all respondents had participated in the activity while in high school (54.5%). This is slightly higher than previously reported by Guzdial, et al [34], who found that 32% had participated in such activities in high school and 16% participated in activities outside of school. Combined, this might reflect a maximum of 48% if there were no duplications in the other study's responses.

Our study also found that 30.2% participated in junior high/middle school, which may be lower than the 28% in school plus 14% out of school (maximum of 42%, again if no duplications in reporting) as reported in the Georgia study [34]. This could indicate a regional component to availability of outreach activities, or it could indicate that there are more activities available in the last few years to K-12 students than there were in previous years. However, one vital difference is that participants in our study were not limited to those currently enrolled in a computing course, while the Georgia study was.

Non-whites were more likely to have participated in high school (60.8%) than whites (51.9%) and less likely to in junior high (25.7% for non-whites and 32.1% for whites) or elementary school (10.1% for non-whites and 14.1% for whites). Historically outreach programs have been more common for high school students than for younger students. These results may indicate that when outreach programs are available in earlier grades that they are not reaching non-white participants as much as they are reaching white participants.

5.2 Perceived Impact on Major

There were 336 respondents who indicated whether the computing outreach programs had impacted their choice of major. Of these 22.3% indicated that their participation had impacted their choice of a computer science major and another 7.1% indicate that it had impacted their choice of a major in game design or development. More (30.1%) indicated that it had a positive effect than that it had a negative effect (5.4%), which is a positive result for outreach programs as a whole.

When the results were considered by race, there were wide variations in the responses. There was a weak correlation for all respondents between having participated in an activity before college and choosing to major or not major in computing, although for non-white respondents the result was not significant. When each subpopulation was considered separately, the only subgroup for which the relationship between participation and a choice of a computing major was significant was white respondents. This is a discouraging result for outreach programs, since the goal of many is to influence the choice of major among participants toward computing. These results suggest that those programs may not be as successful as the organizers might desire.

Another discouraging result was the difference between responses for the statement "I felt like I was a welcome part of the group participating in the activities." Whites were more likely to agree with this statement (M=4.04) than non-whites (M=3.76). Given that many outreach programs are designed with non-white participants in mind, this suggests that they may not be successful in making all participants feel equally welcome.

There were also significant differences for responses to the statement "The majority of participants were boys." Blacks and African Americans were more likely to agree with the statement (M=4.68) than Asians (M=3.68), whites (M=4.14), or Hispanics (M=4.11). It is difficult to determine without further information whether these differences were an accurate reporting of the populations represented, which would indicate that programs with African Americans were more likely to have male participants and Asians were more likely to have girls in their programs, or whether the various groups simply had different perceptions of the participants in the programs they attended.

5.3 Considering Program Type

It is difficult to compare our results due to the lack of studies that consider the long-term impact of outreach programs. Worth noting is that, unlike the Guzdial, et al, study [34], we did not collect data on the types of programs that were reviewed nor the impact on self-efficacy or knowledge that the participants may have experienced. In fact, we were unable to distinguish between programs that may have had a stronger influence than others. Previous research indicates that a culturally relevant pedagogy, including culturally diverse content, role models, teacher professional development, and recruitment, among others, all play an important role in creating a solid program that may have more immediate impact on students, which may lead to more long-term impact [6, 17, 21, 26, 32, 34, 35]. However, without any long-term studies tracking activity participants, we can only rely on indicators from anecdotal data or data collected from long-term memories of participants, both of which are poor substitutes for quantitative analysis on a variety of measures.

6. CONCLUSION

Given the duration of the problem of underrepresentation of racial and ethnic minorities in the computing field and the decades-long interest of the computer science community in addressing the issue, it is interesting to consider the long-term impact of computing outreach programs on ethnic diversity in the field. The Taulbee data suggests that things have improved at the undergraduate level [81]. However, a decline in AP computer science courses and the lack of test-takers who are ethnic minorities remains a problem in the U.S. [26]

Though a study that requires respondents to recall participation in an activity from roughly a decade ago cannot replace data collected during participation, this study found results that differed significantly among several ethnic groups. There are a variety of variables that may also impact accurate recollection, such as support of computing careers by parents and peers. However, based on the data, whites and non-whites recall different experiences with these activities that are worth further consideration.

The data reflects on activities put into place over the last decade and may not accurately reflect the impact that current activities may have. Despite these limitations, this study has two important implications. First, the data confirms a need for longitudinal studies to determine whether or not the countless hours put into such activities are not only effective, but also in how they are most effective across various ethnic groups.

Second, the data provides awareness of the potential inequities in activities across various ethnic groups. This alone can be very powerful when seeking to ensure that youth have equal access and opportunities to pursue computing careers. Knowing that there are large discrepancies in when different ethnicities participate in these activities and how different ethnicities perceive their impact may provide more motivation to create such programs that counter these past trends.

Further, future research requiring recall and/or is constructed as a longitudinal study can benefit by consideration of the following:

- Construct a sample size that more accurately represents the representation of the various groups in college,
- Students who participated in these activities but then did not choose to attend a four-year higher education institution,
- Variables of the computing activities (length of time, type of instruction, type of activity, etc.), and
- Self-efficacy as a variable in context with ethnicity.

Likewise, researching differences within ethnic groups and understanding why a black student, for example, chooses to major in computing while another black student chooses not to do so can more finely distinguish variables that may have influenced each students' decision.

7. REFERENCES

[1] Adams, J.C. 2010. Scratching middle schoolers' creative itch. In Proc of the 41st ACM tech symp on Comp Sci Ed. ACM, 356-360.

[2] Adrion, W.R., Fall, R. et al. 2010. Integrating evaluation into program development: benefits of baselining a NSF-BPC alliance. In Proc of the 41st ACM tech symp on Comp Sci Ed. ACM, 27-31.

[3] Al-Bow, M., Austin, D., Edgington, J., et al. 2009. Using game creation for teaching computer programming to high school students and teachers. In Proc of the 14th ACM SIGCSE conf on Innovation and tech in comp sci ed (ITiCSE '09). ACM, 104-108.

[4] Andrews, G. R. 1994. 1993-1994 CRA Taulbee Survey. http://archive.cra.org/Activities/workshops/broadening.participation/cra/Taulbee/1993-1994.pdf

[5] Basawapatna, A.R., Koh, K.H. et al. 2010. Using scalable game design to teach computer science from middle school to graduate school. In Proc of ITiCSE '10 ACM, New York, NY, 224-228.

[6] Bell, T., Rosamond, F., Casey, N. 2012. Computer Science Unplugged and Related Projects in Math and Computer Science Popularization. *Lecture Notes in Computer Science*, 7370, 398-456.

[7] Benotti, L., Martínez, M.C. and Chapachnik, F. 2014. Engaging high school students using chatbots. In Proc of the 2014 conf on Innov & tech in comp sci ed (ITiCSE '14). ACM, New York, NY, 63-68.

[8] Bruckman, A., Biggers, M., Ericson, B., et al. 2009. "Georgia computes!": improving the computing education pipeline. In Proc of the 40th ACM tech symp on Comp sci ed. ACM, 86-90.

[9] Burge, J.E., Gannod, G.C., Doyle, M. et al. 2013. Girls on the go: a CS summer camp to attract and inspire female high school students. In Proc of the 44th ACM tech symp on Comp sci ed. ACM, 615-620.

[10] Carter, E., Blank, G. and Walz, J. 2012. Bringing the breadth of computer science to middle schools. In Proc of the 43rd ACM tech symp on Comp Sci Ed (SIGCSE '12). ACM, New York, 203-208.

[11] Cavender, A.C., Ladner, R.E. and Roth, R.I. 2009. The summer academy for advancing deaf and hard of hearing in computing. In Proc of SIGCSE '09. ACM, New York, NY, USA, 514-518.

[12] Cheung, J.C.Y., Ngai, G. et al. 2009. Filling the gap in programming instruction: a text-enhanced graphical programming environment for junior high students. In Proc of SIGCSE '09. ACM, 276-280.

[13] Cottam, J.A., Foley, S.S. and Menzel, S. 2010. Do roadshows work?: examining the effectiveness of just be. In Proc of the 41st ACM tech symp on Comp Sci Ed (SIGCSE '10). ACM, New York, NY, 17-21.

[14] Craig, A., Coldwell-Neilson, J. and Beekhuyzen, J. 2013. Are IT interventions for girls a special case?. In Proc of the 44th ACM tech symp on Comp sci ed (SIGCSE '13). ACM, New York, 451-456.

[15] Craig, M. and Horton, D. 2009. Gr8 designs for Gr8 girls: a middle-school program and its evaluation. SIGCSE Bull. 41, 1 (March 2009), 221-225.

[16] Creswell, J.W. 2008. *Educational Research. Planning, Conducting, and Evaluating Quantitative and Qualitative Research*. Pearson Education, Upper Saddle River, New Jersey.

[17] Crutchfield, O.S.L., Harrison, C.D., et al. 2011. Berkeley Foundation for Opportunities in Information Technology: A Decade of Broadening Participation. Trans. Comput. Educ. 11, 3, Art 15, 24 pg.

[18] Curzon, P., McOwan, P.W., Cutts, Q. I. et al. 2009. Enthusing & inspiring with reusable kinaesthetic activities. SIGCSE Bull. 41, 3 (July 2009), 94-98.

[19] Dahlberg, T., Barnes, T., Buch, K. et al. 2011. The STARS Alliance: Viable Strategies for Broadening Participation in Computing. Trans. Comput. Educ. 11, 3, Article 18, 25 pages.

[20] Daily, S.B., Leonard, A.E., Jörg, S., et al. 2014. Dancing alice: exploring embodied pedagogical strategies for learning computational thinking. In Proc of SIGCSE '14. ACM, 91-96.

[21] Doerschuk, P., Liu, J., and Mann, J. 2010. INSPIRED Broadening Participation in Computing: Most successful strategies and lessons learned. In 40th ASEE/IEEE Front in Ed Conf, Washington, DC, Oct 27-30, 2010, T2H-1-T2H-6.

[22] Doerschuk, P., Liu, J. and Mann, J. 2011. INSPIRED High School Computing Academies. Trans. Comput. Educ. 11, 2, Art 7, 18 pages.

[23] Doerschuk, P., Liu, J., and Mann, J. 2012. An INSPIRED game programming academy for high school students. 2012 Frontiers in Education Conf (FIE 2012), Seattle, WA, October 3-6, 2012, 1-6.

[24] Egan, M.A.L. and Lederman, T. 2011. The impact of IMPACT: assessing students' perceptions after a day of computer exploration. In Proc ITiCSE '11 ACM, New York, NY, USA, 318-322.

[25] Eglash, R., Krishnamoorthy, M., Sanchez, J., et al. 2011. Fractal Simulations of African Design in Pre-College Computing Education. Trans. Comput. Educ. 11, 3, Art 17, 14 pages.

[26] Ericson, B. and Guzdial, M. 2014. Measuring demographics and performance in computer science education at a nationwide scale using AP CS data. In Proc SIGCSE '14. ACM, New York, 217-222.

[27] Ericson, B. and McKlin, T. 2012. Effective and sustainable computing summer camps. In Proc of the 43rd ACM tech symp on Comp Sci Ed (SIGCSE '12). ACM, New York, NY, USA, 289-294.

[28] Feaster, Y., Segars, L., Wahba, S.K. et al. 2011. Teaching CS unplugged in the high school (with limited success). In Proc of the 16th conf on Innov and tech in comp sci ed. ACM, 248-252.

[29] Franklin, D., Conrad, P., Aldana, G. et al. 2011. Animal tlatoque: attracting middle school students to computing through culturally-relevant themes. In Proc SIGCSE '11. ACM, New York, 453-458.

[30] Freeman, J., Magerko, B. et al. 2014. Engaging underrepresented groups in high school introductory computing through computational remixing with EarSketch. In Proc of SIGCSE '14. ACM, 85-90.

[31] Gasser, M., Yung-Hsiang Lu, and Cheng-Kok Koh. 2010. Outreach project introducing computer engineering to high school students. In 40th ASEE/IEEE Frontiers in Education Conference (FIE 2010), Washington, DC, October 27-30, 2010, F2E-1-F2E-5.

[32] Goode, J. 2008. Increasing diversity in k-12 computer science: strategies from the field. In Proc of the 39th SIGCSE tech symp on Comp sci ed (SIGCSE '08). ACM, New York, NY, USA, 362-366.

[33] Goode, J. and Margolis, J. 2011. Exploring Computer Science: A Case Study of School Reform. Trans. Comput. Educ. 11, 2, Article 12 (July 2011), 16 pages.

[34] Guzdial, M., Ericson, B. J. et al. 2012. A statewide survey on computing education pathways and influences: factors in broadening participation in computing. In Proc of ICER '12. ACM, 143-150.

[35] Guzdial, M., Ericson, B., Mcklin, T. et al. 2014. Georgia Computes! An Intervention in a US State, with Formal and Informal Education in a Policy Context. Trans. Comput. Educ. 14, 2, Article 13, 29 pgs.

[36] Harriger, A., Magana, A.J., and Lovan, R. 2012. Identifying the impact of the SPIRIT program in student knowledge, attitudes, and perceptions toward computing careers. 2012 Frontiers in Education Conference (FIE 2012), Seattle, WA, October 3-6, 2012, 1-6.

[37] Hart, M.L. 2010. Making contact with the forgotten k-12 influence: are you smarter than your 5th grader?. In Proc of the 41st ACM tech symp on Comp Sci Ed (SIGCSE '10). ACM, New York, 254-258.

[38] Hulsey, C., Pence, T.B. and Hodges, L.F. 2014. Camp CyberGirls: using a virtual world to introduce computing concepts to middle school girls. In Proc of SIGCSE '14. ACM, New York, 331-336.

[39] Isomöttönen, V., Lakanen, A. and Lappalainen, V. 2011. K-12 game programming course concept using textual programming. In Proc of the 42nd ACM tech symp on Comp sci ed. ACM, 459-464.

[40] Kacmarcik, G. and Giral Kacmarcik, S. 2009. Introducing computer programming via gameboy advance homebrew. In Proc of the 40th ACM tech symp on Comp sci ed (SIGCSE '09). ACM, 281-285.

[41] Kafai, Y., Griffin, J., Burke, Q. et al. 2013. A cascading mentoring pedagogy in a CS service learning course to broaden participation and perceptions. In Proc of SIGCSE '13. ACM, New York, 101-106.

[42] Kafai, Y.B., Searle, K., Kaplan, E., et al. 2013. Cupcake cushions, scooby doo shirts, and soft boomboxes: e-textiles in high school to promote computational concepts, practices, and perceptions. In Proc of the 44th ACM tech symp on Comp sci ed. ACM, 311-316.

[43] Karp, T. and Schneider, A. 2011. Evaluation of a K-8 LEGO robotics program. In 41st ASEE/IEEE Frontiers in Education Conf (FIE 2011), Rapids City, SD, Oct 12-15, 2011, T1D-1-T1D-6.

[44] Khan, K.S., Kunz, R., Kleijnen, J., Antes, G. 2003. Five steps to conducting a systematic review. *J R Soc Med*. 96, 3, 118–121. http://www.ncbi.nlm.nih.gov/pmc/articles/PMC539417/

[45] Lakanen, A. and Isomöttönen, V. 2013. High school students' perspective to university CS1. In Proc of the 18th ACM conf on Innov and tech in comp sci ed. ACM, New York, 261-266.

[46] Lakanen, A., Isomöttönen, V. and Lappalainen, V. 2014. Five years of game programming outreach: understanding student differences. In Proc of SIGCSE '14. ACM, New York, NY, USA, 647-652.

[47] Lakanen, A., Isomöttönen, V. and Lappalainen, V. 2014. Understanding differences among coding club students. In Proc of ITiCSE '14. ACM, New York, NY, USA, 159-164.

[48] Lakanen, A., Isomöttönen, V., and Lappalainen, V. 2012. Life two years after a game programming course: longitudinal viewpoints on K-12 outreach. In Proc of SIGCSE '12. ACM, New York, 481-486.

[49] Lang, C., Craig, A., Fisher, J. et al. 2010. Creating digital divas: scaffolding perception change through secondary school and university alliances. In Proc of ITiCSE '10. ACM, 38-42.

[50] Larkins, D.B., Moore, J.C., Rubbo, L.J. et al. 2013. Application of the cognitive apprenticeship framework to a middle school robotics camp. In Proc of the 44th ACM tech symp on Comp sci ed. 89-94.

[51] Lau, W.W.Y, Ngai, G. et al. 2009. Learning programming through fashion and design: a pilot summer course in wearable computing for middle school students. SIGCSE Bull. 41, 1 (March 2009), 504-508.

[52] Layer, R., Sherriff, M., and Tychonievich, L. 2012. "Inform, Experience, Implement" Teaching an intensive high school summer course. 2012 Frontiers in Ed Conf, Seattle, WA, Oct 3-6, 2012, 1-6.

[53] Lewis, C.M. 2011. Is pair programming more effective than other forms of collaboration for young students? Computer Science Education. 21, 2 (June 2011), 105-134.

[54] Liebenberg, J., Mentz, E. and Breed, B. 2012. Pair programming and secondary school girls' enjoyment of programming and the subject Information Technology (IT). Computer Sci Ed. 22, 3, 219-236.

[55] Ludi, S. and Reichlmayr, T. 2011. The Use of Robotics to Promote Computing to Pre-College Students with Visual Impairments. Trans. Comput. Educ. 11, 3, Article 20 (October 2011), 20 pages.

[56] Mano, C., Allan, V., and Cooley, D. 2010. Effective in-class activities for middle school outreach programs. In 40th ASEE/IEEE Front in Ed Conf, Washington, DC, Oct 27-30, 2010, F2E-1-F2E-6.

[57] Marcu, G., Kaufman, S.J., Lee, J.K., et al. 2010. Design and evaluation of a computer science and engineering course for middle school girls. In Proc of SIGCSE '10. ACM, New York, NY, 234-238.

[58] Maxim, B.R. and Elenbogen, B.S. 2009. Attracting K-12 students to study computing. In 39th IEEE Frontiers in Education Conference (FIE '09). San Antonio, TX, October 18-21, 2009, M1H-1-M1H-5.

[59] Meerbaum-Salant, O., Armoni, M. and Ben-Ari, M. 2013. Learning computer science concepts with Scratch. Computer Science Education. 23, 3 (Sept 2013), 239-264.

[60] Morreale, P., Kurkovsky, S. and Chang, G. 2009. Methodology for successful undergraduate recruiting in computer science at comprehensive public universities. In Proc SIGCSE '09. 91-95.

[61] National Center for Education Statistics. 2012. Digest of Education Statistics: 2012, http://nces.ed.gov/programs/digest/d12/tables/dt12_263.asp?referrer=report.

[62] Nugent, G., Barker, B., Grandgenett, N., et al. 2009. The use of digital manipulatives in k-12: robotics, GPS/GIS and programming. In 39th IEEE Frontiers in Education Conference (FIE '09). San Antonio, TX, October 18-21, 2009, M2H-1-M2H-6.

[63] Ouyang, Y. and Hayden, K. 2010. A technology infused science summer camp to prepare student leaders in 8th grade classrooms. In Proc of the 41st ACM tech symp on Comp Sci Ed. ACM, 229-233.

[64] Pivkina, I., Pontelli, E., Jensen, R. et al. 2009. Young women in computing: lessons learned from an educational & outreach program. In Proc of SIGCSE '09. ACM, New York, NY, USA, 509-513.

[65] Rheingans, P., Brodsky, A., Scheibler, J. et al. 2011. The Role of Majority Groups in Diversity Programs. Trans. Comput. Educ. 11, 2, Article 11 (July 2011), 15 pages.

[66] Robertson, J. 2013. The influence of a game-making project on male and female learners' attitudes to computing. Computer Science Education. 23, 1(Apr 2013), 58-83.

[67] Robinson, A. and Pérez-Quiñones, M.A. 2014. Underrepresented middle school girls: on the path to computer science through paper prototyping. In Proc of SIGCSE '14. ACM, New York, NY, 97-102.

[68] Rodger, S.H., Hayes, J., Lezin, G., et al. 2009. Engaging middle school teachers and students with alice in a diverse set of subjects. SIGCSE Bull. 41, 1 (March 2009), 271-275.

[69] Rosson, M.B., Ioujanina, A., Paone, T. et al. 2009. A scaffolded introduction to dynamic website development for female high school students. SIGCSE Bull. 41, 1 (March 2009), 226-230.

[70] Roy, K. 2012. App inventor for android: report from a summer camp. In Proc of the 43rd ACM tech symp on Comp Sci Ed (SIGCSE '12). ACM, New York, NY, USA, 283-288.

[71] Searle, K.A., Fields, D.A., Lui, D.A. et al. 2014. Diversifying high school students' views about computing with electronic textiles. In Proc of the 10th conf on Int comp ed res (ICER '14). ACM, 75-82.

[72] Sundaram, R. 2011.Set up and delivery of electrical and computer engineering projects at undergraduate engineering universities for outreach and partnership with K-12 STEM schools. In 41st ASEE/IEEE Frontiers in Education Conference (FIE 2011), Rapids City, SD, October 12-15, 2011, F4D-1-F4D-5.

[73] Taub, R., Armoni, M. and Ben-Ari, M. 2012. CS Unplugged and Middle-School Students' Views, Attitudes, and Intentions Regarding CS. Trans. Comput. Educ. 12, 2, Article 8 (April 2012), 29 pages.

[74] Taub, R., Ben-Ari, M., and Armoni, M. 2009. The effect of CS unplugged on middle-school students' views of CS. SIGCSE Bull. 41, 3 (July 2009), 99-103.

[75] "Testing for Equivalence with confidence intervals or P values." GraphPad Software, Inc. Retrieved 15 Dec 2015 from http://www.graphpad.com/guide/prism/6/statistics/index.htm?stat_testing_for_equivalence_with_c.htm

[76] US Census Bureau. 2006. Martin, Elizabeth. "Survey questionnaire construction." Survey methodology. 2006 (2006): 13.

[77] Van Wart, S.J., Vakil, S. and Parikh, T.S. 2014. Apps for social justice: motivating computer science learning with design and real-world problem solving. In Proc of ITiCSE '14. ACM, 123-128.

[78] Wagner, A., Gray, J., Corley, J. et al. 2013. Using app inventor in a K-12 summer camp. In Proc of the 44th ACM tech symp on Comp sci ed (SIGCSE '13). ACM, New York, 621-626.

[79] Webb, H. and Rosson, M.B. 2013. Using scaffolded examples to teach computational thinking concepts. In Proc of the 44th ACM tech symp on Comp sci ed (SIGCSE '13). ACM, New York, 95-100.

[80] Webb, H.C. and Rosson, M.B. 2011. Exploring careers while learning Alice 3D: a summer camp for middle school girls. In Proc of the 42nd ACM tech symp on Comp sci ed. ACM, 377-382.

[81] Welleck, S. 2002. Testing Statistical Hypotheses of Equivalence. Chapman and Hall, London/CRC, Boca Raton (in press).

[82] Wolz, U., Stone, M., Pearson, K., et al. 2011. Computational Thinking and Expository Writing in the Middle School. Trans. Comput. Educ. 11, 2, Article 9, 22 pgs.

[83] Zimmerman, T. G., Johnson, D., et al. 2011. Why Latino High School Students Select Computer Science as a Major: Analysis of a Success Story. Trans. Comput. Educ. 11, 2, Art 10, 17 pgs.

[84] Zweben, S., Aspray, W. 2003 Taulbee Survey, May 2004, http://archive.cra.org/statistics/survey/03/03.pdf

[85] Zweben, S., Bizot,B. 2013. Taulbee Survey, May 2014, http://cra.org/uploads/documents/resources/crndocs/2013-Taulbee-Survey.pdf

ACM Curriculum Reports: A Pedagogic Perspective

Sebastian Dziallas
School of Computing
University of Kent
Canterbury, CT2 7NF, England
+44 1227 827684
sd485@kent.ac.uk

Sally Fincher
School of Computing
University of Kent
Canterbury, CT2 7NF, England
+44 1227 824061
S.A.Fincher@kent.ac.uk

ABSTRACT
In this paper, we illuminate themes that emerged in interviews with participants in the major curriculum recommendation efforts: we characterize the way the computing community interacts with and influences these reports and introduce the term "pedagogic projection" to describe implicit assumptions of how these reports will be used in practice. We then illuminate how this perceived use has changed over time and may affect future reports.

Categories and Subject Descriptors
K.3.2 [**Computers and Education**]: Computer and Information Science Education – *curriculum, computer science education.*

General Terms
Standardization

Keywords
Computing Curriculum Guidelines, Computing Education Research

1. INTRODUCTION
In 1968, the ACM curriculum committee delivered the first curriculum report of its kind: a series of recommendations and guidelines for academic programs in computer science. Since then, the ACM has published curriculum reports roughly once every decade, as of 1991 in conjunction with the IEEE Computer Society. (The first curriculum recommendations were produced by the ACM curriculum committee. Subsequent efforts from 1991 through 2008 referred to the group of authors as task force. The most recent 2013 report dropped this in favor of the term steering committee.) These reports have become an institution; with each new iteration, chairs are chosen, task forces formed, disciplinary groups engaged, drafts produced and then posted on websites and presented at conferences to solicit community feedback. Over the years, these committees and these documents have provided course descriptions, articulated learning outcomes, and taken views on what is – and is not – computer science. In the process, they have inherently shaped the academic discipline.

The reports are documents that reflect their time. And yet, as written records, they cannot fully capture the context of their time. [14] While some reports explicitly respond to pressing contemporary concerns (such as "the computing crisis" in the 2008 interim report), they do not reveal the rich discourse that is exchanged between committee members and that is engaged more widely in the academic community, that the reports ultimately represent. This dialogue includes the reports' joint and several authors, but also other, less central participants, such as those who contribute perspectives to individual knowledge areas; those who provide sample courses and curricula; and those who provide oversight on the ACM Education Board.

2. METHODOLOGY
We initially reviewed each of the major ACM and IEEE[1] curriculum reports to identify emerging themes in the texts. In a second stage, we interviewed participants in these efforts: chairs of the reports, knowledge area contributors, members of the ACM Education Board and educators who contributed additional material (such as curriculum exemplars). Semi-structured interviews were conducted remotely via video chat and each lasted no longer than an hour. Throughout our conversations, we were looking to illuminate the following key questions:

- How did the work of the committee come about and progress? How was their work situated within the larger community? How (if at all) do these aspects differ between the various reports?

- Within the larger societal context, what factors, developments, and pressures were influencing the creation of the respective reports?

- What did each committee try to achieve with its report? What were their goals?

- Did they look to effect particular changes? What were they?

Inspired by work on narrative journalism we also introduced a question at the end of each interview: "Who else should we talk to?" [11] For such a slight intervention, this proved to be rich and valuable, and through it we discovered participants who we otherwise would not have known to interview, or not have considered as having a perspective to contribute. Our approach, then, was exploratory: we expanded our reach and conducted additional interviews based on the conversations we had.

---

[1] The IEEE Computer Society independently published model curricula in 1977 and 1983. The 1983 report influenced the creation of the subsequent joint report in 1991, for instance through its detailed laboratory materials. While we included these reports in our review, we didn't explicitly interview participants in these efforts.

Table 1: Study Participants

Curriculum Report	Study Participants		
Curriculum '68	Werner Rheinboldt[2]		
Curriculum '78	Richard Austing[3]	Gerald Engel[3]	
Computing as a Discipline	Peter Denning		
Computing Curricula 1991	Allen Tucker	Kim Bruce	
Computing Curricula 2001	Eric Roberts	Bob Sloan	Shai Simonson
Computer Science Curriculum 2008	Andrew McGettrick	Lillian Cassel	
Computer Science Curricula 2013	Mehran Sahami	Dan Grossman	Kathleen Fisher
	Henry Walker	Simon Thompson	

Table 2: Major Changes Between Reports

Curriculum Report	Major Changes
Curriculum '68	first report; focused on defining the subject and provided a suggested curriculum structure
Curriculum '78	significantly raised the profile of programming; introduced CS1-CS8 course sequence
Computing as a Discipline	aimed to distinguish computing from other disciplines; argued for a view beyond programming, including, e.g., design
Computing Curricula 1991	introduced knowledge units & breadth-first curriculum; first joint ACM & IEEE-CS curriculum report
Computing Curricula 2001	reduced the size of the body of knowledge; returned to a more specific approach to course descriptions & included learning objectives
Computer Science Curriculum 2008	interim report; minor updates, including a section on security and "the computing crisis"
Computer Science Curricula 2013	advocated flexibility in relation to other disciplines; introduced curricular exemplars & division of core into tier 1 and 2; refined learning objectives by levels of mastery

For each of these interviews, with two exceptions, both authors were present. One of us (Dziallas) guided the conversation, while the other (Fincher) captured observations and followed up with questions. Immediately after the interview, we debriefed by comparing notes. [15] The completed interviews were then professionally transcribed and analyzed using methods of grounded theory. [4]

In a few instances where participants on the respective committees could not be reached, we relied on previous publications, such as the *Computing Educators Oral History Project*. Whilst those interviews were not centrally concerned with participants' work on the curriculum reports, their reflections on their contributions nevertheless provided additional context for this work.

Not all of the people we interviewed were involved as part of the task forces and steering committees. Indeed, we interviewed some of them for their perspective on the periphery of the effort, whether as contributors to individual knowledge areas or for their work on the implementation of the curriculum.

In the interview excerpts below, we identify participants by the year of their contribution. While some of them have contributed to multiple instances of the curriculum recommendations, we identify them by the report we interviewed them for, as indicated in table 1. (We refer to the *Computing as a Discipline* report by its release date in 1989.)

We want to highlight three themes that emerged in our analysis: perceived use and pedagogic projection; community involvement and influence; and contrasting visions for the future of these reports.

---

[2] Werner Rheinboldt submitted written responses to our questions.

[3] Neither Richard Austing nor Gerald Engel participated directly in this study. However, both of them took part in oral history interviews which we used to include their accounts. [16, 22]

3. PERCEIVED USE & PEDAGOGIC PROJECTION

Implicit in these reports is their perceived use: that is, committee members' assumptions and perceptions about how a report will be used, that are reflected in decisions about its approach and structure.

I think the real issue… is how people want to use [it] or whether they want to use it. [2001]

3.1 Actual use

Some committees have conducted surveys, or undertaken polls as to their projected use. One of the most common reported uses is reassurance: that is, to pick up the document, match it against current practice and say "yes: close enough".

…as part of our survey of department chairs before we started CS2013, we did a survey asking how had they used CC2001, or 2008. It was kind of a multiple choice. They had five answers which was everything from, A was "Didn't use it at all," B was "We kind of looked at it but didn't really pay a lot of attention to it." C was, "We used it as guidance. We read the report, we understood what it said, but we weren't going to implement everything in it but we wanted to understand the trends so that could influence our curriculum." D was, "We implemented significant portions of it, but not necessarily the whole thing." E was, "We did the whole thing." As you can imagine, that distribution across those five choices looks like a bell curve. The biggest one was, "We used it as guidance, but it wasn't going to just dictate what our curriculum was." [2013]

Others cited numbers of downloads as a metric of use, or the quantity of textbooks that are based on a curriculum, or which cite it.

3.2 Curriculum as weapon

In the early years of the discipline, the committees aimed to take a formative stance, providing guidance as institutions established their computing programs.

> ...in the older days the field was not well defined and people really needed some help figuring out what to do. [2008]

The role of the early reports could be seen as *curriculum as weapon*, in defining disciplinary boundaries, as what was – and what was not – to be counted as "computing" or "computer science", and how that might be distinctively different from other subjects.

> ...we were able to answer the nagging education questions of the day, is computer science engineering? Science? Mathematics? Where does it fit in a university? [1989]

It was a weapon to be wielded by Department Chairs in arguing for resource, or in establishing programmes. As Peter Denning, the chair of the *Computing as a Discipline* report, recalled:

> I just did not want us to become the victim of other people's stories about us. There was so much we could do for ourselves. I wanted to help computing find its own voice. I think that our report was the beginning of finding our voice. We were able to say who we are, why we are new and not part of older more familiar fields. I think other people began to see what was different about computing and why we are not a subfield of mathematics, science, or engineering. We certainly have much to offer to mathematics, science, and engineering, but we are different because computing deals with information processes and machines that transform them. No other field has that as a focus of concern. [1989]

The role of disciplinary maturity runs through this paper, as it has run through the coeval period this paper covers. The need for *curriculum as weapon* inevitably decreases as computing has become an established – even dominant – offer in Universities over the last 50 years.

3.3 Curriculum as prescription

A second perceived use is curriculum as prescription, either *what should be taught at all* or *what should be taught everywhere*.

> In our discussions of the many common problems, we soon identified as a major concern ... the selection of the material that should be taught. [1968]

Notably, the focus of early curricula was on *what* should be taught, and not *how*. The 1978 report was particularly prescriptive, and consisted of a largely pre-defined course sequence, from CS1 to CS8 in the core (with an additional ten elective courses) that formed an orderly progression of material from first introduction to graduation. The degree of prescription, however, was not unwelcome and widely adopted; indeed, terminology it introduced persists in many universities who still call their introductory course "CS1".

> I think '78 had the most impact. It really redefined the field. '68 would have had impact, except that there's not that much computer science going on, you know, it's an early effort. '78 was the sort of basis on which all future reports would be built, and had enormous impact. [2001]

The Curriculum 78 report, for instance, created the term 'CS1'. That's where it came from, that report, and every single course was numbered CS1, CS2, CS7, whatever. For quite a long time, courses were referred to by reference to that report and the number in that report. CS1/CS2 are the lingering numbers; I don't think anything else remains in common use. [2008]

3.4 Curriculum as permission

As computer science matured as discipline in its own right, the curriculum perception changed: it became less important that everyone had to be exposed to the same material in the same order, that there was only one way that computer science could be taught (and learned). It became more important that the range and diversity of possible content in a computer science degree was represented. Thus, the 1991 report departed from the previous approach of outlining an entire computing curriculum. Instead, it introduced "knowledge units" which, when combined in various ways, constituted the requirements for undergraduate computing education.

> We wanted to present a single curriculum model that could be embraced by the widest range of undergraduate CS programs, from small colleges to universities to engineering schools. For that reason, we invented the notions of a "knowledge area" and a "knowledge unit" with the idea that knowledge units (KU's) could be repackaged in different ways to fit the goals of different types of programs. We also felt [that] there should be an alternative to the standard way of organizing the CS1 and CS2 courses, so as to present students with a sense of the richness of the discipline beyond just programming. We called it the "Breadth-First Curriculum.... [1991]

As the level of prescription diminished, the perception of use changed. In 1991, the more permissive approach to subject matter content, went hand-in-hand with ideas of how the content could be combined: the "breadth first" approach suggesting a new way of presenting computer science to a new end, displaying "the richness of the discipline".

In this paradigm the curriculum is as much about *how* to teach as it is about *what* to teach.

> So the body of knowledge [of the 2013 report] was very much written in a general 'leave room for innovation' 'support all comers as long as they are hitting the learning outcomes' sort of way. I think all of them were, maybe all the knowledge areas... [2013]

The UK equivalent to the US curriculum reports (called benchmark statements) is another such example of a permissive stance:

> They saw their view as being one where they would try and encompass everything ... at a high level. [2013]

3.5 Curriculum as authority

The relationship between curriculum and textbooks is oft-cited. The idea that textbooks and curriculum inhabit the same space, as resources for classroom practitioners is widespread, although it takes on different characteristics. Sometimes, it is seen as a beneficial symbiotic relationship:

> the other outcome ... is to drive publishers to name books as covering particular courses. And that's critical, because most people want the textbook from

which to teach, and having a name of a course that's standard and not specific to an institution means that publishers can design for that market. [2001]

Certainly I've seen, in my reviews of book proposals, people will talk about how they fit the Curriculum 2001 model. [2001]

In this view, textbook and curriculum proceed hand-in-hand, supporting each other's effort, and when this breaks down, it is to mutual disadvantage:

...'91 was harder to take off the shelf. It was a bunch of, you know, "Choose one from column A," sorts of things, and build it yourself. And that ... gave no guidance to publishers, you couldn't cover a particular course or something in '91, it didn't have the impact. [2001]

For others, the curriculum/textbook relationship is not seen a mutually beneficial, but rather more parasitic:

...what is core and what's not ... determines what people put in their textbooks, and what people therefore teach. [2013]

The implicit workflow is that curriculum comes first and the publishers/authors latch onto that.

Textbook authors wanted us to lay out a series of courses so they could write books ... It makes perfectly good sense from their point of view. [1991]

In another framing of the parasitic relationship, the for-profit motives of the publishers mean that textbooks represent but a poor resource, and the curriculum must exist as redress for educators, a reliable source of content:

A non-specialist will not have ... examples at their fingertips. ... They would be, if you will, at the mercy of the author of the textbook who is not necessarily thinking what's best because there's some commerce involved there. [2001]

A third view is that, by drawing on diverse talents, the curriculum provides deep expertise in every area which the average academic doesn't have the time or resource to access individually:

*Because in a large university, even in a small college, for the most part you're going to be judged on how much work you're publishing. Secondarily—even in teaching school—**secondarily** on your teaching. So to take a very strong interest in making sure that when you teach a non-specialised course, you're actually teaching something that is authentic and really good for the students, takes a lot of initiative. [2001]*

As well as the symbiotic and parasitic framings, there are more subtle interactions between the two estates. Sometimes the curriculum committee become the most knowledgeable, most appropriate textbook authors.

As it turned out, some of the people on the committee afterward contributed to a series of books in this breadth-first approach.... [1991]

And sometimes, the influence is the other way around: the textbooks, and their perception of how knowledge is arranged, are the inspiration for (parts of) the curriculum:

As an area, there's less uniformity in the way courses are taught than in some of the other areas. In AI, a huge number of institutions, particularly in North

America, use the Russell and Norvig text. ... [other areas] have not achieved that uniformity. ... I didn't have three standard textbooks to go to and reverse engineer, we really did it more from scratch. [2013]

So there are perceived uses of a stipulated curriculum document from within and outwith the committees that construct them. However, there is a category of use that comes alongside the construction of the curriculum. This is the implicit notion of how the committee think the curriculum will be used by teachers in their practice, of course design or in teaching, We call this "pedagogic projection".

3.6 Pedagogic projection

Pedagogic projection differs between the different curriculum reports, sometimes reflecting the perceived use. So, for the early years, 1968 and 1978, the pedagogic projection is that an educator will pick up the course sequence and deliver it as constructed. Associated with this is the view that the people who are designing the curriculum know more than those who will use it, that the teachers who pick it up will be less skilled or less expert than the designers.

This becomes problematic when the intended recipients feel themselves to be seen as deficient or lacking in some respect.

I think the impression that many of us had [of the 1978 effort] was [that] it simply wrote down what people in large universities were doing that day. [1991]

In 1991, the pedagogic projection was different; it expressly defined a mix-and-match freedom that expected educators to be engaged with the construction of their own curriculum. It recognised that "Each curriculum will be site-specific, shaped by those responsible for the program who must consider factors such as institutional goals, opportunities and constraints, local resources, and the prior preparation of students." [19]

By 2001 the Knowledge Units introduced in 1991 had become the normal way expression of the Body of Knowledge. The 2001 committee also put together a series of model ways the units could be combined, in made-up sequences. Any one of six introductory courses (Imperative-first, Breadth-first, Functional-first; Objects-first, Algorithms-first, Hardware-first) could be followed by any intermediate approach (Topics-based, Compressed, Systems-based, Web-based) and finished with "additional courses to complete the undergraduate curriculum". Whilst this illustrated the flexibility that the authors wanted, the projections were generic and fell between prescription and permission: institutions found it hard to see themselves represented. [10]

The 2013 committee took a very different view. Their pedagogic projection of the relationship between curriculum and classroom was one of professional discussion. This was underpinned by the belief that educators knew their own context best, and knew what would work within that context. What permitted discussion were examples of how curriculum was differently arranged in other contexts, similar or dissimilar in their construction and constraints: so teachers could see courses from colleges that were "the same" as theirs, and those typical of other types of institution. The Steering Committee devised a common template and solicited authentic examples of how the curriculum (in part or whole) was delivered in a wide range of institutional contexts. They called these *course exemplars* and *curricula exemplars* and appended 84 and 6 of these, respectively, in Appendices C and D of the final report. As the authors write: "These exemplars are not meant to be prescriptive with respect to curricular design, nor are they meant to define a standard curriculum for all institutions. Rather they are provided to give educators examples of different ways that the Body of Knowledge may be organized into courses, to provide comparative breadth, and to spur new thinking for future course design." [10]

The different levels of abstraction at which these documents project their pedagogic use are reminiscent of the "ladder of abstraction", a model of communication where each rung represents a different degree of abstraction. Terms on the bottom of the ladder are concrete, while those at the top are most abstract. "…we create meaning at the top of the ladder and exemplify that meaning at the bottom of the ladder." [11]

The most successful communication needs to work on both ends of the ladder of abstraction, while avoiding the middle. For example:

Participants at school board meetings never discuss critical issues such as literacy or the development of young citizens who can participate in democratic life – ideas at the top of the ladder. Nor is there discussion about the children trying with difficulty to decode the reading in Miss Gallagher's first grade classroom – the bottom of the ladder. Instead, it's a world where teachers are referred to as "instructional units," while the conversation is about the "scope and sequencing of the language arts curriculum" – the middle of the ladder.

We contend that curriculum recommendations, too, can be seen stepped between the struggles of "Jo the Computer Science Teacher" and the desirability that "Graduates need understanding of a number of recurring themes, such as abstraction, complexity, and evolutionary change, and a set of general principles, such as sharing a common resource, security, and concurrency." [10] – and that they, too, work best when they avoid the dangerous middle.

4. COMMUNITY INVOLVEMENT & INFLUENCE

Curriculum reports are produced by committees. But committees are not isolated, they do not do their work in purdah, they are jointly and severally part of the wider computing community. Committee members incorporate perspectives from their own, specific subject (mathematics, programming languages, human-computer interaction, etc.) and institutional communities (liberal arts, engineering, etc.). During the course of its construction, each curriculum is periodically exposed for comment. Here, we first characterize the general processes employed to ensure that the curriculum is acceptable. Then, we describe two examples of communities working to influence the creation of a report.

4.1 Creating a Curriculum: How it is Done

By 2013, the way a curriculum committee was expected to engage the wider community was well established. Committee members were each associated with a knowledge area, and each knowledge area formed small working groups, with expert membership outside of the main committee to formulate guidelines and review drafts. For the overall document, drafts of reports were prepared and presented at conferences, such as the SIGCSE symposium.

There's a report regularly; interim reports are available. There is a straw-man version of the report produced. It's put out for public comment. In 2013 that was put on the Ensemble site as a community, so that's where the comments and feedback were gathered. All

of that was taken into account and they go through the various iterations until they get to the final draft....

[Interviewer] Is that process of iteration mandated, or is it just down to each committee to decide how to do that?

That's a good question. It's always done. I don't know that it's written down officially as a rule, but it always is. [2008]

For earlier efforts, though, this was not always done, and there were less formal ways in which recommendations emerged. As universities across the United States were establishing computing centers in the 50s and 60s, the need to incorporate computing into university curricula emerged in largely informal conversations among their directors. These conversations eventually led to the formation of a committee, the solicitation of input from community members, multiple writing sessions hosted at IBM and others, and to the release of "Recommendations for Academic Programs in Computer Science" in 1968. [1]

In the years following the publication, some institutions played more significant roles than others in the development of curriculum reports. Of particular note was the University of Maryland. The first director of the computing center at Maryland was Werner Rheinboldt (a member of the 1968 committee). In 1963 he hired Earl Schweppe, the secretary of the '68 committee, and Richard Austing, who would become one of authors of the '78 report. And in 1966, William Atchison, the chair of the '68 curriculum report, joined the University to become the second director of its computing center. [13] While the University of Maryland didn't establish its own computer science department until 1973, it was certainly a hotbed for curriculum development in computer science at the time.

... I just kind of got mixed up in that with Atchison, Rheinboldt, and Schweppe. Deeply involved. And I certainly am not going to claim any contribution to it all, but I certainly benefited personally from it. And it certainly spiked my interest in combining my interest in education with the field itself. I feel kind of on the ground floor of a lot of that. And in some sense ... Bill Atchison was really a mentor in that regards. He saw my interest in it and his interest corresponded to that and he ... opened the doors a bit, which was very helpful. And so ... [I] got into the ACM through him and into the education operation through him. [1978]

The personal nature of the community is very evident here. And personality and personal networks remain influential in a pre-formal craft approach to getting the job done.

That [at Stanford] is where actually I first met Eric Roberts.... We got to know each other. I think those kind of personal interactions make a big impact along the way, ... [he] was the person who was one of the driving forces for saying, "Hey, you should go do the CS2013 curricular effort." [2013]

4.2 Engaging the community

All reports have (more or less formally) solicited input from outside the committee membership, sometimes individually, sometimes in a cascade of participation. The 1968 curriculum committee engaged community members, who were referred to as "consultants". [17] And in preparation for the 1978 report, Gerald Engel and Richard Austing arranged for subcommittees and prepared a series of papers and working reports. The 2001 report had a number of unique features with regard to engagement: it brought all of its participants together in a room.

> *Probably our most successful meeting around the curriculum was an NSF-funded workshop, where we able to invite all of the people who were on our knowledge task force working groups to a meeting ... where they would make the case for the larger number of required units.... [2001]*

It employed a devolved structure consisting of 14 knowledge focus groups and, for the first time, 6 pedagogy focus groups.

> *There was, I imagine, someone in charge of the whole thing and then someone in charge of the whole theory area.... And then, whoever was in charge of that area then distributed it again and refined it, and in the end I personally was in charge of the discrete structures part of that area. That was my major responsibility, where I effectively wrote the document and then everybody else would check and edit, and suggest. And then there would be some discussion and argument about that. [2001]*

These "focus group" contributors also helped review and edit other areas.

> *My role in other areas in theory was to do the suggesting, the editing, and the checking – rather than the initial proposal. Basically, one person was in charge of the original write up, just like two people collaborating on some sort of a writing project. One person typically comes up with a first draft and the other one revises it, then it goes back and forth. That's what it was here, where one person was the lead in a certain area and the rest acted as editors and a panel. [2001]*

4.3 Influencing the Curriculum: Unwritten Rules

The processes of consultation are visible, but not transparent to the outside. Aside from open solicitation of comments, and trust that the committee will take heed of them, there is no specification for how particular issues can be raised, or particular change affected. Interest groups negotiate these paths differently, and we examine two instances here.

4.3.1 Liberal Arts

One of the groups that has played a role in shaping these reports since their inception is a (more or less formalized) coalition of Liberal Arts colleges. As Henry Walker and Charles Kelemen observed, the problem for the Liberal Arts was that the reports "...treated all institutions as being similar; the same recommendations were to apply to technical schools, research-oriented universities, and liberal arts colleges." [20]

Liberal Arts institutions began establishing computer science programs around the time the '78 curriculum report was released. In fact, both Richard Austing and Gerald Engel recalled in their oral history interviews the desire to develop a curriculum applicable to smaller colleges[4] as part of their work on the 1978 curriculum report.

> *I felt large colleges, large universities could kind of fend for themselves, get their own faculty, etc. Small colleges at the time were struggling like crazy ... a lot them realized the need... that a lot of students wanted to get into computing and so they had to build up something ... So I felt that I was around at the right time and could take some of that background and information I had into their curriculum. [1978]*

And yet, despite this sensitivity, the 1978 curriculum makes few references to such institutions. Indeed, a number of educators at liberal arts institutions published experience reports in the early 1980s, many of which included suggested changes to adapt the '78 curriculum to a liberal arts context. [8, 18, 21] Liberal Arts colleges, then, were unsatisfied with the status quo of curricular guidelines available to them. A session at the 1984 SIGCSE conference particularly reinforced this issue.

> *...the basic theme was: "How would small colleges have to water down curricula in order to do something" Or rather, it [the curriculum] wasn't going to be very good [for them], but at least they could do **something**. This did not resonate well with many people, as you might expect... [2013]*

This lack of an appropriate solution for their context led to the emergence of the Liberal Arts Computer Science Consortium (LACS), an alliance of concerned individuals from Liberal Arts institutions. In 1986, with support from the Sloan Foundation, they published the first "Model Curriculum for a Liberal Arts Degree in Computer Science". [9] It provided suggestions for how an institution with a small computer science faculty would be able to offer a B.A. degree. The curriculum was highly prescriptive, even including a detailed description of a teaching load distribution for departments with as little as three faculty members.

The group aimed to provide others with the resources to establish their own computer science programs at Liberal Arts institutions. Among the initial list of questions to be discussed by the members of LACS were: [3]

- What kind of curriculum would be appropriate and realistic in the small liberal arts college environment?

- How could we attract faculty to this kind of environment?

These questions, as the larger liberal arts agenda in the early days, speak to the notion of *curriculum as prescription* and *as a weapon*.

The subsequent 1991 ACM/IEEE-CS curriculum report faced difficulties in bridging differences between engineering and liberal arts programs: differences in participants' backgrounds lead to differences in perspectives, which contributed to tensions within the group. For instance, opinions on when to introduce concepts such as P/NP or whether physics should be a compulsory course for computing students varied widely based on institutional background.

> *The notion that one might have a curriculum that was more flexible and had lower requirements than is typical in an engineering school, some of them found that difficult to accept and thought that it just meant*

---

[4] The influence we refer to in this section is generally characterized by liberal arts institutions and specifically by the Liberal Arts Computer Science Consortium (LACS). While liberal arts and small colleges don't necessarily describe the same type of institution, we employ the terms used by the participants in our study.

you were watering things down, that it wasn't a real curriculum, and so there were a number of strains. The ACM and the IEEE people tended to have different points of view. Obviously, there was a range in there, but there was often a fair amount of tension. [1991]

Dissatisfied, this led LACS to release another set of its own recommendations specifically for liberal arts institutions in 1996. And again, the 2001 ACM curriculum was symmetrically followed by the release of LACS recommendations in 2007. (See [3] for an overview the three curriculum models released by LACS.)

In the 2001 there was an effort in the task force to be broader and think of more perspectives. But ultimately LACS concluded it was a nice effort, but it really didn't get the job done in terms of what would make sense in a liberal arts perspective. [2013]

For liberal arts institutions, with limited number of available course hours and instructors, one of the central concerns had been the size of the curriculum. That is, how they would be able to cover a computer science curriculum as defined. The 2001 task force explicitly worked to reduce the size of the body of knowledge:

The most common reaction that we got when we had a survey of what were the problems with '91, which was one of the first things that we did, was that people felt that it was just too large; you know, that there was no way that that institution, particularly if it had limitations of resources, or if it was a small faculty, could cover all the material that was in the desired set of knowledge units from '91. So ours is considerably smaller. [2001]

And in 2013, this issue was addressed early on.

Something we were very cognisant of from the beginning is how do we create these guidelines that contain new material, but can't require more hours of instruction? That is what creates some of the real challenge: if you're putting new stuff in, what's the old stuff that comes out? You're always going to upset someone when you take old stuff out, because if it's their stuff, they're going to be upset. But luckily, we found a structure with this tiered structure that worked. [2013]

Indeed, the 2013 curriculum report introduced a two-tiered structure. While previous reports had distinguished between core and elective materials in the body of knowledge, the 2013 report further separated the core into tier 1 and 2.

*...when I read that 2001 document with fresh eyes— having never read one before—the language that bothered me a lot was pieces about... "you **must** do this", "you **have** to do this", "**every** undergraduate program must", "**every** student", "**every** hour of the core".*

And I looked at that and I said "this is bogus". I mean it's not reality. It's not fair. You can't tell me that a strong computer science program that happens to have a curriculum that covers 273 of the 280 hours is somehow not a computer science program. It's not believable. And that was the genesis for me to say "We've got to relax some of the language." [2013]

Material in tier 1 is seen as fundamental to any degree program in computing, and thus essential. At the same time, the 2013 report acknowledges that not every degree program may necessarily include the content in tier 2 in its entirety. The response to the 2013 report has been notably different.

For the 2013, with two of the three curricula exemplars for four-year programmes coming from Liberal Arts, we're really pretty pleased that our perspectives are represented in a meaningful way. I don't believe there's expectation there will be a follow-up consortial [LACS] response, because effectively then that's been incorporated already into what's there. [2013]

Over decades, the liberal arts agenda was represented to the various curriculum committees to get their perspective embodied in the curriculum. Sometimes this was directly espoused by members of the main committee, even the committee chairs. In this respect one might claim that the liberal arts agenda had enormous, and persistent, influence. And yet the group still felt the need to regularly create its own guidelines. A contrasting example of community influence is the effort of the programming languages group.

4.3.2 Programming Languages

The 1978 curriculum recommendations had included a significant amount of programming. This was something the 1991 report reversed, in part in response to the 1989 *Computing as a Discipline* report.

Whenever someone asked "What is computer science?" our main answers were about programming computers. Many in our field celebrated great programming as the epitome of computing. ... I think our report gave us a way of talking about our discipline that made clear we have strong elements of mathematics, science, and engineering, blended in a new way, and that we are not simply coders or technology hackers. We wanted to overcome the disconnect between the public view of computing and the real guts of our field. Characterising the field as a field of programmers is just a giant mistake. [1989]

The next effort in 2001 initially didn't include a representative from the programming languages on its task force, and the programming languages knowledge area focus group was only established at a later point. A draft of the curriculum had significantly reduced the number of core hours allocated to programming languages. The programming languages knowledge area focus group published an article soliciting comments from the community in the SIGPLAN Notices in response [2], and the SIGPLAN executive committee released a letter to the curriculum task force. [6] While ultimately changes were made in time for the final curriculum report, it left the programming languages community dissatisfied.

As part of the work leading up to the 2008 curriculum recommendations, an interim revision of the 2001 report, the programming languages group then argued for additional material to be included. However, the task force at the time decided not to incorporate substantial changes until the next major revision.

And people sent in 100 comments saying "You need to fix this, we've been mad since 2001; fix it, fix it, fix it!" And the 2008 group decided – it was a very close call – that it was too significant a change for what 2008 was trying to accomplish. [2013]

So, the consultation route had not succeeded, perhaps in similar ways that it had not succeeded for the liberal arts. In 2008, the SIGPLAN community established its own education board. [7] During the 2013 effort, two representatives from SIGPLAN were on the report's steering committee and the SIGPLAN education board effectively became part of the programming languages knowledge area working group. They re-wrote the programming languages section from the ground up, and in this way the group was able to effect change within a single curricular iteration.

If you have someone who is willing to do a lot of the work, they can have a great impact on things, so whoever is the driving force. The Curriculum Committee, certainly in my experience, the people who are willing to do a lot of the work can have a major impact. [1991]

We have illustrated some ways in which interest groups have been able to influence the curriculum, and there is clearly no one "right way" to achieve this. Indeed, both the liberal arts and programming languages groups' efforts were successful in 2013. The formal mechanisms of consultation and review are important; the informal mechanisms of friendship and group membership are important; models of activism and organization are important. Community members need to be able to have influence in the system, but, at least as importantly, the system has to be malleable to allow that influence to take effect.

5. IMPLICATIONS FOR FUTURE REPORTS

In our interviews with community members, we discovered contrasting narratives about the future of these curriculum recommendations. Visions for the future are necessarily grounded in the perceived use of the reports, and one narrative views the mission of these curriculum reports as accomplished: if their goal was to provide guidance in the early years of the discipline, future reports may not be necessary.

It's an interesting question: what will happen in the future? Computer science is now a more or less grown up discipline ... as recently as the late '90s ... computer science was still an adolescent and needed extra things. Computer science is finally growing up, and this year - this decade a superstar! - growing up. Are we going to keep needing this stuff? Beats me.

That's the thought that comes to my mind from reflecting back and thinking about where we are today. How much of the need was because it was a young, new field with many of the educators being converted from their training before computing training was widely available to being a mature field? Is the one that just came out the last one? [2001]

A second set of observations take a more apocalyptic vision of the continued growth of the discipline, along with an inherent increase in subject matter knowledge (SMK).

...one of the real worries ... was after CC2001 and 2008, was it even possible to do another curricular volume? Was there just so much work to do because the field had expanded so much? It had been so much work [in 2001] that he wasn't even sure it was possible to do it again. [2013]

This view stands on the notion that a single undergraduate degree can and should still encompass the whole field. All the while, the number of available course hours in an undergraduate degree has not changed. A second view is that this increase in SMK is driven by a focus on technological developments.

...I believe the historical progression of focus on computing as a series of technologies has begun to outlive its usefulness. It's certainly true that computing has been a driving force in technology advancement and the agent of many major advances and innovations. We do not want to throw away the technology history we are. But my fear is that our curriculum has gotten so technology oriented that it's short-changing important parts of the field, especially the many growing interactions with other fields and the rising importance of design in our field. [1989]

The vision of a vastly restricted curriculum comes from other voices, too, not with the intention of excising bloat, but rather with the twin aims of identifying an essential core and empirical examination of authentic practice.

I actually think that [we were] unsuccessful to some extent ... tier 1 is too big ... there are a lot of things in tier 1 that belong in tier 2. ... There are perfectly reasonable high quality computer science program that aren't quite doing everything in tier 1. Hopefully over time -- in ten years from now – we'll be able to revisit that again and say, "Well, we've evidence that they aren't doing that, that there are good programs out there that aren't covering this material". [2013]

This radically restricted approach is already in practice at some institutions. As Downey and Stein observe: "Compressing the core of the CS curriculum is a necessity at many schools, but may be a virtue at others. By relieving the obligation of coverage, it facilitates other kinds of innovation." [5] It may be a way to address both ends of the ladder of abstraction – by providing an abstract description of the essential core of the discipline, as well as an exploration of authentic practice through, for instance, course exemplars.

6. SUMMARY

Curricula are texts, and as such they are passive and silent. [12] But these curriculum recommendations emerge from the joint collaborative effort of the community and from networks of influence. We have given voice to these threads and documented their interplay in this paper. This exploration concerns only the production (and embedded in it, the implicit perception of use) of the various reports, and not how they were received, read, or acted upon.

These are complex documents: their production is a complex endeavor, involving multiple authors and multiple influences. They also have historicity; that is, individual reports don't stand alone. They are located in time, and placed in the larger sequence of curriculum reports. Indeed, participants in our study often referred to previous and subsequent efforts. Through our interviews with them, in this paper, we have illuminated themes that span these efforts.

7. ACKNOWLEDGEMENTS

We are grateful for the support of this work through the award of a 2015 ACM History Fellowship, to the *Computing Educators Oral History Project* for allowing us to include parts of their interview with Richard Austing, and to the anonymous reviewers for their helpful comments.

8. REFERENCES

[1] Atchison, W.F., Conte, S.D., Hamblen, J.W., Hull, T.E., Keenan, T.A., Kehl, W.B., McCluskey, E.J., Navarro, S.O., Rheinboldt, W.C., Schweppe, E.J., Viavant, W. and Young, D.M., Jr. 1968. Curriculum 68: Recommendations for Academic Programs in Computer Science: A Report of the ACM Curriculum Committee on Computer Science. *Commun. ACM.* 11, 3 (Mar. 1968), 151–197.

[2] Bruce, K.B. 2000. Curriculum 2001 Draft Found Lacking in Programming Languages. *SIGPLAN Not.* 35, 4 (Apr. 2000), 26–28.

[3] Bruce, K.B., Cupper, R.D. and Drysdale, R.L.S. 2010. A History of the Liberal Arts Computer Science Consortium and Its Model Curricula. *Trans. Comput. Educ.* 10, 1 (Mar. 2010), 3:1–3:12.

[4] Charmaz, K. 2011. *Constructing grounded theory: a practical guide through qualitative analysis*. SAGE.

[5] Downey, A.B. and Stein, L.A. 2006. Designing a small-footprint curriculum in computer science. *Frontiers in Education Conference, 36th Annual* (Oct. 2006), 21–26.

[6] Fenwick, J., Norris, C., Cytron, R. and Felleisen, M. 2001. Computing Curricula 2001 Draft. *SIGPLAN Not.* 36, 4 (Apr. 2001), 3–4.

[7] Fisher, K. and Krintz, C. 2008. SIGPLAN Programming Language Curriculum Workshop: Workshop Organization. *SIGPLAN Not.* 43, 11 (Nov. 2008), 1–6.

[8] Fosberg, M.D.H. 1982. Adapting Curriculum 78 to a Small University Environment. *Proceedings of the Thirteenth SIGCSE Technical Symposium on Computer Science Education* (New York, NY, USA, 1982), 179–183.

[9] Gibbs, N.E. and Tucker, A.B. 1986. A Model Curriculum for a Liberal Arts Degree in Computer Science. *Commun. ACM.* 29, 3 (Mar. 1986), 202–210.

[10] Joint Task Force on Computing Curricula, A. for C.M. (ACM) and Society, I.C. 2013. *Computer Science Curricula 2013: Curriculum Guidelines for Undergraduate Degree Programs in Computer Science*. ACM.

[11] Kramer, M. and Call, W. eds. 2007. *Telling True Stories: A Nonfiction Writers' Guide from the Nieman Foundation at Harvard University*. Plume.

[12] McGann, J.J. 1991. *The Textual Condition*. Princeton University Press.

[13] Minker, J. 2007. Forming a Computer Science Center at the University of Maryland. *IEEE Annals of the History of Computing*. 29, 1 (Jan. 2007), 49–64.

[14] Mishler, E.G. 1991. *Research Interviewing: Context and Narrative*. Harvard University Press.

[15] Portigal, S. 2013. *Interviewing Users: How to Uncover Compelling Insights*. Rosenfeld Media.

[16] Russell, A.L. 2013. An Interview with Gerald L. Engel. IEEE Computer Society Leaders Oral History Project.

[17] Schweppe, E.J. 1990. On the Genesis of Curriculum 68. (Washington, DC, 1990).

[18] Smith, J. 1979. The Small Liberal Arts College: A Challenge for Computer Science. *Proceedings of the Tenth SIGCSE Technical Symposium on Computer Science Education* (New York, NY, USA, 1979), 220–223.

[19] Tucker, A.B. ed. 1991. Computing Curricula 1991. *Commun. ACM.* 34, 6 (Jun. 1991), 68–84.

[20] Walker, H.M. and Kelemen, C. 2010. Computer Science and the Liberal Arts: A Philosophical Examination. *Trans. Comput. Educ.* 10, 1 (Mar. 2010), 2:1–2:10.

[21] Worlana, P.B. 1978. Using the ACM Computer Science Curriculum Recommendations in a Liberal Arts College. *SIGCSE Bull.* 10, 4 (Dec. 1978), 16–19.

[22] Young, A. 2006. An Interview with Richard (Dick) Austing. Computing Educators Oral History Project.

Comparing Textual and Block Interfaces in a Novice Programming Environment

Thomas W. Price
North Carolina State University
890 Oval Drive
Raleigh, NC
twprice@ncsu.edu

Tiffany Barnes
North Carolina State University
890 Oval Drive
Raleigh, NC
tmbarnes@ncsu.edu

ABSTRACT

Visual, block-based programming environments present an alternative way of teaching programming to novices and have proven successful in classrooms and informal learning settings. However, few studies have been able to attribute this success to specific features of the environment. In this study, we isolate the most fundamental feature of these environments, the block interface, and compare it directly to its textual counterpart. We present analysis from a study of two groups of novice programmers, one assigned to each interface, as they completed a simple programming activity. We found that while the interface did not seem to affect users' attitudes or perceived difficulty, students using the block interface spent less time off task and completed more of the activity's goals in less time.

Categories and Subject Descriptors

K.3.2 [**Computers and Education**]: Computer and Information Science Education; D.1.7 [**Programming Techniques**]: Visual Programming

Keywords

Block programming, drag-and-drop, programming interface

1. INTRODUCTION

Programming is a challenging subject to learn, and educators have investigated many strategies for making it more accessible to students [17]. Much of this effort has been directed towards creating better programming environments for novices, resulting in many new systems [13, 18]. A common feature in many modern novice programming environments is the use of drag-and-drop blocks of code, which fit together to form a program, minimizing the possibility of syntax errors and the need to memorize procedure names. While this feature can be traced at least as far back as the LogoBlocks environment [3], it has become prevalent in many more recent environments [1, 8, 10, 16, 29], which have

been evaluated in classrooms [24, 25, 26], summer camps [21, 31] and after-school programs [22].

In this paper, we will use the term Block-Based Programming Environment (BBPE) to refer to those environments that allow users to construct and execute computer programs by composing atomic blocks of code together to produce program structure. These code blocks may additionally have slots, which can be filled by other blocks; for example, a function call block may have slots for each of its parameters. These blocks may represent high-level structures, such as methods or loops, or low-level operators such as multiplication or equality comparison. An example is shown in Figure 1. There exist a variety of programming environments which use the block metaphor, but here we limit our use of the term BBPE to those that use *procedural* languages. For a more thorough introduction to one BBPE, see [29].

Much work has gone into the evaluation of BBPEs. Previous studies have identified what programming concepts students use in BBPEs [22], measured learning gains from classes based on BBPEs [24, 26], and investigated the ease of transitioning from these environments to textual programming [9, 31]. However, these studies evaluate entire programming environments, or even whole curricula, and thus it is difficult to attribute success or failure to any specific aspect of the environment.

This study seeks to isolate the effects of a block interface on the experience of novices when learning to program. To do this, we created two instances of a programming environment, differing only in that one uses a textual programming interface, and one uses a block interface. We collected data from novice, middle-school programmers as they used one of the two interfaces, and analyzed it to answer the following research questions. When compared to a textual interface, how will a block interface:

RQ1. Affect students' attitudes towards computing?

RQ2. Affect their perceived difficulty of programming?

RQ3. Affect their performance on a programming activity?

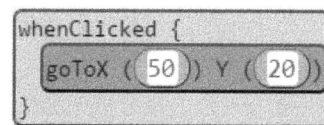

Figure 1: An example of a simple block program, consisting of a procedure call with two literal arguments, nested inside of of an event block.

To the best of our knowledge, this is the first study to directly compare block and textual programming interfaces in an otherwise controlled setting. Our results contribute to a better understanding of the role that block interfaces play in students' experiences in BBPEs. The following sections cover related work, detail the methodology of this study, and present results, analysis and discussion of the data.

2. RELATED WORK

2.1 Block-based Environments

There are a variety of BBPEs available, many appearing within the last 5-10 years. While most of these environments are developed in academic settings, others, such as Google's Blockly [1] and LEGO Mindstorms [2] emerged from industry. A full review of BBPEs is beyond the scope of this paper, but we highlight two examples, Scratch and Alice, which capture the common characteristics of BBPEs and have been evaluated in a number of setting.

Scratch [29], developed by researchers at MIT, is one of the best-known BBPEs. It was designed to be "more tinkerable, more meaningful and more social" than previous novice programming environments, such as LOGO [27]. To that end, Scratch features primarily graphical output, allowing users to create and manipulate 2D sprites, while adding music, animation and interactivity. The Scratch website allows users to upload, share and remix each other's programs, adding a social element to the environment. Scratch is also notable for its use of executable program fragments. Scratch programs can be built in small chunks, and any piece of Scratch code can be individually executed, with its effects immediately visible. Scratch has become a widely used programming language. As of June 2015, it ranks 25th on the TIOBE index[1], which measures programming languages' popularity based on search engine results.

Scratch has been evaluated in a number of contexts. Meerbaum-Salant et al. [24] designed a two-hour Scratch curriculum and observed its implementation in two ninth grade classrooms. An analysis of student scores on a pre- and post-test of CS concepts showed significant improvement after using Scratch, though students did struggle with more abstract concepts such as initialization, variables and concurrency. Maloney et al. [22] describe their experience using Scratch in an urban after-school center and their analysis of the programs created. Scratch was popular, with students using it voluntarily and more frequently than any other available design software. While around 20% of the projects included only media manipulation without code, about half of the remaining programs employed loops and user interaction, with another quarter using conditional and synchronization statements. Students produced programs of increasing complexity over time.

Alice 2 [8], and its successor Alice 3 [9], are BBPEs which allow users to program within a 3D environment. Alice was one of the first novice programming environments to adopt a drag-and-drop interface. It employs an event-based, object-oriented paradigm, allowing users to add objects to their scene, manipulate the objects' attributes and call their methods. Alice offers a library of 3D objects, animations and sounds, making it a media-rich experience. Alice uses drag-and-drop controls for manipulating lines of code and

some expressions, but relies more heavily on menus to give the user access to the many manipulable properties of each object. Alice's interface shares the goal of many BBPEs of simplifying programming by removing the capacity for syntax errors.

Moskal et al. [26] developed an introductory college curriculum using Alice. They compared students who underwent this course prior to, or concurrently with, their first CS1 course to students who took only the CS1 course. They found that the Alice course significantly improved students' grades in the CS1 course, as well as retention in CS over a two year period. They found these trends more apparent with "high-risk" students, who had less math experience and no programming experience prior to college. A similar study by Cooper et al. [8] supports these findings, showing that an Alice-based curriculum helped achieve improved grades and retention. Kelleher et al. [19] found that Alice could be further adapted to young female students by adding features to facilitate storytelling programs, such as easier animations and more character-driven methods.

Other popular BBPEs include MIT App Inventor [28], which allows users to design and program Android apps in a web application. It has been evaluated in K-12 classrooms and summer camps, suggesting it is a powerful, motivational and accessible tool [25], which can serve as a bridge to textual coding in Java [31]. The block interface of App Inventor was turned into a standalone project called Google Blockly [1], which was designed to allow developers to create visual interfaces for their applications. LEGO Mindstorms NXT are customizable LEGO robotics, which can be programmed using a simple block programming environment that employs both procedural and data-flow paradigms. LEGO Mindstorms have been used to teach programming to middle school students [6] and in introductory undergraduate CS courses [7]. Harvey and Mönig created Snap (formerly BYOB) [15], a web-based BBPE based on Scratch, which is being used as the environment of choice for a pilot of an upcoming AP CS Principles course [14].

In addition to their block interfaces, many BBPEs share the following characteristics as well:

- They target novice programmers [8, 15, 28], often younger children during primary or secondary education [9, 19, 25, 29, 31].

- Their programs reflect the syntax and structure of existing programming languages [8, 15, 16].

- They situate programming in a multi-media context, with a focus on cultural relevance [30]. Users can integrate art, music and interactivity into their projects [21, 22], leading to the creation of games [31], stories [19] and apps [28].

We present these *characteristics* separately from our definition of BBPEs, which is concerned only with the block interface. There exist textual programming environments which emphasize these features (e.g. Greenfoot [20]), and BBPEs which do not (e.g. Blockly [1]).

2.2 Comparing Block and Textual Languages

Some studies do compare block and textual programming environments to each other. Lewis [21] compared two groups of 5th grade students participating in a computing summer

---

[1] http://www.tiobe.com/

camp, over the course of 6 days. One group was taught using Scratch, and the other was given similar lessons using Logo, a textual language. The course was designed to teach "making music, movies and games using computers," and as such its lessons were media-rich. Contrary to the author's hypothesis that Scratch's lack of syntax errors would make learning programming easier, students found the exercises equally difficult in both groups. Students in the Logo condition also expressed more confidence in their computing ability after the activities. Both languages seemed better suited to teaching specific constructs, with Logo students showing a better understanding of loops and Scratch students showing a better understanding of conditionals.

Booth and Stumpf [5] studied adults as they learned to program for Arduino, an electronics platform, through two 20-minute exercises. They compared two conditions, which respectively used a Java-based textual editor and a block-based editor called Modkit, which the authors compare to Scratch. Their results suggest that the block-based editor may have improved completion rates, and that these effects were more pronounced in the activity in which participants were modifying an existing program, rather than creating a new one. They found that the Modkit group found their experience more user friendly and had a lower perceived workload and higher perceived success. While the authors also support their conclusions with quotations from participants, they had a small sample size and did no statistical analysis.

McKay and Kölling [23] used predictive modeling to compare a variety of block and textual programming environments used for education, including Scratch, Alice, Greenfoot, LEGO Mindstorms NXT and Python. Using a prototyping tool called CogTool, they modeled the execution time of a variety of programming tasks in each environment. The results suggest that textual languages are better suited to some tasks, such as insertion and replacement, while block languages are better suited to deletion and movement. Importantly, they also show that there is large variance among block languages, and features such as how the language handles instantiating literals can have a large effect on task time. The authors note that their model does not account for time spent thinking or designing the program, and it is possible that some languages facilitate this better than others.

Other work has investigated the *transition* from BBPEs to textual programming. Wagner et al. [31] introduced K-12 students at a summer camp to programming through MIT App Inventor, but transitioned after two days to the Java Bridge, a Java implementation of the App Inventor API. They found that by repeating exercises first using a block interface and then a textual interface, students were able to mentally map familiar block procedures to the new textual procedures. Dann et al. [9] used Alice 3 in an introductory undergraduate CS course, and transitioned from Alice's original block interface to a Java implementation of the Alice API. Students were given a test at the end of the course, which used Java code in its questions. The authors compared students' scores with those of the previous, all-Java version of the course. They found that the Alice classes performed on average at least one grade level higher than the previous pure Java classes on each section of the test. These studies are important both because they show that skills learned in a BBPE can be transferred to a textual environment, and because they serve as examples of textual

environments that can offer the same media-rich features of BBPEs without a block interface.

2.3 Visual Programming Languages

The programming languages employed by BBPEs are often classified under the larger category of Visual Programming Languages (VPLs). In their taxonomy of novice programming environments, Kelleher and Pausch [18] categorize Alice 2 and other early BBPEs like LogoBlocks [3] as environments trying to "find alternatives to typing programs," specifically by "constructing programs using graphical... objects." A number of authors also refer to specific BBPEs as visual programming languages or environments [5, 21, 22, 31]. While we agree that BBPEs are visual, we find it important to distinguish them from more traditional VPLs, such as spreadsheets, flowcharts and the LabView language [32]. This distinction is important due to the body of research comparing these VPLs to textual languages, which may not be applicable to BBPEs.

Historically, the evidence supporting VPLs has been mixed [32]. For instance, Greene and Petre [11] compared programmers' ability to read and comprehend LabView with a simple textual programming language. They found that VPL comprehension was slower for all programmers, regardless of whether their past experience was with LabView or a textual language. The authors later analyzed two dataflow VPLs along a cognitive dimensions framework [12], finding them lacking in a number of dimensions compared to their textual alternatives. For example, they found that the VPLs had higher *Viscosity*, the amount of effort required to make a small change to a program, and that they forced *Premature Commitment*, making users commit to code structure before their programs are fully formulated. We reference these studies to differentiate their work on *dataflow* VPLs from more modern research on BBPEs.

3. METHOD

While many studies have evaluated BBPEs for their effectiveness in engaging students, making programming accessible, or teaching CS concepts, these studies have evaluated the environments holistically. This makes it difficult to assign success to any single aspect of the environment, including the block interface. Since many BBPEs employ a media-rich environment, for instance, perhaps their success is due primarily to this fact, and not to their novel interfaces. Even those studies which control for content when comparing BBPEs with their textual counterparts [5, 21] are still comparing two different programming environments (e.g. Scratch and Logo), which may differ in a number of ways outside of their programming interfaces that could account for different outcomes. To address this, our methodology was designed to isolate the effect of the programming interface on novice students as they learned to program.

3.1 The Environment

For our programming environment, we chose Tiled Grace [16], a web-based environment that implements both block and textual programming interfaces, and even allows the user to switch between the two when working. The "tiled" version of Grace supports the usual features of a BBPE, with drag-and-drop code blocks. These blocks correspond directly to constructs in the Grace programming language, which is also supported by the editor. A program written with either interface will consist of the same text in the same general layout, but in the block interface this text is contained within blocks. We created two versions of the Tiled Grace environment, which were locked into either the block or textual interface, but were otherwise identical. Both versions of the environment can be seen in Figure 2.

We also performed some minor changes to the environment to make the block interface more similar to other BBPEs. The authors of Tiled Grace note that the coloring of their blocks was essentially arbitrary, so we colored blocks by functionality, as is done in other BBPEs (e.g. one color for control structures, variable manipulation, etc.). The authors also note that while other BBPEs use block and hole shapes to indicate how blocks should fit together, the authors leave this for future work. As a simple improvement, we added rounded corners to expression blocks (such as literals or functions that return a value), to indicate that these block could be placed into parameter holes. The shapes were only guidelines, and any block could still be placed in any hole, which is not true of some BBPEs. While Tiled Grace offers a palette of usable blocks, there is no equivalent for textual coding. To keep the two interfaces as similar as possible, we also added a "Code Palette," consisting of equivalent blocks of sample code. Where the blocks had holes to indicate where other blocks should be placed, the Code Palette snippets had dummy values for method parameters and comments indicating where lines of code could be added. Expression code snippets had a blue background, similar to the rounded corers of the block interface. We found these to be additions that a novice textual programming environment could reasonably implement for a specified domain.

Since our goal was to evaluate the interface in the context of novice programmers, we developed a programming exercise based on an Hour of Code activity from the Snap website [15], a tutorial designed to introduce novices to programming for the first time. The exercise had users create a simple web-based game, similar to whack-a-mole, in which users attempt to click on a sprite as it jumps around the screen to win points. Many BBPEs support the creation of similar, simple games. The exercise was split into 9 sections, with tutorial text introducing each one. Each section introduced a new goal, which often built off of previous goals. The tutorial text was the same for both versions of Tiled Grace, except where the differing interfaces necessitated changes (referring to "blocks" instead of "code"). A finished project required the use of various programming concepts, including events, loops, variables and conditionals.

3.2 Procedure

This study took place as part of a middle school STEM outreach program called SPARCS [6]. The program, which meets for half-day sessions approximately once a month during the school year, consists of lessons designed and taught by undergraduate and graduate students to promote technical literacy. We worked with a group of sixth graders, who were randomly assigned to use the block interface, and a group of 7th graders, who were assigned to use the textual interface. We chose to assign the conditions by classroom, rather than by student, to avoid confusion from students within a classroom seeing different interfaces. The Block group consisted of 17 6th grade students (12 male, 5 female). The Text group consisted of 14 7th grade students, (11 male, 3 female). We took measures to test for population

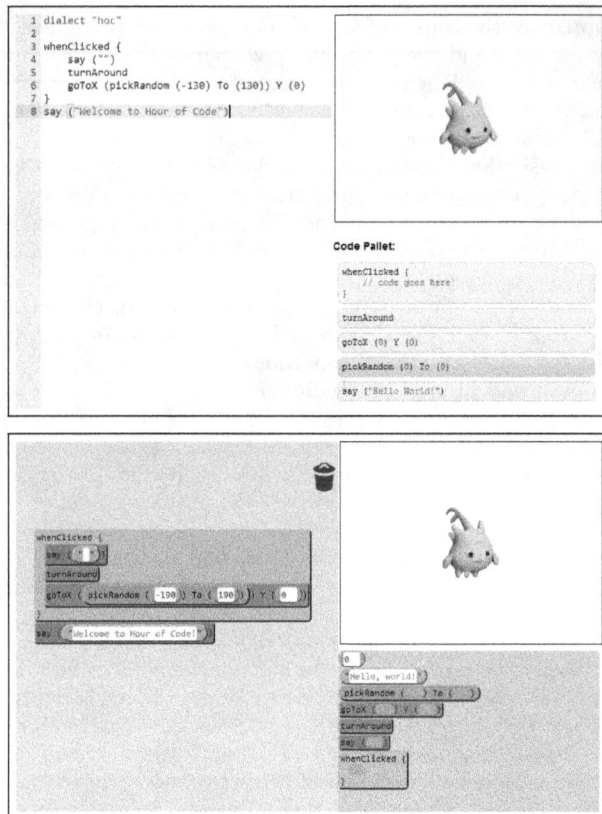

Figure 2: A comparison of the textual (top) and block (bottom) interfaces. The coding interface for both consists of a work area (left), an output canvas where the game can be played (top-right) and a palette of usable blocks or code (bottom-right).

differences between the classrooms, which are explained in Section 5. The Block group participated in the study in the late morning, while the Text group held an unrelated lesson on security, with no content that addressed programming. The text group participated in the study approximately 3 hours later, in the early afternoon. The students in both groups had participated in previous SPARCS sessions that semester, but none had participated in previous years.

In each classroom, the first author led the study. Before starting, the students were directed to complete a brief pre-survey (covered in Section 4.1). The programming exercise was then explained to the students. The students were allowed to go through the exercise at their own pace. If they had questions, the students were allowed to ask for help from the student volunteers, and the volunteers made a note of the type and duration of assistance offered. After finishing the exercise, the students were allowed to continue to work on their game. After 45 minutes, the students were directed to take a post-survey (covered in Section 4.1). The programming environment was instrumented to log most student interactions, such as button presses, block drags and compilations. Snapshots of each student's code were saved at regular intervals and each time it was run.

Occasional technical issues did occur in both groups. One student in each group had severe technical issues, and these students were excluded from analysis (and are not reflected

94

Efficacy: Please say how confident you are that you can do each of the following tasks. I can:
  Use a computer to solve a problem
  Write a computer program
  Create something interesting using a computer
  Explain how a computer works
Choices: Strongly Disagree, Somewhat Disagree, Neutral, Somewhat Agree, Strongly Agree

Interest: Please say how likely you think you are to do each of the following in the future:
  Take a programming or Computer Science class
  Create a computer program, app or game for fun
  Learn more about programming on your own
Choices: Very Unlikely, Somewhat Unlikely, Undecided, Somewhat Likely, Very Likely

Table 1: Efficacy and Interest survey questions.

```
var x := 7
x := x + 2
print(x)
```

```
var y := 8
if (y > 4) then {
  y := y - 5
}
print(y)
```

```
var z:= 0
forever {
  if (z < 5) then {
    print z
  }
  z := z + 1
}
```

Figure 3: Students were asked to determine the output of these programs in the pre- and post-surveys.

Type (Group)	Pre	Post	Change
Efficacy (B)	3.51 (0.90)	3.88 (0.73)	0.250 (0.50)
Efficacy (T)	3.59 (0.70)	3.75 (0.93)	0.167 (0.57)
Interest (B)	4.24 (0.70)	4.26 (0.53)	0.128 (0.42)
Interest (T)	3.76 (0.71)	3.93 (0.81)	-0.037 (0.42)
Knowledge (B)	1.53 (0.94)	1.30 (0.95)	0.100 (0.99)
Knowledge (T)	1.14 (0.86)	1.13 (0.99)	0.125 (0.64)

Table 2: Results (and standard deviations) from the pre- and post-survey. Efficacy and Interest scales were from 1-5. Knowledge scores range from 0-3. The Post and Change columns are computed only for the students who took the post-survey. B and T indicate Block and Text groups.

in the counts above). Further, one student in the Text group had a parent present (this is not typical), who offered significant help, and this student's data was also excluded from analysis. Some students in the Block group arrived late, and the group was given more time to compensate; however, only the first 45 minutes of any given student's work is analyzed (not including time spent taking the pre-survey).

4. RESULTS

4.1 Survey Results

One set of survey questions was presented to students in both the pre- and post-survey. This was done to account for initial differences in attitudes towards computing between the two groups. This set of questions consisted of three sections. The first section assessed students' self-efficacy with regards to computing, and the second assessed students interest in computing in the future. These sections consisted of 3-4 Likert items, which are presented in Table 1. The last section consisted of three knowledge-based questions, in which students were asked to evaluate the output of a code routine. The code was presented as blocks or text to match the interface the student was using. The code used in these questions is presented in Figure 3. The questions were identical in the pre- and post-surveys, except that the Knowledge questions had numeric values changed on the post-survey. We calculated averages from the Likert questions to produce a numeric value for each student (1-5) for Efficacy and Interest questions in both the pre- and post-survey. We also calculated the number of correct answers in the Knowledge section (0-3) for both surveys. A summary of the results is presented in Table 2.

Since SPARCS is a voluntary program, we could not force students to take the surveys. In order to start the activity, the students did have to complete the pre-survey, but despite strong encouragement, some chose not to complete part or all of the post-survey. In the Block group, 15 of 17 students completed part or all of the post-survey, and in the Text group, 9 of 14 students did so. Students who failed to complete the post-survey were excluded from our analysis of survey results but were included in log data analysis.

A second set of questions was asked of both groups only in the post-survey. These questions assessed the user's experi-

ence when performing the activity, and asked them to rate their difficulty performing certain tasks within the activity. Both groups of questions received very similar ratings across conditions. The results of the difficulty questions can be seen in Figure 4. Finally, demographic data was collected, along with questions about the students' access to technology.

4.2 Logged Interactions

Each time the student performed an action within the environment, it was timestamped and logged to a database. Some actions were specific to one interface, such as drag and drop actions. Other actions, such as advancing to the next section of the tutorial, were used in both interfaces. From these logs, the time spent on each section of the tutorial was calculated for each student. Students were able to skip ahead and revisit sections, so the time spent on a given section may be divided among multiple visits. Idle time, defined as going more than 60 seconds without modifying code, was also calculated for each student. Though students were strongly encouraged to use all available time, some students also chose to end the activity early. The duration each student spent in the activity was also calculated.

The students' programs were also saved to the database after each edit. An ideal finished program (not from the collected data) is shown in Figure 5. Programs were analyzed for goal completion, as explained in Section 5.2.

5. ANALYSIS

We compared pre-survey and demographic data from both conditions to determine if there were significant differences between groups. In this analysis we did include students who did not finish the post-survey. We investigated results from each of the questions presented in Table 1, and the data did not appear normally distributed; therefore, a

95

Difficulty Ratings by Condition and Type

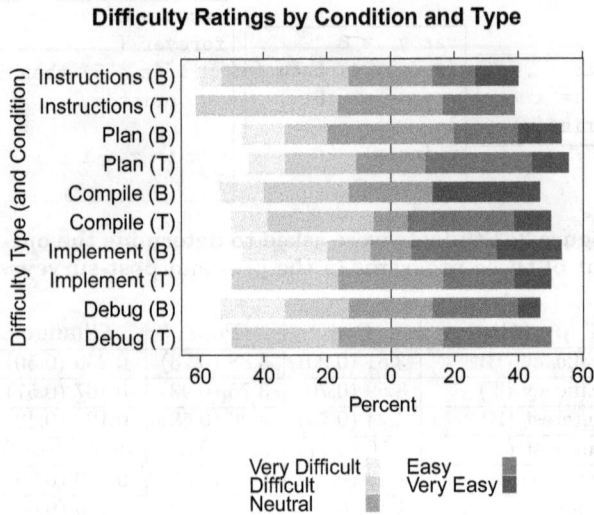

Figure 4: The distribution of difficulty ratings given by students in each condition. The questions, in order, asked users to rate their difficulty understanding instructions, deciding what to do, getting the program to run (compile), implementing a solution and figuring out what went wrong (debugging).

```
1  dialect "hoc"
2                          Goals:  1 2 3 4 5 6 7 8 9
                           Colors:
   var delay := 2
   var score := 0
   var maxScore := 0
   whenClicked {
       say ""
       delay := delay - 0.1
       score := score + 10
       if (maxScore < score) then {
           maxScore := score
           clear
       }
       forever {
           goToX( pickRandom (-190) To (190) )
               Y ( pickRandom (-130) To (130) )
           turnAround
           if (score > 0) then {
               score := score - 1
           }
           wait (delay)
       }
   }
24
25 goToX (-190) Y (130)
   say ("Welcome to the hour of code")
   penDown
```

Figure 5: The target finished program. Colors indicate the goals to which each line of code corresponds.

Mann-Whitney U Test was performed[2] to determine if one group had significantly higher average ratings on any of the three questions. The Block group did have a significantly higher Interest rating ($W = 163$, $p = 0.040$). No other differences between the groups were significant.

Demographic information included questions about access to computers, frequency of computer use and past computing experiences. These questions had similar results between groups, and no differences were significant. Lastly, both groups received an almost identical amount of volunteer assistance during the experiment. Since there were few differences between the two groups, we determined that they could be compared directly, but the difference in Interest ratings should be noted. We performed three primary analyses, covered in the following sections.

5.1 Survey Analysis

The survey questions shown in Figure 1 were repeated in both the pre- and post-survey. We first wanted to determine if the activity had an effect on participants' answers to these questions. Only the Efficacy scale shows a meaningful improvement. The data did not appear normally distributed, so we performed a Wilcoxon Signed-Rank Test and found the improvement to be significant ($V = 102$, $p < 0.040$, Cohen's $d = 0.289$). Note that this effect is present when considering both conditions together, but not strong enough to be significant in either condition alone. The effect is more pronounced in the Block group, and we compared the improvements of both groups using a Mann-Whitney U Test, but the difference was not significant ($W = 62$, $p = 0.412$).

We investigated the Efficacy Likert items individually to determine which contributed to the improvement. We tested each item using a Wlxocon Signed-Rank Test and used the

---

[2] All statistical analysis was performed using the R statistical software package.

Benjamini-Hochberg procedure [4] to control the False Discovery Rate (FDR) at 0.05. The items which showed a significant improvement were Item 2, "I can write a computer program" ($V = 16.5$, $p = 0.006$), and Item 4, "I can explain how a computer works" ($V = 4.5$, $p = 0.005$). Surprisingly Item 3, "I can create something interesting using a computer," showed a significant decline ($V = 24.5$, $p = 0.035$). This may be in part the result of very high pre-suvey ratings. The distributions of each question can be seen in Figure 6.

The remaining questions were only present in the post-survey, as they were about the completed activity. This included questions about the user's experience using the interface, and their difficulty completing the activity. Responses appeared to have similar distributions in both conditions, and Mann-Whitney U Tests confirmed that there were no significant differences between conditions.

These analyses suggest that the activity did have some positive impact on students' self-efficacy regarding computing, though for such a short activity it is not surprising that no other effects were observed. Still, the results offer little evidence to support a claim that the interface affected students' attitudes towards computing. Most surprising is that it seems to have had no impact on students' perceived difficulty, despite pronounced differences in student behaviors in the system, as explored in the following sections.

5.2 Time Analysis

As discussed in Section 4.2, the time each student spent on the activity was calculated, including how much of that time was spent active or idle. Results are shown in Table 3. While the interface did not appear to affect the duration

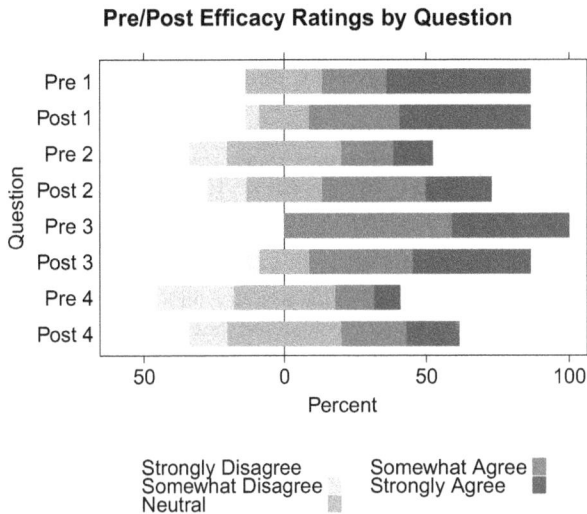

Figure 6: The distribution of ratings given by students in the pre- and post-survey for each Efficacy item (see Figure 1 for the items' text).

Value	Block	Text	p	d
Total	2273.9 (596.4)	2208.0 (427.1)	0.851	–
Idle	407.2 (238.9)	793.5 (368.3)	0.002	1.27
Active	1866.8 (617.4)	1414.5 (463.1)	0.014	0.82

Table 3: Average total, idle and active time in seconds for both groups (with standard deviations). The differences in idle and active time are significant, and Cohen's d is given.

spent on the activity, it did have a significant effect on both idle and active time.

5.3 Completion Analysis

Each section of the activity had a goal, stated in the instructions, which could be uniquely accomplished with the blocks and concepts introduced in that section. Snapshots of each participant's program were analyzed to determine if and when each of the sections' goals were met. Goal specifications were designed to be independent of the rest of the program; thus, a student could accomplish a section's goals even after skipping previous sections of the activity, which did occur. Since programs with syntax errors are inherently ambiguous and could not be tested by students, only compilable snapshots of programs were analyzed. While we believe this requirement to be reasonable, it likely had a disproportionate effect on textual programs. The analysis was automated, but we checked it for correctness manually on 1/8 of the students. While at least one student completed each goal, no students completed the 8th or 9th goal within the first 45 minutes analyzed here.

Figure 7 shows the percentage of students who completed each goal, as well as the percentage who viewed that goal for at least 10 seconds. The Block group outperformed the Text group in all respects by these measures. Of particular interest is Goal 4, which introduced loops. A nearly equivalent percent of participants from both groups viewed the problem, but many more from the Block group completed the

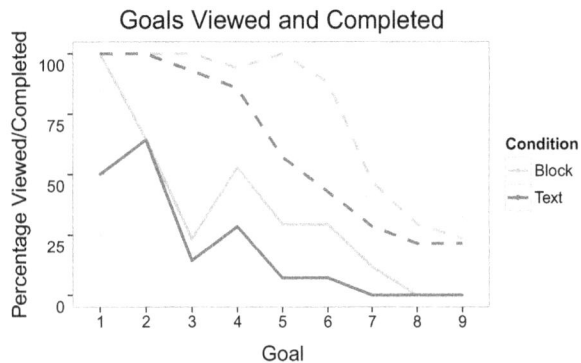

Figure 7: For each condition, the solid line shows the percentage of students who completed each goal. The dashed line shows the percentage of students who viewed each goal for at least 10 seconds.

goal to specification. Goal 5 then shows a marked dropoff in viewers for the Text group, but an increase for the Block group. This implies a logical relationship between the completion of a goal and viewing the next goal.

Figure 8 shows the average total time that had passed before students completed each goal. Each bar only includes the students who completed the given goal. On sections where at least 25% of students in both conditions completed the goal, a Mann-Whitney U Test was performed (data did not appear normally distributed) to determine if the difference in completion time was significant, with the FDR controlled at 0.05. For each of these goals it was significant: Goals 1 ($W = 13, p < 0.001$), 2 ($W = 21.5, p = 0.018$) and 4 ($W = 4, p = 0.017$). This seems sufficient evidence to assert that the interface significantly increased the rate at which students completed programming goals.

Pearson correlations were calculated between the number of goals completed and a variety of the survey questions, including pre- and post-survey Efficacy, Interest and Knowledge scores, and reported difficulty, and none appeared meaningful, or had a magnitude greater than 0.35.

6. DISCUSSION

We now revisit our original research questions. Compared with the textual interface, how did the block interface:

RQ1 *Affect students' attitudes towards computing?* This question was addressed primarily by the Efficacy and Interest questions in the pre- and post-surveys. While we did observe significantly improved responses to the Efficacy questions as a whole after the activity, two items primarily accounted for this shift. The most relevant item, "I can write a computer program," was one of these. It is unclear why one item, "I can create something interesting using a computer," showed a decline. It may be a reflection of the students' opinion of the programming activity, more than their self-efficacy with regards to computing. Regardless, there was no significant difference in improvement on these questions between conditions. It is quite possible that the effect was simply too small to be observed in the relatively small sample size of this study. It is also possible that a longer activity would have produced more pronounced changes, and these would have been more dependent on the programming in-

Average Time of Completion Per Goal

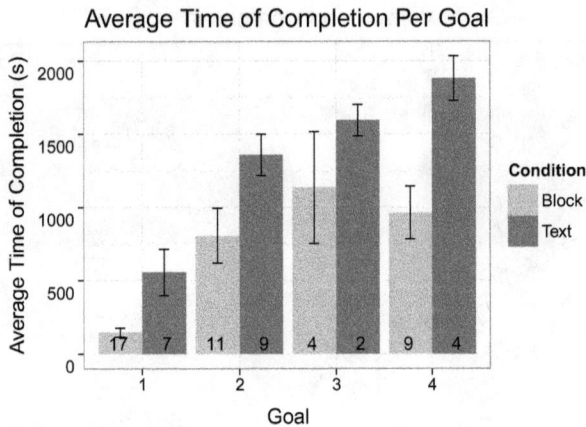

Figure 8: The average total time spent in the activity before completing each goal, with bars indicating standard error. The numbers at the bottom of each bar indicate the number of students who completed the goal. Values are not strictly increasing, in part because goals could be completed out of order. Goals 5-9 are not shown, as at most 1 student from the Text group completed them.

terface. Interpretation is further complicated by the higher pre-survey Interest ratings in the Block group. While we certainly cannot argue against the possibility that the interface has an impact on user attitudes towards computing, we can offer no evidence to support it.

RQ2 *Affect students' perceived difficulty of programming?* There is no survey evidence to support the claim that the Block group experienced less difficulty than the Text group, either in general or on specific aspects of programming. This matches similar findings in previous work [21]. Interestingly, there was little correlation between perceived difficulty and goal completion. One possible explanation for both of these observations is that the free-form nature of the exercise allowed students to progress until they hit an aspect of the activity that was challenging, and that is where they spent the majority of their time. Even if the block interface helped students overcome confusion about the language's syntax, perhaps they simply moved on to other, equally challenging, aspects of programming. In this case, one might still expect students to emphasize the difficulty of different aspects of programming, depending on their interface, and this was not observed. This may be due to novices' inability to distinguish sources of difficulty in programming.

RQ3 *Affect students' performance on a programming activity?* Whether measured by self-pacing, completion, efficiency or time on task, the Block group did demonstrate increased performance. Not all of these observations are easily quantified or statistically tested, but in combination they seem to conclusively show that the block interface did improve performance.

6.1 Limitations

It is worth stating that none of the findings in this paper should be casually generalized to other contexts. The findings with regard to RQ3 are likely the most robust, but some limitations should be considered.

Tiled Grace lacks some of the common features of other block-based languages, such as "jigsaw" pieces that only snap into legal locations. Conversely, while Grace was designed to teach CS, it might be considered more complex syntactically than other textual languages, due to its use of meaningful whitespace and method names which are split between arguments (e.g. `goToX( 10 )Y( 20 )`). However, these differences are likely no more extreme than those between most programming languages.

The activity studied here was adapted from one designed for a BBPE. It is possible this activity unfairly emphasizes aspects of programming which are advantageous for BBPEs. For instance, the first section of the activity used event handling, which was syntactically trivial in Tiled Grace, but involved nesting one command inside of another, which is much more complex in textual Grace. This is evidenced by the lack of completion of Goal 1 by the Text group, as shown in Figure 7. Even if the activity highlighted advantages in block interfaces, this means that such advantages do exist, which is still a meaningful finding.

The lack of responses to the post-survey make it difficult to draw strong conclusions from it. It is also likely that some students did not take the surveys seriously, but this is difficult to verify. Further, the survey questions, while typical of validated instruments, were not themselves validated. They were also kept short to avoid survey fatigue. This may explain why we observed contradictory responses to the Efficacy Likert items and why the surveys do not seem to reflect the differences observed in the log data.

Finally, it should be noted that the Text group was a full grade higher than the Block group. While this makes the success of the Block group more notable, it may have impacted the study in unforeseen ways. The Block group also had significantly higher Interest ratings in the pre-survey.

6.2 Future Work

Inconclusive results from the survey questions indicate the need for further study of the effect of a block interface on students' perceptions of programming, specifically with improved survey design and larger samples. The discrepancy between students' performance on the activity and their perceived difficulty with the activity merits further investigation, as well.

Though this study does support the claim that block interfaces improve programming performance in novices, it would be useful to investigate whether this remains true for first or second year programmers. Further, while this study does show that block interfaces reduce idle time and increase goal completion, it does not suggest a mechanism for these changes. While some answers may seem intuitive, an investigation of *how* block interfaces reduce idle time, or facilitate goal completion would be fruitful, as a better understanding of the underlying causal relationships could lead to the creation of better BBPEs in the future.

7. CONCLUSION

This study supports the claim that block programming interfaces can significantly improve novice performance on some programming activities, specifically through increased time on task and quicker, more frequent achievement of programming goals. The study suggests that the block interface is an important component of BBPEs, which is worthy of future study and development.

8. REFERENCES

[1] Google Blockly. A Visual Programming Editor. http://code.google.com/p/blockly/.

[2] LEGO Mindstorms. http://mindstorms.lego.com.

[3] A. Begel. LogoBlocks: A graphical programming language for interacting with the world. *Electrical Engineering and Computer Science Department, MIT, Boston, MA*, 1996.

[4] Y. Benjamini and Y. Hochberg. Controlling the false discovery rate: a practical and powerful approach to multiple testing. *Journal of the Royal Statistical Society. Series B (Methodological)*, pages 289–300, 1995.

[5] T. Booth and S. Stumpf. End-user experiences of visual and textual programming environments for Arduino. *End-User Development*, pages 25–39, 2013.

[6] V. Cateté, K. Wassell, and T. Barnes. Use and development of entertainment technologies in after school STEM program. In *Proceedings of the 45th ACM technical symposium on Computer science education*, pages 163–168, 2014.

[7] D. C. Cliburn. Experiences with the LEGO Mindstorms throughout the Undergraduate Computer Science Curriculum. In *Frontiers in Education Conference, 36th Annual*, pages 1–6, 2006.

[8] S. Cooper, W. Dann, and R. Pausch. Teaching objects-first in introductory computer science. *ACM SIGCSE Bulletin*, 2003.

[9] W. Dann, D. Cosgrove, and D. Slater. Mediated transfer: Alice 3 to java. In *Proceedings of the 43rd ACM technical symposium on Computer Science Education*, pages 141–146, 2012.

[10] D. Garcia, B. Harvey, L. Segars, and C. How. AP CS Principles Pilot at University of California, Berkeley. *ACM Inroads*, 3(2), 2012.

[11] T. Green and M. Petre. When visual programs are harder to read than textual programs. In *Tasks and Organisation, Proceedings of ECCE-6 (6th European Conference on Cognitive Ergonomics)*, 1992.

[12] T. Green and M. Petre. Usability analysis of visual programming environments: a 'cognitive dimensions' framework. *Journal of Visual Languages & Computing*, 1996.

[13] M. Guzdial. Programming environments for novices. In S. Fincher and M. Petre, editors, *Computer Science Education Research*, pages 127–154. Taylor & Francis, 2004.

[14] B. Harvey. The Beauty and Joy of Computing: Computer Science for Everyone. In *Proceedings of Constructionism*, pages 33–39, 2012.

[15] B. Harvey and J. Mönig. Bringing "No Ceiling" to Scratch: Can One Language Serve Kids and Computer Scientists? In *Proceedings of Constructionism*, pages 1–10, 2010.

[16] M. Homer and J. Noble. Combining Tiled and Textual Views of Code. In *Proceedings of 2nd IEEE Working Conference on Software Visualization*, 2014.

[17] T. Jenkins. On the difficulty of learning to program. In *Proceedings of the 3rd Annual Conference of the LTSN Centre for Information and Computer Sciences*, 2002.

[18] C. Kelleher and R. Pausch. Lowering the Barriers to Programming: A Taxonomy of Programming Environments and Languages for Novice Programmers. *ACM Computing Surveys*, 37(2):83–137, June 2005.

[19] C. Kelleher, R. Pausch, and S. Kiesler. Storytelling alice motivates middle school girls to learn computer programming. *Proceedings of the SIGCHI conference on Human Computer Interaction*, 2007.

[20] M. Kölling. Greenfoot - A Highly Graphical IDE for Learning Object-Oriented Programming. *Journal of Computer Science*, 13:60558, 2008.

[21] C. Lewis. How programming environment shapes perception, learning and goals: logo vs. scratch. In *Proceedings of the 41st ACM technical symposium on Computer science education*, pages 346–350, 2010.

[22] J. Maloney, K. Peppler, Y. Kafai, M. Resnick, and N. Rusk. Programming by choice: urban youth learning programming with scratch. *ACM SIGCSE Bulletin*, 40(1):367–371, 2008.

[23] F. McKay and M. Kölling. Predictive modelling for HCI problems in novice program editors. In *Proceedings of the 27th International BCS Human Computer Interaction Conference.*, pages 35–41, 2013.

[24] O. Meerbaum-Salant, M. Armoni, and M. Ben-Ari. Learning computer science concepts with scratch. In *International Computing Education Research Conference 2010 (ICER '10)*, pages 69–76, 2010.

[25] R. Morelli, T. de Lanerolle, and P. Lake. Can android app inventor bring computational thinking to k-12. In *ACM technical symposium on Computer science education (SIGCSE'11)*, 2011.

[26] B. Moskal, D. Lurie, and S. Cooper. Evaluating the effectiveness of a new instructional approach. *ACM SIGCSE Bulletin*, 36(1):75–79, 2004.

[27] S. Papert. *Logo Philosophy and Implementation*. Logo Computer Systems Inc., 1999.

[28] S. Pokress and J. Veiga. MIT App Inventor: Enabling personal mobile computing. In *Workshop on Programming for Mobile and Touch*, 2013.

[29] M. Resnick, J. Maloney, H. Andrés, N. Rusk, E. Eastmond, K. Brennan, A. Millner, E. Rosenbaum, J. Silver, B. Silverman, and Y. Kafai. Scratch: programming for all. *Communications of the ACM*, 52(11):60–67, 2009.

[30] I. Utting, S. Cooper, and M. Kölling. Alice, Greenfoot, and Scratch–a discussion. *ACM Transactions on Computing Education (TOCE)*, 10(4), 2010.

[31] A. Wagner, J. Gray, J. Corley, and D. Wolber. Using app inventor in a K-12 summer camp. In *Proceeding of the 44th ACM technical symposium on Computer science education*, 2013.

[32] K. Whitley. Visual programming languages and the empirical evidence for and against. *Journal of Visual Languages & Computing*, 8(1), 1997.

Using Commutative Assessments to Compare Conceptual Understanding in Blocks-based and Text-based Programs

David Weintrop
Northwestern University
2120 Campus Drive, Suite 332
Evanston, Illinois 60628
dweintrop@u.northwestern.edu

Uri Wilensky
Northwestern University
2120 Campus Drive, Suite 337
Evanston, Illinois 60628
uri@northwestern.edu

ABSTRACT

Blocks-based programming environments are becoming increasingly common in introductory programming courses, but to date, little comparative work has been done to understand if and how this approach affects students' emerging understanding of fundamental programming concepts. In an effort to understand how tools like Scratch and Blockly differ from more conventional text-based introductory programming languages with respect to conceptual understanding, we developed a set of "commutative" assessments. Each multiple-choice question on the assessment includes a short program that can be displayed in either a blocks-based or text-based form. The set of potential answers for each question includes the correct answer along with choices informed by prior research on novice programming misconceptions. In this paper we introduce the Commutative Assessment, discuss the theoretical and practical motivations for the assessment, and present findings from a study that used the assessment. The study had 90 high school students take the assessment at three points over the course of the first ten weeks of an introduction to programming course, alternating the modality (blocks vs. text) for each question over the course of the three administrations of the assessment. Our analysis reveals differences on performance between blocks-based and text-based questions as well as differences in the frequency of misconceptions based on the modality. Future work, potential implications, and limitations of these findings are also discussed.

Categories and Subject Descriptors

D.1.7 [Visual Programming]. K.3.2 [Computer and Information Science Education]:Computer science education.

General Terms

Measurement, Design, Human Factors, Languages

Keywords

Introductory Programming Environments; High School Computer Science Education; Blocks-based Programming; Assessment

1. INTRODUCTION

A long-standing question faced by computer science educators is what language to use to introduce learners to programming. Ask this question to a room of ten teachers and you are likely to hear more than ten languages mentioned, many of which will carry qualifiers describing under what conditions a given language is the best choice. These so called 'language wars' have been raging for as long as computer science has been taught, with little in the way of consensus emerging and with potentially detrimental effects [58]. Much work has been done attempting to empirically answer the question of which text-based language is best for novices, or at least identify features that make a language more or less accessible to beginners. While there is much to show for this effort, an alternative to conventional text-based languages is emerging in novice programming classrooms that brings a new dimension to introductory tools. Graphical blocks-based programming tools like Scratch [49], Blockly [23], and Alice [13] are becoming commonplace in introductory programming contexts, with a growing number of new curricula utilizing blocks-based programming tools in their materials, including the CS Principles project, the Exploring Computer Science program, and the materials being developed by code.org. The introduction of blocks-based programming environments changes the landscape of introductory tools, replacing questions of syntactic features of textual languages with the larger question of if text-based programming altogether is the best way to introduce novices to programming. Despite the increasing use of blocks-based tools in formal computer science learning contexts, relatively little work has investigated the cognitive affordances and drawbacks to the use of the graphical, blocks-based modality in classrooms. Similarly, few side-by-side studies have compared blocks-based and text-based tools directly (a notable exception being [32]). In their review of assessments of introductory programming, Gross and Powers [26] found that "one of the least studied questions are those that focus on how the environments impact a student's learning process and understanding from a formative perspective." In this paper, we set out to begin the process of filling in these gaps in the literature, specifically, we seek to answer the following two research questions:

1. How can we comparatively assess student understanding in blocks-based and text-based programming environments?

2. Does modality (blocks-based versus text-based) affect novice programmers' understanding of basic programming concepts? And if so, how does it differ by concept?

To answer to the first question, we created the Commutative Assessment, a novel programming assessment designed to measure students' understanding of programming concepts in both blocks-based and text-based modalities. Each question on the assessment requires the learner to read a short program (usually 4 or 5 lines) then answer a question about the outcome of the script. The key feature of the assessment is that every question can be asked with either a blocks-based or text-based program. In pursuit of our second question, the assessments were given three times over the course of a ten-week study in three introductory high

ICER '15, August 9-13, 2015, Omaha, NE, USA.
Copyright is held by the owner/author(s). Publication rights licensed to ACM.
ACM 978-1-4503-3630-7/15/08...$15.00.
DOI: http://dx.doi.org/10.1145/2787622.2787721

school programming courses. By administering the assessment at three points, students answered each question in both modalities. In this paper, we present the Commutative Assessment and share findings from its use as part of a larger study on the relationship between modality and student understanding.

2. Previous Research

2.1 Representations and Learning

"The tools we use have a profound (and devious!) influence on our thinking habits, and, therefore, on our thinking abilities." [16]

As stated by the Turing Award winning computer scientist Edsger Dijkstra in the quote above, the tools we use, in this case the programming languages and development environments, have a profound, and often unforeseen, impact on how and what we think. diSessa [17] calls this material intelligence, arguing for close ties between the internal cognitive process and the external representations that support them: "we don't always have ideas and then express them in the medium. We have ideas *with* the medium" [17 emphasis in the original]. He continues: "thinking in the presence of a medium that is manipulated to support your thought is simply different from unsupported thinking" [17]. The recognition that mental activity is mediated by tools and signs is one of the major contributions of the work of Vygotsky [65, 66] who argued that it is the external world that shapes internal cognitive functioning [72]. This perspective, coupled with Piaget's constructivist learning theory, which contributes an interactionist perspective to learning that foregrounds the mutual dynamic of tools and thought [46], informs why it is so crucial to understand the relationship between the growing family of graphical programming representations and the understandings and practices they promote.

The role of representations in cognition has been studied across a variety of representational systems and their influence on various cognitive tasks. One large body of work that has emerged from studying this question is identifying the relationship between language, literacy and thought [33, 41, 66, 73], but as we are primarily concerned with the use of symbolic formalisms, we focus our review on scholarship looking at the role of arithmetic representation in supporting thought. The recognition that a learner's own knowledge and experience influences the representations used and how it is understood and evaluated has been a recurring idea within the Learning Sciences [18, 31, 39, 52, 69]. For example, focusing on concepts from physics and investigating the use of conventional algebraic notation as compared to programmatic representations, Sherin [51] found that differing representational forms had different affordances with respect to students learning physics concepts and, as result, affected their conceptualization of the concepts learned. "Algebra physics trains students to seek out equilibria in the world. Programming encourages students to look for time-varying phenomena, and supports certain types of causal explanations, as well as the segmenting of the world into processes" [51]. Similar investigations have been done between programming languages. For example, Gilmore and Green [25] compared declarative and procedural notations and found that each notation afforded different types of reasoning. The procedural notation was superior for answering sequential questions while the declarative notation was better for answering circumstantial questions. This lead them to conclude that "the structure of a notation affects the ease with which information can be extracted both from the printed page and from recall" [25].

Wilensky and Papert [74] use the term structuration to describe this relationship between the representational infrastructure used within a knowledge domain and the knowledge and understanding that the infrastructure enables and promotes. While often thought of as static, the structurations that underpin a discipline can change as new technologies and ideas emerge. Wilensky and Papert document a number of restructurations - shifts in representational infrastructure - including the move from Roman numerals to Hindu-Arabic numerals [61], the use of the Logo programming language to serve as a representational system to explore geometry [1], and the use of agent-based modeling to representation various biological, physical, and social systems [8, 50, 67, 75]. These shifts, and the new possibilities they enable, highlight the importance of studying representational systems, as restructurations can profoundly change the expressiveness, learnability, and communicability of ideas within a domain. While we are not claiming that the introduction of blocks-based tools constitutes a restructuration of programming knowledge, the recognition of the influence of representational infrastructure motivates this work and frames our larger program of research.

2.2 Programming Languages for Learners

Early on it was recognized that the design of a programming language itself can support or hinder students in their quest to master programming, which resulted in early efforts to develop more accessible programming languages [36]. Lead by Logo [22], which was explicitly designed with mathematics learning in mind, a number of languages emerged with the goal of serving as an introduction to the field of computer science. An early, influential language designed for novices was BASIC, whose acronym stands for Beginner's All-purpose Symbolic Instruction Code. BASIC included a relatively small instruction set, removed all unnecessary syntax, and was designed to support short turn around times between composition and execution of programs, which collectively made it more accessible to novices.

As the field of computer science education matured, new languages and strategies emerged that were designed to serve as introductory tools and prepare learners for more powerful, fully featured languages. Languages such as Blue [30] and JJ [37] simplified syntax and provided tools to allow learners to focus on programming fundamentals before progressing to professional languages. Mini-languages, which are small languages designed to support the first steps in learning to program, are another approach for introductory languages [11]. These languages often center around specific activities and provided only the commands necessary to accomplish the immediate task, such as Karel the Robot, which has learners write short programs to control an on-screen robot [44]. Mini-languages are not intended for general purpose programming, they instead tailor the language around specific tasks, narrowing the gap between the objective and the representations in which intentions are encoded [15].

A final strategy that speaks directly to the work we are pursing here is the creation of languages that try and address the documented issues that novices have with the syntax of programming languages. Research has found language syntax, the seemingly esoteric punctuation and formatting rules that must be followed when composing programs, can a serious barrier for novice programmers [14, 59]. Through a serious of controlled experiments that had novices use one of a variety of languages that demonstrated various syntactic features, Stefik and Siebert [59] found that characteristics of syntax directly influence a language's learnability. One solution to the problem of syntax is the creation of visual programming tools that visually represent syntactic information of commands, making it easier to compose programs without encountering syntax errors.

2.3 Blocks-based Programming

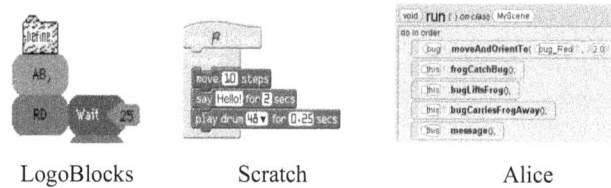

| LogoBlocks | Scratch | Alice |

Figure 1. Three examples of blocks-based programming tools.

The blocks-based approach of visual programming (Figure 1), while not a recent innovation, has become widespread in recent years with the emergence of a new generation of tools, lead by the popularity of Scratch [49], Alice [13]Snap! [28], and Blockly [23]. These programming tools are a subset of the larger group of editors called *structured editors* [19] that make the atomic unit of composition a node in the abstract syntax tree (AST) of the program, as opposed to a smaller element (i.e. a character) or a larger element (like a fully formed functional unit). In making these AST elements the building blocks, then providing constraints to ensure nodes can only be added to the program's AST in valid ways, the environment can prevent syntax errors. Blocks-based programming environments leverage a programming-primitive-as-puzzle-piece metaphor that provides visual cues to the user about how and where commands can be used as their means of constraining program composition. Programming in these environments takes the form of dragging blocks into a composition area and snapping them together to form scripts. If two blocks cannot be joined to form a valid syntactic statement, the environment prevents them from snapping together, thus helping to alleviate difficulties with syntax while retaining the practice of assembling programs instruction-by-instruction. This feature is especially relevant to the proposed study, as graphical programming proponents argue that visual depiction of syntax information is a key feature that contributes to its appropriateness for novice programmers [49]. However, other researchers are finding this approach does not solve the syntax problem, but merely delays it [43, 48]. Along with using block shape to denote usage, there are other visual cues to help novices, including color coding blocks by conceptual use, and nesting blocks to denote scope. Blocks-based programming has been found to be perceived as easier by learners, with a number of these visual features cited for its relative ease-of-use [70].

Early version of this interlocking approach include LogoBlocks [6] and BridgeTalk [9], which helped formulate the programming approach which has since grown to be used in dozens of applications. Alice [13], an influential and widely used environment in introductory programming classes, uses a very similar interface and has been the focus of much scholarship evaluating the merits of the approach at the undergraduate level. In addition to being used in more conventional computer science contexts, a growing number of environments have adopted the blocks-based programming approach to lower the barrier to programing across a variety of domains including mobile app development with MIT App Inventor and Pocket Code [53], modeling and simulation tools like StarLogo TNG [7], DeltaTick [76], NetTango [40] and EvoBuild [67], creative and artistic tools like Turtle Art and PicoBlocks, commercial educational tools like

Tynker and Hopscotch, game-based learning environments like RoboBuilder [68] and CodeSpells [21], and the activities included in Code.org's Hour of Code, and Google's Made with Code.

2.4 Programming assessments

Across educational research broadly there is a recognized need for high quality and validated assessments, a position echoed in computer science education circles [62]. Towards this end, a number of assessments have been developed and validated with the goal of improving our ability to evaluate and measure student learning across a variety of languages, environments, and contexts [27]. Related work has sought to define the process one follows to develop quality computer science assessments, beginning with identifying the goals of the assessment and the material to cover, through validating, piloting, and refining the instrument [12]. Additionally, new techniques are being developed and applied to programming assessments to improve accuracy and build confidence in new assessments [60]. One notable example of a rigorous, validated assessment is the Foundational CS1 assessment (FCS1) [64], which is a language independent instrument designed to decouple concepts from the language used to represent them. This makes it possible to be used with learners regardless of the language used during instruction. This is in contrast to most validated programming assessments developed by testing boards, like the Advanced Placement (AP) CS exam and the A-level General Certificate of Education in Computing, both of which are currently designed for the Java language.

There are a growing number of projects working towards developing assessments for the blocks-based approach to programming that we are investigating herein. Much of this work looks to assess not programming specifically, but computational thinking more broadly [27]. For example, the Fairy assessment [71], designed for middle school aged learners, uses Alice and presents learners with partially completed, or buggy, programs that need to be fixed in order for in-world characters to accomplish a specific task. In taking this approach, the Fairy assessment evaluates both comprehension (learners understanding of what a written program does) as well as gives learners a chance to problem solve, design and implement algorithmic solutions to assessment tasks. This design addresses the critique that process is often lost in conventional assessments of programming knowledge [47]. Another innovative assessment approach to computational thinking comes out of the Scalable Game Design group that developed an automated way to measure the frequency of computational thinking patterns in student-authored programs as a way to assess learning [29].

2.5 Evaluating Blocks-based Programming

A small, but growing body of literature is investigating the learning that happens with blocks-based programming tools. To date, most of this work has focused on Scratch and Alice, as these two environments have the widest use in contemporary computer science education. While both Alice and Scratch have been used in formal education environments, it is important to keep in mind that the two projects initially had different goals and targeted different age groups. Scratch from its inception, was focused on younger learners and informal settings [49], while Alice was targeted at more conventional computer science learning contexts and, as such, has a been the focus of more initiatives to evaluate student learning of programming concepts [13].

Ben-Ari and colleagues have conducted a number of studies on the use of Scratch for teaching computer science in formal contexts [3, 4, 34, 35]. Meerbaum-Salant et al. [35] found that Scratch could successfully be used to introduce learners to central computer science concepts including variables, conditional and iterative logic, and concurrency. While students did perform well on the post-test evaluation in this project, a closer look at the programming practices learners developed while working in Scratch gave pause to the excitement around the results. The researchers found that students developed some undesirable programming habits, including a totally bottom-up programming approach, a tendency towards extremely fine-grained programming, and often unconventional, non-optimal usages of programming structures [34]. In a continuation of this study, the researchers concluded that students who learned Scratch in middle school more quickly grasped concepts in text-based languages when they reached high school (although they did not perform better on content assessments) [4]. Other work looking at comparing blocks-based to text-based programming using Scratch found that Scratch can be an effective way to introduce learners to programming concepts, although it is not universally more effective than comparable text languages [32]. There is also a growing body of work suggesting that the transition from blocks-based to text-based programming contexts is not as smooth as had once been assumed [24, 43, 48]. This suggests there are cognitive differences between these two programming modalities and is at the heart of the questions we pursuing here.

3. The Commutative Assessment

In pursuit of our first research question, we developed the Commutative Assessment as a way to evaluate if and how programming modality affects learnability. Each question on the assessment includes a short program for the student to read that can be expressed either in a blocks-based or text-based form. This means that no question relies on a construct unique to either modality, so for example, there are no questions that use blocks related to motion that students familiar with Scratch would recognize, as these instructions are not native to JavaScript. For each administration of the assessment, half of the questions are presented with blocks-based code and the other half use the text-based modality. The design of the Commutative Assessment makes it possible to group the responses along a number of dimensions that collectively yield insight into the relationship between modality and emerging understanding and provides data to support or refute claims about whether one modality is easier to interpret than another with respect to the various concepts.

To decide what concepts to include in our assessment, we primarily drew on two resources: the recently released 2013 CS Curriculum [2] and the work of Tew and Guzdial [63, 64]. In making the FCS1 assessment, Tew and Guzdial reviewed the contents of 12 introductory computer science textbooks along with other published curricula to establish a list of ten core CS1 concepts. Of this list, we chose to include five concepts in our assessment: fundamentals (variables, assignment, etc.), selection statements (conditional logic), definite loops (for loops), indefinite loops (while loops), and function/method parameters. Based on our review of the CS2013 Curriculum and what it emphasizes for introductory courses, we decided to add two additional content categories: program comprehension and algorithms (natural language descriptions of steps to be followed to solve a problem). As the algorithm questions do not include blocks-based or text-based programs, they are not discussed here.

The Commutative Assessment includes 28 questions, five each for conditional logic, loops, functions, and algorithms, and four

from the categories of variables and comprehension. While we would have liked to include a larger number of questions, we were constrained by the length of class and an awareness of testing fatigue effects from long assessments. All of the questions are multiple choice or true/false and, with the exception of the algorithm questions, take the form of a short piece of code that students are asked to interpret. The multiple choice answers were informed by misconceptions that have been identified in the literature (see appendix A of [56] for a summary of misconceptions). Figure 2 shows a sample variable question from the assessment. When taking the assessment, students see either the text version or the blocks version of the program.

```
var x = 10;
var y = x;          vs.
x = (x + 5);
```

What will be the value of x and y after this script is run?

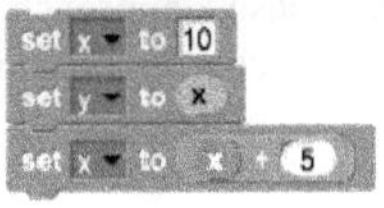

A) x is equal to 15 and y is equal to 15
B) x is equal to 5 and y is equal to 10
C) x is equal to 15 and y is equal to 10
D) x is equal to "x + 5" and y is equal to "x"
E) x is equal to 10, 15 and y is equal to 10

Figure 2. A question from the Commutative Assessment.

The set of available choices includes the correct answer as well as responses drawn from the literature on misconceptions around variable assignment. Option A would be chosen by a student that holds the misconception that when one variable is assigned to another, the two values are linked and that whatever happens to one, happens to the other [10]. If a student incorrectly thinks that a value gets passed from one variable to another (i.e. the variable does not retain its value if another variable is set to it), then the student would choose option B. Option D would be chosen by a student who thinks expressions do not get evaluated during assignment [5, 55]. Finally, option E would be chosen by students who think that variables "remember" prior values [10, 20]. We also choose to write out "is equal to" instead of using an equals sign to be explicit about the meaning of the choices. Throughout the assessment we tried to follow this approach as much as possible to shed light on potential misconceptions conveyed or supported by the different modalities.

It is important to note that while the goal of this assessment is to understand the effect of programming modality on learning, there are other factors complicating the issue, most notably, differences in the language itself. For example, in Figure 2, the syntax and keywords used in variable declaration and assignment are different between the two modalities, making the difference between the two forms of the question more than just a shift in modality. This is a constant challenge with this work as a feature of the blocks-based modality is the ability to support more conversational and readable commands [70]. We will return to this challenge through the paper.

4. Methods and Participants

The data presented in this paper are part of a larger study comparing blocks-based, text-based, and hybrid blocks/text programming environments at a selective enrollment public high school in a Midwestern city. We followed students in three sections of an elective introductory programming course for the first 10 weeks of the school year. Each class spent the first five weeks of the course working in a blocks-based programming environment. The students then transition to Java for the next five weeks of the study and then continued with Java for the remainder of the year. Two teachers participated in this study (one teacher taught two of the classes), both of whom had over five years of computer science teaching experience at the high school level.

The Commutative Assessment was administered online during class time at three points over the course of the 10-week study: at the outset, at the midpoint (end of week 5), and the conclusion of the study (end of week 10). Each time students took the assessment, they were asked the same set of 28 questions but the order and the modality (blocks vs. text) changed between administrations. The questions on the second content assessment used the opposite modality from the first assessment, so after taking the content assessment twice, all students had seen every question in both modalities. For the third assessment, two version of the assessment were created that asked question in the same order, but varied modality. Students were then randomly given one of the two versions of the third assessment.

For the first five weeks of the course, each class used a slightly different programming environment based on Snap! [15]. Snap! is a blocks-based programming tool that is very similar to Scratch, but adds a few features (notably Snap! has first-class functions), and is implemented in JavaScript. The first class used a version of Snap! that gave students the ability to right-click on any block or script to see a JavaScript implementation of the program (Figure 3). In this tool, students were able to read, but not edit or write, text-based versions of the programs they constructed with the blocks. The second class used a version of Snap! that allowed students to read their programs in text and added the ability to define the behavior of new custom blocks in JavaScript. This served as a hybrid blocks/text read/write environment, as students could both read a text-based version of their own blocks, as well as write the behaviors of new blocks in JavaScript. The final class served as a control and used an unmodified version of Snap! All three classes followed the same curriculum based on UC Berkeley's Beauty and Joy of Computing course, which covers all concepts included in the Commutative Assessment.

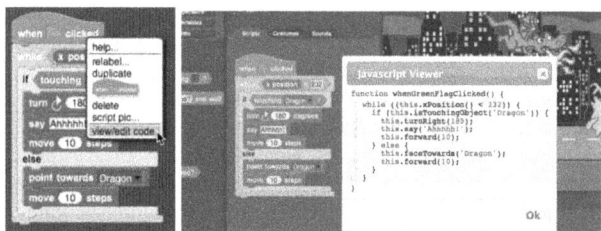

Figure 3. Side-by-side blocks and text in our version of Snap!

At the conclusion of the 5-week blocks-based introduction, the students transitioned to Java, following an objects-first curriculum. During the Java portion of the study, the topics covered in class included how to compile and run Java programs, simple data input and output, and the basics of defining and calling functions. While Java and JavaScript have syntactic differences, few of these differences were encountered by students during the five weeks of Java, the notable exception being the existence of variable types in Java as opposed to JavaScript's weak typing. This difference was discussed by the teachers and was not identified as problematic by students during the study.

The school we worked with was chosen as it has a large computer science department, offering three sections of their Programming I course. A total of 90 students across three sections of the course participated in the study, which included 67 male students and 23 female students. The students participating in the study were 43% Hispanic, 29% White, 10% Asian, 6% African American, and 10% Multi-racial - a breakdown comparable to the larger student body. The classes included one student in eighth grade, three high school freshman, 43 sophomores, 18 juniors, and 25 high school seniors. Two-thirds of the students in the study speak a language other than English in their homes.

5. Results

As our research questions focus on the relationship between modality and concept, the first step of our analysis was to come up with a score for each concept/modality pair for every participant in the study. This means for each student we had 10 unique scores, one for each concept/modality tuple (variable/text; variables/blocks; loops/text, loops/blocks, etc.), resulting in 180 data points for each concept (90 students * 2 modalities). These scores were calculated by averaging together the student's score for every question that fell into the tuple. Grouping this way helps us control for features of specific questions, and gives us a more accurate within-participant score for conceptual understanding by modality. These scores were then aggregated across the full set of participants to determine the relationship between concept and modality. We do not present a breakdown of responses by condition or time period. As this is our first analysis of data from the Commutative Assessment, we chose to focus on general outcomes, specifically looking for patterns and differences in student responses by concept/modality. Figure 4 shows the difference found for each concept.

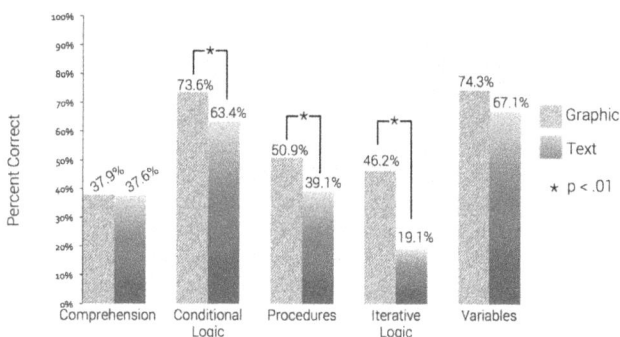

Figure 4. Student performance on the Commutative Assessment grouped by modality and concept.

Looking across the five conceptual categories covered in the Commutative Assessment using paired-samples t-tests shows that students in the graphical condition perform significantly better with the blocks-based modality on questions related to iterative logic t(178) = 10.40, p < .001, d = 1.57, conditional logic t(178) = 2.82, p < .01, d = .41 and functions t(178) = 2.89, p < .01, d = .41. Students also performed better in the graphical condition on variable questions, but not significantly so, t(178) = 1.66, p = .10, d = .25. Interestingly, there was almost no difference in how students performed on the comprehension questions between the two modalities t(178) = .094, p = .92, d = .01. These data suggest that the answer to the first part of our second research question is yes, modality does affect novice programmers' understanding of basic programming concepts. Further, these data show that the effect is not uniform across concepts and does not seem to influence comprehension of programs in the same way it effects basic understanding of what a construct does within a program. Seeing that a difference does exist, we now further investigate each category to answer the second part of our second research question, looking at how specific concepts are differentially influenced by modality and if they can be explained by misconceptions from the literature.

5.1 Iterative Logic Questions

While iterative logic showed the largest difference in scores between blocks-based and text-based questions, a closer analysis of the questions shows that a majority of this difference can be attributed to the difficulty students have with the structure of for loops [10]. Two of our five iterative logic questions compared a graphical repeat block to a text-based for loop (Figure 5).

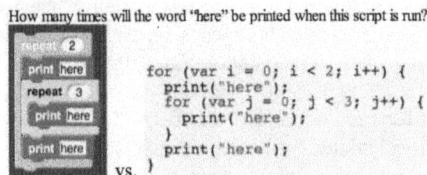

Figure 5. A sample iterative logic question.

On these two questions, students performed significantly better in the graphical condition (83% correct) versus the text-based for loop version of the question (16.1% correct). This provides compelling evidence for the finding that students find the repeat command common to blocks-based languages easier to understand than text-based for loops, a finding already documented in the literature [57, 59]. By examining the incorrect responses given by students, we can glean additional information about how students understand the concepts with respect to the way they are presented. For example, on the text-based for loop questions, almost half of the students (49.3%) chose an answer that had each command inside the for loop run once and only once – suggesting it was not clear that any looping was going to occur. When answering the same questions with the graphical repeat blocks, only 1.5% of students chose those options. Second, in the text-based conditions, 20.7% of students chose the answer that suggested the number of times a given for loop would run was variable, and would be different each time it was executed. In the graphical repeat versions of the questions, only one student chose this option. The Commutative Assessment includes one looping question that compared a blocks-based version of a for loop to a text-based version (Figure 6).

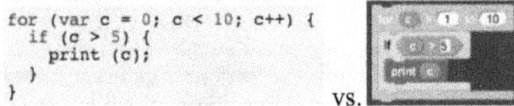

Figure 6. Comparing blocks-based and text-based for loops.

On this question, students performed comparably, answering the question correctly 19.6% percent of the time in the graphical condition and 18.0% of the time in the text-based condition. One possible explanation for the lack of difference on this question compared to what we saw on the two questions that use repeat is the confusion around the use of the term "for" to capture the concept of looping and the lack of transparency in how for loops behave based on this conventional representation [10, 57]. This outcome, along with the other for loop questions adds to the

evidence that students find the word "for" unintuitive, and that "repeat" better describes the looping behavior. As there are languages that utilize the keyword "repeat" (Logo in particular comes to mind), this finding speaks more to language design than features of the modality.

The two indefinite loop questions use the while construct. There was little difference in performance between the blocks-based and text-based versions of these questions. For both questions, students' performance was very similar (a difference of .6% and 2.3% for the two questions). A closer investigation of the answers given (include incorrect answers) does not show a systematic difference between the types of representations used. This suggests that on indefinite loops, the blocks-based representation does not seem to provide any distinct advantage over a comparable text-based implementation. The lack of a difference between the two modalities when using comparable syntax/keywords, both with while loops and for loops, matches the finding from Lewis [32], who found no significant difference in accuracy between questions asked using the repeat block in Scratch and the repeat command in Logo. This suggests that for iterative logic, the blocks-based representation does not provide additional conceptual support; meaning the nested scoping and visual syntactic information did not better support student comprehension. A closer analysis of the five iterative logic questions only reinforces what we already know about the difficulty learners have with for loop syntax.

5.2 Conditional Logic questions

Students performed significantly better in the blocks-based modality on three of the five conditional logic questions. On one question the students performed comparably (.34% better on the blocks-based form), and on the last question students performed slightly better on text, scoring only 2.72% higher. On this final question, students were asked about the overall behavior of the script, as opposed to just the output, making it closer to our comprehension questions than the others, which may in part explain the better performance for the text-based representation - we will return to this issue later in the paper. On the three questions where students performed better in the graphical condition, two patterns emerged in analyzing the incorrect responses, revealing a slight systematic bias. First, on the two questions where the test of an if/else statement evaluated to true, students in the text condition were more likely to think both the if and the else branches would execute (11.5% for text versus 7.1% in the graphical case). This misconception has been identified in the literature [54] and is part of the work showing the if/else construct to be challenging for learners. In the current version of the Commutative Assessment only one of our five questions exposes this misconception, so we cannot make a strong claim about this error being alleviated by the blocks-based representation, but we plan on addressing this shortcoming in the next iteration of the assessment. Second, we found that students in the text condition were more likely to think the last statement is the one that is evaluated regardless of the outcome of the conditional logic surrounding it. On all three questions where this was a possible incorrect answer, students were more likely to choose it in the text-based condition (10.7% for text, versus 3.5% in blocks). This could be explained a number of ways, including students thinking that the body of a conditional statement gets executed regardless of the outcome of the conditional test, thinking the else outcome is always evaluated (which matches the first misconception identified and could explain two of the three questions we saw this error in), or not know how or when conditions evaluate to true so defaulting to falling through to the last statement. Overall, the finding that students performed better on blocks-based conditional logic questions matches Lewis' pervious work [32].

5.3 Variables Questions

Like with the two previous conceptual categories, students performed better (although not at a statistically significant level) on the variable questions when they were presented in the blocks-based form. A more detailed look reveals that students only performed better on the graphical case on three of the four questions in this category. On the one question that students performed better in the textual modality (Figure 7), one difference stands out from the others: variables are set then used, but never re-assigned, making it the simplest of the four questions.

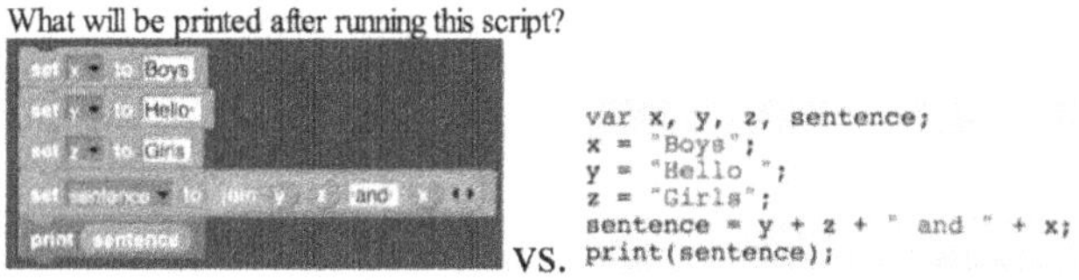

What will be printed after running this script?

```
var x, y, z, sentence;
x = "Boys";
y = "Hello ";
z = "Girls";
sentence = y + z + " and " + x;
vs.  print(sentence);
```

Figure 7. The variable question that students performed better in the text condition than the blocks-based condition.

This suggests that the text-based representation is comparable to the blocks-based version for simple variable assignment and usage, but that as statements and programs get more sophisticated (i.e. variables are assigned to other variables or variable values are set then reset), that the blocks-based modality is more intuitive for learners. As this is only a single question, we only mention is as a potential finding and plan to further investigate this in the future.

Looking at the incorrect responses given by students across the four variable questions reveals three findings that link modality to the existing misconceptions literature on variables. First, all four questions included an option that would be chosen by students who mistakenly thought expressions do not get evaluated as part of assignment (option D in Figure 2) and for all four questions, this incorrect option was chosen slightly more often in text form (7.3% of text responses, 5.3% of graphical). This could potentially be explained by the text form not providing visual hints about how to parse the statement. Second, we found that on text-based questions, students were more likely to incorrectly choose the answer that would result if variables held their initial values, meaning the values do not get overwritten (30.6% in text, 14.5% in graphical). We have not previously encountered this misconception in the literature. Our hypothesis is that in the case where students do not know what is supposed to happen when a variable that already contains a value has a new value set to it, the assumed behavior is for nothing to happen, i.e. the new value is ignored and the original value retained. Finally, students were also slightly more likely to choose answers that fit with the linked variables misconception (option A in figure 2) in the text questions (23.4% of text responses, 17.4% of graphical).

5.4 Function Questions

The fourth category of questions asked students about the outcome of running programs that contained function calls (Figure 8). On these questions, students performed better on the blocks-based version on four of the five questions we asked. Looking at the errors students made, we see a few cases where

students show signs of displaying documented misconceptions and other patterns that seem systematic, but are new to this work and can, at least partially, be explained by features of the modality. First, in one of our questions, we intentionally wrote a program that would output

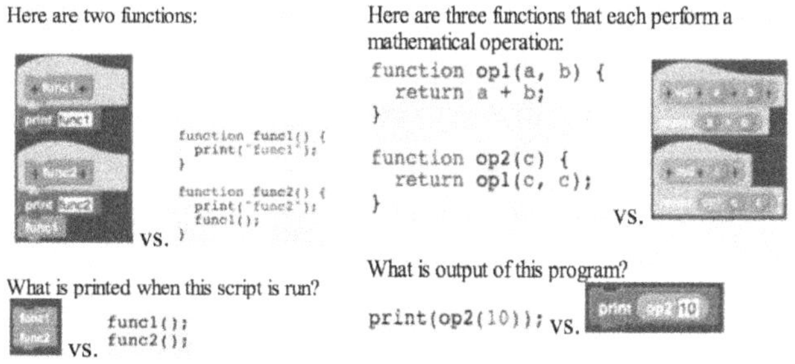

Here are two functions:

```
function func1() {
    print("func1");
}
function func2() {
    print("func2");
    func1();
vs. }
```

What is printed when this script is run?

```
func1();
vs.  func2();
```

Here are three functions that each perform a mathematical operation:

```
function op1(a, b) {
    return a + b;
}

function op2(c) {
    return op1(c, c);
}                        vs.
```

What is output of this program?

```
print(op2(10)); vs.
```

(a) (b)

Figure 8. Two sample function questions.

the same word twice in a row, meaning the correct answer included the duplicated word while other choices included what students might assume was intended. Over half of the students (57%) in the text version of the question incorrectly chose the non-duplicated responses, compared to 38.6% of responses in the blocks-based version of the question. This suggests students found it easier to trace the flow in the blocks-based modality and were less likely to fall victim to what Pea [45] calls an "intentionality bug", where the learner assumes the computer knows the programmer's intention. A second systematic finding from analyzing these questions reinforces a trend observed in the variables questions, that students answering text-based questions were more likely to think that expressions do not get evaluated, but instead retain the expanded form (44% for text versus 31% of graphical responses). A third trend we found is that students were twice as likely (50% compared to 22%) to think that an unbounded recursive function stopped after a fixed number of calls in the text-based form than the blocks-based modality. Finally, two of our questions included functions that return values (`report` is the keyword used in the graphical form). Figure 8b provides an example of this type of question. Across these two questions, students were almost twice as likely to think the `return` command would cause an error in the text-based form (24.5% of responses) than the blocks-based alternative (13.2% of responses). In this case, we can point to a feature of the blocks-based modality that can account for this difference. In the blocks-based language, functions that return values are depicted as ovals or hexagons that need to be nested inside another block (like `op2` in Figure 8b), whereas functions that do not have return statements take the shape of the interlocking blocks (like the `func1` block in figure 8a). This visual difference at the place where the function is being invoked, and the ability for the blocks-based representation to enforce syntactic validity, provide a pair of scaffolds for the learner that potentially explains this difference in student responses in the two modalities.

5.5 Comprehension Questions

The final type of question on the assessment is program comprehension. These questions, unlike the others, focus more on what the purpose of a script is, as opposed to specific outcomes. In each case, the question students must answer is: what does the following script do? These questions require students to mentally run the program, often for different sets of potential inputs, and then interpret that behavior into a natural language description of the behavior. Figure 9 shows two examples of these questions, with the correct answer being that the program swaps two values (left) and returns the largest of the three numbers (right).

Across the full set of questions, students performed comparably on the comprehension questions by modality (a difference of less then 1%). Looking at the questions individually, we see outcomes

a, b and tmp are variables. What does this script do?

The function op4 takes in 3 numbers. What does op4 function do?

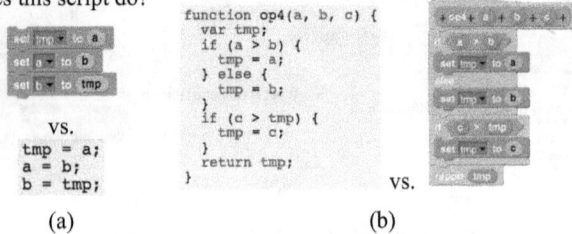

vs.

```
tmp = a;
a = b;
b = tmp;
```

```
function op4(a, b, c) {
    var tmp;
    if (a > b) {
        tmp = a;
    } else {
        tmp = b;
    }
    if (c > tmp) {
        tmp = c;
    }
    return tmp;
}
```

vs.

(a)   (b)

Figure 9. Two comprehension questions

that correlate with the trends of how students did on questions from the conceptual category of the constructs used in the question. So, for example, question b in Figure 9, involves conditional logic and we found students performed better on the graphical versions of the question. Conversely, on a comprehension question that included a `while` loop, students performed better in the text condition. Because these questions involve the additional step of interpreting the behavior of scripts and the intention of the author, it becomes more difficult to map incorrect responses to specific misconceptions from the literature. Additionally, the small difference in performance between blocks-based and text-based questions is also interesting as it is the only category for which this is true, which leads to some potentially interesting conclusions. Notably, this suggests that while the graphical representation supports students in understanding what a construct does (i.e. what the output from using it is), that support does not better facilitate learners in understanding how to use that construct.

6. Discussion

The first research question we posed was how to comparatively assess understandings in two different modalities as part of the larger goal of studying the relationship between programming modality and understandings. The Commutative Assessment is our answer to that question. This assessment gives us the ability to directly compare responses to questions based on modality and concept and by giving the assessment at multiple time points, we are able to do both within and across student analyses of responses. Additionally, by providing responses based on misconceptions in the literature, we can link representational features of modalities with understandings that novices hold.

On three of our four conceptual categories we found significant differences in performance between modality, with the fourth category showing a similar, though less pronounced, trend. Three features of the blocks-based modality in particular stand out as possible explanations for this result. First, the graphical nesting of the blocks to denote scope appears to be an effective way to depict this concept, as we saw fewer errors made on blocks-based versions of questions where such misconceptions might be found. For example, students incorrectly thinking both branches of an `if/else` statement will be run was more prevalent in the text-based condition. The difference between {}s and visually nested commands provides one plausible explanation for this. Second,

the fact that the blocks-based modality allows for statements that can be closer to natural language can, in part, explain some of the differences we found. Notably, the command to assign values to variables takes the form of `set __ to __`, which is a closer description to what the command does than the comparable text-based language command of `var __ = __`. This difference is not a feature of the blocks-based modality, but instead an example of the language designer taking advantage of the more conversational format that the block-based modality enables. This difference can explain at least part of the differences we saw in the variable questions. Finally, the different shape of commands that return values from those that carry out actions in the blocks-based modality provides a compelling explanation for some of the differences we found in the function questions.

One of the more interesting outcomes from this work is the lack of difference between student performance on the comprehension questions. There are a few possible ways to explain this. One explanation is that the gains learners get from the graphical affordances of the blocks-based modality that support conceptual understanding of specific constructs does not carry over to slightly more challenging comprehension tasks. A second possible explanation is that it takes longer than the time allotted in the study for the gains from the graphical layout to apply to these types of questions. If this were the case, we would expect that if given more time, we would see similar gaps in performance emerge. A third possible explanation is that the modality has little effect on student comprehension. Although prior research would suggest otherwise, we continue to test this possibility. Teasing out which of these explanations is most accurate, or developing a potentially new explanation for this outcome is one direction this work is heading.

While we think the Commutative Assessment is a productive approach and can shed some light on the stated research questions, it is important to note what is not assessed by this work – the composition of programs. As such, the work we presented above only begins to answer our second research question on the relationship between modality and understanding. To more fully understand the relationship, additional data and complementary methods need to be applied. As part of this study we also conducted semi-structured clinical interviews with student and gathered log data of student programs. Our next step for this project is to use those data to triangulate patterns and relationships between the modalities and their cognitive affordances that we identified here. Additionally, the analyses presented herein did not account for time period or by Snap! condition. These are two dimensions we will pursue in future work. Finally, as previously mentioned, on some questions in the current form of the Commutative Assessment there is a conflation of modality and language features. While it is difficult to completely disentangle these characteristics of a programming language, in our next iteration of this study, we intend on using an environment where the language used in the blocks-based and text-based interfaces is syntactically more similar and uses a shared set of keywords and update the assessment with images from the new environment.

7. Conclusion

With the increasing presence of blocks-based programming in both formal and informal educational computing contexts, it is becoming increasingly important for us as educators and designers to more fully understand the effects of this modality on learners' conceptual understanding. The Commutative

Assessment allows us to systematically compare student understanding of fundamental concepts in blocks-based and text-based modalities, which in turn can give us insight into how learners are making sense of concepts using different representational tools. Through analyzing student responses, both correct and incorrect, we are starting to learn how blocks-based languages influence learners' emerging understandings and identify how modality can elicit or suppress misconceptions. The next step is to apply these findings to design new environments that will prepare the next generation of learners for the computational futures that await them.

8. References

[1] Abelson, H. and DiSessa, A.A. 1986. *Turtle geometry: The computer as a medium for exploring mathematics.* MIT Press.

[2] ACM/IEEE-CS Joint Task Force on Computing Curricula 2013. *Computer Science Curricula 2013.* ACM Press and IEEE Computer Society Press.

[3] Armoni, M. and Ben-Ari, M. 2010. *Computer Science Concepts in Scratch.*

[4] Armoni, M., Meerbaum-Salant, O. and Ben-Ari, M. 2015. From Scratch to "Real" Programming. *ACM Transactions on Computing Education.* 14, 4 (2015), 25.

[5] Bayman, P. and Mayer, R.E. 1983. A diagnosis of beginning programmers' misconceptions of BASIC programming statements. *Comm. of the ACM.* 26, 9 (1983), 677–679.

[6] Begel, A. 1996. *LogoBlocks: A graphical programming language for interacting with the world.* Electrical Engineering and Computer Science Department. MIT.

[7] Begel, A. and Klopfer, E. 2007. Starlogo TNG: An introduction to game development. *Journal of E-Learning.* (2007).

[8] Blikstein, P. and Wilensky, U. 2009. An Atom is Known by the Company it Keeps: A Constructionist Learning Environment for Materials Science Using Agent-Based Modeling. *Int. Journal of Computers for Mathematical Learning.* 14, 2 (2009), 81–119.

[9] Bonar, J. and Liffick, B.W. 1987. A visual programming language for novices. *Principles of Visual Programming Systems.* S.K. Chang, ed. Prentice-Hall, Inc.

[10] Du Boulay, B. 1986. Some difficulties of learning to program. *Journal of Educational Computing Research.* 2, 1 (1986), 57–73.

[11] Brusilovsky, P., Calabrese, E., Hvorecky, J., Kouchnirenko, A. and Miller, P. 1997. Mini-languages: a way to learn programming principles. *Education and Information Technologies.* 2, 1 (1997), 65–83.

[12] Buffum, P.S., Lobene, E.V., Frankosky, M.H., Boyer, K.E., Wiebe, E.N. and Lester, J.C. 2015. A Practical Guide to Developing and Validating Computer Science Knowledge Assessments with Application to Middle School. (2015).

[13] Cooper, S., Dann, W. and Pausch, R. 2000. Alice: a 3-D tool for introductory programming concepts. *Journal of Computing Sciences in Colleges.* 15, 5 (2000), 107–116.

[14] Denny, P., Luxton-Reilly, A., Tempero, E. and Hendrickx, J. 2011. Understanding the syntax barrier for novices. *Proc. of the 16th Annual ITiCSE* (2011), 208–212.

[15] Van Deursen, A., Klint, P. and Visser, J. 2000. Domain-specific languages: An annotated bibliography. *ACM Sigplan Notices.* 35, 6 (2000), 26–36.

[16] Dijkstra, E.W. 1982. How do we tell truths that might hurt? *Selected Writings on Computing: A Personal Perspective.* Springer. 129–131.

[17] diSessa, A.A. 2000. *Changing minds: Computers, learning, and literacy.* MIT Press.

[18] diSessa, A.A., Hammer, D., Sherin, B.L. and Kolpakowski, T. 1991. Inventing graphing: Meta-representational expertise. *Journal of Mathematical Behavior.* 10, (1991), 117–160.

[19] Donzeau-Gouge, V., Huet, G., Lang, B. and Kahn, G. 1984. Programming environments based on structured editors: The MENTOR experience. *Interactive Programming Environments.* McGraw Hill.

[20] Doukakis, D., Grigoriadou, M. and Tsaganou, G. 2007. Understanding the programming variable concept with animated interactive analogies. *Proc. of the 8th HERCMA Conference* (2007).

[21] Esper, S., Foster, S.R. and Griswold, W.G. 2013. CodeSpells: embodying the metaphor of wizardry for programming. *Proc. of the 18th annual ITiCSE conference* (2013), 249–254.

[22] Feurzeig, W., Papert, S., Bloom, M., Grant, R. and Solomon, C. 1970. Programming-languages as a conceptual framework for teaching mathematics. *SIGCUE Outlook.* 4(1970), 13–17.

[23] Fraser, N. 2013. *Blockly.* Google.

[24] Garlick, R. and Cankaya, E.C. 2010. Using Alice in CS1: A quantitative experiment. *Proc. of the 15th Annual ITiCSE Conference* (2010), 165–168.

[25] Gilmore, D.J. and Green, T.R.G. 1984. Comprehension and recall of miniature programs. *Int. Journal of Man-Machine Studies.* 21, 1 (1984), 31–48.

[26] Gross, P. and Powers, K. 2005. Evaluating Assessments of Novice Programming Environments. *Proc. of the 1st Annual ICER Conference* (NY, USA, 2005), 99–110.

[27] Grover, S., Cooper, S. and Pea, R. 2014. Assessing computational learning in K-12. (2014), 57–62.

[28] Harvey, B. and Mönig, J. 2010. Bringing "no ceiling" to Scratch: Can one language serve kids and computer scientists? *Proc. of Constructionism 2010* (Paris, Fr.), 1–10.

[29] Koh, K.H., Basawapatna, A., Nickerson, H. and Repenning, A. 2014. Real Time Assessment of Computational Thinking. *Visual Languages and Human-Centric Computing,* 49–52.

[30] Kölling, M. and Rosenberg, J. 1996. Blue—a language for teaching object-oriented programming. *ACM SIGCSE Bulletin* (1996), 190–194.

[31] Lave, J. 1988. *Cognition in practice: Mind, mathematics, and culture in everyday life.* Cambridge Univ Press.

[32] Lewis, C.M. 2010. How programming environment shapes perception, learning and goals: Logo vs. Scratch. *Proc. of the 41st Annual ACM SIGCSE Conference* (NY, 2010), 346–350.

[33] Luria, A.R. 1982. *Language and cognition.* Winston ; Wiley, Washington, D.C. : New York ; Chichester :

[34] Meerbaum-Salant, O., Armoni, M. and Ben-Ari, M. 2011. Habits of programming in Scratch. *Proc. of the 16th Annual ITiCSE Conference* (Darmstadt, Germany, 2011), 168–172.

[35] Meerbaum-Salant, O., Armoni, M. and Ben-Ari, M.M. 2010. Learning computer science concepts with scratch. *Proc. of the 6th Annual ICER Conference* (2010), 69–76.

[36] Mendelsohn, P., Green, T.R.G. and Brna, P. 1990. *Programming languages in education: The search for an easy start.* Academic Press London.

[37] Motil, J. and Epstein, D. 1998. JJ: a Language Designed for Beginners.

[38] Nemirovsky, R. 1994. On ways of symbolizing: The case of Laura and the velocity sign. *The Journal of Mathematical Behavior*. 13, 4 (1994), 389–422.

[39] Noss, R. and Hoyles, C. 1996. *Windows on mathematical meanings: Learning cultures and computers*. Kluwer.

[40] Olson, I.C. and Horn, M.S. 2011. Modeling on the table: agent-based modeling in elementary school with NetTango. *Proc. of the 10th Annual IDC Conference*. (2011), 189–192.

[41] Ong, W. 1982. *Orality and Literacy: The technologizing of the world*. Routledge.

[42] Palmer, S.E. 1978. Fundamental aspects of cognitive representation. *Cognition and categorization*. E. Rosch and B.B. Lloyd, eds. Lawrence Erlbaum Associates. 259–303.

[43] Parsons, D. and Haden, P. 2007. Programming osmosis: Knowledge transfer from imperative to visual programming environments. *Proc.of The 12th Annual NACCQ Conference* (Hamilton, New Zealand, 2007), 209–215.

[44] Pattis, R.E. 1981. *Karel the robot: a gentle introduction to the art of programming*. John Wiley & Sons, Inc.

[45] Pea, R.D. 1986. Language-independent conceptual" bugs" in novice programming. *Journal of Educational Computing Research*. 2, 1 (1986), 25–36.

[46] Piaget, J. 1952. *The origins of intelligence in children*. International Universities Press, Inc.

[47] Piech, C., Sahami, M., Koller, D., Cooper, S. and Blikstein, P. 2012. Modeling how students learn to program. *Proc.of the 43rd ACM SIGCSE Conference* (2012), 153–160.

[48] Powers, K., Ecott, S. and Hirshfield, L.M. 2007. Through the looking glass: teaching CS0 with Alice. *ACM SIGCSE Bulletin*. 39, 1 (2007), 213–217.

[49] Resnick, M. et al. 2009. Scratch: Programming for all. *Comm. of the ACM*. 52, 11 (2009), 60.

[50] Sengupta, P. and Wilensky, U. 2009. Learning Electricity with NIELS: Thinking with Electrons and Thinking in Levels. *Int. Journal of Computers for Mathematical Learning*. 14, 1 (2009), 21–50.

[51] Sherin, B.L. 2001. A comparison of programming languages and algebraic notation as expressive languages for physics. *Int. Journal of Computers for Mathematical Learning*. 6, 1 (2001), 1–61.

[52] Sherin, B.L. 2000. How students invent representations of motion: A genetic account. *The Journal of Mathematical Behavior*. 19, 4 (2000), 399–441.

[53] Slany, W. 2014. Tinkering with Pocket Code, a Scratch-like programming app for your smartphone. *Proc. of Constructionism 2014* (Vienna, Austria, 2014).

[54] Sleeman, D., Putnam, R.T., Baxter, J. and Kuspa, L. 1986. Pascal and high school students: A study of errors. *Journal of Educational Computing Research*. 2, 1 (1986), 5–23.

[55] Sorva, J. 2008. The same but different students' understandings of primitive and object variables. *Proc. of the 8th Annual ICER Conference* (2008), 5–15.

[56] Sorva, J. 2012. *Visual Program Simulation in Introductory Programming Education*. Aalto University.

[57] Stefik, A. and Gellenbeck, E. 2011. Empirical studies on programming language stimuli. *Software Quality Journal*. 19, 1 (2011), 65–99.

[58] Stefik, A. and Hanenberg, S. 2014. The Programming Language Wars: Questions and Responsibilities for the Programming Language Community. *Proc. of the 2014 Int. Symposium on New Ideas, New Paradigms, and Reflections on Programming* (NY, USA, 2014), 283–299.

[59] Stefik, A. and Siebert, S. 2013. An Empirical Investigation into Programming Language Syntax. *ACM Transactions on Computing Education*. 13, 4 (2013), 1–40.

[60] Sudol, L.A. and Studer, C. 2010. Analyzing Test Items: Using Item Response Theory to Validate Assessments. *Proc. of the 41st ACM SIGCSE Conference* (NY, 2010), 436–440.

[61] Swetz, F. 1989. *Capitalism and arithmetic: The new math of the 15th century*. Open Court.

[62] Tew, A.E. and Dorn, B. 2013. The Case for Validated Tools in Computer Science Education Research. *Computer*. 46, 9 (2013), 60–66.

[63] Tew, A.E. and Guzdial, M. 2010. Developing a validated assessment of fundamental CS1 concepts. *Proc. of the 41st Annual ACM SIGCSE Conference* (2010), 97–101.

[64] Tew, A.E. and Guzdial, M. 2011. The FCS1: a language independent assessment of CS1 knowledge. *Proc. of the 42nd Annual ACM SIGCSE Conference* (2011), 111–116.

[65] Vygotsky, L. 1978. *Mind in society: The development of higher psychological processes*. Harvard University Press.

[66] Vygotsky, L. 1986. *Thought and language*. MIT Press.

[67] Wagh, A. and Wilensky, U. 2012. Evolution in blocks: Building models of evolution using blocks. *Proc. of Constructionism 2012* (Athens, Gr, 2012).

[68] Weintrop, D. and Wilensky, U. 2012. RoboBuilder: A program-to-play constructionist video game. *Proc. of Constructionism 2012* (Athens, Gr, 2012).

[69] Weintrop, D. and Wilensky, U. 2014. Situating programming abstractions in a constructionist video game. *Proc. of Constructionism 2014* (Vienna, Au, 2014).

[70] Weintrop, D. and Wilensky, U. 2015. To Block or not to Block, That is the Question: Students' Perceptions of Blocks-based Programming. *Proc. of the 14th Annual IDC Conference* (Boston, MA, 2015).

[71] Werner, L., Denner, J., Campe, S. and Kawamoto, D.C. 2012. The fairy performance assessment: measuring computational thinking in middle school. *Proc. of the 43rd Annual ACM SIGC Conference* (2012), 215–220.

[72] Wertsch, J.V. 1991. *Voices of the mind: A sociocultural approach to mediated action*. Harvard University Press.

[73] Whorf, B.L., Carroll, J.B. and Chase, S. 1956. *Language, thought, and reality: Selected writings of Benjamin Lee Whorf*. MIT press Cambridge, MA.

[74] Wilensky, U. and Papert, S. 2010. Restructurations: Reformulating knowledge disciplines through new representational forms. *Proc. of Constructionism 2010* (Paris, Fr., 2010).

[75] Wilensky, U. and Reisman, K. 2006. Thinking like a wolf, a sheep, or a firefly: Learning biology through constructing and testing computational theories— an embodied modeling approach. *Cognition and Instruction*. 24, 2 (2006), 171–209.

[76] Wilkerson-Jerde, M.H. and Wilensky, U. 2010. Restructuring Change, Interpreting Changes: The DeltaTick Modeling and Analysis Toolkit. *Proc. of Constructionism 2010* (Paris, Fr, 2010).

Fourth Grade Students Reading Block-Based Programs: Predictions, Visual Cues, and Affordances

Hilary Dwyer[1], Charlotte Hill[2], Alexandria Hansen[1], Ashley Iveland[1],
Diana Franklin[2], & Danielle Harlow[1]

[1] Gevirtz Graduate School of Education
University of California
Santa Barbara, CA 93106
{hdwyer, akillian, aockey, dharlow}@education.ucsb.edu

[2] Department of Computer Science
University of California
Santa Barbara, CA 93106
{charlottehill, franklin}@cs.ucsb.edu

ABSTRACT

Visual block-based programming environments allow elementary school students to create their own programs in ways that are more accessible than in textual programming environments. These environments help students write code by removing syntax errors and reducing typing. Students create code by dragging, dropping, and snapping constructs together (e.g. blocks) that are organized by lists, colors, shape, images, etc. However, programming in visual block-based environments is not always simple; in fact, it can become complex quickly. In addition to elements that create code, the visual aspects of these environments provide readers information about what happens, when, and how. Here, we focus on how students used visual cues when reading programs in our block-based programming environment, LaPlaya, a variant of Scratch. Specifically we identified the visual cues students noticed and acted upon. These included not only those that were intended by designers (perceptible affordances), but also those that were not intended by designers (false affordances). Through a detailed content analysis of 13 focus groups with fourth graders we created an initial taxonomy of visual cues in our programming environment and explored how students used these cues to make predictions about provided code, and the types of affordances such cues offered students.

Categories and Subject Descriptors

D.1.7 [**Programming Techniques**]: Visual Programming; K.3.2 [**Computer and Information Science Education**]: Computer Science Education.

General Terms

Design, Human Factors, Languages.

Keywords

Block based languages; graphical programming; computer science education; elementary school; novice programming environments

1. INTRODUCTION

Block-based programming environments have become increasingly popular over the past decade particularly with children and novice programmers. These environments offer

colorful, reactive interfaces that reduce the amount of typing needed to write a program, making them well suited for tablet computers and other touch screen devices. Many block-based environments such as Scratch [1] and LaPlaya [2] are centered on characters, or "sprites". In these environments, programs are composed of multiple scripts (segments of code) that are organized by sprite. Not all scripts are visible to the programmer. When programming, the programmer will see four primary areas: a palette of commands (e.g. block lists); the scripting area (e.g. where the programmer connects blocks together); a menu of sprites (e.g. characters available in the program); and a stage (e.g. display visual output). The command palette includes categories of commands organized and displayed into lists by function such as motion or looks. The number of commands available is usually smaller than in textual languages. Next to this area is the scripting area. Scripts are organized by sprite and only those of the selected sprite are displayed.

Many block-based environments are event-driven and implement parallel programming. This means that scripts are programmed to begin when something else happens—a user clicks on a key, or another sprite does something. Often events trigger multiple actions across multiple sprites simultaneously. This means that programmers must keep track of the ways that scripts interact as they work, and how different events trigger action.

Reading and remixing others' programs has increasingly become part of block-based programming environments. Online communities encourage users to view and experiment with others' codes. Scratch [1], Hopscotch [3] and other block-based environments are more than just editors: they also serve as platforms for programmers to easily share their projects online. Scratch's online community encourages "remixing" projects, where users modify another's project. Additionally, programmers may use these online environments to follow coding tutorials, such as "The Hour of Code" on Code.org [4], and modify or expand code snippets provided in the lessons. In the curriculum and interface we designed, students were given sample scripts or partially completed programs to revise or complete [5]. Whether remixing others' code or completing partial code, being able to read block-based programs is as important as being able to create new code.

Reading programs in block-based environments differs considerably both from textual programming environments (e.g., C++ or Python) and other types of reading that children encounter. Block-based programming environments include visual information that may contribute to or, in some cases, hinder comprehension. Children also need to attend to complex and hidden structures that control the flow of the story or game programmed. As a result, we wanted to explore how students understood and read existing code using the visual cues provided by our block-based programming environment (including the scripts and a still picture of the output).

In this paper, we investigated how fourth graders read and made predictions about block-based programs written by other people. Fourth-graders from two schools participating in our computational thinking curriculum—Kids Engaged in Learning Programming and Computer Science (KELP-CS)—made predictions about projects in our programming environment, LaPlaya [2]. We interviewed 13 pairs of students from two local schools about projects conceptually at or slightly above the level they had reached in the curriculum. We asked them to use the information provided to predict and figure out what would happen when a provided program ran.

Here, we present a preliminary taxonomy of the features in LaPlaya that students used to predict what would occur on the stage (the output of a program), functions of individual blocks, functions of individual scripts, and how scripts and sprites were coordinated (understanding of the overall program). Students used the visual features in both expected and unexpected ways. We further analyzed students' explanations through Gaver's construct of technology affordances [6] to identify visual cues that students recognized and acted on, those they failed to notice, and those that they acted on in ways unintended by the developers.

Our analysis demonstrates that, while visual block-based environments reduce syntax errors and typing requirements, they are definitely not simple. As Petre [7] wrote about visual programming more generally:

> Both graphics and text have their uses – and their limitations. Pictorial and graphic media can carry considerable information in what may be a convenient and attractive form, but incorporating graphics into programming notations requires us to understand the precise contribution that graphical representations might make to the job at hand (p. 33).

In block-based programming environments, almost all information and constructs are graphical representations and as yet little research has demonstrated how students use these visuals to aid in program comprehension. In LaPlaya, students utilize a number of intended and unintended visual cues to interpret provided code. We found that, in addition to the scripts and blocks, students used the layout of the stage and characteristics of the sprites to predict program results. Further, students used visual attributes of the programming blocks such as color, shape, and arguments (e.g., words embedded in blocks) to predict how the block or script would function.

2. RELATED WORK

Learning how to program is much like learning how to read: both consist of multiple aspects of literacy such as knowing basic vocabulary, identifying key words, comprehending how series of words construct meaning, and ultimately composing text [8, 9]. Learning to program encompasses the same attributes of learning to read with the added context and structure of the interface and programming language.

Block-based programming environments offer innovative ways to analyze how young students and novices read programs and understand computational concepts (e.g., sequences, events, and operators), practices (e.g., testing, debugging, or reusing), and perspectives (e.g., expressing, connecting, and questioning) [10]. Some work has already demonstrated that students understand programming concepts differently depending on the visual-nature of a particular block-based programming environment. Lewis [11] found that 6th grade students (ages 10-12 years old) appeared to better understand loop construct when using Logo, but the construct of conditionals better in Scratch.

The spatial organization of block-based programming environments makes it easier for programmers to view the output while looking at the scripts. Gross and Kelleher looked at how university students with little to no programming experience understood and reused code in Storytelling Alice [12]. Although participants were not able to fully read and understand the scripts, they were able to match the output to the scripts to find the desired portions of the program. Ferriera et al. [13] found that ninth graders in Brazil using AgentSheets attributed agency to objects (such as an image of a shark) inside of the program, and interpreted the program differently when looking at a program report versus running the program. The program report allowed users to see the whole set of program elements, not just parts associated with a single object/character. Without the visible program report, participants did not understand or notice all the underlying logic and agent in the program. Rader, Brand and Lewis [14] looked at students' understanding of programs in KidSim and found misconceptions stemming from students' views of the objects: children expected objects to behave as they do in the real world and expected the computer to understand the way objects looked (e.g., a picture of a fish) the same way that the children understood the object. Similarly, Pea [15] found that students expected computers to understand programs like people did: remembering code previously executed while running later portions of the program, looking at multiple parts of the program simultaneously, and having implicit knowledge of the program's overall goal.

Though block-based programming environments limit syntax errors and typing requirements, they are complex learning environment and assessing student learning can be challenging [10]. Schulte [9] proposed a Block Model to aid teachers and researchers in identifying different learning paths students may take when comprehending programs "bottom up"—first reading words or text, then making inferences about the relations between blocks, and lastly understanding the overall program structure. This model organized elements of a program by their structure and function. Atoms were language elements and operations of statements. Blocks were regions of interest that syntactically built a unit. Relations referred to connections between blocks. Lastly macrostructure was the overall structure, goal, and purpose of the program. Schultz tested this model with a small sample of potential teachers at one university.

Our work builds on the Schulte's work [9] by examining program and reading comprehension of young students from an ecological perspective. Ecological perspectives [16] assume that objects have actionable qualities that can be acted upon by individuals with the appropriate cognitive and physical resources. For example, a chair has the affordance of being sat in, but only for individuals of the appropriate size. An adult may not be able to sit in a child's high chair, and thus a high chair does not have this affordance for an adult. Affordances are an interaction between the user and the object. In some cases, the actionable qualities are not clear. Norman [17] introduced the term signifier to indicate visual cues to the individual about the affordances of an object. "Push" signs on doors are examples of signifiers, indicating how to access the affordance of opening the door. Gaver [6] applied this work to technology and proposed the idea of perceptible, hidden, and false affordances.

Affordances are, in the context of block-based programming, objects that have possibilities for action. Visual cues provide information about the possible actions. For example, the shape of a block is a visual cue that may indicate which blocks it can connect to or how commands can be linked (affordances). If a child noticed this feature and acted on it, it would be considered a perceptible affordance (from the child's perspective) and an appropriate visual cue. If a child did not notice the feature or did not think that the visual feature had meaning attached to it, it would be considered a hidden affordance. In contrast, students sometimes attach meaning to features that were not intended to impart value such as acting upon visual cues that were not designed to impart information. For example a child might assume (falsely) that the sprite on the far left of the stage would always be the first to act. In reality, the position of sprites is not related to the order in which they appear or act in the program. If this were the case, then position of sprites would constitute a false affordance meaning that students found information that was not actually present.

3. RESEARCH DESIGN

We asked the question, "What perceptible, hidden, and false affordances of a block-based programming environment do students use to read block-based programs?" To answer this question, we conducted focus group interviews in which we presented LaPlaya programs and asked students to predict the outcome.

We interviewed 13 pairs of fourth grade students at two schools, Aguacate and Cabrillo Elementary (pseudonyms), participating in our computational thinking curriculum. Students were interviewed in same-sex pairs: eight pairs of girls and five pairs of boys. Each pair shared a computer and answered questions about and modified three programs written in LaPlaya, the block-based environment used in their computational thinking curriculum.

3.1 Research Context

The fourth graders at both schools, Aguacate and Cabrillo, were participating in our computer science curriculum related to computational thinking and programming. The curriculum includes on-computer and off-computer components: the on-computer exercises are activities in LaPlaya [2] and the off-computer activities relate computational thinking and programming concepts back to every-day life examples.

LaPlaya is based on Snap! [18] and Scratch [1]: students use multiple *blocks* of code to create *scripts* that control *sprites*, images of animals or people that students draw or import. In our curriculum, students were given partially completed projects in LaPlaya that already contained some sprites and scripts. LaPlaya allows project designers to hide elements of the programming environment—such as sprites, scripts, or block options—to focus students' attention on specific computer science concepts and reduce the cognitive load required to program. As students moved through the curriculum, more blocks and LaPlaya features were made available to them.

3.2 Participants

We interviewed 26 students in pairs at Aguacate Elementary (n = 16 students) and Cabrillo Elementary (n = 10) over several weeks. We paired students by gender, and together they worked on three

programming projects in LaPlaya with an interviewer, a graduate or undergraduate student in computer science or education. The participants and interviewers were familiar with the programming interface. At the time of the interviews, the students had completed 3-4 hours of curricular time with the interface.

3.3 Data Collection

We used two sets of interview protocols each containing three projects: the same introductory project followed by two different projects. For this study, we only analyzed students' actions and discourse in the introductory activity, which was identical for all students. In this activity, the interviewer asked students to predict what the program would do if they ran it. Students explored the program while the interviewer asked follow-up probes to further clarify and expand upon what students were saying.

Figure 1. Layout of the first project

Figure 1 shows what students saw when they opened the introductory project. On the stage were three sprites: a bat, unicorn, and dragon. Because the bat sprite was selected at the onset, only the scripts for the bat sprite were initially visible. To see the scripts for the unicorn and dragon, the students needed to click on each sprite individually in the sprite corral (lower right of screen). The interviewer would then ask students to describe what they expected the program to do when it ran. Students were encouraged to interact with the program as long as they did nothing to prompt action on the stage (e.g., click sprites or the green flag).

This activity took approximately 10 minutes to complete, though the complete interview lasted 30 minutes. We captured students interacting with the computer through a combination of video, table microphones and screen recordings of the interface. We combined the video and screen recordings for each pair of students, transcribed the interviews verbatim, and coded the transcripts to find common threads throughout the interviews.

3.4 Data Analysis

We analyzed the focus groups in three iterations examining smaller parts of the transcripts at each juncture. In the first and second rounds (what students were predicting and student tools for making predictions), we analyzed whole transcripts. In the third round (affordances), we analyzed only the introductory activity, and isolated individual instances of visual cues. This impacted our results directly as the activity selected constrained what visual cues could have been discussed and the types of predictions that students made.

3.4.1 What students were predicting

In our first round of analysis, we focused on the ways students responded to the interviewer's probes about what would happen when the program ran. We open-coded the transcripts and created a domain analysis described by Spradley [19]. Using Spradley's specific analytic steps, we identified cover terms and terms related in specific semantic ways to the cover terms. While Spradley's approach to analysis was created to interpret ethnographic studies, we found it appropriate for understanding the programming interface. Like ethnographers, we were trying to describe an emic perspective. That is, our goal was to understand the programming environment from the child's perspective.

In this process, we identified multiple levels of the program that students made predictions about: individual blocks, single scripts, collections of scripts, and the program as a whole. Figure 2 demonstrates our first semantic relationship. We collapsed these terms to align with the functional structure of LaPlaya. This left us with four codes [20] to describe what student made predictions about in LaPlaya: individual blocks, single scripts, multiple scripts, and the output (actions and timing of sprites for program).

```
X is a predictable attribute of a LaPlaya Program
X may include:
    • How sprites will act (actions)
    • When sprites will act (timing)
    • What a script will do
    • What blocks will do
    • How programs are run
```

Figure 2. Semantic Relationship - Attribution

3.4.2 Student tools for making predictions

In our second analytic cycle, we developed semantic relationships [16] for each of the codes developed in our first round of analysis. Each took the form, "X is a tool for predicting Y," where X was an aspect of LaPlaya and Y was one of the predictable attributes listed above. We created a list of terms related to this semantic relationship for each of the four predictable attributes (blocks, single scripts, multiple scripts, and output). As we developed these lists, we realized that many of the tools children used were not necessarily related to the scripts or blocks; rather, the tools related to some visual cue embedded in the interface (e.g., physical characteristics of a sprite).

With this notion of visual cues in mind, we created a summative table relating visual cues to what students were predicting. The visual cues listed in this table were developed both through our group conversations about what was possible, and what students actually talked about in the focus groups with this specific activity. Through multiple rounds of systematic coding [20] and discussion, we reduced, added, and combined visual cues into categories until the group reached consensus.

3.4.3 Affordances

In our third analytic cycle, we systematically coded [20] transcripts again by when students made predictions and what tools they drew on to make those predictions using the construct of affordance [6]. For each prediction, we coded for visual cue and type of affordance (perceptible, false, and hidden). Perceptible affordances occurred when students identified an attribute that developers intended to be useful. False affordances occurred when students interpreted a visual element as useful when that aspect did not in fact contain useful information. Hidden affordances occurred when students overlooked an attribute that developers intended to be useful. Due to methodological limitations, we were not always able to determine hidden affordances as students did not see these attributes. If they did not see a tool, they likely did not discuss it during the focus groups and it would not be captured in the transcripts.

3.4.4 Final analysis

Taken together, our final coding scheme included the taxonomy created in the first two rounds of analysis, and the affordances in round three. Researchers coded transcripts by hand as they watched video and screen recordings for each pair of students. They identified each instance when students made predictions about how a program ran and then identified the visual cue or tool used, what aspects of LaPlaya students were making predictions about (block, single script, multiple scripts, and output) and the type of affordance offered (perceptible, hidden, or false).

Four researchers coded transcripts together until internal consistency was reached with this coding scheme about student predications, tools drawn on on to make predictions, and the intended use of the tool [20]. Then two researchers (one each from computer science education) coded transcripts independently. Pairs resolved discrepancies in coding through discussion and at times with the entire group until consensus was reached. Then, transcripts were uploaded into the qualitative data analysis software Dedoose [21] to aid in the development of findings.

4. RESULTS

Our analyses led to the development of two sets of findings. In the first finding, we describe a taxonomy of visual cues embedded in our visual block-based programming environment, LaPlaya. We developed this taxonomy through several iterations of domain analysis [15], group discussions about theoretically possible visual cues, and visual cues that students discussed during the focus groups. We then outline how this taxonomy linked to what students made predictions about in the focus groups during the introductory activity (block, single scripts, multiple scripts, and output).

In our second finding, we connect the visual cues students discussed with the construct of technology affordances [6]. We provide examples from the focus group transcripts of students acting upon affordances when reading provided code in the activity.

4.1 Taxonomy of Visual Cues in LaPlaya

Using our domain analysis, group discussions, and transcripts we created a taxonomy of visual cues embedded in LaPlaya (see left-hand side of Table 1 and Figure 3 as a reference).

We further sorted these tools into categories based on their function in LaPlaya (blocks, scripts, stage, and interface) and subcategories as necessary. Visual cues in parentheses signaled tools that did not impact how a program ran and thus were categorically false affordances (see following section). For example, in Scratch, whether a programmer places a script in the upper right corner of the scripting area or in the bottom left corner has no bearing on when or how that script is run. Thus interpreting the layout of scripts as providing information is always false. Across the top of Table 2, we listed the aspect of LaPlaya that students could make predictions about (blocks, single scripts, multiple scripts, and output). An "X" signified that students cited a visual cue when making a prediction during the introductory activity. Note that there are two shaded columns with no X's (Single Script and Multiple Scripts). This is because our analysis could not identify these types of predictions but they will be part of future work

Table 1. How Students Used Visual Cues in LaPlaya to Predict Aspects of a Program

Visual Cues in LaPlaya			Block	Single Script	Multiple Scripts	Output
				What Students Were Predicting		
Blocks	Word choice	Prior experience with word	X			X
		Word's everyday meaning				X
	Block layout	Block argument	X			X
		Color				
		Shape				
	Same block, other script		X			X
Scripts	Ordering of blocks within scripts		X			X
	(Layout of scripts)					X
	Other blocks in script					
	Other scripts					X
Stage	(Sprites on the stage)	(Physical characteristics)	X			X
		(Orientation)				X
		(Stage position)				X
	(Background)					
Interface	Sprite corral		X			X
	(Costume tab)					X
	(Costume images)		X			X
	(Instruction tab)					X

Note: Parentheses distinguish visual cues that were categorically false affordances. "X" signifies that students used a visual cue when making predictions during the introductory activity. Both "Single Script" and "Multiple Scripts" columns are shaded because the introductory activity did not provide students with opportunities to predict single or multiple scripts though each emerged in the other focus group activities.

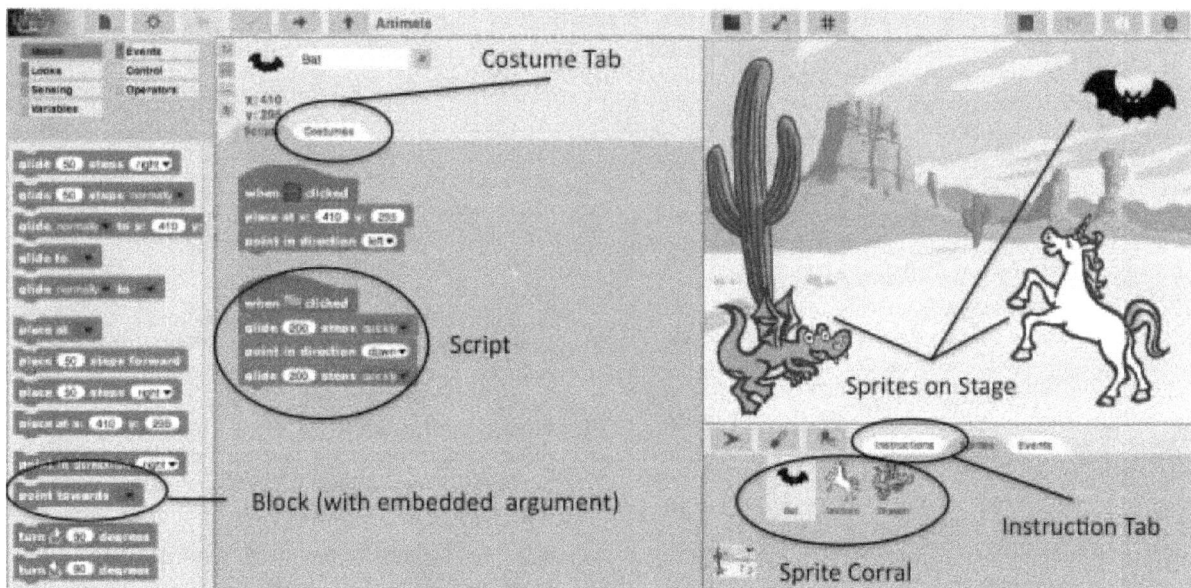

Figure 3. Overview of LaPlaya Interface

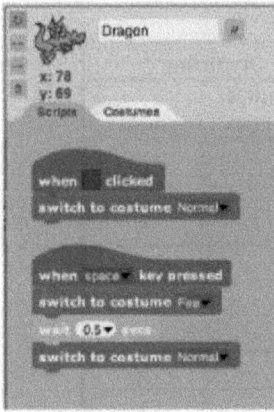

Figure 4. Scripts for Dragon Sprite

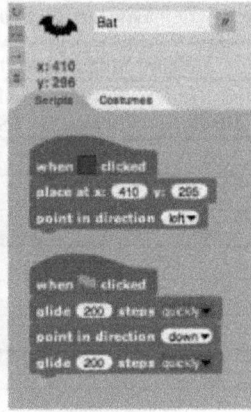

Figure 5. Scripts for Bat Sprite

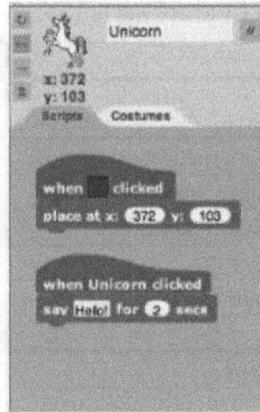

Figure 6. Scripts for Unicorn Sprite

Figure 7. Stage for Introductory Activity

4.1.1 Categories of Visual Cues

Block-level visual cues focused on attributes of blocks such as color, shape, and argument. Users could infer block function by the words embedded in a block (e.g. "glide"). Block argument included information that could be passed through the program such as when a user selected from a dropdown menu or wrote in his or her own text (e.g., "say ___ for ___ sec"). Users could look at how a block functioned elsewhere in a project (same block, other script).

Script-level visual cues related to multiple blocks connected together into single or multiple scripts. Users could look at the order of blocks within script or more generally what other blocks were included in a script. They could also get information based on where the scripts were located (layout of scripts) and the way a script functioned in other instances such as under another sprite.

Stage-level visual cues related to the screen in the upper right-hand corner of LaPlaya. Here, users could see sprites (characters) and different backgrounds depending on a project. Users could make predictions based on attributes of the sprites such as physical characteristics (image or icon used for a sprite), orientation (e.g., whether a sprite faced up or down), and stage position (where on the stage a sprite started). Users could also get information from the image displayed in the background. These visual cues were categorically false affordances; attributes of sprite images do not functionally impact a program.

Lastly, interface-level visual cues related to the ways users engaged with the LaPlaya environment not captured in the other categories. The sprite corral was located in the lower right corner and displayed all active sprites by small images or icons. Users clicked on each image to create code for a particular sprite. Within each sprite, users could manipulate the iteration of an image (costumes). Costumes used in sequence create animation on the stage and were listed as icons for each sprite. Users could gain information both from the costume tab listing the costumes, and the particular image for a costume. Finally, LaPlaya included instructions in the lower right-hand side of the interface. These visual cues were categorically false affordances as they did not functionally impact how a LaPlaya program ran.

4.1.2 Linking Visual Cues to Student Predictions

The introductory project we selected to analyze constrained what students could make predictions about and what visual cues they discussed. The introductory activity included six

scripts total (two for each sprite). One script initialized each sprite and the second script created output on the stage (e.g. action for each sprite). Thus, we could not distinguish when students discussed a single script or output, and we did not provide opportunities for students to make predictions about multiple scripts in the first activity. As a result, these two columns in Table 2, single script and multiple scripts, were blank but still theoretically possible were we to analyze other focus group activities.

In most cases, students used the cues we identified as potential sources of information. For example, when predicting the function of blocks, students discussed the embedded text and arguments in blocks, or how the block was used elsewhere in a program. However, we were also surprised by what visual cues students drew upon to make predictions. When making predictions about blocks, students talked about physical attributes of a sprite, the images of sprites in the sprite corral, and the different costume images provided for a sprite. Though students attributed meaning and acted upon these visual cues, none directly connected to block functionality in LaPlaya.

We found similar patterns when students made predictions about the output of the project – what would happen when the program ran. Students discussed the words and arguments embedded in blocks, and how blocks or scripts were used elsewhere. As we expected, they also read blocks sequentially within a script. However, they attributed meaning to visual cues in unexpected ways. They predicted that some scripts would run first or more quickly depending on where they were located in relation to each other (upper right or left-hand area of scripting area). As well, they used features of particular sprite images to predict the output: physical characteristics, orientation, and position on the stage. They also discussed multiple interface features such as the sprite corral, costume tab, costume images, and instruction tab. In the following section we provide more detailed examples of these different types of visual cues.

4.2 Affordances and Visual Cues

In this section, we provide examples of how students used visual cues to make predictions during the focus groups. We organized these examples by the three types of affordances. Perceptible affordances were visual cues that students recognized and acted on. False affordances were those that students acted on in ways unintended by the developers. Hidden affordances were those they failed to notice. For each type, we provide multiple vignettes demonstrating how students discussed a visual cue and used it to read provided code. All student names are pseudonyms.

4.2.1 Perceptible Affordances

Scripts in LaPlaya are triggered by events. The most common way to run scripts is to click the green flag button, but scripts can also be programmed to run when a user clicks a sprite or presses a key. In the following example, the interviewer asked Kaylee and Ivy to predict what would happen without running the program (clicking the green flag). The students read the embedded argument in visible blocks to predict the output (see Figure 4). This was a perceptible affordance as the students read the blocks and scripts in ways that developers intended.

> Interviewer: What do you think will happen when you click the green flag?
> Kaylee: Ready. Go. [Program will run].
> Ivy: It [the program] will go [run].
> Interviewer: It will go [run] …does anything else make the program run?
> Kaylee: Maybe clicking on the dragon because it says…oh, no! Space key.
> Interviewer: How did you figure out the space key?
> Kaylee: Because it [the block] says "When Space Key Pressed."

Kaylee quickly recognized by reading the provided scripts that the "When Space Key Pressed" block controlled how to run that script. This was an example of students using block arguments to make predictions because "space key" was a dropdown option that also included other keys on the keyboard.

In the next example, Richard and Bryan predicted the output of the program by reading the blocks sequentially for all three sprites. Richard also recognized that he needed to click through the different sprites to see the visible scripts (e.g., sprite corral). Both students used block arguments (e.g. number of steps and direction) and words embedded in blocks (e.g. costume "fire") to make predictions.

> Interviewer: … So before you click on anything, without running the code, what do you think the sprites will do?
> Richard: … with just reading them?
> Interviewer: Yep, just reading the code.
> Richard: Well first of all … can we go through each one [sprite in the sprite corral]?
> Interviewer: Yep! Go through each one [sprite].
> Richard: … when you click the [get] ready [button], they [the sprites] all go back to where they are …When you click the [green] flag, the bat will glide, to right here [points to stage] –
> Bryan: [overlap] 200 steps.
> Richard: Yeah and [move] down, and then [move] over right here. And then the unicorn will say hello and get placed back here like that and say hello. And then the dragon, when you click it, it'll go back to where it is and then it'll switch to fire I'm guessing, and then it'll wait point five, like half a second and then switch back to [].

Richard and Bryan used multiple, perceptible affordances to make predictions about how the program ran. These visual cues (block word choice, block argument, ordering of blocks within scripts, and sprite corral) were intended to be useful when reading LaPlaya programs, and both students acted upon the affordances in expected ways.

4.2.2 False Affordances

Students also acted on visual cues in ways unintended by the developers. These visual cues such as the sprites on the stage or parts of the interface imparted information to students as they made predictions. However, in most cases these visual cues did not functionally impact the program.

In the following, Kaylee and Ivy were predicting what the dragon, unicorn, and bat sprite would do when the program ran (see Figure 4, 5, 6, and 7 for visible scripts and stage setup). Both students looked at the sprites, their attributes, and their location on the stage – instead of the scripts – to predict what they would eventually do when running the program.

> Interviewer: Ok. So, how did you figure out which ones doing what?
> Ivy: …This one's [the bat's] the highest, so I assumed that it must be going down. And, this [the dragon] must be gliding. And this is the only one [the unicorn] that's actually stepping.
> Interviewer: So, they look like they're about to do something?
> Kaylee: Yeah.

As illustrated in the transcript, Ivy predicted that the bat would move downwards because it was positioned in the background's sky (stage location and orientation of sprite on stage). Also, she predicted that the unicorn would take a step because its feet were in the air (physical characteristics of sprite on stage).

In the following, Ethan and Luis also made predictions using attributes of the sprites rather than reading the scripts.

> Interviewer: … So without running the code in this activity, what do you think will happen? What will the sprites do?
> Ethan: I think the bat will start flying to the cactus.
> Luis: The dragon's gonna eat the horse. I think that dragon wants to eat, needs to get to the horse [points to unicorn]

Ethan predicted that the bat sprite would fly across the stage because already located in the upper, right corner of the stage. As well, since the sprite was a bat he concluded that it would "start flying to the cactus" located on the left side of the stage (physical characteristics and stage location of sprite on stage). Luis described how the dragon would move to the unicorn. Since the dragon sprite appeared predatory, he inferred that the dragon would "need to get to the horse" (physical characteristics and stage position of sprite on stage).

The attributes of sprites on the stage do not functionally impact how the program ran, only the associated scripts impart change. However, as these examples demonstrate, students associated the actual image (bat, dragon, or unicorn) with their prior knowledge of each character. They then used this prior knowledge to predict how the program ran. These were all false affordances because students were acting on visual cues not intended to be useful by designers.

4.2.3 Hidden Affordances

Hidden affordances were challenging to identify methodologically with our research design. Hidden affordances existed when a child did not notice a LaPlaya feature or did not think that the visual cue had meaning attached to it – in both cases, evidence of the hidden affordance would be the absence of student talk. As well, we as environment and curriculum developers possessed subjective, insider perspective about what visual tools students should or could be using as they read code.

As a result, there may have been more hidden affordances than we found in this particular analysis. Below we provide one vignette in which students overlooked a LaPlaya feature initially and later in the interview decided that feature was helpful in making predictions. Because they found the tool later, they could articulate that they had not identified it earlier, a rare instance of students describing hidden affordances.

In the following, Kevin did not originally perceive that he could click on sprite icons in the sprite corral to view individual sprites' scripts. He was originally confused about the visible scripts, and how to associate scripts with a particular sprite. He overlooked the affordance of clicking on the sprite icons in the sprite corral. It was not until the moderator asked what the unicorn would do that Kyle eventually realized what he had overlooked. In this event, Kyle vocalized his confusion, allowing us to label this a hidden affordance.

> Interviewer: … Ok, what do you think it [the bat] will do?
> Kevin: I'm not sure if it [bat] will do anything because, well…I don't know which one [script] will be the bat.
> Ben: This one [script] is [for] the bat.
> Kevin: No, but like, on there [points to scripts]. Are they all for the bat?
> Ben: ….(overlapping) That one [script]. This is the dragon and this is the bat.
> Kevin: So I think the bat might not do anything. [Kevin does not associate scripts for the bat sprite]
> Kevin: Maybe.
> Ben: Yeah, maybe we point the dragon to the bat and the bat is going to … go away.
> Interviewer: … so what do you guys think the unicorn is going to do?
> Kevin: Point left and then, maybe just, might not do anything because it's already pointing left.
> Ben: Left is on the (??) and right is to the – right here. And this is right.
> Interviewer: So for the sprites, it's easier- this is one is for the (bat) right?
> Kevin: Oh! It's all for the bat. [Kevin recognizes all scripts refer to bat]
> Interviewer: Yes, so how do you see what the unicorn will do?
> Kevin: Oh, you have to click on the unicorn.
> Interviewer: So what do you think will happen when you click on the unicorn?
> Kevin: It will say hello.

In this example, the students initially overlooked that they could click through sprites in the sprite corral. Kevin did not use this feature as designers had intended, a false affordance. As the interview progressed however he realized that he could click through the different icons and change what scripts were visible.

5.   DISCUSSION

Students in our focus groups recognized that blocks and scripts were important tools in predicting what would happen in a visual block-based program. They read provided scripts to inform their predictions; and nearly always, they recognized that the scripts held information that would aid in figuring out what would happen in the program. However, students did not use scripts as the only tool or even as their first tool. Students attempted to use information on the stage (e.g., placement of sprites), to imagine what the characters could do based on sprite characteristics (e.g., a bat image flies horizontally), and visual

information related to blocks (e.g., whether it contained a dropdown menu). In some cases this information was effective and provided information that was usable. In other cases, the visual cues were distracting.

We analyzed how students read code in our block-based programming environment – LaPlaya – that had been adapted from Scratch for our particular student population and learning objectives. The taxonomy we created reflects the particular visual cues and affordances embedded in our interface. However, since LaPlaya was a variant of Scratch, the taxonomy may reflect tools in comparable Scratch-based environments. Many of the attributes implemented in LaPlaya (e.g., blocks, sprites, scripts, and stage) are available in other environments.

Though our specific findings are LaPlaya or Scratch specific, they offer two major contributions more generally to the computer science research community. First, reading code in visual block-based programming environments is complex. There are many components to a single program that could be analyzed (e.g. single blocks, single scripts, single scripts with multiple sprites, multiple scripts across multiple sprites, etc.). Young students like those in this study may be better able to discern, interpret, and read individual aspects of a visual blocked-based program but not all. Young students reading these programs may need explicit instruction about how the different attributes work independently and together alongside the development of their own programs.

Second, students use the visual nature of block-based programming environments in both intended and unintended ways. In many of these environments, users create code (e.g., scripts) alongside the output (e.g., stage) within a single interface. As designers and developers add features to the interface in the hopes of facilitating the creation of code (e.g., such as listing sprites by images) they are also creating sources of (mis)information for users. In some cases young students may overlook provided features (hidden affordances); in other cases, they act upon features that do not have actual use in the environment (false affordances). Curriculum developers and researchers should consider all visual cues and affordances – hidden, false, and perceptible – when analyzing how novices and young students read projects in these environments.

Our goal was to understand the information on the screen that a typical student might interpret as useful to understand the program. Here, our unit of analysis was the interface, not individual children. So while we described vignettes from individual focus groups to elaborate on our findings, the findings were not used to describe how well an individual or pair of students understood the LaPlaya programming environment. We sought to illuminate the complexities within a block-based programming environment for young students reading projects. To simplify the analysis, we also focused on a single project in LaPlaya that constrained the visual tools students could discuss during the interviews. Next steps in this area could focus on using a variety of projects that align with particular aspects of a taxonomy like the one described we created. As well, future work could focus on which visual cues are used most commonly used by different groups of students such as by age, background in programming, and gender.

6.   ACKNOWLEDGMENTS

This work was supported by the National Science Foundation CE21 Award CNS-1240985. We are grateful to the teachers and children who participated in this project.

7. REFERENCES

[1] Resnick, M., Maloney, J., Monroy-Hernandez, A., Rusk, N., Eastmond, E., Brennan, K., Millner, A., Rosenbaum, E., Silver, J., Silverman, B., Kafai, Y. (2009). Scratch: Programming for all. *Commun ACM*, 52, 11, 60-67.

[2] Hill, C., Dwyer, H. A., Martinez, T., Harlow, D., & Franklin, D. (2015). Floors and flexibility: Designing a programming environment for 4th – 6th grade classrooms. In *SIGCSE '15*. Kansas City, MO: ACM.

[3] Hopscotch Technologies. (2015). Hopscotch – Programming made easy! Make games, stories, animations and more! (Version 2.12) [Mobile application software]. Retrieved from https://www.gethopscotch.com

[4] Alvarado, C. (2014). CS Ed Week 2013: The hour of code. *ACM SIGCSE Bull*, *46*(1), 2-4.

[5] Franklin, D., Harlow, D., Dwyer, H., Henken, J., Hill, C., Iveland, A., Killian, A., & Development Staff. (2014). *Kids enjoying learning programming and computer science (KELP-CS)- Module 1 Digital Storytelling*. Available at https://discover.cs.ucsb.edu/kelpcs/educators.html

[6] Gaver, W. W. (1992). Technology affordances. In *CHI '91*. New York, NY: ACM.

[7] Petre, M. (1995). Why looking isn't always seeing: Readership skills and graphical programming. *Commun ACM*, *38*(6), 33-44.

[8] Pea, R., D. & Kurland, D., M. (1984). On the cognitive effects of learning computer programming. *New Ideas Psychol, 2* (2), pp. 137-168.

[9] Schulte, C. (2008). Block model – an eductional model of program comprehension as a tool for a scholarly approach to teaching. In *ICER '08*. Sydney, Australia: ACM.

[10] Brennan, K., & Resnick, K. (2012). *New frameworks for studying and assessing the development of computational thinking*. Presented at AERA '12. Vancouver, BC.

[11] Lewis, C. M. (2010). How programming environment shapes perception, learning and goals: Logo vs. Scratch. In *SIGCSE '10*. Milwaukee, WI: ACM.

[12] Gross, P., & Kelleher, C. (2009). Non-programmers identifying functionality in unfamiliar code: Strategies and Barriers. *J Visual Lang Comp, 21*(5), 263-276.

[13] Ferreira , J. J., de Souza, C. S., de Castro Salgado, L. C., Slaviero, C., Leitão , C. F., de F. Moreira, F. (2012). Combining cognitive, semiotic and discourse analysis to explore the power of notations in visual programming. In *VL/HCC '12*. Innsbruck, Austria: IEEE.

[14] Rader, C., Brand, C. & Lewis, C. (1997). Degrees of comprehension: Children's understanding visual programming environment. In *CHI '97*. Los Angeles, CA: ACM.

[15] Pea, R. D. (1986). Language-independent conceptual "bugs" in novice programming. *J Educ Comput Res, 2*(1), 25-36.

[16] Gibson, J. J. (1979). *The ecological approach to visual perception*. New York, NY: Houghton Mifflin.

[17] Norman, D. (2002). *The design of everyday things*. New York, NY: Basic Books.

[18] Garcia, D., Segars, L. & Paley, J. (2012). Snap! (build your own blocks): tutorial presentation. *J Comput Sci Coll 27*(4), pp. 120-121.

[19] Spradley (1979). *The ethnographic interview*. Forth Worth, TX: Hancourt Brace.

[20] Saldana, J. (2013). *The coding manual for qualiative researchers* (2nd ed.). Thousand Oaks, CA: SAGE Publications, Inc.

[21] Dedoose. (2014). Web application for managing, analyzing, and presenting qualitative and mixed method data (Version 5.0.11). Los Angeles, CA: SocioCultural Research Consultants, LLC. Retrieved from www.dedoose.com

Exploring Machine Learning Methods to Automatically Identify Students in Need of Assistance

Alireza Ahadi and Raymond Lister
University of Technology, Sydney
Australia
alireza.ahadi@uts.edu.au
raymond.lister@uts.edu.au

Heikki Haapala and Arto Vihavainen
Department of Computer Science
University of Helsinki
Finland
heikki.haapala@cs.helsinki.fi
arto.vihavainen@cs.helsinki.fi

ABSTRACT

Methods for automatically identifying students in need of assistance have been studied for decades. Initially, the work was based on somewhat static factors such as students' educational background and results from various questionnaires, while more recently, constantly accumulating data such as progress with course assignments and behavior in lectures has gained attention. We contribute to this work with results on early detection of students in need of assistance, and provide a starting point for using machine learning techniques on naturally accumulating programming process data.

When combining source code snapshot data that is recorded from students' programming process with machine learning methods, we are able to detect high- and low-performing students with high accuracy already after the very first week of an introductory programming course. Comparison of our results to the prominent methods for predicting students' performance using source code snapshot data is also provided.

This early information on students' performance is beneficial from multiple viewpoints. Instructors can target their guidance to struggling students early on, and provide more challenging assignments for high-performing students. Moreover, students that perform poorly in the introductory programming course, but who nevertheless pass, can be monitored more closely in their future studies.

Categories and Subject Descriptors

K.3.2 [**Computer and Information Science Education**]: Computer science education; H.2.8 [**Database Applications**]: Data mining

Keywords

introductory programming; source code snapshot analysis; programming behavior; educational data mining; learning analytics; novice programmers; detecting students in need of assistance

ICER '15 August 9 – 13, 2015, Omaha, Nebraska, USA
Copyright 2015 ACM 978-1-4503-3630-7/15/08 ...$15.00.
DOI: http://dx.doi.org/10.1145/2787622.2787717.

1. INTRODUCTION

Every year, tens of thousands of students fail introductory programming courses world-wide, and numerous students pass their courses with substandard knowledge. As a consequence, studies are retaken and postponed, careers are reconsidered, and substantial capital is invested into student counseling and support. World-wide, on average one third of students fail their introductory programming course [4, 40]. Even when looking at statistics describing pass rates after teaching interventions, as many as one quarter of the students still fail the courses [38].

One of the challenges in organizing teaching interventions is that any change is likely to also affect students for whom the prevalent situation is more suitable. For example, if a student is already at a stage where she could work on more challenging projects on her own, mandatory excessively structured learning activities that everyone needs to follow may even be counterproductive for her [16, 31]. To provide another example, while collaborative learning practices such as pair programming [45] have been highlighted as efficient teaching approaches for introductory programming [23, 38], there are contexts in which students mostly work from a distance and rarely attend an institution.

This diversity of institutions, students, and teaching approaches is the setting upon which our work builds. We believe that the appropriate next step in teaching interventions is the transition towards interventions that address only those students that are in need of guidance, and work towards that goal by analyzing methods for detecting such students as early as possible. More specifically, in this work, we explore methods for detecting high- and low-performing students in an introductory programming course already based on the performance during the very first week of the course. Variants of the topic have been investigated previously, for example, by Jadud, who proposed an approach to quantify students' ability to solve errors using source code snapshots [15], Ahadi et al., who measured students' knowledge using tests [1, 2], and Porter et al., who used in-class clicker data as a lens into students' performance [24, 25].

This work is organized as follows. First, in Section 2, we provide an overview of the evolution of the field of understanding factors that contribute to students' performance in introductory programming. Then, in Sections 3 and 4 we outline our research questions and data in more detail, as well as explain the methodology and outline the results. The results are discussed in Section 5, and finally, Section 6 concludes the work and outlines future research questions.

2. BACKGROUND

In the article *"What best predicts computer proficiency"* [9], Evans and Simkin describe early advances into understanding attributes that contribute to the ability of learning to program. This ability, *programming aptitude*, is often defined as the student's ability to succeed in an introductory programming course, and is measured through e.g. the course grade or a finer-grained measure such as within-course point accumulation. Before 1975, the research focused mainly on demographic factors such as educational background and scores from previous courses, while by the end of the 1970s, the focus moved slowly to evaluating static tests that measure programming aptitude. This was followed by research that started to investigate the effect of cognitive factors such as abstraction ability and the ability to follow more complex processes and algorithms [9]. Such research has continued to this day by introducing factors related to study behavior, learning styles and cognitive factors [42]. However, recently, dynamically accumulating data from students' learning process has gained researchers' attention [15, 25, 37, 41].

Overall, this stream of research has been motivated by multiple viewpoints, which include identification of students that have an aptitude for CS-related studies (e.g. [35]); studying and identifying measures of programming aptitude as well as combining them (e.g. [3, 5, 30, 43]); improvement of education and the comparison of teaching methodologies (e.g. [34, 36]); and identifying at-risk students and predicting course outcomes (e.g. [15, 41]).

Next, we outline some of this work in more depth. We begin by focusing on factors that do not change at all or change very slowly, and continue towards dynamic factors that change more rapidly and where new information may be constantly accumulated.

2.1 Gender

Studies in past often investigated gender as one of the factors that may explain programming aptitude – one of the reasons may be that the field of computing is at times seen as being dominated by males, and thus exhibits a male-oriented culture. However, the results show no clear trend. For example, in an analysis of introductory programming course grade and gender, Werth found no significant correlation ($r = 0.080$) [43]. In a similar study, Byrne and Lyons found that female participants in introductory programming course had a marginally higher point average than their male counterparts, but the difference was not statistically significant [6]. The role of gender was also investigated by Ventura, who studied the effect of gender by comparing students' programming assignment, exam, and overall course points, and found no effect that could be explained by gender [36].

Studies exist that suggest a referential connection between programming aptitude and gender. For example, in a small study ($n = 11$), Bergin and Reilly observed that female students had statistically significant and strong correlations ($r = 0.72 - 0.93$) between an Irish high-school leaving certificate test and programming course scores [5] – an effect that was not visible among male counterparts.

2.2 Academic Performance

The connection between students' academic performance and programming aptitude has been investigated in several studies. For example, Werth analyzed the connection between the amount of tertiary education mathematics courses and programming aptitude, but found no significant correlation ($r = -0.019; p > 0.1$). She suggested that a large amount of mathematics courses in tertiary education may actually be an indicator of improving a weak mathematics background [43]. Other studies have found connections between mathematics and introductory programming. For example, Stein studied the connection between Calculus and Discrete Mathematics and the grade from an introductory programming course. The correlations, overall, were weak (Calculus: $r = 0.244$; Discrete Math: $r = 0.162$) [34]. Watson, Li and Goldwin did a similar study, and, similarly, found no significant correlation between the Discrete Math and the introductory programming grade ($r = 0.06; p > 0.05$). However, there was a mediocre albeit not statistically significant effect between the Calculus course grade and programming course points ($r = 0.37; p = 0.06$) [42].

In addition to mathematics, factors such as language performance and overall grade averages have also been studied. For example, Leeper and Silver studied students' English language scores and the score of the verbal part of the SAT test. In their study, only the verbal SAT score had a mediocre correlation with the introductory programming course grade ($r = 0.3777$) [19]. Werth found no significant correlation between secondary education grade average and the grade achieved in an introductory programming course ($r = 0.074; p > 0.1$), but she did find a weak correlation between university-level grade average and the introductory programming course grade ($r = 0.252; p < 0.01$) [43]. Similarly, Watson et al. studied correlations between various secondary education courses and course averages, but found no statistically significant correlations [42].

2.3 Past Programming Experience

It is natural to assume that past programming experience influences programming course scores, and thus, the connection has been studied in a number of contexts, albeit with contradictory results. Hagan and Markham found that students with previous programming experience received considerably higher course marks than the students with no programming experience [10]. Wilson and Shrock utilized five variables related to programming and computer use, such as formal programming education, the use of internet, and the amount of time spent on gaming. The combination of these variables had a significant correlation with the midterm score in an introductory programming course ($r = 0.387; p < 0.01$) [7]. Similarly, in 2004, Wiedenbeck et al. reported on a study in which the number of ICT courses taken by students, the number of programming courses taken, the number of programming languages students had used, the number of programs students had written, and the length of those programs were combined into a single factor. The combination had a weak but significant correlation with the introductory programming score ($r = 0.25; p < 0.05$) [44].

While multiple studies indicate a positive correlation between past programming experience and introductory programming course outcomes, somewhat contradictory results also exist. For example, Bergin and Reilly found that students with no previous programming experience had a marginally higher mean overall score in an introductory programming course, and found no statistically significant difference between students with and without previous programming experience [5]. In another study, Watson et al. found that while students with past programming experience had significantly higher overall course points than those with no previous programming experience [42], programming experience in years had a weak but statistically insignificant negative correlation with the course points ($r = -0.20$) [42].

2.4 Behavior in Lectures and Labs

Rodrigo et al. studied students' observed behavior in programming labs [26]. They studied students' gestures, outbursts, and other factors including collaboration with other students, and sought to identify factors that are potentially related to students' success. In addition, they collected source code snapshots from students' programming process. Six statistically significant factors ($p < 0.05$) that had a mediocre correlation with an introductory programming course midterm score were identified. Four of them were related to students' behaviors; confusion ($r = -0.432$), boredom ($r = -0.389$), focus ($r = 0.346$), and discussion about the programming environment (-0.316), while two were related to snapshots. The number of consecutive snapshots with errors ($r = -0.326$) and compilation events in which the student had worked on the same area in the source code ($r = -0.336$) were both negatively correlated with the midterm score [26].

Another angle at studying students behavior was recently proposed by Porter et al. [25], who studied students' responses to clicker questions in a peer instruction setting. In their study, they identified that the percentage of correct clicker answers from the first three weeks of a course was strongly correlated with overall course performance ($r = 0.61; p < 0.05$).

2.5 Source Code Snapshots

In "*Methods and Tools for Exploring Novice Compiling Behaviour*" [15], Jadud presents a method to quantify a student's tendency to create and fix errors, which he called the *error quotient*. In his study, the correlation between the error quotient and the average score from programming assignments was mediocre and statistically significant ($r = 0.36; p = 0.012$), while the correlation between the error quotient and the grade from a course exam was high ($r = 0.52; p = 0.0002$) [15]. Rodrigo et al. used an alternative version of Jadud's error quotient, and found that in their context the correlation between the error quotient and the midterm score of an introductory programming course was strong and statistically significant ($r = -0.54; p < 0.001$) [27]. In essence, this suggests that the less programming errors a student makes, and the better she solves them, the higher her midterm grade will tend to be [27].

Watson et al. also conducted a study using Jadud's error quotient, and found a significant correlation between the error quotient and their programming course scores ($r = 0.44$) [41]. They proposed that the amount of time that students spend on programming assignments should be taken into account, and that one should consider the files that a student is editing as a part of the error quotient calculation [41]. They proposed an improvement to the error quotient called *Watwin*, and found that with this improvement the correlation increased from ($r = 0.44$) to ($r = 0.51$) [41]. They also noted that a simple measure, the average amount of time that a student spends on a programming error, is strongly correlated with programming course scores ($r = -0.53; p < 0.01$).

Source code snapshots have been used to elicit information in finer detail as well. For example, Piech et al. [22] studied students' approaches to solving two programming tasks, and found that students' solution patterns are indicative of course midterm scores. Programming patterns were also studied by Hosseini et al., who identified students' behaviors within a programming course – some students were more inclined to build their code step by step, while others started from larger quantities of code, and reduced their code in order to reach a solution [14]. Another approach recently proposed by Yudelson et al. was to use fine-grained concepts extracted from source code snapshots, and to model students' understanding of these concepts as they proceed [46].

Next, we explore some of these methods for source code snapshot analysis, as well as provide researchers with an outline for performing such studies.

3. RESEARCH DESIGN

This study is driven by the question of identifying high- and low-performing students as early as possible in a programming course to provide better support for them. By high- and low-performing students, we mean students in the upper- and lower-half of course scores, and by early, we mean after the very first week of the programming course. This means that instructors could plan and provide additional guidance to specifically selected students already during the second week of the course.

For the task, we explore previously proposed methods for predicting students' performance from source code snapshots, and evaluate a number of machine learning techniques that have previously received little attention for the task at hand.

3.1 Research Questions

Our research questions for this study are as follows.

RQ1 Given our dataset, how do the methods proposed by Jadud and Watson et al. perform for detecting high- and low-performing students?

RQ2 Given our dataset, how do standard machine learning techniques perform for detecting high- and low-performing students?

To answer the first question, we have implemented the algorithms described in [15, 41], and evaluate their performance on our data. For the second question, we first identify relevant features from a single semester, then evaluate different machine learning techniques to build a predictive model using the extracted features to determine a top-performing approach. Finally, the top-performing predictive model is evaluated on a dataset from a separate semester to determine cross-semester performance of the selected model.

3.2 Data

The data for the study comes from two semesters of an introductory programming course organized at the University of Helsinki. The course lasts six weeks, is taught in Java, and uses a blended online textbook that covers variables, basic I/O, methods, conditionals, loops, lists, arrays, elementary search algorithms and elementary objects. In the programming course, the main focus is on working on practical programming assignments, accompanied by a weekly two-hour lecture that covers the basics needed to get started with the work. Support is available in open computer labs, where teaching assistants and course instructors are available some 20-30 hours each week (see [18] for details).

Although no socio-economic factors were available for this study, the studied population is relatively homogenic, and the educational system in the context is socially inclusive, meaning that there is both a minimal underrepresentation of students from low education background and a minimal overrepresentation of students from high education background [21]. There are also no tuition fees, and students receive student benefits such as direct funding from the state, assuming that they progress in their degree work.

For the purposes of this study, students' programming process was recorded using Test My Code [39] that is used for automatically assessing students' work in the course. For each student that consented to having their programming process recorded, every key-press and related information such as time and assignment details was stored. The students used the same programming environment both from home and at the university. Students were asked to provide information on whether they had prior programming experience, and access to information on students' age, gender, grade average, and major was given for the researchers for the purposes of this study. In the studied context, major is selected before enrollment, and in both semesters, over 50% of the students had other subjects than computer science as their major – for students with CS as a major, the studied course is the first course that they take.

In the first semester (spring), a total of 86 students participated in the study, and in the second semester (fall), a total of 210 students participated in the study. Full fine-grained key-log data is available only for the first semester, while for the second semester, only higher level actions such as saves, compilation events, run events and test events are available.

While attendance in the course activities is not mandatory, 50% of total course points comes from completing programming assignments. The rest of the course points comes from a written exam, where students answer both essay-type questions as well as programming questions. To pass the course, the students have to receive at least half of the points from the exam as well as half of the points from the programming assignments, while the highest grade in the course can be received by gathering over 90% of the course points.

4. METHODOLOGY AND RESULTS

The students were divided into groups based on their performance in (1) an algorithmic programming question given in the exam, (2) the overall course, and (3) a combination of the two. The first division into groups is motivated by students' struggling with writing programs even at a later phase of their studies [20], and has also been the focus in related studies, such as the work by Porter et al. [25]. The algorithmic programming question is a variant of the Rainfall Problem [32], where students have to create a program that reads numbers, possibly filters them, and prints attributes such as the average of the accepted numbers. The second division into groups outlines the students' overall performance, and the third division combines the previous. Table 1 shows student counts in these groups for the dataset that is used to evaluate the algorithms in RQ1, and to train the predictive model for RQ2.

4.1 Research Question 1

To answer the first research question, *"Given our dataset, how do the methods proposed by Jadud and Watson et al. perform for detecting high- and low-performing students?"*, we implemented these algorithm's as they were described [15, 41]. Both algorithms use a set of successive compilation event

Table 1: Student counts for the studied population, binned based on the predicted variable.

Target class	Median or Above	Below Median
Exam Question	47	39
Final Grade	48	38
Combined	43	43

pairings to quantify the students' ability to fix syntactic errors in the programs that they are writing. The main difference between Jadud's error quotient and the Watwin-algorithm is that the Watwin-algorithm also considers the possibility that students may be working on multiple files, where one file has errors, and the other does not. Thus, changing from one file to the other is not seen as if the user fixed the errors. Moreover, the Watwin algorithm also takes into account the amount of time that students spend on fixing errors.

Unlike the data used by Jadud and Watson et al., the data recorded from standard programming environments do not have explicit compilation events as the environments continuously compile the code and highlight errors to developers. To approximate these explicit compilation events for Jadud EQ and Watwin algorithm, two options were evaluated: (1) use only snapshots where students perform an action that does not involve changing the code, i.e. run their code, test their code, or submit the code to the assessment server (i.e. *action* in Table 2), and (2) use only snapshot pairs between which the students have taken at least a ten second pause from programming (*pause* in Table 2). The value for the pause was determined by evaluating the algorithms with 60, 30, 10 and 5 second pauses, after which the value which resulted in the best average performance was selected. Our rationale for the use of actions is that in such cases, the students want explicit feedback from the system, while the rationale for pauses is that the students have stopped to, for example, debug their program. Option (2) is only available for the first semester, as fine-grained key-log data is not available for the second studied semester.

Pearson correlation coefficients between the predicted variables (Table 1) and Jadud's error quotient and Watwin-score are given in Table 2. The correlations are given as absolute values, and are all low ($r < 0.3$).

Table 2: Pearson Correlation coefficients for between the Jadud's error quotient, the Watwin-score, and the predicted variables.

Variable	Semester	Jadud action	pause	Watwin action	pause
Exam Quest.	First	.15	.21	.25	.18
	Second	.20	-	.09	-
Final Grade	First	.03	.08	.01	.13
	Second	.10	-	.005	-
Combined	First	.02	.08	.01	.13
	Second	.12	-	.01	-

4.2 Research Question 2

To answer the second research question, *"Given our dataset, how do standard machine learning techniques perform for detecting high- and low-performing students?"*, the problem was approached as a supervised learning task, where existing data is used to infer a function that can be used to categorize incoming data into groups [13].

First, features were extracted from the dataset. Then, to avoid the use of irrelevant or redundant features, feature selection was used to identify relevant features. Once a relevant subset of features had been selected, we evaluated a number of classifiers. Finally, when a classifier had been selected from the evaluated classifiers, we tested the model against a data set from a separate semester. Feature selection and classifier evaluation was performed using the WEKA Data Mining toolkit [11].

Feature Extraction

For the study, we extracted two types of attributes: (a) Attributes based on previously studied success factors, such as previous academic performance (tertiary education) and past programming experience; (b) programming assignment specific Source-code snapshot attributes that potentially reflect students' persistence and success with the course assignments. For each assignment, the number of steps that a student took, measured in key-presses and other actions, as well as the maximum achieved correctness when measured by automated tests was extracted. The Source-code snapshot attributes were programmatically extracted from the programming process data, which is recorded by Test My Code as students are working on the assignments. An overview of the used attributes is given in the Table 3. The datasets were also normalized.

Table 3: Features extracted for the study

Features	Type
Gender	Categorical
Major	Categorical
Grade Average	Numerical
Age	Numerical
Programming experience	Binary
Maximum obtained correctness for each programming assignment	Numerical $[0 - 1]$
Amount of steps taken in each of the programming assignment	Numerical $[0-\infty]$

Feature Selection

After the feature extraction phase, there was a total of 53 features. To reduce the amount of overlapping features, possible over fitting, and to potentially improve predictive accuracy of the feature set, feature selection was performed. We used correlation-based feature subset selection [12], where individual predictive ability of each feature along with the degree of redundancy between them was evaluated using three methods; (1) genetic search, (2) best first method and (3) greedy stepwise method. Results of the feature selection phase are given in Table 4.

After this phase, the information gain of each feature was measured to reveal features that had little or no predictive value. Information gain, or Kullback-Leibler divergence [17], is used to measure the amount of information that the feature brings about a predicted value, assuming that they are the only two existing variables, and is measured by the difference of two probability distributions (in our case, e.g., the difference of the probability distributions of the exam question results and grade average). After measuring information gain for each of the features and predicted value, the low-contributing features were removed. The features above the line in Table 5 were retained in the training set.

Table 5: Information gain of the features. Features below the line were excluded from further use.

Feature	Exam question	Grade	Both
Grade Average	0.34	0.36	0.44
Correctness of a20	0.40	0.40	0.38
Steps for a23	0.44	0.32	0.29
Steps for a21	0.23	0.20	0.20
Steps for a22	0.22	0.16	0.19
Major	0.17	0.11	0.13
Steps for a17	0.27	0.15	0.12
Steps for a20	0.26	0.15	0.12
Steps for a18	0.14	0.15	0.12
Steps for a19	0.23	0.13	0.11
Age	0.11	-	0.11
Prog. Exp	-	0.05	0.07
Gender	0.01	0.008	0.003

Classifier Evaluation

As is typical for studies that explore machine learning methodologies, a number of classifiers were evaluated. In our case, we evaluated three families of classifiers; Bayesian classifiers, Rule-learners, and Decision tree -based classifiers, and chose a total of nine classifiers from these three families. All of these approaches are commonly used for classifying students [28, 29]. The evaluation was performed using two separate validation options: k-fold cross validation (with k=10), and percentage split (2/3 of the dataset used for training and 1/3 for testing). This means that during the classifier training and evaluation phase, parts of the data was hidden during the training, and was then used for the evaluation. Table 6 presents the results for the classification algorithms that were investigated in this study.

As can be seen in Table 6, the overall accuracy of decision trees is higher than that of the other two classifier families. Among decision trees, Random Forest has on average the highest accuracy for all predictive variables with 86%, 90% and 90% accuracy for predicting Exam question, Final Grade and the combination of both. To show the predictive accuracy in more detail, Table 7 shows the confusion matrix of the Random Forest classifier when predicting the combination of the Exam Question and Final grade, when using 10-fold cross-validation on the training data set.

Table 7: Confusion matrix of Random Forest on predicting whether students are equal-to-or-above or below the median score on the combination of exam question and final grade

	Predicted above	Predicted below
Actual above	38	5
Actual below	3	40

Thus, we selected the Random Forest as the classifier that is used to evaluate students' performance. More detailed evaluation of the performance of the Random Forest classifier is given in Table 8. The F1-Measure, which represents the balanced precision-recall, shows that Random Forest provides a strong result in this prediction task. Moreover, the Receiver operating characteristic value (*ROC*) suggests that the classifier still performs well when the classification threshold is changed from the median, i.e. if we would rather

Table 4: Features selected during feature selection. The left-hand side describes the feature selection method, and the columns describe the features selected for the different predictive variables. *Steps* **denotes the number of recorded events for a student on a specific programming assignment.** *Correctness* **denotes the percentage of tests passed by a student on a specific programming assignment.**

Method	Exam question	Final Grade	Both
Best First	Age; Grade Average; Steps for a17, a21, and a23	Grade Average; Steps for a21 and a23; Correctness for a23	Grade Average; Steps for a21 and a23; Correctness for a20
Genetic Search	Age; Grade Average; Steps for e17, e19, e20, e21, and e23; Correctness for e2, e6, e11, and e12	Grade Average; Steps for e20, e21, and e23; Correctness for e23	Grade Average; Steps for e21, and e23; Correctness for e20
Greedy Stepwise	Age; Grade Average; Steps for e17, e21, and e23	Grade Average; Steps for e21 and e23; Correctness for e23	Grade Average; Steps for e21 and e23; Correctness for e20

Table 6: Classifier accuracy when performing evaluation of the classifiers on the training set from a single semester. The highest accuracies are marked with bold. Exam question is shown as Q in the Table.

Classifier	Family	10-fold cross-validation accuracy			percentage split accuracy		
		Q	Final grade	Q + Final grade	Q	Final grade	Q + Final grade
Naive Bayes	Bayesian	80%	80%	77%	86%	86%	86%
Bayesian Network	Bayesian	81%	77%	76%	82%	76%	72%
Decision Table	Rule Learner	78%	73%	84%	86%	76%	90%
Conjective Rule	Rule Learner	73%	80%	83%	72%	86%	90%
PART	Rule Learner	85%	79%	**93%**	90%	76%	82%
ADTree	Decision Tree	80%	85%	86%	90%	83%	83%
J48	Decision Tree	83%	82%	**93%**	**93%**	89%	83%
Random Forest	Decision Tree	**86%**	**90%**	90%	90%	**90%**	**93%**
Decision Stump	Decision Tree	73%	76%	84%	83%	**90%**	90%

seek to identify the lowest performing quartile of students, and the Matthews correlation coefficient (MCC) shows a high correlation ($r = 0.71 - 0.81$) between the classifier and the predicted values.

Evaluation on a Separate Semester

As the data that is produced within educational settings varies between semesters, due to variations in student cohorts and course changes, the generalizability of the model needs to be evaluated using data from a separate semester. Accordingly, we evaluated the Random Forest -classifier (i.e. our best performing classifier from above) on data from a separate semester with $n = 210$ students. We found that the Random Forest -classifier was able to categorize students on the Exam Question, the Final Grade, and the combination of both with the accuracy of 80%, 73%, and 71% respectively, when the training of the model was performed on the data from the first semester with $n = 86$ students.

5. DISCUSSION

5.1 Research Question 1

To answer research question one, "Given our dataset, how do the methods proposed by Jadud and Watson et al. perform for detecting high- and low-performing students?", the performance of the approaches differs from the studies in which the algorithms have traditionally been evaluated. Next, we discuss factors which may explain this result.

First, we use data from a considerably shorter period than Jadud and Watson et al. use in their studies. The first results in the article by Watson et al. [41] are given after three weeks into the course, and at that time, the correlation coefficients are near 0.3 for both Watwin-score

and Jadud's error quotient – marginally better than our results. Moreover, in Watson et al.'s work, the analysis is performed against overall coursework mark, that is, the overall score from programming assignments [41], and not against the performance in a written exam.

Second, the programming environment used in the studies by Jadud and Watson et al. expects the student to take an extra step for her to receive information on whether her code compiles or not, while such a step is not necessary in current programming environments. It is possible that such a feature stimulates specific working behavior, which in turn may have contributed to previously observed outcomes.

A third factor is related to the quantity and type of the programming assignments. In the context of our study, the students work on a relatively large number of programming assignments during the very first week. Many of the assignments are relatively straightforward, and have been designed to help students gain confidence. This means that it is possible that the predictive approaches that are based on students' programming errors may also be dependent on the programming assignments being non-trivial for the students, which is not always the case in the studied context. These details from the contexts of Jadud and Watwin are not at our disposal.

Finally, the fourth factor is the guidance that students receive during the course. For example, in the context of Watson et al. [41], the students have specific and limited lab hours during which they can receive support on the programming assignments, while in the context that we studied, the labs are open most of the time, and anyone can attend. It is also possible that the type of guidance provided in labs differs.

Table 8: Statistical measures for the Random Forest -classifier when predicting the considered target variables. TPR stands for True Positive Rate, FPR stands for False Positive Rate, ROC stands for Receiver Operating Characteristic, and MCC stands for Matthews Correlation Coefficient.

Class	TPR	FPR	Precision	Recall	F1-Measure	ROC	MCC
Exam question	0.86	0.14	0.86	0.86	0.86	0.92	0.71
Final grade	0.89	0.10	0.89	0.89	0.89	0.92	0.78
Exam question & Final grade	0.90	0.09	0.90	0.90	0.90	0.95	0.81

5.2 Research Question 2

To answer research question two, "Given our dataset, how do standard machine learning techniques perform for detecting high- and low-performing students?", we both described the workflow of creating and evaluating machine learning algorithms as well as outlined the results. The process starts with feature extraction, continues with feature selection that is followed by classifier evaluation, and finally concludes with evaluation with a separate data set – in our study, from a separate semester. While the performance of the classifier was high when evaluating the approach within a single semester, ranging from 86% to 90% accuracy with 10-fold cross-validation, the performance was lower (ranging from 71% to 80%) when the predictive model was evaluated on data from a separate semester.

When extracting and selecting the most important features, it was observed that most *a priori* features such as past programming experience, age, and gender made relatively little contribution to the predicted values. This is in line with previous research, which was discussed in Section 2. The information provided by *a priori* features was lower than that of the performance in the actual programming assignments. The most important features were students' grade average, the maximum percentage of automated tests that a student's solution to a specific programming assignment reached, number of steps that students took in a number of programming assignments, and the students' major. Note that for the students who have CS as their major, no grade average was available as the programming course was the very first course that they took – tree-based models handle this well.

5.3 Analysis of Programming Assignments

The feature selection process selected a number of programming assignments as important for the predictive process. All of the programming assignments were from the later part of the week – assignments 17 to 23 were selected, out of a total of 24 assignments in the first week. In all of these programming assignments from the first week, students were given a class that had an empty main-method. In the assignments leading to assignment 17, students had practiced producing different kinds of outputs, the use of variables such as `int` and `String`, reading input from the keyboard, simple comparisons with `if` and `if-else` structures, and combinations of these. Instructions for assignments 17 to 23 are given in Table 9. In addition to what is shown in the table, students had one or two examples of the program output. Also, assignment 23 had an API description of the visualization library.

As with assignments 1-16, assignments 17 and onwards introduce new concepts step-by-step. For example, in assignment 17, the students practice the use of an `else if` structure for the first time, and in assignment 18, the stu-

Table 9: Programming assignments that were highlighted during the feature selection process. Examples of input/output were also given to students.

#	assignment instructions
17	Write a program that reads in two numbers from the user, and prints the larger of them. If the numbers are equal, the program should output "they are equal."
18	Write a program that reads in a number between 0 and 60, and transforms it to a grade using the following rules: 0-35 should be F, 36-40 D, 41-45 C, 46-50 B, and 51-60 A.
19	Write a program that reads in a number and checks that it is a valid age [0-120]. If the number is within the range, the program should output "OK!", otherwise the program should output "Impossible!".
20	Write a program that reads an username and a password, and compares them to user credentials that are given with the assignment. The program should print "correct", if the credentials are correct, otherwise, "false".
21	Write a program that reads in a number, and determines whether it is a leap year or not.
22	Write a program that continuously asks for a password until the user types in the right password.
23	Write a program that continuously reads in numbers, if the numbers are between [-30, 40], they are to be added to a plot (a ready library given). The program execution should never end.

dents are expected to use multiple `else if` statements. In assignment 19, the students are practicing the same concepts as in assignment 18, but with a different task and a smaller number of cases that need to be taken into account. Assignment 20 is the first assignment in which the students compare String variables. Assignments 21 is more algorithmic in nature than earlier assignments. Finally, assignments 22 and 23 are programs that require the student to use a loop for the first time. These are concepts that are known not to be easy in other contexts as well (see e.g. [8]).

It is somewhat surprising that assignment 20 was the only assignment for which the student's maximum achieved correctness, i.e. the percentage of tests passed, was highlighted as an important feature. Upon further analysis, as the students were accustomed to comparing numbers, many had initially challenges with comparing strings and the use of the `equals` method, which was needed in the assignment. Most of the students eventually did tackle this, and some of those that did not seemed to be confused with comparing multiple strings at the same time; even if not completing the assignment, students eventually moved forward. At the same time, a persistent student could work through the assignments with the support from the programming environment and course staff, given that she would not start too late, which likely also explains parts of the correctness not being important. From the viewpoint of a material designer, the first finding could imply that it might be beneficial to consider an assignment with simpler string comparisons at first, e.g. by comparing just a single string, instead of the first assignment being one where two strings are compared at the same time. However, this was no longer an issue in assignment 22, where the students combined the same behavior with a loop construct.

Overall, when considering the number of steps that the students took to reach a solution, the students in the high-performing group took more steps on average than the students in the low-performing group. While initially one would assume that this would be explained simply by the low-performing students not attempting the assignments, this was not the case. It simply seems that the students in the high-performing group, when generalized, tried out more than a single approach and were not always content with simply reaching a working solution. Such behavior was also encouraged by the course staff.

5.4 Misclassified Students

We also performed an analysis of the students who were misclassified, i.e. students who were classified into another category than that to which they belonged. When considering the students who were classified as high-performing but belonged to the low-performing group, a number of them had adopted a work behavior where they diligently worked through the assignments by battling their way through the automatic tests. This is likely due to a result that has been previously pointed out by Spacco, i.e., if students are given full test results, they may adopt the habit of *"programming by 'Brownian motion', where students make a series of small, seemingly random changes to the code in the hopes of making their program pass the next test case"* [33] – currently, the programming environment used does not provide ways to battle this behavior.

Similarly, when considering the students who were classified as low-performing, but were high-performing, some of them used copy-paste in a quantity that had the classifier consider them as students who did not explore the solutions at length. Note that this does not mean that these students were plagiarizing their solutions from others, but seemed to extensively utilize their solutions from previous assignments.

5.5 Practical Implications

Our work implies that one can differentiate between the high- and low-performing students in a programming class already based on the performance of a single week with a relatively high accuracy. This means that instructors may, potentially, provide targeted interventions already during the second week. Practices such as additional rehearsals could be introduced for low-performing students, while high-performing students may benefit from additional challenges.

The results also indicate that students' programming behavior during the class is more important than background variables such as age, gender, or past programming experience, which is in line with previous studies. Moreover, in the studied context, the correctness of the students' solutions was not as important as the effort. That is, students who simply pushed towards a solution did not benefit from the programming tasks as much as the students who did additional experiments. It is plausible that such information on students' behavior can also be used to guide students towards more productive learning strategies.

5.6 Limitations of work

Predictive models are generalizations over a dataset gathered during a single or a number of semesters, and should always be validated using an additional dataset. As is evident in our case, the new dataset, when gathered within the same context but during a different semester, had different results than those from the initial evaluation. At the same time, the comparison was strict as we compared the performance of a model built on data from a spring semester against data from a fall semester. This effectively demonstrates that if the teaching approach, materials, or other related variables change, the performance of the predictive model may also change. That is, the predictive model is tuned to a specific context and dataset, and thus, it should be adjusted if the context changes.

Naturally, while the machine learning approach described in this article generalizes to other contexts, one should not assume that the same features would be the best features in other contexts as well. That is, the process should be started from the first step, i.e. extracting features, and followed as described in this article. That is, the predictive model that works on our data set would likely be different from a predictive model from other data sets – how different is a question that is left for future work. This is likely similar for all related studies.

6. CONCLUSIONS AND FUTURE WORK

In this work, we explored methods for early identification of students to guide from naturally accumulating programming process data. Such information can be useful for instructors and course designers, and can be used to create targeted interventions and to adjust materials accordingly. For example, the students who are performing well in the course may benefit from additional, more challenging tasks, while the students who are performing poorly are likely to benefit from rehearsal tasks as well as other activities that are typically used to help at-risk students.

The three main contributions of this article are as follows: (1) Analysis of the performance of existing source code snapshot-based methods for identifying high- and low-performing students in a new context; (2) Exploration of machine learning techniques for identifying high- and low-performing students; and (3) Analysis of cross-semester performance of the predictive models.

When analyzing the performance of the methods proposed by Jadud and Watson et al., we observed that the approaches had relatively poor performance on the data at our disposal. When exploring the performance of the machine learning techniques, the within-dataset performance was higher than that of the cross-semester performance, which was measured based on the predictive performance during a separate semester. This is explainable by the natural variance between semesters and student populations. Even so, with the cross-semester accuracy that ranges between 70% and 80%, reaching many of the right students is possible.

As a part of our future work, we are tuning the predictive models using additional data, seeking to further understand the students' behavior by delving deeper into their programming process, and conducting interviews that hopefully will shed further light on students' working practices as well as to those students who were misclassified. We are also performing targeted interventions within the studied context.

7. REFERENCES

[1] A. Ahadi and R. Lister. Geek genes, prior knowledge, stumbling points and learning edge momentum: Parts of the one elephant? In *Proceedings of the Ninth Annual International ACM Conference on International Computing Education Research*, ICER '13, pages 123–128, New York, NY, USA, 2013. ACM.

[2] A. Ahadi, R. Lister, and D. Teague. Falling behind early and staying behind when learning to program. In *Proceedings of the 25th Psychology of Programming Conference*, PPIG '14, 2014.

[3] J. Bennedsen and M. E. Caspersen. Abstraction ability as an indicator of success for learning object-oriented programming? *ACM SIGCSE Bulletin*, 38(2):39–43, 2006.

[4] J. Bennedsen and M. E. Caspersen. Failure rates in introductory programming. *ACM SIGCSE Bulletin*, 39(2):32–36, 2007.

[5] S. Bergin and R. Reilly. Programming: factors that influence success. *ACM SIGCSE Bulletin*, 37(1):411–415, 2005.

[6] P. Byrne and G. Lyons. The effect of student attributes on success in programming. In *ACM SIGCSE Bulletin*, volume 33, pages 49–52. ACM, 2001.

[7] B. Cantwell Wilson and S. Shrock. Contributing to success in an introductory computer science course: a study of twelve factors. In *ACM SIGCSE Bulletin*, volume 33, pages 184–188. ACM, 2001.

[8] Y. Cherenkova, D. Zingaro, and A. Petersen. Identifying challenging CS1 concepts in a large problem dataset. In *Proceedings of the 45th ACM Technical Symposium on Computer Science Education*, SIGCSE '14, pages 695–700, New York, NY, USA, 2014. ACM.

[9] G. E. Evans and M. G. Simkin. What best predicts computer proficiency? *Communications of the ACM*, 32(11):1322–1327, 1989.

[10] D. Hagan and S. Markham. Does it help to have some programming experience before beginning a computing degree program? *ACM SIGCSE Bulletin*, 32(3):25–28, 2000.

[11] M. Hall, E. Frank, G. Holmes, B. Pfahringer, P. Reutemann, and I. H. Witten. The WEKA data mining software: an update. *ACM SIGKDD explorations newsletter*, 11(1):10–18, 2009.

[12] M. A. Hall. *Correlation-based feature selection for machine learning*. PhD thesis, The University of Waikato, 1999.

[13] T. Hastie, R. Tibshirani, J. Friedman, T. Hastie, J. Friedman, and R. Tibshirani. *The elements of statistical learning*, volume 2. Springer, 2009.

[14] R. Hosseini, A. Vihavainen, and P. Brusilovsky. Exploring problem solving paths in a Java programming course. In *Proceedings of the 25th Workshop of the Psychology of Programming Interest Group*, 2014.

[15] M. C. Jadud. Methods and tools for exploring novice compilation behaviour. In *Proceedings of the second international workshop on Computing education research*, pages 73–84. ACM, 2006.

[16] H. Jang, J. Reeve, and E. L. Deci. Engaging students in learning activities: It is not autonomy support or structure but autonomy support and structure. *Journal of Educational Psychology*, 102(3):588, 2010.

[17] S. Kullback and R. A. Leibler. On information and sufficiency. *Ann. Math. Statist.*, 22(1):79–86, 03 1951.

[18] J. Kurhila and A. Vihavainen. Management, structures and tools to scale up personal advising in large programming courses. In *Proceedings of the 2011 Conference on Information Technology Education*, SIGITE '11, pages 3–8, New York, NY, USA, 2011. ACM.

[19] R. Leeper and J. Silver. Predicting success in a first programming course. In *ACM SIGCSE Bulletin*, volume 14, pages 147–150. ACM, 1982.

[20] M. McCracken, V. Almstrum, D. Diaz, M. Guzdial, D. Hagan, Y. B.-D. Kolikant, C. Laxer, L. Thomas, I. Utting, and T. Wilusz. A multi-national, multi-institutional study of assessment of programming skills of first-year CS students. *SIGCSE Bull.*, 33(4):125–180, Dec. 2001.

[21] D. Orr, C. Gwosć, and N. Netz. *Social and economic conditions of student life in Europe: synopsis of indicators; final report; Eurostudent IV 2008-2011*. W. Bertelsmann Verlag, 2011.

[22] C. Piech, M. Sahami, D. Koller, S. Cooper, and P. Blikstein. Modeling how students learn to program. In *Proceedings of the 43rd ACM Technical Symposium on Computer Science Education*, SIGCSE '12, pages 153–160, New York, NY, USA, 2012. ACM.

[23] L. Porter, M. Guzdial, C. McDowell, and B. Simon. Success in introductory programming: What works? *Communications of the ACM*, 56(8):34–36, 2013.

[24] L. Porter and D. Zingaro. Importance of early performance in CS1: Two conflicting assessment stories. In *Proceedings of the 45th ACM Technical Symposium on Computer Science Education*, SIGCSE '14, pages 295–300, New York, NY, USA, 2014. ACM.

[25] L. Porter, D. Zingaro, and R. Lister. Predicting student success using fine grain clicker data. In *Proceedings of the tenth annual conference on International computing education research*, pages 51–58. ACM, 2014.

[26] M. M. T. Rodrigo, R. S. Baker, M. C. Jadud, A. C. M. Amarra, T. Dy, M. B. V. Espejo-Lahoz, S. A. L. Lim, S. A. Pascua, J. O. Sugay, and E. S. Tabanao. Affective and behavioral predictors of novice programmer achievement. *ACM SIGCSE Bulletin*, 41(3):156–160, 2009.

[27] M. M. T. Rodrigo, E. Tabanao, M. B. E. Lahoz, and M. C. Jadud. Analyzing online protocols to characterize novice Java programmers. *Philippine Journal of Science*, 138(2):177–190, 2009.

[28] C. Romero and S. Ventura. Educational data mining: a review of the state of the art. *Systems, Man, and Cybernetics, Part C: Applications and Reviews, IEEE Transactions on*, 40(6):601–618, 2010.

[29] C. Romero, S. Ventura, P. G. Espejo, and C. Hervás. Data mining algorithms to classify students. *Educational Data Mining 2008*.

[30] N. Rountree, J. Rountree, A. Robins, and R. Hannah. Interacting factors that predict success and failure in a CS1 course. In *ACM SIGCSE Bulletin*, volume 36, pages 101–104. ACM, 2004.

[31] E. Sierens, M. Vansteenkiste, L. Goossens, B. Soenens, and F. Dochy. The synergistic relationship of perceived autonomy support and structure in the prediction of self-regulated learning. *British Journal of Educational Psychology*, 79(1):57–68, 2009.

[32] E. Soloway. Learning to program = learning to construct mechanisms and explanations. *Commun. ACM*, 29(9):850–858, Sept. 1986.

[33] J. Spacco. *Marmoset: a programming project assignment framework to improve the feedback cycle for students, faculty and researchers*. PhD thesis, 2006.

[34] M. V. Stein. Mathematical preparation as a basis for success in CS-II. *Journal of Computing Sciences in Colleges*, 17(4):28–38, 2002.

[35] M. Tukiainen and E. Mönkkönen. Programming aptitude testing as a prediction of learning to program. In *Proc. 14th Workshop of the Psychology of Programming Interest Group*, pages 45–57, 2002.

[36] P. R. Ventura Jr. Identifying predictors of success for an objects-first CS1. 2005.

[37] A. Vihavainen. Predicting students' performance in an introductory programming course using data from students' own programming process. In *Advanced Learning Technologies (ICALT), 2013 IEEE 13th International Conference on*. IEEE, 2013.

[38] A. Vihavainen, J. Airaksinen, and C. Watson. A systematic review of approaches for teaching introductory programming and their influence on success. In *Proceedings of the Tenth Annual Conference on International Computing Education Research*, ICER '14, pages 19–26, New York, NY, USA, 2014. ACM.

[39] A. Vihavainen, T. Vikberg, M. Luukkainen, and M. Pärtel. Scaffolding students' learning using Test My Code. In *Proceedings of the 18th ACM conference on Innovation and technology in computer science education*, pages 117–122. ACM, 2013.

[40] C. Watson and F. W. Li. Failure rates in introductory programming revisited. In *Proceedings of the 2014 conference on Innovation & technology in computer science education*, pages 39–44. ACM, 2014.

[41] C. Watson, F. W. Li, and J. L. Godwin. Predicting performance in an introductory programming course by logging and analyzing student programming behavior. In *Advanced Learning Technologies (ICALT), 2013 IEEE 13th International Conference on*, pages 319–323. IEEE, 2013.

[42] C. Watson, F. W. Li, and J. L. Godwin. No tests required: comparing traditional and dynamic predictors of programming success. In *Proceedings of the 45th ACM technical symposium on Computer science education*, pages 469–474. ACM, 2014.

[43] L. H. Werth. *Predicting student performance in a beginning computer science class*, volume 18. ACM, 1986.

[44] S. Wiedenbeck, D. Labelle, and V. N. Kain. Factors affecting course outcomes in introductory programming. In *16th Annual Workshop of the Psychology of Programming Interest Group*, pages 97–109, 2004.

[45] L. Williams, C. McDowell, N. Nagappan, J. Fernald, and L. Werner. Building pair programming knowledge through a family of experiments. In *Proc. Empirical Software Engineering*, pages 143–152. IEEE.

[46] M. Yudelson, R. Hosseini, A. Vihavainen, and P. Brusilovsky. Investigating automated student modeling in a Java MOOC. In *Proceedings of The Seventh International Conference on Educational Data Mining 2014*, 2014.

Aggregate Compilation Behavior: Findings and Implications from 27,698 Users

Matthew C. Jadud
Berea College
Berea, KY 40403
matthew.c@jadud.com

Brian Dorn
University of Nebraska at Omaha
Omaha, NE 68182
bdorn@unomaha.edu

ABSTRACT

The error quotient (EQ) was first reported in 2006 as a behavioral measure of novice programmers. The EQ scores how well students deal with correcting syntax errors (or not) in their programs. The original studies were carried out on data collected using BlueJ, a pedagogic Java programming environment; today, newly installed instances of BlueJ capture data similar to these early studies automatically, meaning data regarding nearly 2 million programmers is captured every year by the Blackbox project. In this paper, we apply Jadud's original error quotient algorithm to this new, massive data set, and discuss our results and analysis in light of related work. Further, we consider the implications of our findings for researchers and educators in applying the EQ to 27,698 users in 10 different countries during the fall term of 2013.

Categories and Subject Descriptors

K.3.2 [**Computers and Education**]: Computer and Information Science Education—*computer science education*

Keywords

novice compilation behavior; Blackbox; BlueJ

1. INTRODUCTION

Novice programmers make mistakes when learning to program. This is, in no small part, due to the challenges that beginners face when trying to express complex ideas in a foreign language that has a strict, formal grammar. In Thomas Green's work regarding the cognitive dimensions of notations, we would say that the programming language, as an "interface" to expressing the semantics of a program, has a horrible abstraction gradient, almost no mapping to the problem at hand, many hidden dependencies, and is extremely error-prone (to speak to just a few of Green's dimensions) [7, 8]. Recent work by Stefik et al. highlights the challenges novices continue to face as a result of syntax features, some 30 years post Green's work [15].

As a pedagogic programming environment, BlueJ attempts to reduce the barriers to success for novices. Highlighting to indicate where code blocks begin and end help the beginner see the significance of the symbols like '{' and '}'. A UML-like diagram provides an alternative view of the relationship between parts of a program. Despite these scaffolds, the novice programmer must still learn to express their ideas in the syntax of the Java programming language, and they must learn to correct syntax errors with little-to-no help from the environment that is wrapped around the compiler—which is designed by and written for experts.

In this study, we replicate elements of previous work carried out by Jadud regarding the use of the *error quotient* (or EQ) as a measure of a student's process when learning to respond to the Java compiler [9]. This algorithm scores and characterizes student programming behavior in terms of their ability to address syntax errors reported by a compiler, interpreter, or similar tool. Our analysis examines data collected as part of the Blackbox effort, a global logging enabled by instrumentation in every BlueJ instance [5]. On one hand, we are replicating prior work; on another, we are carrying out new analyses of a large, and largely unexplored, data set.

We have been guided by three questions in this work:

1. Is the EQ a reasonable proxy for student performance (in the absence of other evaluative data)?
2. Does the EQ correlate with behavioral measures for which there was inadequate data in previous studies?
3. Given the scale of the Blackbox data, are there significant similarities (or differences) that can be seen in the behavior of users from different countries, and does the EQ help us find them?

These questions frame a series of explorations that ultimately challenge the error quotient as a behavioral measure of novice programmers. Our work here explores how the EQ, as a non-dimensional measure of novice programmers, belies more complexity than was previously known. Specifically, we find that the (significantly) larger sample size suggests new distributions of data and opens the door for new interpretations that were not possible in previous studies. To explore these ideas, we begin by discussing underlying assumptions in our work and the danger of those in light of the opportunistic nature of the Blackbox data set (Section 2), followed by our approach to handling the data (Section 3). We then focus on an aggregate anslysis of a subset of the Blackbox data (Section 4), present a possible theoretical bridge from the aggregate data to the individual (Section 5), and close our analysis by investigating of some individual behavioral characteristics (Section 6). Finally, we discuss our findings and future work in the context of related studies (Section 7), and conclude with possible threats to validity (Section 8) and our findings (Section 9).

2. UNDERLYING ASSUMPTIONS

The original work regarding the error quotient involved a well-defined set of subjects who agreed to take part in a study that would link their programming behavior to traditional measures of performance (eg. grades) [9]. Replications of this work similarly correlated the EQ from a well-defined population to traditional measures [16, 17, 18] as well as other observational data (eg. student affect) [13, 14].

When we consider the Blackbox data as a "replication" of the data collected in earlier studies, we need to be cognizant of how little we know about the subjects who agree to take part in the Blackbox data collection. We do not know:

- if the users are students
- if a user shows up multiple times in the data set by using multiple computers
- if the user is an instructor or teaching assistant grading the work of others
- if the user is working in a laboratory setting, at home, or somewhere else

Perhaps most significantly, the scale of the data is different from previous studies. Jadud's original study included about 42,000 compilation events from 96 subjects generated over the course of an academic year. The Blackbox data set includes nearly 78,000,000 compilation events at the time of this paper's writing. Looking at unique users, we find that the UK has roughly 2100 unique users (with at least 50 compilation events) between August 15th, 2013 and December 25th, 2013, and the US has just over 14,000 unique users during the same time frame (and with the same conditions). In this analysis we chose "fall term" data, largely from the northern hemisphere, so as to roughly align with (and maintain a modicum of comparability to) previous studies.

Were we to engage in a direct comparison of the populations from earlier studies and this data set, these orders-of-magnitude differences would be a source of statistical concern. Because of the opportunistic nature of the Blackbox data, we will take it on its own terms; in doing so, we will not be making any direct statistical comparisons with prior data sets, instead leveraging the scale of the Blackbox data to examine more users with more interactions with BlueJ than in any previous related study.

3. METHOD

Our analysis of the Blackbox data began as an exploration; our starting point was the *error quotient*, a simple algorithm developed by Jadud for characterizing the behavior of a novice programmer as they interact with the compiler as mediated by the BlueJ pedagogic IDE [10]. At the outset our rationale was that the EQ has been shown to correlate with traditional academic measures, and therefore we might use it as a crude performance metric as we investigated this large, anonymous data set. By the end of the analysis, we instead found that we had developed a much richer understanding of the EQ, how it might relate to student behavior, and how programmer behavior varies from one cultural context to another.

We begin by discussing our methodology for calculating the error quotient, and how some of our earlier assumptions played out in our analysis.

3.1 Calculating the EQ

The error quotient is determined by a simple algorithm. As reported by Jadud, for a given ordered sequence of compilation events, we score each pair of events [9]. If the events (e_i, e_{i+1}) are either both syntax free, progress from error to correct code, or correct code that progresses to an error, we give it a score of zero. If both events are syntax errors, we score them as $8/11$ if they are different error types, and 1 if they are the same error type. These scoring values were used in the original (and subsequent replication) studies of the EQ, and were used here for consistency.

After scoring each pair of events, the mean is taken, yielding an EQ score in the range of 0 to 1. Based on multiple studies that have replicated this analysis on student behavior correlated with traditional assessment metrics (graded homework, examination, and so on), our intent was to use this measure as a means for categorizing subjects within the Blackbox data set. While EQ does not correlate *strongly* with traditional measures of student success, it is adequate for saying that subjects with high EQ scores (meaning they had many compilation event pairs that began and ended with an error) probably struggle with learning to program (and therefore perform less well on tests and the like), while students with low EQ scores (meaning they more often corrected errors and/or had error-free compilations) likely performed reasonably well on traditional metrics.

3.2 Filtering Subjects

As reported in Brown et al., the daily opt-in rate for participation in Blackbox data collection was 42% in November of 2013 [5]. Based on the minimum (43%) and maximum (48%) reported at that time, we can begin by assuming that our data includes between $4/10$ and $5/10$ users of BlueJ.

Beyond self-selection on the part of the subject, our primary filtering of subjects is threefold. First, we chose to present our data on a country-by-country basis; the information enabling this was added to Blackbox's researcher-facing database in March of 2015. Second, we filter by date: we chose to work with compilation events logged between the 15th of August and the 25th of December in 2013 to align approximately with one academic term. Finally, we limited our analysis to subjects for whom at least 50 compilation events were logged; as we discovered, and in contrast to earlier work, this turns out to be a paucity of data regarding a subject's programming behavior. As a result, some of our later analyses will focus on subjects for whom we have at least 800 compilation events available (Section 6).

Once subjects were filtered on these criteria, we saw a linear correlation between the number of subjects and number of events for each of the countries studied (see Figure 1 and Table 1). This was a useful first "sanity check" of the Blackbox data; no one country generated (significantly) proportionally more (or fewer) events than any other. Germany appears to be a slight outlier, but not enough so for us to be concerned; there are still over 4,000 subjects and 1M events captured from German users of BlueJ during the time period covered by our study.

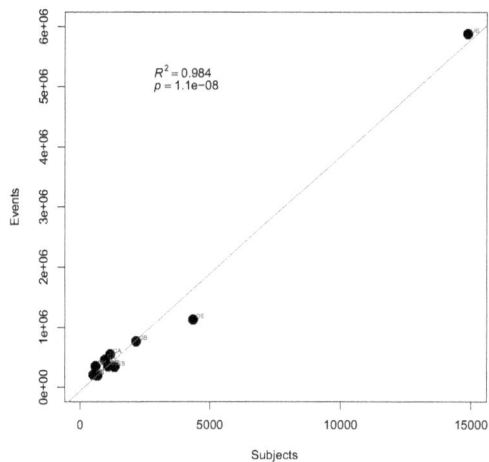

Figure 1: Users vs. events on a per-country basis.

Using these filtering criteria, we examined a total of 27,698 subjects who generated 10,193,432 compilation events between August 15th and December 25th, 2013.

3.3 Check Against Prior Work

Before beginning any deeper analyses, the final check of our methodology was to examine the distribution of EQ values for the entire population and the individual countries. We did this primarily to see if the normality claims of prior work still hold; in Figure 2a, we see the distribution of all EQs for all 27,698 in this study. At a glance, it appears normal, but has a slight tail to the right. This is confirmed by the kurtosis and skewness metrics for this distribution (0.825 and 0.519, respectively). The kurtosis measure speaks to the "peaky-ness" of the distribution, and when skewness is positive it indicates a tail on the right side of the distribution.

We do not consider this an alarming departure from previous work regarding the EQ. Instead, we see this as a refinement on previous studies. Given the small number of subjects and events available in previous work, it would have been extremely difficult to characterize the distribution of EQ scores across a population to this degree of precision. The consistency begs two questions: is it consistent across all of the countries included in our study, and what might that suggest about the metric's "ecological validity" and its interpretation? We will proceed to investigate both of these questions in the sections that follow. First, we explore the question of similarity and difference across countries in the next section, and we will close by painting a picture of the behavior of individuals and their relationship to their EQ score in Section 6.

4. AGGREGATE ANALYSIS

To investigate the question of how EQ scores vary (or not) worldwide, we extracted data for all compilation events for the fall 2013 term (Aug. 15th–Dec 25th) for 10 different northern-hemisphere countries, primarily from North America and Europe. We focus on the northern hemisphere in an effort to minimize (to the extent possible) noise in the data

caused by markedly different academic terms arising from opposite seasons. These particular countries were selected from those with the greatest number of unique BlueJ users during this time period. Descriptive statistics for the 10 sampled countries can be found in Table 1.

The volume of data collected by Blackbox varied greatly by country in this time interval, with users from the United States generating the majority. Individual users in most countries generated between 300 and 450 compilation events each during the period of study; however, a one-way ANOVA test suggests statistically significant differences in the number of events generated per user ($F(9, 27688) = 32.54; p < 0.001$). TukeyHSD post-hoc pairwise comparisons revealed Danish users as significantly more active than those from all other countries except for the Czech Republic, though this may be due (at least in part) to a single outlying Danish user who generated nearly 60,000 compilation events. German and Spanish users were markedly less active than those from most other countries. Of course, we recognize that academic terms may not have been uniform across these countries, and this may account for some degree of spread in the event activity levels. Even so, the pairwise analysis revealed overlapping boundaries between groups, and did not uncover differences forcing us to question the validity of EQ computations for users from a particular country.

We then computed the cumulative EQ for users from each country, and examined the EQ distributions for differences. EQ distribution densities are visualized in Figure 2b. In general, these distributions roughly resemble normal distributions with bounded ranges, have means near 0.31, and exhibit varying degrees of right skew. Denmark and the Czech Republic demonstrate more peaked distributions than others. In Jadud's dissertation, the original study of 96 had a mean of 0.41, which is high compared to the data presented here. Based on our "reading" of individual user's programming history (Section 6), we suspect this is because of the greater number of users who engage briefly with BlueJ, generate at least 50 events (that are largely correct—most likely by starting with a starter file of some sort), and then never interact with BlueJ (under that unique user identifier) for the duration under study.

While the range of values for mean EQ by country only ranged from 0.29 to 0.36, a one way ANOVA for EQ by country was significant ($F(9, 27688) = 65.4; p < 0.001$). Further, post hoc pairwise comparisons using the TukeyHSD method and a 95% family-wise confidence level identified three mutually exclusive clusters of EQ distributions [12]. At the high end were Spain and Israel, each with mean EQs of 0.36. Five countries (Canada, Denmark, the United States, France, and the Czech Republic) were grouped with mean EQs of about 0.30 and below. The remaining three countries (the United Kingdom, Belgium, and Germany) all had EQs near 0.33. Figure 2c presents EQ densities for each of these three groups separately to highlight their differences.

Perhaps the most striking statistics from Table 1 are those related to the number of active days logged by BlueJ users during the nearly 19 week data collection window for fall 2013. Worldwide, the mean number of active days per user ranged from as few as 7 to around 14. The histogram shown in Figure 3 illustrates the stark reality of student activity. 80.6% of users engaged in compilation activities fewer than 19 times—roughly once a week, and the majority (55.6%) compiled code on 9 or fewer separate occasions. This is

Table 1: Summary statistics for selected countries and users with ≥ 50 sessions, ordered by decreasing EQ

Country	# Users	# Events	Events per User	Mean EQ (σ)		Max	Mean Active Days (σ)	
Israel	665	195,703	294.3	0.36	(0.16)	0.86	8.5	(7.4)
Spain	1,332	339,242	254.7	0.36	(0.16)	0.81	7.8	(7.1)
United Kingdom	2,160	760,047	351.9	0.33	(0.14)	0.77	9.1	(8.0)
Belgium	1,072	346,403	323.1	0.33	(0.14)	0.79	8.8	(8.3)
Germany	4,368	1,123,530	257.2	0.32	(0.16)	0.82	7.3	(6.8)
Canada	1,161	543,487	468.1	0.30	(0.13)	0.76	13.3	(11.8)
Denmark	594	346,417	583.2	0.29	(0.12)	0.72	14.2	(9.6)
United States	14,877	5,878,907	395.2	0.29	(0.14)	0.82	14.3	(12.8)
France	517	206,242	398.9	0.29	(0.14)	0.74	8.7	(9.3)
Czech Republic	952	453,454	476.3	0.29	(0.13)	0.76	11.0	(9.4)

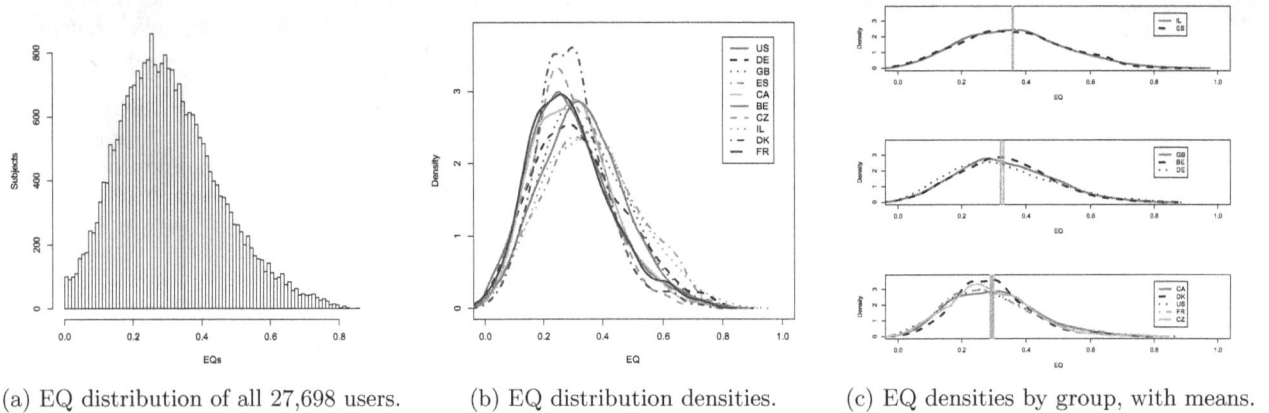

(a) EQ distribution of all 27,698 users.   (b) EQ distribution densities.   (c) EQ densities by group, with means.

Figure 2: Summary data for entire population and per-country populations.

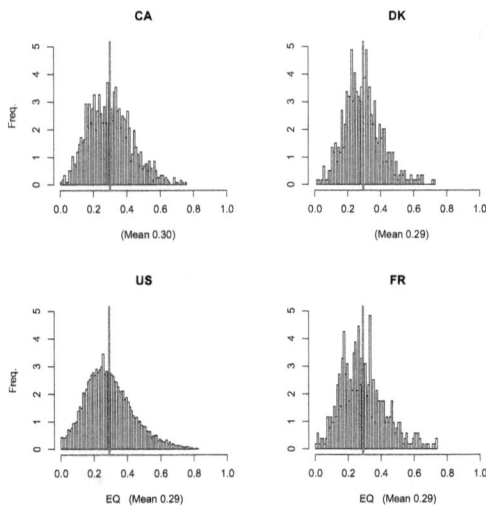

Figure 4: EQ densities for CA, DK, US, and FR.

especially concerning when most instructors' primary goal is for students to gain hands-on practice and build expertise in the skill of programming and debugging. These patterns are generally uniform across the countries examined here.

Overall these data illustrate the robustness of the EQ measure. Across 10 different countries, the cumulative value and ranges are reasonably consistent. However, as we look more closely at the distributions of EQ and its variation in density from one country to the next, the notion that there is *surface consistency* is not entirely satisfying. Canada, Denmark, the US, and France all have EQ values with means within 0.01 of each-other, and yet, the distributions look slightly different, and we know there are (sometimes significant) differences in their educational systems. While the distribution of EQ values speaks to the aggregate behavior of the subjects in this study (and in a given country), it leaves us wondering: what do these distributions mean, and how do they come about on a user-by-user basis?

5. FROM AGGREGATE TO INDIVIDUAL

Our analysis so far has focused on the large-scale behavior of entire populations. We see distributions that are hill-shaped and resemble normal distributions, but are skewed and tailed (to some degree). The "peakyness" and skew in these distributions actually tells us something (in the large) about our population's behavior, and helps us begin to see how the users in this study are engaging with BlueJ on an event-by-event basis. To explore this more fully, we will briefly consider an analogy to batting averages in the game of baseball.

Players' batting averages can be characterized by a family of distributions known as *beta distributions* [1]. Beta distributions are bounded on the range [0,1], and are described by two shape parameters, α and β. These parameters determine the shape of the distribution; a normal curve is actually in the family of beta distributions, with shape parameters $\alpha = 1$ and $\beta = 1$ [11]. Because of the large number of users in

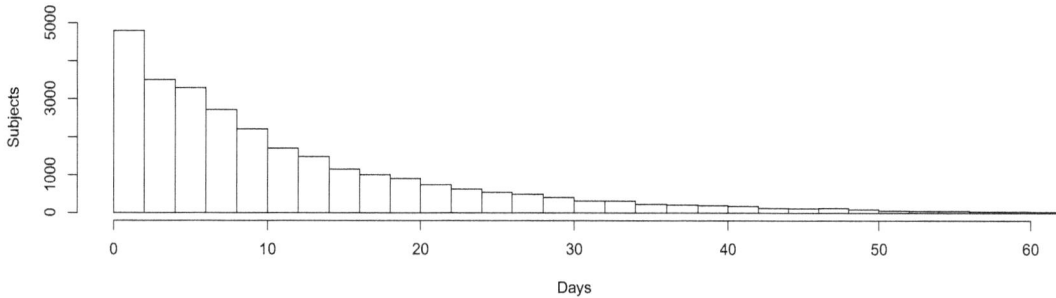

Figure 3: Days users spent editing code, worldwide.

the Blackbox data, the EQ fits a normal distribution reasonably; however, using parameter fitting we can find α and β parameters for beta distributions that fit each country's EQ data even more accurately. Given that our data is bounded on the range [0,1], and is characterized by a tail on the side of increasing EQ values, we believe that using a beta distribution is a better way to characterize the EQ of users in this study.

Two questions become important to consider at this point. First, what is the significance that this data is best described as a beta distribution, and what relationships exist between the populations we are considering here? To consider the first question (the "beta? so what?" question), we will consider our analogy to baseball more closely, and the notion of batting averages, which also follow a beta distribution.

5.1 Batting Averages and EQs

In the U.S.A., a baseball player's *batting average* is the number of hits they get divided by the number of times they are at bat. A batting average of less than 0.200 is considered exceedingly poor; an average of more than 0.300 is considered excellent. How this number comes to be, over time, is important. Consider:

- A batter might begin their career by being striking out their first three at-bats. Their batting average will, therefore, be zero. This is horrendous!

- A batter might begin their career by getting three hits in a row, thus batting 1.000. This is astounding!

Put simply, a batting average does not mean a great deal given only a small number of data points; the first few data points are not a strong predictor of a batter's ability. However, as the number of at-bats grows, the predictive power of the distribution increases. Likewise, each individual at-bat has less impact on the batting average overall. Put another way, a batter with 10 at-bats is unpredictable; a batter with 500 at-bats is a known quantity.

We posit that the EQ is not unlike this value; each attempted compilation is equivalent to an "at bat." It is scored as either 0, $^8/_{11}$, or 1. A student who opens BlueJ, opens a syntactically correct starter file, and then hits compile (without changing anything) three times will have an outstanding EQ score of 0.000. Contrariwise, another student might open BlueJ, make some changes to the same starter,

get a syntax error, and spend one minute attempting to fix it. In the process, they compile twice more—and, in failing to do so, gets the same error both times. Their EQ is now an abysmal 1.000.

These early compilations have little overall predictive power. However, the number events grow, the EQ begins to look a lot like a batting average: it becomes increasingly representative of a student's "lifetime behavior," individual events have a decreasing impact on the distribution overall, and the majority of EQ values for any given population span a relatively small range of possible values. At the same time, it is the trajectory of these values—the "running average" of the error quotient—that provides a lens into the interesting behavior of individuals within this massive population.

6. BEHAVIORAL ANALYSIS

If Davinci said that "art is never finished, only abandoned," then the subjects in our study would possibly claim their code as art. Despite a study period that covers 132 days (just shy of 19 full weeks), and intended to span the traditional period of a semester or term in the northern hemisphere, we see surprisingly little engagement with code amongst the users in our study. Recall from Table 1:

Country	Days	σ	Country	Days	σ
DK	14	10	FR	9	9
US	14	13	UK	9	8
CA	13	12	ES	8	7
CZ	11	9	IL	8	7
BE	9	8	DE	7	7

In Denmark and the United States of America, we see that students spend, on average, 14 days of the 132 in our study programming; that number varies greatly, however, as the standard deviations for those distributions are quite high. However, what it says is that users typically spend (on average) one day per week programming in the US during the time considered; in the UK, they spend just over half that—9 days in the period considered—working in BlueJ.

Figure 5 shows four users from the study pool—specifically, each plot illustrates the running average of each user's EQ over the total events captured. As can be seen, the EQ is quite dynamic in the first 100-200 events—like the batter early in their career, the average fluctuates greatly with each new event. However, as the number of events increases,

135

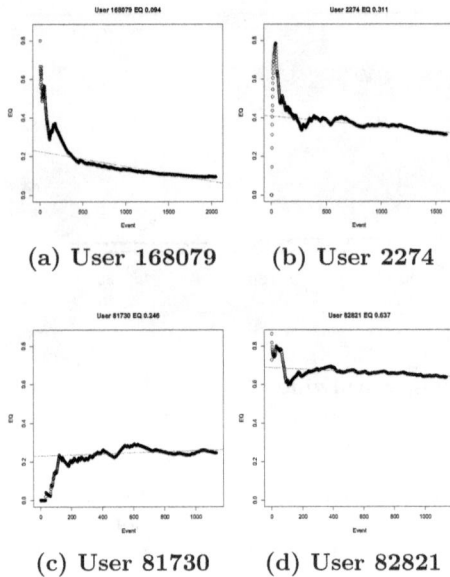

(a) User 168079   (b) User 2274

(c) User 81730   (d) User 82821

Figure 5: UK EQ event trajectories; x-axis = event number.

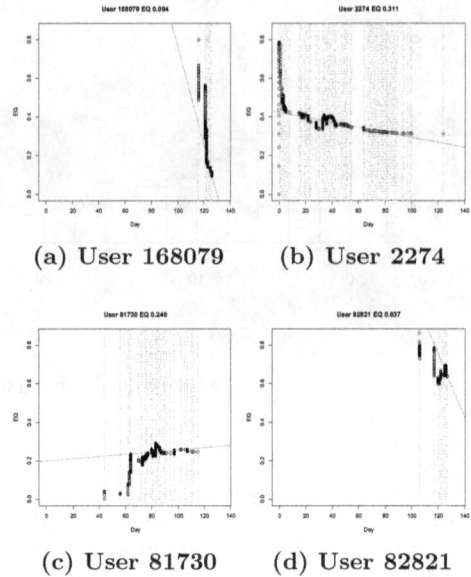

(a) User 168079   (b) User 2274

(c) User 81730   (d) User 82821

Figure 6: UK EQ event trajectories; x-axis = day of event.

the EQ begins to stabilize, and ultimately approaches the average for the entire session; the average EQ for that user is, therefore, the rightmost point in these plots. In each case, the unique ID of the user within the Blackbox data set is used as a plot label.

User 168079 has an EQ of 0.094—quite low; their average quickly drops and stabilizes around this value. User 2274 has a mean EQ of 0.31, which is just below the mean for the UK subset of the data. On the other hand, user 82821 has a very high EQ at 0.637; in previous studies, this would have suggested that the user might perform poorly if their work was in a classroom context. In each case, a linear fit has been overlaid on the data. This fit was computed by ignoring the first 200 points in the data; in the case of these four users, that means it was a fit against the last 800+ events they generated during the period of observation. These fits are reasonably good, and give us the impression that the students EQ is either holding steady (a good thing, if it is low), or generally trending downward, which would suggest they are fixing more errors than repeating them.

Because event trajectories in Figure 5 are agnostic as to exactly *when* the programming took place, we get the impression of a stream of events that are contiguous and equal in measure. However, the picture looks very different when we change the x-axis to represent the actual day in our time period (indexed from 0) that an event was recorded. Whereas we plotted all events on an equal timescale in Figure 5, the x-axis in Figure 6 now ranges from 0 to 140, capturing the 132 days of our study. Multiple events might be plotted on a single day, and we mark the days with green dashed lines to indicate where programming activity is taking place within the BlueJ environment. This means, in some cases, that 100 or more events might take place on a single day.

Our impression of user behavior is changed drastically by this change in measure. User 168079 has a remarkably low EQ, but he/she did not show up in the study until very late

in the period covered. This could be for any number of reasons: he/she may have never been part of the study before, he/she may have been working on a different computer most of the term, or (perhaps more disturbing) he/she may have done little-to-no work all term. Given the low EQ, we wonder if this user recently switched computers, as we do not want to believe he/she just began programming so late in the term (and so well), but it is hypothetically possible.

We are more inclined to believe, if these are students enrolled in university in the UK, that user 82821 might have truly decided to do no work until the very end of the term. He/she has a very high EQ, and shows little sign of bringing it down during the 1000+ events on record (as indicated by poor trendline fit). He/she, too, showed up in the last weeks of the study, much like 168079, but the EQ suggests a very different level of skill when it comes to dealing with syntax errors in Java.

Both user 2274 and user 81730 show more balanced profiles of engagement; with EQ values of 0.31 and 0.25 (respectively), neither is likely to be dealing with too many errors in sequence as part of their EQ profile. User 2274 worked consistently throughout the term, programming 3-4 times per week throughout the first $3/4$s of the term. User 81730 started a bit later in the term (perhaps before a midterm?), and engaged nearly as consistently through the remainder of the period studied.

6.1 Quantifying Trajectories

Our intuition as educators is that the EQ, taken as a rolling average, represents a notional measure for the development of expertise. As students see more syntax errors (or, in some cases, see the same errors over-and-over), we would like it if they became more proficient at fixing the common errors they encounter and, likewise, deal more gracefully with new errors as they appear throughout their exploration of the Java programming language.

To test this, we took our population of users with at least 800 events, calculated a best-fit linear regression to the last 600 events in their running EQ, and categorized the slope as downward-, even-, or upward-trending. (Any slope within 1σ of the population mean was considered even-trending.) We then looked for correlations between a user's EQ (a static, post-hoc mean) and the slope, or trend, of the evolution of their EQ over time.

We carried these explorations out because we thought there might be a correlation between downward-trending EQ values and a low, overall EQ score. In short, our intuition was that a downward trend would represent a kind of "improvement" for users within the data set. At this time, we have not found any substantive correlations between the EQ and the path that students take to get there. In addition, our intuition that days spent programming should correlate with EQ—where "days spent programming" might stand in for a notional measure of "time on task"—we found this not the case. While statistically significant due to large sample size, the global correlation between EQ and active days is very weak (r=-0.120, p<0.001), as is that between EQ and number of compilation events (r=-0.053, p<0.001). In none of the data sets for the countries described here have we identified any correlations that match our intuition as educators with the EQ, our (possibly questionable) proxy for student programming performance.

6.2 Social/Cultural Markers

Perhaps the most interesting thing about the large-scale data and its connection to the individual behavior of users is how some *cultural affinity* between countries may be percolating to the surface. By this, we mean that there are cultural commonalities that likely hold for all of the users in a given country, and they are (consciously/structurally or unconsciously) impacted by those cultural factors. For example, we see a significant difference in the average number of days spent programming between the US and UK data sets, but little difference between the United States of America and Canada. This may be due to cultural similarities between the institutions in the US and CA (for example) that are using BlueJ in their classrooms. It is common to have homework that is graded on a weekly basis in the US and Canada, and therefore we would expect that the users (assuming they are students) would be programming on a weekly basis. This might be contrasted with the data we see from the UK, where there might be more weight placed on a final examination, or possibly a midterm and final. The side effect of this could be that student interaction with BlueJ would then decrease.

Ultimately, we would like to see a quantifiable measure that brings together more of the behavioral qualities and quantities that we see in this data. A structural or multivariate model that takes into account more user behavior might give us this measure. This is just one of several possible points for future work and consideration that our exploration of the Blackbox data set has inspired.

7. DISCUSSION & FUTURE WORK

The Blackbox data, in its breadth and variability, presents both opportunities and challenges for the researcher interested in the behavior of novice programmers learning Java "objects first" with BlueJ (e.g., [3, 10]). We believe three of these opportunities/challenges are particularly important as

this (and similar) data is mined for relevance and meaning in the future.

7.1 Objective Measures of Success

The Blackbox data does not contain any (obvious, external) measures of success. Whereas previous work correlated grades or in-class observations to a student's EQ score, the Blackbox data only provides fine-grained behavioral data regarding the user and their interactions with the environment and their code. As a result, at least one of two steps might happen if we want to develop a measure that correlates with some objective measure of success on the part of the user:

Integrate with other environments. The BlueJ environment can, for example, interact with the Web-CAT automated assessment environment[6]. If a connection were made between these two environments, it would be possible to assess how many unit tests (for example) a student's code was passing on any given (syntax-error free) compilation event.

Extract known endpoints. The Blackbox data set does recognize the hashes for the projects in the Barnes and Kölling text *Objects First with Java* [3]. It would be possible to write a test suite for the projects in the book, and limit the scope of analysis to those trajectories that are moving towards a known solution-space. This would provide an external measure of success for a (possibly large) subset of the users captured in this data collection effort.

While there are other possibilities, these appear to be the most direct pathways to improving the Blackbox data for the mining of student programming behavior and its connection to traditional measures of success.

7.2 Connection to Intuition

It was our intuition that the EQ, when applied to a larger data set, would help us explore our intuitions quantitatively. Instead, we found that we were missing information that might have made our explorations more profitable. It is possible that the addition of objective measures of success might help us in these explorations, or it might be that the EQ is only a step towards a useful behavioral measure of novice programmers. Given the analyses we have carried out so far, it is difficult to say which is the case.

Our intuition is that our students are intentional, goal-oriented people who want to learn (and can be objectively evaluated), and that instructors are intentional people who want to help students achieve those goals. If (and perhaps it is too large an "if") these intuitions are true, we believe it should be observable in data like that collected in projects like Blackbox.

Future work might, in addition to leveraging objective external measures, begin exploring some of the patterns we saw in this study. For example, we have barely begun to scratch the surface on the EQ as a "batting average." We can see, in the event traces, that user EQ goes up-and-down, often corresponding with a new day. In other words, we might begin "chunking" our data on a day-by-day basis, and think about what those individual sessions might mean. Is a spike in EQ common at the start of *every* session, or just some? Does the nature of the spike change over time, as users improve? If we expand our study to encompass an entire year, will change be more observable, or will we find something that further challenges our intuitions as educators in this web-scale data (as was the case with [2, 4])?

7.3 Mining Expert Behavior

There is no information available regarding how experts fare when examined in this way. It is, of course, possible that very capable programmers are using BlueJ, and they are part of our data analysis—we have no way of knowing. We can imagine an interesting possible study where 1) "expert" programmers develop solutions to problems assigned to beginners, 2) that data is tagged within the Blackbox data set, and 3) modern machine learning techniques are used to find other users who are "similar" to those experts. This may require additional (objective) measures of success, or it may be possible to extract richer, more interesting behavioral data from the Blackbox data set as it stands.

8. THREATS TO VALIDITY

We have attempted, repeatedly, to remind ourselves that every user in this study is not necessarily a student in a traditional classroom context. The behaviors observed may, or may not, be the result of processes that we have intuitions about. As educators, we see "binge" or "crunch-time" behavior at the end of a "term," and naturally assume that this is a student attempting to catch up on many weeks worth of learning in a short period of time. It could be that the user in question is just encountering BlueJ for the first time—but the analyses presented in this paper do not attempt to assess this (admittedly complex, and possibly unanswerable) criterion within the scope of this study.

With that repeated concern regarding assumptions restated, we acknowledge several clear threats to validity that future work in this vein can address.

Completeness. We would like to include all countries (northern and southern hemisphere) for which we have data, as well as the first and second terms of both the '13–'14 and '14–'15 academic years. Extracting and processing this data will require substantial time on the Blackbox servers, given that the '14–'15 data is typically 60-70% larger than the data presented here (but, at first glance, comparable in character).

Term Dates. We made assumptions about term start and end times. In the UK, terms tend to start in September, while in India, the term schedule is rather different; our dates would not quite bisect a typical term in that country. Some institutions are on trimesters or quarters, and yet others run year-round. At the least, we could calibrate our academic start/end times to be more appropriate on a per-country basis.

Day Trippers. We have many subjects who only show up in the database for one or two days; should they be part of our analysis? Given the direction of the analyses presented here, it is tempting to drop subjects for whom we have very few days on record. That said, we have many events for these users, and the average (on a country-by-country basis) is between 9 and 14 unique programming days... these low numbers may not be "outliers" so much as "reality." Alternatively, they might be an artifact of computer lab images that are reset regularly, erasing students' BlueJ profiles each time.

The Extremes. There is a user in Denmark who, in 132 days, compiled their code nearly 60,000 times. It is difficult to imagine how they could average 452 events *per day* during our study period. Was this an automated process? Was this an entire institution using a single, shared installation of BlueJ? These and other outliers demand further exploration; at the least, they skew "typical" (or "fathomable") data, or may be meritorious of further investigation unto themselves.

Language. Not all students work in English, regardless of the country of origin of a given compilation event. Improving our analytical tools to accomodate language localizations is necessary so as to reduce the number of "unknown" compilation errors we find in this large-scale data set.

9. CONCLUSION

We have investigated both the large-scale aggregate behavior of 27,698 from 10 countries from the fall of 2013, the first academic semester during which the Blackbox data collection effort took place. This data represents approximately 40% of all BlueJ users during that time period, and our analysis examined the similarities and differences, in the aggregate and at the level of individuals. We found that:

- The EQ is not-quite-normally distributed, and we have postulated a new interpretive framing for this kind of behavioral data as it changes over time.

- Users in a given country appear to exhibit some degree of cultural affinity for each-other, and these differences show up in the aggregate as statistically significant, quantifiable measures.

- Important work remains to connect behaviors believed to be valuable in learning (e.g. "time on task") to behaviors that are observable within this data (e.g. days spent programming).

- External, objective measures of student performance, whether integrated at the time of learning or applied post-hoc, are likely to radically transform our understanding of novice programming behavior in the small and in the large.

Three questions guided our explorations, and they begot more questions than were answered. The EQ may yet serve as a proxy for traditional measures of performance, but it must be validated against additional objective quantifiers before this is possible (Q1). The EQ does not appear to correlate against intuitive, observable measures like days spent programming (Q2). Finally, while there are statistical differences in mean EQ on a country-by-country basis, we cannot speak to the significance of this finding at this time (Q3).

ACKNOWLEDGMENTS

We thank the entire BlueJ/Blackbox team for both the infrastructure that made this analysis possible and their willingness to help external research teams investigate new questions. In particular, Dr. Neil Brown's help was especially important in enabling country-level analyses.

References

[1] J. Albert and R. H. Koning. *Statistical thinking in sports*. CRC Press, 2007.

[2] A. Altadmri and N. C. Brown. 37 million compilations: Investigating novice programming mistakes in large-scale student data. In *Proceedings of the 46th ACM Technical Symposium on Computer Science Education*, SIGCSE '15, pages 522–527, New York, NY, USA, 2015. ACM.

[3] D. J. Barnes and M. Kölling. *Objects First with Java: A Practical Introduction Using BlueJ*. Prentice Hall Press, Upper Saddle River, NJ, USA, 5th edition, 2011.

[4] N. C. Brown and A. Altadmri. Investigating novice programming mistakes: Educator beliefs vs. student data. In *Proceedings of the Tenth Annual Conference on International Computing Education Research*, ICER '14, pages 43–50, 2014.

[5] N. C. C. Brown, M. Kölling, D. McCall, and I. Utting. Blackbox: A large scale repository of novice programmers' activity. In *Proceedings of the 45th ACM Technical Symposium on Computer Science Education*, SIGCSE '14, pages 223–228, 2014.

[6] S. H. Edwards and M. A. Perez-Quinones. Web-cat: automatically grading programming assignments. In *ACM SIGCSE Bulletin*, volume 40, pages 328–328. ACM, 2008.

[7] T. R. Green. Cognitive dimensions of notations. *A. Sutcliffe and Macaulay, editors, People and Computers V*, pages 443–460, 1989.

[8] T. R. G. Green and M. Petre. Usability analysis of visual programming environments: a 'cognitive dimensions' framework. *Journal of Visual Languages & Computing*, 7(2):131–174, 1996.

[9] M. C. Jadud. Methods and tools for exploring novice compilation behaviour. In *Proceedings of the Second International Workshop on Computing Education Research*, ICER '06, pages 73–84, 2006.

[10] M. Kölling, B. Quig, A. Patterson, and J. Rosenberg. The bluej system and its pedagogy. *Computer Science Education*, 13(4):249–268, 2003.

[11] K. Pearson. Contributions to the mathematical theory of evolution. ii. skew variation in homogeneous material. *Philosophical Transactions of the Royal Society of London. A*, pages 343–414, 1895.

[12] R Core Team. *R: A Language and Environment for Statistical Computing*. R Foundation for Statistical Computing, Vienna, Austria, 2013.

[13] M. M. T. Rodrigo, T. C. S. Andallaza, F. E. V. G. Castro, M. L. V. Armenta, T. T. Dy, and M. C. Jadud. An analysis of java programming behaviors, affect, perceptions, and syntax errors among low-achieving, average, and high-achieving novice programmers. *Journal of Educational Computing Research*, 49(3):293–325, 2013.

[14] M. M. T. Rodrigo, R. S. Baker, M. C. Jadud, A. C. M. Amarra, T. Dy, M. B. V. Espejo-Lahoz, S. A. L. Lim, S. A. Pascua, J. O. Sugay, and E. S. Tabanao. Affective and behavioral predictors of novice programmer achievement. In *Proceedings of the 14th Annual ACM SIGCSE Conference on Innovation and Technology in Computer Science Education*, ITiCSE '09, pages 156–160, New York, NY, USA, 2009. ACM.

[15] A. Stefik and S. Siebert. An empirical investigation into programming language syntax. *ACM Transactions on Computing Education (TOCE)*, 13(4):19, 2013.

[16] E. S. Tabanao, M. M. T. Rodrigo, and M. C. Jadud. Predicting at-risk novice java programmers through the analysis of online protocols. In *Proceedings of the Seventh International Workshop on Computing Education Research*, ICER '11, pages 85–92, 2011.

[17] C. Watson, F. W. Li, and J. L. Godwin. Predicting performance in an introductory programming course by logging and analyzing student programming behavior. In *Advanced Learning Technologies (ICALT), 2013 IEEE 13th International Conference on*, pages 319–323. IEEE, 2013.

[18] C. Watson, F. W. Li, and J. L. Godwin. No tests required: Comparing traditional and dynamic predictors of programming success. In *Proceedings of the 45th ACM Technical Symposium on Computer Science Education*, SIGCSE '14, pages 469–474, 2014.

The Normalized Programming State Model: Predicting Student Performance in Computing Courses Based on Programming Behavior

Adam S. Carter*, Christopher D. Hundhausen*, and Olusola Adesope[†]

Human-centered Environments for Learning and Programming (HELP) Lab
*School of Electrical Engineering and Computer Science
[†]College of Education
Washington State University
Pullman, WA 99164
+1 509-335-6602

cartera@wsu.edu, hundhaus@wsu.edu, olusola.adesope@wsu.edu

ABSTRACT

Educators stand to benefit from advance predictions of their students' course performance based on learning process data collected in their courses. Indeed, such predictions can help educators not only to identify at-risk students, but also to better tailor their instructional methods. In computing education, at least two different measures, the Error Quotient [14, 23] and Watwin Score [26, 27], have achieved modest success at predicting student course performance based solely on students' compilation attempts. We hypothesize that one can achieve even greater predictive power by considering students' programming activities more holistically. To that end, we derive the Normalized Programming State Model (NPSM), which characterizes students' programming activity in terms of the dynamically-changing syntactic and semantic correctness of their programs. In an empirical study, the NPSM accounted for 41% of the variance in students' programming assignment grades, and 36% of the variance in students' final course grades. We identify the components of the NPSM that contribute to its explanatory power, and derive a formula capable of predicting students' course programming performance with between 36 and 67 percent accuracy, depending on the quantity of programming process data.

Categories and Subject Descriptors

K.3.2 [**Computer and Information Science Education**]: *Computer science education.* D.2.8 [**Metrics**]: Performance measures, Process metrics, Product metrics.

Keywords

Error Quotient, Watwin Score, Normalized Programming State Model, Predictive measures of student performance and achievement, Learning analytics, Educational data mining

1. INTRODUCTION

By collecting a stream of learning process data in their courses, educators create opportunities to continuously assess their students learning processes and progress. Using techniques from

the fields of educational data mining and learning analytics [3, 24], educators can analyze these data in order to identify ways in which learning patterns and attitudes relate to learning outcomes. Such analyses open up new opportunities to better tailor instruction to individual learners, and ultimately to improve student learning outcomes, especially among at-risk learners.

In computing education, employing educational data mining and learning analytics techniques would appear to be particularly appropriate, given computing education's "grand challenge" problem of improving student retention, especially in early computing courses (see, e.g., [6, 9, 28]. Indeed, if computing educators are able to identify, at an early stage in a computing course, students who are at risk of dropping out or failing the course, then they are in a better position to improve retention by tailoring or adapting their instructional approaches.

Recognizing this potential, computing education researchers have become increasingly interested in collecting log data on students' programming processes as they work on course assignments [2]. Two predictive measures in this line of research—the Error Quotient [14] and the Watwin Score [27]—focus exclusively on differences between successive compilation attempts. These metrics associate improved learning outcomes with an ability to quickly remove compilation errors from a program.

While these measures have achieved modest success at predicting student performance in early computing courses, they have at least two shortcomings. First, their narrow focus on compilation behavior ignores other programming behaviors—most notably, debugging [1]—that might be associated with learning success. Second, both measures have been derived within one particular programming course (CS1), language (Java) and novice programming environment (BlueJ); their predictive power has not been tested in other courses, programming languages and environments. These limitations raise two key research questions:

RQ1:	*How is the predictive power of the Error Quotient and Watwin Score affected by different courses, languages, and programming environments?*
RQ2:	*How well can a more holistic model of students' programming processes predict performance?*

By presenting preliminary research that addresses these questions, this paper makes two key contributions. First, we perform a replication study of the Error Quotient and Watwin Score studies, using a different student population (CS2 instead of CS1), different programming language (C/C++ vs. Java), and different programming environment (Visual Studio® vs. BlueJ). Second,

ICER '15, August 9--13, 2015, Omaha, Nebraska, USA.
© 2015 ACM. ISBN 978-1-4503-3630-7/15/08…$15.00
DOI: http://dx.doi.org/10.1145/2787622.2787710

we propose the Normalized Programming State Model (NPSM) as a more holistic characterization of students' programming processes. In an empirical study, the NPSM achieved over eight times the explanatory power of the Error Quotient, and over three times the explanatory power of the Watwin Score. In a follow-up study, we use the NPSM to derive a formula that is capable of predicting students' course performance based on the programming process data available at any point in a course.

2. BACKGROUND AND RELATED WORK

A large body of educational research has explored the extent to which various learner variables are able to predict learning outcomes or future learning behaviors. These variables include the learner's background (e.g., [5, 15]), prior knowledge (e.g., [5, 18]), cognitive abilities (e.g., [20]), time-on-task (e.g., [21]) and learning attitudes (e.g., [4]). In computing education, for example, Rosson et al. [19] found strong positive correlations between a number of attitudinal variables, including self-efficacy, and a learner's orientation towards the computing discipline. While this line of research shares our interest in predicting student learning outcomes, it differs in that it relies on only a limited number of data snapshots to make its predictions. Thus, it lacks the ability to furnish predictions of student performance that are dynamic, robust and continuously updated throughout a course.

The research presented here analyzes a continuous stream of data in order to identify patterns of learning associated with positive learning outcomes. As such, it falls within the emerging areas of educational data mining and learning analytics [3, 24], which, in many STEM fields, have been used to gain insights into the processes that underlie student learning, and ultimately to better tailor instruction. A foundational idea is to build learner models that infer learners' background knowledge, learning strategies, and motivations from learning process data [18]. In turn, such models are used to adapt instruction to learner needs.

Within computing education, a legacy of research has studied students' programming processes using think-aloud protocols (e.g., [16, 22]), video analysis (e.g., [12]), and software logs (e.g., [8, 10]). These studies have had a variety of goals, ranging from better understanding how novices approach programming and debugging (e.g., [1]), to developing cognitive models of student programming knowledge (e.g., [16, 22]), to evaluating novice programming environments [8, 10, 12] While carrying forward its interest in studying students' programming processes in detail, our work differs from this line of work in that it aims to make accurate advance predictions of course performance.

Most closely related to the work presented here are the Error Quotient [14, 23] and Watwin Score [26, 27], which have been proposed as predictive measures of student performance based on programming behavior. Both measures focus on quantifying a student's ability to recover from compilation errors. This is accomplished by examining successive pairs of compilation attempts and awarding points based on whether or not later compilation attempts remove errors identified in earlier compilation attempts. In past studies, the Watwin Score has generally outperformed the Error Quotient as a predictive measure. While the Error Quotient was able to account for between 19% [26] and 25% [14] of the variance of final course grades, the Watwin score was able to account for between 36% [26] and 42% [27] of the variance in final course grades. However, a refinement of the Error Quotient published more recently appears to raise the Error Quotient's predictive power to nearly 30% [23]. The NPSM presented here can be seen as an expansion of the Error Quotient and Watwin Score—one that

aims to harness greater predictive power by considering the programming process more holistically.

3. A PROGRAMMING STATE MODEL

Both the Error Quotient and Watwin Score focus exclusively on students' compilation activities: students who quickly and accurately fix syntax errors in their programs are predicted to perform better than those who do not. While the ability to eliminate syntax errors from a program is an important programming skill, it is widely acknowledged that programming success also hinges on one's ability to identify, diagnose, and repair runtime (semantic) errors (see, e.g., [1]). Thus, one would expect that an ability to eliminate semantic errors would also correlate positively with performance in a computing course.

This observation motivates a more holistic predictive model of student performance rooted in a students' ability to develop both *syntactically* and *semantically*-correct programs. Our proposed model aims to approximate the syntactic and semantic correctness of a programming solution at any given point in time (see Table 1). Given a stream of programming data, we map a student's current programming solution to one of the four states in this 2 × 2 space. We can determine the syntactic correctness of a program based on whether the last compilation attempt yielded an error.

In contrast, semantic correctness is impossible to determine unequivocally. All we have is a rough proxy: the presence or absence of runtime exceptions in the last execution attempt. If the last execution attempt yielded a runtime exception, we classify the program as *semantically incorrect*. If the last execution attempt did not yield a runtime exception, we classify the program as *semantically unknown*. Clearly, our proxy for semantic correctness has significant limitations. For instance, a student's program could meet the assignment specification (and hence be "semantically correct" for the purpose of the assignment), but still raise a runtime exception if it encounters input data that it is not required to process. Conversely, a student's program could run without raising a runtime exception, but its output could be incorrect. Likewise, the student could have failed to test key boundary cases that would have raised a runtime exception.

Figure 1 presents a state-transition diagram that maps our model to the stream of programming log data made available to us by Microsoft® Visual Studio® [25], the IDE used in our study. Note that Visual Studio does *not* report runtime exceptions that occur outside of debug mode. Thus, our log data do not contain two potentially important transitions: those between RN/RU and YN/YU. For this reason, we are forced to determine the current state based on the results of the student's last compilation and *debug* attempt. In order to switch from a syntactically incorrect state (NU and NN) to a syntactically correct state (YN and YU), the student's last compilation attempt must have been free of build errors. Likewise, a student switches from a semantically unknown

Table 1. Dimensions of Program Correctness That Can Be Approximated from Programming Log Data

		Syntax	
		Correct	*Incorrect*
Semantics	*Incorrect*	Syntactically correct/ Semantically incorrect	Syntactically incorrect/ Semantically incorrect
	Unknown	Syntactically correct/ Semantically unknown	Syntactically incorrect/ Semantically unknown

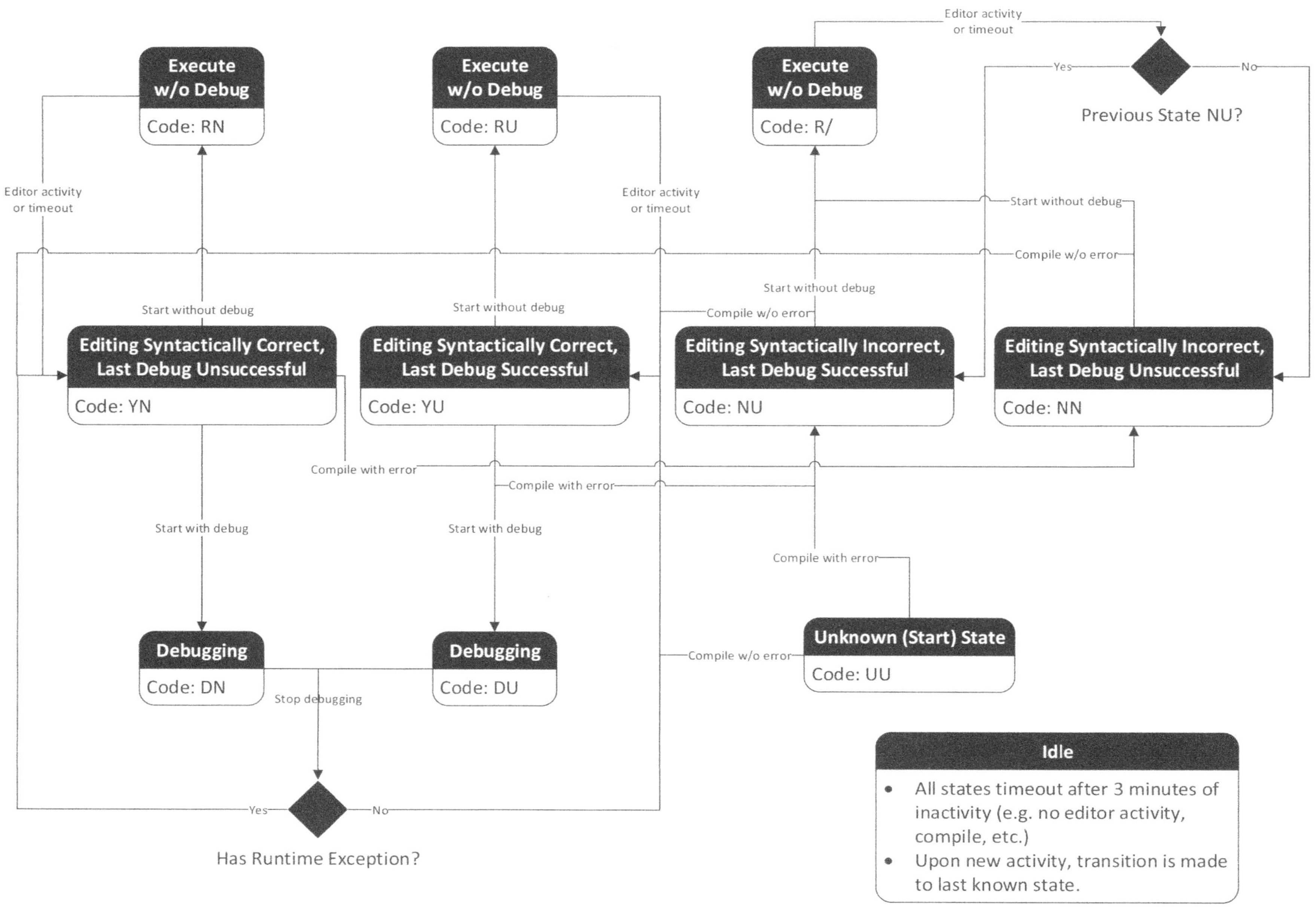

Figure 1: Programming State Transition Diagram

143

state (NU and NN) to a semantically incorrect state (YN and YU) only if the last debug attempt yielded a runtime exception.

Observe that intermediate execution states are also captured in this state transition diagram. If the student's program is syntactically correct, it can be executed either with or without the debugger in Visual Studio. This leads to the four left-most "Execute" states in the diagram (RN, RU, DN, DU). In contrast, if the student's program is syntactically incorrect, it is not possible to execute it in debug mode. However, in Visual Studio, it is possible to execute the last successful build of a program. This leads to the right-most "Execute" state (R/).

Lastly, two additional states are necessary in this model. First, it is impossible to determine the state if no compilation or execution attempts have been made. To account for this situation, which commonly occurs at the beginning of a programming session, we define an additional state called "Unknown (Start) State" (UU). Second, a prolonged period of inactivity (three minutes) in any state leads to a transition to the Idle state, in which the next editing activity causes a transition back to the previous state.

3.1 Relating States to Student Performance

The four editing states in the model just presented (YN, YU, NU, NN) serve as a rough proxy for the syntactic and semantic status of the program being edited. We speculate that students who spend more of their time in syntactically correct and semantically unknown states will tend to outperform students who spend more of their time in syntactically and semantically incorrect states.

The relationship between the five execution states in the model (RN, RU, DN, DU, R/) and student performance is murkier. Students in the RN and DN states appear to be asking the question, "Why doesn't my program work?" However, students who are in state DN may be approaching that question from a more powerful position, since they are using the debugger. In a similar vein, students in the RU and DU states seem to be asking the question, "Does my program work?" Once again, those who choose to use the debugger (in the DU state) appear to be asking that question from a more powerful position. Finally, it is difficult to say just what students in the R/ state are up to. We suspect many of them may not realize that they are actually executing a *previous* build of the program. As such, we speculate that time spent in this state may indicate that a student is struggling; we would not expect time spent in this state to be positively associated with course performance.

3.2 Deriving an Explanatory Model: NPSM

The programming model just presented maps, on a moment-to-moment basis, a student's programming activity to one of the 11 different states shown in Figure 1. Given our intuitions about how states might correlate with student performance, how can the model be used as a basis for explaining the variance in student achievement? We adopt the most straightforward approach: For each student, we record the amount of time spent in each state, and then normalize the times relative to the total time the student spent programming.

In a preliminary analysis of data generated from this model, we observed that the Idle state tended to dominate student activity; students tended to spend most of their day *not* programming. As we wanted to focus exclusively on the time students spent programming, we decided to eliminate the Idle state from the normalization process. In addition, since our normalization is based on the total amount of time students spent programming, we decided to include time-on-task as a variable in the model. We were left with ten state variables plus time-on-task, for a total of 11 data points per student. These 11 data points form the Normalized Programming State Model (NPSM).

4. STUDY I: EVALUATING EXPLANATORY POWER

The goal of our first empirical study was two-fold: (1) to address RQ1 by exploring whether the results of previous studies of the Error Quotient and Watwin Score could be replicated using a different student population, programming language, and programming environment, and (2) to address RQ2 by exploring the explanatory power of the NPSM.

We conducted Study I in a 15-week CS 2 course at Washington State University. Taught by the first author, the course used C++ as its instructional language, and required students to use the Microsoft® Visual Studio® programming environment [25] for course assignments. The course revolved around three weekly 50-minute lectures and one weekly 170-minute lab. We collected programming process and grade data, and used those data as input to the Error Quotient, Watwin Score, and NPSM.

4.1 Participants

The spring 2014 offering of CptS 122, the CS 2 course at Washington State University, enrolled 140 students, of whom 129 completed the course. Of these, 95 students (87 male, 8 female) consented to release their programming log data and course grades for analysis in this study.

4.2 Data Collection Materials and Procedure

Students' programming activities were collected using OSBIDE [7], a plugin for Microsoft® Visual Studio®. We hired a professional programmer to write the software for computing the Error Quotient, Watwin Score, and state transition network on which the NPSM is based. The first author aggregated the state transition data into the eleven variables that make up the NPSM.

Because of a key difference between BlueJ and Visual Studio® (BlueJ only displays one build error at a time, whereas Visual Studio® displays all build errors), we had the programmer create two versions of the Watwin Score: One that mimics the originally-published algorithm by considering only one error at time, and another that considers all build errors. Both versions of the Watwin Score are considered in the analysis that follows.

Three performance indicators were used for the analysis: (1) students' grades on individual assignments; (2) students' overall assignment average, and (3) students' final grades, which were based on the grades received on programming assignments (35%), labs (10%), participation (5%), in-class quizzes (10%), midterm exams (20%), and a final exam (20%). Predictions of individual assignment grades were based exclusively on the programming log data generated while the corresponding assignment was open. (The length of each assignment varied between ten and twenty three days). Predictions of students' overall assignment averages and final grades, in contrast, were based on programming log data generated throughout the entire semester.

4.3 Results

4.3.1 Predictions of Individual Assignment Grades

To evaluate the ability of the three measures to explain the variance in individual assignment grades, we performed a linear regression, with measure (Error Quotient, Watwin Score, NPSM) as the predictor variable and individual assignment grades as the outcome variable (see Table 2). Because the NPSM relies on *normalized* time values, students who spend little time on an assignment are likely to skew the explanatory model. With that in mind, we ran a secondary analysis that considered only students who spent at least one hour on each programming assignment. The results of this analysis, in which 63 out of 665 data points were thrown out, are also presented in Table 2. Significant factors in the multivariate regression run on all data points are presented in Table 3, while Table 4 shows the significant factors in the multivariate regression run on only those data points corresponding to students who were active for at least an hour.

As indicated in Table 2, all measures were significant but weak predictors of individual assignment scores. If we filter out data corresponding to students who spent less than an hour of programming time on an assignment, the NPSM model accounted for the most variance ($r^2 = 0.11$) in assignment grades. Interestingly, setting a minimum time limit of one hour altered three of the five significant contributing factors in the NPSM.

4.3.2 Predictions of Overall Assignment Averages
We next aggregated an entire semester's worth of IDE data and correlated these data with students' overall assignment averages. Results for each measure are presented in Table 5. Significant contributors in the NPSM model are shown in Table 6.

By considering an entire semester's worth of data, two of the three predictive measures improved. The Error Quotient's explanatory power decreased, whereas the Watwin Score increased its explanatory power by a factor of five, and the NPSM increased its explanatory power by more than a factor of three. In absolute terms, the NPSM was a substantially better predictor than the other two measures, nearly quadrupling the explanatory power of its closest rival (the Watwin Score).

Interestingly, when the input dataset was expanded to include all data collected throughout the semester, the number of NPSM variables that made significant contributions shrank from three (NU, UU, RU) to two (UU, NU) (see Table 6). Moreover, both of these variables (UU and NU) were *negatively* correlated with performance. Recall that the UU state is used when students first begin programming. It makes sense that the longer students go without compiling or running their programs, the more likely it is that they will do poorly on the assignment. Likewise, it makes sense that students who spend large proportions of time in the NU state would tend to do worse on assignments, since students in that state are grappling with syntax errors, and may not ever be able to execute their programs. Indeed, the significance of NU as an explanatory factor aligns well with the Error Quotient and Watwin Score, both of which can be seen as quantifying the rate at which students leave the NU state.

4.3.3 Predictions of Final Grades
Lastly, we consider each measure's ability to explain the variance in students' final course grades. As was the case with assignment averages, we used students' programming behavior over the entire semester as input to each measure. The results of this analysis are presented in Table 7. Significant factors in the NPSM are shown in Table 8. As can be seen in Table 7, the Error Quotient was the only measure that did not significantly correlate with students' final grades. The Watwin Score appears to be slightly better at explaining the variance in final grades than it was at explaining the variance in assignment scores. In contrast, the NPSM appears slightly worse at accounting for the variance in final grades than at accounting for the variance in average assignment scores. As before, however, the NPSM did a substantially better job in absolute terms, furnishing three times the explanatory power of the Watwin Score, its closest competitor. Finally, we note that the

Table 2. Explanation of Variance in Individual Assignment Grades

Measure	df	F	p	Adj. R^2
Error Quotient	1, 679	53.65	< 0.01	0.07
Watwin Score (one)	1, 662	13.61	< 0.01	0.02
Watwin Score (all)	1, 662	14.63	< 0.01	0.02
NPSM (no min. time)	11, 653	8.92	< 0.01	0.08
NPSM (>1 hr)	10, 591	8.92	< 0.01	0.11

Table 3. Significant Predictors in NPSM for Individual Assignment Grades (no minimum time)

Variable	β	t	p
YN	0.32	2.03	0.04
RU	0.31	3.77	<0.01
RN	0.18	2.98	<0.01
R/	0.12	2.92	<0.01
Time on task	0.09	2.45	0.02

Table 4. Significant Predictors in NPSM for Individual Assignment Grades (at least 1 hr of programming time)

Variable	β	t	p
NU	-0.17	-3.80	< 0.01
UU	-0.15	-3.45	< 0.01
RU	0.14	2.95	< 0.01
Time on task	0.11	2.57	0.01

Table 5. Explanation of Variance in Average Assignment Grades

Measure	df	F	p	Adj. R^2
Error Quotient	1, 94	7.16	<0.01	0.06
Watwin Score (one)	1, 94	11.50	< 0.01	0.10
Watwin Score (all)	1, 94	10.93	< 0.01	0.10
NPSM	10, 84	7.00	< 0.01	0.39

Table 6. Significant Predictors in NPSM for Assignment Average Grades

Variable	β	t	p
UU	-0.44	-3.88	<0.01
NU	-0.22	-2.28	0.03

two significant factors in the NPSM (UU and NU) remained the same in its correlations with assignment average and final grade.

5. STUDY II: DERIVING A PREDICTVE MEASURE
The previous study showed that the NPSM was able to account for substantially more variation in student performance than both the Error Quotient and Watwin Scores. Given this potential, it makes sense to derive a predictive measure that can be used *in situ* to predict performance, rather than *post hoc* to explain variance.

Table 7. Explanation of Variance in Final Grades

Measure	df	F	p	Adj. R^2
Error Quotient	1, 94	3.68	0.06	0.03
Watwin Score (single error)	1, 94	14.26	< 0.01	0.12
Watwin Score (all errors)	1, 94	14.40	< 0.01	0.12
NPSM	10, 84	6.63	< 0.01	0.36

Table 8. Significant Predictors in NPSM for Final Grades

Variable	β	t	p
UU	-0.30	-2.55	0.01
NU	-0.27	-2.74	<0.01

We now present a follow-up study that uses the results of the previous study to derive a predictive formula rooted in the NPSM.

Given that the NPSM includes eleven predictors, the ideal sample size for achieving full statistical power when deriving a predictive measure would be approximately 220 students (see, e.g. [11, 29]). While it is still possible to detect strong effects on a smaller sample size, running eleven predictors against our sample size of 95 students increases the probability of producing a significant model without any significant predictors. For this reason, we restricted ourselves to the development of a four-variable model—the most appropriate size, given the size of our dataset [11, 29].

We began by examining the seven significant variables identified in Study I: YN, RU, RN, R/, NU, UU, and time on task. A preliminary data analysis using datasets of varying sizes (see Figure 2) revealed a sporadic level of significance for YN, R/, and time on task. Therefore, we decided to drop these variables from further consideration, and settled on the variables UU, NU, RU, and RN for our predictive model.

5.1 Method
For Study II, we used the same programming log data and grade data as were used in Study I. However, for this study, we evaluated the NPSM using seven input data sets whose sizes were systematically varied, as illustrated in Figure 2. The first data set consisted solely of the data collected during the first programming assignment. The final six data sets each added an additional assignment's grades and programming data. Therefore, starting with the second, data set, the outcome variable was the average of all the programming assignment scores received up to that point in time. It follows that the final data set included all programming data from the semester, matching the dataset reported in Table 5.

5.2 Results
For each of the seven data sets, a multivariate regression was performed using UU, NU, RU, and RN as predictor variables and assignment averages as outcome variables. Table 9 provides the individual contribution of each predictive variable. The bottom two rows of the table compute the average value and weighted average value of each coefficient.

In examining the coefficients listed in Table 9, we see that the RU and RN variables are consistently significant regardless of the amount of data considered. In contrast, the UU and NU variables only became significant as the amount of data considered increases. However, in examining the standardized beta

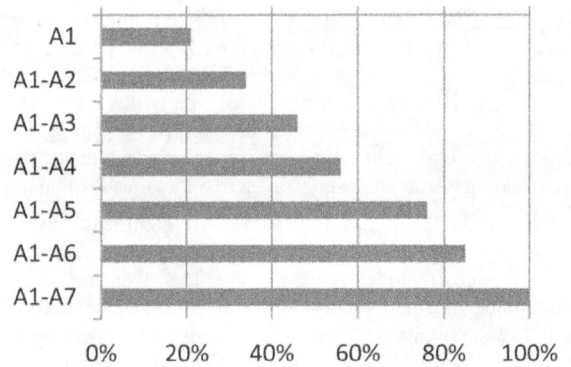

Figure 2. Seven Programming Data sets of Increasing Size as a Percentage of All Programming Data

coefficients, we see that the relative contributions of RU and RN decrease as the size of the data increases, whereas the relative contributions of UU and NU increase as the size of the data increases. Finally, we see a drop in the amount of variance explained when adding data associated with the last assignment. Whether this represents a true ceiling in the NPSM's predictive power remains an interesting question for future research.

5.3 A Predictive Formula
Running the NPSM model with the variables UU, NU, RU, and RN across the seven overlapping data sets reveals a general trend in which the amount of variance increases with the size of the data set. We now use the coefficients from these results in order to formulate two predictive measures. The first is obtained by averaging the unstandardized beta coefficients of each predictor variable across the data sets considered. The second model is obtained by using a weighted averaged of each predictor variable's unstandardized beta coefficients. Recall that the weighted average is formulated based on the overall model's variance numbers. Using the averaged coefficient values reported in Table 9, we arrive at the following formula:

$$NPSM\ Score = 69.78 + (1.75 * RN) + (0.66 * RU) - (0.63 * UU) - (0.43 * NU)$$

Using the weighted coefficient values yields a slightly different formula:

$$NPSM\ Score = 73.42 + (1.58 * RN) + (0.61 * RU) - (0.84 * UU) - (0.45 * NU)$$

To verify the accuracy of each formula, we calculated the predicted score for each dataset using both formulas. Next, we performed a linear regression using this predicted score as the predictor variable and the student's actual assignment score as the outcome variable. We deemed a formula to be successful if it closely mirrored the total amount of variance explained by the overall NPSM model. The amount of variance accounted for by each formula, as well as the overall NPSM model, is listed in Table 10. Inspection of Table 10 reveals that both formulas closely mirror each other (within +/- 2%), and that both are close to the overall NPSM model in terms of explanatory power. As such, it would appear that either formula does a good job of transforming the NPSM data into a usable predictive measure.

6. DISCUSSION
We now turn to a detailed discussion of our results, organized around the two research questions we posed for this research.

Table 9: NSPM Predictive Power and Coefficients for Seven Datasets of Increasing Size (* = sig. at p < 0.05)

Dataset	Variance Explained	Constant	Unstandardized β Coefficients				Standardized β Coefficients			
			UU	NU	RU	RN	UU	NU	RU	RN
A1	13%	50.01	0.09	-0.25	0.87*	2.33*	0.02	-0.08	0.25*	0.34*
A1-A2	15%	58.43	-0.05	-0.16	0.81*	2.54*	-0.02	-0.06	0.28*	0.36*
A1-A3	20%	65.57	-0.07	-0.50*	0.79*	2.17*	-0.03	-0.20*	0.29*	0.33*
A1-A4	26%	75.32	-0.45	-0.62*	0.63*	1.56*	-0.15	-0.26*	0.27*	0.27*
A1-A5	37%	77.54	-1.12*	-0.51*	0.58*	1.48*	-0.34*	-0.22*	0.24*	0.25*
A1-A6	45%	80.80	-1.45*	-0.44*	0.53*	1.16*	-0.45*	-0.19*	0.22*	0.19*
A1-A7	41%	80.79	-1.34*	-0.52*	0.41*	1.02*	-0.43*	-0.23*	0.19*	0.18*
Average	N/A	69.78	-0.63	-0.43	0.66	1.75	-0.20	-0.18	0.25	0.27
Weighted Avg.	N/A	73.42	-0.84	-0.45	0.61	1.58	-0.27	-0.19	0.24	0.25

6.1 RQ1: Do Prior Results Generalize to Different Populations and Programming Languages/Environments?

The results for the Error Quotient and Watwin measures differ drastically from the results presented in prior research. For example, a recent study of both the Error Quotient and Watwin measures accounted for 18% and 36% of the variance in students' final grades [26] as compared to merely 3% and 12% in our study. How can we account for this large discrepancy? We offer two possible explanations.

First, differences in the instructional emphasis of the courses studied might have contributed to the differences in the Error Quotient and Watwin Score observed across the studies. In previous studies in which the Error Quotient Watwin Score were calculated, student homework was worth just 25% of the overall grade. In contrast, in our study, student homework accounted for 35% of the overall grade.

Second, the discrepancies in Error Quotient and Watwin Score measures might be related to key differences in the programming environments and languages used in the studies. Previous studies focused on the BlueJ [17] and the Java programming language. This study collected data on Microsoft® Visual Studio® and the C++ programming language. Both the Error Quotient and Watwin Score rely on the processing of compilation error messages. Given that C++ compilers tend to produce terser and/or more obtuse compilation error messages, it seems plausible that differences could have occurred with respect to students' compilation behaviors in the two environments. For example, forgetting a semi-colon in BlueJ and Java results in the error message, *"error: ';' expected,"* followed by the exact line on which a semi-colon is missing. In contrast, forgetting a semi-colon in Visual Studio® and C++ results in nine error messages. The first message is a red-herring referencing an illegal usage of a type as an expression. For the actual cause, the user must look to the second error message, which states, *"syntax error: missing ';' before identifier <x>,"* with <x> being the line below the statement on which a semi-colon is missing.

Of these two explanations, we find the second one to be the most compelling. Recall that both the Error Quotient and Watwin Score assign penalty points when subsequent compilation attempts either result in more errors, or contain the same error messages as previous compilation attempts. Given that Visual Studio® and C++ generate more error messages per compilation, it stands to

Table 10: Variance Explained by Overall NPSM Model, Averaged NPSM Formula, and Weighted NPSM Formula

Dataset	NPSM Model	Averaged Coefficient Formula	Weighted Coefficient Formula
A1	13%	13%	13%
A1-A2	15%	15%	13%
A1-A3	20%	20%	18%
A1-A4	26%	28%	27%
A1-A5	37%	38%	39%
A1-A6	45%	43%	45%
A1-A7	41%	39%	41%

reason that the Error Quotient and Watwin would artificially inflate the base penalty assigned to students for each failed compilation. Furthermore, in Visual Studio®/C++, the possibility that both the Error Quotient and Watwin Score will generate false positives (matched compilations that have the same error message but for different reasons) increases. In contrast, the coarser approach taken by the NPSM is not affected by these differences: an error state is an error state, regardless of whether a student generated one or one hundred errors in a given compilation.

Even though the amount of variance accounted for by the Error Quotient and Watwin Score in this analysis is much lower than what has been previously reported, it is still possible to make comparisons with prior studies. For example, in their first study, Watson et al. [27] found that the predictive power of both the Error Quotient and Watwin Score increased as a function of the size of the input data. When they considered only a single assignment's worth of data (roughly 2-3 weeks), the variance explained by both Error Quotient and Watwin was fairly low: 10% for Error Quotient and 6% for Watwin. However, by the end of the term, the variance explained by Error Quotient and Watwin had increased to 19% and 42% respectively. Using relative magnitudes, we see that, in their study, Error Quotient increased by a factor of two and Watwin by a factor of seven.

These results are somewhat consistent with the results of this study, which found that the Error Quotient performed best with smaller data sets, and that the Watwin Score performed best with larger data sets. However, unlike in previously published studies, the variance explained by the Error Quotient in our study actually decreased as the size of the input data set increased. That the relative trend in the amount of variance explained by the Watwin Score is similar across studies, whereas the relative trend in the amount of variance explained by the Error Quotient is not, lends further credence to the idea that these predictive measures do not perform consistently when applied to different programming environments and languages. However, in order to increase our confidence in this claim, we would need to conduct additional studies of the Error Quotient, Watwin Score, and NPSM using a variety of programming environments and languages.

6.2 RQ2: How Well Can a More Holistic Programming Model Predict Performance?

In this paper, we developed the NPSM, a predictive model based on the time spent in a set of programming states derived from a program's syntactic and semantic correctness. Given the configuration of instructor, assignments, exams and IDE we studied, the NPSM outperformed models that only consider compilation behavior. At the level of individual programming assignments, the NPSM accounted for four times as much variance as the Watwin Score, but only slightly more variance (1%) than the Error Quotient. With respect to students' overall assignment averages, the NPSM accounted for nearly four times as much variance as the Watwin Score, and over six times the variance accounted for by the Error Quotient. With respect to final course grades, the NPSM accounted for three times as much variance as the Watwin Score, and 12 times as much variance as the Error Quotient.

In Study II, we developed a predictive formula based on four NPSM states. RN (execute a semantically incorrect program) and RU (execute a semantically unknown program) were found to be positive contributors to student success. Conversely, UU (default state before first compilation/execution action is taken in a programming session) and NU (syntactically incorrect program) were found to be negative contributors to a student's success. This seems to indicate that toying with a program's runtime behavior, regardless of semantic correctness, is a successful programming approach. In contrast, writing large portions of code without attempting to compile (UU) is not conducive to success. Indeed, it is easy to imagine that when these students finally do compile, they quickly find themselves in NU, the other state negatively correlated with performance. It is also worth noting that editing states that precede runtime exceptions (YN, NN) were not significant predictors. Therefore, it might be worthwhile to drop this distinction in a future version of our model.

As revealed by our study, the calculations performed by both the Error Quotient and Watwin measures are based on the least weighted significant contributor in the NPSM model: NU. Interestingly, performing a linear regression with NU as the sole predictor variable explains more variance than either the Error Quotient or Watwin Score for both assignment average, $F(1,93 = 15.06)$, $p < 0.01$, $Adj. R^2 = 0.13$, and final grade, $F(1,93 = 23.676)$, $p < 0.01$, $Adj. R^2 = 0.19$. This strongly suggests that any measurement based on programming behaviors would do well to look beyond compilation behavior.

Finally, we note that the aggregation method used in the NPSM is only one possible approach to quantifying **Error! Reference source not found.**'s state diagram. It is possible that other approaches, such as one that quantifying the number and types of transitions, would yield better results. Exploring this possibility would be an interesting direction for future research.

7. CONCLUSION AND FUTURE WORK

This paper introduced the NPSM, a holistic model of student programming behavior; compared its explanatory power against two previously established measures; and derived a formula for predicting student performance given a set of programming process data. Our results indicate that, at least in the population considered in this paper, the NPSM is much better at predicting student performance than the Error Quotient and Watwin Score.

Our preliminary research into the NPSM suggests several directions for future work. First, future studies should examine the robustness of the NPSM by performing a replication study with a larger student population under similar classroom conditions. This would allow researchers to test the predictive NPSM formula against a population different from the population used to derive it. Furthermore, the increased power that accompanies an increase in sample size might allow for the discovery of additional significant factors within the NPSM.

Second, future research should examine the suitability of the NPSM as a predictive measure under conditions not considered in our study. This includes applying the NPSM to different programming languages, environments, and computing courses. It will be especially important to explore the predictive power of the NPSM as applied to different programming environments, given that the NPSM includes states that are unreachable in novice programming environments. For example, novice programming environments often do not allow a program to be executed unless it is syntactically correct (i.e., there is no R\ state), and have only one mode of execution (i.e., there is no distinction between RN and DN, and between RU and DU). Might a modified NPSM, with some states eliminated and other states combined, yield the same predictive power as was observed in this study?

Third, one should consider expanding the scope of the NPSM by incorporating predictors that are not based on programming behavior. For example, in ongoing work, we are exploring how a student's online social behavior (see, e.g. [13]) might impact the predictive capabilities of the NPSM.

Lastly, we plan to explore how the NPSM might serve as a foundation for pedagogical interventions derived from a student's NPSM state. For example, a student who appears to be stuck in an unhelpful state (e.g. NU) might be prompted to ask for help. Alternatively, we might be able to use programming behavior to encourage students to improve their programming techniques. For example, for students who spend a lot of time in the RN (execute without debug) state, an intervention could suggest using the debugger (DN) to troubleshoot semantic issues.

For instructors, we envision an online dashboard that could present continuously-updated information on students' NPSM states and programming progress. Using this information, instructors could check in on struggling students, or perhaps devote additional lecture time to topics or strategies that the dashboard indicates may be problematic for many students.

8. ACKNOWLEDGMENTS

This project is funded by the National Science Foundation under grant no IIS-1321045.

9. REFERENCES

[1]   Ahmadzadeh, M., Elliman, D. and Higgins, C. 2005. An analysis of patterns of debugging among novice computer science students. *ITiCSE '05: Proceedings of the 10th*

annual SIGCSE conference on Innovation and technology in computer science education. ACM Press. 84–88.

[2] Altadmri, A. and Brown, N.C.C. 2015. 37 Million Compilations: Investigating Novice Programming Mistakes in Large-Scale Student Data. *Proceedings of the 46th ACM Technical Symposium on Computer Science Education* (Kansas City, MO, USA, 2015), 522–527.

[3] Baker, R.S.J. and Siemens, G. 2014. Educational data mining and learning analytics. *The Cambridge Handbook of the Learning Sciences.* Cambridge University Press. 253–274.

[4] Bergin, S., Reilly, R. and Traynor, D. 2005. Examining the role of self-regulated learning on introductory programming performance. *Proc. 2005 ACM International Computing Education Research Workshop.* ACM Press. 81–86.

[5] Bransford, J., Brown, A.L. and Cocking, R.R. eds. 1999. *How people learn: Brain, mind, experience, and school.* National Academy Press.

[6] Campbell, P.F. and McCabe, G.P. 1984. Predicting the Success of Freshmen in a Computer Science Major. *Commun. ACM.* 27, 11 (1984), 1108–1113.

[7] Carter, A.S. 2012. Supporting the virtual design studio through social programming environments. *Proceedings of the ninth annual international conference on International computing education researc* (Auckland, New Zealand, 2012), 157–158.

[8] Goldenson, D.R. and Wang, B.J. 1991. Use of structure editing tools by novice programmers. *Empirical Studies of Programmers: Fourth Workshop.* Ablex. 99–120.

[9] Graham, M.J., Federick, J., Byers-Winston, A., Hunber, A.B. and Handelsman, J. 2013. Increasing persistence of college students in STEM. *Science.* 341, 27 Sept. (2013), 1455–56.

[10] Guzdial, M. 1994. Software-realized scaffolding to facilitate programming for science learning. *Interactive learning Environments.* 4, 1 (1994), 1–44.

[11] Harrell, F.E. 2001. *Regression Modeling Strategies: With Applications to Linear Models, Logistic Regression, and Survival Analysis.* Springer.

[12] Hundhausen, C.D., Brown, J.L., Farley, S. and Skarpas, D. 2006. A methodology for analyzing the temporal evolution of novice programs based on semantic components. *Proceedings of the 2006 ACM International Computing Education Research Workshop.* ACM Press. 45–56.

[13] Hundhausen, C.D., Carter, A.S. and Adesope, O. 2015. Supporting Programming Assignments with Activity Streams: An Empirical Study. *Proc. 2015 SIGCSE Symposium on Computer Science Education* (New York, 2015).

[14] Jadud, M.C. 2006. Methods and tools for exploring novice compilation behaviour. *Proce. Second International Workshop on Computing Education Research.* ACM. 73–84.

[15] Jeske, D., Stamov-Rossnagel, C. and Backhaus, J. 2014. Learner characteristics predict performance and confidence in e-Learning: An analysis of user behavior and self-evaluation. *Journal of Interactive Learning Research.* 25, 4 (2014), 509–529.

[16] Kessler, C.M. and Anderson, J.R. 1986. A Model of Novice Debugging in LISP. *Empirical Studies of Programmers.* 198–212.

[17] Kölling, M., Quig, B., Patterson, A. and Rosenberg, J. 2003. The BlueJ system and its pedagogy. *Journal of Compuer Science Education.* 13, 4 (2003), 249–268.

[18] Ma, W., Adesope, O.O., Nesbit, J.C. and Liu, Q. 2014. Intelligent tutoring systems and learning outcomes: A meta-analytic survey. *Journal of Educational Psychology.* 106, 2007 (2014), 901–918.

[19] Rosson, M.B., Carroll, J.M. and Sinha, H. 2011. Orientation of Undergraduates Toward Careers in the Computer and Information Sciences: Gender, Self-Efficacy and Social Support. *ACM Transactions on Computing Education.* 11, 3 (Oct. 2011), 1–23.

[20] Schunk, D.H. 2012. *Learning theories: An educational perspective.* Merrill Prentice Hall.

[21] Slavin, R.E. 2011. *Educational psychology: Theory and practice.* Pearson Education.

[22] Spohrer, J.C. 1992. *MARCEL: Simulating the novice programmer.* Ablex.

[23] Tabano, E.S., Rodrigo, M.M.T. and Jadud, M.C. 2011. Predicting at-risk novice Java programmers through the analysis of online protocols. *Proceedings of the seventh international workshop on Computing education research* (Providence, Rhode Island, USA, 2011), 85–92.

[24] U.S. Department of Education, Office of Educational Technology 2012. *Enhancing Teaching and Learning through Educational Data Mining and Learning Analytics: An Issue Brief.*

[25] Visual Studio® - Microsoft® Developer Tools: 2015. *http://www.visualstudio.com.* Accessed: 2015-04-20.

[26] Watson, C., Li, F.W.B. and Godwin, J.L. 2014. No tests required: comparing traditional and dynmaic predictors of programming success. *Proceedings of the 45th ACM Technical Symposium on Computer Science Education* (2014), 469–474.

[27] Watson, C., Li, F.W.B. and Godwin, J.L. 2013. Predicting Performance in an Introductory Programming Course by Logging and Analyzing Student Programming Behavior. *Proceedings of the 2013 IEEE 13th International Conference on Advanced Learning Technologies* (2013), 319–323.

[28] Wilson, B.C. and Shrock, S. 2001. Contributing to Success in an Introductory Computer Science Course: A Study of Twelve Factors. *SIGCSE Bull.* 33, 1 (2001), 184–188.

[29] Wilson, C.R., Voorhis, V. and Morgan, B.L. 2007. Understanding power and rules of thumb for determining sample sizes. *Tutorials in Quantitative Methods for Psychology.* 3, 2 (2007), 43–50.

School/Work: Development of Computing Students' Professional Identity at University

Robert McCartney
Department of Computer Science and Engineering
University of Connecticut
Storrs, CT USA
robert@engr.uconn.edu

Kate Sanders
Mathematics and Computer Science Department
Rhode Island College
Providence, RI USA
ksanders@ric.edu

ABSTRACT

When students talk about their university experiences, they identify particular events as being significant in their development. We look at the experiences relating to coursework and career of two students who were interviewed throughout their undergraduate degree programs. We found that they shared some of the significant events but not all, and the reactions to the shared events were sometimes quite different.

Categories and Subject Descriptors

K.3.2 [**Computers and Education**]: Computers and Information Science Education—*Computer Science Education*

General Terms

Measurement, Human Factors, Experimentation

Keywords

longitudinal; intellectual development

1. INTRODUCTION

Earning a university degree in computing is a multi-year process. Students generally enter with varied computer science backgrounds, generally (in the US at least) with little or no formal training, and are expected to be ready to join the workforce or take graduate degrees in four years. We design curricula to make this possible, so students progress from introductory to advanced courses in computing, and gradually attain the necessary expertise to enter a career in the discipline.

How does this development occur? To examine this, we have interviewed a group of computing majors from a single cohort over the last five years. Having sets of interviews from the same individuals over time allows us to look at how individual students changed during their college years.

ICER'15, August 9–13, 2015, Omaha, Nebraska, USA.
© 2015 ACM. ISBN 978-1-4503-3630-7/15/08 ...$15.00.
DOI: http://dx.doi.org/10.1145/2787622.2787732.

These interviews covered a number of set topics, but some of these were quite open-ended, and there was room to expand and follow up on any of these topics in each interview.

In this paper, we examine the events that students chose to discuss in their interviews that relate to coursework and jobs. In many of the interviews these were things that students chose to emphasize, and so it can be assumed that the students saw these as significant parts of their experience. The specific research questions that we address are

1. What are significant school- and job-related events that affect computing students' professional identity?

2. How do these events affect the computing students who experience them?

Although these students experience many of the same events in a significant way, the effects of these events are fairly specific to the individual. For example, two students may be strongly affected by taking Data Structures, but the effect on one is is to become comfortable with abstraction rather than implementation, while the effect on the other is to change his or her focus toward hardware systems. Similarly, internships can lead to different results: a student may gain a sense of identity as a professional and focus more strongly on career, or find out that a particular kind of job is just a bad fit.

2. BACKGROUND

Our longitudinal study was inspired by the work of William Perry at Harvard in the 1960s. Perry [6] studied the development of university students and observed certain characteristics in first-year students, notably that they start with something close to a "dualist" perspective, that is, there are right and wrong answers, and that the teacher knows (and represents) the absolute truth and will impart that truth to the student. He presents a nine-step path of development from seeing knowledge as an absolute, to seeing knowledge as relative and contextual, to ultimately developing a personal identity within this relative world.

More recently, Stevens et al. reported on a longitudinal study of engineering students at four different universities. [10] They identified three "dimensions" of becoming an engineer:

- acquiring "accountable disciplinary knowledge" (ADK). Different forms of knowledge count as disciplinary knowledge in different contexts. The kinds of knowledge that freshmen and seniors are expected to display may be significantly different, and may in turn be different from the knowledge they must use on the job. Students take exams; they will rarely take exams on the job (though they may be asked to take one as part of a job interview). Freshmen are generally expected to work alone on well defined problems; by the time they're seniors, they're more likely to be working in teams on open-ended ill-defined problems. Knowledge is situated in a way that is not captured, for example, by simply giving a novice and an expert the same task.

- developing a professional identity as an engineer. Identity includes both the way you see yourself and the way you are seen by others.

- "navigating" through their university education. Every university program has certain requirements: courses to be taken, often in a particular order, assignments and exams to be completed, advisors to be met with, paperwork to be filled out, etc. There are usually official pathways through these requirements, made explicit by advisors and on webpages. There also exist *unofficial* pathways. For example, students in the know might take a particularly difficult course at another school and transfer it back to their home institution.

This framework has been shown to be a helpful way to think about the value of having students develop portfolios. [3, 11] It abstracts away from the details of any particular major, however. One of the questions we investigate is how the specific details of a particular major can be fit into – and perhaps illuminate – Stevens et al.'s broad picture.

Peters has begun a longitudinal study of computing students. A preliminary research design was presented in 2013. [7] The following year, she and others reported on a phenomenographic outcome space of freshman computing students' experience of participation in computing, based on an analysis of the first year's data. [8] The categories in the outcome space included using, inquiry, creating things, systematic problem solving, creating for others, continuous development, and doing research. Peters's project will likely address questions similar to those of the work described in this paper, but so far has taken a different and complementary approach.

Finally, Pierrakos et al. have proposed a model, based on a study of freshman engineers, of "persisters" and "switchers". [9] The "persisters" (students who continued in engineering through at least the end of their first year) had more knowledge of and exposure to engineering before university: someone in their family or someone they knew well was an engineer, or they had taken relevant classes in secondary school, attended engineering summer camps, etc. The "switchers" (students who left) had weaker exposure to engineering. Someone such as a family member, friend, or school counselor – not an engineer – may have suggested that they try engineering, for example. Persisters formed stronger social networks with faculty and peers in engineering; switchers made fewer social contacts, or made them in the major they switched into instead of in engineering. Of the two students examined in detail in this paper, one exhibited the "switcher" characteristics and the other the "persister" characteristics, but they both graduated. We will discuss the nuances of their stories further below.

3. METHODOLOGY

In this paper, we are examining the individual experience of computing majors as they progress through their university degree program. We have chosen to do this by means of case studies. This is appropriate for a number of reasons: [12]

- The questions of interest ask "How?" and "Why?" development happens;

- The examination is contemporary with the phenomena of interest: the development is taking place during the study; and

- Development (in the sense we use the term) is individual and cannot easily be separated from experience; in terms of epistemology it is relativist and contextualized.

Case studies have been used in computing education research, for example to illustrate a middle school student's debugging techniques [4] and the possible positive (or at least non-negative) value of the nerd stereotype of computing majors. [1]. Stevens et al. explain their choice of a similarly narrative approach by saying that they want to "get at the whole person's experience ... to recover engineering students moving through their undergraduate educations" and capture "their individual pathways and experiences as engineers-in-the-making." [10, pp. 355-356]

The cases in the study are the individuals who are studied over time. The expectation is that individual changes in attitude can be identified and explained in context, from the perspectives of the individual students – within-case analysis. Given this, we can further analyze the data across cases to characterize both the commonalities and the variation.

3.1 Data Collection

The data used in this study consist of a series of interviews, all with the same interviewer, Robert McCartney. The original goal was to interview 12 computing students at the end of each of their academic years at the University of Connecticut (UConn). Students were recruited for the interviews by email sent to all freshmen computing majors who started in Fall, 2010. The first round of volunteers was all male, so a second request was sent to all of the female students to get a more gender-diverse pool. These students were all in the engineering school; all had declared computing majors: eight in Computer Science and Engineering, four in Computer Science.[1] Two students had second majors, one in Cognitive Science, one in Mathematics. All were between 18 and 20 years old; nine were male, three female; eight were Caucasian, three Asian or Asian-American, one African-American. The first set of interviews took place in late April, 2011.

The interviews were semi-structured, based on a script that covered the topics shown in Figure 1. The emphasis varied, depending on the students' responses: for example, if a student had never learned anything informally we did not discuss that experience in depth. The interviews ranged from 24 to 67 minutes in length, with an average of approximately 45 minutes. The average length increased from 36 minutes in 2011 to 57 minutes in 2014. The interviews were

[1]At UConn both the Computer Science and Engineering and the Computer Science degrees are in the Computer Science and Engineering (CSE) department.

1. What does the discipline of CS entail? (important topics, skills needed, follow-up on topic/skill)

2. Is there anything about computing that you learned informally, i.e. not in a class (if not: what was most interesting/important thing you learned this year) (why this, how did you do it, were there others involved, compare with formal,what did you learn from the experience, what advice would you give to others)

3. Who is it that contributes to your education? (follow up: assess the relative contribution of your individual efforts, the efforts of your instructors, and the efforts of your peers? How are your lectures and labs?)

4. Why did you choose to major in CS? (influenced by others, background before university, how do you think you are doing)

5. What do you hope/expect to do when you graduate? What do you expect to see/do in your career?

6. Reflecting on this year at university: What have you learned? Has the experience been what you expected? Have your views of your education changed? Was there a point where you became stuck or discouraged – how did you deal with it?

7. How could we (the department) improve things for students?

Figure 1: Outline of the interview script, by topic. Possible follow-up areas in parentheses.

Table 1: Interviews and Graduations by academic year, 2011-2015.

	10-11	11-12	12-13	13-14	14-15	Graduated
Andrew	x			x		May 2014
Benjamin	x	x	x	x		May 2014
Charles	x	x	x	x	x	May 2015
Daniel	x	x	x	x		May 2014
Edward	x	Left program 2012				
Frank	x	x	x	x	x	May 2016[a]
George	x	x	x	x		May 2014
Henry	x	x	x	x		May 2014
Ian	x	x		x	x	Dec. 2014
Judy	x	x	Left program 2013			
Karen	x	x	x	x		May 2014
Louisa	x			x		May 2014

recorded and then transcribed by a commercial trancription service.

For various reasons, not every student was interviewed every year. Two students left the computing degree program, one before the second interview, one before the third. Two students missed interviews while they were studying abroad. Three students chose not to participate for a year during the study for other reasons (each interview was voluntary). The interviews given and graduation dates are given in Table 1. Nine of the students have graduated with computing degrees, one is scheduled to graduate in May 2016, and two left the computing major before finishing. All but one of these interviews was face-to-face in the interviewer's office; one interview was done over Skype when a student was studying abroad.

3.2 Data Analysis

Each case (or *unit of analysis* [12]) corresponds to an individual student. The data related to each case consist of a sequence of transcripts taken from annual interviews with a particular student, starting in the student's first academic year and continuing through the year he or she graduates or leaves the program.

Our primary analytic approach is within-case analysis, comparing school-work attitudes both within and between each person's interviews. This necessitated reading the transcripts in each case multiple times, to identify the individual

context as it changed over the years, and the "big picture" view of the individual's time in school. Doing this for multiple individuals illustrated that many of the changes were related to school- and work-related events; it also illustrated that the specifics – the events and how they affected the students – were quite dependent on the individual.

Once this big picture was constructed, we loaded the transcripts into a QDA tool for tagging and memoing. This was done for individual students across years rather than across students in an attempt to capture the individual experiences. Further examining the data by category over time allowed us to identify both general characteristics of the individual that did not change over time, as well as those that did, and identify *critical incidents* (defined in Section 4.2) associated with these changes.

In this paper, we focus on two individuals, which allows us to present their cases in sufficient detail. These two were chosen in part because their backgrounds and experiences have much in common – both males, neither having programming experience before university, both finishing in four academic years – but also because they illustrate how students faced with similar events can have different experiences and responses. For each of these individuals, we present a timeline of critical incidents and responses to illustrate their individual development, then compare the incidents and responses between these two individuals to identify similarities and differences.

4. RESULTS

The results of the analysis are the within-case and cross-case analyses of school- and work-related events for two individuals, Benjamin and George.[2] First, to set the context, we summarize the cases used in these analyses. These summaries are presented as the "stories" of these two individuals, Benjamin and George.

4.1 The case synopses

4.1.1 Benjamin

Benjamin entered the university as an Engineering Physics major; he knew he wanted to be an engineer, but was unsure about which particular discipline. His mother is a soft-

---

[2]All subjects are referred to by pseudonyms chosen to reflect their gender.

ware engineer. During his first semester he changed majors from Engineering Physics to Computer Science & Engineering while taking a programming class required for all engineers. He enjoyed programming, which he had not done before, and "could see myself" doing programming for a job. In addition, he believed that programming would be in demand for any kind of engineering, giving him a wide variety of opportunities.

By the end of his second year, Benjamin had changed majors again, from Computer Science & Engineering to Computer Engineering. During that year, he took a mixture of courses, some oriented toward software (Data Structures, Software Engineering), some toward hardware (Digital Logic, Electrical Circuits). While he did reasonably well in all of these, he really enjoyed (and was more comfortable in) his hardware classes, so he switched to a major that was more hardware-oriented but still in the general area of computing. In the summer after his second year he had an internship in a large aerospace company providing Excel and database support.

In the spring of his third year, Benjamin obtained an internship with a local engineering firm that tested buried power lines to locate faults and focus on specific areas that need repair. A year later, at the end of his fourth year, he was proud to report that he'd accepted a permanent position with that company. The fact that he knew both software and hardware helped him with his salary negotiations and also gave him the opportunity to work on a wider variety of different projects.

Benjamin was transformed during his four years in engineering school. He chose engineering because he was told that he should, but he didn't know exactly what he wanted to do and didn't know if he could succeed. He wanted to be competent, to be able to see a problem and solve it without step-by-step instructions of the kind he'd been given in his freshman-year assignments. By the end of his fourth year, he had achieved that goal. During his internship, his supervisors expected him to work independently: "They don't even want to be involved in the project. That's the reason they gave it to you." By this point, however, he was confident that he could do it. He believed that he was "prepared to enter the workforce."

4.1.2 George

George came to university from an urban, economically-disadvantaged area. He graduated near the top of his high-school class, where he never had to work at academics, and was a fairly serious skateboarder. He was encouraged to go to engineering school because he was good at math and science, but he had little or no exposure to engineering and no programming experience. He selected CSE because he thought it was "cool". The purpose of university, in George's view, was to prepare for a job.

George found university to be a fairly rough transition. His first-year courses were more difficult than he expected, and his grades were lower than he wanted. He responded by developing a strong social network: getting help from instructors and TAs and working with peers in study groups. He noted optimistically, "There's plenty of help that can be found."

George, like Benjamin, took Data Structures in the fall of his second year. Like Benjamin, he found it challeng-

ing. He considered switching majors to Business, but unlike Benjamin, he stuck with CSE.

During his third year, George made some changes to his work habits – he stopped studying with others, and began handing in assignments early. He also became more strategic with his studying, trying to predict what would be on exams. His grades improved greatly in his last three semesters; he received an academic prize his last year given to people who attain an impressive grade point average (GPA) of at least 3.7 out of 4 in consecutive semesters. This achievement enabled him to raise his cumulative GPA from about 2.5 to over 3.0 by graduation. In his fourth year, George took the year-long Senior Design course, where his team developed an iPhone app for planning and promoting social events, and re-took Data Structures, largely as a way to improve his performance at interviews.

George's work history includes an internship after his third year with an engineering firm, doing non-computing work. He interviewed for a software internship elsewhere, but did not get it. Just before graduation, he had accepted a job as a consultant, but as his start had been delayed he was considering looking for a software developer job.

Certain characteristics pervade all of George's interviews. He shows awareness of and concern over the cost of attending university. He discusses the importance of getting a job to support himself. Every year he talks about the need to work even harder, and finds his academic program to be stressful. He is strongly motivated to succeed by grades, the need to get a job, and the desire to avoid wasting his parents' money. These extrinsic motivations fight with his long-held dream of owning a skateboard shop. It wasn't until his senior year that he found something about computing that he really enjoyed: the year-long senior project. He spoke at length about how much fun the project was, took it to interviews to show prospective employers, and envisioned himself being happy with a job doing that type of software development.

4.2 Critical Incidents

Within the stories the students have told us about their years of undergraduate study, we focus on the critical incidents. "Critical incidents" are defined by Miles and Huberman as "those events seen as critical, influential, or decisive in the course of some process." [5, p. 115] In the case of our participants, these events include particular courses, projects, exams, job interviews, internships, and research experiences. These were things that either the participant emphasized in an interview or identified as something that caused a change. Generally, once mentioned, these were mentioned again in future years' interviews.

A number of critical incidents were common to many of the cases, including Benjamin and George. These included things related to coursework (specific required courses, grades, and the senior design project) and events relating to work outside the university: interviews, internships, and finding (permanent) jobs.

Courses and Grades can affect students beyond the expected gain in knowledge. The effects were occasioned by different factors: the difficulty of the course, the appreciation of the material, specific interactions with instructors, or how they fit with the students' other courses or interests. The Senior Design course, a year-long team project that all engineering students take at UConn in their last year, can be particularly influen-

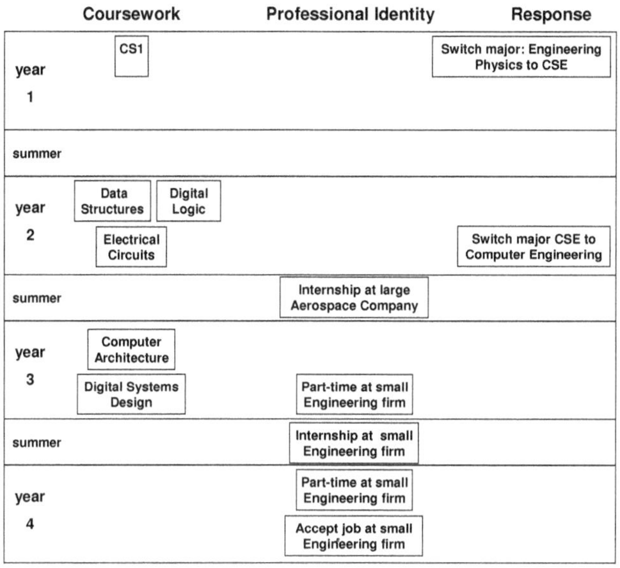

Figure 2: Benjamin's critical incidents over time, organized by Coursework, Professional Identity, and Response.

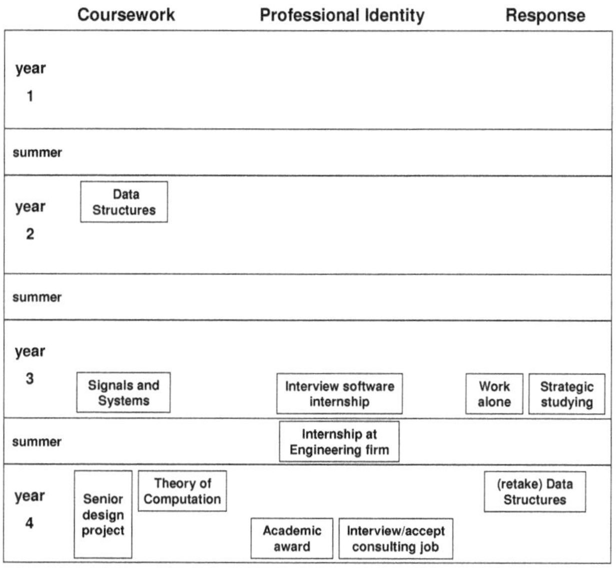

Figure 3: George's critical incidents over time, organized by Coursework, Professional Identity, and Response.

tial, as it is meant to pull together all that the students have learned, and involves greater autonomy and less structure than other courses.

Internships, Interviews and Jobs Expectations and attitudes toward career are a part of each student's professional identity, and we can see critical events and changes in these attitudes over the four years. Many students find the interviews stressful, especially since they have become such a cultural obsession in computing.

The critical incidents for Benjamin and George are summarized in Critical Incident Charts in Figures 2 and 3 respectively.

4.2.1 Benjamin's Critical Incidents

Courses and Grades

Benjamin's first critical incident was changing degree programs from Engineering Physics to Computer Science & Engineering. Largely this was due to his CS1 course, a course using MATLAB taught to all engineering students. He liked programming, and saw that it could be applied to a broad range of engineering disciplines.

In his second year, however, his computing coursework changed. He found Data Structures to be both difficult and time-consuming. His first-year computing courses had programming assignments that provided a lot of guidance on how things should be implemented – what classes to write, what methods they should have, and so forth – but in Data Structures more was left to the student, described by Benjamin as "Do this very high level description." While he understood the concepts, he had a difficult time coding, and spent about three-quarters of his total effort on that one class. He expected to fail the course; he ultimately received a grade of B+ (relatively high), which he attributes to the concept-focused exams and "a massive curve." He projected his discomfort with coding to whether he could do that for the rest of his life.

He mentioned this course again in his interview two years later, when he reflected:

> *2014:* I was just talking before about how nothing is too difficult, but when I took Data Structures and Algorithms, I kind of fell off. That's one of the things that kind of pushed me away ... that class and sophomore year in general is really what separates people who think that they can write MATLAB code and then the people who are writing actual code out in the real world.

Also in his second year, Benjamin took courses in Digital Logic (fall) and Electrical Circuits (spring), both required for Computer Science & Engineering. He really liked these courses, unlike Data Structures, and felt he would rather design hardware than software. He contemplated switching his major to Electrical Engineering, but decided on Computer Engineering as well – in part because of his "investment" of time in Data Structures, but also because he still wanted to work with computing, but at the hardware level.

His attitude toward programming changed somewhat as a result of his third year courses in Computer Architecture, where he programmed in assembly, and in Digital System Design, where he programmed in VHDL. He found that he liked programming at a lower level, where "I can see where the bits are going in the hardware." He further explained that he would have to be more well-rounded than only designing circuits, and programming would be part of that.

Internships, Interviews, and Jobs

From the first year on, Benjamin relates his education to his ultimate career: his goals are to both get a degree and be good at what he does.

The critical incident of Benjamin's first year, his change from Engineering Physics to Computer Science, was motivated in part by job concerns: his belief that Computer Science would leave more options open. His change to Computer Engineering after his second year was motivated by an interaction between courses and job concerns. After Data Structures and Circuits, he saw himself as a weak coder but good with circuits. Reflecting on the two major changes:

> *2012:* From Engineering Physics to Computer Science was purely me thinking about my job after. And I didn't really know quite what Engineering Physics would prepare me for.
>
> I'm glad that I'm in Computer Engineering over Electrical Engineering, not just because of the classes I've taken. Because, when I graduate, I want to work on devices. I want to work on computers. The electrical components, but I want to work on that. I don't think I'd be interested in Power Systems, or the larger stuff in Electric Engineering. So I'm happy with my decision.

Benjamin had internships after his second and third years. The first was at a large aerospace firm, where he applied to work with the VLSI group, but was hired to provide spreadsheet and database support in a less technical group. Among the lessons learned was that people in large companies tend to be quite specialized, working on narrow slices of projects.

In his third year, he obtained an internship doing Electrical Engineering for a relatively small tech company specializing in power-cable testing, which involves designing hardware and software, collecting data on-site, and analysis. He stayed on part-time through his fourth year at school, and accepted a full-time position as an R&D Engineer when he graduated. He did a variety of things as an intern, including power electronics, analog measurement circuitry, and digital data acquisition, the last including coding. He compared his experience there with his experience at the large aerospace firm, noting that in the small firm people could design and implement prototypes from the ground up: design, fabrication, programming, and testing, whereas in the large firm such work would be spread across the various specialists. As he values his versatility, he sees his current environment as a positive.

4.2.2 George's Critical Incidents

Courses and Grades

George also found Data Structures to be challenging; it was quite a transition from his previous programming courses, one he described as from "I'm going to help you through this" to "do this." He was unsure about his programming skills, and observed that a number of students "just dropped it after the first homework assignment and switched majors."

He talked more about people leaving because of Data Structures in his third year interview, noting that the people that changed majors then (in their second year) could still graduate in four years. He had considered changing majors himself, and was concerned that he would not be able to finish on time. He was also concerned with his programming skills, and referred to Data Structures as one of the three most important courses in the curriculum, with Algorithms and Software Engineering, for those people who wanted to become software developers.

Data Structures is an important theme of George's relative to internships and jobs as well, so we will return to this topic later.

In his third year, experience in a course (Signals and Systems) led to a change in his study habits. The specific event was getting a relatively low grade on a test after having studied a lot, exacerbated by his roommate getting a high score. His responses were 1) to try and be more strategic with studying, to try and figure out what topics are likely to be covered by being more observant at help and review sessions and making sure to study them, and 2) to stop studying and doing homework with others. This was a big change, as he had been studying with others since high school, but he realized that he was relying on others too much, and not adequately learning the material.

George was also influenced by other particular courses, although not necessarily by their content. While taking a Theory of Computation course in his fourth year, George did poorly on the first exam, then spent more time with the instructor in office hours, then did poorly on the second exam. The instructor gave him a candid assessment:

> *2014:* He helped me realize that sometimes you have to work harder than everyone else in order to do well. And he didn't do it in the way of, "Oh, you're going to do good. Just study really hard." He did it in the way of, "You've got to get this right or else this is what your grade is going to be." I ended up, I don't know what happened on the final, and ended up getting an A- in his class.

In Senior Design, George worked with a team of computer science students to build an iPhone app for scheduling social events. As it was not a sponsored project, the team had a great deal of freedom to include whatever features they wanted. They chose to include a number of "social" features: the ability to comment on events, to post pictures, to send invitations, to access maps, to incorporate texts. It was developed in Objective-C and XCode, and made extensive use of storyboards in development. After eight months of development and testing, they were able to demonstrate their system at the design-project demonstration day, a public event held at the end of the year that included students from all of the departments in the engineering school.

The project was a positive experience for a number of reasons. It was "fun" to work on, and it allowed George to learn Objective-C and Xcode. It allowed independence as well, as the team was responsible for planning the work, setting milestones, and dealing with new (to them) technologies.

Internships, Interviews, and Jobs

George's view of work is also apparent from his first year on. He talks about learning the things he needs to do (and keep) his job. He has a pragmatic view of work, that "you have to have a job that pays before you can do what you really want to do." He describes college as an option that you are paying for, and that the purpose of going to college is getting a job, an attitude that colors his view of students who don't put forth effort in their classes.

But he has conflicting goals, in that he doesn't want to give up on his avocation, skateboarding. He talks about somehow tying in his job with skateboarding; when things are academically rough for him at the end of the second year he talks about switching to a Business major, with the goal of opening a skateboard shop.

After his third year, George was more specific about jobs and interviews, but had not done any. He assessed his programming skills as "not too strong", which might mean working in a more hardware-related job. He showed some anxiety about the interview process ahead, particularly during his senior year:

> *2013:* I'm going to have to go to these career fairs and have to meet people and make first impressions and set up phone interviews and dress nice and – it's a lot of pressure.

Subsequent to the 2013 interview, George interviewed for an internship with a software company. It did not go well; they asked him a number of relatively straightforward data structures questions – reverse a string, write a recursive method for a node class – that he was not able to answer. He did not get the job. He was able to get a job at an engineering firm that had nothing to do with computing, and although the pay was good, it was not the sort of job that he wanted for the future, "reading diagrams and walking around the site and picking out if these pipes were installed the right way."

As a response to his interview problems and weakness as a programmer, George re-took Data Structures in his fourth year, so he could perform better on interviews. This strategy paid off, as he was able to perform well in interviews, and had accepted a job as a consultant before graduation. He attributed his ability to answer the interview questions to his taking Data Structures again.

Job issues were a strong motivator for getting better grades as well. He was concerned that his GPA would cause him to get screened out when applying for jobs, and so he became a highly effective student in his third and fourth year, raising his GPA significantly, from around 2.5 to over 3.0 (out of 4). He received an award in his fourth year for having semester grades averaging over 3.7 for consecutive semesters. His improved GPA gave George more confidence:

> *2014:* Employers ask me, "Why don't you have a 3.5?" I'm like, "Well, that's a good question to be asking," as opposed to, "Why don't you even have a 3.0?"

4.2.3 Comparing Benjamin's and George's Critical Incidents

Benjamin and George had some of the same critical incidents. For both, taking Data Structures changed their perspectives, leading them to characterize themselves as weak programmers. Their responses, however were different: Benjamin switched to a major more focused on hardware; George ultimately changed his view of himself by retaking Data Structures and successfully completing some software projects, including his Senior Design project. Both students took Digital Logic and Electrical Circuits, but they were only critical for Benjamin, who really liked hardware.

Both had summer internships that were outside of their desired areas, but at different times. Benjamin, who failed to get his VLSI design internship, seemed to be unaffected by that rejection as it was after his second year ("Obviously I expected that.."), whereas George failed to get a computer science internship after his third year, and had the extra disappointment of an unsuccessful interview. Both learned from these experiences: Benjamin that he did not want to work at a large firm where everyone is specialized, and George that he needed to work hard to improve his interview performance (and that he didn't want a job like his internship).

There are significant differences in how these two were affected by job-related incidents. Benjamin found a work environment in his internship and subsequent part-time work that gave him confidence that he would be successful. George was stressed that he couldn't deal with interviews and recruiters, and that his grades needed to be improved significantly to be hired. George's retaking Data Structures, plus his experience in his senior design project, improved his confidence and contributed to his successful job search.

One thing that was critical for George but *not* critical for Benjamin was the senior design course. Benjamin discussed his, but it didn't seem to be a big deal, even as he suggested that we should institute a sophomore-level course on that model. A likely explanation is that Benjamin was already getting the benefits that the senior design experience imparts from his internship and part-time job – he was getting authentic team-based design experience already. George's senior design benefits look a lot like Benjamin's job benefits.

Finally, some critical incidents are simply different between the two. Benjamin was affected by course content that changed his view of programming. George was strongly affected by course incidents, but the effects on his work and study habits was not related to the specific course content.

5. DISCUSSION

This project extends previous work on persisters and switchers and on the ways in which students become engineers. It also has implications, both for teaching and for future research. We consider each of these in turn.

5.1 Comparison with other studies

These case studies suggest a more nuanced view of Pierrakos et al.'s persisters and switchers. According to the original theory, George had many characteristics of a switcher: he came into computing because he was good at math and science, without any real exposure to engineering or any programming background. Until his final year, his only motivations were extrinsic: getting good grades, getting a job, pleasing his parents, not wasting the money his parents were providing for his support. He was well aware that something was lacking in his attitude towards engineering: the passion that he felt for skateboarding. Yet he did not switch.

Why was George able to persist? There were numerous reasons. First, he was very strongly motivated to succeed. Second, in Dweck's terms, he had a "growth mindset" [2]: he believed that if he just worked harder and smarter, he could improve his results. Perhaps because of that mindset, he was able to listen to and learn from negative feedback, for example when he re-took Data Structures to improve his performance in job interviews. Third, he had remarkable emotional intelligence. He was able to manage his own emotions, recognizing that it was important to keep calm and not panic during exams, and he established a very strong social network starting in his first year, working with his instructors, his TAs, and his peers.

Fourth, he continually refined and improved his study strategies. As time went on, he spent less time working in study groups. He continued to take advantage of professor's office hours, however, and learned to combine hard work with people skills when preparing for exams. He studied the material carefully before review sessions and then carefully observed what happened during the review session:

2014: When you [the professor] get to the topics that are on the exam you're kind of quiet. When a student pinpoints exactly what the quote unquote curveball or section is. You kind of give it away. But it takes a person who is studying the class a lot to realize that. You can't figure that out if you're not even looking at the material.

Fifth, in his senior year, he finally found an intrinsic reason to continue: he really enjoyed his work on his senior design project. The only one of these factors that was included in the Pierrakos et al. model was the formation of social ties within the major.

Similarly, our case studies both agree with and augment Stevens et al.'s three-dimensional model of becoming an engineer. We consider their three dimensions in turn.

Accountable Domain Knowledge. Like the students in Stevens et al.'s study, our students experienced a shift from very well defined assignments, to assignments with more gaps to be filled in, to very open-ended senior projects. Because we focused on a particular major, we are able to identify particular courses where these transitions occurred: Data Structures and the two-semester capstone course (Senior Design). Moreover, we can see how differently students respond to the same course (taken in the same semester with the same instructor).

Identity. A professional identity includes both your own view of yourself and outside recognition. For these students, the primary sources of outside recognition (other than successfully obtaining a diploma) are related to jobs. Imagining future jobs in their major (or being unable to) was a key part of their developing individual identity as well. They began to talk about the importance of jobs in their freshman interviews, and internships, interviews, and jobs were prominent topics throughout. Surprisingly, jobs were downplayed in Stevens et al.

Navigation. Like the students in Stevens et al.'s study, George and Benjamin also had to learn to find a path from freshman year to graduation. Due to institutional differences, however, the shoals they were required to navigate and the possible strategies were different. Unlike UConn, the university in the earlier study did not officially admit students to the engineering program until their third year, so the need to be admitted dominated their thinking.

Instead, our students discuss three navigation challenges: choosing a major within engineering, succeeding within the major, and finding a job (first summer, and then permanent). Choosing a major was easier for George than for Benjamin. Benjamin moved from Engineering Physics to Computer Science & Engineering, before finally settling on Computer Engineering. He kept looking for a field that he could see himself working in. George, on the other hand, chose a major and never changed. He didn't seem to expect his major to make him happy. He considered switching to Business, but only when he was unsure of his ability to succeed in CSE. His focus was on the second challenge, finding a way to succeed within the major, and he continually revised his study strategies to that end.

Finally, both students discussed their job search. Benjamin explored both a large and a small company, before concluding that he preferred the broad range of opportunities open to him at the smaller company. George was unsuccessful in his first interviews. He found that, like many CS interviews, they involved answering Data Structures questions. He took the unusual (and successful) step of re-taking Data Structures to improve his performance in interviews.

5.2 Implications for Teaching

Consistent with Stevens et al., we saw the progression from very well-defined assignments to more open-ended ones as students progressed from freshmen to seniors. Because we focused on a single discipline, we were able to observe that students did not experience this as a gradual transition; rather there were specific identifiable courses where multiple students experienced an abrupt change. By identifying such courses in their programs, instructors could help prepare their students and help them through these transitions.

5.3 Threats to Validity

These results are based on interviews; it is possible that the students told the interviewer what they thought he wanted to hear rather than what they believed. It is also possible that the students avoided talking about things that cast themselves in an unfavorable light. The interviewer may have directed the conversations in ways that support his theories. These seem unlikely. The students seemed both open and comfortable. Indeed, they seemed to enjoy returning each year and reflecting on their goals and experiences.

6. CONCLUSIONS AND IMPLICATIONS FOR RESEARCH

In this study, we identified a number of events that occurred during two students' university training in computing that had significant effects on their development as professionals. Both students faced a transition, sometimes abrupt, from clearly defined assignments to increasingly under-specified, open-ended tasks. Both had to choose majors within engineering, find a way to succeed in their majors, and search for jobs. Even though their experiences were very similar, their responses were sometimes quite different.

The approach of using case studies to do individual analysis worked well here, as it allowed us to examine the events and responses without losing the context of the individuals. Comparing these results across individuals allowed us to see commonalities and differences.

In both cases, external job-related factors (internships, interviews, and jobs) seemed to be more important than previously reported. In addition, there is a complex relationship between these factors and coursework, with courses influencing students' beliefs about the work world and their ability to succeed there, and actual job interviews and work experiences influencing what they want from their education.

Finally, we saw an example of a student who entered without any programming background, without previous exposure to engineering, and with only extrinsic motivations – grades, getting a job, pleasing his parents, etc. – who nevertheless succeeded.

The next step in building on this work is to expand the analysis to include a detailed examination of the other students in our dataset. Second, a closer examination of the interplay between school- and job-related events would be of interest. We saw evidence in these two cases that job-related events could affect the response to school-related events, and vice-versa; understanding the interactions of these two may lead to a better understanding of each area. Finally, this study supports further investigation of why students persist and succeed in engineering.

7. REFERENCES

[1] D. Davis, T. Yuen, and M. Berland. Multiple case study of nerd identity in a CS1 class. In *Proceedings of the 45th ACM Technical Symposium on Computer Science Education*, SIGCSE '14, pages 325–330, New York, NY, USA, 2014. ACM. Available from World Wide Web: http://doi.acm.org/10.1145/2538862.2538960.

[2] C. S. Dweck. *Self-Theories: their role in motivation, personality, and development*. Taylor & Francis, 1999.

[3] M. Eliot and J. Turns. Constructing professional portfolios: sense-making and professional identity development for engineering undergraduates. *Journal of Engineering Education*, 100:630–654, 2011.

[4] C. M. Lewis. The importance of students' attention to program state: A case study of debugging behavior. In *Proceedings of the Ninth Annual International Conference on International Computing Education Research*, ICER '12, pages 127–134, New York, NY, USA, 2012. ACM. Available from World Wide Web: http://doi.acm.org/10.1145/2361276.2361301.

[5] M. B. Miles and A. M. Huberman. *Qualitative Data Analysis: an expanded sourcebook*. Sage Publications, Thousand Oaks, California, 2d edition, 1994.

[6] W. G. Perry. *Forms of Intellectual and Ethical Development in the College Years: A Scheme*. Holt, Reinhart and Winston, Inc., New York, 1970.

[7] A.-K. Peters. Identity development of CS and IT students: What's the role of higher education? In *Proceedings of the Ninth Annual International ACM Conference on International Computing Education Research*, ICER '13, pages 187–188, 2013. Available from World Wide Web: http://doi.acm.org/10.1145/2493394.2493427.

[8] A.-K. Peters, A. Berglund, A. Eckerdal, and A. Pears. First year computer science and IT students' experience of participation in the discipline. In *Proceedings of the 2014 International Conference on Teaching and Learning in Computing and Engineering*, LATICE '14, pages 1–8, 2014. Available from World Wide Web: http://dx.doi.org/10.1109/LaTiCE.2014.9.

[9] O. Pierrakos, T. K. Beam, J. Constantz, A. Johri, and R. Anderson. On the development of a professional identity: Engineering persisters vs engineering switchers. In *Proceedings of the 39th IEEE International Conference on Frontiers in Education Conference*, FIE'09, pages 599–604, 2009. Available from World Wide Web: http://dl.acm.org/citation.cfm?id=1733663.1733804.

[10] R. Stevens, K. O'Connor, L. Garrison, A. Jocuns, and D. Amos. Becoming an engineer: toward a three dimensional view of engineering learning. *Journal of Engineering Education*, pages 355–368, July 2008.

[11] J. Turns, B. Sattler, and D. Kilgore. Disciplinary knowledge, identity, and navigation: The contributions of portfolio construction. In *Proceedings of the 9th International Conference of the Learning Sciences - Volume 1*, ICLS '10, pages 818–825, 2010. Available from World Wide Web: http://dl.acm.org/citation.cfm?id=1854360.1854465.

[12] R. K. Yin. *Case Study Research: design and methods*. Sage Publications, Thousand Oaks, California, 5th edition, 2014.

Exploring Changes in Computer Science Students' Implicit Theories of Intelligence across the Semester

Abraham E. Flanigan
Markeya S. Peteranetz
Duane F. Shell
University of Nebraska-Lincoln
114 Teachers College Hall
Lincoln, Nebraska 68588
1-402-472-8331
abrahamflanigan@gmail.com,
markeya.dubbs@huskers.unl.edu,
dshell2@unl.edu

Leen-Kiat Soh
University of Nebraska-Lincoln
122E Avery Hall
Lincoln, Nebraska 68588
1-402-472-6738
lksoh@cse.unl.edu

ABSTRACT

Our study was based on exploring CS1 students' implicit theories of intelligence. Referencing Dweck and Leggett's [5] framework for implicit theories of intelligence, we investigated (1) how students' implicit theories changed over the course of a semester, (2) how these changes differed as a function of course enrollment and students' self-regulation profiles, and (3) whether or not implicit theories predicted standardized course grades and performance on a computational thinking knowledge test. For all students, there were significant increases in entity theory (fixed mindset) and significant decreases in incremental theory (growth mindset) across the semester. However, results showed that students had higher scores for incremental than entity theory of intelligence at both the beginning and end of the semester. Furthermore, both incremental and entity theory, but not semester change in intelligence theory, differed based on students' self-regulation profiles. Also, semester change in entity theory differed across courses. Finally, students' achievement outcomes were weakly predicted by their implicit theories of intelligence. Implications for student motivation and retention in CS and other STEM courses are also discussed.

Categories and Subject Descriptors

K.3.2. [**Computers and Education**]: Computer and Information Science Education

General Terms

Performance, Human factors, Theory

Keywords

Implicit learning theories; CS1; Profiling

1. INTRODUCTION

Student achievement and retention in science, technology, engineering, and mathematics (STEM) courses have been the focal point of much research. STEM-related fields will grow at nearly twice the rate as opportunities in non-STEM fields between 2008 and 2018 [13]. Additionally, the number of jobs in STEM fields grew at nearly three times the rate as the number of jobs in non-STEM fields during the first decade of the 21st century [13]. However, research has demonstrated that retention rates of students pursuing STEM majors fall short of meeting the workforce's demands. For example, studies have shown that approximately 44% of STEM majors change to a non-STEM major before graduation [21]. As a result, a major concern for postsecondary administrators is increasing the number of students who declare a STEM-related major and retaining those students in the major until they graduate and enter the workforce.

A significant body of literature has investigated the factors that influence achievement and retention in STEM courses and majors [2, 12, 29]. Studies have demonstrated how STEM students' goal orientation [10], quality of instruction received [20], gender [27], strategic self-regulation [21], performance/enrollment in introductory ("gatekeeper") courses [2], and the perceived difficulty and usefulness of STEM courses [16] predict achievement and attrition in undergraduate STEM courses such as Computer Science (CS).

Meanwhile, *implicit intelligence theories* have remained a relatively understudied aspect of students' learning, achievement, and persistence in STEM courses. According to Dweck [4], implicit intelligence theories refer to *peoples' general theories about whether their intelligence is a fixed trait (entity theory) or a malleable quality that can be enhanced through learning and effort (incremental theory)*. Commonly known as fixed (entity theory) and growth (incremental theory) mindsets, Dweck and Leggett's [5] framework for implicit theories of intelligence has received widespread attention in research. Students' implicit theories about their intelligence have been shown to influence the types of goals they pursue [11], persistence in the face of difficulty [15], academic success [1], and attributions for their successes and failures [19]. However, little research has examined changes in implicit intelligence theories across a single semester.

The present study sought to help fill this gap in the literature by exploring changes in CS students' implicit intelligence theories across a semester in an introductory CS (CS1) course. In this

ICER'15, August 9-13, 2015, Omaha, NE, USA.
© 2015 ACM. ISBN 978-1-4503-3630-7/15/08…$15.00.
DOI: http://dx.doi.org/10.1145/2787622.2787722

study, the profiling approach advocated by several educational researchers was used [17, 25]. In educational research, profile approaches are used to identify distinctly different clusters of students based on their motivation and self-regulated learning behaviors. According to Nelson et al. [17], "Using the profile approach, researchers can consider interactions among many independent, well-established psychological constructs" (p. 76). Instead of exploring how individual motivational constructs (e.g., self-efficacy) predict specific outcomes (e.g., course grades) in a piecemeal fashion, profile approaches utilize a multivariate approach to understand students' outcomes. In the present study, changes in students' implicit intelligence theories across the semester were explored as a function of their motivational and self-regulation profile, as well as their gender and the CS1 course in which they were enrolled.

1.1 Implicit Theories of Intelligence

A significant body of literature explores how students' implicit theories about the nature of their intelligence influence their achievement and motivation. Largely, the literature has shown that students of all ages and grade levels can be classified as being either *entity* or *incremental* learning theorists [5, 4]. *Entity theorists* believe intelligence is a fixed entity (i.e., either you are born intelligent or you are not). Entity theorists believe no matter how much time and effort they put into learning, they are bounded by their natural level of intelligence and their intellectual ability cannot be increased through their own efforts [5]. Conversely, *incremental theorists* believe intelligence is a malleable trait that can be enhanced through learning, time, and effort. Incremental theorists believe their intellectual ability can be cultivated and increased through their own efforts [5].

Differential outcomes have been associated with each of these implicit intelligence theories. Students who possess an entity theory about their intelligence tend to focus more on their performance outcomes (e.g., getting a passing grade or appearing smart to one's classmates), attribute failure to a lack of ability, and believe that working hard reflects a lack of ability rather than a commitment to improvement [6]. For entity theorists, poor performance reflects inadequacies in their intelligence; in their eyes, giving a purposeful effort to improve would only confirm their inadequacies to their classmates. Alternatively, incremental theorists set mastery goals geared towards gaining a complete understanding of the course material, believe effort is a means to becoming more intelligent, and view failure as an opportunity for improvement [6]. For incremental theorists, poor performance does not indicate an intelligence inadequacy that cannot be overcome. Instead, with sufficient effort, improvements can be made and performance can be enhanced. Differential performance outcomes have also been associated with being an entity or incremental theorist. Specifically, it has been found that students who possess an incremental theory of intelligence tend to receive higher grades than those who possess an entity theory [1].

Although literature related to implicit intelligence theories in STEM courses remains sparse, a couple of studies exist. Reid and Ferguson [18] found that freshman engineering students demonstrated a non-significant increase in entity mindset from the beginning until the end of their first year. Additionally, they found that implementing a team-based project designed to enhance students' incremental theories in a first-year engineering course caused no significant changes in incremental or entity theories

across the school year. A study by Simon et al. [26] found that training CS, computer engineering, and non-CS engineering students to adopt an incremental theory of intelligence did not significantly increase students' incremental theories. In summary, the existing STEM and CS literature suggests that these students may have a tendency to shift towards an entity theory of intelligence across the first-year of college. However, this literature lacks significant results. Thus, more research is needed to understand how implicit intelligence theories change for CS (and other STEM) students across time.

The implicit intelligence theories literature suggests that students who believe intelligence in a domain can be enhanced through time and effort tend to experience enhanced levels of motivation and success. Meanwhile, students who believe their intelligence is outside of their control tend to give up in the face of difficulty. The relationship between implicit intelligence theories and persistence in the face of difficulty could inform an approach for increasing retention and enrollment in STEM and CS courses. Exploring changes in STEM and CS students' implicit intelligence theories over time may help educators understand the difficulty in retaining students and how to address it.

1.2 Profile Approach

Although many factors influence undergraduate students' success, these factors have historically been studied individually, in a piecemeal fashion. For example, studies may look at the relationship between students' mathematical self-efficacy and performance on exams or explore the relationship between intrinsic motivation and persistence on difficult tasks. At most, according to Nelson et al. [17], studies may look at the way these factors interact, through methods such as a multiple regression or analysis of variance. For example, predicting students' final course grades using their self-efficacy, intrinsic motivation, and goal orientation. An alternative approach to studying students' outcomes is by focusing on the coordinated pattern of specific factors, such as students' motivation and self-regulated learning tendencies.

This was the approach taken by Shell and Husman [24] when they attempted to understand differences in motivation and strategic self-regulation among college undergraduates taking an elective psychology course. In this study, participants completed a battery of measures to assess their self-efficacy for self-regulation, expectancy for success, causal attributions, locus of control, goal orientation, future time perspective, course affect and anxiety, strategic self-regulation, and study time. Five profiles were identified: (a) a *strategic* learner who demonstrates a high level of self-regulation and aspires to master course-content and achieve highly in the classroom, (b) an *apathetic* learner who demonstrates low levels of self-regulation, as well as low levels of mastery and performance orientations, (c) a *knowledge builder* who aspires to master the course content but places less emphasis on utilizing traditional learning strategies, (d) a *surface* learner who sees little value in the course, applies the lowest amount of self-regulation, and seeks to do the minimum amount required to pass a class, and (e) *learned helpless* students who ineffectively attempt to be good students, eventually causing them to lose confidence in their own academic abilities. Recent studies have replicated the presence of these five profiles among undergraduate CS, engineering, and other STEM students taking introductory computer science courses [17, 25].

Profile research has yielded interesting results and discussions for those concerned with STEM education, specifically CS education for purposes of the present study. First, researchers have argued that profile adoption may be course specific [7, 22]. In other words, a student may adopt a more motivated, goal-directed approach in her biology courses, but take a more surface learning approach towards her history courses. For those concerned with CS education, it is important to understand whether or not students possess the motivation and self-regulation necessary to enhance their computational thinking and ability including problem solving via computer programming. Second, some profiles are more adaptive than others. Research has shown that the strategic learning and knowledge building profiles are more adaptive than the other three profiles. For example, students adopting the strategic learning and knowledge building profiles score more highly on achievement measures [17], demonstrate higher mastery goal orientations [10], and see greater value in their CS courses [25] than students adopting the apathetic, surface learning, and learned helpless profiles. Finally, research has found that profile adoption tends to be relatively stable over time, with only one-third of students changing profiles across the course of an academic year [9, 26]. Thus, *it is important for educators to be proactive about impacting the learning orientation students take towards CS courses before students commit to a maladaptive approach to learning CS.*

2. THE PRESENT STUDY

The present study sought to contribute to the CS education community's understanding of the dynamic nature of student learning theories by exploring how CS students' implicit intelligence theories changed across the semester. The central research question guiding this study was: ***Do CS students' implicit intelligence theories change from the beginning to the end of the semester?*** Additionally, the following sub-questions served to compliment the central research question:

1. Do changes in implicit intelligence theories across the semester differ as a function of student profiles (strategic, knowledge building, apathetic, surface learning, and learned helpless) or the CS1 course they are enrolled in?

2. How does change in implicit intelligence theories across the semester relate to students' learning outcomes in CS1 courses?

3. METHODS
3.1 Participants

Participants for this study were 621 undergraduate students (538 males; 83 females) from CS1 courses at a large Midwestern state university. Two hundred and ninety-seven participants were freshmen, 184 were sophomores, 72 were juniors, 51 were seniors, and 17 identified as other. Of these participants, 443 (380 males; 63 females) provided complete data and were included in the profile analysis. The CS1 courses, from which the participants were recruited, catered to different undergraduate student populations: one course consisted of CS majors, one course consisted of engineering majors, one course consisted of a combination of computer, engineering, and physical science majors, one course consisted of humanities majors, and one course consisted of interdisciplinary business-CS honors students.

3.2 Instruments
3.2.1 Implicit Intelligence Theories
Participants' implicit intelligence theories were assessed using the Implicit Theories of Intelligence Scale [4, 30] which contains eight Likert-type items with response options ranging from 1 *(strongly disagree)* to 6 *(strongly agree)*. Two separate four-item scales measure students' incremental theory that intelligence can be increased (e.g., "You can always substantially change how intelligent you are") and their entity theory that intelligence is unalterable (e.g., "You have a certain amount of intelligence, and you can't really do much to change it"). This measure operationalizes intelligence as a general construct and is not specific to CS1 or other courses. For the present study, an alpha level of .92 was obtained for the incremental scale and an alpha level of .91 was obtained for the entity scale.

3.2.2 Profile Measures
For Profile Analysis a battery of assessments of students' motivation and strategic self-regulation were used. Students' motivation was assessed with a battery of instruments consisting of (1) students goal orientation for the class; (2) students' future time perspective consisting of their ratings of the connectedness between their academic coursework and a STEM career and the perceived instrumentality of their specific course work for attaining STEM academic and career goals; and (3) students' emotional/affective reactions to the course. Students' strategic self-regulation was assessed with four scales from the Student Perceptions of Classroom Knowledge Building instrument (SPOCK) that assessed metacognitive self-regulation, knowledge building, question asking, and lack of engagement. Students' study time and study effort also were assessed. Details on these measures can be found in [24, 25, 17]

3.3 Procedures
This study took place as part of a larger NSF-funded study geared towards improving students' abilities to learn computational thinking by incorporating computational and creative thinking exercises into undergraduate CS courses [14]. Participants completed the beginning of the semester Implicit Theories of Intelligence Scale, future time perspective measures, and additional assessments not used in this study during lab or lecture sessions during the first week of the semester. End of semester surveys were done in lab or lecture sessions during the last two weeks of the semester. Participants repeated the beginning of semester instruments, except for the connectedness scale, along with the SPOCK, emotion/affect, and studying measures and additional scales to assess their computational thinking knowledge and to evaluate the course activities. All of the surveys were completed using the Survey Monkey® online survey tool.

3.4 Analysis Procedures
All data analysis was performed using SPSS v. 21 and 22. ANOVA were done using the General Linear Model repeated measures procedure. Regression was done using the linear regression procedure. Profile analysis was done using the two-step cluster analysis procedure.

4. RESULTS
The present study explored (a) whether CS1 students' implicit intelligence theories changed across the course of the semester, (b) the factors that potentially mediate changes in students'

Table 1. Five Profile Solution

	Strategic	Knowledge Building	Surface Learning	Apathetic	Learned Helpless
SPOCK Self-Regulation	3.84	3.02	3.38	2.32	3.31
SPOCK Knowledge Building	3.70	2.89	2.72	1.87	3.20
SPOCK Lack of Regulation	2.62	2.63	3.25	3.20	3.06
SPOCK High-Level Question Asking	3.50	2.30	2.57	1.67	3.20
SPOCK Low-Level Question Asking	3.44	2.28	2.89	1.85	3.23
Study Time	3.80	2.60	4.68	2.43	3.04
Study Effort	3.33	2.87	3.67	2.63	2.81
Learning-Approach Goal Orientation	4.57	4.15	3.48	3.45	3.20
Learning-Avoidance Goal Orientation	2.03	2.33	3.78	3.55	2.84
Task-Approach Goal Orientation	4.69	4.54	4.66	4.26	3.21
Task-Avoidance Goal Orientation	2.05	2.53	2.86	3.28	2.83
Performance-Approach Goal Orientation	3.33	3.14	2.98	2.39	2.76
Performance-Avoidance Goal Orientation	2.72	2.98	2.91	2.74	2.90
Endogenous Instrumentality	4.42	3.82	2.54	2.50	3.22
Exogenous Instrumentality	1.71	2.03	3.60	3.37	3.01
Future Time Perspective Career	4.23	4.14	4.19	4.01	3.82
Positive Affect	3.82	3.04	2.56	2.21	2.83

implicit intelligence theories (e.g., student profile, gender, and course enrollment), and (c) how changes in implicit intelligence theories could be used to predict course achievement, as measured by standardized course grades and computational thinking knowledge-test scores. Changes in sample sizes reflect changes in the number of participants who provided relevant data at each time point.

4.1 Profile Analysis

Profile analysis was conducted following methods used in [25, 17]. A five-cluster solution (Table 1) was identified consistent with the strategic, knowledge building, apathetic, surface learning, and learned helpless profiles found previously [24, 25, 17]. As in these previous studies, alternative three-, four-, and six-cluster solutions were examined and both aggregate fit indicators and theoretical interpretability favored the five-profile solution.

4.2 Do CS students' implicit intelligence theories change from the beginning until the end of the semester in CS1 courses?

To determine whether participants' fixed theories changed from the beginning to the end of the semester, a repeated measures ANOVA was conducted. Overall for all participants, their entity theory increased significantly from the beginning of the semester until the end (Wilks' $\lambda=.987$, $F(1, 440)=5.602$, $p=.018$, partial Eta^2=.013). Entity theory scores increased from a mean of 2.62 at the beginning of the semester to 2.81 at the end. A second repeated measures ANOVA was conducted to determine whether participants' incremental theories changed from the beginning to the end of the semester. Overall for all participants, incremental theories decreased significantly from the beginning of the semester until the end (Wilks' $\lambda=.971$, $F(1, 440)=13.101$, $p<.001$, partial Eta ^{2}=.029). Incremental theory scores decreased from a mean of 4.28 at the beginning of the semester to 4.05 at the end. Taken altogether, these findings suggest that students' implicit intelligence theories change significantly over the course of a semester. Interestingly, participants' theories that intelligence is a fixed, unalterable entity increased over the course of the semester while

their theories that intelligence can be grown incrementally decreased.

4.3 Do changes in implicit intelligence theories differ as a function of student profile and/or course enrollment?

Mixed ANOVA was used to test whether changes identified in students' entity intelligence theory differed as a function of profile cluster. As shown in Table 2, entity intelligence theory was significantly different across different profiles ($F(4, 436)=5.263$, $p<.001$, partial Eta^2=.046); however, the interaction between profile and change across the semester was not significant ($F(3,436)=1.713$, $p=.146$, partial Eta^2=.015) indicating that across semester change in entity intelligence theory was not affected by profile membership.

Table 2. Changes in Entity Theory

		Beginning of Semester		End of Semester	
	N	M	SD	M	SD
Profile	441	2.62	1.08	2.74	1.12
Strategic	132	2.38	1.08	2.49	1.16
Knowledge Building	98	2.54	0.98	2.69	1.13
Apathetic	70	2.75	1.22	2.70	1.10
Learned Helpless	54	2.79	0.87	3.21	0.89
Surface Learning	87	2.90	1.09	2.93	1.08
Course	435	2.63	1.08	2.75	1.12
CS majors	68	2.65	1.24	2.58	1.23
CS/PS majors	107	2.79	1.16	2.80	1.19
Engineering majors	205	2.58	0.98	2.70	1.04
Business/CS Honors program	55	2.50	1.03	3.01	1.10

A second mixed ANOVA was used to test whether changes identified in students incremental intelligence theory differed as a function of profile cluster. As shown in Table 3, incremental intelligence theory was significantly different across different profiles ($F(4, 436)=7.354$, $p<.001$, partial $Eta^2=.063$); however, the interaction between profile and change in incremental intelligence theory across the semester was not significant ($F(3,431)=2.079$, $p=.102$, partial $Eta^2=.016$) indicating that across semester change in incremental intelligence theory was not affected by profile membership.

Mixed ANOVA was used to test whether changes identified in students' entity intelligence theory differed as a function of course enrollment. As shown in Table 2, entity intelligence theory was not significantly different across different courses ($F(3, 431)=.817$, $p=.485$, partial $Eta^2=.006$); however, the interaction between course enrollment and change in entity theories was significant ($F(3, 431)=3.634$, $p=.013$, partial $Eta^2=.025$; see Figure 1), indicating that change in entity intelligence theory across the semester was different in different courses. An analysis of simple main effects revealed that students in the honor's CS1 course started the semester with the lowest entity theory scores and finished the semester with the highest entity theory scores.

Mixed ANOVA was used to test whether changes identified in students' incremental intelligence theory differed as a function of course enrollment. As shown in Table 3, incremental intelligence theory was not significantly different across different courses ($F(3, 431)=2.311$, $p=.076$, partial $Eta^2=.016$). Also, the interaction between course and change in incremental intelligence theory across the semester was not significant ($F(3,431)=2.079$, $p=.102$, partial $Eta^2=.014$).

Table 3. Changes in Incremental Theory

		Beginning of Semester		End of Semester	
	N	*M*	*SD*	*M*	*SD*
Profile	441	4.29	1.02	4.12	1.09
Strategic	132	4.63	0.92	4.42	1.02
Knowledge Building	98	4.28	0.93	4.14	1.15
Apathetic	70	4.12	1.19	4.18	1.07
Learned Helpless	54	4.17	0.81	3.77	0.84
Surface Learning	87	4.01	1.10	3.83	1.14
Course	435	4.29	1.02	4.12	1.09
CS majors	68	4.48	1.09	4.44	1.12
CS/PS majors	107	4.14	1.14	4.03	1.15
Engineering majors	205	4.27	0.93	4.09	1.04
Business/CS Honors program	55	4.42	0.96	3.96	1.03

4.4 Do changes in implicit intelligence theories predict CS1 course learning outcomes?

Multiple linear regression analysis was used to examine the relationships between participants' initial intelligence theories, the change in their theories across the semester, and course achievement (as measured by standardized final course grades). Changes in theories were calculated by subtracting participants' beginning of semester scores from their end of semester scores, so that positive values indicate a strong endorsement of the theory at the end of the semester. The overall model was significant ($R^2=.025$, $F(4, 430)=2.741$, $p=.028$). Initial incremental theory ($\beta=-.253$, $t=-2.862$, $p=.004$) and change in incremental theory ($\beta=-.135$, $t=-2.017$, $p=.044$) were both significant predictors of students' standardized course grades. This indicates that the theory that intelligence can be incrementally developed over time has significant implications for CS students' final grades. Taken together, it appears students' initial incremental theories about intelligence and the degree to which those theories change across the semester are significantly related to course grades. However, contrary to prior research [18], having an incremental theory of intelligence and increasing in belief in an incremental theory of intelligence both were associated with lower course grades. No significant relationships were found for their initial entity theory or the change in entity theory across the semester.

Figure 1. Change in Entity Theory by Course

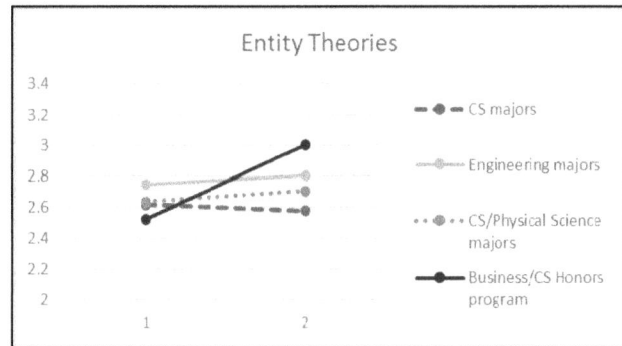

A parallel analysis was conducted using computational thinking knowledge-test scores as the criterion variable. The overall model was significant ($R^2=.023$, $F(4, 409)=2.431$, $p=.047$). Only initial entity theory ($\beta=-.185$, $t=-2.032$, $p=.043$) and initial incremental theory ($\beta=-.217$, $t=-2.403$, $p=.017$) were significant predictors. These findings suggest that the theories about intelligence students possess when they enter into a CS1 course has a significant relationship with their learning of computational thinking knowledge and skill during the semester. Although entity theory, as expected from prior research and theory [1, 4], predicted lower learning, incremental theory, contrary to expectations [1, 3], predicted lower learning.

5. DISCUSSION

5.1 Grand Summary of Findings

Our results indicate that the implicit intelligence theories of undergraduate CS1 students change across the semester. These findings differ from conventional literature that posits the stable nature of implicit intelligence theories across time [19].

First, *regardless of student profile, incremental theory decreased from the beginning until the end of the semester.* Interestingly, although the decrease in incremental theories was significant for all participants, significant decreases were only detected for the Strategic and Learned Helpless profiles. For the Learned Helpless profile, this change seems comprehensible. These students apply themselves in a purposeful effort to self-regulate their learning, but struggle to do so effectively. As a result of the incongruence between effort and achievement, these students may "lose faith" that their learning outcomes are a result of their effort. For the Strategic Learners, this decrease is more perplexing. This profile is typified by high levels of motivation, effective learning strategies, and achievement. Why these students come to view their intelligence as less malleable over the course of a semester warrants future investigation. However, a tentative explanation does exist. Perhaps the strategies employed in other courses do not readily translate to success in CS courses. If this explanation is correct, then perhaps Strategic Learners who enter into CS courses have their incremental theories challenged by the difficulty of transferring their learning strategies into CS.

Second, *regardless of student profile, entity theory increased from the beginning until the end of the semester.* Similar to the change in incremental theory from beginning until end of the semester, the increase in entity theory was significant for all participants overall, but a significant increase was only detected for the Learned Helpless profile. Again, based on the characteristics of this profile, the change makes sense. As the Learned Helpless begin to see their efforts as futile, they may begin to view intelligence as less malleable and more as a pre-determined trait outside of their control.

However, it is important to note that, overall, CS1 students began the semester scoring highly on incremental theory of intelligence ($M=$ 4.29). Furthermore, CS1 students scored more highly on incremental than entity theories of intelligence at both the beginning and end of the semester. Thus, even though incremental theory decreased and entity theory increased throughout the course of the semester, *incremental theory was still more strongly endorsed by CS1 students across the semester.* These findings suggest that promoting incremental theory of intelligence in CS1 students should *not* be CS educators' main concern. Instead, CS educators should concern themselves with helping their students sustain their belief in the implicit theory that intelligence is a malleable trait within one's own control.

Third, *course enrollment was related to students' implicit intelligence theories across the semester.* Specifically, students in the CS1 course offered to members of a prestigious honors program for business and CS double-majors exhibited significant changes in their incremental and entity theories from the beginning until the end of the semester. These students tended to be more motivated and higher achieving than the students in other CS1 courses. However, the pattern of change experienced by these students matched the general pattern for all students (increased entity theory and decreased incremental theory), but this group had the greatest increase in entity theory. So, even for students with the highest levels of motivation and achievement in our sample, their theories of intelligence still shifted away from a malleable trait and more towards a fixed entity. A potential explanation for this shift may exist. Honors students are used to experiencing high levels of academic achievement, which may lead them to attribute their success to being a "smart" person. As a result, their high

performance in CS1 and other courses may only serve to confirm their theory that intelligence is a fixed entity—an entity which they possess. Future research is warranted to explore this tentative explanation.

Finally, implicit intelligence theories weakly predicted standardized final course grades and performance on an end-of-semester computational thinking knowledge test. *Decreases in incremental intelligence theory were associated with higher standardized course grades.* This is opposite of what is expected for incremental theory, but may be due to range restriction. Most students scored highly on incremental theory, but a large drop in incremental theory in a few high achieving students could strongly impact the statistical relationship between intelligence theories and course achievement. This is what occurred with the honors course: the most successful students experienced the largest decrease in incremental theory from beginning to end of the semester. These students still scored more highly on incremental than entity theories, but scored so highly at the beginning of the semester there was seemingly nowhere else for their score to go but down. Thus, the relationship between intelligence theories and standardized course grades may have been distorted. Additionally, the relationship between intelligence theories and achievement was weak. Although previous research has detected more pronounced relationships between students' implicit intelligence theories and grades [1], the present study only found a weak relationship between implicit theories and performance outcomes (final standardized course grades and computational thinking knowledge test). At least for CS1 courses, the present study suggests that *the relationship between implicit intelligence theories and performance outcomes may be weaker than previous research suggests.*

5.2 Implications for CS Educators

STEM educators have long been concerned with attracting and retaining students in STEM-related majors [21, 29], including CS educators. Given this concern, it is important for educators to be aware of the pitfalls associated with students' entity theories of intelligence. As has been noted, possession of an entity theory of intelligence reduces motivation, performance, and the desire to give purposeful effort when attempting to learn or overcome an obstacle [6]. Given the difficult nature of CS courses, research [1, 8] suggests that students who possess an entity theory of intelligence and do not view themselves as "naturally intelligent" may be in danger of giving up in the face of difficulty, withdrawing from CS courses, and switching to a different major.

The present study found that students' inclinations towards an entity theory of intelligence increased over the course of a semester, a finding that has important implications for CS educators and students. While literature has shown that setting performance and mastery approach goals [10], persisting in the face of difficulty [16], and academic achievement [2] are all positively associated with retention in CS and other STEM courses, possessing an entity theory of intelligence is associated with a decrease in all of these factors influencing retention [1, 11, 20]. Thus, *it is important that CS educators explore the relationship between entity theory of intelligence, and persistence in CS related courses, and investigate the impact that this can have on subsequent enrollment.* Better understanding would allow CS educators to better design their courses, assignments, and other activities to check students' conceptual models about intelligence and learning.

Fortunately, CS educators have tools at their disposal to help students maintain the high levels of incremental theories they possess at the outset of the semester. First, research has shown how the type of praise and feedback educators provide to their students impacts the theories of intelligence their students adopt. Specifically, Mueller and Dweck [15] demonstrated how praising students' intelligence (e.g. "You're a very smart student when it comes to reading code.") can actually diminish their motivation and performance. Additionally, students who receive intelligence-based praise or feedback may be more likely to view intelligence as a fixed entity (e.g. "The instructor focused her feedback on intelligence. This must be something either I have or I don't have"). Instead of providing intelligence-based praise or feedback, these researchers found that focusing on effort (e.g., "You did great work. I can tell you applied yourself on this assignment.") enhanced students' performance, motivation, and incremental theories of intelligence. For CS educators, centering praise or feedback on effort may help to combat against the growth of entity theories across the course of the semester and help students sustain their initial incremental theories of intelligence. Second, [3] advocated that instructors emphasize how meaningful learning often takes an extended period of time. Instead of creating a classroom atmosphere where immediate mastery of content is expected, Dweck [3] suggests that instructors instill within students the mindset that it often takes time to understand information at a deeper level. Doing so would allow CS students to understand that just because they do not "get it" right away does not mean they lack intelligence. Rather, deep learning often takes an extended period of time and they can "get it" with more time and effort. Research suggests that creating such a climate in CS classrooms can enhance students' performance, motivation, and incremental theories of intelligence.

6. CONCLUSION

Our findings contrast with existing literature that posits implicit intelligence theories as stable across time [19] and significant predictors of students' learning outcomes [1]. Rather, we found students' implicit theories change from the beginning to the end of the semester, in introductory CS courses included in our study. Although students' scored more highly on incremental theories of intelligence at the beginning and end of the semester, these implicit theories were decreasing. Meanwhile, students' implicit theories that intelligence is a fixed, unalterable entity increased across the semester. Both students' entity and incremental intelligence theories were different across different motivated self-regulatory profiles; but change during the semester in these was not different across profiles. Although both incremental and entity theories of intelligence did not differ as a function of the course the student was in, change in entity theory of intelligence across the semester was different in different courses. This suggests that at least some aspects of students' implicit intelligence beliefs are impacted by what occurs in the classroom during the course. Implicit intelligence theories were only weakly predictive of achievement outcomes. Both initial incremental theories of intelligence and the change in incremental theories of intelligence were predictive of standardized course grades, whereas initial incremental and entity theories of intelligence were predicative of computational thinking knowledge test scores.

Given the emphasis placed on increasing retention in STEM-related (including CS) courses [2] we believe it is important for CS educators to understand the pitfalls commonly associated with the theories that one's own intelligence and learning capabilities are largely stable and outside of his or her control. By incorporating instructional practices into their courses to combat against the growth of entity theories of intelligence and taking steps to help students maintain their incremental theories of intelligence, CS educators may be able to positively impact student motivation, achievement, and retention in CS courses and computing-related majors.

Future research is needed to identify (a) why changes in implicit theories of intelligence occur across the semester, (b) how changes in implicit intelligence theories impact subsequent enrollment in CS (and STEM) courses, (c) the relationship between implicit theories and retention in CS majors, and (d) whether similar shifts in implicit intelligence theories across the semester occur in other STEM courses and majors aside from introductory-level computer science.

7. ACKNOWLEDGMENTS

This material is based upon work supported by the National Science Foundation under grant nos. 1431874 and 1122956.

8. REFERENCES

[1] Blackwell, L. S., Trzesniewski, K. H., and Dweck, C. S. 2007. Implicit theories of intelligence predict achievement across an adolescent transition: A longitudinal study and an intervention. *Child Dev.* 78, 1 (Jan./Feb. 2007), 246-263.

[2] Crisp, G., Nora, A., and Taggart, A. 2009. Student characteristics, pre-college, college, and environmental factors as predictors of majoring in and earning a STEM degree: An analysis of students attending a Hispanic serving institution. *Am Educ Res J.* 46, 4 (Dec. 2009), 924-942. DOI= 10.3102/0002831209349460.

[3] Dweck, C. S. 2007. Boosting achievement with messages that motivate. *Educ Can.* 47, 2 (Apr. 2007), 6-10.

[4] Dweck, C.S. 1999. *Self-theories: Their role in motivation, personality, and development.* Psychology Press, Philadelphia.

[5] Dweck, C.S. and Legget, E.L. 1988. A social-cognitive approach to motivation and personality. *Psychol Rev.* 95, 2 (Oct. 1987), 256-273.

[6] Dweck, C.S. and Molden, D.C. 2005. Self-theories: Their impact on competence motivation and acquisition. In Elliot, A.J. and Dweck, C.S. ed. *Handbook of Competence and Motivation,* Guilford Press, New York City, 2005, 122-141.

[7] Entwistle, N., and McCune, V. 2004. The conceptual bases of study strategy inventories. *Educ Psychol Rev.* 16, 4 (Dec. 2004), 325-345.

[8] Gonida, E., Kiosseoglou, G., and Leondari, A. 2006. Implicit theories of intelligence, perceived academic competence, and school achievement: Testing alternative models. *Am J Psychol.* 119, 2 (Summer, 2006), 223-238.

[9] Hayenga, A. O. and Corpus, J. H. 2010. Profiles of intrinsic and extrinsic motivations: A person-centered approach to motivation and achievement in middle school. *Motiv Emotion.* 34, 4 (Aug. 2010), 371-383.

[10] Hazley, M.P., Shell, D.F., Soh, L.K., Miller, L.D., Chiriacescu, V., and Ingraham, E. 2014. Changes in student goal orientations across the semester in undergraduate computer sci-

ence courses in *Proc Front Educ Conf,* (Madrid, Spain, 2014), IEEE, 1-7.

[11] Hong, Y.Y., Chi, C.Y., Dweck, C.S., Lin, D.M., and Wan, W. 1999. Implicit theories, attributions, and coping: A meaning system approach. *J Pers Soc Psychol.* 77, 3 (Feb. 1999), 588-599.

[12] Koenig, K., Schen, M., Edwards, M., and Bao, L. 2012. Addressing STEM retention through a scientific thought and methods course. *J Coll Sci Teac.* 41, 4 (Jan/Feb. 2012), 23-29.

[13] Langdon, D., McKittrick, G., Beede, D., Khan, B., and Doms, M. 2011. STEM: Good jobs now and for the future. Technical Report. Economics and Statistics Administration, Washington, D.C.

[14] Miller, L.D., Soh, L.K., Chiriacescu, V., Ingraham, E., Shell, D.F., and Hazley, M.P. 2014. Integrating computational and creative thinking to improve learning and performance in CS1. in *SIGCSE* (New York, NY, 2014), ACM, 475-480. DOI= http://dx.doi.org/10/1145/2538862.2538940.

[15] Mueller, C.M. and Dweck, C.S. 1998. Praise for intelligence can undermine children's motivation and performance. *J Pers Soc Psychol.* 75, 1 (July. 1998), 33-52.

[16] National Science Foundation, Education and Human Resources Advisory Committee. 1996. *Shaping the future: New expectations for undergraduate education in science, mathematics, engineering, and technology,* NSF, Arlington, VA.

[17] Nelson, K.G., Shell, D.F., Husman, J., Fishman, E.J., and Soh, L.K. 2015. Motivational and self-regulated learning profiles of students taking a foundational engineering course. *J Eng Educ.* 104, 1 (Jan, 2015), 74-100. DOI= 10.1002/jee.20066

[18] Reid, K.J. and Ferguson, D.M. 2014. Assessing changes in mindset of freshman engineers. In *Proceedings of the 2014 ASEE North Central Section Conference* (Rochester, Michigan, April 04-05, 2014). NCS '14.

[19] Robins, R.W. and Pals, J.L. 2002. Implicit self-theories in the academic domain: Implications for goal orientation, attributions, affect, and self-esteem change. *Self Identity,* 78, 1 (2002), 246-263. DOI= 10.1080/15298860290106805

[20] Seymour, E. 1995. Why undergraduates leave the sciences. *Am J Phys.* 63, 3 (1995), 199-202.

[21] Seymour, E. and Hewitt, N.M. 1997. *Talking about leaving: Why undergraduates leave the sciences.* Westview Press, Boulder, CO.

[22] Shell, D.F., Brooks, D.W., Trainin, G., Wilson, K.M., Kauffman, D.F., and Herr, L.M. 2010. *The unified learning model: How motivational, cognitive, and neurobiological sciences inform best teaching practices.* Springer, New York.

[23] Shell, D.F., Hazley, M.P., Soh, L.K., Ingraham, E., and Ramsay, S. 2013. Associations of students' creativity, motivation, and self-regulation with learning and achievement in college computer science courses in *Proc Front Educ Conf,* (Oklahoma City, Oklahoma, 2013), IEEE, 1637-1643.

[24] Shell, D.F. and Husman, J. 2008. Control, motivation, affect, and strategic self-regulation in the college classroom: A multidimensional phenomenon. *J Educ Psychol.* 100, 2 (May. 2008), 443-459. DOI= 10.1037/0022-0663.100.2.443

[25] Shell, D.F. and Soh, L.K. 2013. Profiles of motivated self-regulation in college computer science courses: Differences in major versus required non-major courses. *J Sci Educ Technol,* 22 (Feb. 2013), 899-913. DOI= 10.1007/s10956-013-9437-9

[26] Simon, B., Hanks, B., Murphy, L., Fitzgerald, S., McCauley, R., Thomas, L., and Zander, C. 2008. Saying isn't necessarily believing: Influencing self-theories in computing. In *Proceedings of the ICER Conference* (Sydney, Australia, September 06-07, 2008). ICER '08. ACM, New York, NY, 173-184. DOI= 10.1145/1404520.1404537

[27] Simpson, J.C. 2001. Segregated by subject—racial differences in the factors influencing academic major between European Americans, Asian Americans, and African, Hispanic, and Native Americans. *J High Educ.* 72, 1 (Jan./Feb. 2001), 63-100.

[28] Tuominen-Soini, H., Salmela-Aro, K. and Niemivirta, M. 2011. Stability and change in achievement goal orientations: A person-centered approach. *Contemp Educ Psychol.* 36, 2 (Apr. 2011), 82-100.

[29] Whalen, D.F. and Shelley, M.C. 2010. Academic success for STEM and non-STEM majors. *J Stem Educ.* 11, 2 (Jan.-June. 2010), 45-60.

[30] Yeager, D. S., and Dweck, C. S. 2012. Mindsets that promote resilience: When students believe that personal characteristics can be developed. *Educ Psychol.* 47, 4 (Oct./Dec. 2012), 302-314

Analysis of Interactive Features Designed to Enhance Learning in an Ebook

Barbara J. Ericson

Georgia Institute of Technology
801 Atlantic Drive
Atlanta, GA, 30332
+1 404 385-2107
ericson@cc.gatech.edu

Mark J. Guzdial

Georgia Institute of Technology
85 Fifth Street NW
Atlanta, GA, 30332
+1 404 894-5618
guzdial@cc.gatech.edu

Briana B. Morrison

Georgia Institute of Technology
85 Fifth Street NW
Atlanta, GA, 30332
bmorrison@gatech.edu

ABSTRACT

Educational psychology findings indicate that active processing (such as self-testing) is more effective for learning than passive reading or even rereading. Electronic books (ebooks) can include much more than static pictures and text. Ebooks can promote better learning by increasing the reader's interaction with the material through multi-modal learning supports, worked examples, and low cognitive load practice activities. For example, multiple choice questions with immediate feedback can help identify misconceptions and gaps in knowledge. Parsons problems, which are mixed up code segments that have to be put in the correct order, require learners to think about the order of the statements in a solution without having to worry about syntax errors. Our research group has been applying concepts from educational psychology to make learning from ebooks more effective and efficient. This paper reports on an observational study and log file analysis on the use of an ebook that incorporates interactive activities. We provide evidence that learners engaged in the interactive activities, but used some types of activities more than others. We also found evidence that learners encountered some "desirable difficulties" which can improve learning. This descriptive study informs a research agenda to improve the quality of instruction in computing education.

Categories and Subject Descriptors

K.3.1 Computer Uses in Education: Computer-managed instruction (CMI) and Distance Learning

General Terms

Design; Experimentation

Keywords

Electronic book; ebook; educational data mining; Parsons problem; learning analytics

1. INTRODUCTION

Several countries are trying to increase the number of computer science teachers at the secondary level including Denmark [13] and the UK [10]. In the United States, the National Science

ICER '15, August 09 - 13, 2015, Omaha, NE, USA.
© 2015 ACM. ISBN 978-1-4503-3630-7/15/08…$15.00.
DOI: http://dx.doi.org/10.1145/2787622.2787731

Foundation has started an effort called CS10K, to prepare 10,000 high school teachers to teach computer science by 2016 [3]. Only approximately 2,500 US high schools offered Advanced Placement Computer Science in 2013-2014 out of about 25,000 high schools in the US [1]. This means that large numbers of secondary teachers in the United States will need to learn how to teach programming by 2016. Because of how CS is classified in the US, most of these teachers will not have had any prior programming experience. Learning to program can be difficult and failure rates can be quite high, especially in large classes at the university level [6].

Our research group believes that electronic books (ebooks) have the potential to help prepare a large number of teachers to teach programming at a low cost. We believe that this approach could also be used with students to improve their success rates in introductory programming courses. Our research group has been applying concepts from educational psychology to make learning from ebooks more effective and efficient.

1.1 Using Educational Psychology Principles to Improve CS Learning

Our challenge is to provide high school teachers effective and efficient learning opportunities in computer science. A recent review of the literature on studying and learning behavior by Bjork et al. [7] tells us that active processing is more effective than simply reading. Learning is enhanced when students are tested, try to solve problems, and even fail – what Bjork calls "desirable difficulties [7]." Activities enhance learning when they cause students to face challenges and make a cognitive effort, which eventually leads to understanding. Physics education research has shown that active engagement is far more effective for physics learning than passively watching a lecture [22].

Traditional computer science education involves a lot of active engagement, in the form of programming activities. However, our study of professionals taking online CS classes shows that the reliance on programming activity is one of the most significant reasons for giving up on the class [5]. If we want teachers and students to be successful in learning programming, we need alternative forms of active engagement.

In our ebook, we are using activities that promote CS learning, but have lower cognitive load than writing programs. We hypothesize that these activities are more likely to be completed by teachers because they can fit into their limited free time. Because they are low cognitive load, the amount of time needed for each problem is predictable and manageable. We hypothesize that an ebook organized around low cognitive load activities will result in teacher learning. In this paper, we describe the activities we are using in our ebook and the educational psychology principles that support their use. We provide evidence that learners utilized these activities and that learners do face "desirable difficulties" when working through these activities. We use an observational study and log file analyses to design principles for more effective use of the activities, with particular emphasis on Parsons Problems [32] as a promising learning activity.

1.2 Why not MOOCs?

Massively Open On-line Courses (MOOCs) could also provide low cost learning at scale. However, most MOOCs are structured around passive consumption of video lectures [19]. Researchers have found that students often do not watch the entire videos, especially if the videos are over 6 minutes in length [19]. One study found that even certificate earners (those that complete all the MOOC requirements) skip 22% of the MOOC content on average [20].

The first trials of CS education MOOCs in Summer 2014 had a 5-10% completion rate [12, 21]. While low completion rates might not be a significant problem for many MOOCs where a large number of learners are just exploring a topic, they are a problem when our goal is to prepare teachers to teach an entire curriculum.

Most MOOC completers have prior knowledge in the subject and are highly motivated to learn the content [33]. Few teachers in the United States have any computer science coursework or experience [3]. Teachers are overworked professionals who have to squeeze their learning into small bits of time [5]. They are willing to learn computer science to help their students, but few are intrinsically motivated to learn computer science [30]. Therefore, professional development opportunities for teachers have to be motivating and have clear value over cost (what educators call *expectancy value*) [16].

Our hypothesis is that we can create an efficient and effective environment for learning programming concepts by applying principles from educational psychology to the design of an ebook, thus achieving the low-cost online advantages of MOOCs, but with better completion rates. We chose a text-centric book structure because it is easier to break into small segments to fit into a teacher's available free time. The educational psychology principles we are using have been effective in controlled studies in a laboratory setting and in interventions in science and mathematics [4]. Our work is an attempt to apply these approaches in computer science instruction where they have rarely been used [26].

2. EDUCATIONAL PSYCHOLOGY PRINCIPLES

The interactive features we added to the ebook platform are based on educational psychology principles, described in the following sections.

2.1 Practice, Feedback, and Testing

As reported by Bransford, Brown, and Cocking learning requires practice with frequent feedback [9]. Students can develop misconceptions that hinder learning so it is important that misconceptions be discovered and addressed as quickly as possible [9]. As reported by Bjork, Dunlosky, and Kornell spaced practice and self-testing are better than massed practice and reading or rereading material [8]. However, most students have not been taught how to learn and tend to believe the opposite [8]. Learners also tend to overestimate how much they have learned [8]. Self-testing helps learners gauge how much they have actually learned.

2.2 Learning from Errors

Another important finding from educational psychology is that people learn from making errors [8]. This is especially true when the learner is very confident in his or her incorrect answer [8]. This means that self-testing problems should contain answers that correspond to common misconceptions in order to bring those misconceptions to the attention of the reader.

2.3 Cognitive Load and Worked Examples

Cognitive load is the effort needed to manage the flow of information during instruction. Working memory is fixed and limited. Poorly designed instruction can cost working memory that is needed to simply understand and learn from content. One way in which we often discount cognitive load is when teaching problem solving. By asking students to problem-solve (e.g., write programs) when they are still learning the content (e.g., the programming language and computer science concepts), we are increasing cognitive load which leads to less learning of both the content and the problem-solving approach [36].

One way to reduce cognitive load is to increase the use of *worked examples*, i.e., completely worked out problems to be studied. Worked examples were shown to be more effective for teaching algebra than simply asking students to solve more algebra problems [37], and have since been used to improve learning in many other domains [4]. The optimal pattern for learning is intermixed worked examples with opportunities to practice [38].

2.4 Use of Multiple Modalities

Educational psychologists know that over-reliance on visual modalities can lead to less learning than using multiple modalities [14]. A diagram with a text description is harder to learn from than a diagram with a narrated description, because of increased load and split attention (looking between the diagram and the text) [27]. By relying more on audio, we can reduce effort and improve learning. Videos certainly are an example of using mixed modalities, but they are also dynamic (as opposed to a static diagram or a program code listing) and can be harder to retain as they can result in the *transience effect* [11].

3. ORIGINAL EBOOK FEATURES

Brad Miller and David Ranum of Luther College created an interactive version [28, 29] of the on-line book "How to Think Like a Computer Scientist" [17] during the summer of 2011. This book was released with a GNU public license, which means that it can be used freely and modified. Their interactive version added several features to the original on-line textbook: embedded videos, embedded code execution, and embedded code visualization.

3.1 Embedded Videos

Miller & Ranum augmented the book by including embedded screencast videos that were 5 to 10 minutes in length. They were displayed as a static thumbnail image that the user could click on. The user then had to click on the play button to play the video. The videos were typically placed at the beginning of a chapter and covered the same material as the chapter.

3.2 Embedded Code Execution: Active Code

The Active Code feature allows Python programs to be executed in the browser window, as a kind of worked example. The programs can be modified in place and executed again. The Python code is compiled to JavaScript at runtime using Skulpt (http://www.skulpt.org) and then run in the JavaScript virtual machine in the browser window. Miller & Ranum included textual descriptions of some of the programs after the Active Code feature.

3.3 Embedded Code Visualization: Code Lens

The Code Lens feature (see Figure 1) allows users to step through the execution of a program and see the state of all of the variables, using Guo's Python program visualizer [18].

The visualizer gives students another way to study a worked example program. Users can step forward or backward through the program. They can also jump to before the first line has executed or after the last line has executed.

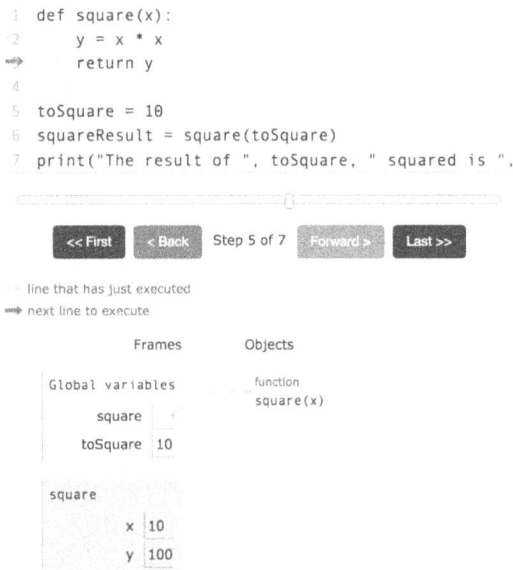

```
1  def square(x):
2      y = x * x
→      return y
4
5  toSquare = 10
6  squareResult = square(toSquare)
7  print("The result of ", toSquare, " squared is ",
```

`<< First`   `< Back`   Step 5 of 7   `Forward >`   `Last >>`

– line that has just executed
→ next line to execute

Frames	Objects
Global variables	function square(x)
square	
toSquare 10	

square	
x	10
y	100

Figure 1. Program visualization with Code Lens

4. NEW EBOOK FEATURES

We added additional interactive features based on educational psychology principles: audio tours of code, multiple choice questions with different feedback for each possible answer, and Parsons problems. These new features allowed us to test the users' current understanding, address misconceptions, provide frequent feedback, and provide low cognitive load practice. We added practice problems (multiple choice questions and/or Parsons problems) after each worked example (Active Code and/or Code Lens) since experiments have shown the best results from interleaved worked examples and practice [38].

4.1 Audio Tours of Code

Audio tours were added to the Active Code feature. They highlight one or more lines of program code as the audio explanation of the line(s) plays. The user can go forward, backward, jump to the beginning, or jump to the end as shown in Figure 2.

Audio tours provide worked examples utilizing the *multi-modality principle* [27]. The multi-modality principle indicates that humans can process more information when using both the audio input channel as well as the visual input channel rather than have two items that both use the visual input channel such as program code and the textual explanation [14].

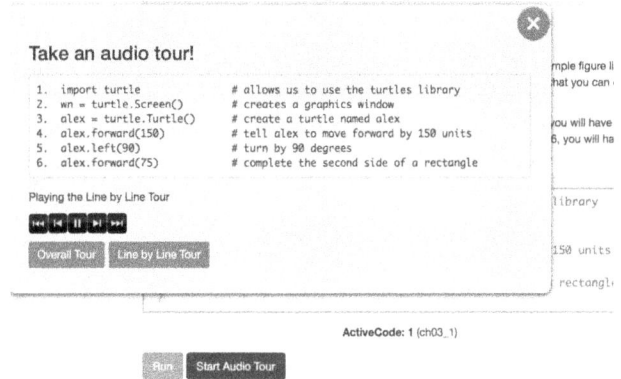

Take an audio tour!

```
1.  import turtle            # allows us to use the turtles library
2.  wn = turtle.Screen()     # creates a graphics window
3.  alex = turtle.Turtle()   # create a turtle named alex
4.  alex.forward(150)        # tell alex to move forward by 150 units
5.  alex.left(90)            # turn by 90 degrees
6.  alex.forward(75)         # complete the second side of a rectangle
```

Playing the Line by Line Tour

`|◀◀ ◀| ▌▌ |▶ ▶▶|`

`Overall Tour`   `Line by Line Tour`

ActiveCode: 1 (ch03_1)

`Run`   `Start Audio Tour`

Figure 2. Audio tour controls

4.2 Multiple Choice Questions

Miller & Ranum's version of the ebook had only a few multiple choice questions. Each question gave the same feedback regardless of the answer selected. Our group added different feedback for each possible answer. We also added many more multiple choice questions in order to have a large number of self-testing problems. The answers to the multiple choice questions included distractors based on common misconceptions and the feedback for those answers tried to address the misconceptions as shown in Figure 3.

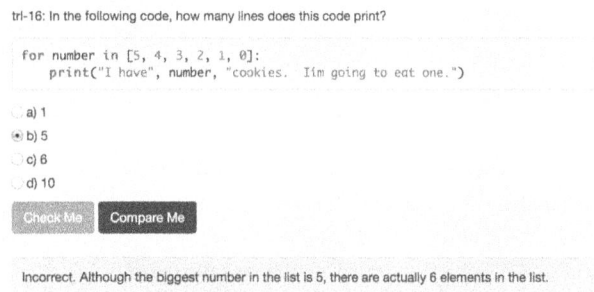

trl-16: In the following code, how many lines does this code print?

```
for number in [5, 4, 3, 2, 1, 0]:
    print("I have", number, "cookies.  Iim going to eat one.")
```

○ a) 1
◉ b) 5
○ c) 6
○ d) 10

`Check Me`   `Compare Me`

Incorrect. Although the biggest number in the list is 5, there are actually 6 elements in the list.

Figure 3. Multiple choice question with feedback based on the answer selected

4.3 Parsons Problems

Parsons problems have correct code that is broken into code blocks that have to be put in the correct order. They were originally created by Dale Parsons and Patricia Haden [32] to provide practice on programming principles in a puzzle-like format. There are several variants of Parsons problems such as including unnecessary code as distractors and requiring students to correctly indent the code. Parsons problems were intended to be an engaging way to give students programming practice without requiring students to type code and encounter syntax errors [32], thus reducing the overall cognitive load on the student when solving the problem. Parsons and Haden found that the majority of students in two first programming courses found Parsons problems useful when first learning Pascal [32]. Parsons and Haden suggested that the appropriate level of difficulty for Parsons problems was that they should be solvable in two or three attempts [32].

We added 11 Parsons problems to the chapter with turtle graphics. Instead of activity diagrams, which were used originally by Parsons and Haden, we used pictures of the intended result to guide the user (see Figure 4). We also specified the steps in a text block above the mixed up code blocks. Students drag the blocks from left to right and then click the *"Check Me"* button to see if they have the correct solution. If the solution is incorrect the first block that is incorrect is highlighted and an error message is displayed. We did not include any distractors in this set of Parsons problems. Other researchers studying Parsons problems have found that distractors increase the difficulty of the problem [15].

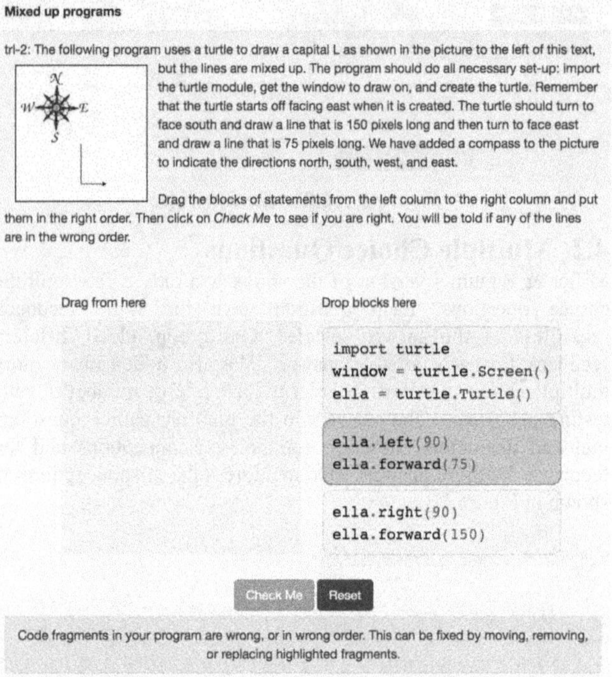

Figure 4. Parsons problem 1 with feedback

The number of blocks for each problem is shown in Table 1 along with a description of the output.

Table 1. Parsons problems information

Num	Blocks	What it Draws
1	3	A capital L
2	5	A checkmark
3	5	A line to the west
4	5	A capital L in white on a blue background
5	5	A capital T in white on a green background
6	5	A capital L in blue with one turtle and a line in orange to the west with another
7	6	A line in blue to the north with one turtle and a line to the east with another
8	6	An equilateral triangle
9	6	A square
10	7	A circle of 10 turtles facing out using the stamp function
11	8	Three turtle stamped in a line

Denny, Luxton-Reilly, and Simon explored using Parsons problems in exams and found that Parsons problems scores highly correlate with code writing scores [15]. This means that Parsons problems provide the opportunity to practice coding with less overall cognitive load. These same researchers suspected that students would be able to solve Parsons problems more quickly than writing the equivalent code, but did not test this hypothesis [15]. Parsons problems eliminate syntax errors and we know that

syntax errors can be a significant reason why CS students learning at a distance give up when programming [5].

While the cognitive load is reduced, Parsons problems can still be challenging. Researchers have found that even though Parsons problems can remove syntax errors, users can get stuck and repeat the same incorrect solution [23].

5. STUDYING USE OF THE EBOOK
Our research questions were 1) would readers use the new features, 2) would some features be used more than others, and 3) were the practice problems at the right level of difficulty? We expected readers to be familiar with multiple choice questions and solve those within a few tries. We wanted to see if readers would attempt the Parsons problems and how many attempts it would take them to get them correct. We wanted the practice problems to be difficult enough to cause errors which improves learning [7], but not so difficult that the readers would give up.

We conducted two studies to examine the use of our added features within the ebook. The first was an observational study of four *teachers* working through one chapter of the ebook after working through the earlier chapters at their own pace. The goal of this study was to observe teacher use of the features as they worked through the chapter to determine what difficulties they encountered that would not be obvious from a log file analysis. This study also allowed us to ask the teachers questions about why they didn't use certain features and what they thought of the features.

The second study was a log file analysis of use of the ebook by *undergraduate and high school students* to determine how many features were actually used, how many students attempted each practice problem, and how many solved each practice problem. The ebook is freely available and is used by several universities and some high schools. The log file analysis was informed by the findings from the observational study.

This paper focuses on user activity within the first four chapters of the ebook. The first chapter is an introduction to algorithms, programming, and errors. The second chapter is about variables, expressions, operators, operands, and statements. The third chapter is about how to avoid debugging and how to debug a program. The fourth chapter introduces turtle graphics (originally created by Seymour Papert [31] for the LOGO programming language), the *for* loop, and the *range* function.

5.1 Teacher Observational Study
We recruited teachers with less than six months of textual programming experience (in languages like Python or Java) to participate in an observational study with the ebook. We had 18 teachers fill out the registration and sign the consent forms. We disqualified two teachers due to too much *textual programming experience* (we allowed longer drag-and-drop programming experience).

We asked the teachers to complete the first three chapters of the ebook at their own pace and then notify us before starting the fourth chapter on turtle graphics and loops. We did the remote observations using the webinar software BlackBoard Collaborate (http://www.blackboard.com/) as the teachers worked through the chapter. We took notes on our observations, but also recorded the sessions so that we could check our notes against the recordings. We instructed the teachers to talk aloud as they worked though the interactive elements and asked what they were thinking if they were silent for more than a few seconds. After they completed the chapter we also asked questions based on our observations. We observed four teachers, since only four teachers notified us that they had completed the first three chapters during the study period. All of the teachers were currently teaching a programming class.

5.1.1 Findings from the Observations

All four teachers interacted with *all* of the worked examples (Active Code and Code Lens) and practice problems (multiple choice and Parsons problems) in chapter four. They also all edited the code when directed to by the ebook. They correctly answered most problems in one try, but a few problems took two attempts. While these teachers didn't have more than six months of textual programming experience, some of them had taken a college course in programming and several had been teaching programming using drag-and-drop languages such as Scratch or Alice for several years.

Only one of the teachers watched all of the videos. Another teacher said that he had watched the videos in the other chapters, but realized that they covered much the same material as in the text and said he thought that he could get through the practice problems without watching them. He said, *"The teacher in me wants to watch them (the videos), but the student in me says see how you do without them."*

Only two of the four teachers listened to any of the audio tours. When we asked the other teachers why they hadn't listened to the audio tours, they told us that they hadn't noticed them. After one teacher noticed the audio tours he said, *"The audio tour was interesting – I think that would be helpful if I wanted things to be explained to me."* At the time of this study the "Start Audio Tour" button was gray and was next to the green "Run" button and above two other gray buttons that let the user save and load modified code. The text did not mention the audio tours.

The teachers solved all of the Parsons problems in 1-2 tries. The most common difficulty we observed was that the teachers did not immediately realize that they had to indent statements in the body of a loop, even though the ebook text explained that Python requires the body of the loop to be indented. The Active Code examples also showed that the body of the loop was indented. The text before the Parson problems said that the user would be told if any of the blocks are in the wrong order *or are incorrectly indented*, but the teachers did not notice that text. One teacher even said, *"These need to be indented but I don't think we can indent here."* After he received the error (shown in Figure 5), he realized he could actually indent the code blocks. Some teachers also got the order of some of the blocks wrong at first, but were able to fix the order in their second attempt. Some teachers read the textual instructions out loud and went back and forth between dragging blocks and reading the instructions. One teacher said, *"I love this. I am curious to see how this works in a classroom."* One teacher said, *"They (the Parsons problems) weren't hard but they gave me a good idea of the flow (import first, name turtle and properties)."*

One teacher dragged code blocks from the left to the right and then dragged some code blocks back to the left before rereading the textual instructions. He used the right side to hold the code segments that he was sure of and the left side to hold the blocks that he still needed to move. This behavior was interesting as we were considering saving space by using just one text area to hold the mixed up code and having the user reorder the blocks within that area rather than have the user drag blocks from left to right. However, it appears that having the two text areas can reduce the cognitive load on the user when solving the Parsons problem. It allows the user to keep track of what has been moved and what

still needs to be moved. This is a type of *distributed cognition* in which some of the cognitive load is offloaded to items in the environment, as described by Hutchins [24].

5.2 Log File Analysis of Ebook Features

Miller and Ranum's "How to Think Like a Computer Scientist" interactive ebook has been in use for several years now by both undergraduate and high school students. We can study *how* more traditional students use the interactive features in order to provide additional insight into the effectiveness of these features. We can expect that teachers and students will have similar difficulties when using the features of an ebook to learn programming. Our earlier pilot studies with teachers and students did show differences between how teachers and students used ebooks [2]. Teachers tended to work through every practice problem in a chapter, while students skipped some practice problems. Teachers also tended to work on practice problems until they got them correct, while some students gave up if they were having difficulty finding the correct answer.

We received an anonymized version of the log file data in the fall of 2014. This file was over 700 MB and contained data for all student use of the ebook from May 17, 2012 to May 26, 2014. Identifying information for both users and courses had been replaced with user and course numbers. A separate file contained information on the courses such as the course number, the type of course (college, community, and high school), and the start date for the course.

5.2.1 Selecting Courses to Analyze

Instructors can create their own course using the ebook. This gives the instructor access to student progress and activity. While many instructors create their own course, others just use the open access version of the book, which anyone can use.

There were 90 courses represented in the log file data. We selected 4 courses that had the highest number of entries on which to conduct further analysis. Table 2 shows the course information and number of log file entries for each of the analyzed courses. In addition to the entries related to these 4 specific courses, we also analyzed the data from the open access version of the book between January 1, 2014 to June 1, 2014. The open access version of the book had over 2,000 unique users during this time period. We chose this time period to correspond to the time period of most of the courses and to examine the book after we had added practice features such as the Parsons problems.

Table 2. Courses that were analyzed

Course #	Start Date	Type	# Entries
1	8/25/2013	College	250,909
2	1/26/2014	Unknown (not selected)	243,362
3	1/6/2014	High School	193,668
4	1/31/2014	College	132,075

5.2.2 Parsons problems

We focused a significant amount of our analysis on Parsons problems, as they are such a good exemplar of our approach. Parsons problems are clearly practice, but with decreased cognitive load as compared to writing code. We looked for evidence in our analysis that Parsons problems were solvable with a reasonable amount of effort, but still challenging. We also looked for clues as to how we might improve Parsons problems, e.g., provide hints if they were challenging, or make them more challenging if they became too easy.

We concentrated our analysis on chapter four since it was the only chapter containing Parsons problems. Across all Parsons problems, the average percent of people that eventually achieved a correct solution was 96.5% (standard deviation of 4.3). The lowest percentage for a correct solution was students in the High School course on problem 8 (83.6%). This is not surprising -- problem 8 is the first Parsons problem that requires indention. After the observational study of teachers using the ebook, our hypothesis was that Parsons problems that require indention would present a greater challenge to the students. This also confirms prior research, which showed that Parsons problems were easier to solve if they gave the structure of the solution (the number of lines and indention) [15]. Figure 5 shows problem 8 with feedback telling the user that the highlighted block is not indented correctly. In Python, a code block is indicated by indention so all code in the body of a loop must be indented. Problems 8-11 all require the user to indent lines in the body of the loop correctly and these were the problems that required the most attempts before getting the problem correct as shown in Table 3.

Figure 5. Parsons problem 8 with feedback

Most students correctly solved most of the Parsons problems after only a couple of attempts. Table 3 shows the number of attempts it took for 50% and 75% of the people to get the problem correct, disaggregated by each Parsons problem. As you can see from this table the last four Parsons problems were the ones that students had the most difficulty solving. This is not surprising since these four problems all require indention and our observational study had shown that problems that required the correct indention were more difficult.

Table 3: Number of tries to correct for Parsons Problems

Num	# tries 50%	# tries 75%	Maximum
1	1	2	42
2	1	2	25
3	1	1	38
4	1	1	29
5	1	2	23
6	1	2	28
7	1	1	24
8	4	7	80
9	1	3	46
10	2	9	109
11	2	4	76

Given that the number of permutations for a Parsons problem with 3 blocks is 6 (since statement order matters) and the maximum number of tries for problem 1 was well over 6 it is obvious that the student repeated incorrect solutions.

It is also interesting to look at the number of attempts users made before giving up on the Parsons problem – those who failed to ever solve the Parsons problem correctly. Table 4 shows the number of attempts before 50% and 75% of the students quit trying to solve each Parsons problem, the maximum number of tries, and the total number of students who quit trying to solve that problem. Again the number of tries that individuals made before quitting is more than expected with a maximum of 183 for problem 10. In comparison, the maximum number of attempts before correctly solving that problem was 109.

Table 4: Number of tries before quitting on Parsons Problems

Num	50%	75%	Max Tries	# Quit
1	2	4	16	151
2	2	5	18	98
3	2	6	76	66
4	4	5	45	25
5	4	7	41	38
6	2	7	33	28
7	3	8	18	18
8	8	15	79	152
9	6	12	69	101
10	9	17	183	183
11	7	13	72	105

Figure 6 takes a closer look at the number of attempts before giving up on problem 10, which appears to have been the most difficult problem.

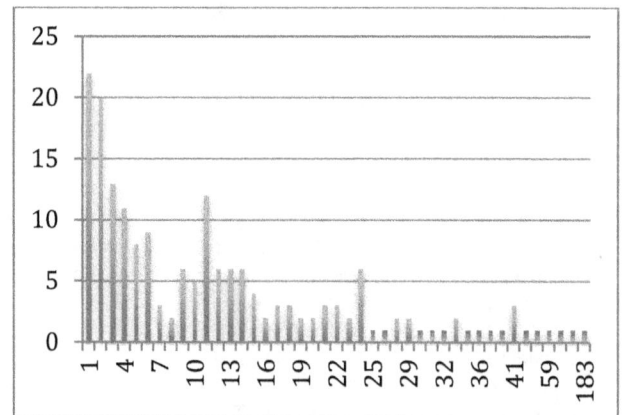

Figure 6. The number of people who quit after each number of attempts for problem 10

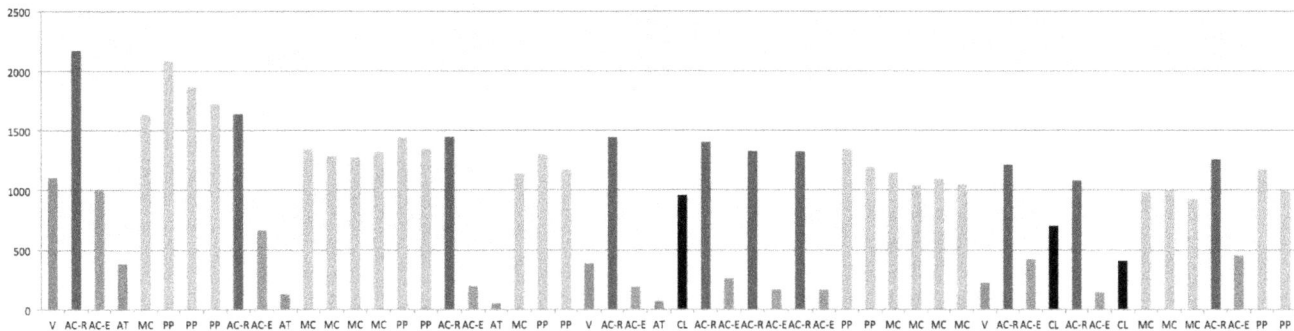

Figure 7. The number of unique users that did each action in Chapter 4 in the open access use of the ebook

The largest number of students quit after just one solution attempt. There are also spikes after 11 and 24 attempts. This information will be useful for deciding when to offer the user help on solving the problem, which we intend to do in future work.

5.2.3 Log File Analysis

For each selected course we calculated the number of unique users who attempted and eventually correctly solved every multiple choice problem and Parsons problem. We also counted the number of unique users that ran and edited each Active Code example, clicked the forward button on a Code Lens, played a video, and played an audio tour. We generated the same data for the open access version of the book as well.

6. Use Across All Features

One of the most interesting explorations of the data was to look at all the features within a specific chapter, chapter 4. We analyzed this data for the open access use of the ebook as well as the four courses. The results for the open access use of the book are shown in Figure 7, though the results for the four courses were similar. Each bar indicates the number of unique users that performed each of the possible actions in chapter 4. Table 5 explains the labels and colors used in Figure 7.

In general we see a drop off in the number of people who perform each activity over the course of the chapter. By the end of the chapter, students do less of *everything*. However, it is important to note that they do *more* of the lower cognitive load practice activities (e.g., multiple choice questions and Parsons problems) than the higher cognitive load (and more traditional) computer science practice activity, editing code. This is interesting because readers were explicitly told to modify the code after the first, second, and last Active Code examples, but less than half of the students did this.

Table 5: Explanation of Labels and Colors for Figure 7

Label	Color	Explanation
AC-E	Light Blue	Editing an Active Code example
AC-R	Dark Blue	Running an Active Code
AT	Red	Playing an Audio tour
CL	Black	Clicking forward on a Code Lens
MC	Orange	Checking a multiple choice answer
PP	Green	Checking a Parsons Problem
V	Purple	Playing a video

We see this same drop off in activity in each of the four courses we analyzed. One possible reason for this drop off is user fatigue. The entire chapter in this version of the ebook was one long HTML page. In the current version of this ebook, the long chapters have now been broken into much smaller sections. It will be interesting to compare the usage data from this new version to the old version to see if the shorter sections encourage more use of the interactive activities toward the end of a chapter. However, we also see the same drop off in activity in each of the first nine chapters of the open access use of the ebook. Another possible explanation for the drop off in activity is that students felt that they had a good grasp on the material and did not need the additional practice. However, students often overestimate the amount they have learned [8].

The activities that the largest number of students performed were running Active Code examples, solving Parsons problems, and answering multiple choice questions. The activities that had the highest percent of continuation from first to last are running Active Code examples, answering multiple choice questions, solving Parsons problems, and editing Active Code examples. Table 6 gives a further breakdown of these data for the open access use of the ebook.

Table 6: The number of people who did the first and last of each activity and the percentage of last versus first.

Activity	# 1st	# Last	%last / first
Active Code–run	2173	1260	58%
Multiple choice	1636	929	57%
Parsons	2087	995	48%
Active Code-edit	1011	453	45%
Code Lens – fwd	961	407	42%
Video	1107	221	20%
Audio tour	383	68	18%

One of the interesting results of the data analysis is that the videos were not viewed as often as expected. Videos are the primary method for presenting information in many MOOCs and often are where learners spend a great deal of time in a MOOC [34]. However, only 51% of the people who ran the first Active Code example (2173) in the chapter also watched the first video (1107) (see Figure 7). By the third video in the chapter only 18% of the people watched the video (221) compared to the number that ran the next Active Code example (1215).

Perhaps the students in the four courses we analyzed were not likely to watch the videos because they also had face-to-face lectures. This may also be the case with the open access use of the book, but while some people use the open access book in their course we would expect that quite a few of the 2000 unique users were working on their own rather than participating in a course. We anticipated that students working on their own would have viewed the videos much like MOOC students do. Another possibility for the low usage of the video feature is that the videos were not engaging. The videos in the ebook were screencasts and not the type of high production videos that you often find in MOOCs. From our teacher observation we learned that at least some teachers stopped watching the videos when they realized that the videos covered the same material as the text. Finally, the videos may not have been played due to the confusing interface that required two clicks to play a video.

The audio tours also had very low usage rates. Only 383 people played the first audio tour compared to 2,173 people that ran the first Active Code example. One possibility is that the user interface made it difficult for people to notice the audio tours and thus they did not use that feature. This possibility is supported by the comments from the teachers in the observational study.

7. Conclusion

Our research questions were 1) would readers use the new features, 2) would some features be used more than others, and 3) were the practice problems at the right level of difficulty? All of the new interactive features in the ebook were used, but some features were used much more than others. The teachers solved all of the practice problems in one or two tries, but the students had more difficulty with some of the Parsons problems. This may be due to the fact that the teachers had more prior programming experience than the students. All of the teachers had been teaching programming using drag and drop environments and one had taken a college-level programming course.

Both students and teachers ran the code examples, attempted the multiple choice questions, and attempted the Parsons problems. Teachers did *all* of these activities in chapter four, but students did more of these at the beginning of the chapter four and less by the end of the chapter. Students show this same pattern of reduced use of the interactive features over the course of a chapter in all of the first nine chapters of the ebook. Teachers edited the code examples when instructed to by the ebook, but less than half of the students did this. Teachers also interacted with all of the Code Lens examples, but less than half of the students used this feature. Both teachers and students made very little use of the videos and Audio Tours. The observational study suggests that the teachers thought that the videos were not necessary since they covered the same material as the text. The observational study also suggests that the user interface made it hard to notice the Audio Tours. We have changed the user interface to highlight the Audio Tours and also added text in a new ebook for teachers to encourage the teachers to try the Audio Tours. It will be interesting to see if these changes improve use.

One interesting finding is that more students attempted to solve the Parsons problems than tried to solve the multiple choice questions after a worked example. This finding is a contribution to the research on Parsons problems since prior studies of Parsons problems [15, 23, 32] didn't compare the use of Parsons problems with other types of practice problems. However, this preference for Parsons problems may be due to a novelty affect if the students had not seen this type of problem before. More research will need to be done to see if this preference for Parsons problems over multiple choice questions continues over time.

Parsons and Haden suggested that Parsons problems are at the appropriate level of difficulty if they are solvable by all students in two to three tries at most [32]. However, we feel that the standard should be if 75% of the students solve the problems in two to three tries, since some students give up quickly. This standard indicates that three of the 11 Parson problems may be too easy since 75% of the students solved them in just one try. Five of the Parsons problems appear to be at the desired level of difficulty since 75% of the students solved them in 2 or 3 tries. However, three of the Parsons problems took more than 3 tries for 75% of the students to solve them, so these might be considered too difficult without additional help. One surprise was the number of attempts that students made before getting the problems correct. It took from 23 to 109 tries for at least one student to get each problem correct. The data on how many tries it took before students gave up on solving Parsons problems will be useful in determining when to offer additional help.

At the ITiCSE 2013 conference, a working group developed a set of requirements and design strategies for ebooks [25]. One of the top features on the "must include" list was the ability for "editing and execution of code segments." Our results suggest that code editing was not actually used much by the students, as compared to other activities. Low cognitive load activities like Parsons problems were much more commonly used. We believe that it's important for ebooks to support editing code. They might be perceived as inauthentic without code editing [35]. However, features that would actually be *used* and be *useful for learning* may not be what we might expect. Other kinds of activities may increase opportunities for engagement while also contributing to learning.

Research in educational psychology suggests that a worked examples plus interleaved practice problems approach leads to effective and efficient learning. This paper contributes to the research on worked examples plus practice by showing that the four teachers interacted with all of the worked examples and practice problems, however future research will have to determine if that interaction led to learning gains. While students didn't use all of the worked examples and practice problems, more of them attempted the low cognitive load practice problems than the higher cognitive task of code editing even though they were instructed to edit the code in the ebook. These studies demonstrate that Parsons problems are a promising type of low cognitive load practice problem, since more students attempted Parson problems than attempted the multiple choice questions after a worked example.

8. ACKNOWLEDGMENTS

We thank our collaborators Brad Miller and David Ranum for their work on both the development environment and the *"How to Think Like a Computer Scientist"* ebook. We thank Christine Alvarado for creating multiple choice questions and for her analysis of the pilot studies. We thank the reviewers for their suggestions on ways to improve the paper. We also thank the teachers who were part of the observational study. The funding for this research came from the National Science Foundation award CNS-1138378. Any opinions, findings, and conclusions or recommendations expressed in this material are those of the authors and do not necessarily reflect the views of the National Science Foundation.

9. REFERENCES

[1] *AP Course Ledger.*
https://apcourseaudit.epiconline.org/ledger/

[2] Alvarado, C., Morrison, B., Ericson, B., Guzdial, M., Miller, B. and Ranum, D. *Performance and use evaluation of an electronic book for introductory Python programming.* Georgia Institute of Technology, 2012.

[3] Astrachan, O., Cuny, J., Stephenson, C. and Wilson, C. The CS10K project: mobilizing the community to transform high school computing. In *Proc. 42nd ACM technical symposium on Computer science education* (2011). ACMTavel, P. 2007. *Modeling and Simulation Design.* AK Peters Ltd., Natick, MA.

[4] Atkinson, R. K., Derry, S. J., Renkl, A. and Wortham, D. Learning from Examples: Instructional Principles from the Worked Examples Research. *Review of Educational Research*, 70, 2 (2000), 181–214.

[5] Benda, K., Bruckman, A. and Guzdial, M. When life and learning do not fit: Challenges of workload and communication in introductory computer science online. *ACM Transactions on Computing Education* (2011).

[6] Bennedsen, J. and Caspersen, M. E. Failure rates in introductory programming. *SIGCSE Bull.*, 39, 2 (2007), 32-36.

[7] Bjork, E. L. and Bjork, R. A. Making things hard on yourself, but in a good way: Creating desirable difficulties to enhance learning. *Psychology and the real world: Essays illustrating fundamental contributions to society* (2011), 56-64.

[8] Bjork, R. A., Dunlosky, J. and Kornell, N. Self-Regulated Learning: Beliefs, Techniques, and Illusions. *Annual Review of Psychology*, 64 (2013), 417-444.

[9] Bransford, J. D., Brown, A. L. and Cocking, R. R. *How People Learn.* NATIONAL ACADEMY PRESS, City, 2000.

[10] Brown, N. C. C., Kölling, M., Crick, T., Jones, S. P., Humphreys, S. and Sentance, S. Bringing computer science back into schools: lessons from the UK. In *Proc. 44th ACM technical symposium on Computer science education* (2013). ACM

[11] Byrne, M. D., Catrambone, R. and Stasko, J. T. Evaluating animations as student aids in learning computer algorithms. *Comput. Educ.*, 33, 4 (1999), 253-278.

[12] Carol, S., Diana, L., Michael, P. R. and Judy, C. Are MOOCs an appropriate pedagogy for training K-12 teachers computer science concepts? *J. Comput. Sci. Coll. %@ 1937-4771*, 30, 5 (2015), 115-125.

[13] Caspersen, M. E. and Nowack, P. Computational thinking and practice: A generic approach to computing in Danish high schools. In *Proc. 15th Australasian Computer Education Conference (ACE 2013)* (2013). Conferences in Research and Practice in Information Technology (CRPIT)

[14] Clark, R. C. and Mayer, R. E. *E-Learning and the Science of Instruction: Proven Guidelines for Consumers and Designers of Multimedia Learning* Pfeiffer, 2011.

[15] Denny, P., Luxton-Reilly, A. and Simon, B. Evaluating a New Exam Question: Parsons Problems. In *Proc. International Computing Education Research Conference* (2008). ACM

[16] Eccles, J. *Expectancies, values, and academic behaviors.* Freeman, City, 1983.

[17] Elkner, J., Downey, A. B. and Meyers, C. *How to Think Like a Computer Scientist*, 2012.

[18] Guo, P. J. Online python tutor: embeddable web-based program visualization for cs education. In *Proc. 44th ACM technical symposium on Computer science education* (2013). ACM

[19] Guo, P. J., Kim, J. and Rubin, R. *How video production affects student engagement: an empirical study of MOOC videos.* ACM, City, 2014.

[20] Guo, P. J. and Reinecke, K. *Demographic differences in how students navigate through MOOCs.* ACM, City, 2014.

[21] Guzdial, M. The State of Computing Education in the World: Report on the 2014 ACM Education Council Meeting. ACM, City, 2014.

[22] Hake, R. R. Interactive-engagement vs traditional methods: A six-thousand-student survey of mechanics test data for instructory physics courses. *American Journal of Physics*, 66 (1998), 64-74.

[23] Helminen, J., Ihantola, P., Karavirta, V. and Malmi, L. How Do Students Solve Parsons Programming Problems? - An Analysis of Ineraction Traces. In *Proc. International Computing Education Research Conference* (2012). ACM

[24] Hutchins, E. How a Cockpit Remembers Its Speed. *Cognitive Science*, 19 (1995), 265-288.

[25] Korhonen, A., Naps, T., Boisvert, C., Crescenzi, P., Karavirta, V., Mannila, L., Miller, B., Morrison, B., Rodger, S. H., Ross, R. and Shaffer, C. A. Requirements and design strategies for open source interactive computer science eBooks. In *Proc. ITiCSE working group reports conference on Innovation and technology in computer science education-working group reports* (2013). ACM

[26] Margulieux, L. E., Guzdial, M. and Catrambone, R. Subgoal labeled worked examples improve K-12 teacher performance in computer programming training. In *Proc. 35th Annual Conference of the Cognitive Science Society* (2013)

[27] Mayer, R. E. *Multimedia Learning.* Cambridge University Press, 2009.

[28] Miller, B. and Ranum, D. *How to Think Like a Computer Scientist Learning with Python: Interactive Edition*, 2013.

[29] Miller, B. N. and Ranum, D. L. *Beyond PDF and ePub: toward an interactive textbook.* ACM, City, 2012.

[30] Morrison, B. B., Ni, L. and Guzdial, M. Adapting the disciplinary commons model for high school teachers: improving recruitment, creating community. In *Proc. ninth annual international conference on International computing education research* (2012). ACM

[31] Papert, S. *Mindstorms: children, computers, and powerful ideas.* Basic Books, Inc., 1980.

[32] Parsons, D. and Haden, P. Parson's programming puzzles: a fun and effective learning tool for first programming courses. In *Proc. 8th Australasian Conference on Computing Education - Volume 52* (2006). Australian Computer Society, Inc.

[33] Perna, L., Ruby, A., Boruch, R., Wang, N., Scull, J., Evans, C. and Ahmad, S. The life cycle of a million MOOC users. In

Proc. MOOC Research Initiative Conferece (2013). Graduate School of Education, University of Pennsylvania

[34] Seaton, D. T., Bergner, Y., Chuang, I., Mitros, P. and Pritchard, D. E. Who does what in a massive open online course? *Commun. ACM*, 57, 4 (2014), 58-65.

[35] Shaffer, D. W. and Resnick, M. "Thick" Authenticity: New Media and Authentic Learning. *Journal of Interactive Learning Research*, 10, 2 (1999), 195-215.

[36] Sweller, J. Cognitive load during problem solving: Effects on learning. *Cognitive Science*, 12 (1988), 257-285.

[37] Sweller, J. and Cooper, G. A. The use of worked examples as a substitute for problem solving in learning algebra. *Cognition and Instruction*, 2 (1985), 58-89.

[38] Trafton, J. G. and Reiser, B. J. The contributions of studying examples and solving problems to skill acquisition. In *Proc. Proceedings of the 15th Annual Conference of the Cognitive Science Society* (1993). Lawrence Erlbaum Associates, Inc.

How Do Students Use Program Visualizations within an Interactive Ebook?

Teemu Sirkiä
Department of Computer Science
Aalto University, School of Science
Espoo, Finland
teemu.sirkia@aalto.fi

Juha Sorva
Department of Computer Science
Aalto University, School of Science
Espoo, Finland
juha.sorva@aalto.fi

ABSTRACT

We investigated students' use of program visualizations (PVs) that were tightly integrated into the electronic book of an introductory course on programming. A quantitative analysis of logs showed that most students, and beginners especially, used the PVs, even where the PV did not directly affect their grade. Students commonly spent more time studying certain steps than others, suggesting they used the PVs attentively. Nevertheless, substantial numbers of students appeared to gloss over some key animation steps, something that future improvements to pedagogy may address. Overall, the results suggest that integrating PVs into an ebook can promote student engagement and has been fairly successful in the studied context. More research is needed to understand the differences between our results and earlier ones, and to assess the generalizability of our findings.

Categories and Subject Descriptors

K.3.2 [**Computers and Education**]: Computer and Information Science Education—*Computer science education*

General Terms

Human factors

Keywords

program visualization, beginner programmers, CS1, ebooks

1. INTRODUCTION

We, the authors, have recently taught a large-class introductory programming course (CS1) that is based on a interactive electronic textbook. Into this ebook, we have integrated several dozen *program visualizations* (PVs; see Figure 1), which animate the dynamics of example programs and combine with the rest of the ebook in other ways. In this article, we quantitatively explore whether, how, and to what extent students make use of these visualizations.

ICER'15, August 9–13, 2015, Omaha, Nebraska, USA.
© 2015 ACM. ISBN 978-1-4503-3630-7/15/08 ...$15.00.
DOI: http://dx.doi.org/10.1145/2787622.2787719

What we already know is that educational PV can help beginners develop a viable understanding of the *notional machine* [8, 44] that runs the programs that they write, and thereby to help them learn to program. More specifically, visualization has the potential to help students avoid and overcome misconceptions about tricky programming concepts such as parameters [22], constructors [34], or recursion [39]. However, students also sometimes find PVs opaque or fail to connect what they learn from PV with programming practice [46], and much is unknown about how to make PVs more attractive and more useful to more students. The present study looks into what students do with PVs that are tightly integrated into an interactive ebook. The results help us evaluate the present approach and point to future improvements to PV-based teaching and learning.

Our research questions are:

RQ1 *Do students use the PVs integrated into the ebook?*

RQ2 *When students view a PV, do they view all of it? Do they return to review any PVs or parts of them?*

RQ3 *Do students view the integrated PVs attentively, e.g., pausing to consider key animation steps longer?*

In terms of research methods, this study explores automatic logs as a source of data about large numbers of PV users.

The rest of this article is structured as follows. Section 2 motivates the use of PV and reviews prior work. Section 3 overviews the course that we studied and the PVs that we used. Section 4 describes how we collected and analyzed data. We present our results in Section 5 and discuss their implications in Section 6. In Section 7, we conclude the article with an examination of the limitations of our study.

2. RELATED WORK

2.1 Motivation: Seeing Structure

Consider this line of code:[1]

```
var test = Buffer("A buffer", "with", "a few", "strings")
```

We might say of it: "It creates a buffer `test`." or "`test` now holds four strings." Even as we say so, it is perhaps obvious to us that, speaking more strictly, `test` is not the name of the buffer itself but of a variable associated with the buffer, much as it is obvious to us that "Kafka" in "She likes to read Kafka." does not refer to a person as such but to the literary works associated with the person. We say such things anyway, often without consciously choosing to do so, because it is convenient and usually works.

---

[1]The code is in Scala, in which buffers are mutable collections similar to the `ArrayList`s of Java.

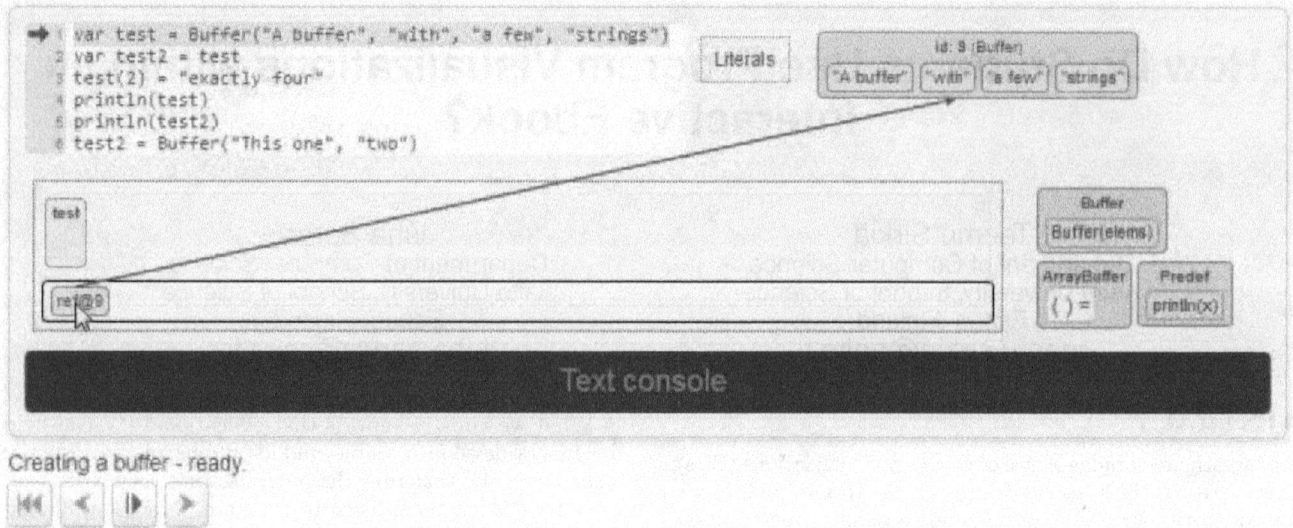

Figure 1: A snippet of Scala code illustrated by the PV tool Jsvee [42]. In this snapshot, the first line has been partially executed: A buffer has been created and a reference to it has been produced (now at cursor) and is just about to be assigned to the variable test. The student can use the controls at the bottom to pace the animation. In the ebook, this is the second PV that features references and the first in which multiple variables (at a later stage) refer to one mutable object. (Image translated from a Finnish-language original.)

Referring to a thing indirectly in the way just discussed, by mentioning an associated thing, is called *metonymy*, and it is something we humans naturally accept and indeed embrace [20, 27]. Metonymy is effortless because of the imaginative nature of human thought [20] and the co-operative nature of human communication [12]. In conversation, we count on our listener not to take us too literally. The listener has implicitly promised to try to make sense of our utterances, and where a literal interpretation would be incongruous, they can decipher the intended meaning through means such as metonymy and metaphor. However, a computer, not being intentional, does not volunteer these imaginative inferences, which is why we spell things out in programs. If we can. Beginner programmers are plagued by various difficulties and misconceptions that may relate to metonymy [27] and, more generally, to the beginners' attempts to instruct a computer in a way that only works with recipients that are co-operative, intentional, and sufficiently informed [30, 48].

According to a theory by de Kleer and Brown [5, 6], to understand a causal system in a way that transfers to other systems and is felicitous for troubleshooting, one must have a *robust mental model* of the system. A robust mental model allows one to reason about each system component separately from the purpose of the overall system: One's understanding of *structure* is untainted by one's understanding of *function*. Following this line of thought, a student's understanding of a piece of code is more useful if they can understand the code in terms of what each of its parts does in isolation.

Metonymy is predicated on a shared ability to discern implicit associations between the thing that is mentioned and the thing that is meant. In our example, "test now holds four strings" is a summary of a *function* of the code, which is that we intend to be able to access certain strings using the word test. If we are to use this phrase with a student, we must consider whether they discern what we left unsaid, that is, the implicit *structure* that involves the name test,

the variable, the reference, and the buffer. If the student does not, our utterance may spark or feed misconceptions such as the conflation of the variable and the buffer into a single entity [15].

To help a student construct a robust mental model of our example code, we can try to draw their attention to its separate structural components. A more detailed description of the code is: "It creates a buffer with four strings. It also creates a variable test and stores within it a reference to the buffer." A description in this vein may help the learner form an understanding that transfers better to code in which multiple variables refer to the same object or in which one variable refers to different objects at different times. A still more detailed description highlights expressions and assignment: "The computer evaluates the expression on the right, producing a reference to a new buffer with four strings. That reference is stored in the variable test." The realization that the right-hand side is an expression, and so can appear in places other than variable initialization, is an example of a further boost to the formation of transferable knowledge.[2]

Reasons such as these, and others [44], have inspired the creation of PV tools that *show* how the computer handles each component of a program.

2.2 Program Visualization as a Medium

There are many PV tools that aim to help beginners reason about program behavior and to nurture the development of programming skill [45]. A nascent trend is to embed PVs within interactive ebooks, in which they illustrate example programs or students' own code [26, 7, 33, 47, 49]; similar initiatives have also arisen in the neighboring field of algorithm visualization [36, 41]. Ebooks that incorporate interactive "smart learning content" [2, 35] such as PVs may be gradually replacing traditional computer science textbooks [19].

---

[2]N.B. We are not suggesting that a single example is sufficient, whichever way it is presented.

Whichever medium is used for delivering educational materials, a key concern is whether students study the materials with care. Mental effort is affected, among other things, by the predispositions that students have about the medium. Studies of educational video, for instance, have shown that videos tend to engender less mental effort than more interactive media [3, 38]. Viewing visualizations can be deceptively easy and give students an illusion of competence that hinders learning [4, 21]. Other pedagogical choices matter, too. A recent study of open online courses found that students were undisposed to watch videos longer than a few minutes and that some types of video (e.g., classroom lecture) were less likely to engage students than others [14].

The potential of PV as a medium for computing education can only be realized if students are motivated to reflect on the visualizations and if they succeed in relating them to programming concepts. Reading a PV is a skill that cannot be taken for granted and needs to be learned [31, 46]. Without guidance, not nearly all students use PV tools in the ways intended by their teachers [18].

Much like researchers of other educational media, PV researchers, too, have identified the need to engage students. It has been proposed that engagement is promoted by concrete activities such as responding to questions or manipulating visual elements [17, 28, 45]. Even though some such endeavors have been qualified successes, challenges remain. One risk is that students are unable to see the connections between programming practice and what they see in PVs, which drains motivation and inhibits transfer [46]. Another risk is that even though students engage in a concrete PV-based activity, their minds are not cognitively engaged. (The failure to distinguish between the two forms of engagement is "the constructivist teaching fallacy" [23].)

One way of mitigating these risks could be to have students visualize code that they wrote themselves and are intrinsically motivated to understand [45]. Another approach is to integrate PV into learning materials so that it is a natural part of learning to program and its practical relevance is easier to grasp; research in science education suggests that dynamic visualizations work better when they are embedded in supportive curriculum materials and when learners grow used to them over a period of time [21, 25]. The use of PV that we study in this article is an example of the latter strategy, as we will explain in Subsection 3.2 below.

2.3 Similar Prior Work

There are not many empirical studies of how CS1 students use PVs embedded in ebooks, but one such study is reported by Alvarado et al. [1]. They studied a college course whose ebook [26] featured embedded PVs that had been created with Online Python Tutor [13] and displayed program execution on a line-by-line basis. Alvarado et al. found that voluntary use of the PV features of the ebook dropped from about 70% of all students in the first week to under 20% by the fourth; students varied greatly in how much they used PV. PV use was positively albeit weakly correlated with performance, perhaps because PV boosted learning, perhaps because of how mostly the stronger students tended to use PV, and perhaps because of both reasons. It is unclear how well the results of Alvarado et al. generalize to other contexts. It is also not known how the various ways in which a visualization may be embedded in a textbook (see below), or other pedagogical choices, may impact on these phenomena.

The present study is not a replication of the one by Alvarado et al., but our first two research questions explore similar topics in a different context.

Our last question concerns whether students watch integrated PVs attentively and whether they gloss over parts of them. These issues are perhaps especially relevant in the context of *expression-level* PV (which we use): Although advancing through each line of code in multiple distinct steps can clarify important concepts such as expressions and return values, such fine-grained PVs tend to require more time to view, may bore students, and run the danger of insights being lost under a barrage of detail [43]. Knowing more about how students step through an animation can help assess the effectiveness of the PV and identify weaknesses such as key events that students fail to notice. As far as we can tell, these questions have not been directly addressed in the literature to date. The quantitative results concerning students' attention during program animations have tended to focus on other aspects and taken place in laboratory settings; consider, as one example, the work of Nevalainen and Sajaniemi [29], who used eye-tracking technology to investigate which areas of a PV display students primarily paid attention to.

3. SETTING

In this section, to help the reader interpret our results, we overview our CS1 and explain how we integrated PV into it.

3.1 The Programming Course

Our study takes place in the context of a large-class CS1 offered by Aalto University. The course, worth 5 ECTS credits [11], has been designed for the first-year students of the university's School of Science; we will refer to them as *main students*. Roughly a third of the main students major in computing. Since Fall 2014, the course has also been available to students from the other schools of Aalto (e.g., Arts, Business) and indeed to anyone else as an open online course; we will refer to all these students as *other students*.

The main students have had good to excellent success at the K-12 level and are usually well motivated to learn to program, to do well in the course, or both. They need the course for their degrees. Roughly half of the main students have no or very little prior experience with programming; the rest are experienced to various extents. The other students are still more varied in all respects, including motivation, expectations, occupation, hours available for studying, prior exposure to computing, etc. The other students do not have access to all the guidance available to the main students.

The course is designed for beginners and aims to help students appreciate and enjoy programming and to learn how to read, modify, and write application programs. Topics typical of an object-oriented CS1 are covered, such as classes, iteration, and inheritance, as well as some less common ones such as higher-order functions. There are longitudinal themes which include abstraction, the notional machine, software quality, roles of variables [37], and (im)mutable state. One of our goals is to lay the foundations for subsequent deeper learning of functional OOP (i.e., OOP with immutable data and higher-order functions) and functional programming more generally. We use the multiparadigm language Scala [9].

The course seeks to provide extensive deliberate practice [10] that is grounded in interesting, concrete programming projects. Program authoring is complemented by other forms of practice that have low cognitive load [32] such as

Table 1: Uses of program visualizations (adapted from [47]). The right-hand column shows the number of PVs with this role in the ebook; the number in parentheses indicates how many of them were part of a small graded assignment (usually one or more MCQs). A few PVs had two distinct roles.

Role of PV	Description	# in ebook
Clarifying a Newly Introduced Concept	Illustrates a concept just introduced in the text, e.g., nested calls. May be accompanied by questions that the PV helps to answer or that guide the learner to interpret the PV.	27 (5)
Clarifying an Example Program	"If you didn't understand that program, you may view this animation of it." Only uses constructs that the students are largely expected to understand already, but uses them in a new combination.	6 (1)
Predictive Tracing	"Can you predict what this code prints out? Then see the animation for the answer." Students may be prompted to write down predicted output and, after viewing, receive formative feedback tailored to their prediction. May also precede a graded multiple-choice or other question.	6 (2)
Clarifying a Solution	Illustrates a solution to an earlier assignment.	4 (n/a)
Hint for Task	Example: "Implement method M. If stuck, view this illustration of the execution of a working implementation with no code shown. Try to write code that matches the PV."	4 (4)
Introducing or Motivating a Construct	The first encounter with a concept is in a PV. Example: Students are tasked to work out from a PV what the keyword `this` is used for. Only then do they proceed to a detailed discussion of it. Or: Students view the execution of a pseudocode loop before learning the loop syntax.	4 (1)
Elaboration Task	Guides students to discover new relationships between concepts they have encountered previously. Example: MCQs prompt students to consider, with the aid of PV, whether formal parameters are local variables, and whether it is possible to have distinct variables with the same name.	3 (3)
Bug Analysis	Example: "Here is a program that crashes when run. Use this visualization to examine the conditions under which it crashes and answer some questions about the reasons."	2 (2)

worked examples, completion problems, and multiple-choice questions (MCQs). Students read a lot of code. Larger programs always come with skeleton code, and the design of applications from scratch to meet ill-specified goals is left to a subsequent course. Principles ("the theory") are often introduced "on demand" as they arise in the context of concrete projects (cf. [16]), but with an emphasis on their generalness. There are barely any lectures. Sorva and Seppälä [47] have elaborated on some aspects of this pedagogy.

An ebook in the form of a web pages has been tailor-made by one of the present authors to suit the course. Apart from text, the ebook contains assignments of various kinds, PVs (see below), other interactive sections, and occasional video. Most programming takes place in an IDE, but the programming assignments intertwine with the text. Students have great freedom in choosing how, where, and when they study, but whether they work in class under the guidance of a teaching assistant, at home, with a pair, or alone, nearly all course activities revolve around the ebook. Students use the ebook on university computers or on their own devices, usually laptops and desktops. The ebook is in Finnish.

92% of 247 main students and 51% of 653 other students passed our CS1 in Fall 2014.[3] The course was exceptionally well received despite the fact that students often described it as being a lot of work: The students who responded to an end-of-course survey gave an average overall feedback mark of about 4.6 (on a scale from 1 to 5) both in the case of main students ($n = 225$) and other students ($n = 227$).

3.2 The Program Visualizations

Fifty-three animated PVs were created using the Jsvee library [42] and embedded into the web pages that form the chapters of the ebook. The ebook gradually introduced the visual notation along with new programming constructs and

elements of a notional machine (e.g. references, stack). The text fairly frequently made reference to the PVs and helped the reader interpret them. PV was used more in the first half of the semester than the second. Some of the PVs were in optional sections, and not all chapters had any PVs.

A typical PV showed a selected snippet of Scala or pseudocode relevant to the topic at hand (lines: $min = 1$, $avg = 8.6$, $max = 28$; steps: $min = 6$, $avg = 44$, $max = 214$). Some of the snippets were parts of larger application programs, while others, such as the one in Figure 1, had no broader context. The student could explore a PV using the given controls and see the program execute. Due to the limitations of the current version of Jsvee, all the PVs were simply user-paced animations of given programs; the students could not visualize code that they wrote or manipulate the PV in other ways. Students had to click to advance at each step: "Just Press Play" was deliberately not supported so that they would be less likely to miss key events [40, 21].

A few of the PVs featured modal popup dialogs that interrupted the animation and highlighted "Don't Miss" steps. However, these alerts were used very sparingly (in 9 of 53 PVs), as viewers tend to find them intrusive. (Jsvee does not support other means of highlighting PVs at present.) Overall, it was largely up to the students to glean what they could from each animation by reading the accompanying section of the ebook, viewing the animation, and attempting to locate important entities and events in the PV.

There are many ways of linking the text and assignments of an ebook with PVs; such links may improve the understandability, perceived relevance, and effectiveness of the PVs. The most common roles for PVs in our ebook were the traditional ones — the clarification of a concept just introduced or an example program — but there were others as well, as shown in Table 1. Some of the PVs in the ebook were connected with multiple-choice questions (with automatic written feedback on correct and incorrect answers) or other small assignments that were worth a minor number of points.

---

[3]These figures do not include the few main students and many other students who dropped out before Week 2.

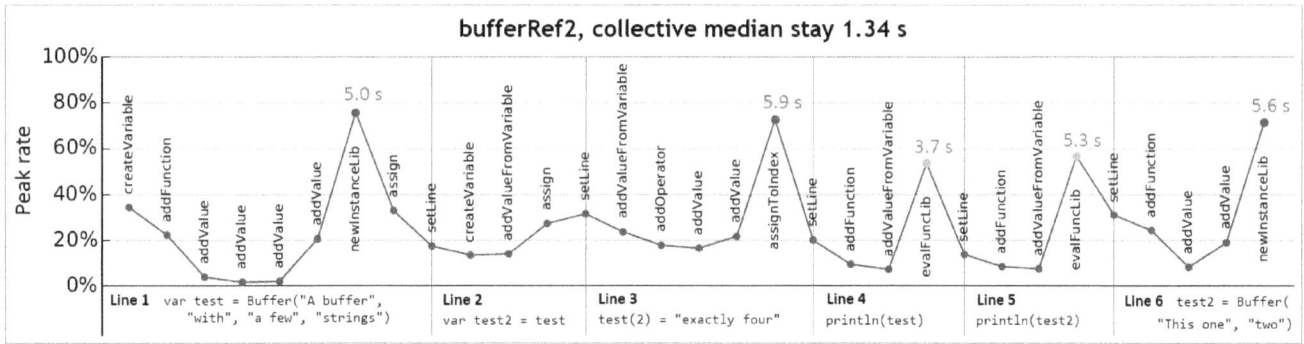

Figure 2: The peak rates of the steps of the PV from Figure 1, indicating how many of the students spent an untypically (for themselves in this PV) long time at each step. High peak rates (red) occur in three places: two where buffers are created and one where a buffer is modified. (Figure 1 shows the PV paused at one of these steps.) Print statements produced medium peak rates (yellow). The average times that students spent at these five collective peaks are also shown.

4. METHOD

4.1 Data Collection

Our main data source is a set of logs of student use of the PVs in our ebook during Fall 2014. A PV *session* was defined as the clicks of the Next, Back, or Start Over controls of a single animation during a single visit to an ebook chapter. Each such event was timed to the precision of a millisecond. If a student stopped for longer than two minutes between events, we assumed they were focusing on something other than the PV; these intervals were discarded.

Only users who had signed in, as students typically had, were logged. In total, we analyzed exactly 34 800 sessions from 1569 students; this includes early dropouts.

For grouping students into beginners and non-beginners, we used their answers to a background questionnaire that they had answered upon enrolling.

4.2 Analysis

We analyzed the data quantitatively using Python scripts and Statistix 9 by Analytical Software.

4.2.1 RQ1: Overall use of the PVs

The overall tendency of students to view the PVs was determined separately for each week of the course that had any PVs. We checked which students had been active during a week by looking at whether they had submitted any graded assignments. We then counted which percentage of those students had also viewed PVs during the week; a PV session was counted as part of a week if it was part of that week's materials in the ebook. To determine whether it was the graded PV-related assignments that made students view the PVs, the analysis was repeated so that only non-assignment PVs were included.

4.2.2 RQ2: Finishing, rewinding, revisiting

We consider a student to have *finished* a PV if they advanced all the way to the final step. The *finish rate* of a PV is the percentage of students who finished it.

A *rewind* was defined as a sequence of one or more consecutive clicks of the Back or Start Over buttons. A *revisit* is a separate PV session (chapter visit) in which the student used a PV they had already used before.

4.2.3 RQ3: Attentive viewing

The steps of a program animation are not equal. Which steps are interesting, important, and worthy of more careful study depends on the student, the program, the design of the PV, and the context in which the student encounters the PV. The other steps provide a backdrop for the key moments and help the learner grow familiar with the graphical notation. Some steps are visually more complex, and so require more time to view attentively in any case.

We explored whether students studied the PVs attentively by looking at the time they spent at each step. Our assumption was that an inattentive student will simply advance at a steady or increasing pace rather than choosing particular steps for more careful study. We expected that if the students had been attentive, we would see clear peaks in stepwise times, both in individual logs and also at the collective level so that certain steps of a PV would attract the interest of more students than the other steps do.

We only included genuine animation steps and excluded the time students spent reading the textual alerts that appeared during a few PVs. (On a related note, we do not know how much time students spent reading PV-related texts in the ebook, looking at the code of the PV before starting the animation, or examining the final state of the PV.)

Each student's *stay* was calculated for each step as the difference between consecutive timestamps. In case the student viewed the step multiple times (rewinding or revisiting), the lengths of the views were summed to produce the stay.

A student's *personal median stay* for a PV was defined as the median of their stays at the steps of the PV. It describes the overall pace at which the student viewed the PV (the higher, the slower). The student cohort's *collective median stay* for a PV was determined by taking the medians of students' stays at each step of the PV and computing the median of those stepwise medians. For each step, only students who had viewed it at least once were included.

We defined a *peak* as a step at which the student's stay is at least 50% greater than their their personal median stay for the PV (an admittedly somewhat arbitrary limit). The *peak rate* of a step is the percentage of students who had a peak at that step. We call a peak rate *low* if it is under 40%, *medium* if it is at least 40% but under 70%, and *high* if it is 70% or greater. A step at which the peak rate is medium or high is a *collective peak*. An example is shown in Figure 2.

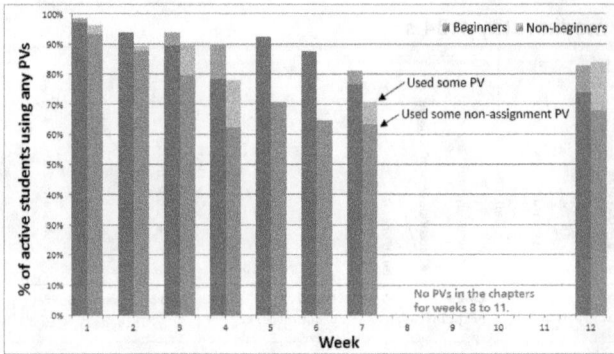

Figure 3: Weekly PV use. The lighter bits at the top correspond to students who had only viewed PVs that were part of a graded task. Only those students who were still active during the week (i.e., submitted something) are included.

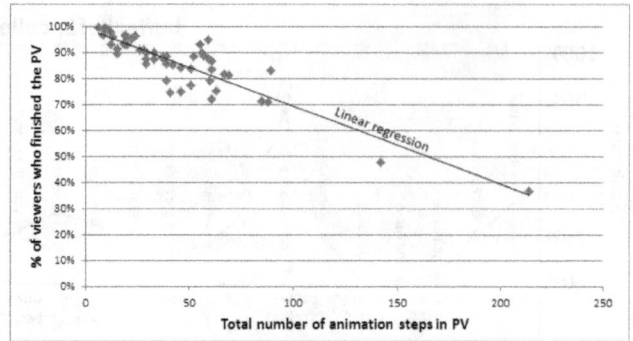

Figure 4: The finish rate of each PV (dot) plotted against the number of animation steps in the PV.

5. RESULTS

5.1 RQ1: Overall Use of the PVs

Figure 3 shows weekly statistics of PV use, separately for beginners and non-beginners. For each week, the percentage of students who viewed at least one PV is shown, ranging between 81% and 98% for beginners and 65% and 96% for non-beginners. Also shown in the figure are the (lower or equal) percentages of students who had viewed, during the week, at least one PV that is not associated with a graded assignment. In each week that had PV, except in weeks 3 and 12, the difference between beginners and non-beginners is significant (z-test for two proportions; p-values < 0.05).

In order to pass the course, students were required to work on assignments in most of the chapters of the ebook. The 567 students who passed the course viewed an average of 34.6 PVs out of 53; the corresponding average is 38.7 for beginners and 33.1 for non-beginners. The students who did not pass viewed fewer chapters in general and their average PV count was also lower: 11.6 PVs.

There was a borderline negligible positive correlation between the total number of points the students scored for course assignments and the number of PVs they viewed ($r = 0.18$, $p = 0.00$). Looking at beginners only, the correlation was slightly higher ($r = 0.26$, $p = 0.00$). Most of the points came from programming assignments. Assignments directly related to PV use were excluded from this analysis.

5.2 RQ2: Finishing, Rewinding, Revisiting

The PV that students finished most often was a 9-step one whose role (as per Table 1) was to Clarify the New Concept of nested expressions. It had a finish rate of 99.6%. The PV with the lowest finish rate (36.5%) was a very long (214-step) optional additional Clarification of a Solution to an earlier program-reading assignment. The median finish rate across all PVs was 88.3%, and only two PVs had a finish rate below 70%. As shown in Figure 4, there was an approximately linear inverse relationship between the lengths and finish rates of the PVs ($r = -0.89$, $p = 0.00$).

Beginners started but did not finish an average of 2.43 PVs during the whole course, non-beginners 2.73; this difference is statistically significant (Wilcoxon rank-sum test, $p = 0.02$).

This is despite the beginners starting more PVs overall. There were a few PVs that non-beginners finished somewhat more frequently than beginners did (e.g., a long PV of a recursive program).

Students rarely used the Back or Start Over controls for rewinding animations. Considering only the students who passed the course, the average beginner rewound a total of 16.8 times during the entire course (median 11.5) — less than once for every two PVs viewed — and the average non-beginner 11.5 times (median 7). We found no correlation between rewinding PVs and assignment scores.

Revisits were rarer still. Beginners revisited a PV an average of 2.4 times during the course (median 2), non-beginners 2.3 times (median 1). The PV that was revisited the most, by 26% of those who ever viewed it, was one that Clarified the New Concept of the call stack. We found no correlation between revisiting PVs and assignment scores.

5.3 RQ3: Attentive Viewing

5.3.1 Overall stepwise statistics

The students' collective median stay was approximately 1.7 seconds in the first PVs but became gradually lower as the course progressed, dropping to only about 0.7 in the final PVs. This means that early-semester PVs were viewed at a slower pace than late-semester ones. Both beginners and non-beginners increased their viewing speed during the course. Beginners' median stays were somewhat higher than non-beginners', especially near the beginning of the course.

Certain types of steps were viewed longer than others. Students spent the most time at steps where glass-box visualizations of function calls returned values to the caller's frame (1.37 s). Jumping to a different line of code (0.81 s) and manipulating operators and simple values (0.82 s), which are fairly routine steps in most PVs, were commonly the fastest.

Steps late within a PV tended to be viewed faster than early ones. As illustrated by Figure 5, there was no clear drop-off point but a roughly linear relationship between the number of a step and time spent ($r = -0.90$, $p = 0.00$). Beginners and non-beginners followed the same pattern.

5.3.2 Peak rates

318 steps (14% of all steps in all PVs) had a peak rate of 40% or higher and were therefore classified as collective

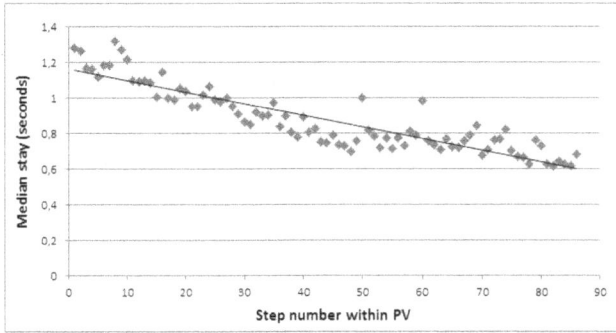

Figure 5: The correlation between the sequence number of a step and the median time that students stayed at steps with that number across PVs. Steps beyond the 86th were not included because only two animations were that long.

peaks. 50 of these steps had a high peak rate of at least 70%. The PVs had an average of 6.0 collective peaks.

The ends of PVs had fewer collective peaks than the beginnings: We calculated, for each step sequence number, the proportion of PVs that had a collective peak at that point, and correlated that percentage with the sequence number. The correlation was strong and negative ($r = -0.59, p = 0.00$).

On average, beginners had a total of 336 personal peaks across all animations and non-beginners 273. Both groups had collective peaks at largely the same places. However, looking at the 318 collective peaks and comparing the beginner and non-beginner populations in terms of whether they had personal peaks there reveals some differences between the groups. There were 50 collective peaks at which beginners were more likely to have a personal peak than non-beginners were (z-test for two proportions; p-values < 0.05), suggesting that beginners in particular paid attention to these steps. An example of such a step is the first print statement (third collective peak) in Figure 2. There were also seven collective peaks where non-beginners were more likely to have a personal peak than beginners were.

We conducted an informal review of how peak rates were distributed in the PVs. It appears to us that collective peaks occurred almost exclusively at steps that are visually complex (in Jsvee), such as returning from a function, and/or interesting in terms of the intended purpose of the PV. We invite the reader to consider Figure 2, for instance. Even so, high peak rates (of 70% or over) were rare, and medium peak rates (40% to 70%) suggest that even though many students found those steps to be pauseworthy, there was a large minority who failed to pause there for any of a number of reasons including inattention and failing to understand the PV.

This informal review of peak rates also drew our attention to a number of missing peaks, that is, low peak rates where we might have expected or hoped to see a medium or high one. A detailed analysis of these cases is beyond the present scope, but we describe one case by way of example: In a PV that illustrated object construction, students were expected to pay attention to the copying of constructor parameters into instance variables to initialize an object. However, the peak rates of these steps were between 12% and 15%, indicating that almost all students had either glossed over them or understood them without pausing there.

6. DISCUSSION

Let us consider the answers to each research question before drawing overall conclusions.

6.1 Main Findings

RQ1 *Do students use the PVs integrated into the ebook?*

Yes. Most students used the PVs throughout the course. Beginners used them somewhat more actively than non-beginners, but use of PVs was common in both groups. Significantly, the students did not only use the PVs that were directly tied to a graded assignment but also viewed the other animations (Figure 3).

In this respect, our results contrast with those of Alvarado et al. [1], who reported substantially lower student use of ebook-embedded PV. This demonstrates that there can be great variation in student adoption of PV between contexts, but does not enable us to identify the reasons behind the contrasting findings. Possible explanations include different degrees of PV integration, other pedagogical choices, and student demographics, among others.

Alvarado et al. found a weak positive correlation between PV use outside class and some aspects of course performance. We found a similar weak correlation between PV use and assignment scores; PV use was high both among high and low achievers.

RQ2 *When students view a PV, do they view all of it?*
Do they return to review any PVs or parts of them?

There was some attrition during the longest PVs especially, but, overall, students tended to view each PV that they started all the way to the end (Figure 4).

Much like the students in the study by Alvarado et al. [1], our students rarely returned to rewatch a PV, and rewinding parts of a PV was also infrequent. We found no connection between course performance and rewinds or revisits.

RQ3 *Do students view the integrated PVs attentively?*

Students tended to move through the PVs at a fairly brisk pace, their median steps quickening from under two seconds near the beginning of the course to under one second near the end. The pickup in viewing speed is understandable, since the students are more familiar with the graphical notation during the later PVs and since the later PVs tended to be longer and sparser in terms of key events. Beginners moved through the PVs somewhat slower than non-beginners.

We had suspected that students might not study the ends of long animations carefully. Indeed, stepwise time usage decreases with step number, fairly slowly and steadily (Figure 5). The sparseness of the longer animations probably affects this result as well.[4]

On the individual level, we see clear peaks and lows in the times that students spend at different steps of the program animations. On the collective level, there are steps where the peak rate is relatively high, that is, where many students slow down. This suggests that a good number of students are paying attention and giving more consideration to certain animation steps than to routine ones. Informally, we observe

---

[4]UI options such as "Run Quickly until Line N", which we did not support, might help students focus on key events, but only if they are able to use the functionality effectively.

that such collective slowdowns seem to happen in reasonable places, that is, at steps that are complex and/or pedagogically relevant. However, at most such steps, there was a sizeable minority of students who did not alter their viewing pace. This raises the suspicion that many students were either not paying attention to the PV or otherwise failed to notice something noticed by other students. We also found steps at which the peak rate was low against our hopes, which way mean that the majority of students failed to learn something from the PV. There may be other partial explanations for these phenomena as well, some of which are specific to step types; for instance, it may not have been as necessary to pause at each print statement because the output remains visible in the text console. Some students may have just quickly checked the PVs for anything surprising.

To summarize, this study tentatively supports the notion that many students viewed the PVs more or less attentively. However, the quick overall pace of PV use and the rarity of high peak rates are a worry: Are students going too fast? Are many of them missing key steps?

6.2 Conclusions and Recommendations

In Section 2, we identified PV as a medium that can help beginners form transferable mental models of programs, the fine print being that students need to engage with the PVs. Moreover, we proposed that integrating PVs into the increasingly common medium of the ebook can boost the perceived utility of PV and make learning from PV more effective.

In this study, we have not directly assessed learning gains. What we can say is that the integrated approach worked to attract interest: Students voted with their mice and viewed the PVs even where no credit was to be directly gained from it. It seems clear that the students felt, at least, that they benefited from the PVs. This conclusion is in keeping with written student feedback collected at various points during the semester: 354 individuals commented on the PVs in a positive tone (e.g., "The animation was a big help."), 81 reported technical issues (e.g., "It was hard to fit the large animation on the screen of my laptop."), 90 wrote negatively about the PVs (e.g., "The animation was incomprehensible."), and 56 offered other PV-related comments.

The students in our study viewed PVs of given programs. This form of interaction ranks low in the engagement taxonomies proposed in the literature [28, 45]. Nevertheless, our results lend tentative support to the conclusion that such use of PV can serve a productive role in a learning environment such as an ebook, if cognitive engagement is promoted by making the PVs an integral part of the environment.

On the basis of our results, we make the following recommendations to programming educators and PV designers.

- Consider adopting PV in CS1. Ebooks seem a natural fit for program animations and other PVs.
- Find ways for PVs, texts, and tasks to interact. Encourage use of the PVs directly and indirectly.
- Find out what students do with the PVs you provide.
- Be wary of program animations that are longer than a few dozen steps. Key events late in a long animation, especially, may be missed. Speaking of which:
- Do not assume learners will find what is important in a PV unaided. Identify difficult parts in PVs. Draw students' attention to key elements and events.

With regard to the final recommendation, it is our intention to develop PV tools that make it more convenient for ebook authors or teachers to furnish automatically generated animations of example programs with annotations that match the needs of particular contexts and goals (cf. [50]). Such elaborations of PV examples might use audio (to exploit modality [24]) and/or graphics; we are initially pursuing the latter option. The present study has suggested that PV is already useful in CS1 ebooks, and it is our hope that such future improvements to program visualization will further help beginners learn to program.

7. LIMITATIONS

Our study, which involves a real student cohort in their actual study environment, has high ecological validity. However, construct validity is a concern, particularly in relation to the research question that addresses students' attentiveness. This is because we have relied on cheap and easy data in the shape of usage logs.

We have studied which PV steps give students pause — but not what they think and do during those pauses. We have assumed that peaks in stepwise time use often indicate germane cognitive activity; this might be confirmed or disconfirmed by a triangulatory observation study, for instance. What is a "long enough" stay at a step is also unclear.

Qualitative methods could be used to dig deeper into what happens as students work with ebook-embedded PV, and why. More work is needed to assess how useful usage logs are for inferring how students engage with visualizations.

Another challenge in the stepwise analysis of program animations is that some kinds of steps are inherently more complex to view and understand than others (e.g., initializing a buffer is more complex than evaluating a plus operation). To estimate whether a student assigned particular importance to a step, one might consider stepwise stays relative to the inherent complexity of the step type, which would, however, require credible estimates of complexity. By comparison, our present analysis is rather homespun: We simply identified peaks in stepwise time use within a PV and argued that their presence is a positive thing. A more detailed analysis is beyond this article, but our results still provide a point of reference against which the effects of future modifications may be gauged.

The work at hand only allows us to discuss the integration of PVs into an ebook in general terms. We are unable at present to comment, for instance, on how students' attention perhaps moved between PVs, text, and PV-related assignments. Additional research would also be needed to determine the relative impact of the different roles that PVs may play in ebooks.

Finally, we are not in a position to tell which other contexts our result transfers to. Using a different ebook, different PVs, or different ways of integrating the two might produce quite different results. Having a less motivated cohort of students certainly might. And so on. Nevertheless, our study contributes to the small body of work on student use of PVs in introductory programming ebooks. Future metastudies or other research may be able to pinpoint the underlying factors and assess generalizability.

ACKNOWLEDGEMENTS

We thank Otto Seppälä for his help with the analysis.

8. REFERENCES

[1] C. Alvarado, B. B. Morrison, B. Ericson, M. Guzdial, B. N. Miller, and D. L. Ranum. Performance and use evaluation of an electronic book for introductory Python programming. Technical Report GT-IC-12-02, Georgia Institute of Technology, 2012.

[2] P. Brusilovsky, S. Edwards, A. Kumar, L. Malmi, L. Benotti, D. Buck, P. Ihantola, R. Prince, T. Sirkiä, S. Sosnovsky, J. Urquiza-Fuentes, A. Vihavainen, and M. Wollowski. Increasing adoption of smart learning content for computer science education. In *ITiCSE 2014 Working Group Reports*, ITiCSE -WGR '14, pages 31–57. ACM, 2014.

[3] K. S. Cennamo. Learning from video: Factors influencing learners' preconceptions and invested mental effort. *Educational Technology Research and Development*, 41(3):33–45, 1993.

[4] J. L. Chiu and M. C. Linn. The role of self-monitoring in learning chemistry with dynamic visualization. In A. Zohar and Y. Dori, editors, *Metacognition and Science Education: Trends in Current Research*, pages 133–163. Springer, 2012.

[5] J. de Kleer and J. S. Brown. Mental models of physical mechanisms and their acquisition. In J. R. Anderson, editor, *Cognitive Skills and Their Acquisition*, pages 285–309. Lawrence Erlbaum, 1981.

[6] J. de Kleer and J. S. Brown. Assumptions and ambiguities in mechanistic mental models. In D. Gentner and A. L. Stevens, editors, *Mental Models*, pages 155–190. Lawrence Erlbaum, 1983.

[7] J. DeNero. Composing Programs (electronic textbook). http://composingprograms.com/, 2015.

[8] B. du Boulay. Some difficulties of learning to program. *Journal of Educational Computing Research*, 2(1):57–73, 1986.

[9] École Polytechnique Fédérale de Lausanne. Scala (programming language web site). http://www.scala-lang.org/, 2015.

[10] K. A. Ericsson, R. T. Krampe, and C. Tesch-Römer. The role of deliberate practice in the acquisition of expert performance. *Psychological Review*, 100(3):363–406, 1993.

[11] European Commission. European Credit Transfer and Accumulation System (ECTS). http://ec.europa.eu/education/ects/ects_en.htm, 2015.

[12] H. P. Grice. Logic and conversation. In P. Cole and J. L. Morgan, editors, *Syntax and Semantics 3: Speect Acts*, pages 41–58. Academic Press, 1975.

[13] P. J. Guo. Online Python Tutor: Embeddable web-based program visualization for CS education. In *Proceedings of the 44th ACM Technical Symposium on Computer Science Education*, SIGCSE '13, pages 579–584. ACM, 2013.

[14] P. J. Guo, J. Kim, and R. Rubin. How video production affects student engagement: An empirical study of MOOC videos. In *Proceedings of the 1st ACM Conference on Learning at Scale*, L@S 2014, pages 41–50. ACM, 2014.

[15] S. Holland, R. Griffiths, and M. Woodman. Avoiding object misconceptions. *SIGCSE Bulletin*, 29(1):131–134, 1997.

[16] L. J. Höök and A. Eckerdal. On the bimodality in an introductory programming course: An analysis of student performance factors. In *2015 International Conference on Learning and Teaching in Computing and Engineering*, LaTiCE '15, pages 79–86, 2015.

[17] C. D. Hundhausen, S. A. Douglas, and J. T. Stasko. A meta-study of algorithm visualization effectiveness. *Journal of Visual Languages and Computing*, 13(3):259–290, 2002.

[18] E. Isohanni and M. Knobelsdorf. Behind the curtain: Students' use of VIP after class. In *Proceedings of the Sixth International Workshop on Computing Education Research*, ICER '10, pages 87–96. ACM, 2010.

[19] A. Korhonen, T. L. Naps, C. R. Boisvert, P. Crescenzi, V. Karavirta, L. Mannila, B. N. Miller, B. B. Morrison, S. H. Rodger, R. J. Ross, and C. A. Shaffer. Requirements and design strategies for open source interactive computer science eBooks. In *ITiCSE 2013 Working Group Reports*, ITiCSE -WGR '13, pages 53–72. ACM, 2013.

[20] G. Lakoff. *Women, Fire, and Dangerous Things: What Categories Reveal about the Mind*. The University of Chicago Press, 1990.

[21] M. C. Linn, H.-Y. Chang, J. L. Chiu, Z. H. Zhang, and K. W. McElhaney. Can desirable difficulties overcome deceptive clarity in scientific visualizations? In A. S. Benjamin, editor, *Successful Remembering and Successful Forgetting: A Festschrift in Honor of Robert A. Bjork*, pages 235—-258. Psychology Press, 2011.

[22] S. Madison and J. Gifford. Parameter passing: The conceptions novices construct. Research Report, AERA. http://eric.ed.gov/PDFS/ED406211.pdf, 1997.

[23] R. E. Mayer. Should there be a three-strikes rule against pure discovery learning? *American Psychologist*, 59(1):14–19, 2004.

[24] R. E. Mayer. *Multimedia Learning*. Cambridge University Press, 2nd edition, 2009.

[25] K. W. McElhaney, H.-Y. Chang, J. L. Chiu, and M. C. Linn. Evidence for effective uses of dynamic visualisations in science curriculum materials. *Studies in Science Education*, 51(1):49–85, 2015.

[26] B. N. Miller and D. L. Ranum. Beyond PDF and ePub: Toward an interactive textbook. In *Proceedings of the 17th ACM Annual Conference on Innovation and Technology in Computer Science Education*, ITICSE '12, pages 150–155. ACM, 2012.

[27] C. S. Miller. Metonymy and reference-point errors in novice programming. *Computer Science Education*, 24(2-3):123–152, 2014.

[28] T. L. Naps, G. Rößling, V. Almstrum, W. Dann, R. Fleischer, C. Hundhausen, A. Korhonen, L. Malmi, M. McNally, S. Rodger, and J. A. Velázquez-Iturbide. Exploring the role of visualization and engagement in computer science education. *SIGCSE Bulletin*, 35(2):131–152, 2003.

[29] S. Nevalainen and J. Sajaniemi. Short-term effects of graphical versus textual visualisation of variables on program perception. In P. Romero, J. Good, E. Acosta-Chaparro, and S. Bryant, editors, *Proceedings of the 17th Workshop of the Psychology of Programming Interest Group*, PPIG'05, pages 77–91. PPIG, 2005.

[30] R. D. Pea. Language-independent conceptual 'bugs' in novice programming. *Journal of Educational Computing Research*, 2(1):25–36, 1986.

[31] M. Petre. Why looking isn't always seeing: Readership skills and graphical programming. *Communications of the ACM*, 38(6):33–44, 1995.

[32] J. L. Plass, R. Moreno, and R. Brünken, editors. *Cognitive Load Theory*. Cambridge University Press, 2010.

[33] D. Pritchard and T. Vasiga. CS Circles: An in-browser Python course for beginners. In *Proceedings of the 44th ACM Technical Symposium on Computer Science Education*, SIGCSE '13, pages 591–596, 2013.

[34] N. Ragonis and M. Ben-Ari. A long-term investigation of the comprehension of OOP concepts by novices. *Computer Science Education*, 15(3):203–221, 2005.

[35] G. Rößling, J. Urquiza-Fuentes, J. A. Velázquez-Iturbide, T. Naps, M. S. Hall, V. Karavirta, A. Kerren, C. Leska, A. Moreno, R. Oechsle, and S. H. Rodger. Merging interactive visualizations with hypertextbooks and course management. *SIGCSE Bulletin*, 38(4):166–181, 2006.

[36] G. Rößling and T. Vellaramkalayil. A visualization-based computer science hypertextbook prototype. *ACM Transactions on Computing Education*, 9(2):1–13, 2009.

[37] J. Sajaniemi. The Roles of Variables Home Page. http://cs.joensuu.fi/~saja/var_roles/, 2008.

[38] G. Salomon. Television is "easy" and print is "tough": The differential investment of mental effort in learning as a function of perceptions and attributions. *Journal of Educational Psychology*, 76(4):647–658, 1984.

[39] I. Sanders, V. Galpin, and T. Götschi. Mental models of recursion revisited. *SIGCSE Bulletin*, 38(3):138–142, 2006.

[40] P. Saraiya, C. A. Shaffer, D. S. McCrickard, and C. North. Effective features of algorithm visualizations. *SIGCSE Bulletin*, 36(1):382–386, 2004.

[41] C. A. Shaffer, V. Karavirta, A. Korhonen, and T. L. Naps. OpenDSA: Beginning a community active-eBook project. In *Proceedings of the 11th Koli Calling International Conference on Computing Education Research*, Koli Calling '11, pages 112–117. ACM, 2011.

[42] T. Sirkiä. A JavaScript library for visualizing program execution. In *Proceedings of the 13th Koli Calling International Conference on Computing Education Research*, Koli Calling '13, pages 189–190. ACM, 2013.

[43] T. Sirkiä. Exploring expression-level program visualization in CS1. In *Proceedings of the 14th Koli Calling International Conference on Computing Education Research*, Koli Calling '14, pages 153–157. ACM, 2014.

[44] J. Sorva. Notional machines and introductory programming education. *ACM Transactions on Computing Education*, 13(2):1–31, 2013.

[45] J. Sorva, V. Karavirta, and L. Malmi. A review of generic program visualization systems for introductory programming education. *ACM Transactions on Computing Education*, 13(4):1–64, 2013.

[46] J. Sorva, J. Lönnberg, and L. Malmi. Students' ways of experiencing visual program simulation. *Computer Science Education*, 23(3):207–238, 2013.

[47] J. Sorva and O. Seppälä. Research-based design of the first weeks of CS1. In *Proceedings of the 14th Koli Calling International Conference on Computing Education Research*, Koli Calling '14, pages 71–80. ACM, 2014.

[48] J. Tenenberg and Y. Ben-David Kolikant. Computer programs, dialogicality, and intentionality. In *Proceedings of the Tenth Annual Conference on International Computing Education Research*, ICER '14, pages 99–106. ACM, 2014.

[49] The CSLearning4U Team at Georgia Tech. The Teacher CSP Ebook. http://ebooks.cc.gatech.edu/TeachCSP-Python/, 2015.

[50] J. P. Träff. *Integrating Visualization Software into Learning Objects*. Bachelor's thesis, Technical University of Denmark, 2011.

What Are We Teaching? Automated Evaluation of CS Curricula Content Using Topic Modeling

Jean Michel Rouly
Department of Computer
Science
George Mason University
Fairfax, Virginia
jrouly@gmu.edu

Huzefa Rangwala
Department of Computer
Science
George Mason University
Fairfax, Virginia
rangwala@cs.gmu.edu

Aditya Johri
Department of Information
Sciences & Technology
George Mason University
Fairfax, Virginia
ajohri3@gmu.edu

ABSTRACT

Identifying the concepts covered in a university course based on a high level description is a necessary step in the evaluation of a university's program of study. To this end, data describing university courses is readily available on the Internet in vast quantities. However, understanding natural language course descriptions requires manual inspection and, often, implicit knowledge of the subject area. Additionally, a holistic approach to curricular evaluation involves analysis of the prerequisite structure within a department, specifically the conceptual overlap between courses in a prerequisite chain. In this work we apply existing topic modeling techniques to sets of course descriptions extracted from publicly available university course catalogs. The inferred topic models correspond to concepts taught in the described courses. The inference process is unsupervised and generates topics without the need for manual inspection. We present an application framework for data ingestion and processing, along with a user-facing web-based application for inferred topic presentation. The software provides tools to view the inferred topics for a university's courses, quickly compare departments by their topic composition, and visually analyze conceptual overlap in departmental prerequisite structures. The tool is available online at `http://edmine.cs.gmu.edu/`.

Keywords

topic modeling; course descriptions; prerequisite chain; web visualization

1. INTRODUCTION

Computer Science education is an increasingly important field of growth at many universities [22, 15]. As departments grow and change, it becomes necessary to automate the comparison and evaluation processes. However, much of the published data about departments is non-standard, natural language text that is not easy to process automatically.

There are many parties impacted by the lack of up to date, automatic, and simple to understand information about the characteristics of universities across the country.

Prospective college students and their parents seek out information on college courses to compare curricula in a meaningful way, based on content, in order to find their best fit. A typical approach to this task is an information gathering and subsequent program comparison process duplicated many thousands of times across the population of rising college-going freshmen. Hewner [10] conducted a qualitative study of CS students and found that students in CS need to make a variety of decisions about what courses they take. Invariably, they have limited knowledge when making these decisions. They also often make these decisions based on whether the classes will be enjoyable and assumed that since courses are required, they will have useful content. We believe that a system such as ours can assist students with making more strategic goal-oriented decisions which many of the students want to take. It will also allow them to better see the connection between courses and if possible make decision based on the skillset they want to develop.

Additionally, accrediting bodies (e.g., ABET) typically require a department to cover a given set of standardized topics as a criterion for evaluation [1]. The accreditation process can take up to 18 months to complete [1]; automating the departmental evaluation process would greatly reduce time spent measuring a CS department's coverage of a specific set of areas.

Programs of study at institutions of higher education can be represented as a chain composed of the courses required to complete a degree. These component courses in turn are composed of the topics or concepts they are intended to cover. Evaluation of the courses within a particular program is necessary for the evaluation of an overall academic curriculum. Analyzing the structure of a program's prerequisite chain, for example, requires an understanding of each constituent course and any overlap of covered topics between courses and their prerequisites. Additionally, inter-institutional curricular comparison requires an aggregate evaluation of the courses within each institution's program. However, comparing and evaluating different courses requires expert knowledge in the relevant field. No two courses can be measured for similarity based only on inherent, measurable properties. A domain expert is required to inspect the description of the courses and determine their conceptual overlap.

Automating the information retrieval process to identify core concepts covered in any particular course removes the need for a domain expert. By analyzing course descriptions from a corpus spanning fields and institutions, topic modeling can provide a method to generate a statistical representation of core course concepts. Specifically, unsupervised latent variable models present a method of identifying the core concepts (i.e., topics) covered in a course. This introduces the possibility of applications in automated course and program evaluation methods. The form of topic modeling employed in this work is Latent Dirichlet allocation (LDA) [6]. As with any automated process of information retrieval, our proposed application of LDA comes with a certain set of limitations, discussed in Section 5.1.

The overall goal of this work is the development of a system to digest large quantities of university course information, specifically academic course descriptions, and to process and ultimately generate interactive descriptions of the core concepts covered within institutional programs as illustrated by inferred topics. Learned topics will be presented in a web-based application allowing inspection from multiple perspectives.

2. BACKGROUND ON LDA

Topic modeling, a form of latent variable modeling, is an unsupervised machine learning method which attempts to recreate the distribution of so-called "topics" an author used to generate a corpus of documents. The term topic is used to describe a frequency distribution of terms within a vocabulary. In this use, a topic can be understood to represent an academic concept covered within the context of a course. This is based on the assumption that the words used in a course description when introducing the course's topics are the same words used within descriptions of the topic itself. The topics discovered in a corpus can be used to categorize documents and provide structure to an otherwise unknown dataset.

Latent Dirichlet allocation (LDA) is a specific type of topic modeling which assumes that a mixture of multiple topics exist within a single document in some proportion (i.e., were used to generate that document) [6]. LDA assumes a generative process where, for each word in the document, the algorithm selects a distribution over topics, selects a topic, and then selects a vocabulary term [6]. Reversing this generative process is significantly more difficult because the topic distributions are unknown; these unknown information is what the "hidden model" or "latent model" refers to.

The computation LDA performs is the determination of the topic distributions over a set of documents. Given the set of documents as input, generating the corpus topics is a probabilistic process. Taking the variables $\theta_{d,k}$ (topic proportion for topic k in document d), $\beta_{1:k}$ (topic k), $z_{d,n}$ (topic assignment for word n in document d), and $w_{d,n}$ (the nth word in document d), LDA estimates the posterior probability in Equation 1 [5].

$$p(\beta_{1:K}, \theta_{1:D}, z_{1:D}|w_{1:D}) = \frac{\beta_{1:K}, \theta_{1:D}, z_{1:D}, w_{1:D}}{w_{1:D}} \quad (1)$$

Gibbs Sampling is used to estimate the denominator (i.e., the evidence) [6]. Running LDA over a document set re-

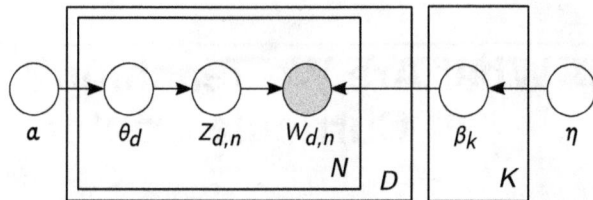

Figure 1: LDA graphical diagram adapted from [5].

sults in a usable set of vocabulary frequency distributions or topics for each document.

A graphical "plate" diagram of LDA's generative process is given in Figure 1, adapted from [6]. Circular nodes represent random variables while rectangular plates represent duplication. The shaded node is the only observed (i.e., evidence) variable, words from the document set.

2.1 Related Work

Our research complements other efforts within Computer Science education that are directed towards categorization of content to improve pedagogy, e.g., Hubwieser et al. [11]. We believe that our project contributes both, by identifying content (i.e., topics) being taught across institutions and by identifying gaps and unique contributions. This information can be compared to teacher competencies and used to design assessment and instruments to measure them. Another area in which this work can assist is in identification of concepts and their classification, especially "threshold concepts" [20]. Overall, we believe our data-driven approach complements other qualitative efforts by building on them and by automating some aspects of the research. The work of [3] discusses a taxonomy related to learning breaking the process down along the cognitive process and knowledge dimensions. Using a richer source of course information that course descriptions our proposed method could be adopted to learn concepts along these dimensions.

Other work has also attempted to extract concept information from course data. Yang et al. employ four distinct techniques to map courses into a conceptual space and then learn prerequisite relationships between similar courses [21]. Two of their conceptual mapping techniques generate latent features, which have the downside of not being human-readable as in LDA. The remaining two techniques generate human-readable topics, but rely either on an outside source (Wikipedia) or simply represent concepts as the vocabulary of the document. The benefit of LDA as an information retrieval tool is its ability to generate pseudo human-readable topics while acting in a fully unsupervised manner on a single, large data set. Our approach naively targets a dataset of fixed universities and customizes web scrapers specifically for their computer science departments. Effland et al. introduces a robust web crawler system to automatically search for, identify, and extract course descriptions from disparate locations on the Internet [9]. Application of similar technology in this work was considered, and would greatly improve the scale of the analyzed data.

3. METHODS

The structure of this work is threefold. First, a dataset of university course descriptions is generated using publicly available data from a number of North American universi-

University	Course Count
American University (AU)	32
George Mason University (GMU)	145
Kansas State University (KSU)	83
Louisiana State University (LSU)	59
Portland State University (PDX)	190
Rensselaer Polytechnic Institute (RPI)	61
University of South Carolina (SC)	64
Stanford University (Stanford)	69
University of Utah (Utah)	142
University of Tennessee, Knoxville (UTK)	29
ACM Exemplar Courses (EC)	68

Table 1: CS program statistics

ties. This process is discussed in Section 3.1. Second, LDA is applied to the collected data and topics are inferred. This step is discussed in Section 3.3. Finally, the collected data and inferred topics are presented in a user-facing web application, described in Section 3.4.

3.1 Data Acquisition

The primary data manipulated in this study are university catalog course descriptions. The current experimental data sources are described in Table 1. Note that only Computer Science departments are included in this dataset, in order to simplify the evaluation process and the required number of inferred topics. Simple web scrapers were written using Python and BeautifulSoup to download publicly available descriptions from university catalogs. These will be made publicly available at http://github.com/jrouly/trajectory. Descriptions and catalog webpages appear in a vast variety of different formats, structures, and HTML correctness, so a parser was written for each university to acquire the unstructured text. This text was then passed through a cleaning procedure to remove abbreviations and non-English characters, as well as common English stop words. Finally the text was passed through a stemmer to strip morphology from the words and eliminate duplicate terms. At the same time, departmental course prerequisite data is collected from the catalog as well. Prerequisites are limited to courses in the database, meaning that references older courses that are no longer present in the catalog are ignored. Non-specific prerequisite references (e.g., 400-level) are ignored as well.

The Python scraping framework developed is structured to allow pluggable web scrapers tooled to specific syllabus repositories. There are a number of existing web scrapers in place pointing to different university course catalogs, but the code can be easily extended in the future to grow the data set. Integrated in the scraping framework is a lightweight relational database layer to store both course description data and university metadata, including names, URLs, and prerequisite information. The database layer also stores inferred topics.

3.2 Preliminary Data Exploration

In addition to LDA, other unsupervised machine learning tools can be applied to the same data set. Simple clustering algorithms (e.g., K-Means) when given the same bag of words corpus as input act to identify groupings of similar documents according to their term frequency vector Eu-

clidean distance [17]. Additional, similar clustering algorithms can be applied in a similar manner.

Preliminary exploratory results are promising. We applied K-Means clustering to a sample dataset of course descriptions selected from the George Mason University Computer Science online catalog across multiple semesters. Using course section IDs as ground-truth labels, we clustered the course descriptions. Table 2 summarizes the metrics computed on the resulting clustering. Homogeneity represents the "same-ness" of a cluster, or the degree to which each cluster contains only members of a single type. Completeness represents the "spread" of courses across clusters, or the degree to which every member of the same type is assigned to the same cluster. V-Measure is simply the harmonic mean of the prior two metrics. For each metric, higher is better, and they are bounded from 0 to 1. A distributed implementation of K-Means available in the Python toolkit scikit-learn was used to perform the clustering.

The high completeness values are promising: this indicates that many of the same course are assigned under the same cluster prototype. The low value of homogeneity is unsurprising given the initialization parameters used: K-Means was initialized to detect only 20 clusters, a far smaller number than the magnitude of distinct course sections available. The number 20 was chosen arbitrarily as a smaller count than the true number of distinct course sections in order to increase cluster size.

Execution time	0.144s
Homogeneity	0.415
Completeness	0.877
V-measure	0.563

Table 2: Preliminary clustering metrics

3.3 Topic Modeling

After the exploratory clustering process, we passed cleaned data into a topic modeling framework by exporting from the database layer to the filesystem in a structured "bucket of files" format. The Java MALLET library is used to perform LDA on the course description data. A data pipeline is constructed using the MALLET API that reads input data, tokenizes it, and trains an LDA topic model. The inferred topics are then exported to a common Comma Seperated Values (CSV) format and read back into the database layer and applied to existing courses. Independent runs of LDA with distinct parameterization are segregated in the database into "Result Sets", allowing sets of inferred topics to sit side by side without interfering. This also allows the presentation of different sets of inferred topics to the end user.

The initialization parameters of MALLET's LDA implementation are summarized in Table 3. Experiments were run varying parameters throughout the experimental range, including the MALLET default values. However, as the number of topics increased greatly beyond 750, and as β decreased greatly below 0.0001, the MALLET framework began to encounter instability and errors. Any runs which encountered infinite or "not-a-number" values were immediately discarded. Ultimately 77 result sets were retained for analysis.

Parameter	Description	Experimental Range	Default
α	Dirichlet concentration parameter.	[1, Iterations]	Iterations
β	Dirichlet concentration parameter.	[0.0001, 0.5]	0.01
Iterations	The number of LDA iterations.	—	3000
Topics	The number of topics to infer.	[100, 1000]	—

Table 3: LDA Initialization Parameters

3.4 Visualization

An interactive, dynamic user visualization of course descriptions and topics has been prototyped. The visualization is a web-based application built upon the Python Flask library. The tool interfaces with the same database layer used by the rest of the application framework to provide an aesthetically pleasing user-facing interface with several primary modules. By default, the web application presents the user with a high level "dashboard" overview of the dataset and available result sets, where a result set is the set of topics inferred after a single run of the LDA module with a distinct initialization set. After selecting a result set, the user can browse the data by course, department, university, or inferred topics. The remainder of this section describes implementation details of the tool's primary features.

3.4.1 Explore Courses

When presented with the complete university dataset, the user may interactively search for a university. Once a university is selected, the user may search through its registered departments and select a course of interest. On selecting a course, the text of its description is displayed in both its original format and its cleaned, stemmed format. Additionally, the course's inferred topics are listed in order of their proportion within the course description. These topics are expandable, and upon interaction present the user with the list of other known courses with that inferred topic. Any topics appearing in a document with proportion under 15% are automatically hidden from the user. This design choice was implemented to reduce visual clutter from inferred topics with low relevance to the class.

3.4.2 Prerequisite Chain Analysis

In addition to the course-specific data, an interactive, collapsible tree visualization of the course' prerequisite chain is displayed. The recursively generated tree visualization provides a high level view of the course's position within a department. Figure 2 details the prerequisite tree visualization. Above this visualization is the prerequisite chain conceptual analysis tool. This tool automatically provides a view of any registered prerequisite courses along with their inferred topics. Any shared topics between the prerequisites and the selected course are highlighted to indicate conceptual overlap.

Observe the course CS 310 "Data Structures" in the upper middle of the prerequisite tree. Table 4 details its topics, along with the topics of its prerequisite courses CS 105 "Computer Ethics and Society" and CS 211 "Object-Oriented Programming". Clearly there is a significant area of overlap between a data structures course and an introductory course in object oriented programming, as illustrated by the two italicized overlapping topics. Specifically, the overlap is in the areas of algorithms and data structures as well as object oriented programming. The ethics course, however, does not share any conceptual overlap with CS 310. Inspecting the context of these courses, however, reveals that CS 105 is a common freshman requirement at George Mason, and many upper level classes depend on its completion. It is intended as a baseline of student maturity rather than a prerequisite because of the concepts it introduces.

3.4.3 Compare Departments

The user may also compare two university departments. Topics inferred from every course in the department are collected and displayed side by side. Topics unique to each department are displayed separately from the intersection set of common topics. Similarity metrics describing the relationship between the two departments are defined as well — Jaccard index, cosine similarity, and Euclidean distance. Defined as $\frac{|A \cap B|}{|A \cup B|}$, the Jaccard index is based on the number of items unique to and shared between each set [12]. The remaining metrics are based on a "topic-vector" representation of each department. The topic-vector is a binary vector where each bit indicates whether a particular topic was inferred for the given department. Features are unweighted and the topic-vector indicates only whether a topic is present in a department's topic set, and not its frequency of occurrence. Interpreting this vector representation geometrically, the Euclidean and cosine distances are calculated.

3.4.4 Evaluate Department

The tool also allows users to easily evaluate university departments against third party benchmarks. The Association of Computing Machinery (ACM) maintains an annual writeup of guidelines for undergraduate computer science education [2]. These guidelines include two important sections, the ACM Exemplar Courses (EC) and Knowledge Areas. The Knowledge Areas are 18 broad topics within Computer Science as put forth by the ACM. EC include real course descriptions from disparate sources compiled by the ACM and manually annotated with the Knowledge Areas they cover. These data sets are used to perform primary evaluation. The benchmarks used in this study are the ACM Knowledge Areas.

The web tool automatically evaluates the performance of a university department. The tool checks for conceptual overlap between courses and ACM Knowledge Areas and predicts Knowledge Area labels where overlap exists. Additionally, if the department has been manually annotated with Knowledge Areas, these "ground truth" labels are compared against the predicted labels, and similarity coefficients between the two sets are computed. The label set similarity coefficient is computed in two ways. First, the Jaccard index of the predicted and ground truth labels is calculated. Then, the percent of the ground truth labels included in the prediction set is calculated. The web visualization provides an automatic interface for performing this evaluation process.

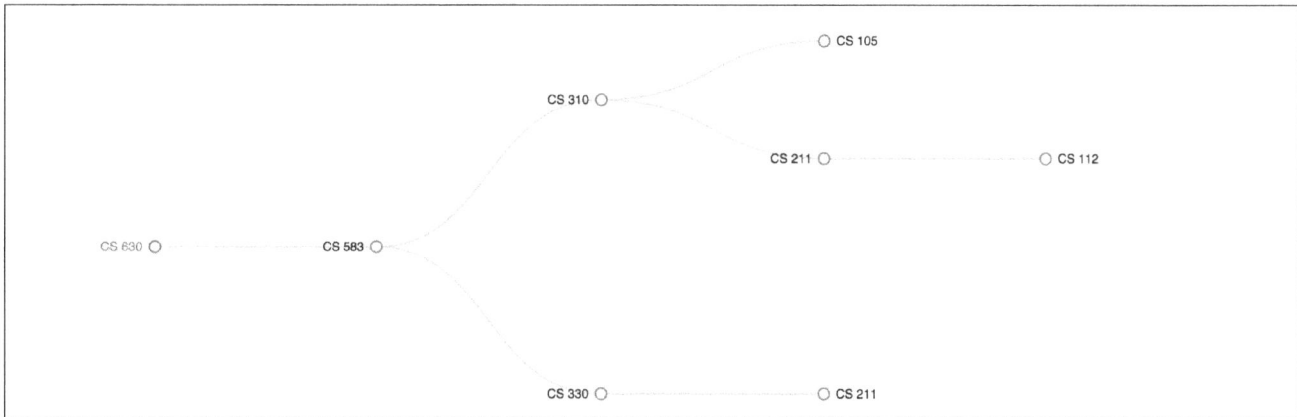

Figure 2: Interactive prerequisite tree visualization tool

GMU CS 310 Topics	Proportion
languag, object, program, orient, includ, type, abstract, design, implement, concept	29.946%
program, problem, solv, algorithm, data, structur, comput, introduct, languag, techniqu	21.461%
includ, design, system, topic, comput, introduct, cover, applic, algorithm, techniqu	26.117%
GMU CS 211 Topics [Prerequisite]	**Proportion**
languag, object, program, orient, includ, type, abstract, design, implement, concept	29.433%
program, problem, solv, algorithm, data, structur, comput, introduct, languag, techniqu	26.772%
code, compil, pars, analysi, optim, gener, languag, lexic, techniqu, construct	18.685%
comput, method, theori, basic, principl, includ, topic, model, cover, scientif	16.076%
GMU CS 105 Topics [Prerequisite]	**Proportion**
ethic, comput, issu, profession, social, technolog, privaci, legal, relat, digit	75.964%

Table 4: Topics of GMU CS 310 and its prerequisite courses, CS 105 and CS 211. Overlapping topics are italicized.

4. CASE STUDIES

In the sequel, three case studies are described in depth to exemplify the main features of the tool. First, Section 4.1 discusses the prerequisite analysis features of the tool, and presents a summary of statistics about the universities included in this study. Second, Section 4.2 closely considers two areas within Computer Science and discusses the inferred topics for courses within those areas. Finally, Section 4.3 details the similarities and differences between pairs of university departments and also presents a summary of comparisons between all the universities in this study.

4.1 Case Study: Prerequisite Analysis

To understand how a course fits into a department, its position in the prerequisite chain must be analyzed. Take, for example, a course in mobile application development. We predict that any course of this nature will most likely be an upper level elective with a moderate number of prerequisite courses. Indeed, we see this is the case with George Mason's CS 477, Portland State's CS 410, and Stanford's 231M. However, many of the topics covered in a mobile development course are niche topics, and specific to that field. Therefore, it might not be the case that any particular lower level courses will cover specific, overlapping topics.

Let us consider George Mason University's CS 477 "Mobile Application Development". The course description discusses mobile platforms and the various software design issues spe-

cific to mobile platforms. There are two inferred topics for this course. The first topic, with 32% proportion, includes the terms "develop", "platform", and "mobile" at high frequency. The second topic, with only 15% proportion, is more generic and includes terms like "system", "computer", and "topic". The course also has two registered prerequisites: CS 310 "Data Structures" and CS 367 "Computer Systems and Programming". Within the context of the department, these two courses are major prerequisites for any upper level course. As expected, neither of the two prerequisite courses share the mobile-specific topic inferred for CS 477. CS 310, however, does overlap with the generic computer systems topic. We therefore conclude that the CS 477 course registers its prerequisites primarily to ensure a baseline level of maturity and skill among its students, rather than because some necessary concepts are introduced at a lower level and expanded upon at the higher level.

To quantify the typical level of conceptual overlap between prerequisites within a department, we introduce a vector representation of a course, the "weighted topic-vector". Like the unweighted topic-vector representation of a department, the weighted topic-vector is a vector of uniform length corresponding to the total number of inferred topics among all known courses. However, the features of a weighted topic-vector represent the proportion with which the particular topic is represented in the course's description. In this way, the weighted topic-vector takes into account the importance

	Prereq$_\mu$	Prereq$_\sigma$
GMU	0.324	0.211
AU	0.278	0.134
KSU	0.273	0.213
Utah	0.257	0.249
UTK	0.201	0.256

Table 5: Level of conceptual overlap between courses and their prerequisites in five universities. Prereq$_\mu$ is the average level of conceptual overlap between prerequisites, Prereq$_\sigma$ is the standard deviation.

of a topic to a course, rather than simply binary topic membership as in the unweighted topic-vector. By computing the average distance between the weighted topic-vectors of a course and its prerequisites, the level of conceptual overlap for that course can be quantified. Averaging these distance measures over every course in the department that has registered prerequisites results in a measure of average prerequisite conceptual overlap within the department. Table 5 summarizes the levels of conceptual overlap for the five universities in the dataset with registered prerequisite trees, where a higher average value of conceptual overlap indicates a closer relationship between courses and their prerequisites. The five universities not included did not have prerequisite relationships in their collected data, and thus this analysis could not be performed.

4.2 Case Study: Topics In Computer Science

4.2.1 Ethics In Computer Science

Computer Science is a wide ranging field, with a number of disparate subfields — according to the ACM, there are 18 distinct Knowledge Areas [2]. At any given university, the Computer Science department will, ideally, cover all or most of these areas. One particular area covered by most universities in this study is "Social Issues and Professional Practice". A clear example of a course within this Knowledge Area is any course in computing and ethics. Take, for example, Kansas State's CIS 415 "Ethics and Computing Technology." The description is brief and to the point, focusing on computing ethics within a professional context. The only topic inferred for this course, at 64% proportion, includes the terms "ethics", "computer", "profession", "issue", and "social" at high frequency. Searching for other courses that teach to the same topic yields 30 courses across nine universities (every university in the study except for Rensselaer Polytechnic). These courses have titles like "Computer Ethics and Society" (GMU CS 105) and "Ethics in Computing" (LSU CSC 1200). This demonstrates the ability of our tool to not only automatically infer relevant concepts from a course description, but to match related courses across universities.

4.2.2 Artificial Intelligence

Another major topic within computer science is the study of Artificial Intelligence (AI). AI itself contains a great number of subfields and areas of specialization, but it is defined in ACM Knowledge Area "Intelligent Systems" as "the study of solutions for problems that are difficult or impractical to solve with traditional methods" [2]. Consider Portland State's CS 441 "Artificial Intelligence." Its course descrip-

tion is highly typical of AI courses included in this study: brief and to the point, it lists a number of subfields within AI that will be touched upon in the course. The only topic inferred for this course, at 86% proportion, includes the terms "intelligence", "knowledge", "artificial", and "agent" at high frequencies. Every other university in this study also contains at least one course which teaches to this topic in some proportion. George Mason's CS 480 "Introduction to Artificial Intelligence", Louisiana State's CSC 4444 "Artificial Intelligence" and University of Utah's CS 6380 "Multi-Agent Systems" to name a few. Indeed, many of these courses share very similar descriptions.

However, one of the most unique examples of a course with this topic is the University of Tennessee's COSC 420 "Biologically-Inspired Computation." The title alone might not suggest that this is an AI based class, and indeed it is not entirely AI. The course description talks about swarm intelligences, multi-agent systems, and other biomimetic computational systems. While the common AI topic discussed prior is inferred at 42%, two other topics, one with terms from biology and one with terms from neural networks, a subfield of AI, appear at proportions 24% and 17% respectively. UTK's COSC 420 is an excellent example of LDA's ability to infer many possibly unrelated topics in a mixture within a document in order to represent the full nature of the text.

4.3 Case Study: Comparing Departments

4.3.1 George Mason vs Stanford

While institutions generally cover a wide range of topics, there are always certain topics that cannot be or are not taught. Take for example George Mason University and Stanford University. The two computer science departments share a lot in common. Of 68 total topics covered between the two, 41 are common to both while only 14 are unique to Stanford and 13 unique to George Mason. The shared topics contain terms that directly relate to similar courses at each school. For example "secure" and "network" are terms in a topic taught in network security classes at both schools. However, a topic containing "linux", "unix", "lab" appears unique to Stanford, covered by CS 1U "Practical Unix", a course that does not exist at George Mason. Similarly, a topic containing "parallel" and "algorithm" appears unique to George Mason. The course GMU CS 683 "Parallel Algorithms" teaches to this topic, with no analogous course at Stanford.

By analyzing the set of unique and shared topics within two departments, simple coefficients can be computed to quantify the degree of similarity. The Jaccard coefficient is computed as the most basic representation of departmental similarity, along with Euclidean and cosine similarity metrics discussed in Section 3.4.3. A pairwise comparison of the universities in this study is presented in Figure 3. In this figure, darker shades of blue represent a higher degree of similarity. Also see Table 6 for the specific computed similarity values.

4.3.2 George Mason vs ACM EC

The EC provide a wide view of different courses from institutions around the world. If we assume the EC to compose a single, hypothetical university's CS department, we can compare existing departments against it in the same fashion as was used in Section 4.3.1. Take George Mason University, for example, to compare against the EC. Both departments share a great deal in common, with 38 overlapping topics. There are additionally not that many topics unique to the two departments, with 14 unique to the EC and 18 unique to GMU. A number of interesting artifacts appear, however, upon closer inspection.

Two topics unique to the EC include the terms "moral" and "religious", one each. Inspecting these topics reveals two members of the EC with the titles "Ethics & the Information Age" and "Technology, Ethics, and Global Society". Both of these courses teach ethics in computation, but from a vastly different perspective than the ethics course at George Mason. These two EC ethics courses include professional ethics, but also moral, religious, and social philosophies of ethical behavior, while the George Mason ethics courses (e.g., CS 105 "Computer Ethics and Society") only discuss professional ethics. This is an important yet subtle distinction to make, which might be overlooked by simply considering course titles.

Another unique topic to the EC includes the terms "design", "circuit", and "digital". The courses which teach to this topic, across institutions, are primarily digital design and logic courses. Inspecting the George Mason CS curriculum reveals that an analogous course is required within the CS degree, ECE 301 "Digital Electronics", but is not contained within the CS department, unlike some other universities. This particular artifact appears because the scope of our data sets include only CS departments. We make the assumption that necessary courses to the CS program at an institution will fall under the heading of Computer Science, which in this case is not true.

Note that included in Figure 3 are the ACM EC. Each course from the EC was entered into the dataset along with every other university course, and had topics inferred by LDA in the same manner. In this way the EC act as control courses with a ground truth label set. High similarity to the EC indicates a high degree of compliance with ACM standards.

5. DISCUSSION

The results of this study are promising. Exploratory K-Means clustering resulted in clusters with a high level of completeness. Even superficial manual analysis of clusters indicated that the collected data were being appropriately grouped. Similar findings were encountered after the application of LDA topic modeling.

Inferred topics generally fall into one of two categories for each course. The first category of topic includes relevant terms and keywords found in the course description. A highly specialized course in a particular subfield might contain a set of these topics that relate to keywords from within the specific domain of the course. The second category of topic includes more generic words common to a large number of courses. Topics in this category often relate to concepts common across courses, e.g., student research or exam and project information.

Take, for example, a computer science course in ethics. At George Mason University the senior level Computer Science ethics course is CS 306. The primary topic inferred for this course in a given run of LDA might look like "ethic, comput, issu, profession, social, impact, privaci, digit, context, technolog." Additionally, the prerequisite course to CS

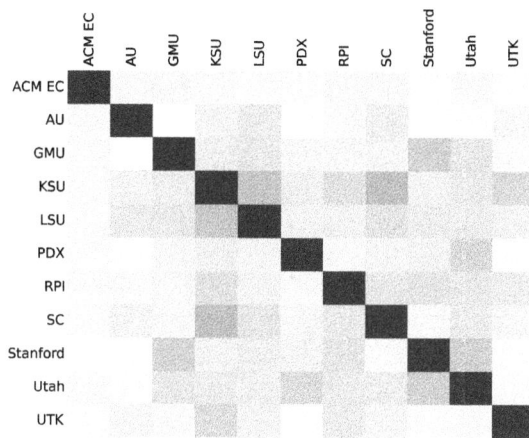

Figure 3: Pairwise similarity of CS departments using the Jaccard index. Darker shades indicate higher similarity. ACM EC refers to the ACM Exemplar Courses (EC). See Table 6 for the specific recorded values.

306, CS 105, shares this same topic. While the topic itself is a frequency distribution over vocabulary, and does not quantifiably evaluate to an "ethics" topic, manual inspection clearly shows that this topic involves ethocs and social issues as they relate to technology professionals.

Our confidence in the applicability of LDA as a course content inference system stems from the appearance of the same or related topics within the same or related courses. Inspecting the same course at different institutions results in the same topics being inferred at each institution. Inspecting prerequisite courses within the same institution illustrates the relationship between the courses by highlighting conceptual overlap, i.e., the appearance of the same topic in both course and prerequisite. As mentioned in Section 3.4.4, third party course descriptions act as an additional evaluative metric for this approach. A high level of consistency is indicated by the same topics being inferred for the same course at multiple institutions, related courses within the same institution, and the third party benchmark course.

5.1 Limitations

We recognize that one of the limitations of our work is that we are focused solely on the formal learning of students [7]. This is an artifact of the data used in the study. We believe that the techniques we use can also be applied to better understand learning in other settings if useful data exists. In a similar vein, that our work focused on course descriptions in English is also simply an artifact of the data used — course description corpora in any other language would be as effectively processed. Additionally, our methodology operates under the assumption that course description data is accurate, up to date, and descriptive of the course topics covered. In truth, this is not always the case. Oftentimes course descriptions do not fully describe the actual content of what is taught in a course, or the course description might only apply to some sections of a given course. It has even been observed that some course descriptions are merely held

	ACM EC	AU	GMU	KSU	LSU	PDX	RPI	SC	Stanford	Utah	UTK
ACM EC	1.000	0.420	0.433	0.426	0.407	0.386	0.433	0.443	0.366	0.427	0.373
AU	0.420	1.000	0.339	0.480	0.522	0.342	0.431	0.500	0.377	0.382	0.462
GMU	0.433	0.339	1.000	0.500	0.532	0.460	0.463	0.471	0.603	0.545	0.439
KSU	0.426	0.480	0.500	1.000	0.623	0.494	0.561	0.655	0.493	0.528	0.587
LSU	0.407	0.522	0.532	0.623	1.000	0.462	0.491	0.554	0.524	0.514	0.500
PDX	0.386	0.342	0.460	0.494	0.462	1.000	0.427	0.469	0.488	0.586	0.347
RPI	0.433	0.431	0.463	0.561	0.491	0.427	1.000	0.525	0.547	0.535	0.532
SC	0.443	0.500	0.471	0.655	0.554	0.469	0.525	1.000	0.443	0.521	0.480
Stanford	0.366	0.377	0.603	0.493	0.524	0.488	0.547	0.443	1.000	0.600	0.407
Utah	0.427	0.382	0.545	0.528	0.514	0.586	0.535	0.521	0.600	1.000	0.409
UTK	0.373	0.462	0.439	0.587	0.500	0.347	0.532	0.480	0.407	0.409	1.000

Table 6: Pairwise similarity of CS departments computed as Jaccard index of department topic sets.

as filler text until a later date, and do not provide any useful information about the course. However, while these circumstances lie outside of our control, we take measures to prevent invalid course descriptions from entering the dataset. The cleaning process described in Section 3.1 removes descriptions that are unlikely to be valid based on length and vocabulary size. It should be noted that this is a general purpose technique which can also be applied to intake other course related information, such as syllabi and assignment data instead of course descriptions. In the case of different data types, it would be similarly necessary to ensure the relevance and descriptiveness of the input text.

Another limitation of our approach is an inability to meaningfully summarize or categorize inferred topics. While the raw topics are used internally for comparison, they do not provide an ideal interface for the end user. This limitation stems from our use of LDA as the primary topic inference tool. We propose a solution in the following Section 6.

6. FUTURE WORK

One of the major benefits and weaknesses of LDA is its unsupervised nature. Beneficially, it allows for the extraction of information from an entirely unknown dataset. In this context, this flexibility allows its application to any number of diverse academic departments. However, the main drawback of this characteristic is the lack of categorical information for the inferred topics. While a topic can be understood via manual inspection of its terms, LDA offers no single comprehensive label to summarize it. A possible solution to this problem might involve a meta-analysis of inferred topics. Each topic could be classified as one of a number of learning outcomes based on its composition and weighting in a description. Mapping the learned topics onto a standardized framework of learning outcomes [16] would allow for immediate integration of the extracted course concepts into existing academic evaluative frameworks based on learning outcome literature.

As educators who often have deficient resources to improve their pedagogy [8] look towards online or virtual mechanisms to support them, the system we have designed can be very useful. Based on ideas discussed by Brown and Kölling [8], one potential we see for future work is the integration of our system with an existing virtual community of CS educators, or the creation of community features around the system we have designed. For instance, we can make it easier for educators to share or request resources from oth-

ers or to learn more about why certain content is or is not covered in specific courses. As more educators provide data to the system, the quality of results will benefit as well.

We also foresee that in the future we will be able to combine course related data with specific course assignments (through learning-management system (LMS) data), thereby providing a better picture of the kinds of experiences students can hope to receive in any given course. This combination of data will also allow a better examination of the effects of different teaching strategies on students' learning [19, 14, 4]. For instance, we will be able to better understand the role of pedagogical techniques, such as problem-based and service-learning, on student outcomes. By aligning with LMS data, we will also be able to learn more about how students perform on different assignments related to a specific competency or course content. In the future we also plan to combine this data with data about student demographics and that can help provide a better picture of performance across gender and race [13, 18]. This can be useful in designing more supportive pedagogical elements.

7. CONCLUSION

Programs of study in higher education differ widely between departments and universities. Because of these discrepancies, program evaluation methodologies are employed with the goal of understanding the contents of a program of study within a standardized framework. However, this process generally requires manual inspection by a domain expert to extract information from large quantities of course descriptions. Automating the digestion and processing of these descriptions will greatly reduce the time and effort required. Probabilistic topic modeling presents a statistical machine learning method to automatically extract the core concepts covered by a course description. Latent Dirichlet allocation (LDA) results in a feasible breakdown of textual descriptions into component concepts. This work has presented a software framework for the ingestion and processing of large volumes of textual course descriptions. Additionally, a web-based visualization tool has been developed to present inferred topics for university programs of study in an accessible format.

8. ACKNOWLEDGMENTS

This material is based on work supported by the National Science Foundation under grant IIS-1447489. Any opinions, findings, and conclusions or recommendations expressed in this material are those of the authors and do not necessarily reflect those of the National Science Foundation.

9. REFERENCES

[1] Accreditation Board for Engineering and Technology. Criteria for accrediting computing programs. Website, 2015.

[2] ACM/IEEE-CS Joint Task Force on Computing Curricula. Computer science curricula 2013. Technical report, ACM Press and IEEE Computer Society Press, December 2013.

[3] P. W. Airasian, K. A. Cruikshank, R. E. Mayer, P. Pintrich, J. Raths, and M. C. Wittrock. A taxonomy for learning, teaching, and assessing: A revision of bloom's taxonomy of educational objectives. *Anderson LW and Krathwohl DR. New York: Addison Wesley Longmann*, 2001.

[4] L. J. Barker and K. Garvin-Doxas. Making visible the behaviors that influence learning environment: A qualitative exploration of computer science classrooms. *Computer Science Education*, 14(2):119–145, 2004.

[5] D. M. Blei. Probabilistic topic models. *Commun. ACM*, 55(4):77–84, Apr. 2012.

[6] D. M. Blei, A. Y. Ng, and M. I. Jordan. Latent dirichlet allocation. *J. Mach. Learn. Res.*, 3:993–1022, Mar. 2003.

[7] J. Boustedt, A. Eckerdal, R. McCartney, K. Sanders, L. Thomas, and C. Zander. Students' perceptions of the differences between formal and informal learning. In *Proceedings of the Seventh International Workshop on Computing Education Research*, ICER '11, pages 61–68, New York, NY, USA, 2011. ACM.

[8] N. C. C. Brown and M. Kölling. A tale of three sites: Resource and knowledge sharing amongst computer science educators. In *Proceedings of the Ninth Annual International ACM Conference on International Computing Education Research*, ICER '13, pages 27–34, New York, NY, USA, 2013. ACM.

[9] T. D. Effland. Focused mining of university course descriptions from highly variable sources. In *Proceedings of the 46th ACM Technical Symposium on Computer Science Education*, SIGCSE '15, pages 716–716, New York, NY, USA, 2015. ACM.

[10] M. Hewner. How cs undergraduates make course choices. In *Proceedings of the tenth annual conference on International computing education research*, pages 115–122. ACM, 2014.

[11] P. Hubwieser, J. Magenheim, A. Mühling, and A. Ruf. Towards a conceptualization of pedagogical content knowledge for computer science. In *Proceedings of the ninth annual international ACM conference on International computing education research*, pages 1–8. ACM, 2013.

[12] P. Jaccard. The distribution of the flora in the alpine zone. 1. *New phytologist*, 11(2):37–50, 1912.

[13] S. Katz, D. Allbritton, J. Aronis, C. Wilson, and M. L. Soffa. Gender, achievement, and persistence in an undergraduate computer science program. *ACM SIGMIS Database*, 37(4):42–57, 2006.

[14] J. Kay, M. Barg, A. Fekete, T. Greening, O. Hollands, J. H. Kingston, and K. Crawford. Problem-based learning for foundation computer science courses. *Computer Science Education*, 10(2):109–128, 2000.

[15] M. Klawe and B. Shneiderman. Crisis and opportunity in computer science. *Communications of the ACM*, 48(11):27–28, 2005.

[16] D. R. Krathwohl. A revision of bloom's taxonomy: An overview. *Theory into practice*, 41(4):212–218, 2002.

[17] S. Lloyd. Least squares quantization in PCM. *Information Theory, IEEE Transactions on*, 28(2):129–137, Mar 1982.

[18] M. Sahami, A. Aiken, and J. Zelenski. Expanding the frontiers of computer science: designing a curriculum to reflect a diverse field. In *Proceedings of the 41st ACM technical symposium on Computer science education*, pages 47–51. ACM, 2010.

[19] P. Sanderson and K. Vollmar. A primer for applying service learning to computer science. In *ACM SIGCSE Bulletin*, volume 32, pages 222–226. ACM, 2000.

[20] D. Shinners-Kennedy and S. A. Fincher. Identifying threshold concepts: From dead end to a new direction. In *Proceedings of the Ninth Annual International ACM Conference on International Computing Education Research*, ICER '13, pages 9–18, New York, NY, USA, 2013. ACM.

[21] Y. Yang, H. Liu, J. Carbonell, and W. Ma. Concept graph learning from educational data. In *Proceedings of the Eighth ACM International Conference on Web Search and Data Mining*, WSDM '15, pages 159–168, New York, NY, USA, 2015. ACM.

[22] S. Zweben. Computing degree and enrollment trends. Technical report, Computing Research Association, 2011.

A Multi-Institutional Study of Learning via Student Involvement in Humanitarian Free and Open Source Software Projects

Gregory W. Hislop
College of Computing and Informatics
Drexel University
Philadelphia, PA
hislop@drexel.edu

Heidi J. C. Ellis
Dept. of CS & IT
Western New England University
Springfield, MA 01119
ellis@wne.edu

S. Monisha Pulimood
Dept. of Computer Science
The College of New Jersey
Ewing, NJ 08628
pulimood@tcnj.edu

Becka Morgan
Dept. of Computer Science
Western Oregon University
Monmouth, OR 97361
morganb@wou.edu

Suzanne Mello-Stark
Dept. of Computer Science
University of Rhode Island
Kingston, RI 02881
suzanne@cs.uri.edu

Ben Coleman
Dept. of Math and CS
Moravian College
Bethlehem, PA 18018
coleman@cs.moravian.edu

Cam Macdonell
Dept. of Computer Science
MacEwan University
Edmonton, AB T5J 4S2
cameron.macdonell@macewan.ca

ABSTRACT
This paper reports on a study of student opinion of the impact of participation in Humanitarian Free and Open Source Software (HFOSS) on motivation, computing learning, and major/career direction. The study builds on an existing body of work in student participation in HFOSS. Six institutions with a variety of profiles are involved in the study and the paper reports on quantitative analysis of Likert survey items. Results of Mann-Whitney U tests on Likert data are mixed. Positive results indicate that students perceived that participating in an HFOSS project made them more comfortable with computing and improved their perceived ability to maintain a project and interact with professionals. Negative results include a perceived decrease in perception of computing skills, which may result from an increased understanding of the complexity of developing a large, real-world project.

Categories and Subject Descriptors
K.3.2 [**Computers and Education**]: Computer and Information Science Education – *Computer Science Education*.

General Terms
Human Factors

ICER '15, August 9-13, 2015, Omaha, Nebraska, USA.
Copyright is held by the owner/author(s). Publication rights licensed to ACM.
ACM 978-1-4503-3630-7/15/08... $15.00
DOI: http://dx.doi.org/10.1145/2787622.2787726

Keywords
HFOSS, Student projects, Computing education

1. BACKGROUND
Free and Open Source Software (FOSS) is developed under open licenses that provide users with the right to run the software for any purpose, and to modify and distribute the software for free. FOSS products such as GNU/Linux have been in widespread use for many years, with use expanding rapidly in business in recent years [35].

The characteristics of FOSS culture provide unique educational opportunities where students can observe and participate in many aspects of software development. In FOSS projects, the community decides the direction of the project, and this community provides students with a group of professionals with whom to interact and from which to learn. Many FOSS projects are eager to embrace students as potential long-term contributors. All project artifacts including code are available, modifiable and long-lived, allowing the history of the project to be examined. This transparency allows students to understand who contributed to various portions of the project, and provides the opportunity for their own contributions to be visible. Open licensing of FOSS indicates that the source code must be available for modification, and avoids the issues of intellectual property and proprietary development that can occur with student involvement in industry projects. Since many FOSS projects are used and developed around the world, students can observe and participate in a globally distributed software team. FOSS operates on a form of meritocracy where responsibilities increase as a contributor demonstrates his or her capabilities. This environment enables students to gain confidence in their abilities and grow professionally. Due to these characteristics, educators have increasingly adopted student involvement in FOSS projects in their courses [11, 25-29, 32, 36, 37].

Humanitarian Free and Open Source Software (HFOSS) is FOSS that benefits the human condition, such as applications for disaster management or managing medical records. Benefits from student participation in HFOSS subsume those of student participation in FOSS such as improving technical and professional skills and understanding complex project development in a distributed environment. In addition, students can see the benefits of using computing skills to aid others and helps prepare students to become contributing members of the community. There is evidence that the aspect of "doing good" is attractive to students [10, 19, 21, 36] and that this characteristic can help attract students, particularly women, to computing majors [1, 3, 4, 38]. Lastly, HFOSS projects are altruistic in nature, which can make the communities more welcoming to new contributors and more helpful to student participants.

While there are significant benefits from student participation in HFOSS, there are also significant challenges for students and instructors. A major challenge is for students and instructors to adjust to a less structured learning environment, where the student must learn from a variety of resources including documentation and by interacting with the professional community, and where the teacher is no longer the sole authority for the material [11].

Students may not be familiar with the tools, approaches or languages used in the project, and may need to learn all these simultaneously. The complexity of the project itself presents another learning curve, as students must learn how to approach and understand an existing project. Students must understand the FOSS culture, including forms and modes of communication, and must often gain significant domain knowledge.

Instructors may face similar learning curves for tools, approaches, FOSS culture, and domain knowledge. In addition, instructors must foster student participation, learn how to create assignments and course deliverables, and create grading rubrics. They must negotiate communication and support with the HFOSS community, for instance identifying what support the community will provide (such as a mentor for the instructor or answering student questions), and what the students will provide, which could include documentation or code fixes. Instructors also need to be mindful of potential FERPA and intellectual property issues.

Project selection is critical when incorporating HFOSS into a course, since the project must fit the learning goals of the course, be open to contributions and welcoming to students, and have good communication mechanisms. Other challenges include synchronizing schedules between the academic calendar and the HFOSS release cycle, and unpredictability where the project may make a major change in its direction mid-term. However, the initial effort can benefit learning activities across a series of courses, not just a single course offering. Several efforts have reported on approaches to FOSS project selection [9, 18, 36].

1.1 Student Involvement in FOSS and HFOSS

Nacimiento et al [33] provide a summary of the use of open source projects in software engineering education that includes courses across the computing disciplines (e.g, software engineering courses in CS programs). Student participation in FOSS projects first appeared in computing education literature in the mid 2000's with a number of efforts involving graduate students [22, 27, 30, 40].

Undergraduate student contributions to FOSS projects also started in the mid 2000's [39]. Results of a survey on student opinion indicate that students perceived that they learned both computing and communication skills via participation in a FOSS project [29]. Gehringer [17] identified best practices for faculty members who involve students in FOSS projects and Kussmaul [24] provides a USABLE model for scaffolding initial student involvement in FOSS projects.

Some of the initial efforts to involve students in HFOSS began as service learning projects [21, 23, 25, 31]. Student learning in HFOSS has the same problems inherent in student involvement in FOSS [28], however the humanitarian nature of the projects has been shown to motivate students [2, 20, 34]. The Humanitarian FOSS effort [31] was founded in 2006 [13-16] and more formal studies of student opinion of motivation and learning resulting from participation in an HFOSS project began in 2009 [12]. Results of an initial study into the impact of student participation in HFOSS projects indicate students feel that they gain software engineering knowledge ranging from tools and techniques to software process to understanding the impact of project size and complexity [10]. The same study, which used a set of Likert scale items, found that women more strongly felt able to plan and participate in an HFOSS project [6]. A similar, more recent study [5] supports the earlier results and indicates that student participation in HFOSS has a positive impact on student motivation to study computing, and also a strong positive impact on perceived learning related to computing.

In another related study, observations on student reflections on participation in HFOSS projects in post-course essays indicates that students felt that they were better prepared to enter industry, were motivated by working within an HFOSS community, and gained an understanding of the need for lifelong learning and how that learning differs from classroom learning [7].

2. CONTEXT OF THE STUDY

The study described in this paper is an expansion of prior work in student participation in HFOSS [5-7, 10]. This enlarged study increases the number of institutions participating and widens the geographical area of participants. The early work involves four Liberal Arts institutions located in New England. This more recent study includes institutions located on both east and west coast. In addition, the survey instrument has been amended to include open-ended questions in a desire to gain a better understanding of student opinion of participation in HFOSS.

The instructors who participated in this study have all taken part in Professor's Open Source Software Experience (POSSE) workshops, funded by NSF and supported by Red Hat. These workshops provide faculty with the opportunity to partner with others in order to learn how to use FOSS tools, to incorporate HFOSS into collegiate courses, and to develop curriculum to involve students in HFOSS [8]. The collaboration of the POSSE cohorts extends beyond the actual workshops as POSSE alumni work together to share resources and help each other develop materials ranging from assignments to entire courses, as well as to conduct research and publish to continue to inform the community of the benefits of supporting student participation in HFOSS. These benefits include the attraction students have to projects that "do good", increased confidence in their abilities and providing real world experiences.

The institutions in this study, described in Table 1 below, are all small to mid-size institutions. Four are public institutions and two are private. Four of the institutions operate on the semester system, a fifth institution is on the quarter system, and one institution offered the course used in the study during a 13-week winter term. Each course is taught focusing on HFOSS project participation at a junior or senior level.

Table 1. Courses in the Study

Title	Term(s)	Students	Length of Term
Software Engineering (WNE)	Fall 2013, Fall 2014	6,8	15 weeks
Software Engineering (URI)	Fall 2014	40	15 weeks
Software Engineering (Mor)	Spring 2014	10	15 weeks
Software Engineering (TCNJ)	Fall 2013	19	15 weeks
Software Engineering (Mac)	Winter 2014	15	13 weeks
Open Source Software Development (WOU)	Winter 2014	20	10 weeks

Western New England University (WNE) is a small, liberal arts institution located in New England. WNE has 2,500 undergraduates and there are approximately 60 Computer Science majors. The CS major generally follows the ACM Curriculum Guidelines. The software engineering course used in the study is a senior-level course that covers major software development topics such as requirements, design, implementation, testing as well as some issues such as estimation and risk. As part of this course, students make contributions to an HFOSS project. The project used during the study is MouseTrap, a GNOME Accessibility project that uses a web-camera to track user head movement to move the cursor on the screen.

University of Rhode Island (URI) is the principal public research university for the state of Rhode Island. URI currently enrolls approximately 13,500 undergraduate and 3,000 graduate students, of which nearly 350 are computer science majors. Students take the software engineering course used in this study in either the sophomore or junior year. In this course, student teams develop a substantial software product from requirements to delivery. An HFOSS project exposes students to open source development tools such as virtual machines, course management tools and bug trackers.

The College of New Jersey (TCNJ) is a public, residential, primarily undergraduate institution with approximately 6,300 students. The Department of Computer Science currently has about 130 majors and minors. The ABET-accredited program provides a comprehensive learning environment through a rigorous curriculum designed to meet the needs of students interested in careers in the industry and graduate school. The software engineering course used in this study is required for all majors and minors and is typically taken in the junior or senior year. In this course, students collaborate on a large project in teams, where they apply concepts learned. In recent semesters, students have been working on an HFOSS, web-based system that manages and provides information about potentially polluted properties for Habitat for Humanity and citizens of the area.

MacEwan University (Mac) is a public undergraduate university in Edmonton, Alberta, Canada. MacEwan is a school of approximately 10,000 students. The Department of Computer

Science offered a 2-year transfer program until 2009 after which it offered its own major for the Bachelor of Science. The department follows the ACM Curriculum Guidelines and currently has over 100 declared majors. The course used in this study is a senior level software engineering required course. The enrolment has increased from 10 to 32 over the past four years. Students are taught a typical software engineering curriculum and apply practical lessons using the Ushahidi platform, an HFOSS project. "Ushahidi", which means "testimony" in Swahili, was a website that was initially developed to map reports of violence in Kenya after the post-election fallout at the beginning of 2008. Since then, the name "Ushahidi" has come to represent the people behind the "Ushahidi Platform".

Western Oregon University (WOU) is a public liberal arts university serving approximately 6,100 undergraduate students and 800 graduate students. Founded in 1980, the Computer Science program is software-oriented and follows the ACM Curriculum Guidelines. The Computer Science program is also closely aligned with the current needs of industry. The course used in this study is a senior level software engineering elective course that applies toward the software engineering track within the CS major. The course uses an existing FOSS project with the goal to engage students in a real world project that will provide job skills that pertain to the "real" world. Although the focus was on the entirety of the project, including documentation, bug triage, activism, and translation, students focused on fixing bugs, testing, or coding to fulfill the software engineering requirement.

Moravian College is residential, liberal arts school with approximately 1,500 students. The course used in this study is the senior capstone experience. Taken by second semester seniors, the course focuses on software engineering principles applied to real-world projects. Students work on an HFOSS project by handling "introductory bugs" (ones that have been prepared by long-term project members), and by participating in weekly project scrum and design meetings. Based on this experience, the students design and implement a small, independent contribution to the overall project. The project used during the study is OpenMRS, an open medical records system originally developed to track AIDS patients in Zimbabwe.

3. THE HFOSS STUDY
The study presented in this paper is an expansion of a study of student perception of the impact of participation in HFOSS projects on motivation and learning [5-7, 10]. The goal of the effort is to gain a better understanding of whether student involvement in HFOSS projects supports computing learning and whether students are motivated by participation in HFOSS. The study has three sets of research hypotheses, each with a null and a direction hypothesis:

$H1_0$: Student participation in an HFOSS project has no impact on student motivation to study computing.

$H1_a$: Student participation in an HFOSS project has a positive impact on student motivation to study computing.

$H2_0$: Student participation in an HFOSS project has no impact on perceived learning related to computing.

$H2_a$: Student participation in an HFOSS project has a positive impact on perceived learning related to computing.

$H3_0$: Student participation in an HFOSS project has no impact on major and career plans.

$H3_a$: Student participation in an HFOSS project has a positive impact on major and career plans.

The study instrument is an anonymous survey that contains three parts. The first part asks about student background including major, race, and gender. The second part contains three sections of Likert scale response questions, one section for each of the three sets of research hypotheses. The Likert scale uses a five-point scale from "strongly disagree" to "strongly agree" with a mid-point value of "neutral". There are also options for "Don't know" and "Not applicable". The last section is one (pre-course) or three (post-course) free response questions. The version of the survey used in this study (v2.2) was revised based on results from an earlier version of the survey. The surveys were administered on paper with the exception of one site that administered the survey using Qualtrix., and one site only included a subset of the computing-related Likert items. Table 2 below contains example Likert items from each of the three sections in that part of the survey. The "H" category indicates items related to the motivation of HFOSS, "SE" items are related to computing, and "G" items are related to general career aspirations (http://foss2serve.org/index.php/Evaluation_Instruments).

Table 2. Sample Likert Items

Item	Explanation
H10	Participating in an HFOSS project made me more comfortable with computing.
SE3	I can use a software process to develop an HFOSS project.
G4	Participation in an HFOSS project has positively reinforced my decision to make computing my major.

4. RESULTS AND DISCUSSION

This section contains a description of the analysis of the data and an explanation of the results. The section begins with an overview of the results. Subsequent sections contain a discussion of the quantitative results of the Likert survey as well as a summary of the qualitative results obtained from student comments.

4.1 Student Profile

As described in Section 2, the study includes data from seven courses from six different institutions. The data was collected over 16 months between Fall 2013 and Fall 2014. The study includes 115 pre-course data points and 94 post-course data points. The participant group contained 75.5% males, 17% females, and 7.5% of study participants declined to indicate gender. The surveys are anonymous with no identifier to match pre- and post-course surveys so only aggregate data is investigated in this study.

Table 3 shows the distribution of majors across the respondents. It should be noted that the "Other" category included majors such as Marine Biology, Biological Sciences, and Applied Math. These results contain a higher percentage of CS majors than prior work, which had 66% CS majors [5].

Table 3. Distribution of Majors - Post

Major	Responses	Percent
CS	77	82%
MIS	8	9%
Comp. Eng.	5	5%
Other	4	4%

Based on the post-course survey, 40% of respondents had some work experience. The median experience across all students was 4 months.

Figure 1 shows students' self-rated programming ability, post-course based on a scale of 1 to 5 where 1 indicated a complete novice and 5 indicated an expert. It is interesting to note that almost half of students (48%) rated themselves as having average programming ability. The median was 3 as was the mode. This differs slightly from prior results [5] where the median was 3 and the mode was 4.

The reported programming ability rose significantly between the pre-course and post-course surveys (Mann-Whitney U, p=.009) with the average rising from 3.08 to 3.38. While this may have been due to other experiences during the study period, it is a possible question for future investigation.

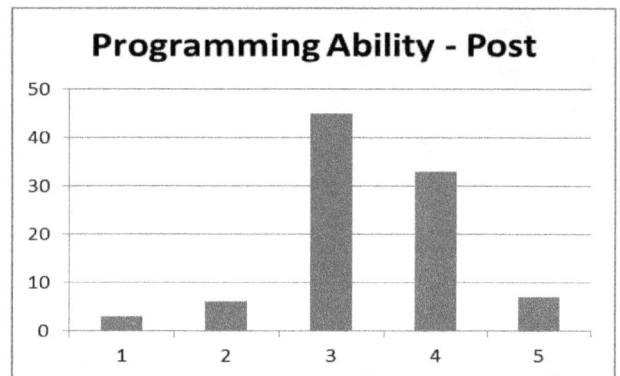

Figure 1. Post-Course Programming Ability

4.2 Comparison of Pre and Post-Course Results

A comparison of student responses between pre-course and post-course surveys provides interesting insights into the impact of student participation in HFOSS projects. The Likert scale responses were converted to ordinal numbers between one and five with one representing "strongly disagree" and five representing "strongly agree". Since a numeric conversion like this may not actually represent interval data, the data were treated as ordinal and the non-parametric Mann-Whitney U was used to test for significant differences using a threshold significance level of $p<=0.05$.

For ease of understanding, the items that showed significant positive difference between pre-test and post-test are grouped into two sets. Each table includes the Mann-Whitney U significance values (p), the post-test average (Post Avg), and the difference between the pre-test and post-test average (Diff).

Table 4 contains the items pertaining to student motivation (H) and student career plans (G). These items provide evidence that HFOSS participation improves motivation and career perspective. Item H10 shows a very significant rise of large magnitude (+2.1). This may reflect student uncertainty about the answer at the pre-test time, but reflects a solid positive perception by post-test. G1 indicates that the interaction with HFOSS communities boosts student confidence. G8 also shows a substantial swing, but it is interesting that the post-test average is still a bit below the neutral point, suggesting a possible area for additional investigation, starting with more narrowly defined questions in this area.

Table 4 Significant Positive Difference in Student Pre/Post Responses (motivation and career)

Q	Description	p-val <	Diff	Post Avg
H10	Participating in an HFOSS project made me more comfortable with computing.	.001	2.1	3.72
G1	I am confident about working with computing professionals	.038	0.24	3.92
G8	I have a high level of experience in the HFOSS subject matter.	.000	0.88	2.89

Table 5 contains the items with significant differences in the area of computing knowledge, which for these courses focused on software engineering topics. In general, the significant items show a substantial shift from near neutral pre-test to solid agreement post-test for each statement. Note that the learning here is mostly related to process, team, and project knowledge rather than technology. In the experience of the authors, learning in these areas is often prized by potential employers and is prominent in discussions of what might get increased emphasis in computing degrees.

Table 5 Significant Positive Difference in Student Pre/Post Responses (computing learning)

Q	Description	p-val <	Diff	Post Avg
SE2	I can list the steps in the software process we used in HFOSS project.	.001	1.02	3.80
SE3	I can use a software process to develop an HFOSS project.	.001	0.75	3.90
SE6	I can describe the impact of project complexity on the approaches used to develop software.	.001	0.50	3.75
SE7	I can describe the impact of project size on the approaches used to develop software.	.001	0.49	3.75
SE9	I can describe the drawbacks and benefits of FOSS to society.	.001	0.64	3.75
SE10	I can use all tools and techniques employed in my HFOSS project.	.001	0.69	3.65
SE11	I can participate in an HFOSS development team's interactions.	.038	0.28	3.83

Table 6 contains items with significant difference in a negative direction. A first note is that all three of these items still indicate student agreement with the statement on the post-test. The difference is that the degree of agreement is less strong. H8 may have limited change potential since most of the students are already CS majors and beyond the early years of their program.

H9 is interesting in combination with the significant rise in self-reported programming ability discussed earlier. One explanation is that the HFOSS experience expands students' horizon as to the true nature of computing ability and they judge themselves as advancing in ability, but are less confident because they realize that they are farther from expert status than they had thought. It is also notable that H9 showed significant positive difference from pre- to post-course survey in prior studies [5].

The negative difference shown by item SE5 supports previous results that also show a negative difference [6]. It should be noted that in both the previous study and this study, item SE5 had a high pre-course average (>4). It is possible that the HFOSS participation gave students a more realistic view of the difficulties of working with a distributed team. The drop in the post-course values may indicate that students had unrealized expectations about interacting with the HFOSS community. Another key to understanding SE5 may be that student comments indicate that many students interacted more with their group than with the HFOSS professionals. So the lower agreement may reflect less interaction than expected pre-course.

Table 6 Significant Negative Difference in Student Pre/Post Responses

Q	Description	p-val <	Diff	Post Avg
H8	Working on an HFOSS project has increased my interest in computing.	.001	-.44	3.69
H9	Working on an HFOSS project has increased my confidence in my computing ability.	.009	-.36	3.79
SE5	I have gained some confidence in collaborating with professionals from a variety of locations and cultures.	.003	-.35	3.65

4.3 Gender and Ethnicity

Comparison of post-test items by gender shows only one significant item. For H2, females indicate stronger agreement than males. (*H2. I have a greater awareness of the potential for computing to benefit society due to working on an HFOSS project.* p = 0.036, average for males = 4.04; average for females = 4.5). Both genders indicate strong agreement with the statement, but the response by the women is particularly noteworthy given that research indicates that an understanding of social benefit is a key element in broadening participation in computing.

Comparison of post-test items by reported ethnicity also indicated one item, Programming Ability, with significant difference between white and non-white students. (p = 0.03, average for white students = 3.0, average for non-white students = 3.5) The reasons for this difference are not clear and further work seems in order.

4.4 Programming Ability

Post-course surveys were grouped by self-reported programming experience, with responses 1-3 being grouped as "beginner" and 4-5 grouped as "advanced." Comparison of post-test responses shows significant differences between the beginner and advanced groups for the items in Table 7.

For all the items with significant differences, the responses for both groups reflect agreement with the statements. For items H5, H6, SE3, and SE4, the students reporting more advanced programming ability also report stronger agreement with the statements. This difference may relate to a stronger sense of confidence by these students in their readiness to perform as members of a software engineering team. SE4 represents this most directly.

For SE1 and SE8, the difference between groups is a matter of distribution of responses rather than the central tendency as represented by the mean. An examination of the data shows that the difference results form a much more scattered set of responses by the beginners and a more coalesced response by the more advanced programmers. A possible explanation is that the more advanced students have developed a better sense of the actual requirements of these tasks (planning, development, and maintenance) and so their answers are more consistent.

Table 7 Significant Positive Difference in Student Responses Based on Programming Ability

Q	Description	p-val <	Diff	Hi Avg
H5	Knowing that my project will help people motivates me to do my best on the HFOSS project.	.017	0.30	3.80
H6	Working with an HFOSS community to develop a project has increased my interest in computing.	.033	0.15	3.98
SE1	I am comfortable that I could participate in the planning and development of a real-world software project.	.019	0.00	4.0
SE3	I can use a software process to develop an HFOSS project.	.030	0.47	4.12
SE4	I am sure that I can actively participate in an HFOSS community to develop a software project.	.002	0.30	3.97
SE8	I am confident that I can maintain an HFOSS project.	.021	-.04	3.73

5. CONCLUSION AND FUTURE WORK

The results presented above provide some substantial support for rejecting the three null hypotheses presented at the beginning of this discussion. In particular:

Student motivation to study computing – The data provide a variety of indicators that HFOSS participation is motivating to students. These are seen most clearly in Tables 4 and 6. Table 6 shows a moderation in strength of agreement, but the items continue to exhibit substantial agreement.

Exploring the basis for reduced strength of agreement is an item for future work. Item G8 (*I have a high level of experience in the HFOSS subject matter.*) is particularly interesting for future work since there was a significant shift toward more agreement but the post-course value is still below neutral. Some better attempt to understand how students are thinking about "experience" and also "subject matter" seems like a good starting point for future work.

Self-perceived learning – The indicators of perceived learning show most clearly in the software engineering topical items listed in Table 5. Students clearly perceive themselves as learning. A next step in the project will be to gather direct learning measures. To some extent, this is a difficult task because participating instructors believe that some of the best learning opportunities provided by HFOSS relate to professional skills rather than factual computing knowledge. For example, directly measuring an item like S2 (*I can list the steps in the software process we used in HFOSS project.*) seems relatively manageable, but directly measuring S11 (*Participation in an HFOSS project will improve my understanding of how to behave like a computing professional.*) is more difficult. Even so, this is a clear future direction.

Plans for career and major – The data provide indirect support for choice of computing as a major via items including H10 (*Participating in an HFOSS project made me more comfortable with computing.*). Given that a substantial majority of the students were already computer science majors, the HFOSS experience provided by this study may be too late to cause much change in intended major. On the other hand, the HFOSS experience was perceived as reinforcing the choice of computing as a major, but without significant change in perception pre-course to post-course. For example, the response for item G4 (*Participation in an HFOSS project has positively reinforced my decision to make computing my major.*) indicated strong agreement both pre-course (mean = 4.04) and post-course (mean = 4.32).

The work presented in this paper is an on-going project to develop and assess student participation in HFOSS. As this approach is extended to more institutions, some more detailed analyses will be possible. Extension to direct measures of learning is a key next step. In addition, the team is discussing use of survey identifiers that would allow pairing of pre-course and post-course surveys while still maintaining anonymity. This would allow analysis to separate different student characteristics as part of the analysis. These expansions in evaluation should add to understanding of HFOSS participation.

6. ACKNOWLEDGMENTS
This material is based on work supported by the National Science Foundation under Grant Nos. - DUE-1225708, DUE-1225738, DUE-1225688, and DUE-1141170. Any opinions, findings and conclusions or recommendations expressed in this material are those of the author(s) and do not necessarily reflect the views of the National Science Foundation (NSF). The authors would also like to thank Debra Wetcher-Hendricks for aiding in the data analysis.

7. REFERENCES
[1] Beyer,S., Rynes, K., and Haller,S. 2004. Deterrents to women taking computer science courses. *IEEE Technology and Society Magazine*. 23, 1, (Spring 2004), 21-28.

[2] Beyer, S. 2008. Predictors of female and male Computer Science students' grades. *Journal of Women and Minorities in Science and Engineering*, 14, 377-409.

[3] Carter, L. 2006. Why students with an apparent aptitude for computer science don't choose to major in computer science. *In SIGCSE Bull*. 38, 1 (March 2006), 27-31. http://doi.acm.org/10.1145/1124706.1121352

[4] Cohoon, J.M. 2002. Recruiting and retaining women in undergraduate computing majors. *SIGCSE Bull.* 34, 2 (June 2002), 48-52. http://doi.acm.org/10.1145/543812.543829

[5] Ellis, H.J.C., Postner, L., Hislop, G.W., and Jackson, S. 2015. Team Project Experiences in Humanitarian Free and Open Source Software (HFOSS). *Special Issue of the ACM Transactions on Computing Education on Team Projects in Computing Education,* in press.

[6] Ellis, H.J.C., Hislop, G.W., Pulimood, S.M., Morgan,B., and Coleman, B. 2015. Software Engineering Learning in HFOSS: A Multi-Institutional Study, In *Proceedings of the 122nd Annual ASEE Conference and Exhibition*, Seattle, WA.

[7] Ellis, H.J.C., Jackson, S., Burdge, D., Postner, L., Hislop, G.W., and Joanie Diggs. 2014. Learning within a professional environment: shared ownership of an HFOSS project. In *Proceedings of the 15th Annual Conference on Information technology education (SIGITE '14).* ACM, New York, NY, USA, 95-100. http://doi.acm.org/10.1145/2656450.2656468

[8] Ellis, H.J.C., Hislop, G.W., Purcell, M., Chua, M., and Dzaillas, S. 2013. Towards a Model of Faculty Development for FOSS in Education, *26th Annual Conference on Software Engineering Education and Training*, San Francisco, May 2013.

[9] Ellis, H.J.C., Purcell, M., and Hislop, G.W. 2012. An approach for evaluating FOSS projects for student participation. In *Proceedings of the 43rd ACM technical symposium on Computer Science Education (SIGCSE '12).* ACM, New York, NY, USA, 415-420. http://doi.acm.org/10.1145/2157136.2157260

[10] Ellis, H.J.C., Hislop, G.W., Rodriguez, J. and Morelli, R.A. 2012. Student Software Engineering Learning via Participation in Humanitarian FOSS Projects. *In Proceedings of the 119th Annual ASEE Conference and Exhibition*, San Antonio, TX.

[11] Ellis, H.J.C., Hislop, G.W., Chua, M. and Dziallas, S. 2011. How to involve students in FOSS projects. In *Proceedings of the 2011 Frontiers in Education Conference (FIE '11).* IEEE Computer Society, Washington, DC, USA, T1H-1-1-T1H-6. http://dx.doi.org/10.1109/FIE.2011.6142994

[12] Ellis, H.J.C. and Hislop, G.W. 2011. Student IT services to support open source software for humanity. In *Proceedings of the 2011 conference on Information technology education (SIGITE '11).* ACM, New York, NY, USA, 307-308. http://doi.acm.org/10.1145/2047594.2047676

[13] Ellis, H.J.C., Hislop, G.W., and Ibanez, L. 2010. Opportunities for Students to Contribute to FOSS Projects," *O'Reilly Open Source Convention (OSCON)*, Portland, OR.

[14] Ellis, H.J.C., Morelli, R.A. and Hislop, G.W. 2008. Support for Educating Software Engineers Through Humanitarian Open Source Projects. *21st Annual Conference on Software Engineering Education and Training*, 14-17.

[15] Ellis, H.J.C., Morelli, R.A., de Lanerolle, T.R., Damon, J. and Raye, J. 2007. Can humanitarian open-source software development draw new students to CS?. In *Proceedings of the 38th SIGCSE technical symposium on Computer science education (SIGCSE '07).* ACM, New York, NY, USA, 551-555. http://doi.acm.org/10.1145/1227310.1227495

[16] Ellis, H.J.C., Morelli, R.A., de Lanerolle, T.R., and Hislop, G.W. 2007. Holistic Software Engineering Education Based on a Humanitarian Open Source Project. *In Proceedings of the 20th Conference on Software Engineering Education & Training (CSEET '07).* IEEE Computer Society, Washington, DC, USA, 327-335. http://dx.doi.org/10.1109/CSEET.2007.26

[17] Gehringer, E.F. 2011. From the manager's perspective: Classroom contributions to open-source projects, in *Frontiers in Education Conference (FIE),* IEEE. F1E–1–F1E–5 (Oct. 2011),

[18] Gokhale, S.S., Smith,T., and McCartney, R. 2012. Integrating open source software into software engineering curriculum: challenges in selecting projects. In *Proceedings of the First International Workshop on Software Engineering Education Based on Real-World Experiences (EduRex '12).* IEEE Press, Piscataway, NJ, USA, 9-12.

[19] Hislop, G.W., Ellis, H.J.C., and Morelli, R.A. 2009. Evaluating student experiences in developing software for humanity. In *Proceedings of the 14th annual ACM SIGCSE conference on Innovation and technology in computer science education (ITiCSE '09).* ACM, New York, NY, USA, 263-267. http://doi.acm.org/10.1145/1562877.1562959

[20] Hodari, A.K., Ong, M. Ko, L.T., and Kachchaf, R.R. 2014. New enactments of mentoring and activism: U.S. women of color in computing education and careers. In *Proceedings of the tenth annual conference on International computing education research (ICER '14).* ACM, New York, NY, USA, 83-90. http://doi.acm.org/10.1145/2632320.2632357

[21] Homkes, R. 2008. Assessing it service-learning. In *Proceedings of the 9th ACM SIGITE conference on Information technology education (SIGITE '08).* ACM, New York, NY, USA, 17-22. DOI=10.1145/1414558.1414564 http://doi.acm.org/10.1145/1414558.1414564

[22] Jaccheri, L., and Osterlie, T. 2007. Open Source Software: A Source of Possibilities for Software Engineering Education and Empirical Software Engineering. In *Proceedings of the First International Workshop on Emerging Trends in FLOSS Research and Development (FLOSS '07).* IEEE Computer Society, Washington, DC, USA, 5-. http://dx.doi.org/10.1109/FLOSS.2007.12

[23] Jacobs, S. 2010. Building an education ecology on serious game design and development for the One Laptop Per Child and Sugar platforms: A service learning course builds a base for peer mentoring, cooperative education internships and sponsored research, *Games Innovations Conference (ICE-GIC), 2010 International IEEE Consumer Electronics Society's.* 1, 6 (Dec. 2010), 21-23. doi: 10.1109/ICEGIC.2010.5716882

[24] Kussmaul, K. 2009. Software Projects Using Free and Open Source Software: Opportunities, Challenges, and Lessons Learned. In *ASEE Proceedings of the 116th Annual ASEE Conference and Exhibition,* Austin, TX.

[25] Liu. C. 2005. Enriching software engineering courses with service-learning projects and the open-source approach. In *27th International Conference on Software Engineering*

(ICSE 2005). IEEE. 2005. 15-21. doi: 10.1109/ICSE.2005.1553612

[26] Ludi, S. 2011. The benefits and challenges of using educational game projects in an undergraduate software engineering course. In *Proceedings of the 1st International Workshop on Games and Software Engineering.* ACM, New York, NY, USA. 13-16. 2011.

[27] Lundell, B., Persson A., and Lings, B. 2007. Learning Through Practical Involvement in the OSS Ecosystem: Experiences from a Masters Assignment in Open Source Development, Adoption and Innovation. *IFIP — The International Federation for Information Processing.* Springer. 234, 289-294. http://dx.doi.org/10.1007/978-0-387-72486-7_30

[28] MacKellar, B.K., Sabin, M., and Tucker, A. 2013. Scaling a framework for client-driven open source software projects: a report from three schools. *J. Comput. Sci. Coll.* 28, 6 (June 2013), 140-147.

[29] Marmorstein, R. 2011. Open Source Contribution as an Effective Software Engineering Class Project. In *Proceedings of the 16th Annual Joint Conference on Innovation and Technology in Computer Science Education, ITiCSE '11,* ACM, New York, NY, USA, 268-272.

[30] Marín Martínez, J.J. 2009. Learning Free Software Development from Real-World Experience, in *International Conference on Intelligent Networking and Collaborative Systems.* IEEE, (Nov. 2009) 417–420.

[31] Morelli, R.A., de Lanerolle, T.R., and Tucker, A. 2012. The Humanitarian Free and Open-Source Software Project: Engaging Students in Service-Learning through Building Software, in Service-Learning in the Computer and Information Sciences, John Wiley & Sons, Inc., 117-136, doi = 10.1002/9781118319130.ch5

[32] Morgan, B and Jensen, C. 2014. Lessons Learned from Teaching Open Source Software Development, Open Source Software: Mobile Open Source Technologies, *IFIP Advances in Information and Communication Technology,* 427, 133-142.

[33] Nascimento, D.M., Cox, K., Almeida, T., Sampaio, W., Bittencourt, R.A., Souza, R., and Chavez, C. 2013. Using Open Source Projects in software engineering education: A systematic mapping study. *In IEEE Frontiers in Education Conference,* 2013 1837,1843, (Oct. 2013) 23-26. doi: 10.1109/FIE.2013.6685155

[34] NCWIT 2007 NCWIT Scorecard 2007: A Report on the Status of Women in Information Technology, National Center for Women and Information Technology, 2007.

[35] Noyes, K. 2011. Open Source Software is Now a Norm in Businesses. PC World, May 18, 2011 http://www.pcworld.com/article/228136/open_source_softwa re_now_a_norm_in_.html Retrieved 11/29/2014

[36] Pulimood, S.M. and Wolz, U. 2008. Problem Solving in Community: A Necessary Shift in CS Pedagogy. In *Proceedings of the 39th SIGCSE Technical Symposium on Computer Science Education* (Portland, OR, USA, March 12 – 15, 2008). SIGCSE '08. ACM, New York, NY, 210-214.

[37] Smith, T.M., McCartney, R., Gokhale, S.S., and Kaczmarczyk, L.C. 2014. Selecting open source software projects to teach software engineering. In *Proceedings of the 45th ACM technical symposium on Computer science education (SIGCSE '14).* ACM, New York, NY, USA, 397-402. DOI=10.1145/2538862.2538932 http://doi.acm.org/10.1145/2538862.2538932

[38] Tillberg, H.K. and Cohoon, J.M. 2005. Attaching Women to the CS Major, *Frontiers: A Journal of Women Studies,* 26, 1, 126-140.

[39] Toth, K. 2006. Experiences with Open Source Software Engineering Tools, *IEEE Software,* 23, 6 (Nov/Dec 2006) 44–52. http://doi.ieeecomputersociety.org/10.1109/MS.2006.158

[40] Xing, G. 2010. Teaching software engineering using open source software. In *Proceedings of the 48th Annual Southeast Regional Conference (ACM SE '10).* ACM, New York, NY, USA, Article 57, 3 pages. http://doi.acm.org/10.1145/1900008.1900085

Grounding Computational Thinking Skill Acquisition Through Contextualized Instruction

Hilarie Nickerson
University of Colorado - Boulder
Department of Computer Science
Boulder, CO 80303
+1 (303) 522-1444
hnickerson@colorado.edu

Catharine Brand
University of Colorado - Boulder
811 University Avenue
Boulder CO 80302
+1 (303) 601-9498
catharine.brand@gmail.com

Alexander Repenning
University of Colorado - Boulder
Department of Computer Science
Boulder, CO 80303
+1 (303) 492-1349
ralex@cs.colorado.edu

ABSTRACT

Computational thinking (CT) involves a broadly applicable and complex set of processes that are often explained by way of the knowledge, attitudes, and general practices that they entail. However, to become facile with CT, learners require instruction that is grounded in concrete, relevant experiences. This paper examines teacher practices that are intended to promote CT skill acquisition through instruction that takes place in two framing contexts. The phenomenological context, which is based on observable patterns of object interaction that recur in games and simulations, is particularly valuable for developing the capacity to think abstractly. Abstraction is the key to recognizing analogous conditions, an ability that is the basis for transferring learning to new situations. The disciplinary context describes areas of application within and across subject areas, including computer science, that can foster proficiency with data representation, problem decomposition, and other CT skills. Using the Scalable Game Design curriculum as a lens to examine classroom practices, we find that teachers both plan and enact CT instruction in these contexts.

Categories and Subject Descriptors

K.3.2 [**Computers and Education**]: Computer and Information Science Education – *curriculum, literacy*

General Terms

Design, Human Factors, Theory

Keywords

Computational Thinking; Contextualization; Scalable Game Design; Computational Thinking Patterns; Phenomenology; Simulation; Abstraction; Computer Science Education; STEM Education

1. INTRODUCTION

Definitions of computational thinking vary, but typical language is succinct and high level. For example, a frequently repeated description is that

"Computational Thinking is the thought processes involved in formulating problems and their solutions so that the solutions are represented in a form that can be effectively carried out by an information-processing agent." [14], as cited in [44]

In an effort to make such definitions more usable, the Computer Science Teachers Association (CSTA) and the International Society for Technology in Education (ISTE) produced a consensus-based list of problem-solving *skills* (e.g., "logically organizing and analyzing data") and *attitudes* (e.g., "tolerance for ambiguity") that characterize computational thinking [13]. The College Board's list of *computational thinking practices* and *big ideas* for the upcoming AP® Computer Science Principles curriculum is similarly abstract for the most part, although a few identifiable technologies are included (e.g., the Internet, the Global Positioning System, 3D printers) [39]. Brennan and Resnick [10] found that children who engage in interactive media development use computational *concepts* and *practices*, and also alter certain *perspectives* (e.g., creative expression, social connection). Overall, these frameworks provide guidance regarding general elements of computational thinking.

As with most subjects, grounding computational thinking instruction within *concrete, relevant application contexts* is expected to enhance learning [29]. Such contexts include courses and units devoted to specific academic disciplines, including computer science and technology education, and to cross-curricular skills. Rich opportunities exist within these settings for students to participate in activities and to work with tools that are intended to develop the desired abilities, knowledge, and habits of mind. To that end, there have been a number of efforts to create context-specific materials for classroom activities that promote computational thinking skill acquisition and application.

Simply having access to pedagogical materials is not necessarily sufficient. Teachers must also learn to use these materials effectively, particularly for computational thinking instruction because it is a new area that is being integrated into their current practice. Although teaching computational thinking does consume class time, the learners' increased ability to solve problems on their own provides a more satisfying experience for both teachers and students. In addition, educational leaders must be prepared to develop and implement supportive policies, working in concert with the computer science community [3].

In this paper we examine the scope of available tools and approaches for computational thinking instruction, describe a framework that relates two contexts used to frame instruction to the potential for learning different sets of computational thinking concepts, and explore how teachers employing a computational thinking curriculum known as Scalable Game Design are using these contexts in their teaching.

2. THE COMPUTATIONAL THINKING INSTRUCTION LANDSCAPE

Over the past few years, programs to instill computational thinking skills in students of all ages have arisen, backed by high profile public and private organizations. Some emphasize computing experiences, while others are drawn from different disciplines. Using visual programming environments to meet selected programmatic objectives is a popular tactic.

2.1 Programmatic Approaches

Instructional materials for K–12 students are available from a variety of sources. For students in high school courses that have a computer science emphasis, several complete curricula are being developed that include focused activities plus ancillary material such as lesson plans and quizzes. For example, *Thriving in Our Digital World* [32] was designed with the support of the National Science Foundation (United States) with the Computer Science Principles framework in mind. In New Zealand, the content of the *NZ Computer Science Field Guide* is based on national standards that were influenced by the 2008 release of the ACM / IEEE-CS computer science curriculum guidelines for undergraduate programs [7]. In these curricula, computational thinking topics may be covered directly or addressed within application areas such as artificial intelligence and computer graphics. Teachers will be able to use these comprehensive resources as provided or select content of interest.

Younger students are more likely to encounter general computational thinking instruction in brief units integrated into other learning experiences such as their elementary school classes or middle school technology courses. The organization Code.org has been spearheading an initiative aimed at K–8 educators to support student exploration of four computational thinking concepts—decomposition, patterns, abstraction, and algorithms—along with computer science familiarization and programming concepts [12]. The lessons incorporate selected activities from Computer Science Unplugged, a set of engaging exercises that teach computing and computational thinking ideas without the use of computers [8].

Students can also acquire computational thinking skills through activities that promote learning in academic subject areas other than computer science and technology. The collection of teacher resources provided by CSTA and ISTE [13] offers numerous brief subject-oriented examples linked to particular grade levels and computational thinking skills as well as nine extended sample lesson plans that emphasize language arts, science, mathematics, social studies, and research skills. In the near future, it is likely that a proliferation of instructional resources prompted by interest in the Next Generation Science Standards (NGSS) [30] will appear. These standards cover essential STEM practices, concepts, and discipline-specific ideas, stipulating how students can demonstrate their understanding of this content. The standards do not prescribe curricular or teaching approaches, which have been left to government bodies and educators to develop over the next several years with the help of emerging professional development resources (e.g., [11, 27]). NGSS competencies relating to computational thinking include the use of data, developing algorithms, and working with and creating simulations.

At the college level, the computer science curricular recommendations that are jointly developed and maintained by ACM and the IEEE Computer Society serve as a recognized international standard [40]. Most recently updated in 2013, these guidelines describe the scope of knowledge and skills that should be mastered by tomorrow's computing practitioners and researchers, including those who will work in non-computing domains, and provide a wealth of implementation ideas for educational institutions. The report suggests in passing that computational thinking concepts can be acquired by college students who take introductory computer science courses intended for non-majors, and subtly implies that students in computer science programs will be exposed to the relevant information. The main reference to computational thinking for majors occurs in the computational science context, an area of knowledge that was added to the recommendations in the most recent revision.

2.2 Learning Environments

Instructors have access to quite a large number of learning environments and tools that have been developed specifically to teach programming, computational thinking, or otherwise introduce computing-related concepts. General categories include 1) authoring environments running on a variety of computing platforms that support visual programming, game design, and simulation development and 2) physical / tangible computing kits for working with robots, microcontrollers, and other devices [17, 23]. This section highlights a subset of authoring environments for which computational thinking connections have been explored in the literature.[1]

The visual programming interfaces provided by Alice, Scratch, and Stagecast Creator are intended to support animated storytelling and related activities such as game creation. Alice's 3D environment is designed to teach object-oriented concepts. Controlling 2D sprites is the essence of Scratch, which includes capabilities for manipulating sound, images, and video to create art and media projects. Additional emphases include learning through experimentation and through social learning, supported by an active content sharing community [35]. Stagecast Creator, which also offers a 2D experience, uses programming by demonstration to create rules for its characters. With appropriate scaffolding provided by instructors and supporting materials, use of these environments is thought to give students practice with several areas of computational thinking suggested by CSTA and ISTE [13]: problem decomposition, abstraction, data analysis and representation, algorithmic thinking, and parallelization [15, 43, 46].

Working with and/or designing simulations adds two more computational thinking skills to the above list: data collection, and modeling and simulation [13]. Although simulations can be created with general visual programming software, purpose-built tools that facilitate the collection and analysis of generated data often enable deeper investigations that make use of computational science techniques. The CTSiM environment offers a dual approach to computational thinking for middle school students, incorporating aspects of program design and scientific inquiry [38]. Currently, agent-based kinematics and ecology simulation modules are available, supporting the development of computational thinking skills through a cycle of model definition, visualization, analysis, and refinement.

Learners working in the AgentSheets (2D) and AgentCubes (3D) environments use visual programming techniques to specify agent behaviors, potentially allowing them to produce a broad range of

---

[1] Additional tools with promise but less formal support include Kodu, Game Maker, and Gamestar Mechanic.

designs ranging from simple games to sophisticated computational science simulations that offer plotting and data export capabilities [33, 34]. An associated curriculum, Scalable Game Design (SGD), recommends skill progression pathways and facilitates progress. SGD researchers have been investigating a paradigm known as *computational thinking patterns* (CTPs)[2] that fosters the growth of transferable computational thinking skills [5].

3. A CONTEXTUALIZATION FRAMEWORK FOR GROUNDING CT LEARNING EXPERIENCES

Although few countries have mandated computer science education, both standards organizations and leading researchers are suggesting that computational thinking should become a required core competency [17, 30, 45]. While it remains to be seen how such a scenario might play out, it is clear that teacher professional development will be a crucial component. Some teachers may be comfortable sorting through the ever-increasing selection of resources and authoring environments on their own, but most will desire a more focused introduction to the topic in order to become familiar with the range of computational thinking competency areas and to identify instructional materials and methods that will be successful in their own classrooms. They will need to learn how ground their instruction in specific application contexts in order to effectively promote student learning.

Through our work offering professional development with the Scalable Game Design curriculum and supporting teachers who are implementing SGD activities, we have identified a framework for thinking about two meaningful application contexts that can be used to frame computational thinking instruction. One is the *phenomenological* context, which is based on observable patterns of object interaction that recur in games and simulations (e.g., collisions). Fun activities in school settings—designing games, for instance—are often thought of as stepping stones to desirable outcomes such as increasing student interest or learning to use a tool or technique that will be applied in a more serious context. We have found that game design on its own is both fun and valuable for developing computational thinking skills. The transferability of phenomenological patterns to interpreting and designing simulations is a bonus. The *disciplinary* context describes areas of application within and across subject areas. As shown by the broad scope of the CSTA / ISTE sample lesson plans [13] mentioned above, it is both possible and constructive to offer computational thinking activities across the curriculum. Depending on which computational thinking constructs are to be learned and what other learning goals are important, teachers may wish to focus on one or both of the above contexts, as explained below.

We believe that this framework will be relevant for thinking about instruction using other creative and computational science-based authoring environments, as well as for teachers who intend to incorporate computational thinking into their classes through the use of standalone activities. This section explains the framework in detail, and the next one reports our findings regarding instructional planning and practices within SGD classrooms as viewed through the framework.

---

[2] As a result of ongoing research in SGD, the list and descriptions of computational thinking patterns are continually being refined (fourteen are listed in the scope and sequence document [36]). Recommended references include [5, 6, 19].

3.1 The Phenomenological Context: Computational Thinking Patterns

Many games and simulations involve physical interactions between objects: Pacman eating a power pill (or predators eating other animals in an ecosystem), a ball hitting a paddle in Breakout (or molecules colliding with the side of a container), the head segment in Centipede pulling body segments behind it (or a tugboat pulling a ship). These kinds of observable phenomena are the basis for Scalable Game Design's computational thinking patterns, which were derived by applying and extending Michotte's work on the perception of causality [25] to the actions found in games and simulations [19]. Patterns are named to make it possible to more easily describe phenomena that recur in multiple situations, providing a scaffold for students to recognize the commonalities among these situations and thereby use the key computational thinking skill of abstraction [17, 22, 24, 45]. The examples above are examples of the patterns called *absorb*, *collision*, and *pull*, respectively.

Like other recurring patterns, computational thinking patterns are a kind of design pattern. First introduced by Christopher Alexander and colleagues in the urban planning and architectural design context [1], design patterns and pattern languages provide information about commonly encountered problems and solutions used by practitioners in a domain. Abstractions identified as design patterns have been applied in other computing-related contexts including software engineering [16] and human-computer interaction [9].

How can a pattern language-like assembly of CTPs support student learning? Identifying a CTP provides an easy way for students to discuss a chunk of code without getting lost in the details. "Do your tunnels absorb properly?" is a meaningful question frequently heard in SGD classrooms. The individual programming constructs in AgentSheets/Cubes can be used in an uncountable number of ways: that's their power for a knowledgeable programmer and their weakness from the point of view of the learner. CTPs provide an intermediate level at which to specify requirements or describe a solution. Without providing students an exact answer to copy, a teacher can employ CTPs to guide learners towards a good solution.

The Scalable Game Design curriculum begins with building the game Frogger, a process that introduces the definitions and underlying rule-based implementations of three fundamental computational thinking patterns that are widely applicable within other games and simulations—generation, absorption, and collision—plus the transport pattern [5]. Tunnels *generate* and *absorb* trucks, which may *collide* with the frog, who is able to be *transported* by logs floating in the river. Students are encouraged to think about the similarities between tunnels and islands, which generate and absorb the river logs.

With respect to pattern implementation, observing that two situations are analogous can be extremely helpful, making the phenomenological context valuable in two ways. First, within a single development environment, knowledge of the technique used to implement a pattern in one situation supports the ability to implement the same pattern when it is needed in a new situation. This holds true for both simple and complex patterns, though students will need to think more deeply about the mapping as complexity increases or the situations become more different. Figure 1 shows how the absorb CTP is implemented with an AgentSheets rule in the Frogger game and in Predator Prey, an ecosystem simulation. Note that the rules are similar except for their referents (truck, tunnel → small fish, large fish).

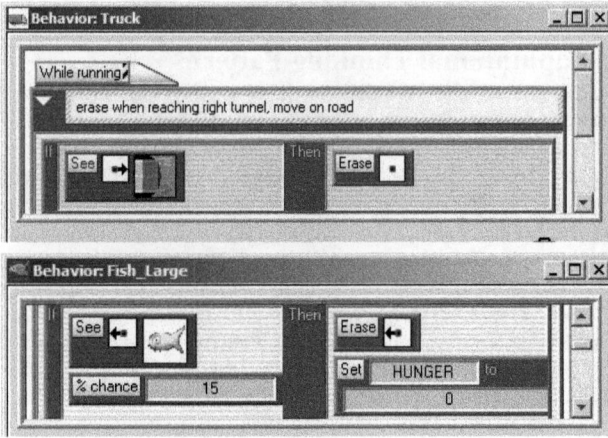

Figure 1. Comparison of implementation rules for the *absorb* computational thinking pattern in a game (Frogger) and simulation (Predator Prey).

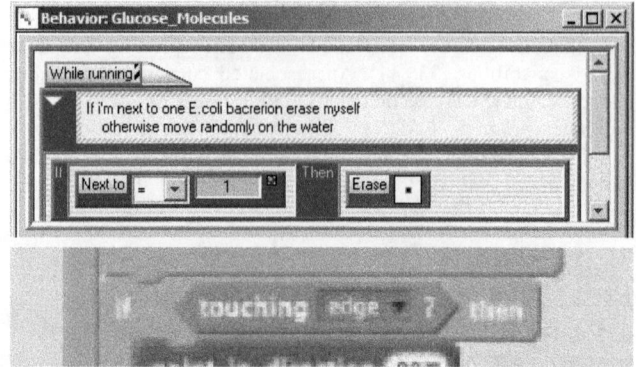

Figure 2. Comparison of implementation rules for the *collision* computational thinking pattern in AgentSheets and Scratch.

In [20] there is an example of student work showing how patterns present in two games, Sokoban and Sims, appeared in combination in a chaos theory simulation subsequently created by the same individual. A later study showed a strong correlation between the ability to incorporate CTPs in the first few projects in a course with the ability demonstrated in the final project [21]. Especially when the implementations of individual patterns is complex, these kinds of outcomes provide strong evidence that the phenomenological context contributes to student success by promoting abstract thinking.

Second, when moving between development environments, understanding the meaning of a computational thinking pattern should allow it to be operationalized more easily in the new setting. Consider the collision CTP, which describes the situation in which two entities run into each other (ball and paddle, molecule and container) and some further action results. In Scratch, *collide* has been identified as one of six *design pattern variables*, which are "contextual proficiencies based around common coding patterns" that can be implemented with varying levels of sophistication [37]. A student who understands the concept underlying collision detection, which is an adjacency test, should recognize that the *next to* condition of AgentSheets/Cubes implements that test (Figure 2a). Moving to Scratch, the student looking for a way to test adjacency should be able to identify the *if touching* block as a suitable option (Figure 2b). More importantly, the student should also be able to implement other CTPs in Scratch for which there are no corresponding design pattern variables.

The above examples of taking what has been learned in one setting and applying it to a second show some potential possibilities for near transfer. Although transfer ought to be facilitated by skill in abstraction learned through experience with the phenomenological context, it is not a given [2, 28]. Transfer is more likely when teachers guide students to develop their understanding rather than presenting prescriptive instructions and when they provide opportunities to see multiple applications of individual CTPs. Becoming a flexible computational thinker in the broader sense depends on mindfully practicing one's skills in a variety of contexts [29].

Computational thinking patterns represent just one level of abstraction. Classifying the patterns in terms of goals that would apply outside the game and simulation design context leads to a

higher level of abstract thinking. For example, one of the more complex patterns is the *hill climbing* CTP, which is typically used in connection with the *diffusion* CTP. Hill climbing can be classified as a form of searching; it is not the only available search algorithm. Note that search itself is a concept, not an algorithm. Also, more advanced students can examine the recommended implementation of diffusion versus a more general mathematical description of diffusion. Through discussion and additional examples, teachers can help students to understand the idea of an algorithm (another important computational thinking construct), explore different kinds of algorithms (e.g., searching, sorting), and consider applications of the hill climbing and diffusion patterns within and beyond the phenomenological context.

It is important to recognize that CTPs have some inherent limitations. Returning to the description of collision provided earlier—*two entities run into each other and some further action results*—it is clear that there is some overlap with absorb. With collision both objects survive, but with absorb one of them vanishes. The existence of adjacency provides some initial information about the phenomenon at hand, and the *running into* in the description implies the type of interaction that humans recognize as collision. In discussions of brief video clips showing real-world activity that is intended to illustrate a particular CTP, we have found that both students and teachers generally identify additional, less prominent phenomena that correspond to other CTPs. Although CTPs are, by nature, not all conceptually orthogonal, this situation does not diminish their usefulness as high-level descriptors.

A second limitation is that the current set of CTPs is merely a starting point. As we observe in classrooms, examine student projects, and monitor the introduction of new software and hardware, we expect to see new CTPs emerge. For example, the possibilities for interaction-related CTPs are expanding. In addition to the original *cursor control* CTP, which is suitable for two-dimensional games with birds-eye or side views, we must now consider the somewhat different behavioral expectations that result from entering a first-person view available only in a three-dimensional environment. For mobile hardware that lacks cursor keys altogether but might offer tilt and gesture sensors, are there new CTPs waiting to be discovered? Clicking on or touching an agent is yet another alternative for interacting with it, and this type of action has not yet been formalized into a CTP.

3.2 The Disciplinary Context: Subject Area Content

"Teaching computational thinking … is to teach [learners] how to think like an economist, a physicist, an artist, and to understand how to use computation to solve their problems, to create, and to discover new questions that can fruitfully be explored." [18]

In addition to the phenomenological context, students experience a disciplinary context surrounding the game or simulation design and development process. As a curriculum that promotes computational thinking and that has high appeal across demographic groups, Scalable Game Design is typically adopted for use during the regular school day and applied within a broad variety of subject areas [4, 42]. While this curriculum is most frequently found in technology education and STEM-focused classes, teachers from art, foreign language, and other fields have also brought SGD to their students. Other visual programming tools are also used in diverse disciplinary settings. The discussion of the phenomenological context showed its relevance to learning about abstraction and algorithms, and the disciplinary context offers the opportunity to consider additional areas of computational thinking such as data representation, problem decomposition, and parallelization.

Recall the three skill areas stressed in the Next Generation Science Standards [29]: data, algorithms, and simulation. Thoughtfully creating and running a simulation in any subject would be expected to provide practice with these areas. Imagine a teacher suggesting that students create a carbon cycle simulation in response to standard HS-ESS3-6: *Use a computational representation to illustrate the relationships among Earth systems and how those relationships are being modified due to human activity.* In completing this assignment, students would gain the desired computational thinking experience while considering which aspects of the cycle to incorporate, how to represent those aspects in the simulation tool, how the movement of the carbon would be controlled, which variables should be included in the simulation, and what the results mean.

Note that design-related activities for both games and simulations can also be used to address disciplinary learning goals that are unrelated or only peripherally related to computational thinking. As an example, a planning activity within the Frogger curriculum [26] suggests that students "identify game objects, called agents, by locating nouns in the game description" (p. 8) and "identify agent interaction by locating verbs in the game description" (p. 9). The verbs describing "agent interaction" are not necessarily the same as the computational thinking patterns that they denote, and teachers are expected to help students acquire the appropriate vocabulary. In a language arts class, the teacher could extend this activity further. A second example of a disciplinary connection involves the use of probability, which we have seen teachers link to instruction in math and other STEM fields. In Frogger, the game is more fun if the pattern of vehicles being generated by the tunnels is unpredictable, which students can accomplish by including a probability condition in the rule for the generation pattern. It is up to teachers to decide how to balance emphasis on computational thinking and on disciplinary constructs in any given activity.

One subject area to keep in mind is computer science (CS), which is present to some extent in when using any game or simulation development software. Students who are scripting and programming learn ideas about computing that increase their general knowledge of the field, including the operation of rule- and object-based systems, local and global variables, iteration, and function calling. Additional CS subject area content includes exposure to disciplinary practices such as debugging and pair programming, which connect nicely to selected computational thinking dispositions in the framework developed by CSTA & ISTE [13]. These are "persistence in working with difficult problems" and "the ability to communicate and work with others to achieve a common goal or solution" (p. 7).

4. SITUATING TEACHER PRACTICE WITHIN THE CONTEXTUALIZATION FRAMEWORK

In order to understand how the above framework might be used to characterize what goes on during computational thinking instruction, we undertook a study that examined two aspects of teacher practice: planning and implementation. In this section we report case study data gleaned by observing Scalable Game Design classrooms, interviewing teachers, and analyzing a selection of instructional planning documents, revealing how teachers and learners are using phenomenological and disciplinary contextualization within SGD-related activities.

Approximately sixty classroom observations were carried out during the 2014–15 school year using an instrument called SCOPE [41] that is designed specifically for data collection relevant to computer science instruction in a physical lab or classroom setting. Use of this tool provides insight into teachers' pedagogical approaches, allowing observers to capture information about the nature of classroom interactions and the degree to which a class is conducted in a teacher- versus student-centered manner. Other portions of the tool address CS and non-CS content emphases and learning goals (e.g., *how* to handle a matter in a particular way, versus *why* to do so). We were able to record the size of instructional groups (individual, small group, or whole class), the types of computing-related activities in which students were engaged (e.g., planning, programming, testing), the nature of instructional resources made available to students, and multiple aspects of discourse among teachers and students including topic generation and uptake, help-seeking behavior, and referencing computational thinking patterns.

The SCOPE form is based on scales, checklists, and short answer fields, supported by optional comment blocks for individual items and general observations. A guide for a brief semi-structured post-observation teacher interview was added midway through the year. The descriptions below combine information captured through SCOPE with additional material provided by observers and interviewers. Observers went to classrooms alone or in teams, often making video recordings for later review. Printed versions of the SCOPE observation forms provided space for field notes, and this information was later entered into an electronic version of the form. Teachers tended to volunteer information that was not on the form, and this information became part of the observers' notes.

Unit and lesson plans serve as another source of information regarding teacher thoughts and practices. An experienced SGD researcher examined materials from thirty teachers / groups, ranging from single pages to entire websites, and found several themes of interest relating to contextualization and computational thinking that are described in section 4.2. These materials were shared with us over a period of several years, typically during our annual professional development event.

4.1 Emphasizing the Phenomenological Context in the Classroom

In this section we offer two examples of teachers who successfully introduced computational thinking patterns to their classes. Like a pattern language, these new language elements gave students ways to describe and evaluate the multiple behaviors of their programs without needing to specify every detail of the code. A visitor to both these teachers' classrooms is struck by the sight of middle school students effectively collaborating in a buzz of quiet conversation as they focus all their efforts on producing colorful and complete video games before the period comes to an end.

MQ teaches the twice-a-week technology class required for all students at a middle school in a small mountain town. A programmer by training, she began as a school district IT specialist and then took a teaching position because she enjoys working with middle school children. Her classroom is decorated with big posters of CTPs that she designed herself (Figure 3). She uses these posters to introduce her students to the language of computational thinking patterns and the phenomena they describe.

When her students reach the point in building a game where they need to use a particular CTP, she has them look at and discuss the relevant poster as a group. Each poster contains a description of the CTP using the objects in the game in which the students will first use it. The natural language description is followed by real world examples, which MQ noted were the most important aspect of the poster to her. Then the code that embodies the CTP appears along with a matching structured English sentence. MQ teaches CTPs by linking the code to the students' everyday experiences and their ordinary non-technical language.

MQ succeeded in teaching her students to describe the behaviors encoded in their programs according to the CTPs that they represent. They internalized the CTPs so well that they could

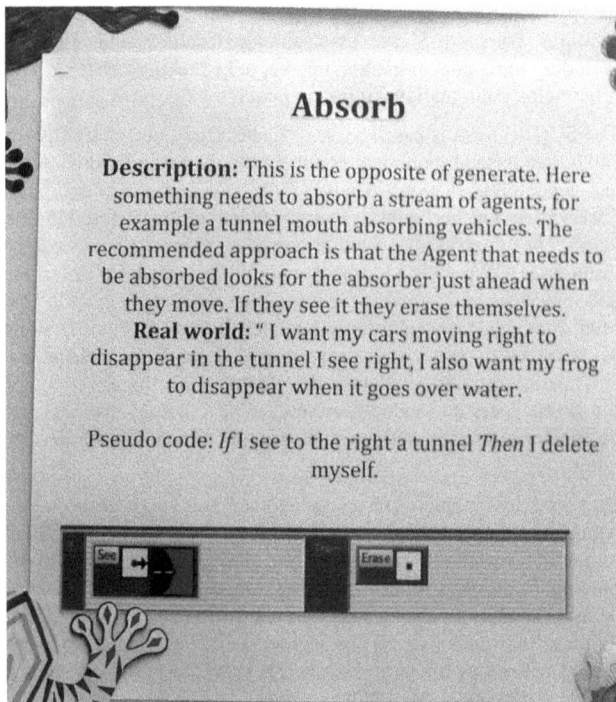

Figure 3. A teacher-created poster describing the Absorb CTP as it is used in the game Frogger. ©MQ

employ them to conduct peer assessments of each other's games. One student would run a game while the assessing student checked off the CTPs that were used correctly in the game. A sample check-off item reads as follows: "8) Turtle agent moves to the left, generates at a reasonable rate, and absorbs at the end of the water." Here, MQ uses the CTPs to specify a solution to a problem without needing to include the details of the code. And her students all understand this language. They were able to complete an assessment with 14 items of this type in twenty minutes.

BW is an art teacher who loves technology and comic book illustration. He teaches elective classes in game design to students at a middle school on a US military base. Less academically-oriented students choose his class instead of a foreign language or instrumental music elective. As the children of parents in the military, they have moved frequently and attended many different schools. Roughly half of the students are Hispanic, African-American or Asian-American.

BW carefully incorporates computational thinking patterns into his students' game building. He begins the first game, Frogger, with direct instruction using a practice project as a low-key fun setting. The students learn to make a simple agent (a colored box with a funny face) move in 4 directions (the key-controlled movement CTP). Agent movement via keystrokes is common to many games, so understanding this CTP as a reusable pattern is extremely helpful. Then BW demonstrates the CTPs that he would like them to create, e.g., a tunnel that generates trucks that run along a road and are absorbed by another tunnel, and challenges them to recreate the behavior in their sandbox project, working in pairs. He projects hints on the screen at regular intervals to help the students move through their task. When a team finishes, the members get up and help other students complete the task. Next, team members are assigned responsibility for different CTPs carried out by the various agents in the actual Frogger game. Each team member must construct a DIY tutorial for their task by copying code drawn from tutorials on the SGD wiki and adding their own explanations. The students use their tutorials to teach their team members how to build part of the game. By the end of this process, every student has a complete Frogger game.

BW tests his students' learning of computational thinking patterns by asking them to create a game, Dungeon Adventure, that employs all the computational thinking patterns that they have learned in a new context. His students are so familiar with the language of CTPs that the rubric can mix ordinary language such as "Monsters die when hit by arrows" (collision CTP) with the verbs closely associated with CTPs such as "Arrows delete when colliding with walls and monsters" (collision CTP again). The students may help each other and use the tutorials that they and their friends have written for earlier games as references. BW troubleshoots hardware problems but does not answer questions about their Dungeon Adventure programs. This semester, the student average grade for this assessment was 86%. Using computational thinking patterns to describe the game behaviors that the students must create narrows the solution space and guides the students towards creating games that function in a similar way. This similarity enables the students to help each other effectively.

A further example of how students are able to rely on abstraction skills learned from the phenomenological context comes from a third grade classroom in which students worked in pairs to build Frogger games. One pair, who had started by creating a standard game with the usual obstacles (road with vehicles, river with logs

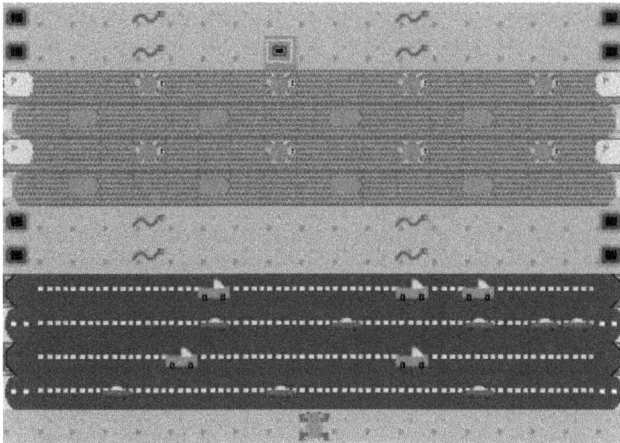

Figure 4. A Frogger game created by elementary students with holes to generate and absorb snakes.

and turtles) went on to invent and add an analogous obstacle to the game that challenged the player with snakes in the grass that are generated and absorbed by holes (Figure 4).

4.2 Implementation Planning for the Disciplinary Context

Although we conducted a few observations of teachers in academic disciplines other than computer science and technology education, our observations occurred while students were still becoming familiar with the software and we saw almost no instances in which teachers emphasized their core subject areas. Therefore, the information reported here regarding the disciplinary context is based on instructional planning documents. Our overall review of these materials was revealing. In addition to the expected mentions of computational thinking patterns, which relate to the phenomenological context, we found an assortment of discipline-related elements, both anticipated and unanticipated. Many teachers referred to relevant standards (perhaps prompted by planning rubrics); planned to develop connections to student experiences in the real world through familiar examples, videos, and hand simulations; and introduced domain-independent STEM concepts (e.g., chaos, variance). The disciplines of computing and gaming were represented through concepts such as design, programming, debugging, artificial intelligence, game objectives, and NPCs (non-player characters). Surprising areas of application included Rock / Paper / Scissors as the basis of a data collection exercise and a supply and demand simulation that brought together economics and history.

As a more detailed example of the disciplinary context in planning, here we 1) report the recommendations of another teacher training organization with respect to the SGD Forest Fire simulation and 2) compare a Forest Fire plan created by an individual teacher who had no connection with that organization. The organization identified cross-disciplinary content, including probability, chaos, and variance, that learners could come to understand through forest fire modeling and simulation. They recommended that classes first review prerequisite math and science concepts and then undertake a hand simulation process using a paper grid and dice, focusing on the probability of unharmed trees catching fire from adjacent burning trees. With the subsequently created computer-based simulation, both the factors affecting the spread of the fire and its effect on animals were to be considered. Teachers were instructed to point out that computer

modeling is helpful for pattern identification. They also suggested having students evaluate each other's work in order to check competency with respect to additional computational thinking concepts (e.g., algorithms, data representation).

The individual teacher, CH, wrote of her plans for a scientific investigation unit in a ninth grade course covering earth and space science. As the first activity, students would repeatedly run a pre-built simulation of how a forest fire spreads and write about their observations. This initial approach is somewhat different from that suggested above, but both offer opportunities for active learning and reflection that are in keeping with the advice of the Next Generation Science Standards [30]. Next, the class would discuss what might control fire spreading behavior (as suggested above) and compare simulations to games to identify similarities and differences. Using their knowledge of computational thinking patterns attained from an earlier SGD experience, the students would then write a specification for their own forest fire simulations. Since unfamiliar computational thinking patterns would be needed, the teacher would provide a worksheet with guiding questions to assist students with programming. Finally, students would propose and test hypotheses about how to minimize spreading under different forest conditions (e.g., moisture levels, forest density, and the presence of fire breaks). Here CH is less explicit regarding the acquisition of specific computational thinking skills, though they are covered.

4.3 Bridging the Contexts

Several of the teachers we work with have come up with clever methods of connecting the disciplinary and phenomenological contexts. Here we highlight two ideas that were shared with us, which are representative of the kinds of experiences that teachers develop for their students. One teacher, MM, explained her plan to introduce the diffusion computational thinking pattern by familiarizing students with its real-world counterpart. She selected a video in which drops of food coloring fall into a glass of water. The video not only demonstrates the phenomenon, but also goes on to show an experiment that helps to answer the question, "What causes diffusion?" by incorporating content from both physics and biology. Once students grasp the phenomenon, MM will move the discussion to the general principles of agent attributes and behavior that would support diffusion and finally to the mathematical representation needed to program diffusion in a game.

As a supplement to the usual SGD curriculum, a second teacher, AR, added a unit that leads her middle school students to consider how games and simulations differ, and developed an accompanying project called Lemmings to provide practice with simulation-oriented approaches to programming. In her class, which as a whole focuses on applications for scientific and mathematical concepts, students first learn to use an assortment of computational thinking patterns by progressing through a series of games. After that they design sophisticated original games before turning to simulation. To begin that discussion, AR shares materials that describe a current event that lends itself to being modeled, such as the spread of the Ebola virus, and shows an AgentSheets simulation of that concept that she has developed. Students then consider how simulations differ from games, brainstorm additional concepts that might or might not lend themselves to being modeled, and reflect on the reasons why.

One feature that often distinguishes simulations from games is that the movement of entities is internally motivated rather than being based on directional control provided by the user. The Lemmings design has both game- and simulation-like characteristics. There is a goal—lemming agents are to move from one area of the board to another—but users do not control this movement directly. While building Lemmings, students discover alternate forms of user interaction that can be used to change a lemming's internal state, which in turn controls its movement. At this point students are ready to develop a model for a construct of personal interest (sometimes based on disciplinary content from another current class) and to create their own simulations with which they gather, display, and interpret data. During her interview, AR expressed her excitement about the value of SGD activities for her students, pointing out that they learn problem-solving skills, understand a software tool that can be used to express their ideas in future endeavors, and are more prepared for career success because computer operation has been demystified.

5. DISCUSSION

The main message of this paper is that learning about computational thinking can be effectively accomplished in contexts that provide scaffolding for learning specific skills. The phenomenological context leads to an understanding of abstraction and algorithms, and the disciplinary context offers a pathway to competency in data representation, problem decomposition, and more.

To support learning in the phenomenological context, we purposefully teach computational thinking patterns to teachers as part of building games and simulations so that they can use this tool effectively with their students. Teachers often worry about how to answer all the questions their students will generate as they learn to use authoring environments such as AgentSheets/Cubes. CTPs provide a means for teachers and students to communicate about the functionality of a program without descending into the finer details of implementation. CTPs also help learners meet the challenge of increasingly difficult programming assignments because each new program does not need to be created *de novo*; instead, familiar CTPs can be combined with new ones to build a more complex program. Learners come to appreciate the flexibility and power of a programming environment as they use familiar CTPs in a new context; e.g., a *hierarchy of needs* can drive the Sims' behavior first and then motivate the animals in an ecosystem. Likewise, the transition from games to simulations can be eased if students have learned simulation-supportive CTPs such as *polling* and *perceive-act* through their game design activities.

A successful exercise in a disciplinary context depends on an individual teacher's background, content knowledge, and creativity. During our professional development activities, we seed teachers' imaginations by providing examples from a wide range of disciplines and offering a Creative Lab day where they can design and build their own games and simulations. At our annual training workshop, teachers who have successfully taught original projects in unusual content areas are invited to present their process and their students' work to event participants.

Disciplinary and computational thinking goals may be pursued in a coordinated fashion, as described above in section 3.2. However, learning subject area content does not necessarily lead to an abiding interest. Beyond increasing proficiency in computational thinking, encouraging students to continue studying computing and STEM fields is an important goal [31]. Having a reason to continue in courses that provide computational thinking benefits through multiple disciplinary contexts (computer science plus subject area) is an exciting possibility from both personal and societal perspectives. In the future we would like to gain a better understanding of differences in computational thinking goals set by technology teachers versus subject area teachers. We also intend to examine the role of contextual information in instructional resources provided to students.

6. ACKNOWLEDGEMENTS

This work is supported by the National Science Foundation under Grant Numbers DLR-0833612, IIP-0848962, and 1312129. Any opinions, findings, and conclusions or recommendations expressed in this material are those of the authors and do not necessarily reflect the views of the National Science Foundation.

7. REFERENCES

[1] Alexander, C. 1977. *A Pattern Language: Towns, Buildings, Construction*. Oxford University Press, New York.

[2] Barnett, S.M. and Ceci, S.J. 2002. When and where do we apply what we learn? A taxonomy for far transfer. *Psychol. Bull.* 128, 4 (Jul 2002), 612-637. DOI= http://dx.doi.org/10.1037/0033-2909.128.4.612.

[3] Barr, V. and Stephenson, C. 2011. Bringing computational thinking to K-12: What is involved and what is the role of the computer science education community? *ACM Inroads*. 2, 1 (Feb 2011), 48-54. DOI= http://dx.doi.org/10.1145/1929887.1929905.

[4] Basawapatna, A., Koh, K.H., Repenning, A., Webb, D.C., and Marshall, K.S. 2011. Recognizing computational thinking patterns. In *Proceedings of the 42nd ACM Technical Symposium on Computer Science Education*. ACM, New York, 245-250. DOI= http://dx.doi.org/10.1145/1953163.1953241.

[5] Basawapatna, A.R., Koh, K.H., and Repenning, A. 2010. Using Scalable Game Design to teach computer science from middle school to graduate school. In *Proceedings of the Fifteenth Annual Conference on Innovation and Technology in Computer Science Education*. ACM, New York, 224-228. DOI= http://dx.doi.org/10.1145/1822090.1822154.

[6] Basawapatna, A.R., Repenning, A., and Lewis, C.H. 2013. The Simulation Creation Toolkit: An initial exploration into making programming accessible while preserving computational thinking. In *Proceeding of the 44th ACM Technical Symposium on Computer Science Education*. ACM, New York, 501-506. DOI= http://dx.doi.org/10.1145/2445196.2445346.

[7] Bell, T., Duncan, C., Jarman, S., and Newton, H. 2014. Presenting computer science concepts to high school students. *Olympiads in Informatics*. 8, (2014), 3-19.

[8] Bell, T.C., Witten, I.H., and Fellows, M.R. 1998. *Computer Science Unplugged: Off-Line Activities and Games for All Ages*. Computer Science Unplugged.

[9] Borchers, J. 2001. *A Pattern Approach to Interaction Design*. Wiley, New York.

[10] Brennan, K. and Resnick, M. 2012. New frameworks for studying and assessing the development of computational thinking. *Proceedings of the 2012 annual meeting of the American Educational Research Association, Vancouver, Canada*.

[11] Bybee, R.W. 2013. *Translating the NGSS for Classroom Instruction*. National Science Teachers Association Press, Arlington, VA.

[12] Code.org 2014. *Teach Our K-8 Intro to Computer Science*. http://code.org/educate/20hr.

[13] Computer Science Teachers Association (CSTA) and International Society for Technology in Education (ISTE) 2011. *Computational Thinking in K–12 Education: Teacher Resources*. Authors, Washington, DC.

[14] Cuny, J., Snyder, L., and Wing, J.M. 2010. *Demystifying Computational Thinking for Non–Computer Scientists (work in progress)*. (2010).

[15] Denner, J., Werner, L., and Ortiz, E. 2012. Computer games created by middle school girls: Can they be used to measure understanding of computer science concepts? *Comput. Educ.* 58, 1 (Jan 2012), 240-249. DOI= http://dx.doi.org/10.1016/j.compedu.2011.08.006.

[16] Gamma, E., Helm, R., Johnson, R., and Vlissides, J. 1995. *Design Patterns: Elements of Reusable Object-Oriented Software*. Addison-Wesley, Reading, MA.

[17] Grover, S. and Pea, R. 2013. Computational Thinking in K–12: A review of the state of the field. *Educational Researcher*. 42, 1 (2013), 38-43. DOI= http://dx.doi.org/10.3102/0013189X12463051.

[18] Hemmendinger, D. 2010. A plea for modesty. *ACM Inroads*. 1, 2 (Jun 2010), 4-7. DOI= http://dx.doi.org/10.1145/1805724.1805725.

[19] Ioannidou, A., Bennett, V., Repenning, A., Koh, K.H., and Basawapatna, A. 2011. Computational Thinking Patterns. *Annual Meeting of the American Educational Research Association (AERA)*.

[20] Koh, K.H., Basawapatna, A., Bennett, V., and Repenning, A. 2010. Towards the automatic recognition of computational thinking for adaptive visual language learning. *2010 IEEE Symposium on Visual Languages and Human-Centric Computing (VL/HCC)*. (Sep 2010), 59-66. DOI= http://dx.doi.org/10.1109/VLHCC.2010.17.

[21] Koh, K.H., Nickerson, H., Basawapatna, A., and Repenning, A. 2014. Early validation of computational thinking pattern analysis. In *Proceedings of the 2014 Conference on Innovation & Technology in Computer Science Education*. ACM, New York, 213-218. DOI= http://dx.doi.org/10.1145/2591708.2591724.

[22] Kramer, J. 2007. Is abstraction the key to computing? *Comm. ACM*. 50, 4 (Apr 2007), 36-42. DOI= http://dx.doi.org/10.1145/1232743.1232745.

[23] Lee, I., Martin, F., Denner, J., Coulter, B., Allan, W., Erickson, J., Malyn-Smith, J., and Werner, L. 2011. Computational thinking for youth in practice. *ACM Inroads*. 2, 1 (Feb 2011), 32-37. DOI= http://dx.doi.org/10.1145/1929887.1929902.

[24] Markman, A.B. and Ross, B.H. 2003. Category use and category learning. *Psychol. Bull.* 129, 4 (Jul 2003), 592-613. DOI= http://dx.doi.org/10.1037/0033-2909.129.4.592.

[25] Michotte, A. 1963. *The Perception of Causality*. Basic Books, New York.

[26] Miller, S. 2014. *Creating "Frogger"*. http://sgd.cs.colorado.edu/wiki/images/a/ac/Frogger_Master_v2.0.pdf.

[27] National Research Council 2015. *Guide to Implementing the Next Generation Science Standards*. National Academies Press, Washington, DC.

[28] National Research Council 2000. *How People Learn: Brain, Mind, Experience, and School: Expanded Edition*. National Academies Press, Washington, DC.

[29] National Research Council 2011. *Report of a Workshop on the Pedagogical Aspects of Computational Thinking*. National Academies Press, Washington, DC.

[30] NGSS Lead States 2013. *Next Generation Science Standards: For States, by States*. National Academies Press, Washington, DC.

[31] President's Council of Advisors on Science and Technology 2010. *Prepare and Inspire: K-12 Education in Science, Technology, Engineering, and Math (STEM) for America's Future*. Office of the President, Washington, DC.

[32] Project Engage 2014. *Thriving in Our Digital World*. http://www.cs.utexas.edu/~engage/.

[33] Repenning, A. 2013. Making programming accessible and exciting. *IEEE Computer*. 46, 6 (Jun 2013), 78-81. DOI= http://dx.doi.org/10.1109/MC.2013.214.

[34] Repenning, A., Webb, D., and Ioannidou, A. 2010. Scalable Game Design and the development of a checklist for getting computational thinking into public schools. In *Proceedings of the 41st ACM Technical Symposium on Computer Science Education*. ACM,265-269. DOI= http://dx.doi.org/10.1145/1734263.1734357.

[35] Resnick, M., Maloney, J., Monroy-Hernández, A., Rusk, N., Eastmond, E., Brennan, K., Millner, A., Rosenbaum, E., Silver, J., Silverman, B., and Kafai, Y. 2009. Scratch: programming for all. *Comm. ACM*. 52, 11 (Nov 2009), 60-67. DOI= http://dx.doi.org/10.1145/1592761.1592779.

[36] Scalable Game Design 2014. *Scope and Sequence v2.0*. http://sgd.cs.colorado.edu/wiki/images/8/86/Scope_and_Sequence_Master_v2.0.pdf.

[37] Seiter, L. and Foreman, B. 2013. Modeling the learning progressions of computational thinking of primary grade students. In *Proceedings of the Ninth Annual International ACM Conference on International Computing Education Research*. ACM, New York, 59-66. DOI= http://dx.doi.org/10.1145/2493394.2493403.

[38] Sengupta, P., Kinnebrew, J.S., Basu, S., Biswas, G., and Clark, D. 2013. Integrating computational thinking with K-12 science education using agent-based computation: A theoretical framework. *Educ. Inform. Tech.* 18, 2 (Jun 2013), 351-380. DOI= http://dx.doi.org/10.1007/s10639-012-9240-x.

[39] The College Board 2014. *AP® Computer Science Principles Curriculum Framework 2016–2017*. Author, New York.

[40] The Joint Task Force on Computing Curricula, Association for Computing Machinery (ACM), and IEEE Computer Society 2013. *Computer Science Curricula 2013: Curriculum Guidelines for Undergraduate Degree Programs in Computer Science*. ACM, New York.

[41] Webb, D.C., Miller, S.B., Nickerson, H., Grover, R., and Gutiérrez, K. 2014. *Student Centered Observation Protocol for computer-science Education (SCOPE)*. University of Colorado Boulder.

[42] Webb, D.C., Repenning, A., and Koh, K.H. 2012. Toward an emergent theory of broadening participation in computer science education. In *Proceedings of the 43rd ACM Technical Symposium on Computer Science Education*. ACM, New York, 173-178. DOI= http://dx.doi.org/10.1145/2157136.2157191.

[43] Werner, L., Denner, J., Campe, S., and Kawamoto, D.C. 2012. The Fairy Performance Assessment: Measuring computational thinking in middle school. In *Proceedings of the 43rd ACM Technical Symposium on Computer Science Education*. ACM, 215-220. DOI= http://dx.doi.org/10.1145/2157136.2157200.

[44] Wing, J.M. 2011. Computational thinking: What and why? *The Link*. 6.0, (2011), 20-23.

[45] Wing, J.M. 2008. Computational thinking and thinking about computing. *Philosophical Transactions of the Royal Society A: Mathematical, Physical and Engineering Sciences*. 366, 1881 (Oct 2008), 3717-3725.

[46] Wu, M.L. and Richards, K. 2011. Facilitating computational thinking through game design. *Edutainment Technologies. Educational Games and Virtual Reality/Augmented Reality Applications*. M. Chang, W.-Y. Hwang, M.-P. Chen and W. Mueller, editor. Springer, Berlin. 220-227.

An Empirical Study of In-Class Laboratories on Student Learning of Linear Data Structures

Sarah Heckman
North Carolina State University
Raleigh, NC
sarah_heckman@ncsu.edu

ABSTRACT

Active learning increases student learning through collaborative engagement with materials during class time. A CS1.5 course at NC State, CSC216, uses active learning lectures involving short simplified think-pair-share in-class exercises to engage students with course materials. However, students still struggle with the course materials and several students do not successfully complete the course on their first attempt. To increase student learning and engagement, we conducted a quasi-experimental study incorporating in-class labs into two sections of CSC216 during the linear data structures unit in the Fall 2014 semester. Both sections completed in-class labs on the Java Collections Framework and iterators. One section completed in-class labs on array-based lists; the other section completed in-class labs on linked lists, in a counter-balanced study design. The active learning lecture delivery was used for the control section and an Exam was administered between the array-based list and linked list topics. Overall, we found no significant difference in student learning on array-based and linked lists as measured by the final exam. Students displayed half as much disengaged behavior during in-class labs and were five times more likely to ask for help from the teaching staff during in-class labs.

Categories and Subject Descriptors

K.3.2 [**Computers and Education**]: Computer and Information Science Education – *computer science education.*

General Terms

Experimentation

Keywords

In-class labs; empirical computer science education; linear data structures; CS1.5

1. INTRODUCTION

Students struggle with the material in CSC216: Programming Concepts – Java, a second semester CS1.5 programming course for computer science majors and minors at North Carolina State University. While a large majority of students successfully complete CSC216 on a first or second attempt, many students report difficulty with the coursework throughout the semester.

ICER '15, August 9-13, 2015, Omaha, NE, USA.
Copyright is held by the owner/author(s). Publication rights licensed to ACM.
ACM 978-1-4503-3630-7/15/08...$15.00.
DOI: http://dx.doi.org/10.1145/2787622.2787713

The prerequisite course of CSC216 is CSC116: Introduction to Programming – Java, a first semester introductory programming course taught in Java[1] with a use objects early, write objects late paradigm. CSC116 is an integrated-lecture lab with at most 33 students in each of seven or eight sections. The class meets twice a week for 110 minutes and one instructor and two TAs are available to help students. CSC216 moves students into two large lecture sections of 70-100 students. There is one instructor per section (sometimes the same instructor for both sections) and three to four TAs pooled for the two sections. A common request on end of semester evaluations for CSC216 is an increase in the amount of in-class programming practice similar to the level in CSC116.

Research has shown that active learning, defined by Freeman et al. [9] as "engaging students in the process of learning through activities and/or discussion in class, as opposed to passively listening to an expert," increases student learning through collaborative engagement with materials during class time [1, 5, 7, 9, 13, 15]. CSC216 currently incorporates a simplified version of the active learning technique, think-pair-share [7, 14], where the emphasis is on the pair and share. However, many students still struggle in the course, and we hypothesize that active learning practices that involve larger problems would increase student learning and engagement.

The study in this paper reports on the use of in-class laboratories, as an inverted or flipped classroom experience [15], for a unit on linear data structures in CSC216. *The goal of our research is to increase student learning and engagement through in-class laboratories on linear data structures.* We conducted a counter-balanced study on the use of in-class laboratories on two sections of CSC216 taught by the author at the same time on different days during the Fall 2014 semester. We found no significant difference in student learning on linear data structure topics; however, we found a large increase in student engagement measured by counts of off topic behavior and student interactions with teaching staff as reported by external observers. However, many of the interactions with students during in-class labs were focused more on the technology used in the course than on the lab topics.

We contribute to the growth of theory in computing education research by building on the foundations of theoretical work [17] in active learning [1, 5, 7, 9, 13, 15]. Additionally, our work builds on a foundation of Bandura's self-efficacy theory [2]. By reporting null-results for learning, we provide more data about the landscape of active learning interventions [21]. The contributions are:

---

[1] Oracle's Java may be found at:
http://www.oracle.com/technetwork/java/index.html

- A replicable study methodology for assessing student learning and engagement when using in-class laboratory assignments.

- Additional data on the effectiveness of active learning activities, like think-pair-share exercises and in-class labs, on student learning and engagement.

This study is the first in a series of interventions focused on increasing student learning, engagement, and eventually completion through the incorporation of various active learning techniques and software engineering best practices into CSC216 coursework.

The rest of this paper is organized as follows: Section 2 describes related work; Section 3 describes the study methodology; Section 4 reports the results; Section 5 provides the threats to validity; Section 6 is a discussion of findings; and Section 7 concludes and presents future work.

2. RELATED WORK

A large meta-analysis on active learning in science, engineering, and mathematics found that active learning activities like think-pair-share [7, 14] and inverted or flipped classrooms support students learning, increase engagement, and reduce failure rates [9]. Freeman et al., [9] found that student performance on exams or concept inventories increased almost half of a standard deviation when using active learning as compared to traditional lecture. Kothiyal et al. [14] report an average 83% student engagement in lecture when using think-pair-share in CS1. These results are useful comparison points for our results.

Our delivery of in-class labs in CSC216 was modeled on the inverted or flipped classroom. Many CS researchers have investigated inverted classroom models in classes at various levels. Amresh et al., [1] conducted a preliminary study on the effectiveness of a flipped classroom in a CS1 for majors and non-majors. They found that students in the flipped sections of the course earned higher average scores. Student efficacy also increased, but the increase may be from other factors than just the course flip. Latulipe et al. [16] included lightweight teams and gamification in a flipped media computation class. Results show that lightweight teams enhanced student learning and increased course engagement. We used randomly assigned teams for in-class lab activities in CS1.5, but not the full lightweight team strategy.

Campbell et al., [5] reported on a study of inverting a CS1 course. They found that while fewer students attended the lectures in the inverted offering, more students completed the preparatory work including videos and quizzes, likely because the preparatory work counted for credit. Students also reported in a survey that they enjoyed the inverted model, but that they felt the course took more time. The authors found no significant difference in learning when compared with a traditional offering of the course. Horton et al., [12] continued the work by comparing a traditional and inverted CS1 course and reported similar pass rates, but a statically significant difference on final exam grade as a measure of student learning. We consider similar metrics for evaluation of our comparison of active learning lectures and in-class labs.

3. STUDY METHODOLOGY

The goal of our research is to increase student learning and engagement through in-class laboratories on linear data structures. We considered the following research questions:

RQ1: Do in-class laboratories on linear data structures increase student learning on linear data structure exam questions when compared to active learning lectures?

RQ2: Do in-class laboratories on linear data structures increase student engagement when compared with active learning lectures?

Several of the artifacts used for the study are available as a partial replication package [20] including the initial survey, observation protocol, and in-class laboratories and related materials [10]. Other materials, including informed consent, exam questions, and projects are available from the author by request.

3.1 Study Context

We conducted the study in CSC216: Programming Concepts – Java during the Fall 2014 semester. CSC216 is a second semester CS1.5 computer science course, which covers advanced object oriented programming, introductory software engineering, linear data structures, finite state machines, recursion, GUIs, sorting, and searching. The class meets twice a week for 75 minutes. Course grades are a combination of three tutorials [11], three two-part programming projects, in-class exercises, and three examinations. The author taught two sections of CSC216 during the Fall 2014 semester. Both sections met in large lecture halls with stationary desks and chairs.

In CSC216 students work with a number of tools to support the learning outcomes related to software engineering. Students develop assignments in the Eclipse Juno[2] integrated development environment using Java v1.7 with a suite of Eclipse plug-ins. Unit tests are written with JUnit v4[3] and coverage is measured by EclEmma[4], which uses the Jacoco[5] code coverage library. Static analysis tools, FindBugs[6], PMD[7], and CheckStyle[8], check for misuse of the Java language and styling problems. Student programming assignments are submitted for evaluation by pushing the project to our university's enterprise GitHub[9]. Student jobs are evaluated automatically with every push to GitHub by using the continuous integration server Jenkins[10]. Each student has a Jenkins job for their project and the job will build the student project, run the student's tests instrumented for coverage, run the static analysis tools, and run a suite of teaching staff unit tests, similar to Web-CAT [6]. Students are introduced to these technologies through a series of tutorials [11].

3.2 Study Participants

Students registered for their section of CSC216 on a first-come, first-served basis. Table 1 provides an overview of each section. We exclude counts on minority students due to low numbers that may lead to identification. The author solicited informed consent from students on the first day of class (NC State IRB #4169). Students opted into or out of the study and completed a survey. After the solicitation for participation, the author left the room and the author's Ph.D. student collected informed consents and

---

[2] Eclipse may be found at: http://www.eclipse.org/.

[3] JUnit may be found at: http://junit.org/.

[4] EclEmma may be found at: http://www.eclemma.org/.

[5] Jacoco may be found at: http://www.eclemma.org/jacoco/.

[6] FindBugs may be found at: http://findbugs.sourceforge.net/

[7] PMD may be found at: http://pmd.sourceforge.net/.

[8] CheckStyle may be found at: http://checkstyle.sourceforge.net/.

[9] GitHub may be found at: https://github.com/.

[10] Jenkins may be found at: https://jenkins-ci.org/.

surveys. To reduce bias, the author's Ph.D. student held all informed consents and surveys until final grade submission.

Table 1: Information about Participants

Metric	Section 001	Section 002
# Enrolled	85	102
Participants (completed course)	49	60
Dropped/Withdrawn (consenting only)	3	4
Women	9	10
Meeting Time	TH 2:05p-3:35p	MW 2:05p-3:35p

Students were given an introductory survey about their background and efficacy when completing informed consent [10]. These measures characterize the consenting populations and show that the participants are similar between the two sections. Table 2 shows the difference between Section 001 and Section 002 percentages on prior experience with using course technology as listed in Section 3.1. A positive number implies that Section 001 had a higher percentage of responses at that level of experience for the given tool and a negative response implies that Section 002 had a higher percentage. A difference of 0% shows that the populations were the same. For each possible Likert response, we characterized the prior experience measure by providing guidelines of the response's meaning in terms of the number of classes and work experience. For most responses, there was less than a 10% difference between sections. The only responses with a greater than 10% difference are shaded in gray. More students in Section 002 responded that they had "some" experience with Eclipse. Students in Section 001 had more students with "no" experience with the Eclipse Debugger and Static Analysis; however the Section 002 experience varies across the categories. These results overall show a relatively common set of prior experiences with course tooling.

Table 2: Prior Experience with Course Tooling

	None	Very Little	Some	Quite a Bit	Very Much
# of Classes	None	< 1	< 2	< 4	> 4
Work Exp.	None	< 6 mos.	< 2 years	< 4 years	> 4 years
Java	0%	0%	0%	0%	0%
Eclipse	9%	5%	-11%	-2%	-2%
Eclipse Debugger	15%	-8%	-5%	0%	-2%
Static Analysis	14%	-7%	-7%	0%	0%
Unit Testing	5%	-2%	-1%	-2%	0%
Code Coverage	8%	-4%	-3%	0%	0%
Version Control	-3%	7%	-3%	-3%	2%
Continuous Integration	-1%	-1%	0%	0%	2%

Another factor of student success is student self-efficacy or self-belief [2]. Bandera defines an efficacy expectation as "the conviction that one can successfully execute the behavior required to produce the outcomes" [2]. Computer science students know the steps to complete a programming assignment successfully, but may not believe that they have the ability to complete the task. Scott and Ghinea [19] found a relationship between a student's self-belief about their programming aptitude and their programming practice behavior, so self-efficacy is important for student success. We surveyed students on their confidence (Table 3). The self-efficacy questions are adapted from examples given

by Bishop-Clark and Dietz-Uhler [4], but future studies may consider a preliminarily validated instrument by Scott and Ghinea [19]. Cells in gray are where there is more than a 10% difference between Sections 001 and 002 on their agreement with a given statement. Agreement with statements A, D, and E suggest confidence while agreement with statements B and C suggest a lack of confidence. The results show that both sections have a similar level of confidence. Section 002 had a higher percentage of students that strongly agree with the statement "I could learn programming and testing". A higher percentage of students in Section 001 were neutral on statements B and C, suggesting that they may have less self-efficacy about their programming skills.

Table 3: Programming and Testing Confidence

	Strongly Agree	Agree	Neutral	Disagree	Strongly Disagree
A	-17%	17%	0%	0%	0%
B	2%	-1%	13%	-13%	-1%
C	0%	-1%	10%	-11%	2%
D	4%	-21%	9%	9%	0%
E	2%	-14%	14%	3%	-5%

A: I am sure that I could learn programming and testing.
B: I am not good at programming and testing.
C: I am not the type to do well at programming and testing.
D: I have a lot of self-confidence when it comes to programming and testing.
E: Generally, I have felt secure about computer programming and testing.

3.3 Study Setup

The use of active learning activities, like think-pair-share exercises and in-class labs, are proven to increase student learning [9, 13]. To minimize the disadvantage to one group of students through the intervention of in-class labs, we used a counter-balanced study design so that each section of the course would have an opportunity to receive the intervention and we could measure student learning on each topic. Six lectures on linear data structures out of the 28 lectures in CSC216 were converted to in-class lab activities (a seventh in-class lab involving code inspection was also done, but it did not directly relate to linear data structures and is not considered in this paper). The linear data structures unit was selected because two of the topics, array-based and linked lists, are very similar and would work well in a counter-balanced study design as shown in Figure 1.

The gray boxes in Figure 1 represent class periods where students participated in the in-class lab intervention. The first and last labs, Lists (an overview of using the Java Collections Framework) and Iterators, were common for both sections. Section 001 received array-based list instruction as in-class labs and linked list instruction with active learning lectures. Section 002 received array-based list instruction with active learning lectures and linked list instruction as in-class labs. The details about active learning lectures are in Section 3.4 and details about the in-class labs are in Section 3.5.

Administration of Exam 1 occurred between the array-based list and linked list class periods. Two parts of the exam assessed student learning of array-based lists. Two parts of Exam 2 assessed learning of linked nodes and linked lists. The final exam included a question on both array-based lists and linked lists.

To assess student engagement, graduate students and a colleague participating in a graduate seminar on Teaching and Learning in Computer Science observed one or more of the class meetings. The observations were conducted on the eight class periods for array-based lists and linked lists – four classes for each section.

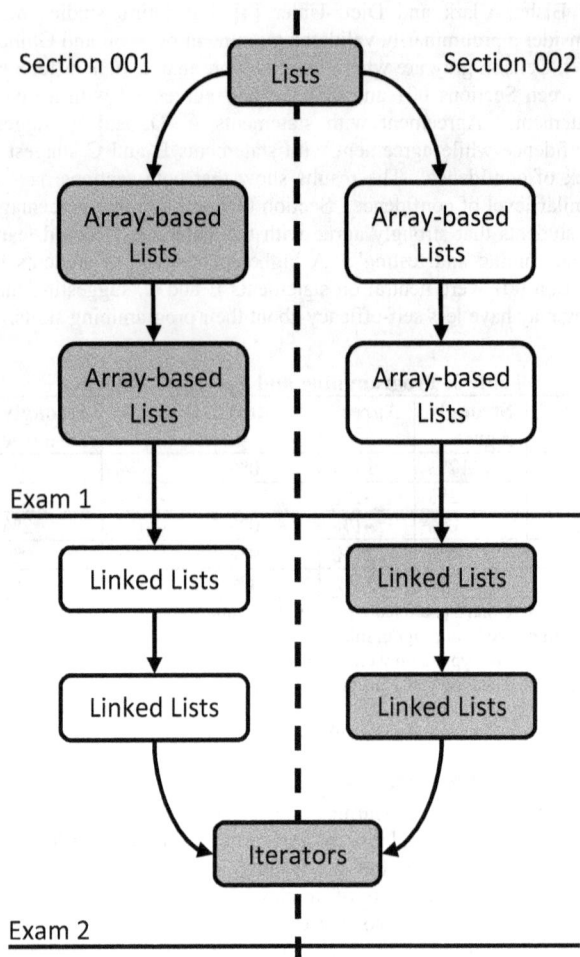

Figure 1: Study Design

Of the eight class periods, seven were observed. The provided observation protocol measured the off topic students and student's engagement with the teaching staff [10]. Off topic behavior was defined as "checking a non-course related website, working on a project or other assignment, checking their cell phone, etc." We asked observers to count the following items:

- number of instances of off topic behavior during lecture portions of the class
- number of instances of off topic behavior during exercise portions of the class
- number of students off topic during lecture
- number of students off topic during exercises
- number of times a member of the teaching staff is called for help
- number of students or student teams asking for help

3.4 Active Learning Lectures
CSC216 classes consist of lectures that are broken up with one or more simplified think-pair-share active learning exercises [7, 13]. Active learning exercises engage students with the materials just covered in lecture. Students are encouraged to work on the exercises with their neighbors (pair) and submit exercise answers through Google Forms (share). The Google spreadsheet backing the form updates automatically with new responses so the instructor can identify student misconceptions and address them after the exercise closes. The active learning exercises count as part of the exercise portion of the student's final grade. Students earn at least half credit for attempting the exercise.

The study control are the active learning lectures on array-based lists and linked lists. Each topic had two class periods devoted to instruction, with seven associated think-pair-share exercises per topic split across the two class periods. The first lecture provides a general overview of the data structure implemented as a list of integers. The second lecture provides instruction about how to implement the data structure using generic types.

3.5 In-class Laboratories
Students completed four of the six in-class laboratories depending on their section. Before the in-class lab, students were expected to watch a short 10-15 minute video about the topic of the lab activity. As students entered the classroom, they joined their groups by finding the paper tent on the desk with their team number on it. The class meeting began with a short lecture introduction to the lab activity, and then students started the lab activity. The class concluded with a reflection exercise and a reminder to complete the activity outside of class. The in-class labs were intended to be counted in the exercise portion of the student's grade, but were excluded by TAs during exercise grade calculation.

Students were randomly placed on teams of three and were assigned a GitHub repository for their in-class lab work separate from their GitHub repositories for submitting projects. Students with missing teammates were reassigned to another team during class to minimize students working on the in-class labs alone.

The design of the in-class laboratories involved development exercises using the software engineering tools for the class. Each lab, except the first lab, was broken into small tasks. The first lab was a Power Point slide, but now the lab is available as a Google doc like all the other labs. At the end of each task, the instructions stated students should run their tests, comment their code, and push to GitHub. All lab materials, including slides, videos, and lab activities are available at [10].

3.5.1 Java Collections Framework In-class Lab
The goal of the Java Collections Framework lab is the creation of a suite of unit tests appropriate for testing a linear data structure. By writing unit tests in the first in-class lab, the students practice test-driven development and can use the tests to evaluate later implementations of linear data structures. Students started with an Eclipse project containing a jar'd implementation of an `ArrayList` of Strings. A unit test skeleton and Javadoc of the `ArrayList` implementation contained the instructions for writing sufficient unit tests for 100% condition coverage of the `ArrayList` implementation. The instructions for this in-class lab were initially provided on a slide projected for both sections. Students struggled with projected instructions, so future labs had more detailed instructions. The Java Collections Framework in-class lab has been revised for future offerings.

Exam Item	Total Points	Section 001			Section 002			W	p-value	Lower CI	Upper CI	Diff. in Loc.
		Mean	SD	Med.	Mean	SD	Med.					
E1 P4 #8	5	3.63	1.56	5	4.35	1.45	5	1064.5	< 0.010	-0.99	-3.7E-6	-5.3E-5
E1 P4 #9	5	4.18	1.07	5	4.57	1.09	5	1167.0	0.016	-5.7E-5	-3.8E-5	-5.0E-5
E1 P4 #10	5	2.63	2.40	2	3.45	2.18	5	1257.5	0.149	-9.9E-6	8.2E-5	-4.7E-6
E1 P4	15	10.45	3.97	10	12.37	3.74	14.5	1054.5	< 0.010	-3.99	-3.3E-5	-1.99
E1 P5	15	17.76	4.00	20	18.25	4.09	20	1294.0	0.233	-4.9E-5	3.5E-5	-5.1E-5
E2 P3	16	8.43	5.85	8	11.80	6.41	16	955.0	< 0.010	-7.99	-4.5E-5	-3.99
E2 P5	20	11.80	4.14	12	12.58	4.21	13	1257.5	0.412	-2.99	0.99	-0.99
E3 Array	10	8.31	2.45	9.5	8.46	2.49	9.5	1096.5	0.313	-0.50	5.9E-5	-1.8E-5
E3 Linked	10	8.36	2.53	9.5	8.81	2.45	10	1069.5	0.221	-0.49	1.8E-5	-4.4E-5
Exam 3	105	85.02	29.17	94.5	87.23	28.92	97.5	1323.0	0.372	-6.00	2.00	-1.50

3.5.2 In-class Lab 1 for Lists

The goal of Part 1 of the ArrayList and LinkedList labs is to write an array-based or linked list of Strings. Students start by copying and refactoring their tests from the Java Collections Framework lab into a new test file for verifying their List implementation. Students then work on standard list functionality, state, constructor, size(), get(), add(), remove(), and set(), with reminders to document their code, run their tests, push to GitHub, and switch drivers.

After implementing the major functions of the List class, students evaluate their test coverage on their solution and work on a stretch goal of writing a program that uses the List.

3.5.3 In-class Lab 2 for Lists

The goal of Part 2 of the ArrayList and LinkedList labs is to write a generic list. Students start from the previous lab's code and refactor both their tests and their implementation to work for any type of object.

3.5.4 Iterators In-class Lab

The goal of the Iterators lab is for students to implement a LinkedList by extending AbstractSequentialList. The standard List methods in AbstractSequentialList are implemented in terms of an Iterator. Students must write a custom Iterator for AbstractSequentialList to work. Students continue to use their tests from the Java Collections Framework lab to verify their solution.

4. STUDY RESULTS

The following sections outline results of the in-class lab activities on student learning of linear data structures and student engagement.

4.1 Learning on Linear Data Structures

Three written examinations measured student knowledge on linear data structures. We only report the summary exam data for consenting students.

We administered Exam 1 between the array-based lists and linked lists portions of the linear data structures unit. Two parts (Part 4 and 5) of Exam 1 assessed student knowledge on array-based lists. Part 4 assessed the ability of students to trace how the contents of an ArrayList are modified when passed to a mystery method. There were three questions in Part 4; each question was evaluated separately and all three were evaluated together. Part 5 assessed the ability of students to write a method for an ArrayList class.

Exam 2 had two parts (Part 3 and Part 5) assessing student knowledge on linked lists. Part 3 evaluated students' ability to

work with linked nodes. Students wrote code to transform a before picture of linked nodes into an after picture of linked nodes. Part 5 assessed the ability of students to write a method for a LinkedList class.

Exam 1 and Exam 2 have similar structure, but the questions differed between sections to minimize sharing of knowledge. For example, Part 5 for Section 001 asked students to write indexOf(); Part 5 for Section 002 asked students to write lastIndexOf(). Both sections took a common final exam, called Exam 3. The final exam included a question on implementing an array-based stack and a linked list-based queue. The final exam grade was also considered as a whole to determine any difference in learning between sections.

Each exam part and sub question were tested for normality using the Shapiro-Wilk Normality Test in the R Project for Statistical Computing [18]. All exam items were nonparametric with p-values < 0.01. Due to the nonparametric distribution of the data sets, a two-sample, non-paired, two-sided Wilcoxon test was used to compare the scores on each exam item between the two sections using R. A two-sided test will determine if there is a difference between the distributions in each section. Table 4 summarizes the results.

The gray cells in Table 4 show the four exam items where the distributions of the sections are different at a statistically significant confidence level of 95%. The first three gray cells are for Part 4 of Exam 1, which was a question about using the data structure as a client and not about implementing part of the data structure. The last gray cell is for Exam 2 Part 3, which was a question about manipulating linked nodes.

For the statistically significant results in Table 4, we ran a one-sided Wilcoxon test to determine if the intervention leads to an increase in exam item scores for the section that received the intervention. Table 5 summarizes the results.

Table 5: One-sided Wilcoxon Test on Significant Exam Items

Exam Item	Test	p-value	Lower CI	Upper CI
E1 P4 #8	001 > 002	0.999	-1.0	Infinity
E1 P4 #9	001 > 002	0.992	-3.0E-5	Infinity
E1 P4	001 > 002	0.996	-3.00	Infinity
E2 P3	001 < 002	< 0.01	-Infinity	-4.01E-5

Our results show that Section 001, which completed the in-class labs on array-based lists did not outperform Section 002 on Exam 1 Part 4. When testing the hypothesis that Section 001 scores were greater than Section 002 scores, the p-value was strongly not significant. A one-sided Wilcoxon test that switches the alternative hypothesis does lead to statistical significance, which means that Section 002 outperformed Section 001 on Exam 1 Part 4. The only place where the alternative hypothesis of a section with the in-class lab intervention outperforming the other section on the related exam material was for Exam 2 Part 3 where Section 002 outperformed Section 001. However, alone, that result is not strong enough to demonstrate higher gains in learning on topics taught using in-class lab activities. Our results show that there was no major difference in student learning as measured by exams when comparing active learning lectures with in-class laboratories.

4.2 Engagement

We measured engagement through classroom observations by graduate students and a colleague participating in a seminar on Teaching and Learning. Each observer used an observation protocol [10]. All students attending class during the observation were observed. The observation protocol included no identifying information about students and consenting students were unknown during the observation period.

Table 6 summarizes the observation counts for the number or average number of instances of off topic behavior during lecture and exercise portions of the class and the number of instances when students engaged with the teaching staff. Each observer used the observation protocol in a slightly different manner. Therefore, each observation period will be described in the following sections followed by a discussion of common metrics and themes. The three observations that considered the average over five-minute intervals, Observations 2, 4, and 8, were completed by the same observer and the summation of the off-topic observations would significantly skew results. The average is more representative of the values reported by other observers.

Table 6: Observation Summary

Obs.	Class Type	# Off Topic Lecture	# Off Topic Exercise	Questions of Teaching Staff
1	Lab	5	7	32
2	Lec.	62	49	12
3	Lab	10	43	50
4	Lec.	46	16	----
5	Lec.	----	----	----
6	Lab	5	10	33
7	Lec.	52	54	2
8	Lab	16	5	-----
Lab Average		9	16.3	38.3
Lec. Average		53.3	39.7	7
Lec. / Lab		5.9	2.4	0.2

4.2.1 Observation 1: Array-Based List 1 In-Class Lab

Section 001 completed the array-based list 1 in-class lab. The observer recorded counts every 5 minutes in two groups: 1) general disengagement and 2) those looking at a Google document. The students in the second group were likely on task since that day's activity was provided in a Google document, so they are not considered in the summary.

During the initial lecture in the first five minutes of class, there were five instances of disengaged behavior. During the in-class lab, there were seven instances of disengaged behavior. Students asked the teaching staff for help 32 times during the class period.

4.2.2 Observation 2: Array-Based List 1 Active Learning Lecture

Section 002 received a standard active learning lecture on the first half of the materials on array-based lists. The observer focused on the number of instances of on and off topic behavior in five-to-ten-minute windows. The window was then marked as lecture or exercise. In a class with attendance of 78 students and with 62 visible laptop screens, an average of 61 students were off topic during lecture and an average of 50 students were off topic during the active learning exercises. The teaching staff was asked for help 12 times during the class period.

4.2.3 Observation 3: Array-Based List 2 In-Class Lab

Section 001 completed the array-based list 2 in-class lab. Two observers attended the class and each recorded notes on one-half of the class. During the initial five-minute lecture portion of the class, there were 10 instances of disengaged behavior. There were 43 instances of disengaged behavior during the in-class lab. Students or student teams asked for help over 50 times.

4.2.4 Observation 4: Array-Based List 2 Active Learning Lecture

Section 002 received a standard active learning lecture on the second half of the materials on array-based lists. The observer focused on an estimate of the number of off topic students by observing screens visible from his spot and creating a class wide estimate of the number of students off topic during five-minute windows. In a class with attendance of 72 students, 65 total screens, and 30 screens used for the estimate, an average of 46 students were disengaged during the lecture portion of the class. An average of 16 students were disengaged during the think-pair-share exercises. Question counts were not recorded.

4.2.5 Observation 5: Linked List 1 Active Learning Lecture

Section 001 received a standard active learning lecture on the first half of materials on linked lists. No observer attended.

4.2.6 Observation 6: Linked List 1 In-Class Lab

Section 002 completed the linked list 1 in-class lab. The observer recorded 5 instances of disengaged behavior during the short introductory lecture and 10 instances of disengaged behavior during the activity and reflection portion of the class. The observer grouped together the likely 25 or more students who were observed as disengaged during the reflection portion of the class as a single incident. There were 33 instances where the teaching staff was called for help.

4.2.7 Observation 7: Linked List 2 Active Learning Lecture

Section 001 received a standard active learning lecture on the second half of materials on linked lists. The observer noted that he could only see half of the class during this observation. Reported numbers are doubled with the assumption that the observed half is indicative of the whole. There were and estimated 52 instances of disengaged behavior during the lecture portion of the course by an estimated 20 unique students. During the exercises, there were an estimated 54 instances of disengaged behavior by an estimated 18 unique students. Only two students asked for help during the class period.

4.2.8 Observation 8: Linked List 2 In-Class Lab

Section 002 completed the linked list 2 in-class lab. The observer counted 57 students with 50 laptops, 26 of which were visible during the observation. The number of disengaged students was estimated from the visible laptops. An average of 16 students were off topic during the lecture portion of the course and an average of 5 students were disengaged during the in-class lab portion of the course. Question counts were not recorded.

4.2.9 Observation Summary

For active learning lectures, students were over five times more likely to display off topic behavior during lecture portions of the class and over two times more likely to display off topic behavior during the exercise portion. During in-class labs, students were over five times more likely to engage with the teaching staff by asking questions.

These results confirm the instructor's reflection on each of the class periods: students engaged with their peers, engaged with the lab activity, and asked more questions of the teaching staff than then in the active learning lectures. However, the observers just counted the number of questions and interactions. The missing piece of the observation is the content of the questions.

Many of the questions, especially for the early in-class labs like the un-observed Java Collections Framework lab, involved technology. The first Java Collections Framework in-class lab had a problem with the provided library. The provided library was compiled and jar'ed using Java 1.8, and many students only had Java 1.7 installed. Due to the volume of questions, the instructor was unable to resolve the issue until the very end of class. The other section had fewer library issues, but had many tool and technology questions. Another common question during the first few in-class lab activities was how to handle a fast-forward error from GitHub. These questions led to the creation of a "Troubleshooting" section at the end of each lab so that the instructor could quickly refer students to the section and move on to answer other questions.

The benefit of the in-class lab experience was that students were able to resolve or consider alternative solutions to problems quickly, especially problems associated with tooling, through the help of their peers and the teaching staff. However, since many of the student questions focused on tooling, students may not have engaged deeply with the covered course topics due to the difficulties with the tools. As the labs progressed, students asked more questions about the lab topics, but no counts of specific question types were recorded during the observed classes. While students were more engaged, as measured by off-topic behavior and teaching staff interactions during in-class labs, the engagement was not solely on the course topics.

5. THREATS TO VALIDITY

Due to the nature of classroom research, there are several threats to validity that constrain the generalizability and application of our results [4, 8].

5.1 External Validity

External validity describes the generalizability of our results for the study population [8]. Our study was restricted to two sections of the same course taught by the same instructor in the same semester and even at the same time of day. While these study constraints allowed for an additional level of control and an increase of internal validity, the constraints do limit the generalizability of this work to other CS1.5 classes, courses, and institutions. Due to the nature of cohorts, there may be differences between results in fall and spring offerings of the same course. Replications of the study in future CSC216 classes, other CS1.5 courses, and at other institutions would increase the

generalizability of the work. A replication package [20] with the study materials is available upon request, but some materials, including labs, initial survey, and observation protocol, that would not affect future studies are available [10].

5.2 Internal Validity

Internal validity is maximized through the reduction of bias and concerns the quality of our conclusions [8]. The study does have selection bias: students selected their own sections. However, an initial survey of students, conducted as part of the collection of informed consent, shows that the characteristics of the sections were roughly the same. Table 2 and Table 3 show each section had participants with similar characteristics, which minimizes sample bias.

There are several possible confounding factors. Students given one intervention may have shared that material with students taught using the control. Additionally, since only a portion of the course incorporated in-class labs, any effect may have been too small to measure. Additional studies with more in-class labs that span the breadth of course topics appropriate for lab exercises would increase internal validity of future studies.

We minimized differential attrition bias by including consenting participants that soft dropped the course. Students that dropped or withdrew did not complete any coursework evaluated in the study.

There is the possibility of experimenter bias because the author created the study and taught both sections of the course. The author tried to reduce experimenter bias by requesting that her Ph.D. student hold all informed consents until the end of the semester so that she would not know who consented to participate in the study. Due to the nature of the classes in the treatment and control, there were differences in how the author presented the materials to each section, but she tried to remove her preferences for lecture success from discussions with the students. Future studies will include other faculty to reduce experimenter bias.

5.3 Construct Validity

Construct validity describes how well the underlying concept of interest, in our case student learning and engagement, are empirically investigated [8]. Exam questions measured student learning. For the first two exams, each section had similar, but different questions. On exam 1, Section 001 wrote the `indexOf()` method and Section 002 wrote the `lastIndeOf()` method for an array-based list. The questions were similar, but iterating through a list in reverse may be conceptually harder. That means the exam questions on Exams 1 and 2 may not equally assess student learning of the topic. Students took a common final, so those questions provide a common comparison point.

Another concern is the exam questions and the grading rubrics themselves. The exam questions and the rubric may not fully evaluate student learning. The department's assessment coordinator has assessed the final exam, and there is no current concern that the exam is not measuring student learning.

The initial survey asked students about their prior experience with tooling and about their self-efficacy when programming and testing [4]. There were additional questions about enjoyment [4], ways of learning, goals, and demographics. The addition of course and time information on the tooling question may provide additional confusion to students about if the relationship is an "and" or an "or" relationship. However, the results of that question were what we expected from courses typically made up of traditional aged college freshman and sophomores. The questions on efficacy and enjoyment were pulled from literature [4], but are not to our knowledge validated instruments. Future studies may consider a preliminarily validated instrument by Scott and Ghinea [19]. All other questions were generated by the author and may be flawed instruments. Further validation of the survey instrument is needed to determine if the questions measure what they are supposed to measure, but those questions do not influence the results of this study.

The intention of the observation protocol was to measure how many times and how many students were off task. Additionally, the protocol measured the number of times the teaching staff engaged with students about course material. However, inconsistent use by observers is a construct threat. Many, but not all, observers measured the counts at five-minute intervals. Future iterations of the protocol will create a timeline for counts and will include summary information like the number of students in attendance. That instrument will allow for better summary results from multiple observations and multiple observers.

6. DISCUSSION
The goal of our research is to increase student learning and engagement through in-class laboratories on linear data structures.

Research question 1 asked do in-class laboratories on linear data structures increase student learning on linear data structure exam questions when compared to active learning lectures? Our results show that in-class laboratories on linear data structures did not lead to an increase in student learning over active learning lectures. Student learning when using in-class labs and active learning lectures is the same as measured by the linear data structure questions on the final exam. Ultimately, the result is not unexpected since both think-pair-share exercises as used in the active learning lectures and in-class labs are both active learning techniques that both lead to increased learning. Overall, the results suggest that using in-class laboratories does no harm to student learning. Future work may formalize the team portion of the in-class labs to use lightweight teams [16], which may increase student learning. Additional studies will strengthen our knowledge.

Research question 2 asked do in-class laboratories on linear data structures increase student engagement when compared with active learning lectures? The observations show that most students engaged with the material during in-class lab sections while a large portion of students were off topic during active learning lectures. Additionally, over five times as many students or student teams asked questions during in-class labs than during active learning lectures. Due to inconsistent and estimated measures during the observations, we cannot attempt any statistical analyses on the data. The raw numbers are highly suggestive that in-class labs were more engaging. However, many of the student questions involved tooling used for the in-class labs rather than questions on in-class lab topics. While students were more engaged during in-class labs, the engagement was not solely on the lab topics, which may contribute to the null-results on student learning. Future studies with better observation protocols, including categorization of student interactions by teaching staff, can further answer our research question.

Prior research on active learning has shown an increase in completion rates [9], where the completion rate is the percentage of students who pass the course. Grade distributions for courses at NC State are protected data, so we cannot compare or comment on how completion rates for the Fall 2014 offerings of CSC216 compare to prior offerings or other core undergraduate computer science courses at NC State. While we cannot compare publically against our own historical data, we can compare with reported completion rates and use these measures as a baseline in future studies that build on this work. Bennedsen and Caspersen [3] report a 67% pass rate for CS1 courses in 2007 and Watson and Li [22] report a similar completion rate of 67.7% for CS1 courses in 2014. We expect that a CS1.5 course would have a similar completion rate due to an overlap with traditional CS1 topics. Freeman et al., [9] found a completion rate of 78.2% with active learning compared to 66.2% completion rate for traditional lecture courses. Seventy-two percent of students completed CSC216 in Fall 2014 with a C or higher. CSC216's completion rate of 72% is lower than the completion rate for active learning classes reported by Freeman et al. [9], but not as low as the completion rate for traditional lecture courses. The completion rate for CSC216 is higher than the completion rates from CS1 literature [3, 22]. Additional reportable data about prior semesters and comparison with future semesters will identify if we are making progress toward increasing the rate of student completion in CSC216.

7. CONCLUSIONS AND FUTURE WORK
Overall, the use of in-class labs was successful in maintaining student learning and increasing student engagement. There were several lessons learned from incorporating in-class labs into CSC216. Students were expected to watch videos about the lecture material before attending class to complete the in-class lab. Based on questions received and the number of students watching the videos at the start of the class, most students did not prepare adequately for class. One solution is to have students take a quiz on the material for a grade [5]. Another solution is to restructure the array-based list and linked list lectures so that the first class period on the topic will be a lecture and the second class period will be devoted to the in-class lab activity for implementing a generic version of the data structure.

We may not have seen gains in student learning since only six lectures of a 28-lecture course were changed to in-class labs. Additional in-class labs will be developed for advanced OO, stacks and queues, FSMs, recursion, and GUIs. Future work will also consider the identification and transfer of the in-class lab software engineering best practices to out-of-class assignments and future coursework.

The introduction of in-class labs addressed a student request in evaluations for more time programming during class, but we would still like to increase student learning with a long term goal for increasing the completion rate. A departmental task force of CSC216 instructors and other undergraduate leadership is working on increasing student support and moving the course to a lab-based delivery mechanism. In-class labs developed or refined for the next academic year will be assessed as a baseline for comparison to the move to a lab-based course in AY16-17.

8. ACKNOWLEDGMENTS
Thanks to Brittany Johnson for survey collection and storage, Jordan Connor for help with data entry and review, and students and colleagues in CSC801-006 for their observations. Thanks to the students who participated in the study. Funding for the study is provided by a NCSU Office of Faculty Development grant and by a Google CS Engagement Award (TFR15-00445).

9. REFERENCES
[1] A. Amresh, A. R. Carberry, J. Femianai, "Evaluating the Effectiveness of Flipped Classrooms for Teaching CS1,"

Frontiers in Education Conference, Oklahoma City, OK, USA, 23-26 Oct. 2013, p. 733-735.

[2] A. Bandura, "Self-efficacy: Toward a Unifying Theory of Behavioral Change," *Psychological Review,* vol. 82, no. 4, pp. 191-215, 1977.

[3] J. Bennedsen and M. E. Caspersen, "Failure Rates in Introductory Programming," *SIGCSE Bulletin*, vol. 39, no. 2, pp. 32-36, 2007.

[4] C. Bishop-Clark and B. Dietz-Uhler, *Engaging in the Scholarship of Teaching and Learning*, Stylus Publishing, Sterling, VA, 2012.

[5] J. Campbell, D. Horton, M. Craig, P. Gries, "Evaluating an Inverted CS1," Proceedings of the 45th ACM Technical Symposium on Computer Science Education, Atlanta, GA, USA, March 3-8, 2014, p. 307-312.

[6] S. H. Edwards, "Improving Student Performance by Evaluating How Well Students Test their Own Programs," *Journal on Educational Resources in Computing*, vol. 3, no. 1, September 2003.

[7] R. M. Felder and R. Brent, "Active Learning: An Introduction," *ASQ Higher Education Brief*, vol. 2, no. 4, August 2009.

[8] S. Fincher and M. Petre, eds., *Computer Science Education Research*, Taylor & Francis, The Netherlands, Lisse, 2004.

[9] S. Freeman et al., "Active Learning Increases Student Performance in Science, Engineering, and Mathematics," *Proceedings of the National Academy of Sciences in the United States of America*, vol. 111, no. 23, p. 8410-8415, June 10, 2014.

[10] S. Heckman, "CSC216 In-class Lab Study Replication Package," [Online]. Available: http://people.engr.ncsu.edu/sesmith5/216-labs/csc216_labs.html

[11] S. Heckman, J. Perry, J. King, E. Gehringer, A. Meneely (2014, August 11) *CS1.5 Tutorials* [Online]. Available: http://courses.ncsu.edu/CS1.5/common/tutorials/.

[12] D. Horton, M. Craig, J. Campbell, P. Gries, D. Zingaro, "Comparing Outcomes in Inverted and Traditional CS1," Proceedings of the 2014 Conference on Innovation & Technology in Computer Science Education, Uppsala, Sweden, June 23-25, 2014, pp. 261-266.

[13] A. King, "From Sage on the Stage to Guide on the Side," *College Teaching*, vol. 41, no. 1, Winter 1993, p. 30-35.

[14] A. Kothiyal, R. Majumdar, S. Murthy, S. Iyer, "Effect of Think-Pair-Share in a Large CS1 Class: 83% Sustained Engagement," Proceedings of the 9th Annual Conference on International Computing Education Research, San Diego, CA, USA, August 12-14, 2013, pp. 137-144.

[15] M. J. Lage, G. J. Platt, M. Treglia, "Inverting the Classroom: A Gateway to Creating an Inclusive Learning Environment," *The Journal of Economic Education*, vol. 31, no. 1, p. 30-43, January 2000.

[16] C. Latulipe, N. B. Long, C. E. Seminario, "Structuring Flipped Classes with Lightweight Teams and Gamification," Proceedings of the 46th ACM Technical Symposium on Computer Science Education, Kansas City, MO, USA, March 4-7, 2015, pp. 392-397.

[17] L. Malmi et al., "Theoretical Underpinning of Computing Education Research – What is the Evidence?," Proceedings of the 10th Annual Conference on International Computing Education Research, Glasgow, United Kingdom, August 11-14, 2014, pp. 27-34.

[18] R Core Team, R: A Language and Environment for Statistical Computing, R Foundation for Statistical Computing, Vienna, Austria, http://www.R-project.org/, 2013.

[19] M. J. Scott, G. Ghinea, "Measuring Enrichment: The Assembly and Validation of an Instrument to Assess Student Self-Beliefs in CS1," Proceedings of the 10th Annual Conference on International Computing Education Research, Glasgow, United Kingdom, August 11-14, 2014, pp. 123-130.

[20] F. Shull, V. Basili, J. Carver, J. C. Maldonado, G. H. Travassos, M. Mendonça, and S. Fabbri, "Replicating Software Engineering Experiments: Addressing the Tacit Knowledge Problem," Proceedings of the 2002 International Symposium on Empirical Software Engineering, Nara, Japan, October 3-4, 2002, pp. 7-16.

[21] A. Vihavainen, J. Airaksinen, C. Watson, "A Systematic Review of Approaches for Teaching Introductory Programming and Their Influence on Success," Proceedings of the 10th Annual Conference on International Computing Education Research, Glasgow, United Kingdom, August 11-14, 2014, pp. 19-26.

[22] C. Watson, F. W. B. Li, "Failure Rates in Introductory Programming Revisited," Proceedings of the 2014 Conference on Innovation & Technology in Computer Science Education, Uppsala, Sweden, June 23-25, 2014, pp. 39-44.

Learning in Distributed Low-Stakes Teams

Stephen MacNeil
Software and Information
Systems
UNC at Charlotte
smacnei2@uncc.edu

Celine Latulipe
Software and Information
Systems
UNC at Charlotte
clatulip@uncc.edu

Aman Yadav
Educational Psychology and
Educational Technology
Michigan State University
ayadav@msu.edu

ABSTRACT

Active learning is important in computer science education, where students often don't have enough opportunities for social learning and development of soft skills. Flipped classrooms can provide social interaction through approaches such as lightweight teams [23], where students collaborate during class in low-stakes peer learning. These teams scaffold positive interdependence [17] by removing high-stakes assignments that heavily impact student's grades.

Given the proliferation of online courses, and MOOCs in particular, it is important to consider whether successful face-to-face pedagogical strategies can be reappropriated for distributed, online contexts. Specifically, we are interested in whether a low-stakes model could provide similar learning benefits when team members collaborate remotely.

This paper presents results from a study that analyzed the efficacy of low-stakes distributed teams. We examined whether low-stakes teams that communicate through Google Hangouts can provide educational benefits, in terms of both engagement and learning outcomes, compared to students who are learning via video in a co-located setting or individually. Results suggest that co-located teams have the highest learning gains, but there are no significant differences between distributed teams and individual work. We discuss implications of these results for practice and future research.

Categories and Subject Descriptors

K.3.2 [**Computer Science Education**]

General Terms

Education

Keywords

lightweight teams, distance learning, cooperative learning, team-based learning, computer science education

ICER'15, August 9–13, 2015, Omaha, Nebraska, USA.
© 2015 ACM. ISBN 978-1-4503-3630-7/15/08 ...$15.00.
DOI: http://dx.doi.org/10.1145/2787622.2787727.

1. INTRODUCTION

The ubiquity of technology in society generates a constant demand for students with computer science skills and consequently enrollment in traditional four-year CS programs is high. Meanwhile, adoption of, and enrollment in MOOC platforms is also significant for CS, as shown by Stanford's 2011 Machine learning course that attracted 104,000 people [41]. Students in CS classes have varying levels of preparedness and diverse backgrounds. In both traditional college classes and MOOCs, the discipline of CS has focused almost exclusively on teaching skills and theory, at the expense of fostering social interaction, peer learning, and soft skills such as teamwork. This lack of soft skills may not only harm graduates when they enter the workforce, but it also means that the learning environments themselves are not optimized to take advantage of the benefits associated with social learning [35, 6, 40].

Fostering social interaction, teamwork, and peer learning in face-to-face courses often involves converting to flipped classrooms, where students consume video lectures online and then engage in active learning in the classroom [36, 37, 19, 22, 11]. Active learning and peer learning provide direct face-to-face interaction with peers and educators and create a much more social and engaging environment. When well-structured, these cooperative learning opportunities have the potential to allow students to leverage their diverse backgrounds and experiences to provide new perspectives.

For online learning, social interaction is limited and happens primarily through discussion boards [4]. Anchored collaboration [14, 9, 33] embeds these discussions into the media to which they correspond and provides support when students first interact with materials online. Asynchronous peer learning is amenable to conflicting schedules and, like face-to-face peer learning, discussion forums can make the diverse backgrounds of CS students an asset rather than a challenge. However, asynchronous peer learning doesn't provide rich face-to-face interaction and may not alleviate feelings of isolation. This isn't to imply a dichotomy where either asynchronous or synchronous learning is better; each have strengths, weaknesses, and use cases [16].

Both flipped classrooms and online classes rely on self-regulated learning without providing support or scaffolding for students who may not possess those essential metacognitive skills. Successful self-regulated learning requires four levels, which begin with observation and imitation and move to self-control and finally self-regulation [32]. However, in online learning and the out-of-class portion of flipped classes, students can't observe how other students interact with material, and therefore can't observe and imitate them.

We hypothesize that synchronous peer interaction, when students first interact with materials, encourages social interaction and allows students to observe and imitate each other's self-regulatory skills. For example, students may engage in collaborative problem decomposition in real-time. In this paper, we extend a pedagogical approach, Lightweight Teams [23], that has been shown to support students socially, mitigate stress associated with teamwork, and scaffold teamwork and communication skills. We test a similar low-stakes teams model that borrows the ideas of positive interdependence and stress-free teamwork but moves them to an online, distributed context where face-to-face communication is mediated by videoconferencing technology.

The contribution of this paper is to evaluate the efficacy of and the challenges associated with online, low-stakes, synchronous, team-based learning. In this work, we conduct a comparative study of co-located teams, distributed teams, and individual learning. The results from our comparative study corroborate previous team-based learning research and discussion-based peer learning research.

2. BACKGROUND

Our work builds on these topics in these ways:

- *Collaborative Learning*: provides a theoretical basis for the efficacy of Lightweight Teams.
- *Flipped Classrooms and MOOCs*: motivates our work and informs how our work could be applied.
- *Distributed Teams and Online Discussion*: prior work that investigates peer learning in an online context.
- *Lightweight Teams*: focus of our comparative study.

2.1 Collaborative Learning

It has been widely argued that students learn best when they actively collaborate on course work in small groups both inside and outside the classroom [35]. Lave et al.'s work on cultivating communities of learners [24] supports this notion, providing evidence that students become more engaged in their activities when they are part of such groups. The social context of learning allows the learners to engage in cognitive processes that would be otherwise unavailable if they were working individually [29, 39]. Specifically, Vygotsky argued that knowledge is constructed through social interaction and interactive talk is a tool mediating the advancement of thinking [39]. From this sociocultural perspective, when an individual interacts with other individuals in a social environment, internal processes occur that support learning. Most tasks, and learning in particular, require social interactions for ideas to develop [6, 40].

Cooperative learning, like collaborative learning, has been found to improve student achievement and self-esteem, and to develop positive race relationships [34]. Peer interaction is also important for scaffolding students' problem-solving processes [12]. In their meta-analysis on effects of small group learning, Springer et al. found that small groups have a positive impact on student outcomes and also increase persistence in STEM courses and programs [35]. Given the push to increase retention rates in MOOCs, synchronous small group learning offers a promising approach to keep students more engaged while learning online.

2.2 Flipped Classrooms

Group work is a common feature in flipped or inverted classrooms, where content delivery occurs outside of the classroom, and in-class time is devoted to active learning activities [36, 37, 19, 22, 11]. The active learning that occurs during class allows students to interact with peers and receive guidance from an instructor. To make this happen, students consume content as homework, so that they are ready to actively interact with content in class.

Post-secondary institutions are increasingly using the flipped class approach for large classes [22, 11, 1]. Large flipped classrooms can be intimidating for students and it can be a challenge to get the students to interact with each other. Dividing the students into smaller groups to collaborate on active learning activities during class time is proving to be a successful approach for increasing student engagement [31] and learning outcomes [15]. The flipped class approach to teaching opens up opportunities for student collaboration and peer learning, given that belonging to a group or a team can have significant positive benefits for individual courses and sustained success in college [2].

2.3 MOOCs

The recent popularity of MOOCs, especially in computing, as a mechanism to offer courses and in some cases, certificates, at no cost to students is changing how people think about higher education. This disruption is cause for both excitement and scrutiny [25]. Researchers who work in academia are particularly intrigued by this disruption that occurs so close to home, and much effort is now being targeted towards studying and understanding how MOOCs work and how effective they are at actually educating people [10, 30, 3]. In particular, it is important to pay attention to the differing communication patterns that emerge in the use of computer-mediated communication, since in the case of MOOCs, face-to-face communication is replaced by digital channels [18, 38]. Consequently, empirical studies are necessary to determine whether and how face-to-face pedagogical techniques translate to these partially or fully online environments.

2.4 Distributed Teams and Online Discussion

To support students working outside of class time or in completely online settings, such as MOOCs, it is important to understand how distance affects teamwork and cohesion. There are known difficulties associated with distributed teamwork and collaborating remotely. Specifically challenging for short-term ad-hoc teams, it is important to establish trust and common ground [26].

Despite these challenges, the benefits of peer learning and global perspectives have encouraged a variety of research around global virtual teams. Recently, Coursera introduced Talkabout[21], which provides students with an online, video-based chatroom for discussing course content. Talkabout enables globally diverse discussions by placing students from different countries into the same chatroom. A similar experiment used Mechanical Turk workers to participate in a synchronous text-based discussion forum [5] where participants answered questions independently, then discussed a short explanation, and finally re-answered the question independently. Coetzee et al. [5] have shown that discussing a question leads to better answers but it isn't clear whether this learning transfers to similar questions.

2.5 Lightweight Teams

In our previous work [23], we defined Lightweight Teams as teams of students who work together in a course but where the work done as a team has minimal direct impact on an individual student's final grade. The idea is to get students talking to each other and engaging around the material in a social way, without forcing the students to work together on large, high-stakes, term-length projects. This means that students get the benefits of social learning, without the stress associated with high-stakes group work. Working with the same team throughout the length of the course gives the students a chance to get to know each other, become comfortable, and learn from one another.

Our lightweight teams were generated randomly and assigned seating, so team members always sat next to each other. Students never had to choose where to sit, who to sit with, or even wonder if someone would sit with them. We used a modified peer instruction method [7] to conduct the clicker quizzes[1]. Students discussed the question and answers with their teams *before* answering, but they were still able to answer individually without forming consensus. All of the clicker quizzes only accounted for 10% of each student's grade. The other peer learning activities included paper problem solving activities, where students were asked to write pseudocode, solve Parson's Problems [8], or create UML class diagrams.

Lightweight teams were used in several large introductory courses, where students worked in small groups during class time. In those classes, a marked change occurred and classrooms became a more friendly, social environment; quite unlike the environment typically associated with large introductory computing lectures. Compared to sections that didn't employ lightweight teams, students from lightweight team sections performed better; although this isn't a fair comparison because the two sections were taught in different languages (C++ and Java). Most importantly, a high percentage of students students indicated that they each made at least 5 new friends. Based on this success, lightweight teams seem to have particular promise as a pedagogical design pattern [13]. However, it is not known how well this design pattern transfers to a distributed online context.

3. INTRODUCING THE DISTRIBUTED LOW-STAKES TEAM

We take inspiration from previous distributed peer learning research, such as the synchronicity of Talkabout and the peer-instruction aspect of Coetzee's Study. We investigated the possibility of extending lightweight teams to an online environment where group members are distributed. In face-to-face (co-located) lightweight teams, students sit together in assigned seating to enable continuous interaction. Outside of class, we envision students using technology, such as Google Hangouts or Skype, to work together synchronously at pre-arranged times. In this experiment, we study low-stakes teams which borrow the low-stress, active learning and positive interdependence aspects of lightweight teams. However the team we study are different from lightweight teams in longevity, in that low-stakes teams meet once and do not have a chance to bond over time.

---

[1]http://www.turningtechnologies.com/higher-education

4. COMPARATIVE STUDY OF LEARNING IN LOW-STAKES TEAMS

This research investigates whether the learning benefits observed from using lightweight teams in a face-to-face setting transfer to an online setting where participants are not co-located. To answer this question, we designed an empirical experiment that presented participants with new material and then asked questions to measure their learning of that material. Participants were split across three different conditions: learning individually, learning as a co-located group, and learning as a distributed group.

4.1 Task and Procedure

The task given to our participants was to learn about using semi-automatic espresso machines. We chose this task because we expected that most participants would be unfamiliar with it, and it is a task that has significant enough complexity to create difficult questions, but low enough complexity that basics can be learned in about 15 minutes. The general procedure of the study was as follows:

Pre-test: Take a web-based test (demographics, attitude and 14 knowledge assessment questions). (10 minutes)

Videos: Watch a series of short YouTube videos about espresso machine operations. (10 minutes)

Learning Quiz: Complete peer-instruction quiz about making espresso. Group conditions discuss questions, but individuals answer them alone. (5-20 minutes)

Post-test: Take a web-based post-test (14 knowledge assessment questions + preferences). (10 minutes)

Watching videos replicates the standard information delivery mechanism for both MOOCs and flipped classrooms. In our experiment, participants were free to watch videos repeatedly, to adjust the video playback speed, to pause and replay parts of the videos, and to skip parts of the videos. The learning quiz was the active learning component, used by lightweight teams in flipped classes, based on the peer instruction methodology [7]. The learning quiz is not for assessment, but rather helps students engage with the material and learn it more deeply. In practice, the learning quiz could be replaced by a different learning task such as paper-prototyping, pair programming, or requirement elicitation. We chose to use the learning quiz because it is the learning task that was used by our lightweight teams. Research has shown that the act of recalling information serves to increase the retention of that information [27]. In addition, synthesizing information to answer complex questions moves learning from simple remembering in Bloom's revised taxonomy to understanding, applying, and analyzing [20].

In the two group conditions, the learning quiz that happens after watching the videos is a form of collaborative test taking [28]. We expected that participants in the group conditions would do better on these quizzes since they are able to talk about the question before answering, based on the 'wisdom of the crowd' effect. We also expected there to be a fair amount of consistency on these answers within each group, although each participant answered the questions individually and the group didn't need to reach consensus. For participants in the individual condition, this learning quiz was completed alone, and so the scores reflected only what the individual understood from watching the videos.

Table 1: Pre- and Post-Test Knowledge Assessment Questions

Question (asked as multiple choice)	Bloom's Category
Describe what it means when your espresso shot is over-extracted.	Comprehension
Choose the boiler type that is most common in coffee shops.	Knowledge
Select the ideal order of steps to make a cappuccino using a single-boiler espresso machine	Analysis
Select the correct amount of time a it should take for a shot to pour	Knowledge
Define a portafilter	Comprehension
Select the ideal temperature for espresso	Knowledge
Indicate a cause of a shot pouring too slowly	Evaluation
Predict what can happen if your shot pours too slowly	Application
Describe the taste of a shot that pours too slowly	Analysis
Describe the taste of a shot that pours too fast	Analysis
Identify the most likely cause of a damp puck	Knowledge
Describe how the shot will pour during the first few seconds of pulling a shot	Comprehension
Describe how you might know that your shot is finished	Comprehension
Choose the benefit typically associated with burr grinders	Knowledge

The pre-test and post-test activities are representative of the types of questions that might be asked on a test in either a flipped course or a MOOC. While it is not standard for students in flipped classes or MOOCs to take a pre-test before being presented with new information about a concept, this was necessary for us to measure learning gains and to control for participants who might already have some knowledge and experience with the subject matter.

4.2 Study Methodology

We used a between groups design with three conditions:

Individual (I) : Participant did all parts of the study in an experiment room by themselves (control condition).

Group Co-located (GC): Participants did the study in a co-located group in an experiment room, working with the participants in their group on all parts of the study except the initial and final learning outcomes tests.

Group Distributed (GD): Participants did the study in individual experiment rooms. They worked individually except during the learning quiz when they discussed questions via Google Hangouts.

4.3 Study Environment

The participants in the co-located group completed the study in a conference room on our campus. The students in the distributed group completed the study from separate conference rooms and offices on our campus. The individual participants completed the study from either an office on campus (14 participants) or from their home (3 participants). Participants used their own equipment (laptop to login to the study, complete the tests and watch the videos); however, we also provided laptops if students were unable to join Google Hangouts. For participants in the distributed condition, this meant that they were using their own computers, microphones, web cams and speakers or headphones to connect to the Google Hangout to participate in the study with their assigned group. While this lead to technical glitches, we felt that this was closest to the real-world situation in which MOOC and distance learning students have to cope with using their own technology to participate.

4.4 Research Question and Hypotheses

Our general research question was whether low-stakes teams could provide educational benefit, in terms of learning outcomes, to students who are learning at a distance. We had the following hypotheses:

H1. Learning outcomes will be highest for the students in the co-located group.

H2. Learning outcomes will be higher for students in the distributed group than for students working alone.

H3. Students in both group conditions will perceive that group interactions improved their learning.

We expected that the best learning outcomes would occur for co-located participants, as current technology for distributed discussion limits interaction in the following ways:

- Videoconferencing technology (VCT) allows people to multitask inconspicuously.
- Gesturing and eye contact aren't as natural in VCT; it may be harder to negotiate who speaks.
- Lags and disconnections in VCT can cause conversations to last longer and fatigue attendees.
- Lags in VCT degrade the quality of the conversation.
- People working remotely do not have the freedom to sketch on paper to share visual ideas as easily.

Despite these technological limitations, we expected that participants in distributed teams would exhibit higher learning outcomes than participants in the individual condition, who had no-one to discuss the material with.

4.5 Data Collection

We created a web-app that allowed participants to take the tests and watch the videos in the same window. The only exception, where students were required to leave the web-app, was when distributed team members discussed questions in the Google Hangout. The investigator was present during the Google Hangout session to ensure that conversation stopped after the learning quiz when participants were required to work independently again. The learning quiz was

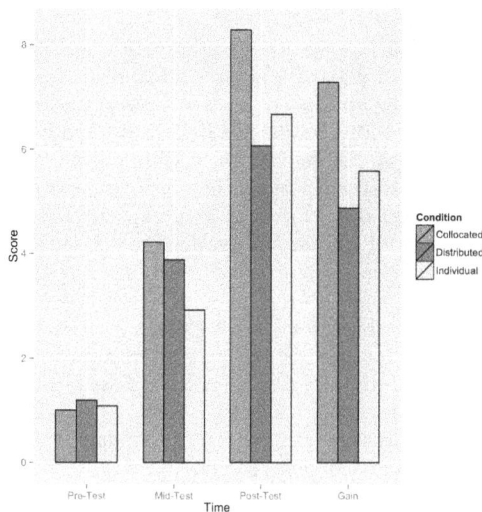

Figure 1: Average scores for the three tests, along with average gain, broken down by condition.

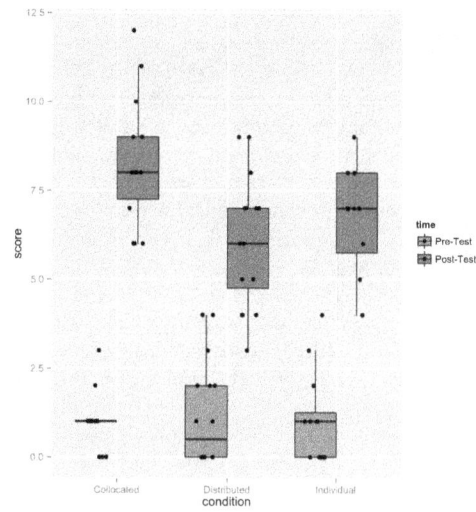

Figure 2: Box plots of pre- and post-test scores grouped by condition. Points are jittered to avoid over-plotting.

audio recorded for both face-to-face discussions and Google Hangout discussions. The web-app monitored the participants' interactions and then updated a server every 15 seconds with results for each section. This prevented participants from losing work and from artificially resetting the timer. All of the questions were optional and some participants did not answer all of the preference questions; however, all participants answered all scored questions.

4.6 Quantitative Data

The quantitative data included the pre- and post-test scores, and included the learning quiz scores. The pre- and post-tests contained 14 identical knowledge assessment questions; shown in Table 1 with their Bloom's taxonomy categorization. The pre-test primed participants on what they should attempt to learn from the videos. Bloom's taxonomy was used to ensure that questions were varied and didn't simply target one type of learning. The difference between pre- and post-scores on these 14 questions represents the learning gain. The demographic information collected included gender, age range, and race. We asked questions on the pre- and post-test to ascertain any affect that our experiment had on participants' preferences; shown in Table 5. Finally, we asked students how they perceived their experience, as summarized in Table 6.

4.7 Qualitative Data

For participants in condition GC, we audio-recorded the session. For participants in the GD condition, we audio-recorded their Google Hangout session. These recordings were used to qualitatively analyze the interactions and also as an archive of what happened during the experiment.

4.8 Participants

We recruited participants from the student population at UNC Charlotte. In total, 53 participants (21 female) participated, and were divided among the three conditions based upon availability to participate during a group slot versus an individual slot. Participants were mainly majoring in com-

puter science or software information systems; although, a few were from Engineering and Bioinformatics. We had four distributed groups (three with five participants each, one with three participants), four co-located groups (two with five participants each, two with four participants), and 17 participants in the individual condition. Participants were compensated for their time (typically 40-60 minutes) with a gift card for a local coffee shop.

4.9 Statistical Analysis

The differences in learning gains between the three conditions were analyzed using a linear mixed effect model (LME) fitted by restricted maximum likelihood. In our model, post-test score was the dependent variable, condition (co-located, distributed, and individual) was a between subjects fixed effect and pre-test was our within subjects term. Participants were treated as random effects. For statistically significant observations ($p < .05$), we performed multiple comparison of means using Tukey contrasts applied to the LME models, which are reported using normally distributed Z values. When performing multiple comparisons, p-values were corrected using single-step method to control for family-wise error rates. We performed this same analysis to analyze scores on the active learning quiz, with learning quiz scores replacing post-test scores as the dependent variable in our model. For each LME analysis, normality and homoscedasticity of standardized residuals were checked using residual-to-predicted plots and Q-Q plots (quantile-quantile).

To corroborate our findings, we performed a simple ANOVA of gain scores (post - pre) as the dependent variable and condition (GC, GD, I) as the independent variable. This approach doesn't account for repeated measures and won't have as much statistical power as our LME, which accounts for repeated measures. ANOVA of gain also assumes equal pre-test scores. For these reasons, we chose to use LME and only report the ANOVA of gain, shown in Table 3, for reference. The results are very similar to those found in our LME models, shown in Table 2. In the following sections, we will only report results from the LME approach.

For preferences, we used a simple ANOVA to compare groups where their preference is the dependent variable. For each ANOVA, we used Levene's Test to ensure homogeneity of variances and this assumption was not violated. For preferences, we observed minor departures from normality. When significant, we performed post-hoc analysis using Tukey HSD test.

After the experiment concluded, we removed 3 participants (two from GC, one from I) because their language barrier was too great, as evidenced by the use of a web-translator during the experiment to answer questions. After removing these 3 participants, but before conducting our analysis, we investigated the distributions of pre-test scores using histograms. We identified outliers and uneven mean values between groups for pre-test scores. To create a fair comparison, we removed all data for participants with pre-tests greater than or equal to 5. The score was chosen because it represents 2 standard deviations from the global pre-score mean. After removing these participants our histograms indicated relatively normal distributions with positive skew and leptokurtosis because many scores existed at one and zero. Similarly, the pre-test scores were comparable between groups: GC (M=1.0, SD=0.8), GD (M=1.2, SD=1.4) and I (M=1.1, SD=1.3). Thus our analysis only includes 16 participants in condition GD, 14 participants in condition GC, and 12 participants in condition I. While this reduced our statistical power, we believe it represents a fairer comparison between groups.

Table 2: LME Learning Gain: Multiple Comparisons of Means Using Tukey Contrasts (single-step corrected: significant if <0.05)

Condition	Estimate	Error	$Pr(>|z|)$
Distributed - Co-located	-2.32	0.61	<0.001
Individual - Co-located	-1.66	0.65	0.029
Individual - Distributed	0.65	0.63	0.550

Table 3: Post-hoc Pairwise Analysis of Learning Gains in Between Condition by ANOVA to Corroborate Our LME Analysis of Gain.

Conditions	Difference	Tukey p-value
Distributed - Co-located	-2.41	0.001
Individual - Co-located	-1.70	0.044
Individual - Distributed	0.71	0.539

Table 4: LME for Learning Quiz: Multiple Comparisons of Means Using Tukey Contrasts (single-step corrected: significant if <0.05)

Condition	Estimate	Error	$Pr(>|z|)$
Distributed - Co-located	-0.37	0.41	0.633
Individual - Co-located	-1.31	0.44	0.008
Individual - Distributed	-0.94	0.43	0.068

4.10 Quantitative Results

Figure 1 shows averages broken down by condition. The box plot in Figure 2 shows the pre-test and post-test score distributions by condition. What is interesting in interpreting these basic results are that the co-located and individual participants saw steady improvement from pre-test to learning quiz to post-test; suggesting that their understanding of espresso improved over time and with exposure to the material. However, for distributed teams, the act of discussing material led to improved scores on the learning quiz, but these did not translate to improved post-test scores.

Our findings for overall learning gains, summarized in Table 2 and corroborated in Table 3, show that co-located teams outperformed both individuals and distributed teams. These findings are statistically significant; however, we did not observe a statistically significant difference between distributed teams and individuals.

For the learning task, shown in Table 4, our results show statistically significant differences between all conditions except for the two team conditions.

These observations corroborate Coetzee's Mechanical Turk study [5] which showed that discussing questions leads to more correct answers; however, for distributed teams this understanding doesn't appear to have carried over to similar questions. This may suggest some aspect of social loafing or an artifact of 'wisdom of the crowd'. This suggests that longitudinal studies involving transfer questions are essential when evaluating distributed teams.

4.10.1 Hypotheses

We began this study with the following three hypotheses:

H1. Learning outcomes will be highest for the students in the co-located group.

H2. Learning outcomes will be higher for students in the distributed group than for students working alone.

H3. Students in both group conditions will perceive that group interactions improved their learning.

Our results support our first hypothesis. GC (co-located) participants outperformed GD (distributed) participants by an average of 2.32 questions answered correctly and outperformed I (individual) participants by 1.67 questions.

We did not obtain statistically significant results to support our second hypothesis. GD participants had similar learning gains to I participants. This result has several possible explanations: GD participants communicated using technology and encountered technical difficulties which were not present in the other two conditions. In our study, many students were using Google Hangouts for the first time. It is also possible that distributed teams have more trouble quickly developing a conversational rapport that is need for this type of learning.

We did not obtain evidence to support our third hypothesis. There was a statistically significant difference between groups for perceived learning (ANOVA $F = 3.5, df = 2, p = 0.039$); however, this difference was between the two group conditions (GC reporting .68 higher than GD on a five-point likert scale). Neither group condition was significantly different from the individual condition. There was also no statistically significant difference for perceived enjoyment.

Table 5: Participant Preferences about Group Work, by Condition. Numbers are counts of participants expressing the preference. For some questions, participants didn't indicate a preference.

Question Statement	I Pre	GD Pre	GC Pre	I Post	GD Post	GC Post	I Dif	GD Dif	GC Dif
I work better in group projects	9	7	10	10	10	9	1	3	-1
I work better alone on projects	5	8	1	4	6	3	-1	-2	2
I learn better in groups	8	7	6	6	12	10	-2	5	4
I learn better alone	6	9	6	8	4	2	2	-5	-4

Table 6: Participant Perception Questions (Likert Scale: 1=Highly Disagree and 5=Highly Agree).

Question Statement	I Average	GD Average	GC Average
I enjoyed learning about espresso machines.	4.2	3.9	4.0
I learned a lot during this experiment.	4.0	3.8	4.4
I would be able to use an espresso machine in real life.	3.6	2.9	3.5

4.10.2 Preferences

Table 5 shows participant preferences regarding learning and working in groups in general, and Table 6 shows their perceptions about their learning in this study. Differences were only significant for perceived learning (ANOVA $F = 3.5, df = 2, p = 0.039$). Co-located participants were significantly more likely to express that they learned more about using an espresso machine than participants in the distributed condition ($p = 0.031$). We also investigated any effect that the experiment had on participant's preferences by comparing differences between participant's pre-test to post-test preferences. We found no significant change in preference related to working in groups; however; we noticed changes in participants' preferences about learning in groups. We observed that typically participants preferred the condition to which they were assigned; likely a 'good participant' artifact.

4.11 Qualitative Observations

Our participants experienced many of the potential difficulties that students typically encounter during traditional courses and more frequently in online and MOOC-based courses. These difficulties include hardware inconsistencies, student language barriers, and scheduling problems.

Technical difficulties were prevalent for distributed teams, where participants used Google Hangouts. In this condition, two of the four groups had microphone issues which forced two members to use Google chat. Without prompting, team-mates read the muted participant's comments to the group and the participant with the "lesser" modality wasn't substantially limited in terms of their ability to contribute. These and other technical difficulties caused distributed teams to take longer to finish the experiment and typically the team took the whole hour. For individuals, the experiment was much faster, sometimes as short as 35 minutes. The distributed groups typically felt rushed because of the technical issues and didn't always fully watch all of the videos. This was in contrast to the co-located groups who all watched all of the videos, and the individuals who all watched all the videos (with one exception - one individual reported that they missed watching one of the videos).

We observed that participants with severe language barriers performed poorly, but their presence did not appear to negatively impact their team-members. In fact, because of the language barrier, these groups discussed each option in depth to help the person with the language barrier understand. Of the participants used in the analysis, we had numerous participants who spoke English as a second language: 7 in co-located, 5 in distributed and 4 in individual.

In general, multiple choice questions elicited more conversation than open-ended questions. There was also substantially more gesturing by participants in co-located teams. Finally, we were surprised that only one of the distributed participants muted his video, despite the fact that most participants didn't know each other.

Multiple perspectives provide students with information that may be missing from course materials. In one example from our study, participants were asked whether steaming milk or making espresso required higher temperatures. A video explained that espresso requires 200 degrees Fahrenheit but didn't mention steaming milk. Participants in group conditions often realized that water becomes steam at 212 degrees and therefore steaming milk requires higher temperatures; however, individual participants often did not.

The team dynamics for the two group conditions were interesting to observe. First, it was difficult to create ad hoc teams for this study, as participants had to be recruited to participate during the same time slot. There were instances of participants being late and one who didn't show up, causing one of our teams to have four instead of five participants. We generally noticed that in each team there were 'power participants' and 'weak participants'. The power participants tended to dominate and their answers, whether right or wrong, tended to be accepted by other group members. In some cases, we saw members 'appease' these power participants and pretend to agree with them, but then choose different answers. The weak participants tended to be ignored, even when their answers were correct. And, due to being ignored, these participants contributed less over time.

5. DISCUSSION

We investigated whether distributed low-stakes teams could provide the same educational benefits, in terms of both engagement and learning outcomes compared to co-located low-stakes teams and individuals.

Our quantitative results show that learning gains are highest for co-located teams; supporting previous team-based learning research and lightweight teams. Results from the learning quiz corroborate findings from Coetzee's Mechanical Turk experiment [5] and suggest that presenting nonidentical post-test questions is necessary for discerning differences between students working in distributed teams. While our quantitative results were not able to support our hypotheses that distributed teams would outperform individuals, our qualitative observations tell a compelling story about the potential for distributed team-based learning.

Despite the language barriers and both hardware and software difficulties, the distributed teams did not perform significantly worse than individuals in our study. This is compelling because compared to individual learning, distributed teams offer many latent benefits, which are not easily measured – such as opportunities for networking and social interaction, an ability to observe and imitate other student's techniques for self regulated learning, and multiple perspectives to solve harder problems.

A few examples from our experiment lead us to believe that these latent benefits could be very important. We describe some of them, such as self-regulated learning, in the introduction and describe others, such as multiple perspectives and helping team-mates with technical difficulties, in the qualitative results section. We believe that these examples show a promising future for distributed teams. These examples show how participants can share their own personal perspective to clarify points of confusion. They demonstrate that teams collaborate to find ways to mitigate and even solve technical difficulties that arise. They suggest that students might feel more connected and create networks of like-minded students that may persist beyond the course.

Our specific design of distributed teams in this study can be considered one point in a large, multi-dimensional design space. If we picked a different point in this space, our distributed team might be larger in size, use Skype voice conference, and meet over successive time periods. Or we might create teams with complementary skills and have them engage using a virtual environment such as Second Life, where there are more affordances for social interaction. Thus, the fact that we did not see larger learning gains by distributed participants in our study does not mean that distributed team learning should be abandoned as a concept. There are many possibilities to explore in this design space, and we suspect that some future instantiation of distributed teams will show significant learning gains for participants.

5.1 Limitations

Having our participants use their own technology for this study is a double-edged sword. This choice lends real-world validity in that students use a variety of hardware and software to participate in online classes, and there are often technical glitches that limit or influence interaction. If we had provided hardware and software to our participants, we could have ensured that everyone had the same equipment and prevented the technical glitches that hampered the interaction of some of our participants. However, we also would have had to deal with some participants being unfamiliar with the systems we provided and that also could have hindered interaction. We opted for real-world validity and the accompanying technical glitches, but that choice does seem to have impacted some of the learning results.

In the flipped classroom deployment of lightweight teams, there is a strong temporal aspect: students get to know each other over the course of the semester and develop a relationship. Our study, consisting of a single session, does not replicate this dimension of lightweight teams. It is possible that the use of distributed low-stakes teams could lead to learning gains that are significant if teams are formed and allowed to work together over multiple sessions.

6. CONCLUSIONS AND FUTURE WORK

Our study showed that the use of co-located teams leads to higher learning gains. In our implementation of distributed teams, we didn't see similar benefits accrue for participants. We believe that the technical difficulties experienced by participants likely explains most of this. Our results support previous co-located team-based learning research and corroborate previous experiments that investigate distributed peer learning.

In future studies, we will provide a training/familiarity phase to ensure that participants are not encumbered by such technical problems. The fact that distributed teams performed similarly to individuals is promising because they additionally allow students to interact socially and develop soft-skills, such as self-regulation and teamwork. Thus, we believe that the use of lightweight teams holds promise outside of class where students may be partially or fully distributed. Clearly, environmental and temporal factors are important and many design decisions need to be investigated to better support distributed collaborative learning.

Because our co-located groups did so well, and there is already a grass-roots effort in many MOOCs to form co-located study groups, it may also be worth investigating ways to foster co-located learning outside of the classroom.

Further research is needed to understand how various factors impact learning outcomes and class engagement for distributed low-stakes teams. In particular, will the learning outcomes and engagement be improved by teams that work together as a group over time, or can teams be thrown together in an ad hoc way, meaning that each time a person joins a team, the team members are different? How does the size of the team impact the outcomes? We could even consider blended teams that are co-located during class and distributed outside of class-time.

And of course, more work is needed to investigate how specific modalities impact team work. Finally, there are reasons to believe that personality, gender and background all have significant impact on team dynamics. There is much work to do in looking at gender-matched teams; creating teams of students with complementary knowledge and skills and complementary personality traits; or creating teams that try to achieve demographic or other types of diversity. All of these factors could be amplified by interaction modalities that are less rich than face-to-face interaction.

7. ACKNOWLEDGMENTS

We would like to thank the members of the HCI lab at UNC Charlotte for piloting this study and providing feedback. This work was partially supported by the U.S. Department of Education under grant P200A130088. Any opinions, findings, conclusions, or recommendations expressed in this material are those of the authors and do not necessarily reflect those of the sponsor.

8. REFERENCES

[1] K. Ash. Educators evaluate flipped classrooms. *Education Week*, 32(2):s6–s8, 2012.

[2] A. W. Astin. What matters in college, 1993.

[3] L. Breslow, D. E. Pritchard, J. DeBoer, G. S. Stump, A. D. Ho, and D. Seaton. Studying learning in the worldwide classroom: Research into edxï£¡s first MOOC. *Research & Practice in Assessment*, 8:13–25, 2013.

[4] D. Coetzee, A. Fox, M. A. Hearst, and B. Hartmann. Chatrooms in moocs: all talk and no action. In *Proceedings of the first ACM conference on Learning@ scale conference*, pages 127–136. ACM, 2014.

[5] D. Coetzee, S. Lim, A. Fox, B. Hartmann, and M. A. Hearst. Structuring interactions for large-scale synchronous peer learning. In *Proceedings of the 18th ACM Conference on Computer Supported Cooperative Work & Social Computing*, CSCW '15. ACM, 2015.

[6] L. A. Coser. *Men of ideas*. Simon and Schuster, 1997.

[7] C. H. Crouch, J. Watkins, A. P. Fagen, and E. Mazur. Peer instruction: Engaging students one-on-one, all at once. *Research-Based Reform of University Physics*, 1(1):40–95, 2007.

[8] P. Denny, A. Luxton-Reilly, and B. Simon. Evaluating a new exam question: Parsons problems. In *Proceedings of the Fourth International Workshop on Computing Education Research*, ICER '08, pages 113–124, New York, NY, USA, 2008. ACM.

[9] B. Dorn, L. B. Schroeder, and A. Stankiewicz. Piloting trace: Exploring spatiotemporal anchored collaboration in asynchronous learning. In *Proceedings of the 18th ACM Conference on Computer Supported Cooperative Work & Social Computing*, CSCW '15, pages 393–403, New York, NY, USA, 2015. ACM.

[10] D. Fisher. Warming up to MOOCs. *Chronicle of Higher Education (Nov. 6, 2012)*, 2012.

[11] J. Foertsch, G. Moses, J. Strikwerda, and M. Litzkow. Reversing the lecture/homework paradigm using eteach® web-based streaming video software. *Journal of Engineering Education-Washington*, 91(3):267–274, 2002.

[12] X. Ge and S. M. Land. Scaffolding studentsï£¡ problem-solving processes in an ill-structured task using question prompts and peer interactions. *Educational Technology Research and Development*, 51(1):21–38, 2003.

[13] P. Goodyear. Educational design and networked learning: Patterns, pattern languages and design practice. *Australasian Journal of Educational Technology*, 21(1):82–101, 2005.

[14] M. Guzdial and J. Turns. Effective discussion through a computer-mediated anchored forum. *The journal of the learning sciences*, 9(4):437–469, 2000.

[15] D. Horton, M. Craig, J. Campbell, P. Gries, and D. Zingaro. Comparing outcomes in inverted and traditional CS1. In *Proceedings of the 2014 Conference on Innovation & Technology in Computer Science Education*, ITiCSE '14, pages 261–266, New York, NY, USA, 2014. ACM.

[16] S. Hrastinski. Asynchronous and synchronous e-learning. *Educause quarterly*, 31(4):51–55, 2008.

[17] D. W. Johnson and R. T. Johnson. Making cooperative learning work. *Theory into practice*, 38(2):67–73, 1999.

[18] D. H. Jonassen and H. Kwon II. Communication patterns in computer mediated versus face-to-face group problem solving. *Educational technology research and development*, 49(1):35–51, 2001.

[19] B. Kelley, S. Miner, and F. Haggar. Technogogy and faculty development. *Academic Exchange Quarterly*, 16(1), 2012.

[20] D. R. Krathwohl. A revision of bloom's taxonomy: An overview. *Theory into practice*, 41(4):212–218, 2002.

[21] C. Kulkarni, J. Cambre, Y. Kotturi, M. S. Bernstein, and S. R. Klemmer. Talkabout: Making distance matter with small groups in massive classes. In *Proceedings of the 18th ACM Conference on Computer Supported Cooperative Work & Social Computing*, CSCW '15, pages 1116–1128. ACM, 2015.

[22] M. Lage, G. Platt, and M. Treglia. Inverting the classroom: A gateway to creating an inclusive learning environment. *The Journal of Economic Education*, 31(1):30–43, 2000.

[23] C. Latulipe, N. B. Long, and C. E. Seminario. Structuring flipped classes with lightweight teams and gamification. In *Proceedings of the 46th ACM Technical Symposium on Computer Science Education*, pages 392–397. ACM, 2015.

[24] J. Lave and E. Wenger. *Situated learning: Legitimate peripheral participation*. Cambridge university press, 1991.

[25] J. Mackness, S. Mak, and R. Williams. The ideals and reality of participating in a MOOC. In *Networked Learning Conference*, pages 266–275. University of Lancaster, 2010.

[26] G. M. Olson and J. S. Olson. Distance matters. *Human-computer interaction*, 15(2):139–178, 2000.

[27] H. L. Roediger and J. D. Karpicke. Test-enhanced learning taking memory tests improves long-term retention. *Psychological science*, 17(3):249–255, 2006.

[28] A. Russo and S. H. Warren. Collaborative test taking. *College Teaching*, 47(1):18–20, 1999.

[29] G. Salomon, D. N. Perkins, and T. Globerson. Partners in cognition: Extending human intelligence with intelligent technologies. *Educational researcher*, 20(3):2–9, 1991.

[30] E. Schneider. Welcome to the MOOCspace: a proposed theory and taxonomy for massive open online courses. In *AIED 2013 Workshops Proceedings Volume*, page 2, 2013.

[31] N. M. Schullery, R. F. Reck, and S. E. Schullery. Toward solving the high enrollment, low engagement dilemma: A case study in introductory business. *International Journal of Business, Humanities and Technology*, 1(2):1–9, 2011.

[32] D. H. Schunk and B. J. Zimmerman. Social origins of self-regulatory competence. *Educational psychologist*, 32(4):195–208, 1997.

[33] V. Singh, C. Latulipe, E. Carroll, and D. Lottridge. The choreographer's notebook: a video annotation system for dancers and choreographers. In *Proceedings*

of the 8th ACM conference on Creativity and cognition, pages 197–206. ACM, 2011.

[34] R. E. Slavin. Cooperative learning. *Review of educational research*, 50(2):315–342, 1980.

[35] L. Springer, M. E. Stanne, and S. S. Donovan. Effects of small-group learning on undergraduates in science, mathematics, engineering, and technology: A meta-analysis. *Review of educational research*, 69(1):21–51, 1999.

[36] J. Strayer. *The effects of the classroom flip on the learning environment: a comparison of learning activity in a traditional classroom and a flip classroom that used an intelligent tutoring system.* PhD thesis, The Ohio State University, 2007.

[37] J. Thornburg. If you build it, will they come?–flipping the classroom. *Mining Key Pedagogical Approaches*, page 79, 2012.

[38] D. Uribe, J. D. Klein, and H. Sullivan. The effect of computer-mediated collaborative learning on solving ill-defined problems. *Educational Technology Research and Development*, 51(1):5–19, 2003.

[39] L. S. Vygotsky. Mind and society: The development of higher mental processes, 1978.

[40] J. Weedman. Conversation and community: The potential of electronic conferences for creating intellectual proximity in distributed learning environments. *Journal of the American Society for Information Science*, 50(10):907–928, 1999.

[41] D. S. Weld, E. Adar, L. Chilton, R. Hoffmann, E. Horvitz, M. Koch, J. Landay, C. H. Lin, and M. Mausam. Personalized online education - a crowdsourcing challenge. In *Workshops at the Twenty-Sixth AAAI Conference on Artificial Intelligence*, pages 1–31, 2012.

Comparing the Effectiveness of Online Learning Approaches on CS1 Learning Outcomes

Michael J. Lee and Andrew J. Ko

Information School I DUB Group
University of Washington
{mjslee, ajko}@uw.edu

ABSTRACT

People are increasingly turning to online resources to learn to code. However, despite their prevalence, it is still unclear how successful these resources are at teaching CS1 programming concepts. Using a pretest-posttest study design, we measured the performance of 60 novices before and after they used one of the following, randomly assigned learning activities: 1) complete a Python course on a website called Codecademy, 2) play through and finish a debugging game called Gidget, or 3) use Gidget's puzzle designer to write programs from scratch. The pre- and post-test exams consisted of 24 multiple choice questions that were selected and validated based on data from 1,494 crowdsourced respondents. All 60 of our novices across the three conditions did poorly on the exams overall in both the pre-tests and post-tests (e.g., the best median post-test score was 50% correct). However, those completing the Codecademy course and those playing through the Gidget game showed over a 100% increase in correct answers when comparing their post-test exam scores to their pre-test exam scores. Those playing Gidget, however, achieved these same learning gains in half the time. This was in contrast to novices that used the puzzle designer, who did not show any measurable learning gains. All participants performed similarly within their own conditions, regardless of gender, age, or education. These findings suggest that discretionary online educational technologies can successfully teach novices introductory programming concepts (to a degree) within a few hours when explicitly guided by a curriculum.

Categories and Subject Descriptors

K.3.2 Computer Science Education: Introductory Programming, D.2.5 Testing and Debugging.

General Terms

Design; Human Factors; Measurement.

Keywords

Programming; debugging; educational game; computing education; learning outcomes; Gidget; Codecademy.

1. INTRODUCTION

In recent years, major efforts such as the Hour of Code and CS Education Week events have attracted millions of people, including celebrities and even the U.S. president, to try programming using many of the discretionary learning resources available for free online [4]. These resource include tutorial websites such as

Figure 1. We examined if novice programmers produced measurable learning outcomes after using the three different types of discretionary, online learning tools shown here.

Codecademy [14] and CodeSchool [17], open-ended creative environments such as Scratch [49] and Alice [19,21], and educational games such as Gidget [30] and LightBot [46]. Users of these systems report that they enjoy these informal resources more than traditional coursework because they allow for flexibility in how they learn, they provide a better sense of retention of the material [7], and they are more motivating, engaging, and interesting than traditional classroom courses [20]. Some of these attitudes can be attributed to these resources' use of game mechanics such as scaffolded materials, structured mastery learning, concrete goals, and extrinsic incentives such as badges [77]. Furthermore, these online resources allow users to learn about programming in a safe environment at their own pace, which gives them the opportunity to clear up any of their negative misconceptions about programming or their ability to learn it, to something more positive [12].

Although all these resources are undoubtably useful at attracting, exposing, and engaging new people in computer programming, few (if any) of these online resources report anything beyond the number of users that have signed up for their services and how many activities their users have completed. We do not know how long it takes learners to complete (or quit) the activities, if they ever come back, or, most importantly, what they are learning, if anything. This lack of evaluation makes it unclear how useful these tools are beyond merely engaging learners for a brief period of time, which resources are actually successful at teaching coding, or what parts of these resources contribute to success or failure. Without this knowledge, we risk designing instructional tools that do not actually instruct learners [28].

To investigate the learning outcomes of these online resources, we conducted a pretest-posttest experiment using three types of online educational technologies (see Figure 1), comparing the learning gains of each. We specifically compared the Python course on Codecademy [14], a debugging puzzle game called Gidget [30], and the open-ended creative environment found in Gidget called the Puzzle Designer [41], which is analogous to other creative development environments such as Scratch [49] and Alice [19,21]. We recruited learners aged 18 and above through Mechanical Turk.

In the rest of this paper, we discuss prior work on educational technologies, detail our test and study design, and discuss our results and their implications for online computing education.

2. RELATED WORK

This paper explores three major areas of work in educational technologies designed to teach beginners programming online: 1) open-ended, creative environments, 2) massively open online courses (MOOCs), and 3) educational games. Although these resources may differ in the way they deliver content and engage their users, there is little doubt that online learning will continue to be a major medium in 21st century computing education. This requires us not only to know about how these different instructional approaches perform in isolation, but also how they compare.

Open-ended, creative environments are largely unstructured and allow users to explore, tinker, and create content that is meaningful for themselves. These attributes align with constructivist theories of learning through hands-on experience [66] and constructionist ideas of learning through construction of meaningful projects [52]. Exemplars of these kinds of environments include Scratch [49] and Alice [19,21]. Prior work has shown that summer camps using these resources are great at engaging their users [10,73], but all of these reports required instructional scaffolding by teachers for learners to succeed.

MOOCs and self-paced learning resources such as CodeSchool [17], Codecademy [14], edX [25], and Khan Academy [35] attract millions of users and are an increasingly popular way for people to learn new skills such as programming. Many people view these approaches as connectivist learning, which is related to social learning theory (learning through social interactions and experiences). However, as Connolly and Stansfield [18] have suggested, many of these resources simply replicate the traditional classroom experience and may be too focused trying to deliver materials over the web rather than on teaching and learning, or motivating and engaging students [64].

Educators have considered games to be a beneficial platform in supporting student learning [55] and have pushed for more educational games to teach STEM (science, technology, engineering, and mathematics) subjects [32,56]. Games have been designed using a range of learning approaches, some constructivist (allowing learners to participate and experiment in non-threatening scenarios), some experiential (learning by doing), and some situated (providing relevant context or setting; for multiplayer, learning takes place alongside social interaction and collaboration). Video games are able to engage learners over extensive periods of time and can also motivate learners to replay the game repeatedly until they have mastered it [36]. This includes educational games such as CodeHunt [16], LightBot [46], CodeCombat [15], and Gidget [30]. Researchers have taken advantage of this interest to improve educational games to be more fun, informative, and educational, prompting more people to use games for both education and entertainment [29,54,76]. Some research focuses on creating games that directly try to teach a skill or subject such as computer programming [24,42,43,44], others focus on adding game-like features to existing teaching systems such as intelligent tutors [34,51], and some focus more generally on creating frameworks for effective evaluation [1,61]. Several works have also attempted to identify the specific parts of games that motivate [48] and attract people to pursue computing education [28,29,48].

Researchers and educators have evaluated the efficacy of many of these systems in isolation (e.g., Scratch [3,27], Alice [68], and edX [9]), and in comparison with other similar systems (e.g. Scratch vs. Karel [59]). However, only a few have examined how to effectively measure the outcomes of educational games [31,61], and very little

is known about how online educational games actually compare to other technologies such as MOOCs and open-ended creative environments in teaching their users introductory programming concepts [13]. We aim to address this gap by comparing the learning outcomes of an open-ended creative environment, a self-paced MOOC, and an educational game.

3. METHOD

The goal of our study was to examine the extent to which adult novices of any age showed measurable learning gains after using one of three online learning technologies. To do this, we first selected three learning activities that are representative of the types of discretionary, online resources that people currently use to learn programming: 1) an online tutorial system using a web-based IDE, where learners go through a didactic, structured curriculum, 2) an educational game using an IDE, where learners go through a problem-based, structured curriculum, and 3) an open-ended creation IDE, where there is no planned curriculum and learners acquire skills by creating with code. Next, we developed a test designed to measure one's knowledge of different introductory programming concepts before and after completing one of the learning activities.

Our null hypothesis was:

> H0: There is no difference in learners' *post-test performance* among the conditions after completing their assigned learning activity.

In the rest of this section, we describe our three learning activities in more detail, explain the design of our pre-post test, and discuss the experiment designed to test our hypothesis.

3.1 Learning Activities

3.1.1. Activity 1: Codecademy Course

Codecademy [14] is a popular online interactive tutorial website that offers free courses in multiple programming languages (see Figure 2). It has had over 24 million users who have completed over 100 million exercises [67]. For our study, learners participated in the introductory "Python Language Skills" course. According to the Codecademy website, over 2.5 million users are enrolled in this course designed for beginners. The website also states that the Python course takes an estimated 13 hours to complete.

Codecademy's course interface consists of a two-pane window split vertically on the screen (see Figure 2). The left pane consists of instructions, examples, and hints for the user to follow. For each activity, it contains a numbered list of explicit instructions for the user to follow (e.g., "01. Set the variable *my_varaiable* equal to the

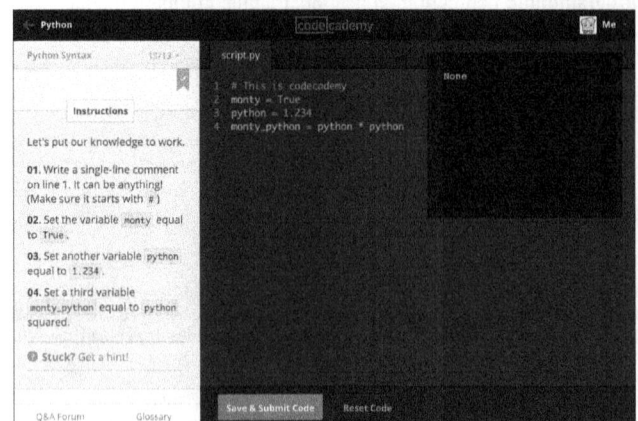

Figure 2. A Codecademy lesson, where users follow step-by-step instructions entering code into a virtual terminal.

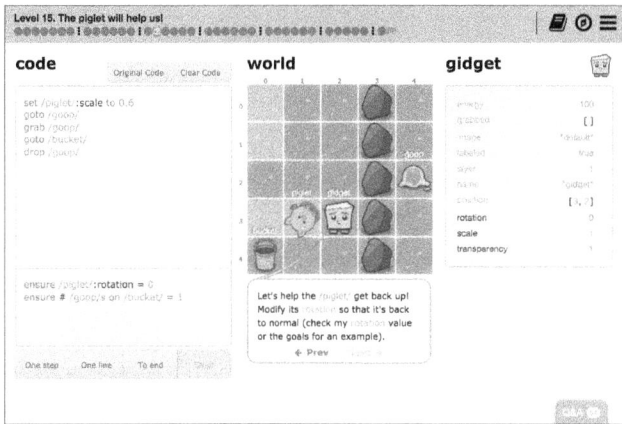

Figure 3. The Gidget game. Where players help a robotic character fix its code to complete 37 missions.

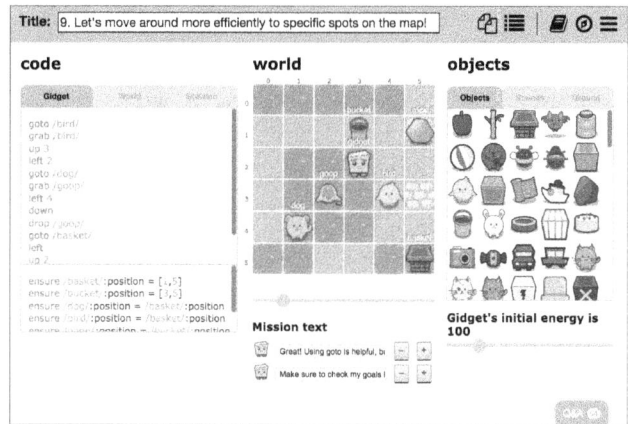

Figure 4. The Gidget Puzzle Designer, which players can use to create their own Gidget levels using a blank canvas.

value *10*" and "02. Click the *Save & Submit* button to run your code."). The right pane is an IDE for users to type in and execute their code, with an overlay on the upper-right corner that shows console output on code execution. In case learners need assistance, there is a "Stuck? Get a hint!" button below the list of instructions on the left pane that users can click to view more help text. The hints are typically explicit instructions (e.g., "All you need to do is type *3* after the equals sign on line 8.") or closely related examples (e.g., "Make sure you're setting your variable like this: *the_machine_goes = 'Ping!' "*.). Finally, the bottom-most area of the left pane includes two buttons that opens up a new browser tab: one labeled "Q&A forum" where fellow Codecademy users can post and answer questions, and another one labeled "glossary," that goes to a dictionary of Python commands and concepts.

The introductory Python course has a total of 12 modules covering the following topics: syntax, variables, mathematical and logical operator, strings, conditionals, control flow, functions, lists and dictionaries, and advanced concepts (e.g., classes and file input/ output). Each module is split into two parts. The first part is designed to teach a specific concept or set of concepts and consists of several activities that subsequently build on the previous activity. The second part of the section is an exercise to practice combining the first part to build something interesting. For example, in the case of the syntax module (where learners are introduced to variable assignment and the use of mathematical operators), the second part of the module tasks users to fill in variables with values to calculate gratuity for a meal.

To ensure that the concepts covered by Codecademy and the Gidget game (described below) were as close as possible, we asked learners to complete only the first 8 of 12 modules before taking our post-test. Although learners would not be tested on these extra advanced concepts on the post-test exam, finishing them would have given them additional practice with many of the previously learned concepts. We asked learners to keep track of the time they spent using Codecademy so that they could report their total time after taking the post-test exam. Since the Codecademy website states it takes around 13 hours to complete the 12 modules in the Python course, we informed our tutorial condition participants it would take approximately 10 hours to complete their assigned 8 modules before they started their activity.

3.1.2. Activity 2: Gidget Game

Gidget is a web application (see Figure 3) that has been played by thousands of people worldwide, with nearly half of its users being female [30,40]. The game was specifically designed to teach and appeal to both youth [41] and adult [12] novices, presenting

debugging tasks as puzzles and using an imperative Python-like programming language. For this study, we asked learners to play through the entire game, which takes approximately 5 hours [41]. In each level of the game, the player must identify the level goals (written as test cases), inspect the given code, then modify and execute it until it satisfies all the level's test cases. Following the mastery learning paradigm [53], each of the game's levels is designed to be passable only if the learner has grasped a particular concept in the game's programming language.

Gidget's interface consists of three vertically-split sections (see Figure 3). The left section consists of the IDE to type in code, the list of goals (written as test cases that are checked after code execution), and the execution buttons. The execution buttons allow the player to control the level of execution (e.g., one compiled instruction, all instructions on one line of code like a breakpoint debugger, or the entire program), or halt the program. The central section shows the graphical representation of all the characters and objects in the game world, and also includes a large speech bubble where the game's protagonist provides detailed explanation of the execution of each statement in the program, highlighting changes in the runtime environment. This serves as the game's primary instructional content, explicitly teaching the language syntax and semantics. Finally, the right section updates after each instruction, showing the current runtime state of all the game's current objects and their respective variables.

The game had a total of 7 modules totaling 37 levels, with each module containing a set of levels focusing on a related set of programming keywords or concepts. The game covered exactly the same topics as the Codecademy modules listed earlier, excluding Python dictionaries and the "advanced topics," which we asked Codecademy participants to skip so the two learning activities would be as similar as possible. Each module was split into two parts, where each level in the first part (between 3-5 levels) had a specific learning objective to familiarize the player with a specific programming concept. The second part of each module included two assessment levels where learners did not have to edit code, but had to answer a question that cumulatively tested the concepts for that module. This was found in prior work to improve adult players' engagement and subsequent level completion speed [44].

Gidget included several ways for players to receive help. After signing up, the game presents the player with a tutorial highlighting and explaining the different parts of the interface and the sequence of steps players should take to proceed through each level. The game also features an in-game reference guide, providing explanations and examples of each command in the language. The reference guide was available as a standalone help guide or as tooltips that appeared when hovering over tokens in the code editor. This was further enhanced by the inclusion of the Idea Garden [11], which analyzed the players' code in real-time and presented context sensitive suggestions if the player requested it, and AnswerDash [2], which allowed players to click on any part of the interface to ask questions about it or read responses to others' queries. Finally, the game's code editor provided keystroke-level feedback about syntax and semantics errors, underlining erroneous code in red and explaining the problem in Gidget's speech bubble.

Based on prior studies [40,41], we told our game condition participants that Gidget would take about 5 hours to complete before they started the activity. We required learners to complete all the levels before taking the post-test. For this specific condition, we automatically logged the time learners took to complete the game.

3.1.3. Activity 3: Gidget Puzzle Designer

The Gidget Puzzle Designer (GPD) is an integrated development environment used to create and edit Gidget levels (see Figure 4). It is normally unlocked after finishing the Gidget game. However, for our study, participants were given access to the GPD without any prior experience playing the Gidget game. This was to mirror other open-ended, creation-oriented learning environments like Scratch [49], Alice [19,21], and others [37], where users are free to explore and tinker to make their own projects.

The interface for the GPD is a modified version of the regular Gidget game interface, allowing modification of previously un-editable code such as the starting world code, the level goals, the dimension of the world grid, and Gidget's introductory dialogue and emotional state at the beginning of the level. In addition, the status pane on the rightmost section is replaced by a tabbed inventory of available characters and objects, ground tiles, and sounds that the learner can use to populate and enrich their programs.

All of the same help tools available in the Gidget game are also available in the GPD. This includes the syntax highlighting, tooltips, dictionary, and Idea Garden suggestions. In addition to the help systems, the learners had access to view and edit all of the regular game levels, giving them pre-designed puzzles to modify for creative purposes. These examples also included the solution (i.e., learners could see both the incorrect code and the correct code) for each level. The assessment levels from the end of each module were excluded, and all the default editable levels were listed in sequential order without indicating which module they belonged to. Similar types of help and examples are available in both Scratch and Alice to help bootstrap learner engagement.

Unlike Codecademy and the Gidget game, the GPD did not have a curriculum or sequence of steps to follow. Therefore, to help orient our GPD users, we showed them a list of directions before they started with their activity. First, we told them their task was to "Use a creative canvas tool to create multiple stories for a robotic character named Gidget." This is based on several works, primarily by Kelleher et al. [38,39], which shows that adding storytelling elements to open-ended creative environments can significantly increase users' engagement [33,60,72]. Second, we told them about the various help features available (see previous paragraph and section 3.1.2), and how to access them. Third, we asked them to "create, explore, and play with the website for at least *several hours* to get the full learning experience" with the activity, to mirror the ideal case of a learner first engaging with an open-ended, creative online environment. For this condition, we automatically logged the time learners spent in the GPD, and collected records of all the levels they created.

3.2 Knowledge Test for C1 Concepts

In order to measure how much participants learned and what they learned, we created and validated a test designed to be taken before and after the learning activities. We adopted this pre-test/post-test design as it widely used in both educational and non-educational contexts to measure change resulting from experimental treatments [6,13,23]. Although we spent considerable time creating and validating the test, its description will mostly be limited to this section as it is not the main contribution of this paper.

First, we determined which concepts to test by comparing the topics that are taught commonly in introductory programming courses [22,26,45,69,78] to the set of concepts that were covered in our Codecademy and Gidget game activities. We chose a total of eight concepts: basics (i.e., variables, mathematical operators, relational operators, Booleans), logical operators, selection statements (i.e., conditionals), arrays, indefinite loops (i.e., while), definite loops (i.e., for), function parameters, and function returns.

We modeled our test questions after Allison Tew's dissertation work on the FCS1, a programming language-independent test using pseudo-code [69]. In her studies, Tew showed that testing introductory programming students in the classroom with their native course language and in pseudo-code were strongly correlated [70] and has the extra benefit of demonstrating transfer of learning [8]. We generated pseudo-code questions using the examples, descriptions, and two-page pseudo-code guide Tew provided [69]. Questions used a verbose style adapted from guides for programmers published by Whitford [75] and Shackelford [62]. To minimize confounding factors in syntax design, we followed the latest evidence on syntax learnability, excluding semi-colons and curly braces, indenting code blocks, upper-casing reserved words, and closing program blocks with explicit keywords [63] (see Figures 5 and 6 for examples).

Based on guidelines and examples from Tew's dissertation, we designed 5 multiple choice questions for each of the concepts

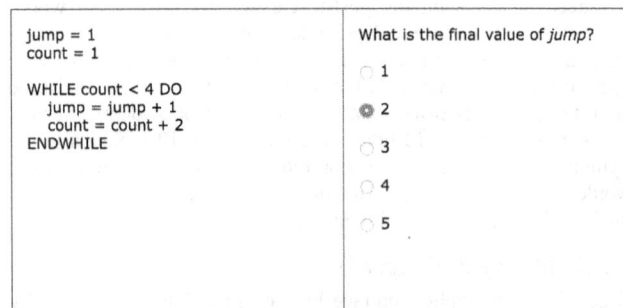

number = 81
 	
IF number >= 90 THEN
    element = 'fire'
ELSE IF number >= 80 THEN
    element = 'water'
ELSE IF number >= 70 THEN
    element = 'metal'
ELSE IF number >= 60 THEN
    element = 'earth'
ELSE
    element = 'wood'
ENDIF
	What is the final value of *element*?
	
	○ fire
	◉ water
	○ metal
	○ earth
	○ wood

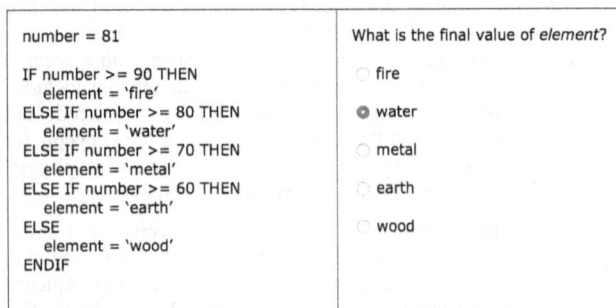

Figure 5. Screenshot of an "if/else" pseudo-code question from the pre- & post-tests with its answer choices.

jump = 1
count = 1
 	
WHILE count < 4 DO
    jump = jump + 1
    count = count + 2
ENDWHILE
	What is the final value of *jump*?
	
	○ 1
	◉ 2
	○ 3
	○ 4
	○ 5

Figure 6. Screenshot of a "while" pseudo-code question from the pre- & post-tests with its answer choices.

Table 1. Demographic summary.

	Tutorial n=20	Game n=20	Canvas n=20
Gender (male : female)	10 : 10	11 : 9	11 : 9
Age (min, median, max)	18, 23, 35	18, 25, 41	19, 23, 29
Max education: high school	5%	0%	0%
Max education: some college	10%	10%	5%
Max education: college degree	85%	85%	90%
Max education: master degree	0%	5%	5%

Table 2. Summary statistics pre-test and post-test scores.

	Tutorial n=20	Game n=20	Canvas n=20
Minimum score on pre-test	2	0	3
Median score on pre-test	5	5	5.5
Maximum score on pre-test	8	6	9
Minimum score on post-test	6	4	3
Median score on post-test	12	10	5
Maximum score on post-test	18	16	9
Percent increase between median pre-test and post-test scores	140%	100%	-9.1%

covered in our learning activities, for a total of 40 questions. All questions had one correct response and four incorrect distractors. We designed distractors to deliberately test for common programming misconceptions [5,71].

To validate our 40 questions, we recruited people on Mechanical Turk (MTurk). MTurk is an online marketplace where individuals aged 18 and over (called "Turkers") can receive micro-payments for doing small tasks. Our Turkers were paid 2 cents to answer one pseudo-code question, indicate their experience with programming, and optionally provide their email address. No additional demographic information was collected. Each Turker could answer up to an additional 39 questions for 2 cents each. In these cases, each additional question would be new, and the Turker did not have to re-enter their answers for programming experience or their e-mail address (if provided previously). To mitigate ordering effects, questions were randomly sequenced each time a participant took the survey. Answer choices for questions that did not require a specific order were randomly arranged as well.

To identify problems with our questions and answer choices, we ran two rounds of pilot tests, with each question getting at least 3 responses for each iteration of testing. We corrected issues dealing with ambiguous/confusing wording, inappropriate distractors, syntax errors, and typos. To achieve this, we looked for data anomalies (e.g., nobody getting the answer correct, or everyone choosing the same answer) and requested open-ended feedback from our respondents. We then ran a full test with 1,494 Turkers and had a total of 8,011 responses to our questions (approximately 200 responses per question). The majority of our Turkers only answered one question, with 11% completing 3 or more questions.

To avoid ceiling and floor effects and to maximize discriminability of the assessment, we categorized our data by splitting responses by the Turkers' self-reported programming experience. We categorized *novices* as those who responded "never" to all of the following statements: 1) "taken a programming course," 2) "written a computer program," and 3) "contributed code towards the development of a computer program." All other respondents were considered *experienced* programmers. For our finalized list of exam questions, we selected the top 3 questions for each concept (for a total of 24) with highest variance between novice and experienced programmers (that is, those that novices tended to get incorrect and those with experience tended to get correct).

3.4 Participants and Procedure

The independent variable in our experiment was the instructional approach, which had three levels: 1) *tutorial* (complete the introductory Python programming tutorial on Codecademy), 2) *game* (play through the Gidget game), or 3) *canvas* (use the GPD to create Gidget levels). To help participants make an informed decision about the time commitment required to participate in our study, we told them that they were allowed seven days to complete

their assigned task, and provided an estimate of the number of hours their task would take (10 hours for the tutorial condition, 5 hours for the game condition, and open-ended for the canvas condition). We emphasized these hours were estimates, and that they could potentially take more or less time than what was listed.

We recruited our participants from Mechanical Turk, specifically sampling adults who self-reported that they had no experience with programming (see previous section). We also required participants to be U.S. residents to minimize English language barriers with the instructions and activities. Participants were compensated $10 for completing their assigned task. This amount was carried over from a previous study [44] and adjusted to account for the extra time required for the pre-test and post-test.

We sent participants an e-mail with a link that randomly assigned them to a condition and redirected them to the web-based pre-test. Each link was uniquely associated with a specific e-mail address, so that we could identify the owner of each test. Like our pilot study (see section 3.2), we randomly ordered our finalized collection of 24 questions to minimize ordering effects, also randomizing the order of the answers, where appropriate. The test only showed one question at a time (see Figures 5 and 6) and it was not possible to go back to a previous question. Each question required a response before being able to move onto the next question. There was a progress indicator on the top of the page showing participants how many questions remained. The system automatically logged each answer choice and the total time to complete the exam(s).

The pre-tests and post-tests were identical across all conditions. There was only one exception to this: the post-test for those in the tutorial condition had two additional questions for the participants to report how many modules they completed, and the time they spent to complete their Codecademy activity. The introductory text for the pre-test briefly explained that participants would be answering coding questions and that they should try their best even though they might not be familiar with the content. The introductory text for the post-test briefly explained that the questions were written in another, related programming language that covered the same concepts available in the learning activity they had completed.

Our study was a between-subjects design, with an even split of 20 people each among the three conditions. Our participants did not differ significantly by gender, age, or education (see Table 1). Consistent with other studies about the demographics of MTurk workers [57], we found that our participants were well-educated, with the majority reporting that they had at least a bachelor's degree (see Table 1).

Table 3. Percent increase between pre & post -test scores. Groupings with a mean >= 100% are in bold. Groupings with a mean >= 150% are also *italicized* in *red*.

Question + Concept (actual question ordered randomly)		(posttest - pretest) / pretest		
		Tutorial	Game	Canvas
Q1	basics	**175%**	60%	-40%
Q2	basics	**120%**	60%	0%
Q3	basics	**100%**	50%	0%
Q4	logical operators	*175%*	**133.3%**	-66.7%
Q5	logical operators	*125%*	**120%**	-40%
Q6	logical operators	*150%*	**166.7%**	-20%
Q7	if / else	**100%**	**100%**	20%
Q8	if / else	**100%**	80%	0%
Q9	if / else	80%	**100%**	0%
Q10	arrays	75%	**100%**	-33.3%
Q11	arrays	60%	50%	-40%
Q12	arrays	**100%**	50%	-33.3%
Q13	while	*225%*	*166.7%*	-60%
Q14	while	*333.3%*	*266.7%*	0%
Q15	while	*266.7%*	*125%*	0%
Q16	for	**100%**	**66.7%**	-50%
Q17	for	**200%**	**133.3%**	0%
Q18	for	80%	**100%**	-40%
Q19	function parameters	*140%*	*166.7%*	25%
Q20	function parameters	*233.3%*	*200%*	0%
Q21	function parameters	*233.3%*	*200%*	25%
Q22	function return	**166.7%**	*200%*	-50%
Q23	function return	80%	*166.7%*	-33.3%
Q24	function return	**125%**	*160%*	0%

4. RESULTS

We provide quantitative results comparing the learning outcomes from our three groups. Throughout this analysis, we use non-parametric Chi-Squared and Wilcoxon rank sums tests with $\alpha=0.01$ confidence, as our data were not normally distributed. For post-hoc analyses, we use the Bonferroni correction for three comparisons: $(\alpha/3 = 0.0033)$.

4.1 Better Post-Scores with Tutorial & Game

Overall, participants did poorly on the pre-test exams, with a median score of 5 out of 24 questions correct (20.8%) across all three conditions (see Table 2). This was expected, as we had selected the questions most difficult for novices from our original set. We compared the pre-test scores across the conditions and found no significant difference, confirming that all of our participants' programming knowledge was roughly equivalent prior to the learning activities.

Participants also did poorly on the post-tests, with the highest median score among the conditions being 12 out of 24 questions correct (50%). However, comparing the post-test scores across the conditions reveal that there is a significant difference in learning gains between conditions $(\chi^2(2,N=60)=27.03,p<.01)$. Post-hoc analysis with Bonferroni correction revealed that two conditional pairs were significantly different: the tutorial vs. canvas conditions $(W=226,Z=-5.00,\ p<.01/3)$ and the game vs. canvas conditions

$(W=272.5,Z=-3.72,\ p<.01/3)$. The scores on the post-test between the tutorial and game conditions did not show a significant difference. Based on these findings, we reject our null hypothesis (see section 3).

These results indicate that though all the participants had approximately the same programming knowledge during the pre-test, participants from the *tutorial* and *game* condition performed significantly better on their post-test, and that their degree of improvement was also significantly greater than that of the *canvas* condition. As seen in Table 2, the effect sizes of learning gains were 140% and 100% increase in scores for the *tutorial* and *game* conditions, respectively, whereas the median score from the *canvas* condition did not change significantly (and were actually 9.1% worse). Since participants had little programming knowledge to start with and there was no difference in demographics, the learning activities are likely the primary cause of the increase in scores for the tutorial and game condition participants.

4.3 Differences in Percent Increase of Scores

Although we had a relatively small sample size of 20 participants per condition, we found consistent patterns, particularly in the tutorial and game conditions, where participants made large percent gains answering questions correctly in their post-tests compared to their pre-tests (see Tables 3 and 4). As we saw in section 4.1, the tutorial and game condition participants performed much better than their canvas condition counterparts. This was particularly true for the basic concepts (i.e., variables, mathematical operators, relational operators, Booleans), logical operators, while loops, for loops, function parameters, and function returns, where participants increased their rate of correct answers by at least 100% in their post-test compared to their pre-test.

Tutorial and game condition participants made the largest improvements (greater than or equal to 150% increase) with *while loop* and *function parameters* concepts. Tutorial condition participants also made these large improvements answering questions about *logical operators*, while the game condition participants also made similarly large improvements answering questions about *function return*s. These results indicate that the tutorial and game conditions' learning activities were successful in helping their participants learn about all the concepts we tested for.

Canvas condition participants did not do well compared to their counterparts. Although we know from section 4.1 that the canvas condition participants did not do significantly worse on their post-tests compared to their pre-tests overall, Table 3 shows that they struggled answering many of the post-test questions, actually performing worse on many concepts in the post-test, despite encountering the identical questions.

Table 4. Summary statistics for activity times.

	Tutorial n=20	Game n=20	Canvas n=20
Minimum time on pre-test	20 min	22 min	20 min
Median time on pre-test	25.5 min	28 min	26 min
Maximum time on pre-test	33 min	31 min	41 min
Minimum time on activity	7.0 hours	3.61 hours	1.25 hours
Median time on activity	9.25 hours	4.76 hours	1.94 hours
Maximum time on activity	14.0 hours	7.22 hours	2.98 hours
Minimum time on post-test	23 min	29 min	19 min
Median time on post-test	35 min	34 min	24 min
Maximum time on post-test	55 min	42 min	35 min

These results indicate that online, educational tutorial and game resources can be successful at teaching users about programming concepts, but that open-ended creative resources in discretionary settings, at least in solitary, are likely not. Tutorial and game condition participants' scores indicate that there are large, measurable learning outcomes (see bolded text in Table 2), and that these learning activities might teach certain concepts better than others (see above and italicized text in Table 3).

4.3 More Time on Exams for Tutorial & Game

During the pre-test, participants from all conditions spent roughly the same amount of time on their exams (see Table 4). However, when we examine the time they spent on their post-test, there is a significant difference in time spent by condition $(\chi^2(2,N=60)=17.87,p<.01)$. Doing post-hoc analysis with Bonferroni correction, we found that the tutorial participants spent significantly more time on the post-test than the canvas condition $(W=288.5, Z=-3.29,p<.01/3)$; the same was true of the game vs. canvas conditions $(W=263.5,Z=-3.96, p<.01/3)$. The time spent on the post-test between the tutorial and game conditions did not show a significant difference.

4.4 Differences on Learning Activity Time

Each of the three learning activities had largely different estimated times for completion (10 hours for Codecademy, 5 hours for Gidget, and open-ended for the GPD). Examining the time spent on each task (see Table 4), we see that there was indeed a significant difference in time participants spent on their respective activities $(\chi^2(2,N=60)=52.34, p<.01)$. With a post-hoc analysis with Bonferroni correction, we found that all pairwise comparisons were significantly different: tutorial vs. canvas $(W=210, Z=-5.40, p<.01/3)$, tutorial vs. game $(W=211, Z=-5.37, p<.01/3)$, and game vs. canvas $(W=210, Z=-5.40, p<.01/3)$.

Combined with the large difference on exam performance in the post-test and pre-test (from section 4.1), this suggests that the *game* condition was the most efficient of the three conditions at improving participants' post-test scores. Examining Table 4 reveals that the tutorial condition participants took nearly twice as long as the game condition participants to complete their assigned learning activity that covered the same materials (see sections 3.1.1 and 3.1.2), but performed similarly in their post-test (from section 4.2), further demonstrating that the game condition participants were most efficient at improving their post-test scores.

4.5 No Demographic Differences in Test Scores

We found that there were no significant differences in learning gains within the groups by gender. This indicates that males and females all performed similarly within their respective conditions.

Next, we used a simple linear regression for each condition's pre-test and post-test to predict test scores based on age. No significant correlation was found between test scores or age for any of the conditions in either of the tests. This indicates everyone performed similarly within their respective conditions, regardless of their age.

For completeness, we also examined if prior education (as measured in Table 1) had an effect on pre-test and post-test scores by condition. We found no significant differences within groups by education. This indicates everyone, regardless of education, performed similarly within their respective conditions.

4.6 No Demographic Differences in Test Time

We examined if gender had any effect on the time participants spent on the pre-tests and post-tests by condition. We found that there were no significant differences within the groups by gender. This indicates that males and females all spent a similar amount of time on their tests within their respective conditions.

Next, we used a simple linear regression for each condition's pre-test and post-test to predict the time spent on tests based on age. No significant correlation was found between the time spent on tests and age for any of the conditions in either of the tests. This indicates everyone spent a comparable amount of time on their tests within their respective conditions regardless of their age.

Finally, we examined if education had any effect on the time spent on the pre-tests and post-tests by condition. We found no significant differences within groups by participants' level of education. This indicates everyone, regardless of their level of education, spent a similar amount of time on their tests within their respective conditions.

5. DISCUSSION

Our findings show that online discretionary resources for computing education such as tutorial websites and games can be successful in teaching adult novices programming concepts without the need for additional external help. Even with relatively small sample sizes, we were able to see large differences in the time players spent on the learning activities, the exams, and their exam scores. All participants performed consistently within their own groups, without any significant differences in the time they spent on either the pre-tests or post-tests, the time on their learning activities, or on their exam scores. This consistency is also reflected in participants' demographics, which showed no differences between males or females, people of different ages, or level of education, within all conditions. This is particularly important for online discretionary learning, because our results indicate that all of our learning activities were gender-neutral, with everyone performing at equal levels within their respective conditions, which does not typically happen in programming-related classroom settings [58,74].

We found that participants in the tutorial and game conditions significantly increased their overall post-test scores by over 100% in comparison to their pre-test scores (see Table 2). These participants showed considerable gains for similar questions (see Table 3), suggesting that the learning activities from both the conditions taught similar concepts and also taught them equally well. Although these participants showed improvements across all the concepts we tested (see Table 3), the highest increases were in: basics, logical operators, while loops, for loops, function parameters, and function returns. Moreover, participants from the tutorial condition appeared to do slightly better on logical operator questions while participants from the game condition did slightly better on the function return questions. We examined the instruction of these two concepts in both Codecademy and the Gidget game, but did not find anything obviously different from the modules teaching those specific concepts from the other concepts within the same learning activity. Like the rest of the interactions within those groups, Codecademy had its users follow step-by-step instructions entering code into its IDE, and the Gidget game required participants to look through, diagnose, and fix broken code like every other level. None of these findings were true for the canvas participants, indicating this condition's learning activity failed to teach the same concepts even though all the necessary help resources were available to users.

We did not find any significant difference in the time participants spent on their pre-test exams. However, participants in the tutorial and game conditions spent significantly more time on their post-tests compared to their canvas condition counterparts. This suggests that those in the tutorial and game condition found more reason to concentrate and take their time on their respective post-test exams, possibly because they were better equipped to answer the questions correctly. Conversely, without clear goals or instruction in the Gidget Puzzle Designer, participants in the canvas condition likely did not learn the concepts necessary for them to engage successfully with the post-test.

Unfortunately, we found that none of the conditions led to substantial learning of the programming concepts (i.e., the highest median score for a post-test was 12 out of 24 questions correct). Although it is understandable that novices scored poorly on the pre-test since it was their first time seeing programming code, examining the overall scores for both the pre-test and post-test exams may give the impression that the exams were too difficult. However, novices performing badly on programming-related concepts they recently learned is not uncommon [5,47,50,65]. Comparable scores were also reported by Tew who administered a similar pseudo-code test to students who had taken entire introductory programming courses [70]. Since our test questions were generated by combining scores from a crowdsourced group of adult novices and experienced programmers, our results suggest that there is a major gap in programming knowledge between beginners and those with more experience, and that one short exposure with code, whether it be an online tutorial, online game, or even a formal high school or university class [70], may be enough to show some learning outcomes, but is still far from mastery of the subject.

There was a large difference in the time people spent on their respective learning activities. Learners spent the most time on the Codecademy course and spent the least amount of time using the Gidget Puzzle Designer. The time participants spent on the Codecademy and Gidget game tasks are not surprising, given that they are close to the developers' estimated time to complete the activity. It is also not too surprising that participants spent the least amount of time on the Gidget Puzzle Designer task. Without any clear goals or instructions, the Gidget Puzzle Designer participants likely lacked the motivation required to go beyond tinkering with the interface a bit. This means that goals are important for engagement with an activity, and that without proper motivation, people are likely to disengage with the activity. This is particularly worrisome for discretionary learning resources, because one negative/boring encounter with programming might cause a lasting impression where a learner decides that computer science is not for them based on this one experience. More generally, it may be that open-ended, but solitary creative learning tasks such as these fail to engage online with more substantial extrinsic motivators, such as teachers, online community, and more directed creative tasks.

5.1 Threats to Validity
Our study has several limitations that may limit its generalizability. First, we recruited all of our participants through MTurk from the USA. Our participants were all adults, aged between 18 to 41 years old. They were also highly educated, with 51 of our 60 participants having a college degree or higher. This may have introduce a sampling bias, which may limit the generalizability of our results to the particular adult populations found on MTurk who want to learn how to code. Since both Codecademy and Gidget were designed for people of all ages, future work could examine a wider demographic, including those without college degrees, youth, and people living outside of the USA.

We gave participants up to 7 days to complete their assigned activity. Although we asked them to refrain from using any other resources to learn or practice programming, participants could have potentially learned coding concepts from other places, even if it was unintentional. Learning or practicing programming concepts outside of the assigned task could have potentially affected exam outcomes, but could have happened in all conditions. However, unlike the numerous resources to get guidance for Python, there are no external resources to get explicit help for Gidget.

Participants spent significantly different times on their task by condition. Although the numbers for the Codecademy and Gidget game are similar to the estimates given by their developers, the extra time they had may have contributed to their performance gains over the GPD. However, we see that Gidget players performed just as well as Codecamy players, even though they spent significantly less time. There is also no evidence that GPD players would have learned anything more by being forced to play longer since the GPD did not provide any guided direction. Codecademy and Gidget users might not have been as successful on their post-tests if they spent less time and/or did not finish their task. However, our data shows that unlike the GPD players, these users were engaged enough to continue through their entire task for hours, and showed improvements in all the concepts that their assigned tasks covered.

Part of our Codecademy data was reliant on self-reported data that participants provided, including the time they spent on the task and how far they got in the course. Although we asked participants to stop at the "advanced concept" modules so the learning interventions were as similar as possible, we had no way of enforcing that since Codecademy is a third-party website.

Finally, there was an economic incentive for participants to participate in the study. We tried to minimize this effect as much as possible. We believe that the economic incentive in our study was minimal, as usage data for both Gidget and Codecademy show that thousands and millions of people have used these systems without being paid to play.

6. CONCLUSIONS & FUTURE WORK
We investigated the learning outcomes of three different types of programming resources designed for beginners. By comparing the test scores of learners before and after their respective learning activities, we found that the learners who took a Codecademy course and the learners who played through the Gidget game showed considerable improvement in their test scores. Though this was true of both cases, learners who played the Gidget game were able to match the post-test performance of learners who completed the Codecademy tutorial, in approximately half the time. Furthermore, we found that participants from both of these groups also spent more time on the post-test exam, suggesting that they found reason to try harder the second time taking the exam. In contrast, those who were assigned to create programs from scratch using the Gidget Puzzle Designer spent approximately the same amount of time on their pre-test and post-test exams, and did not show significant improvements in their post-test exam scores. In addition to these differences, we found that performance by demographics was consistent within all the conditions, meaning our learning activities had a similar impact regardless of gender, age, or level of education.

These findings raise many questions for future work. How might creativity-oriented online learning environments such as Scratch better support learners? Is it really the case that creative environments need a teacher, or can they be designed to teach effectively without human teachers? How might these findings apply to other forms of discretionary computing education such as MOOCs that are modeled more like traditional classroom settings? With the rising interest in learning to program, and the proliferation of resources to do so, we believe that knowledge about the interaction between the design of these resources and engagement and learning will be essential for learner retention and effective pedagogy.

7. ACKNOWLEDGEMENTS
We thank our participants. This work was supported in part by the National Science Foundation (NSF) under grants CNS-1240786, CNS-1240957, CNS-1339131, CCF-0952733, CCF-1339131, IIS-1314399, IIS-1314384, and OISE-1210205. Any opinions, findings, conclusions or recommendations are those of the authors and do not necessarily reflect the views of NSF.

8. REFERENCES

1. Aleven, V., Myers, E., Easterday, M., & Ogan, A. (2010). Toward a framework for the analysis and design of educational games. *IEEE DIGITEL*, 69-76.
2. Answerdash. http://www.answerdash.com. Accessed: 2015-03-26.
3. Armoni, M., Meerbaum-Salant, O., & Ben-Ari, M. (2015). From scratch to "real" programming. *ACM TOCE*, 14(4), 25.
4. Beres, D. (2014). Obama Writes His First Line Of Code. Retrieved 2015-02-08, from http://www.huffingtonpost.com/2014/12/09/obama-code_n_6294036.html
5. Bonar, J., & Soloway, E. (1985). Preprogramming knowledge: A major source of misconceptions in novice programmers. *Human–Computer Interaction*, 1(2), 133-161.
6. Bonate, P.L. (2000). Analysis of pretest-posttest designs. *CRC Press*.
7. Boustedt, J., Eckerdal, A., McCartney, R., Sanders, K., Thomas, L., & Zander C. (2011). Students' perceptions of the differences between formal and informal learning. *ACM ICER*, 61–68
8. Bransford, J.D., Brown, A.L., & Cocking, R.R. (1999). How people learn: Brain, mind, experience, and school. *National Academy Press*.
9. Breslow, L., Pritchard, D.E., DeBoer, J., Stump, G.S., Ho, A. D., & Seaton, D.T. (2013). Studying learning in the worldwide classroom: Research into edX's first MOOC. *Research & Practice in Assessment*, 8(1), 13-25.
10. Bruckman, A., Biggers, M., Ericson, B., et al. (2009). Georgia computes!: Improving the computing education pipeline. *ACM SIGCSE Bulletin*, 41(1), 86-90.
11. Cao, J., Kwan, I., White, R., Fleming, S.D., Burnett, M., & Scaffidi, C. (2012). From barriers to learning in the Idea Garden: An empirical study. *IEEE VL/HCC*, 59-66.
12. Charters, P., Lee, M.J., Ko, A.J., & Loksa, D. (2014). Challenging stereotypes and changing attitudes: the effect of a brief programming encounter on adults' attitudes toward programming. *ACM SIGCSE*, 653-658.
13. Chumley-Jones, H.S., Dobbie, A., & Alford, C.L. (2002). Web–based learning: Sound educational method or hype? A review of the evaluation literature. *Academic medicine*, 77(10), S86-S93.
14. Codecademy. http://www.codecademy.com. Accessed: 2015-03-26.
15. Code Combat. http://www.codecombat.com. Accessed: 2015-03-26.
16. Code Hunt. http://www.codehunt.com. Accessed: 2015-03-26.
17. Code School. http://www.codeschool.com. Accessed: 2015-03-26.
18. Connolly, T.M., & Stansfield, M.H. (2006). Enhancing eLearning: Using Computer Games to Teach Requirements Collection and Analysis. WG HCI & UE of the Austrian Computer Society.
19. Cooper, S., Dann, W., & Pausch, R. (2000). Alice: a 3-D tool for introductory programming concepts. *J. of Computing Sciences in Colleges*, 15(5), 107-116.
20. Cross, J. (2006). Informal learning: rediscovering the natural pathways that inspire innovation and performance. *San Francisco, CA: Pfeiffer.*
21. Dann, W.P., Cooper, S., & Pausch, R. (2011). Learning to Program with Alice. *Prentice Hall Press*.
22. Deitel, H., & Deitel, P. (2005). C++: How to program (5th ed.). *Upper Saddle River, NJ: Prentice Hall.*

23. Dimitrov, D.M., & Rumrill, Jr, P.D. (2003). Pretest-posttest designs and measurement of change. *Work: A Journal of Prevention, Assessment and Rehabilitation*, 20(2), 159-165.
24. Eagle, M., & Barnes, T. (2009). Experimental evaluation of an educational game for improved learning in introductory computing. *ACM SIGCSE Bulletin*, 41(1), 321-325.
25. edX. https://www.edx.org. Accessed: 2015-03-26.
26. Felleisen, M., Findler, R. B., Flatt, M., & Krishnamurthi, S. (2001). How to design programs: An introduction to programming and computing. *Cambridge, MA: MIT Press.*
27. Franklin, D., Conrad, P., Boe, B., et al. (2013). Assessment of computer science learning in a scratch-based outreach program. *ACM SIGCSE*, 371-376.
28. Garris, R., Ahlers, R., & Driskell, J.E. (2002). Games, motivation, and learning: A research and practice model. *Simulation & Gaming*, 4, 441–467.
29. Gee, J.P. (2014). What video games have to teach us about learning and literacy. *Macmillan.*
30. Gidget. http://www.helpgidget.org. Accessed: 2015-03-26.
31. Hamari, J., Koivisto, J., & Sarsa, H. (2014). Does gamification work? – a literature review of empirical studies on gamification. *HICSS*, 3025-3034.
32. Hays, R.T. (2005). *The effectiveness of instructional games: A literature review and discussion* (Technical Report 2005-004). Naval air warfare ctr. training systems division. Orlando, FL.
33. Ivala, E., Gachago, D., Condy, J., & Chigona, A. (2013). Enhancing student engagement with their studies: a digital storytelling approach. *Creative Education*, 4(10), 82.
34. Kapp, K.M. (2012). The gamification of learning and instruction: game-based methods and strategies for training and education. *San Francisco, CA: Pfeiffer.*
35. Khan Academy. http://www.kahnacademy.com. Accessed: 2015-03-26.
36. Kirriemuir, J., & McFarlane, A. (2004). Literature Review in Games and Learning. Report 8, NESTA, Futurelab, Bristol.
37. Kelleher, C., & Pausch, R. (2005). Lowering the barriers to programming: A taxonomy of programming environments and languages for novice programmers. *ACM CSUR*, 37(2), 83-137.
38. Kelleher, C., & Pausch, R. (2007). Using storytelling to motivate programming. *Comm. of the ACM*, 50(7), 58-64.
39. Kelleher, C., Pausch, R., & Kiesler, S. (2007). Storytelling Alice Motivates Middle School Girls to Learn Computer Programming. *ACM CHI*, 1455-1464.
40. Lee, M.J. (2015). Teaching and Engaging with Debugging Puzzles. *PhD dissertation, University of Washington.*
41. Lee, M.J, Bahmani, F., Kwan, I., Laferte, J., Charters, P., Horvath, A., Luor, F., Cao, J., Law, C., Beswetherick, M., Long, S., Burnett, M., & Ko, A.J. (2014). Principles of a Debugging-First Puzzle Game for Computing Education. *IEEE VL/HCC*, 57-64.
42. Lee, M.J., & Ko, A.J. (2011). Personifying programming tool feedback improves novice programmers' learning. *ACM ICER*, 109-116.
43. Lee, M.J., & Ko, A.J. (2012). Investigating the role of purposeful goals on novices' engagement in a programming game. *IEEE VL/HCC*, 163-166.
44. Lee, M.J., Ko, A.J., & Kwan, I. (2013). In-game assessments increase novice programmers' engagement and level completion speed. *ACM ICER*, 153-160.
45. Lewis, J., & Loftus, W. (2005). Java software solutions (Java 5.0 version): Foundations of program design (4th ed.). *Boston, MA: Addison Wesley.*
46. Lightbot. http://www.lightbot.com. Accessed: 2015-03-26.

47. Lister, R., Adams, E.S., Fitzgerald, S., Fone, W., Hamer, J., Lindholm, M., McCartney, et al. (2004). A multi-national study of reading and tracing skills in novice programmers. *ACM SIGCSE Bulletin*, 36(4), 119-150.

48. Malone, T.W. (1981). What Makes Things Fun to Learn? A Study of Intrinsically Motivating Computer Games. *Palo Alto, CA: Xerox*.

49. Maloney, J., Resnick, M., Rusk, N., Silverman, B., & Eastmond, E. (2010). The scratch programming language and environment. ACM TOCE, 10(4), 16.

50. McCracken, M., Almstrum, V., Diaz, D., Guzdial, M., Hagan, D., Kolikant, Y.B.D., Laxer, C., Thomas, L., Utting, I. & Wilusz, T. (2001). A multi-national, multi-institutional study of assessment of programming skills of first-year CS students. *ACM SIGCSE Bulletin*, 33(4), 125-180.

51. McNamara, D., Jackson, G., Graesser, A. (2009) Intelligent tutoring and games. *Artificial Intelligence in Education,* 1–10.

52. Papert, S., & Harel, I. (1991). Situating constructionism. *Constructionism*, 36, 1-11.

53. Pear, J.J. (2004). Enhanced feedback using computer-aided personalized system of instruction. In W. Buskist, V.W. Hevern, B.K. Saville, & T. Zinn, (Eds.), *Essays from excellence in teaching* (Chapter 11).

54. Prensky, M. (2003). Digital game-based learning. *Computers in Entertainment*, 1(1), 21-21.

55. Prensky, M. (2006). Don't Bother Me, Mom, I'm Learning!: How Computer and Video Games Are Preparing Your Kids for 21st Century Success and How You Can Help. *Saint Paul, Paragon House*.

56. Randel, J.M., Morris, B.A., Wetzel, C.D., & Whitehill, B.V. (1992). The effectiveness of games for educational purposes: A review of recent research. *Simulation & Gaming*, 23(3), 261-276.

57. Ross, J., Irani, L., Silberman, M., Zaldivar, A., & Tomlinson, B. (2010). Who are the crowdworkers?: shifting demographics in mechanical turk. *ACM CHI*, 2863-2872.

58. Rubio, M.A., Romero-Zaliz, R., Mañoso, C., & Angel, P. (2015). Closing the gender gap in an introductory programming course. *Computers & Education*, 82, 409-420.

59. Ruf, A., Mühling, A., & Hubwieser, P. (2014). Scratch vs. Karel: impact on learning outcomes and motivation. *ACM WiPCSE*, 50-59.

60. Ryokai, K., Lee, M.J., & Breitbart, J.M. (2009). Children's storytelling and programming with robotic characters. *ACM Creativity & Cognition*, 19-28.

61. Shute, V.J., Ventura, M., Bauer, M., & Zapata-Rivera, D. (2009). Melding the power of serious games and embedded assessment to monitor and foster learning. *Serious games: Mechanisms and Effects*, 295-321.

62. Shackelford, R. L. (1997). Introduction to computing and algorithms. *Boston, MA: Addison Wesley*.

63. Sime, M., Green, T., & Guest, D. (1976). Scope marking in computer conditionals: A psychological evaluation. *International Journal of Man-Machine Studies*, 9, 107–118.

64. Soflano, M., Connolly, T.M., & Hainey, T. (2015). An Application of Adaptive Games-Based Learning based on Learning Style to Teach SQL. *Computers & Education*.

65. Soloway, E. (1986). Learning to program = learning to construct mechanisms and explanations. *Communications of the ACM*, 29(9), 850-858.

66. Steffe, L.P., & Gale, J. E. (Eds.). (1995). Constructivism in education. *Hillsdale, NJ: Lawrence Erlbaum,* 159.

67. Summers, N. (n.d.) Codecademy surpasses 24 million unique users for its free online coding courses. *The Next Web*. Retrieved 23 April 2014.

68. Sykes, E.R. (2007). Determining the effectiveness of the 3D Alice programming environment at the computer science I level. *Journal of Educational Computing Research*, 36(2), 223-244.

69. Tew, A.E. (2010). Assessing fundamental introductory computing concept knowledge in a language independent manner. *PhD dissertation, Georgia Institute of Technology*.

70. Tew, A.E., & Guzdial, M. (2011). The FCS1: A language independent assessment of CS1 knowledge. *ACM SIGCSE*, 111-116.

71. Thompson, S.M. (2006). An Exploratory Study of Novice Programming Experiences and Errors. *Thesis., University of Victoria, Victoria*.

72. Umaschi, M. (1997). Soft toys with computer hearts: Building personal storytelling environments. *ACM CHI*, 20-21.

73. Webb, H. C., & Rosson, M. B. (2011). Exploring careers while learning Alice 3D: a summer camp for middle school girls. *ACM SIGCSE*, 377-382.

74. Werner, L L., Hanks, B., & McDowell, C. (2004). Pair-programming helps female computer science students. *Journal on Educational Resources in Computing*, 4(1).

75. Whitfort, T. (n.d.). Pseudo code guide [web page]. http://ironbark.bendigo.latrobe.edu.au/subjects/PE/2005s1/other_resources/pseudocode_ guide.html.

76. Williamson, B. (2009). Computer games, schools, and young people: A report for educators on using games for learning. *Bristol: Futurelab*.

77. Young, J. (2008). "Badges" earned online pose challenge to traditional college diplomas. *Chronicle of Higher Education*.

78. Zelle, J. M. (2004). Python programming: An introduction to computer science. *Wilsonville, OR: Franklin Beedle*.

Leveraging Narrative Interactivity to Foster Computer Science Identities

Philip Sheridan Buffum

North Carolina State University
Department of Computer Science
Raleigh, NC, 27606, USA
psbuffum@ncsu.edu

ABSTRACT

There is growing recognition in the computer science education research community that supporting students in identity formation for computer science is an essential step toward broadening participation in computing. Because students begin establishing their career aspiration identity at an early age, research into computing identity formation in K-8 education is particularly important. Research suggests that narrative-centered learning environments hold great promise for fostering identity formation. My proposed dissertation research focuses on bringing narrative-centered learning environment technology to bear on supporting computer science learners in middle school. I am particularly interested in how we can make these learning environments more equitable for all learners, especially for underrepresented students.

Categories and Subject Descriptors

K.3.2 [**Computers and Education**]: Computer and Information Science Education – *computer science education.*

Keywords

Identity Formation, Middle School, Narrative, Equity.

1. PROGRAM CONTEXT

I have recently completed the third year of PhD studies in computer science at North Carolina State University. This past semester I completed the Written Preliminary Exam, presenting work that I conducted on using a virtual learning companion to bring gender equity to an educational game for computer science. I have already begun building on this work by further developing the system and conducting a series of small user studies. This fall, I plan on conducting a full classroom study that will yield the data for my dissertation. I then hope to complete the Oral Preliminary Exam (the dissertation proposal) the following semester, and graduate in December 2016. As my proposed research questions are not finalized yet, this ICER Doctoral Consortium comes at an excellent time to help shape my dissertation research.

2. CONTEXT AND MOTIVATION

The importance of developing effective interventions for middle school learners has been well established. At this age students first

start developing subject-specific skills in the pursuit of career aspirations [8]. Indeed, researchers have specifically traced the underproduction and underrepresentation issues in undergraduate computer science departments back to lack of exposure as early as middle school [10]. With effective computer science learning experiences during students' formative years, there is the potential to leave a lasting positive impact on the student.

Motivated by this great promise, my colleagues at NCSU and I have created a narrative-centered learning environment, ENGAGE, that aims to help middle school students learn computational thinking. In ENGAGE, students play the role of computer scientists solving a socially relevant mystery. The game's narrative provides a form of scaffolding, with students developing computational thinking skills as they progress through the multi-week intervention. Building off of a rich theoretical background on narrative-centered learning, ENGAGE also hopes to leverage the narrative element's potential for facilitating *identity formation*. Little research has been done, however, on the specifics of how such narrative-centered learning environments can most effectively foster identity formation. My dissertation work addresses this open research question, with particular attention on identity formation among students traditionally underrepresented in computer science.

3. BACKGROUND & RELATED WORK

Narratives – both those we tell and those we consume, both about ourselves and about others – shape our identities in powerful, long-lasting ways. Some have suggested that we can fully equate the identity of an individual with the narratives about that individual [9]. The importance of narrative appears in most, if not all, theories in the learning sciences. In the cultural-historical perspective, for example, we can see adults interpreting their past experiences to project probable futures for their children [5]. The situative perspective on learning, meanwhile, emphasizes the importance of contextualizing knowledge, which can be accomplished through narrative [7].

Narrative-centered learning environments aim to take advantage of the transformative power of narrative. These immersive environments afford multiple perspectives, situate learning, and facilitate transfer [6]. Indeed, the theory of *transformational play* takes us beyond any broad claims about the potential of games to make learning "fun", and provides more concrete guidance on how to design game-based learning environments that can positively impact students in ways unique to games [1]. In this model, the student takes on the role of a protagonist and, using newly acquired domain knowledge, transforms (a) the fictional context of the game environment, (b) her understanding of the domain knowledge, and (c) herself as someone who uses that domain knowledge to solve socially relevant problems.

Much of the research on narrative-centered learning has been done in the context of middle school science [1, 6], although narrative-centered learning environments have also been used in other subjects, such as language arts [1]. This technology may especially benefit fields such as computer science that struggle to attract diverse students due to pervasive negative stereotypes. My research aims to explore this hypothesis.

4. STATEMENT OF THESIS/PROBLEM

I seek to understand how narrative interactivity in an educational game can improve a student's ability to identify as a computer scientist. I will investigate how students' computer science attitudes evolve while interacting in the narrative-centered learning environment, paying attention to demographic differences. I am particularly interested in how students traditionally underrepresented in computer science respond to varying degrees of narrative interactivity.

5. RESEARCH GOALS & METHODS

My dissertation research includes the following goals:

i. Establish how player actions within the existing educational game map to prior (and evolving) computer science attitudes.

ii. Determine how varying degrees of narrative interactivity affect a student's computer science attitudes.

iii. Discover if this has a measurable impact on a student's ability to identify as a computer scientist or, if it does not, how we could improve its impact.

Toward the first goal, we conducted a full classroom study of ENGAGE during the 2014-15 academic year, with approximately 200 middle school students. We administered a computer science attitudes survey (pre- and post-intervention), engagement survey (post-intervention) and a knowledge assessment (pre- and post-intervention). We also collected game trace data. I plan on using computational methods to analyze the game trace data, with the goal of identifying how player actions differ between students who scored highly on the computer science attitudes survey versus those who scored less highly. I will also look for differences based on engagement and knowledge gains.

We also plan to conduct a new study with modifications to the narrative-centered learning environment. I have already developed a prototype of a virtual learning companion that can add varying degrees of narrative interactivity to ENGAGE. I will fully integrate this pedagogical agent with the existing game, and then conduct a study with at least 100 middle school students. For this new study, I will follow a similar method as previous ones to ensure as representative a participant pool as possible. This will help me achieve my second goal. To achieve the third goal, meanwhile, we will need to supplement the study with focus groups and qualitative analysis. I believe a mixed methods approach is the only way to fully study the complex topic of "identity" in middle school computer science education.

6. DISSERTATION STATUS

The research goals articulated above build on my completed work investigating how the narrative interactivity of a prototype virtual learning companion can improve the gender equity of a game for middle school computer science education [4]. I have also worked on using narrative to teach new concepts such as "big data" to middle school students [3], developing and validating a knowledge assessment for a narrative-centered learning environment [2], and using collaboration in a narrative-centered learning environment to improve its gender equity (under review).

With regard to my upcoming research goals, I have already conducted some analyses of the survey data. Specifically I have looked at gender differences in the engagement post-survey and in the knowledge assessment. Analyzing the game trace data is the next step for understanding how learning unfolds in this narrative-centered learning environment. As for preparing for the next study, our team has completed development of the game environment and I have completed building the next iteration of the virtual learning companion. We will conduct the next study during the 2015-16 academic year. My participation in the Doctoral Consortium at ICER would be perfectly timed to help clarify the design of that study and to help shape my upcoming dissertation proposal.

7. EXPECTED CONTRIBUTIONS

My dissertation research will lead to better understanding how we can leverage narrative interactivity to foster computer science identity formation. Enabling young students to identify as computer scientists is key to seeing them persisting in the field, and therefore important to the grand goal of broadening participation in computing. This research will establish how we can pursue this goal through the use of narrative.

8. REFERENCES

[1] Barab, S.A. et al. 2010. Transformational Play: Using Games to Position Person, Content, and Context. *Educational Researcher*. 39, 7 (2010), 525–536.

[2] Buffum, P.S. et al. 2015. A Practical Guide to Developing and Validating Computer Science Knowledge Assessments with Application to Middle School. *Proceedings of SIGCSE '15*, 622–627.

[3] Buffum, P.S. et al. 2014. CS Principles Goes to Middle School: Learning How to Teach "Big Data." *Proceedings of SIGCSE '14*, 151–156.

[4] Buffum, P.S. et al. 2015. Mind the Gap: Improving Gender Equity in Game-based Learning Environments with Learning Companions. *Proceedings of the 17th International conference on Artificial Intelligence in Education - AIED '15* (2015), To appear.

[5] Cole, M. and Engeström, Y. 1993. A Cultural-Historical Approach to Distributed Cognition. *Distributed Cognitions: Psychological and Educational Considerations*. 1–46.

[6] Dede, C. 2009. Immersive interfaces for engagement and learning. *Science (New York, N.Y.)*. 323, 5910 (Jan. 2009), 66–9.

[7] Lave, J. and Wenger, E. 1991. *Situated Learning: Legitimate Peripheral Participation*.

[8] Lent, R.W. et al. 1994. Toward a unifying social cognitive theory of career and academic interest, choice, and performance. *Journal of Vocational Behavior*. 45, (1994), 79–122.

[9] Sfard, A. and Prusak, A. 2005. Telling identities: In Search of an Analytic Tool for Investigating Learning as a Culturally Shaped Activity. *Educational Researcher*. 34, (2005), 14–22.

[10] Webb, H.C. 2011. Injecting computational thinking into career explorations for middle school girls. *2011 IEEE Symposium on Visual Languages and HumanCentric Computing VLHCC*. (2011), 237–238.

Investigating Novice Programmers' Plan Composition Strategies

Francisco Enrique Vicente G. Castro
Worcester Polytechnic Institute
Department of Computer Science
Worcester, Massachusetts, 01609, USA
fgcastro@wpi.edu

ABSTRACT

Problem solving through effective plan decomposition and composition continues to be exceedingly difficult for novice programmers. This is exacerbated by the fact that these strategies are usually implicit in instruction: students are left to figure out their own problem solving strategies. My research investigates ways to elicit and improve students' plan decomposition and composition strategies.

Categories and Subject Descriptors

K.3.2 [**Computers and Education**]: Computers and Information Science Education—*Computer Science Education*.

Keywords

Novice programmers, problem solving, plan composition

1. PROGRAM CONTEXT

I am beginning the second year of my PhD program in Computer Science at WPI. I am a full-time PhD student and research assistant under the supervision of Dr. Kathi Fisler. I anticipate completing my research qualifying milestone by Fall 2015 and my PhD breadth requirement by Spring 2016 (to gain candidacy). To inform my research, I have included learning science courses in my program coursework. I completed my master's degree in 2014.

As part of my research qualifier, I have completed an initial study of plan composition behavior of CS1 students at WPI. The study and preliminary findings will contribute to the development of a full dissertation proposal around this topic in the coming academic year.

2. CONTEXT AND MOTIVATION

A problem being explored in computing education is plan composition: how students analyze a problem, decompose it into finite subproblems, and finally weave solutions to these subproblems into a coherent, working program. Most introductory courses emphasize using programming concepts in code, usually through extensive sets of exercises [1, 4]. Students are then expected to develop general problem solving strategies, yet they often do not know where or how to start [8]. They are unable to identify problem components and relevant algorithmic structures, as well as the interactions between these components [1, 4, 5, 6].

These difficulties are often not due to students' lack of understanding of how to use language constructs. The problem stems from the fact that problem solving and plan composition strategies are usually implicit in instruction; students are left to figure out their own plan composition strategies [1, 4]. Soloway's study on the Rainfall problem [8] highlights the exceeding difficulty students experience in carrying out plan composition effectively; the problems that underlie plan composition [9] continue to be evident even now.

3. BACKGROUND & RELATED WORK

Literature highlights that novices not only need to be taught programming language syntax and semantics, but also need explicit instruction on design skills, problem solving, and plan composition [8, 10]. Spohrer and Soloway identify both novices' language construct-based difficulties and an extensive list of problems that make plan composition complicated for novices [9]. Their findings suggest that the occurrence of bugs are due to students' inability to effectively organize and integrate the goals and plans that underlie program code, a sentiment echoed by Pirolli et. al. in their study on learning recursive programming [7]. Both of these projects assume that people approach new problems by recalling and modifying solutions to similar problems [7, 10]. These and later projects try to give plans explicit labels to help students recognize (a) concrete goals of individual subproblems and (b) patterns across similar problems [6, 8].

How to Design Programs (HTDP) [2] is an introductory computing curriculum that approaches similarity differently from the projects discussed previously. HTDP teaches students to produce a common code shape based on the structure of the input data, then to use examples to tailor the common shape to a specific problem. Fisler [3] investigated plan composition behavior in HTDP students. These students made fewer errors than in earlier Rainfall studies, but several still struggled with plan composition. My work will explore how the combination of HTDP's data-driven methodology and others' labeling oriented approaches might be used together to improve students' plan composition skills.

ICER'15, August 9–13, 2015, Omaha, Nebraska, USA.
ACM 978-1-4503-3630-7/15/08.
http://dx.doi.org/10.1145/2787622.2787735 .

4. STATEMENT OF THESIS/PROBLEM

The context and and related work informs and guides my research question: When and how do students' task decomposition and code composition instances emerge in their programming process and how can we influence them to do it better? Interesting sub-questions include:

1. Do students: *a*) decompose a problem into smaller plans, implement the individual tasks, and then recompose; *b*) implement a task-related piece of code and then patch around it; or *c*) pull out related code (possibly from prior work done), modify the code to adapt to the problem context, and then build around it?

2. What role can design-based approaches like HTDP play in how students implement task decomposition and code composition strategies?

5. RESEARCH GOALS & METHODS

Methods I expect to use include:

Elicit students' problem solving strategies. We're interested both in the code students produce and more talk-aloud style data. Students' programming activity will be video captured for analysis. I will analyze these for instances of plan decomposition, recomposition, and other relevant problem-solving behavior. I will also use a combination of surveys or other free-form input to understand how students are approaching these problems. My initial study used a combination of these methods.

Elicit program design principles students use in plan composition. How students think about composition can be reflected both in the code they write and on how they comprehend solutions others have written. Data on a combination of problems on writing code and comprehending code will be collected from several educational institutions to understand students' perceptions of composition.

Investigate the role of cognitive factors in plan composition strategies. Because learning programming imposes cognitive load upon the learner, further review of literature will be done to consider how cognitive factors play a role in problem solving.

6. DISSERTATION STATUS

For my research qualifier, I have completed an exploratory study of the edits students made while working on a plan composition problem. We video captured the programming activity of CS1 students at WPI. Preliminary results suggest that while students' programming is informed by HTDP and students recognize the need for plan decomposition, they struggle with the process of how to decompose the problem into coherent plans and eventually recompose solutions. In the cohort that was analyzed, plan decomposition was very minimal, tests were used to confirm code outputs instead of informing the design of solutions, and recomposition could not be effectively carried out due to the ineffective ways with which plans were developed in the first place. The study involved the development of a coding scheme which will be modified as the research progresses.

From the doctoral consortium, I hope to gain insight from commentaries of my research topic and the initial study I have conducted, as well as suggestions to methodology and additional ideas and perspectives of the subject matter that I may have not examined so far. Likewise, feedback may help refine my research questions. Findings from future data analyses using new data to be collected from other institutions will be used for the dissertation proposal which I hope to submit and defend within the year.

7. EXPECTED CONTRIBUTIONS

The contributions of this work to the computing education community include the identification of students' plan decomposition and composition methodologies and techniques that might influence these methodologies. The findings from this research may further inform the development of future computing education curricula and pedagogy.

8. REFERENCES

[1] M. de Raadt, M. Toleman, and R. Watson. Training Strategic Problem Solvers. *SIGCSE Bull.*, 36(2):48–51, June 2004.

[2] M. Felleisen, R. B. Findler, M. Flatt, and S. Krishnamurthi. *How to Design Programs: An Introduction to Programming and Computing.* The MIT Press, Cambridge, Mass, Feb. 2001.

[3] K. Fisler. The Recurring Rainfall Problem. In *Proceedings of the Tenth Annual Conference on International Computing Education Research*, ICER '14, pages 35–42, New York, NY, USA, 2014. ACM.

[4] A. Keen and K. Mammen. Program Decomposition and Complexity in CS1. In *Proceedings of the 46th ACM Technical Symposium on Computer Science Education*, SIGCSE '15, pages 48–53, New York, NY, USA, 2015. ACM.

[5] J. Mead, S. Gray, J. Hamer, R. James, J. Sorva, C. S. Clair, and L. Thomas. A Cognitive Approach to Identifying Measurable Milestones for Programming Skill Acquisition. In *Working Group Reports on ITiCSE on Innovation and Technology in Computer Science Education*, ITiCSE-WGR '06, pages 182–194, New York, NY, USA, 2006. ACM.

[6] O. Muller, D. Ginat, and B. Haberman. Pattern-oriented Instruction and Its Influence on Problem Decomposition and Solution Construction. In *Proceedings of the 12th Annual SIGCSE Conference on Innovation and Technology in Computer Science Education*, ITiCSE '07, pages 151–155, New York, NY, USA, 2007. ACM.

[7] P. L. Pirolli, J. R. Anderson, and R. G. Farrell. Learning to program recursion. In *Proceedings of the Sixth Annual Cognitive Science Meetings*, pages 277–280, 1984.

[8] E. Soloway. Learning to Program = Learning to Construct Mechanisms and Explanations. *Commun. ACM*, 29(9):850–858, Sept. 1986.

[9] J. C. Spohrer and E. Soloway. Novice Mistakes: Are the Folk Wisdoms Correct? *Communications of the ACM*, 29(7):624–632, July 1986.

[10] J. C. Spohrer and E. Soloway. Simulating Student Programmers. In *Proceedings of the 11th International Joint Conference on Artificial Intelligence - Volume 1*, IJCAI'89, pages 543–549, San Francisco, CA, USA, 1989. Morgan Kaufmann Publishers Inc.

Understanding Collaborative Computational Thinking

Bushra Chowdhury
Doctoral Student
Department of Engineering Education
Virginia Tech
Blacksburg, VA, 24061, USA
bushrac@vt.edu

ABSTRACT

In this paper I discuss my doctoral research which aims to better understand collaborative computational thinking (CT). In order to be successful in the 21st century, skills such CT (understanding and applying computational concepts) are indispensable for people across all ages and disciplines. One can learn computational concepts by taking a traditional course offered in a school or by self-guided learning through an online platform. Whatever the form of learning, computational concepts can be difficult to fully comprehend for novices. Collaborative learning has been considered effective in reducing learner's anxiety and in helping struggling learners overcome common learning difficulties. The proposed dissertation study aims to investigate how collaboration impacts learning of CT across both classroom setting and in an online learning community. This paper briefly describes the motivation and outline of my proposed dissertation study, the overarching research questions, the data currently collected, and my data analysis methodologies.

Categories and Subject Descriptors

[**Computers and Education**]: Applied Computing-Education-Collaborative learning

Keywords

Computational Thinking, collaborative learning, novice learner, social interactions

1. PROGRAM CONTEXT

I am a third year doctoral student in the Department of Engineering Education at Virginia Tech. I have passed my Qualifier and Preliminary Examinations. The purpose of the Preliminary Examination was to assess my readiness to pursue creative, original, independent research at a level typically expected of PhD students. Now as a PhD candidate, I am developing my research proposal which describes the background, purpose, and methods of the proposed dissertation study, the anticipated outcomes, and the contribution to the field. I have conducted a pilot study (in a CT general education class) in Fall 2014. At that same time I was also part of a separate study that investigated how a physical sculpture consisting of multiple Raspberry Pi computers can teach parallel computing concepts to non-CS students [1]. Recently, In Spring 2015, I have collected data of novice learners collaboratively learning computational

ICER '15, August 9-13, 2015, Omaha, Nebraska, USA.
ACM 978-1-4503-3630-7/15/08.
http://dx.doi.org/10.1145/2787622.2787736

concepts in a classroom setting. Separately, I have also explored the data set of an open online learning environment – Scratch (http://scratch.mit.edu).

2. CONTEXT AND MOTIVATION

Digitization has significantly shaped our professional and personal lives and computation and communication are at the core of this transformation. Computer modeling, simulation and visualization software, Smart grid, and Software Defined Radio, are few examples where computation has allowed us to tackle problems from varied perspectives. With even more integration of our physical and digital infrastructure, there is a great potential for discovery and mapping of new domains powered by CT, which provides the ability to find the right technology for a problem and apply technology to resolve the problem [2].

As the use of computation spreads across domains, learners of all ages and backgrounds are being urged to master fundamental computer science concepts (e.g. abstraction, iteration, conditional logic, algorithms, functions, and parallelization). However, novice learners struggle to learn and apply some of these concepts [3]. As educators in computer science, it is important for us to determine effective pedagogical approaches to familiarize novice learners to fundamental concepts of computer science.

Collaborative learning has been considered effective in reducing learner's anxiety and in helping struggling learners to overcome common learning difficulties [4]. However, there is limited understanding as to how collaborative learning processes impact learning in the context of CT. One way of understanding the collaborative dimension of learning is by analyzing the social interactions among members of a group of learners; for instance, by understanding how a group of students code and debug a program together in a class or when students share, comment or reuse pre-existing code from each other in an online learning platform. The proposed dissertation study intents to analyze the social interactions between members in groups in order to better understand what novice learners struggle with and how collaborating with others influence their learning.

3. BACKGROUND & RELATED WORK

The definitions of CT provided by Wing [2] and the operationalized versions emphasize CT as an ability to formulate and solve problems using information representations and automated processing. Abstractions, iterations, conditional logic, algorithmic thinking, and parallel computing are considered fundamental concepts of CT.

Different initiatives for integrating CT within existing curricula have started to gain footing. Most initiatives have been at the K12 level. However, some universities are integrating CT modules throughout their undergraduate program whereas others are offering it as a semester long course. Few of these courses are being offered with a particular discipline viewpoint while others as a general education course designed for all non-computers science majors. Online learning platforms (e.g. learning communities of Scratch, Alice, and Blockly) have also been considered to foster learning of CT. The emphasis of teaching has ranged from learning CT in contexts versus learning across context, a cognitive ability versus an application of skills, as a problem-solving tool or an alternative approach to creatively express one's ideas. Along with high-level programming languages, e.g. Python, CT courses also use block based programming languages such as Blockly, Alice, or Scratch to make CT easier for novice learners. The pedagogical approaches seem to be limited to solving programming problems, digital storytelling, and game design. Students learn CT individually as well in groups. However, assessment related to CT has mostly been done at the individual level.

4. STATEMENT OF THESIS/PROBLEM

The overarching goal of the proposed dissertation study is to better understand the collaborative process of learning CT. In order to do so, the proposed dissertation study aims to look into CT from three perspectives. The following paragraphs describe each of these, the data that will be used, and the proposed analysis methods.

The first part of the study will synthesize the implications and pedagogical approaches of learning and assessing CT (particularly at the university level) by investigating the existing literature. Data: Literature review

The second part of the study will investigate the collaborative aspect of learning CT in a classroom setting. This qualitative study will focus on better understanding how social interactions within a group of learners impact learning of CT. Data used for this study will be video recordings of 3 student groups collaboratively learning in an undergraduate general education CT course. Total of 6 class sessions (each session is 20 minutes; total of 120 minutes have already been recorded). I have conducted preliminary analysis of video recordings of collaborative groups. Event based analysis of encounters will be done on the video recording based on an observation check list and also using Chi's framework of differentiating learning activities [5]. The observation check list used for analysis will illustrate the patterns of social interactions exhibited by members within a group while learning CT. Additionally, Chi's framework would allow collaborative CT activities to be categorized as active-constructive-iterative. According to Chi, interactive activities are better than constructive activities and constructive activities are better than active activities.

The third part of the study will investigate the collaborative aspect of learning CT in an open online community. The focus of this part of the study is to better understand how social interactions (e.g. following, commenting) and re-using another user's code impact a learner's ability to create independent projects (a creation made in Scratch program) using computational blocks (puzzle-piece shapes that are used to create code). The dataset of Scratch online community will be used for third part of the proposed dissertation manuscript. Scratch (www. Scratch.mit.edu) is an online community and social networking forum. In this platform, youth (ages 8-16 years) code games, animations, and stories using media-based programming language. Scratch has been designed to support the development of CT in young people. The dataset includes 1.9 million projects of 1 million users. Project codes are available for years 2007 through 2012.

Analysis method: Exploratory factor analysis (based on type and no. of blocks used, no. projects created, no. of remixed projects of a user, user's community age). Also applying network analysis (different visualizing layouts, setting different path lengths, node size, betweeness centrality).

5. DISSERTATION STATUS

I have completed a draft of the literature review (first part) of my dissertation study.

For the classroom part (second part of my dissertation) I have collected video recordings of 3 groups (each group has 4 to 6 students) for 6 days and interviewed 8 students individually. Initial coding of student interactions has been completed. Initial findings suggest that self-explanation/thinking out loud while learning CT helps students to better understand the concepts. Being able ask questions to someone who is at the same level of learning helps students understand concepts in a way they can easily relate to. Learning CT is like learning a new language. Novice learners become frustrated while writing code because they have to be extremely precise.

For the online learning environment (Scratch data) I have created initial relationship tables and have generated basic statistical reports. Initial findings suggest that novice Scratch users tend to remix others' codes and make minor adjustment to the code. I have not yet generated or tested any hypothesis.

I have completed a draft of my dissertation proposal which describes the background, purpose, and methods of my proposed dissertation study, the outcome anticipated, and the contribution to the field. I plan to defend my dissertation proposal in August, 2015, and defend May, 2016.

6. EXPECTED CONTRIBUTIONS

The outcome of this research will explain what novice learners struggle with while learning CT and how social interactions impact their learning in two different settings. The study will also provide a framework that illustrates the collaborative aspect of learning CT.

7. REFERENCES

[1] B. Chowdhury, S.Blanchard . Kirk W. Cameron, A.Johri, SeeMore: An Interactive Kinetic Sculpture Designed to Teach Parallel Computational Thinking, Proceedings of ASEE Annual Conference, 2015

[2] NRC,Report of a Workshop on the Scope and Nature of Computational Thinking. 2010: National Academies Press.

[3] Brown, N.C. and A. Altadmri. Investigating novice programming mistakes: educator beliefs vs. student data. in Proceedings of the tenth annual conference on International computing education research. 2014. ACM.

[4] Hmelo-Silver, C.E., The international handbook of collaborative learning. 2013: Routledge.

[5] Chi, M.T., Active-constructive-interactive: A conceptual framework for differentiating learning activities. Topics in Cognitive Science, 2009. 1(1): p. 73-105.

On Pre-requisite Skills for Universal Computational Thinking Education

Elizabeth Cole
School of Computing Science
University of Glasgow
Glasgow, G12 8RZ, Scotland
e.cole.2@research.gla.ac.uk

ABSTRACT

Computational thinking (CT) has been hailed as valuable to everyone in the population, and if so, it should be taught to all. This research builds on existing work identifying pre-requisite skills for developing CT skills, referred to here as *foundational CT* skills. To add weight to the validity of the "CT for all" claim, this research attempts to determine whether foundational CT skills are of value to non-IT industry and for pupils elsewhere in their studies. The foundational CT skills will be trialled with pupils in the 5-8 yr age range and evaluated for their contribution to the pupils' ongoing education. Findings will be used to inform the curriculum and help to develop worthwhile computational thinking skills irrespective of the child's chosen career.

Categories and Subject Descriptors

K.3.2 [**Computers and Education**]: Computer and Information Science Education – *computer science education*. Language Constructs and Features – *abstract data types, polymorphism, control structures*

Keywords

computational thinking, early years, value, industry, primary

1. PROGRAM CONTEXT

I am currently mid-way through year 1 of the University of Glasgow part-time PhD programme, which typically takes around five years. My academic work is supervised primarily through the School of Computing Science with additional supervision from the School of Education. This collaboration across two schools within the university could have a significant effect on the field of computer science education at both school and university levels.

2. CONTEXT AND MOTIVATION

Jeanette Wing (2006) proposes that CT has value for *all*, a view instrumental in the growing interest in computer science. There is limited research directly assessing the value of CT outwith computer science, particularly in non-IT industry, and this study aims to determine whether there is such value. If it is found, the potential criticism that Wing's view has may have academic acceptance without underpinning rigor can be dispelled.

A national review of Scotland's technologies curriculum identified the need for schools to review their approach in developing children's skills, knowledge and understanding in computing science, age 3 to 18. In addition, the government commissioned a national group to review the computing science curriculum and its delivery. This research comes at a critical time to ensure changes over the next 3-4 years are well-informed. In Scottish education, as in other education systems, initiatives are regularly introduced to improve outcomes for school pupils. Already evidence shows more primary schools have a greater awareness of computer science. With the resurgence of computer science in curricula both in Scotland and worldwide, there is a need for robust academic research to ensure the right foundations for every school pupil.

3. BACKGROUND & RELATED WORK

To demonstrate the subject's worth, academic literature on CT builds on Wing's view that CT is valuable to all [2,3,4]. Brown et al. [1] claim governments and industries are convinced of the wider value of computational thinking and the transferable skills it develops, while highlighting the clear need for teacher confidence and training in the subject to deliver high quality learning and teaching.

Current CT research spans mainly across two categories. The first category highlights CT in its broader sense as a set of problem solving skills [2]; the second focuses on the narrower view linked primarily to coding skills [3][4].

Dierbach, C., et al. [2] discuss CT in its broader sense. Their research aims to demonstrate the intrinsic importance of computational thinking as part of the general education at university level. This work shows valuable applications across disciplines. Rather than computer scientists identifying where CT could be applied across subjects, experts in each field highlight the benefit of computation within their discipline. This yields a range and quality of contexts. It includes evidence supporting Brown et al.'s [1] belief that there is still confusion between ICT and computer science. For example, the English expert suggests using Facebook for students to create profiles for *Romeo and Juliet* highlighting the significant events within the play. While this is undoubtedly a motivational context for using technology, it is not exercising the deeper creative skills CT aims to develop. Their paper provides a clear set of objectives (Fig 3 in [2]) for non-subject specialists applicable across disciplines.

The second emerging category and more narrow view is that of literature exploring computational thinking through the context of coding [3,4]. This view is a concern if adopted by non-subject specialists to satisfy a CT learning outcome and introduce coding too early. Without considered application, the complexities underlying coding may be counter productive and demotivate children. Commendably, Seiter et al.'s. [3] work aligns the view of brain development with a child's ability to acquire certain skills. Coding through the Scratch environment relies on natural language reading skills and the PhD thesis will establish if and how the ability to read affects the ability to code. It also supports Cutts and Connor's [5] view that the introduction of coding for most should be after plentiful experience of CT through play and unplugged activities in the early years.

Cutts and Connor [5] argue for a position between CT as problem solving skills and CT as coding. They propose a progressive CT curriculum from age 3 onwards, founded on knowledge of information and process and the skills of modeling and reasoning. They argue that the early stages of this curriculum are largely overlooked in early formal education, and also in typical CT curricula. These early stages will be referred to as *foundational CT*.

4. STATEMENT OF THESIS/PROBLEM

The thesis statement is as follows: There are foundational CT concepts and skills, of value to non-IT industry and non-CS school subjects alike, that are not currently being taught to 3-8 yr olds, but could be.

5. RESEARCH GOALS & METHODS

Particular research questions are:

- What skills does non-IT industry value in its most effective employees?

- Do the skills of value to non-IT industry overlap with foundational CT skills?

- Is there an overlap between foundational CT skills and the core intellectual skills of other school subjects?

- Can foundational CT skills be developed in the early years of education?

The tasks in process or envisaged are as follows:

- Determine the skills and core competencies of employees that are of most value to non-IT industries.

- Define foundational CT concepts and audit their presence in the early stages of other subject areas.

- Develop an age-appropriate assessment for foundational CT concepts. Include assessing their natural language reading skills.

- Apply the assessment to 7-8 year olds about to engage in a typical primary computer science course, e.g. Scratch. Establish those sampled have no prior CT experience through school.

- Record achievements in Scratch through data capture. Determine whether there is a correlation between the results using the author's assessment tool and the achievements in Scratch.

- Concurrently with the tasks listed above, develop and pilot a series of learning and teaching activities for the foundational CT concepts and skills, to be introduced with 5-7 yr olds.

- Assess pupils' progress using the CT assessment tool and their achievements in Scratch at 7-8 years of age. Compare scores to those pupils without prior CT training.

6. DISSERTATION STATUS

I have carried out a study to determine the most valued skills within the non-digital industries. I led 35 interviews with staff across these industries, focusing mainly on the question of the qualities of their most valued employees. A thematic analysis of the interviews is underway. Being able to create and reflect on process models is emerging from every interview as one of the most highly valued skills. I am undertaking a literature review to synthesise an overarching view of the many brands of computational thinking evident in the literature, as well as to draw out underpinning or pre-requisite skills.

7. EXPECTED CONTRIBUTIONS

This work will provide the pre-requisites for the successful development of CT skills. It will be made available to those interested in reviewing computing science and an interest in delivering the highest quality computing science provision for pupils. Ultimately, it will provide much needed guidance for the development of computer science curricula for all learners. The foundational CT curriculum will develop highly valued skills for those continuing to specialise within computer science related courses or those pursuing a non-IT related course.

8. REFERENCES

[1] Brown, C., Sentance, S., Crick, T. and Humphreys, S., BCS, Restart: The resurgence of Computer Science in UK Schools NEIL The Chartered Institute for IT ACM Transactions on Computing Education, Vol 14, No. 2, Article 9 NY (2014)

[2] Dierbach,C., Hochheiser,H., Collins,S., Jerome, G, Ariza,C., Kellevher,T., Kelinsasser,W., Dehlinger, J., Siddharth, K.,. A model for piloting pathways for computational thinking in general education. SIGCSE '11 Proceedings of the 42nd ACM technical symposium on computer science education. Pgs 257-262 NY (2011)

[3] Seiter,L., Foreman,B. and Carroll,J. Modeling the Learning Progressions of Computational Thinking of Primary Grade Students. Proceedings of the ninth annual international ACM conference on International computing education research pgs 59-66 NY (2013).

[4] Rusak, G., and Lim, D "Come code with codester":an educational app that teaches computer science to K-6 students. Journal of Computing Sciences in College. Vol. 29 Issue 6, pgs 135-143 USA June 2014

[5] Cutts, Q. and Connor, R. A Developmental Framework for Computational Thinking *submitted for publication.*

Modeling-First Approach for Computer Science Instruction

Karen Doore
University of Texas at Dallas
800 W. Campbell Rd.
Richardson, TX, 75080, USA
kdoore@utdallas.edu

ABSTRACT

A Modeling-based pedagogical approach for curriculum design can provide useful framework for teaching computing concepts, particularly in courses that target novices. While modeling is a foundational pillar of computing, it is not typically a focus of introductory computing curricula. Our research proposes that modeling can provide a valuable conceptual framework for teaching abstract computing concepts when student learning is guided along a progression of increasingly formalized models. Our research focuses on student-constructed models to encourage collaborative discourse, which can help surface inconsistencies in student conceptual understanding. After exploring computing concepts through model-mediated activities, students can then extend their understanding through construction of creative representations of the target computing concepts. We are re-designing introductory computing curricula for students majoring in animation, game, and interaction design using this methodology. We argue that this pedagogical approach can be broadly applied, but may be particularly beneficial when designing curricula for students majoring in non-computing domains.

Categories and Subject Descriptors

K.3.2 [**Computers and Education**]: Computer and Information Science Education – *computer science education.*

Keywords

Model, Model-based, Curriculum design, Pedagogy.

1. PROGRAM CONTEXT

I am currently a PhD candidate in the Computer Science (CS) department at the University of Texas at Dallas (UTD). I received my Masters Degree at UTD as a student in the Intelligent Systems track from 2006-2008. I started my PhD studies in January of 2012, and have completed my qualifier exams and required coursework. My research is focused on enhancing CS educational experience for non-majors. Over the past 2 years, I have designed curriculum and taught introductory CS courses for UTD Art & Technology (ATEC) students. I am working as part of an

ICER'15, August 9-13, 2015, Omaha, Nebraska, USA.
ACM 978-1-4503-3630-7/15/08.
http://dx.doi.org/10.1145/2787622.2787738

interdisciplinary team to re-design the curriculum for the CS programming sequence: CS0, CS1, and CS2 for ATEC students.

2. CONTEXT AND MOTIVATION

Designing curriculum for introductory CS courses for non-major students is difficult. CS education research has shown that a wide variety of factors should be considered when designing introductory CS curriculum. Based on the current curriculum re-design process for required CS courses our Arts and Technology (ATEC) students, we propose that a modeling-focused instructional design strategy to support improved student-learning outcomes. In particular, we utilize visual, diagrammatic models and then guide students in construction of dynamic visual representations. Together, these function as learning artifacts to support discussions about abstract computing concepts. For one course, we use this curricula design approach to teach OOP concepts using the processing language. However, this approach is not dependent on using any particular programming language; in fact, it does not require that programming be used at all. For example, we are also researching the use of this curriculum design strategy as an approach to integrate computing in K-12 curriculum. Our research suggests that instructional modules should be designed to include these focal components:

- Observation - Identify processes or concepts from relevant and meaningful contexts, so students have an intuitive understanding of the target concept they will be modeling.

- Modeling - A modeling progression should be designed to guide students in developing a series of conceptual models that can support development of student mental models that are consistent with observed phenomena.

- Representation & Construction. – Design programming or other activities that can be used to create programs, simulations, and creative or artistic representations of learned concepts.

In essence, we are arguing that curriculum design should begin with an analysis of models and model-types, which align with the students' discipline and domain-specific concepts. Then, the curriculum design process should focus on aligning computing concepts to support understanding in the context of these domain-specific models, however we are also arguing that it is important to teach students the domain models as well as the computing concepts. A simple example is teaching finite state machines (FSM) to support game-design students in learning to design buttons in an OOP application. Whereas FSM models are not typically taught to non-major students, we argue that ATEC students benefit from learning models like FSMs as they provide students understanding of concepts of events, states, transitions, and memory, which can be used to represent game-design concepts. In addition, it is important integrate teaching of these concepts using contextually relevant content such as designing a button-type of game element.

3. BACKGROUND & RELATED WORK

Computing education researchers have explored a variety of pedagogical approaches, programming language options and environments designed to support novices in understanding computing concepts [5]. However, limited research has explored the benefit of student-constructed models as a primary curriculum focus for introductory courses. Fishwick [1] defines computer science as 'the study of information dynamics within discrete and continuous space.' Based on this definition, he argues that 'Models' are language constructs that play analogical or metaphorical roles in our understanding of phenomena. He further notes that 'in order to learn about a system, we must first build a model and then make it run' [2].

Our pedagogical approach builds on previous research in CS education, cognitive science, physics education research and other learning-science related disciplines. Hundhausen et al. [5] recommend a studio-based pedagogy, which stresses student-constructed representations of algorithms, which serve as 'meditational' artifacts to scaffold learning. Grover et al. [4] recommend a computing curriculum design strategy, which uses discourse-intensive pedagogical practices where knowledge-building discussions are integrated with computationally rich activities. Hestenes has conducted extensive research, which shows that the use of a modeling-focused instructional strategy is effective for teaching abstract concepts like physics [6]. Research has shown that having a mental-model with consistent and explicit mappings from the conceptual level to the program implementation level is critical in computer program comprehension and understanding [3].

4. STATEMENT OF THESIS/PROBLEM

Does a modeling-based pedagogy for introductory computing curriculum design improve student-learning outcomes?

RQ1. How can computing learning objectives be integrated into a modeling-focused instructional activity to support deep learning and transfer?

RQ2. Does a model-based pedagogy result in improved student understanding of these introductory computing learning objectives?

RQ3. What is the impact of this modeling-based approach on student-perceived relevance, engagement and motivation to learn computing concepts?

5. RESEARCH GOALS & METHODS

The initial phase of this research has been the design of several CS0 and CS1 learning modules, which use a modeling-based approach. After initial teaching episodes, we are re-evaluating and redesigning these modules.

To address RQ1, we are developing a series of curriculum modules, which can serve as guidelines for implementing this pedagogical approach in across a range of computing learning objectives.

To address RQ2, we will are evaluating and refining the design of these modules. We will be designing pre and post-test instruments to assess learning of key computing concepts and skills.

To address RQ3, we are developing pre and post course surveys to analyze the perceptions and experiences of students in these courses.

6. DISSERTATION STATUS

I am currently working on my dissertation proposal based on literature reviews and experience with curriculum design, teaching, and student feedback for our initial use of this pedagogical approach. I am working to design an assessment instrument and surveys to analyze learning gains and student perceptions of the course materials.

7. EXPECTED CONTRIBUTIONS

The use of modeling-focused approach to curriculum design can enable computing concepts to be more easily integrated across a range of contexts. We are currently using this curriculum design approach at the graduate, undergraduate and K-5 levels to guide curriculum design. It allows for integration of computing into any curriculum independent of target computing concepts or technologies such as programming languages, environment etc. Modeling is a foundational pillar of computing, it can be viewed as a fundamental language of computing, however, in the past, modeling has not been leveraged as pedagogical support for designing introductory computing curricula.

8. REFERENCES

[1] Fishwick, P. 2014. Computing As Model-based Empirical Science. In *Proceedings of the 2nd ACM SIGSIM/PADS Conference on Principles of Advanced Discrete Simulation* (New York, NY, USA, 2014), 205–212.

[2] Fishwick, P. A. 1995. *Simulation Model Design and Execution: Building Digital Worlds.* Englewood Cliffs, New Jersey, Prentice Hall, Inc.

[3] Fix, V., Wiedenbeck, S. and Scholtz, J. 1993. Mental representations of programs by novices and experts. In *Proceedings of the INTERCHI'93 Conference on Human Factors in Computing Systems* (Amsterdam, The Netherlands, April 24-29, 1993). IOS Press, Amsterdam, The Netherlands, 74–79.

[4] Grover, S. and Pea, R. 2013. Using a discourse- intensive pedagogy and android's app inventor for introducing computational concepts to middle school students. In *Proceeding of the 44th ACM technical symposium on Computer science education (2013)*, 723–728.

[5] Hundhausen, C.D., Narayanan, N.H. and Crosby, M.E. 2008. Exploring studio-based instructional models for computing education. *ACM SIGCSE Bulletin.* 40, 1 (2008), 392–396.

[6] Hestenes, D. 2006. Notes for a modeling theory. In *Proceedings of the 2006 GIREP conference: Modeling in physics and physics education* (2006), 2.

Characterizing Graduateness in Computing Education

Sebastian Dziallas
School of Computing
University of Kent
Canterbury, CT2 7NF, England
sd485@kent.ac.uk

ABSTRACT

In my research, I employ a highly qualitative, narrative methodology to explore the sense students make of their own educational experiences within their wider learning trajectories. By taking such a holistic perspective on a Computing Education, I hope to be able to identify and distil aspects of successful Computing programs, whose effects may only emerge over time.

Categories and Subject Descriptors

K.3.2 [**Computers and Education**]: Computer and Information Science Education – *computer science education.*

Keywords

qualitative research, narrative methodology, student experience

1. PROGRAM CONTEXT

I am a PhD student in the first year of my program in computer science in the School of Computing at the University of Kent and am part of the local computing education research group. To date, I have identified my area of research, conducted a pilot study with students at my undergraduate institution, and worked over the past few months to better understand the context of my work. My next steps going into the fall will include recruiting and conducting interviews with participants from the university here.

2. CONTEXT AND MOTIVATION

Computing is a notoriously fast-moving discipline, where large technical advancements can quickly alter relevant disciplinary knowledge. The ACM curriculum recommendations, for instance, highlight the importance of lifelong learning: "Curricula must prepare students for lifelong learning and must include professional practice (e.g., communication skills, teamwork, ethics) as components of the undergraduate experience." [3] Indeed, graduates will be unlikely to use many of the specific applications and techniques they learn after they leave University, although the intellectual utility of algorithms, theories and principles will persist.

At the same time, it is hard for academic departments to understand the cumulative effect of the undergraduate experience they provide. Educators only have access to immediate, short-cycle, feedback on separate modules through end-of-year outcomes and surveys. There is little opportunity to either reflect

ICER '15, August 09-13, 2015, Omaha, NE, USA
ACM 978-1-4503-3630-7/15/08.
http://dx.doi.org/10.1145/2787622.2787739

on, or gather data on, the totality of an undergraduate education. Consequently, it is hard for educators and departments to make informed decisions about large-scale changes to curriculum or environment and, when such decisions are made, they are based on partial, time-bound evidence.

Nevertheless, student trajectories are, without doubt, influenced and shaped by educational institutions: different institutions yield different characteristics in different graduates. The goal of this study then is to leverage students' conception of their own education to characterize "graduateness". Graduateness, as a concept, is defined as encompassing disciplinary knowledge, skills related to the type of discipline studied, and generic capabilities (of cognition or presentation for example). With this work, however, I am proposing a more nuanced examination of meaning and contribution of an undergraduate education as a whole in the diverse and changing discipline.

3. BACKGROUND & RELATED WORK

The question of just how students change in college has been a frequent topic of research. Pascarella and Terenzini, for instance, published what is now a third decade of research in their "How College Affects Students" series. Their comprehensive, albeit quantitative, review exposes the reader to a large number of studies – with the goal of identifying effects that are uniquely caused by college. [6]

Indeed, for many students, college is a time of fundamental personal growth and identity development. And "the prevalent institutional culture, navigation of identity, and development of skills are among the factors contributing to the individual growth of students." [1] However, as Pascarella and Terenzini contend, "rendering tone, tint, texture, and nuance [of the college experience] may require the finer brushstrokes characteristic of qualitative approaches". I take such an approach in my work by employing a highly qualitative, narrative methodology.

This approach is grounded in the work of psychologist Dan McAdams, who posed the question "what do we know when we know a person?" [5] According to his research, there are multiple levels at which differences in personality may be described. One of them is the *life story* that we, as adults, "[continue] to author and revise over time to make sense, for [ourselves] and others, of [our] own life in time." Eliciting this life story, then, permits us to explore how students make sense of their own experiences – including those pertaining to education.

Of course, a multitude of factors affect the process of constructing this story. For example, master narratives, which are embedded in the prevalent culture in which the narrative is told, provide scripts that serve as scaffold for stories. [2] In his work, Phil Hammack describes a model of identity that bridges cognitive, social, and cultural perspectives. He argues that we construct personal narratives to make sense of our experiences by integrating stories of culture (that is, cultural scripts available to members of a particular group) with our daily experiences. It is, in his words, "an enculturated, socially situated, and fully contextualized person that [this] research approach seeks to illuminate".

Another approach relevant to this work is Smith's concept of *institutional ethnography*. [7] Smith broadly examines how work in institutions is coordinated through texts and discourse. She describes how readers interact with and interpret texts (which are otherwise passive), become their voices and agents. She also highlights how institutional categories established by these texts may stand in sharp contrast to people's lived experiences.

These two approaches, master narratives and institutional ethnography, will serve as frameworks for analysis in my work and will provide a lens into students' personal experiences, as well as into the larger, institutional and disciplinary contexts.

4. PROBLEMS, GOALS, AND METHODS

The aims of this work are to:

- investigate Computing students' conception of their undergraduate education, within their wider learning trajectories,

- discover what sense individuals make of their education, of their own "graduateness", and

- distil and disseminate guidelines on (otherwise unapparent) aspects of policy and practice that characterize graduates of successful Computing programs.

I focus on students' lived experience and seek to uncover a rich, integrated, view of their relationship to their learning over time, closely situated within a disciplinary context. These aims are not well-suited to quantitative investigation and so this study is designed using a narrative methodology, and comprises two related studies, one focussed and one broad. Both studies will draw on a protocol adapted from Dan McAdams [4], which was first used with teachers in the context of the Sharing Practice project (www.sharingpractice.ac.uk) and subsequently piloted with students at Olin College in a 2013 summer internship project.

The **focussed study** will concentrate on a single Computing department. Two cohorts will initially be recruited:

  a. final-year students in the Computer Science degree at the University of Kent, and

  b. alumni of the same program.

I plan to undertake narrative interviews with participants from each group to detail their "learning trajectories". Using a narrative approach is a significant methodology in this context as it uniquely allows individual sensemaking. Investigating two cohorts allows me to ask questions both of disciplinary content and student experience, and the importance of each over time. It may be that different aspects become prominent whilst others diminish.

The **broad study** takes advantage of social media and distributed data gathering. This will comprise a web-based version of the protocol which may be completed remotely. It will be publicized on Computing-specific mailing lists and through social media such as Facebook groups. This will inevitably represent multi-institutional data as respondents may come from any Universities and any Computing degree program. The broad study will provide

a wider contextualization, both for the data from the focussed study and of the general nature of Computing graduateness.

As in all interpretive work, this project is structured, but not constrained, by its aims. The data may suggest quite other avenues for investigation and I will be open to them.

5. DISSERTATION STATUS

At this point, I have:

- Conducted a pilot study with undergraduate students at Olin College. We explored these students' learning trajectories and identified a number of developmental themes. [1] I am looking to return to these participants and interview them again within a year's time.

- Undertaken a literature review on narrative approaches, which provides methodological grounding for my work.

- Worked to understand the context of a computing education over time by interviewing participants of the major ACM curriculum reports over the past five decades. And in a publication currently under review, my supervisor and I explore how these reports are crafted through community involvement, and what pedagogic perspectives they have taken over the years.

Both the research into methodology and the exploration of context will each form a chapter in my dissertation. Going forward, I plan to recruit and interview participants for the focussed study next.

6. EXPECTED CONTRIBUTIONS

There are two ways this work may directly benefit practice. Firstly, it will provide a deep investigation of a degree program over time, indicating strengths (and weaknesses) that are otherwise invisible. At the moment, what parts of their education students value when they are embarked on their careers is unknown. Secondly, it will permit interrogation of "what works". While we may not be able to apprehend components of successful degree programs immediately, they may come to prominence over time, in the years after students' graduation. If such features are identified, they will be distilled to guidelines and more widely disseminated to the educational Computing community.

7. REFERENCES

[1] Dziallas, S. and Fincher, S. 2014. Learning to Learn: The Co-Evolution of an Institution and its Students. (Madrid, Oct. 2014), 852–858.

[2] Hammack, P.L. 2008. Narrative and the Cultural Psychology of Identity. *Personality and Social Psychology Review*. 12, 3 (Aug. 2008), 222–247.

[3] Joint Task Force on Computing Curricula 2013. *Computer Science Curricula 2013: Curriculum Guidelines for Undergraduate Degree Programs in Computer Science*. ACM.

[4] McAdams, D.P. 1997. *The stories we live by: personal myths and the making of the self*. Guilford Press.

[5] McAdams, D.P. 1995. What Do We Know When We Know a Person? *Journal of Personality*. 63, 3 (Sep. 1995), 365–396.

[6] Pascarella, E.T. and Terenzini, P.T. 2005. *How College Affects Students: A Third Decade of Research*. Jossey-Bass.

[7] Smith, D.E. 2005. *Institutional Ethnography: A Sociology for People*. AltaMira Press.

Adaptive Parsons Problems with Discourse Rules

Barbara J. Ericson
Georgia Institute of Technology
801 Atlantic Drive
Atlanta, GA, 30332, USA
+1-404.385.2107
ericson@cc.gatech.edu

ABSTRACT

Parsons problems are code segments that must be placed in the correct order with the correct indention. Research on Parsons problems suggests that they might be a more effective and efficient learning approach than writing equivalent code, especially for time-strapped secondary teachers. I intend to explore this hypothesis with empirical experiments, observations, and log file analysis.

Categories and Subject Descriptors

K.3.2 [**Computers and Education**]: Computer and Information Science Education – *computer science education.*

General Terms

Design, Experimentation, Measurement

Keywords

Parsons problems; Learning programming

1. RESEARCH SITUATION

I have just completed the 3rd year of my Human-Centered Computing (HCC) PhD program. I am working on my PhD part-time while working full-time. I just finished taking my last required course in the spring of 2015. I passed my written and oral qualifying exams in the spring of 2014. I hope to complete my research proposal by fall 2015 and my PhD defense by fall 2017.

My research group is creating and testing features for e-books to help people learn programming. One of the features that I have focused on is Parsons problems [8]. Parsons problems are code segments that are mixed up and have to be placed into the correct order and may have to be indented correctly as well. I created 11 Parsons problems for a chapter of the *How to Think Like a Computer Scientist – Interactive Edition* Python e-book. Log file analysis of this ebook showed that more people attempted Parsons problems than attempted multiple-choice questions. While most people got most of the Parsons problem right in one or two tries there were four questions that took three to nine tries for 75% of the people to get correct. Some people did as many as 109 tries before correctly solving one problem. We also found that for

some of the easier problems 50% of the people who gave up did so after only 2 tries. For harder problems 50% of the people who gave up did so after six to nine tries. I also created Parsons problems for an ebook for CS Principles teachers and another one to help students prepare for the Advanced Placement Computer Science A exam. Advanced Placement courses are high school (secondary) courses intended to be equivalent to introductory university courses.

2. CONTEXT AND MOTIVATION

The National Science Foundation (NSF) wants to prepare 10,000 United States of America high school teachers to teach a new course, Advanced Placement (AP) Computer Science Principles (CS-P), by the beginning of the 2016-2017 school year. This effort is called the CS 10K effort. Many researchers in the computer science education community are focusing on this effort, including the members of the CS Learning 4U project at Georgia Tech.

The new AP CS-P course covers several big ideas in computing, including programming. It would be very expensive and difficult to provide face-to-face professional development for thousands of teachers before 2016. Much of the professional development will have to be done using distance learning.

One of the difficulties in preparing teachers to teach programming is that programming can be difficult to learn. Reported failure rates in introductory computer science courses at the university level are as high as 90% [2]. A large multi-institutional study found that many undergraduate students can't program as well as expected after either their first or second computer science course [7]. Studies of expert programmers show that experts recognize and apply many "programming plans" as well as "rules of programming discourse" [9]. Teachers who are new to programming will need to learn these "programming plans" and "rules of programming discourse". Soloway and Guzdial recommend using scaffolding to support learners as they learn a new task [10]. Examples include providing hints, correcting mistakes, and coaching. As the learner progresses, scaffolding can fade.

The pace of on-line learning can be problematic for teachers. A study of adult learners in two online introductory computer science university courses found that success in the course was dependent on having sufficient time to dedicate to the course work and that working adults often did not have sufficient time [1]. Students had difficulty in learning to program and the time it took to create working programs was unpredictable. Even simple syntax errors like having a comma out of place could take hours to fix [1].

3. BACKGROUND & RELATED WORK

One way to make the learning of computer science more efficient and effective is to reduce the amount of time that teachers struggle with syntax errors. One approach is to use Parsons problems [8]. There are several variants of Parsons problems, such as including extra code as distractors.

Work in this area [4] has found that Parsons problem scores highly correlate with code writing scores. This means that Parsons problems might be a more effective and efficient way to learn than the traditional approach, which requires teachers to spend an unpredictable number of hours writing code. Denny, Luxton-Reilly et al. suggested that students should be able to solve the Parsons problems more quickly than writing the equivalent code, but they did not test this hypothesis. They also tested several variants of Parsons problems and found that students had the most trouble with Parsons problems with one distractor per code block and had the easiest time solving Parsons problems when they were given the structure of the solution (the number of lines in each code block and the indention).

In the e-books we are using an open-source tool called js-parons. Researchers using this tool have found that even though Parsons problems remove syntax errors, users can get stuck and repeat the same incorrect solution [5]. Some users also exhibit a "trial and error" approach. They drag a single code block into the solution area and ask for feedback to see if it is in the correct place.

One group, [6] who also used js-parsons, tried to limit "trial and error" behavior by restricting the use of feedback if this behavior was detected. They wanted students to think about the solution rather than just try different combinations. They informed the user if the user repeated the same incorrect solution. The feedback they gave was "Your current code is identical to one you had previously. You might to stop going in circles and think carefully about the feedback shown here".

Research on learning highlights the importance of explanatory feedback [3]. Rather than simply recommending that the user "think carefully" I propose exploring adaptive Parsons problems in an on-line e-book where the difficulty of the problem is adjusted dynamically depending on the teachers' performance. I will also add hints to help a teacher learn the "discourse rules" that guide placement of the code block, such as "declarations are usually done near the top of a method".

4. STATEMENT OF THESIS/PROBLEM

Do adaptable Parsons problems with discourse rule feedback help students, and particularly teachers, learn programming effectively and efficiently? I will extend the js-parsons tool to allow for adaptive Parsons problems with discourse rule feedback. I will test if solving these Parsons problems is more efficient than writing the equivalent code and leads to similar learning outcomes.

5. DISSERTATION STATUS

I created one set of Parsons problems and observed teachers solving those problems. We used log file analysis of student use of the same ebook to measure how many people attempted the problems, how many tries it took to solve the problems, and how many attempts people made before giving up. I created two more

sets of Parsons problems for two more ebooks. We will examine the log files for these ebooks as well to create a set of Parsons problems that people have had difficulty solving. I will start revising the js-parsons software this summer to add hints and make the Parson problems adaptable.

6. EXPECTED CONTRIBUTIONS

Research on Parsons problems suggests that they might be a more effective and efficient learning approach than writing equivalent computer programs. However, more research is needed to solidify this claim and to test methods to help students who use "trial and error" approaches or get stuck. If this research helps teachers learn programming on-line in an efficient and effective manner, it could provide a scalable solution to allow the US to prepare 10,000 computing teachers by 2016-2017.

7. ACKNOWLEDGEMENT

This work is supported by the National Science Foundation grant CNS-1138378.

8. REFERENCES

[1] Benda, K. and A. Bruckman (2012). "When life and learning do not fit: Challenges of workload and communication in introductory computer science online." ACM Transactions on Computing Education.

[2] Bennedsen, J. and M. E. Caspersen (2007). "Failure rates in introductory programming." SIGCSE Bull. 39(2): 32-36.

[3] Clark, R. C. and R. E. Mayer (2011). E-Learning and the Science of Instruction: Proven Guidelines for Consumers and Designers of Multimedia Learning. , Pfeiffer.

[4] Denny, P., et al. (2008). Evaluating a New Exam Question: Parsons Problems. International Computing Education Research Conference. Sydney, Australia, ACM.

[5] Helminen, J., et al. (2012). How Do Students Solve Parsons Programming Problems? - An Analysis of Ineraction Traces. International Computing Education Research Conference. Aukland, New Zealand, ACM: 119-126.

[6] Karavirta, V., et al. (2012). A mobile learning application for parsons problems with automatic feedback. Proceedings of the 12th Koli Calling International Conference on Computing Education Research. Koli, Finland, ACM: 11-18.

[7] McCracken, M., et al. (2001). "A multi-national, multi-institutional study of assessment of programming skills of first-year CS students." SIGCSE Bull. 33(4): 125-180.

[8] Parsons, D. and P. Haden (2006). Parson's programming puzzles: a fun and effective learning tool for first programming courses. Proceedings of the 8th Australasian Conference on Computing Education - Volume 52. Hobart, Australia, Australian Computer Society, Inc.: 157-163.

[9] Soloway, E. and K. Ehrlich (1984). "Empirical Studies of Programming Knowledge." IEEE Transactions on Software Engineering SE-10(5): 595–609.

[10] Soloway, E., et al. (1994). "Learner-Centered Design: The Challenge For HCI In The 21st Century." Interactions 1(2) 36-48

Worked Examples with Errors
for Computer Science Education

Jean Griffin
Temple University
1301 Cecil B. Moore Ave.
Shamada Resource Center Suite 150
Philadelphia PA 19122 USA
jean.griffin@temple.edu

ABSTRACT

Numerous studies document the value of worked examples in mathematics education and provide guidance regarding effective instructional design choices. The research described here draws on that body of work, research on learning from errors, and computer science education research, to study worked examples with errors for computer science education. I describe my prototype instructional designs using three programming languages and my two preliminary studies – a quantitative study using worked examples in a college computer science class, and a qualitative study of a high school computing class. These innovations and experiments inform my doctoral research study.

Categories and Subject Descriptors

K.3.2 [**Computers and Education**]: Computer and Information Science Education – *Computer Science Education, Curriculum*; D.2.5 [**Software Engineering**]: Testing and Debugging – *Tracing.*

Keywords

Computer Science Education, Worked Examples, Debugging, Tracing

1. PROGRAM CONTEXT

I have completed my second year as a full time Ph.D. student at Temple University in the College of Education's Interdisciplinary Doctoral Program in Math and Science Education. While the faculty members of this program specialize in mathematics education, science education, technology education, and education psychology, but not computer science (CS) education, they encourage me to explore my interest in CS education for course projects and papers, and for my dissertation. Two of the faculty members, Julie Booth and Kristie Newton, have research experience using worked examples with errors for mathematics education [1], which aligns with my interest in using similar worked examples for CS education. I plan to complete the required coursework and research apprenticeships by August 2015 and the other non-dissertation degree requirements by December 2015 (a comprehensive exam consisting of a literature review related to my dissertation, and my dissertation proposal).

The purpose of my research is to find guidelines for instructional designs that facilitate the analytical process of learning how to code in a time-efficient manner. The research builds on prior work with worked examples in mathematics education. It also incorporates a theory of learning from errors, which manifests in this research as instructional designs for worked examples that consist of series of short segments of computer code, some of which have strategically placed bugs that are logic errors.

2. CONTEXT AND MOTIVATION

Historically, computer science education has evolved top-down from the college/university level, where courses tend to have a primary focus on problem solving. In the 1980's the contrasting learning theory of Constructionism, which promotes learning by creating personally meaningful computational artifacts and sharing them in a public setting, was popularized by Seymour Papert [2]. Constructionism took root in the early grades and in out-of-school-time settings, with educational technologies designed for young children. In the current century, with the emergence of a plethora of educational technologies for creative computing that are more intellectually engaging, Constructionism is percolating up in to high school and college CS classes. One reason this trend is worth encouraging is because it holds the potential for increasing diversity in the field. In the United States, for example, the AP Computer Science curriculum, which has a primary focus on problem solving, has proved to be generally unappealing to females and students from racial and ethnic minorities. The CS Principles project aims to disrupt this imbalance, in large part through the infusion of Constructionism into the normative culture of high school computing [3], [4].

Teachers struggle to effectively interleave problem-solving activities with creative computing activities in ways that promote learning while maintaining student interest. Instructional designs that are lightweight (short and simple), that provide effective scaffolding, and that focus on key analytical computing concepts, can help to realize this goal. The work described here is intended to research guiding principles for such instructional designs.

3. BACKGROUND & RELATED WORK

My theoretical framework draws from research in cognitive science, education psychology, computer science education, and social constructivism. John Sweller's work on cognitive load theory and schema acquisition provides the underpinnings for research on worked examples [5]. Research related to instructional designs with worked examples (e.g. the use of fading, self explanations, sequencing, and errors) also informs my work. While most of the research on worked examples involves mathematics education, studies related to computer science education have been conducted since the inception of the idea, and the topic is experiencing renewed interest by computer science education researchers [6].

Ohlsson's theory of learning from errors across multiple domains is useful in framing my research [7]. Specific to computer science, researchers have investigated the efficacy of learning CS through the process of debugging [8]. (Related, but less relevant are studies that address how people learn debugging skills.) Finally, social constructivism informs my research. Rather than studying how learners engage with worked examples alone (e.g. with a cognitive tutor) I plan to study how they work with a partner, informed by evidence-based research on pair programming [9].

4. HYPOTHESES

1. Novice learners of CS who engage with worked examples that incorporate fading, comparison, tags, self-explanations, and errors will demonstrate higher learning gains than students who spend a comparable amount of time on problem solving with problems similar to those used in the worked examples.
2. Learning gains in the worked examples group will be most pronounced for lower performing students.
3. Students in the worked examples group will be more confident about their understanding of the computing concepts addressed than students in the other group.

5. RESEARCH GOALS & METHODS

My research goals are:
- Conduct an in-depth literature review.
- Create a series of worked examples for CS, including ones with errors, based on lessons learned from the literature review, using a language widely applicable to CS classes.
- Create a research design to compare learning gains and attitudes between treatment and control groups.
- Find diverse settings in which to conduct interventions.
- Conduct the interventions.
- Analyze within-case and across-case results.

6. DISSERTATION STATUS

I wrote a draft literature review in Fall 2014. I will revise it as I complete my comprehensive exam in Fall 2015. In 2012 I wrote about my experiments with teaching CS using Scratch programs with bugs [10]. In Fall 2013 I created a series of worked examples using MIT App Inventor for Android and *quizly*, an online quiz system [11]. For my dissertation work I plan to use Python because of its simplicity, general utility, and (arguably) standard treatment of function definitions.

In Fall 2014 I conducted a pilot study using a quasi-experimental design with roughly 60 students in a CS course that I co-taught at Haverford College in Haverford Pennsylvania USA. I created a series of worked examples on paper worksheets (with fading, comparison, tags, self explanations, and errors) for learning imperative programming with Python. Approximately half of the students worked alone; the others worked with a partner. Students completed pre-tests and post-tests individually. My research question for this study was whether the learning gains for the two groups would differ. Although I am unable to publish the results because the study did not go through an institutional review board process, the results inform my plans for future experiments. The worksheets and pre/post-tests can be re-used with minor revision.

For my dissertation, I plan to conduct a similar intervention in Spring 2016, this time to compare the learning gains and attitudes of students who engage with worked examples (in pairs) to those who work on problem-solving (in pairs). I plan to conduct this intervention at an urban high-minority high school close to Temple University. In preparation I am currently conducting a qualitative study of the high school teacher in whose course I will conduct the intervention. I will analyze the results of the intervention using MANCOVA testing in Summer 2016. If possible I will conduct a similar experiment at another school, in which case I will compare and contrast the results of the two experiments qualitatively and quantitatively.

7. EXPECTED CONTRIBUTIONS

The field of computer science education research will be enriched by this research which seeks to incorporate lessons learned from mathematics education research on worked examples and to replicate some of its successes with regard to student achievement and attitudes. At the same time, the body of research on learning from debugging in computer science will be deepened. Practical guidelines for instructional designs to support problem solving in computing will be contributed, which may be applicable to educational materials using a variety of programming languages and technologies. Suggestions for tailoring and enacting such curricula for varying student populations will also be contributed.

8. REFERENCES

[1] J. L. Booth, K. E. Lange, K. R. Koedinger, and K. J. Newton, "Using example problems to improve student learning in algebra: Differentiating between correct and incorrect examples," *Learn. Instr.*, vol. 25, pp. 24–34, 2013.

[2] S. Papert, *Mindstorms: children, computers, and powerful ideas*. Basic Books, Inc., 1980.

[3] O. Astrachan and A. Briggs, "The CS Principles Project," *ACM Inroads*, vol. 3, no. 2, pp. 38–42, 2012.

[4] R. Kick and F. P. Trees, "AP CS Principles : Engaging , Challenging , and Rewarding," *ACM Inroads*, vol. 6, no. 1, pp. 42–45, 2015.

[5] J. Sweller, "Cognitive Load During Problem Solving: Effects on Learning," *Cogn. Sci.*, vol. 12, no. 2, pp. 257–285, 1988.

[6] B. Skudder and A. Luxton-Reilly, "Worked Examples in Computer Science," in *Sixteenth Australasian Computing Education Conference*, 2014, pp. 59–64.

[7] S. Ohlsson, "Learning from error and the design of task environments," *Int. J. Educ. Res.*, vol. 25, no. 5, pp. 419–448, 1996.

[8] D. Klahr and S. M. Carver, "Cognitive objectives in a LOGO debugging curriculum: Instruction, learning, and transfer," *Cognitive Psychology*, vol. 20, no. 3. pp. 362–404, 1988.

[9] G. Braught, T. Wahls, and L. M. Eby, "The Case for Pair Programming in the Computer Science Classroom," *ACM Transactions on Computing Education*, vol. 11, no. 1. pp. 1–21, 2011.

[10] J. Griffin, E. Kaplan, and Q. Burke, "Debug'ems and other Deconstruction Kits for STEM learning ," in *Integrated STEM Education Conference (ISEC), IEEE 2nd*, 2012, pp. 1–4.

[11] Ralph Morelli, "quizly." [Online]. Available: https://code.google.com/p/quizly/. [Accessed: 05-May-2015].

Learning Together: Expanding the One-To-One ITS Model for Computer Science Education

Rachel Harsley
University of Illinois at Chicago
851 South Morgan, Chicago, IL, 60607, USA
rharsl2@uic.edu

ABSTRACT

The standard paradigm of an intelligent tutoring system (ITS) affords one-on-one learning between a student and a computer tutor. My work shifts this paradigm to accommodate multiple-student computer-mediated learning. The work is grounded in Computer Supported Collaborative Learning, ITS, and the emerging computing industry standard of peer programming. My current research is motivated by my personal experience as an underrepresented student in the field with a strong desire to be connected to others as I learn Computer Science (CS). CS is a discipline not known for collaborative exercises at the introductory level, however, there are promising opportunities for advancement.

Categories and Subject Descriptors

K.3.2 [**Computers and Education**]: Computer and Information Science Education – *computer science education.*

Keywords

intelligent tutoring systems, collaborative environments, computer supported learning, pair programming

1. PROGRAM CONTEXT

I am pursuing my PhD in Computer Science as a current member of the Natural Language Processing Group at the University of Illinois at Chicago. I work under the direction of Professor Barbara Di Eugenio. My research focus is to reconceptualize an intelligent tutoring system (ITS) for Computer Science (CS) education known as ChiQat (formerly iList) [3]; and develop its collaborative counterpart, collaborative-ChiQat. An ITS aims to provide individual, user-adapted support during problem-solving processes in a manner resembling of a human tutor[9]. Our intelligent tutoring system, ChiQat, interacts with students as they learn core CS topics and practice programming in a non-traditional graphical environment. The system is used in introductory computer science classrooms at the undergraduate level.

2. CONTEXT AND MOTIVATION

Recently, the question of why more people do not pursue computer science education has received much publicity from the White House down [8]. The demand for workers with CS skills is

ICER '15, August 9-13, 2015, Omaha, Nebraska, USA.
ACM 978-1-4503-3630-7/15/08.
DOI: http://dx.doi.org/10.1145/2787622.2787742.

at an all-time high. Tech leaders across the industry, including Facebook CEO Mark Zuckerberg, have been quite vocal and supportive of the need for computer science education in K-12 schooling[8].

One factor that contributes to low retention of CS students is the difficulty in understanding foundational CS concepts including basic data structures and the algorithms used to manipulate them [5]. These concepts include linked lists, binary search trees, and recursion. To most students, acquiring an understanding of these topics comes with a learning curve.

My work within the NLP Lab at UIC is exploring how to address this issue. Our intelligent tutoring system, ChiQat, interacts with students as they learn these core CS topics and practice programming. Our reported learning gains are comparable to that of human tutors [3].

3. BACKGROUND & RELATED WORK

Much of my motivation in pursuing this research stems from my personal experience as a trailblazer in a field that lacks representation in both the minority and female populations. Yet, the research documenting the benefits of collaborative learning as a whole provide justification for further exploration in the context of an ITS for CS Education. Thus my research focuses on merging the affordances of both ITS and Computer Supported Collaborative Learning (CSCL).

Longstanding research in and outside of the area of CSCL has shown that both cooperative and collaborative interactions among students are beneficial to learning [7]. In fact, the learning gains are often more profound than those achieved by the best of individual learners [1]. Furthermore, in recent years, the computing industry as a whole has embraced a shift in culture to incorporate collaborative interactions during the software development lifecycle. It is not uncommon for industry professionals to practice "pair programming", a system by which two programmers work on a shared workstation to review and write code. Pair programming in computer science classrooms has also been shown to benefit student learning [2].

Traditional ITSs allow for student learning to be guided and ameliorated in a manor similar to a human tutor. Namely, the ITS provides automatic adaptation to the student and often personalized and responsive interaction.

Both the CSCL and ITS communities shape the current context of technology-enhanced learning. However, the combination of CSCL and ITS research as a single intervention, CITS, is a relatively new area of exploration with opportunities for new advancement. CITS have been created to tutor areas including math, health, and physics among other topics [1, 6, 10]. The learning results have varied along with the means and method of supporting collaboration. Thus, a foundational focus of my research has been to create a uniform system for categorizing CITS that can be used for their design and evaluation [4].

4. RESEARCH OUTLINE

My research objective is to capture and analyze collaborative behavior in CS pair programming groups and redesign our current ITS, ChiQat, to accommodate effective collaborative learning. In particular, my research hopes to address three primary questions:

1. What are the salient aspects of unstructured pair programming collaboration within a computer science ITS session that correlate to student learning?

2. How can we expand the current student model of a computer science ITS to support peer learning, particularly via peer programming?

3. How do different types of collaboration structures, implemented in a computer science ITS, affect student learning?

In order to investigate these questions, I will conduct an experimental classroom study comparing the three types of CITS classifications as implemented in collaborative-ChiQat: unstructured, semi-structured, and fully structured CITS classifications [4]. The classification provides a structure for how CITS may be designed with respect to important themes in CSCL and ITS including: modeling of the student and domain, group dynamics, collaboration and pedagogical guidance, and technology. I expect that students in the fully structured condition will learn more than the unstructured and semi-structured conditions due to the collaboration guidance and also learn more than the individual ChiQat users of past experiments due to the richness of collaboration. For all conditions, students will be faced with the same domain-learning task, which is to solve linked list problems. For example, a prompt may be "Change the list L1 so it represents the concatenation of L1 & L2". As standard for pair programming, one student will serve as driver (keyboard operator) while the other serves as navigator.

The means of measurement for the system will encompasses individual learning via pre-, post-, and delayed posttest as well as analysis of the collaborative process. This necessitates logging of all peer-to-peer and student-tutor interactions. This includes, but is not limited to, speech interactions; turn taking behavior, interface interactions, and problem solving steps.

The conditions will be created and tested iteratively with respect to progression in CITS structure. The data from each study will be used for interaction analysis to understand both the collaborative and learning process and implement the subsequent conditions. Additionally, data mining and statistical analysis of logged (and coded) data may yield a deeper understanding of features that correlate to learning. Once discovered, I will be able to incorporate these features in a student model for peer learning. Finally, I can evaluate my hypothesis in regards to the most effective CITS classification for the CS learning domain. This is an intentional caveat as it should be noted that the most effective CITS structure might depend on domain and learning goals of the intervention. Yet, this research will provide additional insight on the benefits and drawbacks of each type of implementation.

5. DISSERTATION STATUS

Thus far, I have created a novel classification scheme for structuring the type of collaboration an ITS accommodates [4].

This method classifies the CITS across major areas grounded in ITS and CSCL research. Pilot studies of the newly adapted collaborative-ChiQat for unstructured collaboration in pair programming groups will begin in Summer 2015. My aim is to use data from this pilot for extraction of important features and then expound on these features in future iterations of collaborative-ChiQat system development.

6. EXPECTED CONTRIBUTIONS

The larger CS Education research community will benefit from a publicly available corpus of CS pair programming interaction data. My research will also advance the breadth of knowledge in regards to CITS, an emergent field that combines the benefits of CSCL and ITS for enhanced student learning. Lastly, it will help to improve CS learning and retention, especially for students looking to connect with others during their studies.

7. REFERENCES

[1] Arroyo, I., Woolf, B.P. and Shanabrook, D. 2012. Casual Collaborations while Learning Mathematics with an Intelligent Tutoring System. *Collaborative Learning Environments Workshop at ITS 2012*. (2012).

[2] Braught, G., Wahls, T. and Eby, L.M. 2011. The Case for Pair Programming in the Computer Science Classroom. *Trans. Comput. Educ.* 11, 1 (Feb. 2011), 2:1–2:21.

[3] Fossati, D. 2013. ChiQat: An intelligent tutoring system for learning computer science. *Qatar Foundation Annual Research Forum Proceedings*. 2013 (Nov. 2013), ICTP 020.

[4] Harsley, R. 2014. Towards a Collaborative Intelligent Tutoring System Classification Scheme,. *Proceedings Of The 11th International Conference On Cognition And Exploratory Learning In The Digital Age (Celda 2014)* (Porto, Portugal, Oct. 2014).

[5] Katz, S., Aronis, J., Allbritton, D., Wilson, C. and Soffa, M.L. 2003. Gender and race in predicting achievement in computer science. *IEEE Technology and Society Magazine*. 22, 3 (Fall 2003), 20–27.

[6] Kumar, R. and Rosé, C.P. 2009. Building Conversational Agents with Basilica. *Proceedings of Human Language Technologies: The 2009 Annual Conference of the North American Chapter of the Association for Computational Linguistics, Companion Volume: Demonstration Session* (Stroudsburg, PA, USA, 2009), 5–8.

[7] Lehtinen, E., Hakkarainen, K., Lipponen, L., Rahikainen, M. and Muukkonen, H. 1999. Computer supported collaborative learning: A review. *The JHGI Giesbers reports on education*. 10, (1999).

[8] Richtel, M. 2014. Reading, Writing, Arithmetic, and Lately, Coding. *The New York Times*.

[9] Tchounikine, P., Rummel, N. and McLaren, B.M. 2010. Computer Supported Collaborative Learning and Intelligent Tutoring Systems. *Advances in Intelligent Tutoring Systems*. Springer. 447–463.

[10] Walker, E., Rummel, N. and Koedinger, K.R. 2009. Integrating Collaboration And Intelligent Tutoring Data In The Evaluation Of A Reciprocal Peer Tutoring Environment. *Research and Practice in Technology Enhanced Learning*. 04, 03 (Nov. 2009), 221–251.

A Prescriptive Software Process for Academic Scenarios

Maíra Marques
Computer Science Department, Universidad de Chile
Beauchef 851, Santiago, Chile
mmarques@dcc.uchile.cl

ABSTRACT

Software engineering has been taught over the years using expositive classes, but learning this discipline requires more than just theory. Lately, universities started teaching software engineering in a theoretical-practical way. Typically, these experiences involve the development of software projects in the academia, using industry-oriented or ad hoc processes. However, most of them are not fully formalized, therefore it is not possible to repeat, measure or improve them. Moreover, it is not clear which project contexts are proper for each ad hoc process. This thesis work proposes to define and formalize a prescriptive software development process for use in undergraduate software engineering courses. We hypothesize that this process can make these experiences repeatable investing an affordable effort and will help produce positive results in student projects. This software process will be evaluated in the context of a second software engineering undergraduate course at the University of Chile, and it will address specific project contexts. This software process could be used in any university that has a similar course context. The proposed process can also be adapted to fit with new contexts.

Categories and Subject Descriptors

K.3.2 [**Computers and Education**]: Computer and Information Science Education – *computer science education.*

Keywords

Software engineering education, software process.

1. PROGRAM CONTEXT

I am completing the third year of the Ph.D. program in Computer Science at the University of Chile. I obtained candidacy status and already presented my late proposal defense with my research plan on November 2014. I plan to submit my dissertation in 2016.

During the two first years of my thesis work I focused on understanding and characterizing the practical approaches to teaching software engineering; therefore, I conducted a systematic literature review [1]. Using historical information, I introduced changes in the software process used in the software engineering II course (offered by the University of Chile), which is the basis for this thesis work. Pursuing an active research approach I followed the impact of the changes on the project's results. After three improvement iterations I expect to obtain the results of the use of the proposed prescriptive software development process.

The evaluation that we are running during this semester shows highly promising results. When the semester closes the data gathered will be analyzed and modifications to the process will be made if needed. Currently, I am completing the design of a formal experiment to be conducted during the next semester in a different university.

2. CONTEXT AND MOTIVATION

Because software engineering grows in importance, there are countries that are already teaching middle school students to code; but knowing how to code is not equivalent to creating good software.. Unfortunately, there is a gap between what universities teach students and what companies are expecting that students know before their graduation. One of these expectations is related to "soft skills" (e.g., teamwork), which are difficult to formally teach.

It is already known that teaching software engineering in the traditional way may not be very effective; because students learn a lot more when they have the opportunity to put in practice what they have learned in theoretical classes. On the other hand, many of these "soft skills" that companies are expecting from students are related to software engineering somehow. Therefore, why not to teach software engineering in a practical way, using a prescriptive software process that helps students develop their engineering and soft skills.

3. BACKGROUND & RELATED WORK

A recent mapping study performed by the author on software engineering education [1] shows that conducting theoretical-practical experiences is an important concern for the universities. The study also shows that there is scant information on how to do it properly. Many of the primary studies found in this study (60%) did not report the software development process being used in their experiences. Those using UPEDU [2] and Praxis [3] reported in detail the use of a software process in an academic scenario. These two software processes were created for academic contexts and have a high degree of formalization. However, these processes have limitations that make them difficult to use it by a software engineering instructor and also by students. For instance, UPEDU needs previous training [4], and various researchers state that the implementation phase starts too late [5]. Praxis was designed for a specific project context, and students need previous experience to use it, as it was designed for use by graduate students with previous industry experience.

The challenge of teaching software engineering in a theoretical-practical way raises a key question: what is the importance of a software development process for the students? This thesis work assumes that students should be able to understand the relevance of using a software process, and that such a process will depend on the context of the project to be addressed. If a software engineering course has a defined and formalized context, so a software process can be followed by students and instructors ,to get successful project results, and improve the process based on the previous experiences.

4. STATEMENT OF THESIS/PROBLEM

There is a clear need of teaching software engineering to students in a theoretical-practical way, but there is no broadly accepted way to do it. Moreover, there are few software processes that can be reused by instructors in academic scenarios, and it is not clear the amount of effort required to use them and the expected successes rate. In order to help address this challenge, this thesis hypothesizes that a prescriptive software process can:

(H1) make these experiences repeatable investing an effort affordable in a course experience.

(H2) help produce positive results in software projects in the academia.

5. RESEARCH GOALS & METHODS

Following an action research strategy, I am developing and evaluating a prescriptive software development process designed for academic contexts. This process should guide students and instructors in software development projects, making their experiences repeatable and involving a workload reasonable for a software engineering course. The process definition considers the following research goals:

Characterization of the software development scenario. An extensive bibliographic review was performed to characterize the software development in the academia. The main goals were to find out experiences of software development in academic scenarios, and collect lessons learned that could be used in the software process proposed in this thesis. Then, a Systematic Mapping Review was conducted, following the model proposed by Kitchenham et al. [6].

Through the use of these previous studies we tried to identify the context variables (evaluating their relevance on researches already published) that can be used to characterize these experiences. This information will allow us to define several scenarios for software development in the academia, but this thesis work will address only some of them.

Identification of the best practices/skills. The literature reports a large amount of software engineering best practices and work capabilities (skills) that should be learned by the students. Addressing all of them is neither feasible nor appropriate for a single software course. Therefore, we are identifying the best practices and skills that are relevant for addressing the software development in the work contexts defined in the previous phase.

Definition of the prescriptive software process. Once, the software development contexts to be addressed and the best practices and skills to be supported are defined, the architecture of the software process should be established. Provided that we are trying to address various (but similar) project contexts, we propose a flexible process.

The process includes activities, workflows, roles, and deliverables, all of which should address both, the professional and instructional aspects of these experiences. Sets of metrics are defined and will be used to measure the projects and products, and also the way in which these metrics will be calculated.

This thesis will have two types of data to be analyzed: qualitative data (student surveys and meeting reports) and quantitative data (grades and metrics). To perform the analysis of the results we will use the concurrent triangulation strategy [7], which mixes action research [8] and ethnography [9]. The action research is about solving a real-world problem, while studying the experience of solving the problem [7]. It aims to intervene in the situation being studied with the purpose of evaluating it and hopefully improving it.

6. EXPECTED CONTRIBUTIONS

This thesis work makes the following contributions: (1) provides information about the existing reports on how software engineering are being taught; (2) provides information about the best software engineering practices being used in software engineering education; (3) defines and evaluates a prescriptive software development process that helps instructors and students follow a repeatable process for getting successful results.

The prescriptive process will be formalized and made public, and therefore, any software engineering instructor will be able to reuse, adjust and improve it.

7. Acknowledgment

The work of Maíra Marques Samary was supported by the PhD Scholarship Program of Conicyt Chile (CONICYT-PCHA/Doctorado Nacional/2012-21120544). This work was also partially supported by the Project Fondef Idea, grant: IT13I20010.

8. REFERENCES

[1] Marques, M., Quispe, A., Ochoa, S. F., "A Systematic Mapping Study on the Characterization of Software Engineering Teaching in Academia". Proc. of the 2014 IEEE Frontiers in Education, (2014).

[2] Robillard, P., Kruchten, P., D'Astous, P. "Yoopeedoo (UPEDU): a Process for Teaching Software Process." Proceedings of the Conference on Software Engineering Education and Training (CSEE&T). IEEE Press, (2001): 18-26.

[3] Wilson Filho, P. P., "A Process-based Software Engineering Course: Some Experimental Results." Proceedings of the 3as Jornadas Iberoamericanas de Ingeniería de Software e Ingeniería del Conocimiento. Valdivia, Chile (2003).

[4] Germain, É., Robillard, P. N. "Towards software process patterns: An empirical analysis of the behavior of student teams." Information and Software Technology vol. 50, no. 11 (2008): 1088-1097.

[5] Germain, É., Robillard, P. N., Dulipovici, M., "Process activities in a project-based course in software engineering." Proceedings of the Frontiers in Education, (2002), Vol. 3. IEEE Press.

[6] Kitchenham, B.A. "Guidelines for performing systematic literature reviews in software engineering version 2.3". Technical Report S.o.C.S.a.M. Software Engineering Group, Keele University and Department of Computer Science, University of Durham, (2007).

[7] Wohlin C., Ohlsson M. Runeson P., Regnell B., Host M. Wesslen A., "Experimentation in Software Engineering", Springer Publishing Company, (2012).

[8] Avison, D, Lau, F., Myers, M. and Nielsen, P., "Action Research", Communications of the ACM, vol. 42, no. 1, (1999): 94-97.

[9] Moss, B. J., "Ethnography and Composition: Studying Language at Home." In G. Kirsch & P. Sullivan (Eds.), Methods and Methodology in Composition Research. (1992), Southern Illinois University Press.

Computer Science Is Different!
Educational Psychology Experiments Do Not Reliably Replicate in Programming Domain

Briana B. Morrison
School of Interactive Computing
Georgia Institute of Technology
85 5th Street NW
Atlanta, GA, 30332-0760
bmorrison@gatech.edu

ABSTRACT

My research explores how learning computer science, specifically programming, differs from learning math or science in relation to educational psychological principles. I have replicated well established experiments from the science and math domains by using instructional design techniques that minimize the cognitive load imposed on the learner. Instead of receiving the expected results confirming that the educational psychology principles also apply to computing, I received unexpected results contrary to the original hypotheses which indicate that merely adapting these principles to a new domain is not enough. I seek to understand what differences exist in learning programming, as compared to the other problem solving domains that explain the confusing experimental results I obtained.

Categories and Subject Descriptors

K.3.2 [**Computers and Education**]: Computer and Information Science Education – *computer science education.*

General Terms

Experimentation, Human Factors

Keywords

Multi-modality code explanation, subgoal labels, worked examples.

1. RESEARCH SITUATION

I have completed four years of my PhD program at Georgia Tech. During this time I have completed all my coursework, all service requirements, and have successfully passed my qualifying exam. I am currently writing my proposal and expect to propose in early fall and defend my dissertation by Spring 2017.

2. CONTEXT AND MOTIVATION

My original research plan involved using known educational psychological principles to inform the instructional design of worked examples for learning introductory programming. I based my work on reducing the cognitive load [2] for the learner by using multimedia instruction principles [6] and worked examples [1, 10]. The first step was developing a reliable measurement for cognitive

ICER '15, August 09-13, 2015, Omaha, NE, USA
ACM 978-1-4503-3630-7/15/08.
http://dx.doi.org/10.1145/2787622.2787744

load for computer science [7]. Then two studies were conducted: one concentrating on the modality of delivering code explanations and one using subgoals for how to program loops.

The results of both studies were contrary to the original hypotheses — the results did not replicate what was expected based on previous research in other academic domains. This begs the question – Why? What is it about learning to program that is different from learning how to solve problems in geometry or physics such that the educational psychology principles do not apply? My dissertation will attempt to develop a theory to explain the results and differences between domains.

3. MODALITY STUDY

The initial study built on Richard Mayer's [3] work. Humans use a dual-mode for learning, utilizing two different channels, eyesight and hearing, for input while learning. These channels operate separately. Providing nonequivalent instruction for both channels simultaneously is better than giving instruction for a single channel or equivalent instruction for both channels. Mayer describes how a diagram accompanied by text description is harder for students to understand and learn than a diagram with audio of the same description [3].

The first experiment was meant to determine the best modality (visual, aural) for code explanations for novice programmers. The best modality for code explanations will maximize the learning potential by reducing the student's cognitive load. Discovering whether students see code segments as text or diagrams determines the best modality for the accompanying explanation.

Participants were randomly assigned to one of three treatments: 1) audio only explanation of the code, 2) text explanation of the code, and 3) audio and text explanation of the code. In all three cases, the content of the explanation is identical. After each presentation, a series of questions asked participants to recall information or solve problems of a similar nature (near transfer for understanding). We expected the results to indicate that the verbal explanations (audio only) would perform best for both recall and near transfer.

Analysis of valid responses indicated that there were no statistically significant differences between the groups in terms of recall, near transfer, or measurements of cognitive load components. In other words, how the code explanations were given to the participants made no statistical difference in how much they remembered or how they performed on the post tests. The participants reported no difference in the cognitive load components (using the cognitive load measurement tool) regardless of the treatment.

This unexpected result raises the questions: What are the causes behind these results? Why did the explanations of code segments not produce results similar to those of physics or geometry?

4. SUBGOAL STUDY

A proven method for enhancing learning is to reduce unnecessary cognitive load on the student while they are trying to learn to solve problems [8]. One way to reduce cognitive load is through the use of worked examples [4], which are an instructional device that provide an expert's problem solution for a learner to study [1]. Sweller and his colleagues have found repeatedly that studying worked examples along with problem solving produce more effective learning (in amount learned and time to learn) than simply solving problems in the domains of mathematics and physics [9, 10].

While these cognitive load reducing techniques have been empirically tested in math and science disciplines, Margulieux et al. [5] were the first to test these with computer science learning, demonstrating learning benefits for subgoal labels with a drag-and-drop programming language. We sought to extend this research using a more traditional textual language, with mixed results.

A quasi-experiment was conducted using instructional material that was created to teach introductory programming students about the process of using and writing a `while` loop to solve programming problems. The treatment conditions for the study can be seen in Table 1. There were either *no* subgoal labels provided, subgoal labels *given*, or participants were asked to *generate* subgoal labels for groups of solution statements. Within each treatment group, participants were randomly assigned to either an *isomorphic* or *contextual transfer* group. This refers to whether the problem to be solved in the worked example-practice problem pair was identical to the worked example in procedural steps and cover story (isomorphic) or if the problem involved the same procedural steps but the cover story and numeric values changed. Participants' learning was measured with performance on novel problem solving tasks and a post-test.

Table 1. Subgoal Study Treatments

		Subgoal Labels		
		None	Given	Generated
Transfer practice problems	Isomorphs	A1	B1	C1
	Contextual transfer	A2	B2	C2

Some results were surprising. The findings continue to support the belief that subgoal labeling does improve learning. Generating those labels also takes more time, and more time does result in more learning. However, being given the labels may result in about the same amount of learning. In terms of efficiency (the most learning for the least amount of resources, including time), being given the subgoal labels may be the best option.

The context shift from example to practice interacts with subgoal labels in a way that is hard to explain. The best performance on the assessments comes from giving students the subgoal labels and requiring contextual transfer, or having students generate the subgoal labels but using only isomorphic transfer from example to practice.

5. DISSERTATION RESEARCH

To help illuminate the causes of the unexpected experiment results, I propose to conduct several qualitative studies exploring the participant's thought process as they use the instructional material to learn. I plan to use a modified cognitive walk-through method, similar to a think-aloud protocol, to explore the learner thought process throughout both the modality study and the subgoal study.

I believe the problem centers around the fact that cognitive load in programming is high due the intrinsic nature of the material. Students have to keep in mind variables, their roles, their own process in problem-solving, and the process of the computer that they are attempting to model and control. Because of this intrinsic load and the differences from other disciplines, we cannot simply assume that findings from these other disciplines will predict learning in computer science.

My research aims to uncover this intrinsic load difference and discover why known educational psychological techniques do not seem to directly apply to computing education. There must be inherent and subtle differences in the domain that may require more specialized techniques to improve learning. We may need other techniques for reducing cognitive load for learners. My contribution would be to define a theory that adequately explains these differences.

6. REFERENCES

[1] Atkinson, R.K., Derry, S.J., Renkl, A., and Wortham, D. 2000. Learning from examples: Instructional principles from the worked examples research. *Review of educational research.* 70, 2 (2000), 181–214.

[2] Chandler, P. and Sweller, J. 1991. Cognitive load theory and the format of instruction. *Cognition and instruction.* 8, 4 (1991), 293–332.

[3] Clark, R.C. and Mayer, R.E. 2011. *E-learning and the science of instruction: Proven guidelines for consumers and designers of multimedia learning.* Pfeiffer.

[4] Leppink, J., Paas, F., van Gog, T., van der Vleuten, C., and van Merriënboer, J., 2014. Effects of pairs of problems and examples on task performance and different types of cognitive load. *Learning and Instruction.* 30, (2014), 32–42.

[5] Margulieux, L.E., Guzdial, M., and Catrambone, R., 2012. Subgoal-labeled instructional material improves performance and transfer in learning to develop mobile applications. *Proceedings of the ninth annual international conference on International computing education research* (2012), 71–78.

[6] Mayer, R.E. and Moreno, R. 2003. Nine Ways to Reduce Cognitive Load in Multimedia Learning. *Educational Psychologist.* 38, 1 (2003), 43–52.

[7] Morrison, B.B. Dorn, B., and Guzdial, M., 2014. Measuring cognitive load in introductory CS: adaptation of an instrument. *Proceedings of the tenth annual conference on International computing education research* (2014), 131–138.

[8] Renkl, A. and Atkinson, R.K. 2003. Structuring the transition from example study to problem solving in cognitive skill acquisition: A cognitive load perspective. *Educational psychologist.* 38, 1 (2003), 15–22.

[9] Sweller, J. and Cooper, G.A. 1985. The use of worked examples as a substitute for problem solving in learning algebra. *Cognition and Instruction.* 2, 1 (1985), 59–89.

[10] Ward, M. and Sweller, J. 1990. Structuring effective worked examples. *Cognition and instruction.* 7, 1 (1990), 1–39.

Measuring Knowledge of Misconceptions in Computer Science Education

Laura Ohrndorf
University of Paderborn
Fürstenallee 11
33102 Paderborn, Germany
laura.ohrndorf@upb.de

ABSTRACT

This document describes the motivation, background and the current state of my PhD research project. I am aiming to develop a test model to measure educators' knowledge about misconceptions in computer science. I will first outline my position as a PhD student and will then illustrate my motivation for my research. This includes a short overview on related work done in this field before. I will continue with my main research questions and an explanation of my methods. This is followed by an overview on what I have already done. At the end, I will summaries what contributions I expect to make to the CSE community.

Categories and Subject Descriptors

K.3.2 [**Computers and Education**]: Computers and Information Science Education—*Computer Science Education*.

Keywords

misconceptions, evaluation, introductory CS courses, CS1

1. PROGRAM CONTEXT

I am a research assistant in the Computer Science Education group at the University of Paderborn (Germany) since November 2014 after working in the same position at the University of Siegen (also Germany) since 2011. I am currently working in two research projects on competency measurement in CSE. Furthermore, I am involved in the lecture in my group. In the spare time, I am working on my PhD thesis.

I am currently in the state that I have build the fundament of my research and am now in the transition to the key part, which is the development of a test instrument and the conduction of the main study. I consider this as the most challenging part as there are many factors that can influence yif an instrument can be used to retrieve valid results or not. This involves a careful selection of topics, good question scenarios and carefully chosen item formats.

Permission to make digital or hard copies of part or all of this work for personal or classroom use is granted without fee provided that copies are not made or distributed for profit or commercial advantage and that copies bear this notice and the full citation on the first page. Copyrights for third-party components of this work must be honored. For all other uses, contact the Owner/Author(s). Copyright is held by the owner/author(s).

ICER'15, August 9–13, 2015, Omaha, Nebraska, USA.
ACM 978-1-4503-3630-7/15/08.
DOI: http://dx.doi.org/10.1145/2787622.2787745.

2. CONTEXT AND MOTIVATION

In my research I am developing a measuring instrument to measure the knowledge of educators concerning misconceptions in CS. Misconceptions are a strong topic in science and math education as they are often constructed from students' everyday experiences and interfere with learning contents. Therefore it's important that they are identified by the teacher and replaced with proper concepts if necessary. Furthermore teaching materials should be developed paying attention to known misconceptions.

Compared to the disciplines mentioned before, misconceptions are not a popular topic in the practical application of CS education. This can be proved through the amount of research done in this field, but also through an analysis of the contents of textbooks used for the education of future teachers. Most of the books for maths and science include at least one chapter with an explanation how misconceptions develop and list typical examples. For CSE I know of only one book with a more in-depth explanation [2].

I believe that misconceptions in CS should receive much more attention. Learners in introductory courses most often have experience using a computer for a couple of years. Starting at a young age they also begin to develop concepts how these work. It is, for example, inevitable that children who play games on a tablet notice that their game data is saved and can be loaded again and hence develop simple models how this works. These models often originate from existing knowledge by building simple analogies. This procedure does not stop at a certain point but continues throughout the learning process - not only in everyday-life situations but also in CS courses.

My motivation is to create a measurement instrument that covers the knowledge about misconceptions concerning the main concepts in introductory CS courses. The results of the evaluation will give worthwhile insights on what CS educators know about misconceptions today. Furthermore, my research will have additional outcomes for CS education. On the one hand, the theoretical background of this instrument can be used as a framework for the creation of teaching material. On the other hand the instrument itself is a good tool to evaluate what future teachers know about misconceptions.

Many researchers who develop and evaluate assessment instruments for CS state that there are no consistent results on what students in a certain phase of their CS education should have learned and what concepts and topics are the most troublesome for them. Besides other factors, that makes it difficult to develop Concept Inventories (CIs), which are a common tool in other disciplines for a generally applicable assessment. This is, for various reasons, a very troublesome task in CSE. However, CSE should take up this challenge. A test instrument to measure the knowledge about existing misconceptions is definitely only a drop in the bucket. Nevertheless, it can arouse interest in this topic and therefore also foster the development of CIs.

3. BACKGROUND & RELATED WORK

There have been several studies on misconceptions in CS. Starting in the early 80s (i.e. [1, 3]), the quality has increased a lot. Research has focused on very small populations and narrow settings in the beginning, but larger and also international studies have been published in the last 10-15 years. However, there is a large focus on object-oriented programming while other fields of CS have not been considered ever [4]. Nevertheless, we can see that the amount of research results for object oriented programming has also encouraged educators to pay special attention to misconceptions here. This confirms the importance of misconception research.

That given, the majority regarding the published research does not represent where most misconceptions are developed in real class situations. Although far from all CS concepts and topics were covered, there are many where a lot of individual misconceptions have been identified and validated. Reading through the published studies and following the references, one can build a considerable collection. Certainly, the misconceptions do not always fit together really well as there were different target groups addressed or they were specific for a programming language. As a result there is no comprehensive collection of those misconceptions. Only Sorva [6] has arranged one for misconceptions about object-oriented programming.

Furthermore, there is also almost no research on the knowledge of CS educators about misconceptions. The topic has been described as important frequently, especially when defining what educators should know. However, to my knowledge, no one has investigated this in more detail yet.

4. STATEMENT OF THESIS/PROBLEM

My main research questions are:

- Which concepts and topics from introductory CS courses are both important but also challenging as students are likely to develop misconceptions about them?

- What do educators know about misconceptions their students have or misconceptions that can be developed by inadequate teaching material?

The most challenging problem in my research is the missing of related research done in CS. It is not possible to develop a valid and comprehensible test instrument without knowing what to measure. The approach to handle this will be described in the next section.

5. RESEARCH GOALS & METHODS

The instrument builds on an empirical study where experts where asked to rate the central concepts for introductory courses from the ACM/IEEE curriculum by means of four criteria concerning their relevance (following the Fundamental Ideas by Schwill [5]) and one criteria concerning misconceptions connected to them. Using the results, concepts which are both relevant and also connected frequently with misconceptions can be identified.

As a last step, the instrument will be used for an initial study with various groups involved in CSE. By analyzing the results it will hopefully be possible to identify what influences the knowledge about misconceptions. Here, the main research focus lies on the comparison of different groups, i.e. CS teachers in schools, in universities and others, which are not involved in any educational issues.

6. DISSERTATION STATUS

I developed the idea of my PhD thesis in 2012 and started to review related work at the end of the year. In 2013 I developed exemplary test items and conducted think-aloud interviews with CS students which helped me to get an idea how I can measure their knowledge of misconceptions. Meanwhile, by analyzing nearly 150 publications about misconceptions in CS and neighbor disciplines (especially maths) I was able to structure the research field. Starting in the middle of 2014, I developed a survey to retrieve a collection of the most important concepts I can focus on in my research. I conducted the aforementioned study with 27 CS professors from German universities. By analyzing the rating results themselves and an additional cluster analysis, I was able to identify 7 important concepts. I am now connecting these concepts to published misconception.

I am currently in the state that the first test items are ready for a pretest and I am still working on others, which are not yet finished.

7. EXPECTED CONTRIBUTIONS

As a contribution to the CSE research community I hope to develop a validated instrument to assess educators' knowledge about misconceptions in introductory CS courses. This will be especially useful in teachers' education. Meanwhile, the application of the instrument will also give valuable results regarding the current knowledge of educators.

8. REFERENCES

[1] B. du Boulay, T. O'Shea, and J. Monk. The black box inside the glass box: presenting computing concepts to novices. pages 237–249, 1981.

[2] O. Hazzan, T. Lapidot, and N. Ragonis. *Guide to Teaching Computer Science - An Activity-Based Approach.* Springer, London, 2011.

[3] R. E. Mayer. The Psychology of How Novices Learn Computer Programming. *ACM Computing Surveys*, 13(1):121–141, Jan. 1981.

[4] W. Paul and J. Vahrenhold. Detecting and Understanding Students' Misconceptions Related to Algorithms and Data Structures. pages 21–26, 2012.

[5] A. Schwill. Fundamental ideas of computer science. *Bulletin-European Association for Theoretical Computer Science*, 53:274, 1994.

[6] J. Sorva. *Visual Program Simulation in Introductory Programming Education.* PhD thesis, Aalto University, 2012.

Exploring Learning Analytics for Computing Education

Daniel Olivares
Human-centered Environments for Learning and Programming (HELP) Lab
School of Electrical Engineering and Computer Science
Washington State University
Pullman, WA, 99164, USA
daniel.olivares@wsu.edu

ABSTRACT

Student retention in STEM disciplines is a growing problem. The number of students receiving undergraduate STEM degrees will need to increase by about 34% annually in order to meet projected needs [6]. One way to address this problem is by leveraging the emerging field of learning analytics, a data-driven approach to designing learning interventions based on continuously-updated data on learning processes and outcomes. Through an iterative, user-centered, design approach, we propose to develop a *learning dashboard* tailored for computing courses. The dashboard will collect, analyze, and present learning process and outcome data to instructors and students, thus providing an empirical basis for automated, teacher-initiated, and learner-initiated interventions to positively influence learning outcomes and retention. Through a series of mixed-method empirical studies, we will determine what data should be made available to instructors, how that data can be best displayed, how effective teaching interventions can be fashioned from the data, and how such interventions affect student grades and persistence in introductory computing science courses.

Categories and Subject Descriptors

K.3.1 [**Computer Users in Education**]: *Collaborative learning;* K.3.2 [**Computer and Information Science Education**]: *Computer science education, Curriculum.*

Keywords

Learning analytics, learning dashboard, social programming, social learning theory, computing education

1. PROGRAM CONTEXT

I am currently in the Washington State University Computer Science Ph.D. program, with a focus area of Human-Computer Interaction. At WSU, Ph.D. students must complete qualifying and preliminary exams (in addition to required coursework), before reaching "all but dissertation" (ABD) status. I have passed the qualifying exam, and I am presently preparing my dissertation proposal for the preliminary exam.

2. CONTEXT AND MOTIVATION

Science, technology, engineering, and mathematics (STEM) fields have notoriously low persistence rates. This is highlighted in the 2012 report by the President's Council of Advisors on Science and Technology (PCAST) [6], which predicts a deficit in the STEM workforce in the next decade. In order to address this issue, we need to consider ways to change students' motivation, confidence, and peer interaction, with an emphasis on active learning [2, 4].

One way to do this is through *formative assessment techniques*, which involve incrementally assessing student learning, in order to adjust teaching and learning approaches [10]. The data generated by learners can be leveraged through learning analytics and educational data mining [3], which collect and analyze data on students' learning processes and progress, thus forming an empirical foundation on which such adjustments can be made. This motivates a key research question: *How can learning analytics and data mining be leveraged to improve learning and persistence in introductory programming courses?*

3. BACKGROUND & RELATED WORK

Learning dashboards, a learning analytics tool, are central to my dissertation research. Verbert et al. [8] analyzes 24 learning dashboards. Key metrics used in many dashboards include artifacts produced, time spent, social interaction, and resource use. Some dashboards have yielded a significant increase in reported student grades, while others have yielded no significant differences. This suggests the need for further research. What, specifically, is the impact learning dashboards can make on learning and teaching success, and how can we make learning dashboards more effective?

In computing education, there has been great interest in collecting log data on students' programming processes [1], and there have been a number of attempts to predict student performance based on these data (e.g., [9]). In addition, student attitudes (e.g. in regard to gender, self-efficacy, and social support) have been shown to be significant predictors of student success in computing curricula [7].

A recent line of work in my lab on which I am directly building has integrated a social networking-style activity stream directly into the programming environment [5]. In addition to collecting log data on students programming activities, this line of research is collecting *social* data on students' posts and replies in the activity stream. Both sources of data have been shown to be valuable predictors of student performance [5, 9].

STATEMENT OF THESIS/PROBLEM

My thesis will explore the design space of learning analytics for computing education. I posit that the data gathered on computing students' learning processes and outcomes can provide powerful resources for understanding students' issues and ultimately better tailoring instruction to meet their needs. In my thesis, I will iteratively develop a learning dashboard to assist in analyzing and visualizing data on computing students' learning processes and outcomes. This dashboard will support both manual and automated adjustments to learning processes, with the goal of positively affecting student interest, learning, and retention in early computing courses. In designing and evaluating such a dashboard

ICER '15, August 09-13, 2015, Omaha, NE, USA
ACM 978-1-4503-3630-7/15/08.
http://dx.doi.org/10.1145/2787622.2787746

and associated learning interventions, I aim to address the following research questions:

RQ 1: What learning data might be useful to instructors and students?

RQ 2: How can that data be best presented?

RQ 3: Can learning data be used as a basis for automated and manual interventions? In what situations might automated vs. manual (i.e., initiated by instructors and/or students) interventions be most effective?

RQ 4: How can instructors improve their instruction (or tailor it) based on a learning dashboard? How can students improve their learning (or tailor it) based on a learning dashboard?

RQ 5: Will such changes based on the dashboard correlate with higher student grades and greater student persistence?

By collecting and analyzing data on students' programming and social behaviors, this research uses a *data-driven* approach to make evidence-based teaching and learning adjustments.

4. RESEARCH GOALS & METHODS

Presently, we are using a OSBIDE [5], a Visual Studio plugin, to collect both social interaction and programming process data. In order to explore the research questions listed above, we will:

1. Design a learning dashboard.
2. Design and evaluate both automated interventions in the IDE, and instructor- and student-initiated interventions rooted in the learning dashboard.

Figure 1 presents a process model of the learning dashboard. Student data will be collected, analyzed, and presented to instructors and students via dashboard visualizations. We will additionally explore *automated interventions* that provide (a) students with learning hints based on the data, e.g., in-IDE alerts strategically prompting a student to compile his/her program, and (b) students and instructors with notifications that could lead to changes in teaching and learning approaches—e.g., a notification that many students are found to be struggling with a particular programming construct could lead the instructor to alter lecture materials or extend deadlines.

This research will be conducted using a mixed-methods approach. To answer RQ1, we will look to past research for factors that are known to be beneficial in informing instructors of student success. Additionally, instructor surveys will be used to gauge instructor interest in various types of learner data. Pilot studies with instructors and students using the dashboard will also provide feedback to further address RQ1–4. To address RQ2, we will survey the information visualization literature, and collect data through surveys and pilot studies. RQ5 will be addressed via pre and post surveys given to students and instructors participating in the pilot studies.

5. DISSERTATION STATUS

We have performed an initial survey of instructor opinions regarding which student process data are important and how they currently monitor student activity. Initial analysis suggests computing instructors are interested in many of the same data as are presently supported by existing learning dashboards. Specifically, useful learning data appear to be time on task, lines of code written, errors obtained (build, run-time), constructs used, debugger use, methods written, average method length, and social activity (questions asked, answers received, helpful answers, number of replies). Currently, the dissertation proposal is somewhere between an outline and a rough draft. The plan is to present the proposal sometime fall 2015. The goal is to complete and defend the dissertation in 2016.

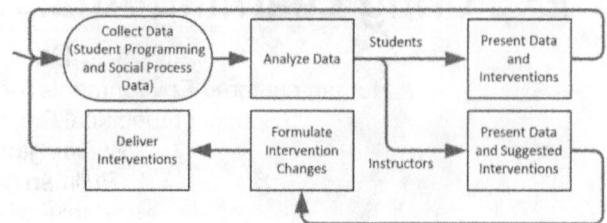

Figure 1: Proposed Learning Dashboard Process Model

6. EXPECTED CONTRIBUTIONS

This research will contribute an implementation of a learning dashboard and automated hints that allow instructors and learners to monitor, assess, and make data-driven teaching and learning adjustments. In addition, based on empirical studies, this research will develop empirically-grounded guidelines for deriving effective interventions from learning process data. Finally, this research should contribute to the literature by providing insight into which student data can be used to improve the CS learning and teaching process, how those data are best displayed, and how teaching and learning changes based on those data affect student learning and persistence in computing education.

7. ACKNOWLEDGEMENTS

This project is funded by the National Science Foundation under grant no IIS-1321045.

8. REFERENCES

[1] Altadmri, A. and Brown, N.C.C. 2015. 37 Million Compilations: Investigating Novice Programming Mistakes in Large-Scale Student Data. *Proceedings of the 46th ACM Technical Symposium on Computer Science Education* (Kansas City, MO, USA, 2015), 522–527.

[2] Barker, L.J., McDowell, C. and Kalahar, K. 2009. Exploring factors that influence computer science introductory course students to persist in the major. *SIGCSE Bull.* 41, 1 (Mar. 2009), 153–157.

[3] Ferguson, R. and Shum, S.B. 2012. Social Learning Analytics: Five Approaches. *Proceedings of the 2Nd International Conference on Learning Analytics and Knowledge* (New York, NY, USA, 2012), 23–33.

[4] Graham, M.J., Federick, J., Byers-Winston, A., Hunber, A.B. and Handelsman, J. 2013. Increasing persistence of college students in STEM. *Science.* 341, 27 (Sept. (2013), 1455–56.

[5] Hundhausen, C.D., Carter, A.S. and Adesope, O. 2015. Supporting Programming Assignments with Activity Streams: An Empirical Study. *Proc. 2015 SIGCSE Symposium on Computer Science Education* (New York, 2015).

[6] Olson, S. and Riordan, D.G. 2012. *Engage to Excel: Producing One Million Additional College Graduates with Degrees in Science, Technology, Engineering, and Mathematics. Report to the President.* Executive Office of the President.

[7] Rosson, M.B., Carroll, J.M. and Sinha, H. 2011. Orientation of Undergraduates Toward Careers in the Computer and Information Sciences: Gender, Self-Efficacy and Social Support. *ACM Transactions on Computing Education.* 11, 3 (Oct. 2011), 1–23.

[8] Verbert, K., Govaerts, S., Duval, E., Santos, J.L., Van Assche, F., Parra, G. and Klerkx, J. 2013. Learning dashboards: an overview and future research opportunities. *Personal and Ubiquitous Computing.* (Nov. 2013).

[9] Watson, C., Li, F.W.B. and Godwin, J.L. 2013. Predicting Performance in an Introductory Programming Course by Logging and Analyzing Student Programming Behavior. *Proceedings of the 2013 IEEE 13th International Conference on Advanced Learning Technologies* (2013), 319–323.

[10] Wilson, M. and Scalise, K. 2006. Assessment to improve learning in higher education: The BEAR Assessment System. *Higher Education.* 52, 4 (Dec. 2006), 635–663.

Privilege and Computer Science Education:
How Can We Level the Playing Field?

Miranda C. Parker
Georgia Institute of Technology
85 5th Street NW
Atlanta, GA 30308
miranda.parker@gatech.edu

ABSTRACT

My research investigates the interaction between privilege and computer science education, and asks what more can be done to level the playing field. Privilege is an unearned, unasked-for advantage gained because of the way society views an aspect of a student's identity, such as race, ethnicity, gender, socioeconomic status, and language. Privilege may provide advantages to some students, and under-privileged students may face unfair barriers to success in education.

Categories and Subject Descriptors

K.3.2 [**Computers and Education**]: Computer and Information Science Education – *computer science education.*

Keywords

Privilege, broadening participation, diversity

1. PROGRAM CONTEXT

I have completed my first year of the Human Centered Computing (HCC) PhD program at Georgia Tech. I anticipate passing my oral and written qualifying exams next spring (2016). I am on track to complete my course work in a timely manner and present my thesis work in the following summer or fall (2017). I expect that I will complete the program by Summer 2019.

I worked on a variety of projects since entering the program. I adapted Allison Elliott Tew's Fundamental assessment of CS1 knowledge (FCS1) [11] to create the Secondary assessment of CS1 knowledge (SCS1). This tool will be made available to the research community to help better assess CS1 students' understanding of the material, regardless of programming language used in the course. Additionally, I ran a three-pronged study to design a student version of an eBook for Computer Science Principles, the new AP Computer Science course. Through a usability study, participatory design, and student reflections, I have gathered data to guide our adaptation of the teacher eBook for use by students. Finally, I wrote a critical research synthesis on issues of privilege in computer science and STEM.

After exposure to a diverse set of projects in the computer science education domain, I am currently determining the feasibility and potential of research questions within the intersection of privilege and computer science education.

2. CONTEXT AND MOTIVATION

"Ultimately, Carlos pinpointed the unfairness of the system, and in doing so, addressed one of the core reasons we explored this topic in the first plac: 'You could have a really smart person who doesn't have any money, or has the potential to be really smart and all that, but because of lack of money they can't get up to the same level as somebody else with the same IQ or whatever, just living in a richer neighborhood.'"
-Margolis et al. (2008), *Stuck in the Shallow End*

There is a problem in computing: not every student is being afforded the same opportunities, which leaves some students who have the *capacity* to learn computing, like Carlos in the quote above, at a *disadvantage* for learning computing [1]. The opposite of a disadvantaged student would be a privileged student [9]. We define privilege as an *unearned, unasked-for advantage* gained because of the way *society* views an aspect of your *identity* [8]. By unearned and unasked-for advantage, we are referring to the opportunities a person is given that they did not earn through work and effort. For example, it is an unearned and unasked-for advantage for a student to live in a better neighborhood than other students. These advantages create an unfair system that Carlos discussed, and this concept runs counter to the idea a meritocracy, where reward is based solely on ability [8]. By definition, privilege does not refer to an advantage that a person *did earn* through work and ability. It is important to note that, in the definition of privilege, society is constantly changing, i.e. our society today is different from our society during the civil rights era or the Civil War. Identity is comprised of different aspects that determine who or what a person is [3]. Aspects of a person's identity can include (but are certainly not limited to): race, ethnicity, sex, gender, socioeconomic status (SES), language, or ability. It is important to note that some aspects of identity are apparent while others are invisible. For example, an individual can typically see race or hear differences in language, whereas an individual may not be able to sense socioeconomic status.

As mentioned previously, privilege interferes with having a level playing field in the classroom. If some students are given advantages due to privilege, those without privilege are (by definition) disadvantaged. Inequities in access to computing education and similar differences in advantage have been identified as critical issues that serve as barriers to women and underrepresented minorities participating more fully in computing

[6, 7]. Addressing the issue of privilege in the classroom will likely help broaden participation in computing. Although privilege is unlikely to ever be completely eliminated, mitigating its impact has the potential to lower barriers to access and increase diversity in the field.

While privilege is an important topic to consider in computing, it is important to recognize the complexity of identity, and thus of privilege. The numerous aspects of an identity (gender, race, SES) cannot be investigated in isolation because they are each intricately connected to one another [8]. For example, some racial groups have higher average household than others. Parrott et al. illustrated the complexity by comparing these issues to streams of water, and "just as waters of separate streams blend, these issues—too often considered separate factors—become blended and difficult to isolate" [10].

3. BACKGROUND & RELATED WORK

Several researchers focus on different aspects of privilege and their effect on computing education [6, 7]. However, most research in privilege and STEM education focus on different individual aspects, rather than the interaction between aspects. My work would try to bridge all aspects of privilege together to fill this gap in the literature.

Additionally, there are two common themes of how privilege is investigated in the community: through its impact, or through interventions. Many research questions ask how gender or race directly or indirectly affects achievement scores, perception, or confidence [4]. There are also many documented interventions to mitigate the effects of privilege, such as through professional development, curriculum changes [5]. I hope to gain clarity through this Consortium as to whether to focus on the impact of privilege, interventions to reduce its effects, or both, for my dissertation research.

4. STATEMENT OF THESIS/PROBLEM

I am currently open to a variety of questions relating to privilege and computing education, most namely:

- How can we study privilege in computer science education at a large scale?

- Do interventions that affect the underprivileged only, or the underprivileged and privileged alike, have greater impact in mitigating the effects of privilege?

5. RESEARCH GOALS & METHODS

The first question can be initially approached by partnering with a national organization that 1) involves computer science education and 2) is willing to collect data related to privilege from organization members or participants. While this partnership is forming, I will need to formulate what questions are best suited to measure the impact of privilege in this context. Once these questions are tested and then implemented by the organization, the task at hand will be analyzing the data in an appropriate manner. If there is no evidence that privilege is affecting the participants, I will further explore what the organization has done to reduce the impact of privilege. If privilege is found to affect the participants, I could continue the project by partnering with the organization to ask what could be done to provide just opportunities to all learners.

The second question can involve the design of a comparative study of two interventions: one that helps everyone in the classroom, and one that is directed at helping the underprivileged learners. Pre- and post-survey data will be collected, including questions that ask about attitudes towards computer science, perception, confidence, and so on. This study will force us to ask the question: can we help the minority by helping everyone, or is it best to focus on the minority? The answer to this question will help the community better direct intervention efforts in the future.

6. DISSERTATION STATUS

My goal is to propose my dissertation in Summer or Fall of 2017. Through my participation in the Consortium I hope to clarify my research questions and begin to design studies to answer them. I would also appreciate assistance in framing my work in preparation for writing my thesis proposal.

7. EXPECTED CONTRIBUTIONS

My work will increase awareness of the existence of privilege in computer science education and provide insight as to how to mitigate the effects of privilege.

8. REFERENCES

[1] Camp, T. (2012). "Computing, We Have a Problem…." *ACM Inroads*, *3*(4), 34–40.

[2] Dahlberg, T., Barnes, T., Buch, K. I. M., & Rorrer, A. (2011). The STARS Alliance: Viable Strategies for Broadening Participation in Computing. *ACM Transactions on Computing Education*, *11*(3). doi:10.1145/2037276.2037282

[3] Erikson, E. (1968). *Youth: Identity and crisis*. New York, NY: WW. doi:10.1002/yd.29

[4] Garvin-Doxas, K., & Barker, L. J. (2005). Communication in Computer Science Classrooms: Understanding Defensive Climates as a Means of Creating Supportive Behaviors. *ACM Journal of Education Resources in Computing*, *4*(1).

[5] Goode, J., Margolis, J., & Chapman, G. (2014). Curriculum is not enough: the educational theory and research foundation of the exploring computer science professional development model. In *SIGCSE* (pp. 493–498). doi:10.1145/2538862.2538948

[6] Margolis, J. (2008). *Stuck in the Shallow End*.

[7] Margolis, J., & Fisher, A. (2003). *Unlocking the clubhouse: Women in computing*. MIT press.

[8] Mcintosh, P. (1988). *White privilege and male privilege: A personal account of coming to see correspondences through work in women's studies* (No. 189).

[9] Mcintosh, P. (1992). White Privilege: Unpacking the Invisible Knapsack. *Multiculturalism*, 30–36.

[10] Parrott, L., Spatig, L., Kusimo, P. S., Carter, C. C., & Keyes, M. (2000). Troubled Waters: Where multiple streams of inequality converge in the math and science experiences of nonprivileged girls. *Journal of Women and Minorities in Science and Engineering*, *6*, 45–71.

[11] Tew, A. E., & Guzdial, M. (2011). The FCS1 : A Language Independent Assessment of CS1 Knowledge. In *Proceedings of the 42nd ACM technical symposium on computer science education* (pp. 111–116).

Integrating Intelligent Feedback into Block Programming Environments

Thomas W. Price
North Carolina State University
890 Oval Drive
Raleigh, NC 27606, USA
twprice@ncsu.edu

ABSTRACT

Block Programming Environments (BPEs) are becoming popular tools for introducing novices to programming, due in part to their connection with students' interests in games, apps and stories. This has led to increasing use of BPEs outside of classroom settings, where knowledgeable instructors are not always available. Intelligent Tutoring Systems (ITSs) can keep students on track in the absence of instructors by providing hints and warnings to students in need of help. Further, data-driven techniques can generate this feedback automatically from previous students' attempts at a problem. This research focuses on the integration of this data-driven, ITS-style feedback into a modern BPE and the evaluation of its impact.

Categories and Subject Descriptors

K.3.2 [**Computers and Education**]: Computers and Information Science Education—*Computer Science Education*.

Keywords

Block programming, Intelligent Tutoring Systems, Hints.

1. PROGRAM CONTEXT

I am a second year PhD student in the Computer Science department at North Carolina State University, working in the Center for Educational Informatics. I have completed my coursework, as well as the first milestone of my program, the written preliminary exam. As part of the exam, I designed and conducted an experiment to compare the effects of textual and block programming interfaces on middle school students' performance and self-efficacy as they completed an introductory programming assignment. I am currently preparing to propose my dissertation research on providing data-driven, intelligent feedback in Block Programming Environments. I have begun initial research and plan to present my proposal in the spring of 2016 and defend my dissertation in spring of 2017.

ICER'15, August 9–13, 2015, Omaha, Nebraska, USA.
ACM 978-1-4503-3630-7/15/08.
DOI: http://dx.doi.org/10.1145/2787622.2787748.

2. CONTEXT AND MOTIVATION

The need for more Computer Science (CS) teachers in K12 schools is well established, with programs such as the NSF's CS10K initiative seeking to train 10,000 high school teachers. Despite these efforts, many students still have little to no access to formal CS education. For these students, the best opportunities to learn CS are informal learning environments, such as after school programs (e.g. [4]) and websites like Code.org that offer self-paced lessons. In these settings, especially in the absence of a trained instructor, it is important that students learn CS in a way that is engaging and supportive.

Block Programming Environments (BPEs), such as Alice, Scratch, MIT App Inventor and Snap are popular tools for introducing CS in informal learning settings [4, 9]. These environments make programming easier by removing syntax errors and the need to memorize procedure names, while allowing students to write code that connects with their interests, such as games, apps and stories. BPEs have been positively evaluated in formal and informal learning settings [2, 4] and have been suggested as tools for broadening participation in Computer Science (CS) [3, 4]. However, these environments generally offer little support to students who get stuck and do not know how to proceed or debug their program. If no instructor is available in these situations, students may give up or lose interest in CS.

Intelligent Tutoring Systems (ITSs) offer a solution to this problem by providing struggling students with automated feedback and guidance. This often takes the form of hints when students are stuck, or warnings if they perform an incorrect step [8]. In fact, this feedback can be generated from past students' solutions to a problem, using data-driven techniques that avoid the need for expensive, hand-authored expert models [7]. This data-driven feedback, in the form of hints, has been successfully generated in many domains, including programming [6].

My research seeks to integrate data-driven, ITS-style feedback into a modern BPE and to evaluate the effect of this feedback on student performance and self-efficacy, in the absence of an instructor.

3. BACKGROUND & RELATED WORK

BPEs have been evaluated in a number of contexts. Dann et al. [2] showed that Alice 3 had great educational benefit in an introductory college CS course, where students later transitioned to a more traditional Java curriculum. Students who took the Alice-to-Java course performed on average a full letter grade higher on the final exam (which was in Java) than historical students taking the Java-only version of the course. Maloney et al. [4] show that BPEs can also be successful in informal settings. They describe the use of Scratch in an urban after-school center, where students used it voluntarily and frequently, despite having no formal instruction. Students picked up some CS concepts, with about half of their programs employing loops and user interaction.

While BPEs generally lack built-in, intelligent feedback, programming ITSs have provided this support for many years. The ACT Programming Tutor [1] uses a Cognitive Model, consisting of hundreds of expert written, language-specific production rules, which model correct (and buggy) actions within the tutor. These rules are used to interpret student actions, recognize mistakes and offer hints. The Hint Factory [7] offers a data-driven alternative to these hand-constructed models, using correct solutions from previous students to build a graphical model of how students can progress through a given problem. This model is used as the basis for hint-generation, directing students in need of help down correct solution paths. The Hint Factory has been extended to work in the domain of programming [6], where a larger space of possible solutions to any given problem makes the task more difficult.

4. PROBLEM, GOALS & METHODS

My hypothesis is that we can adapt the Hint Factory to generate data-driven, on-demand hints for students working in BPEs, and that these hints will improve students' performance and self-efficacy in the environment. Specifically, my goal is to integrate this functionality into the SNAP[1] programming environment, with a focus on supporting open-ended tasks such as creating games, apps and stories.

As a concrete example, imagine a student working on simple game, similar to Whack-a-Mole, which requires the use of variables, loops, conditionals and calls to a simple API to control the position of sprites onscreen. The student can make the mole appear, but is having trouble randomizing its location. After requesting a hint, the student receives a message instructing her to replace her hard-coded coordinates with a call to a `random` function.

I will start by instrumenting the SNAP environment and collecting detailed snapshots from students, who will also serve as a control group, as they complete an open-ended programming activity without instructor assistance. I will work to adapt the Hint Factory to the complexities of this open-ended domain, drawing on previous work [6], and generate hints from the previously collected data. I will integrate these hints into SNAP and collect data from a second group of students completing the same activity with hints available. I will compare the two groups' performance in the environment, as measured by completion of the activity's subgoals, and their change in self-efficacy regarding computing, measured by pre- and post-surveys.

5. DISSERTATION STATUS

I have collected a preliminary dataset from students working with both block and textual programming interfaces on an open-ended problem. I have compared their performance, and confirmed that the block interface does improve student performance. I have explored the application of existing data-driven techniques to this dataset and identified areas

that will require extension [5]. I am currently using these findings to explore possible modifications to the Hint Factory algorithm, and preparing for the initial data collection.

I am in the initial stages of drafting my dissertation proposal, but have not yet started writing the dissertation itself. I intend to complete the initial data collection, analysis and proposal by spring of 2016. The hint generation and evaluation should be completed by the fall of 2016 and the document itself should be finished by spring of 2017.

From this DC I would like guidance on the design of the programming activity, the appropriate setting for data collection, and if there are additional performance measures I should consider collecting. I am also interested in what additional feedback and guidance the programming environment should ideally provide to students, besides on-demand hints.

6. EXPECTED CONTRIBUTIONS

Practically, this work seeks to improve BPEs, common tools for introducing novices to programming, by increasing their accessibility and efficacy outside of a formal learning environment. The data-driven techniques explored here will be important progress toward automated hint generation in ill-defined domains, such as open-ended programming. This work is an important first step towards integrating two successful tools for learning: ITSs and BPEs.

7. REFERENCES

[1] A. T. Corbett. Cognitive Mastery Learning in the ACT Programming Tutor. Technical report, 2000.

[2] W. Dann, D. Cosgrove, and D. Slater. Mediated transfer: Alice 3 to java. In *Proceedings of the 43rd ACM technical symposium on Computer Science Education*, pages 141–146, 2012.

[3] C. Kelleher, R. Pausch, and S. Kiesler. Storytelling alice motivates middle school girls to learn computer programming. *Proceedings of the SIGCHI conference on Human Computer Interaction*, 2007.

[4] J. Maloney, K. Peppler, Y. Kafai, M. Resnick, and N. Rusk. Programming by choice: urban youth learning programming with scratch. *ACM SIGCSE Bulletin*, 40(1):367–371, 2008.

[5] T. W. Price and T. Barnes. An Exploration of Data-Driven Hint Generation in an Open-Ended Programming Problem. In *Workshop on Graph-Based Data Mining held at Educational Data Mining (EDM)*, 2015, forthcoming.

[6] K. Rivers and K. Koedinger. Automatic generation of programming feedback: A data-driven approach. In *The First Workshop on AI-supported Education for Computer Science (AIEDCS 2013)*, 2013.

[7] J. Stamper, M. Eagle, T. Barnes, and M. Croy. Experimental evaluation of automatic hint generation for a logic tutor. *Artificial Intelligence in Education (AIED)*, 22(1):3–17, 2013.

[8] K. Vanlehn. The behavior of tutoring systems. *International Journal of Artifical Intelligence in Education*, 16(3):227–265, 2006.

[9] A. Wagner, J. Gray, J. Corley, and D. Wolber. Using app inventor in a K-12 summer camp. In *Proceeding of the 44th ACM Technical Symposium on Computer Ccience Education*, 2013.

---

[1]snap.berkeley.edu

Designing a Data-Driven Tutor Authoring Tool for CS Educators

Kelly Rivers
Carnegie Mellon University
5000 Forbes Ave.
Pittsburgh, PA, 15213, USA
krivers@cs.cmu.edu

ABSTRACT

Intelligent Tutoring Systems are highly effective at helping students learn, but have required intensive amounts of development time in the past, keeping teachers from making their own. Data-driven tutoring has made it possible to build these tutors more efficiently. For my thesis work, I intend to build an authoring tool for data-driven tutors that is designed to be used by computer science teachers. I plan to design this system based on data gathered in interviews with CS educators and evaluate it on its usability for new users.

Categories and Subject Descriptors

K.3.2 [**Computers and Education**]: Computer and Information Science Education – *computer science education.*

Keywords

data-driven tutoring, teacher adoption of technology, usability, intelligent tutoring system authoring tools

1. PROGRAM CONTEXT

I have just completed the fourth year of my PhD program in Human-Computer Interaction at Carnegie Mellon University. This program has a primary focus in HCI, but also has a large contingent of researchers that specialize in the learning sciences, especially intelligent tutoring systems (ITSs). I have completed all of my classes and teaching requirements, and I intend to propose my thesis in late summer/early fall 2015.

In the past four years I have worked with my advisor, Ken Koedinger, to design and build the Intelligent Teaching Assistant for Programming (ITAP). This system uses collected student solutions to automatically generate hints for code-writing programming problems. I have done a technical evaluation of ITAP by testing its performance on old student data, and I've run a small lab study to determine how students interact with hints in a programming editor. For future work, I plan to continue the development of ITAP, test it empirically with large in-class studies, and explore the potential for practical tutor development in the field by designing an authoring tool for teachers.

ICER '15, August 09-13, 2015, Omaha, NE, USA
ACM 978-1-4503-3630-7/15/08.
http://dx.doi.org/10.1145/2787622.2787749

2. CONTEXT AND MOTIVATION

Writing code is an essential skill that every novice programmer needs to learn. The process of learning to write code is filled with many struggles, but students do better when they get help with the 'insurmountable' problems, especially when that help arrives quickly [3]. However, teachers cannot spend every moment of their time with their studsents helping them get unstuck. Having an automated source of assistance might, therefore, greatly assist students who are learning how to program.

ITSs have been shown to be very effective in assisting students, and have even helped students learn programming more quickly and thoroughly in the past [1]. However, the time and effort required to build a tutoring system is prohibitively large, and almost all of the tutors that have been created so far have been made by research groups or companies, not teachers [4]. Perhaps this is why ITSs have not been widely adopted in introductory programming classes, despite their great potential.

My advisor and I have designed ITAP, a new kind of intelligent tutoring system for programming which can generate hints automatically for students in open-ended code writing environments [8]. This system has the potential to assist students who are working on practice problems, and can help students get 'un-stuck' by giving them next-step hints that move them closer to a correct state. It can also be used to generate tutored problems rapidly with little author input needed. Now that we have developed ITAP to the point that it is usable in real classroom settings, we want to determine whether it can be used to help teachers extend the amount of automated support provided in their classrooms.

3. BACKGROUND & RELATED WORK

Data-driven tutoring for programming has been expanding as a subfield of intelligent tutoring systems over the past few years, with many different researchers creating new techniques to automatically generate hints. However, most of the systems (including ours) have only been evaluated on collected student problem-solving traces, and the ones that are being tested on real students are implemented in online learning environments such as MOOCs [6,7], not in individual classrooms.

In the broader field of ITS authoring by teachers, there have been a few attempts to make tutor authoring more accessible. The introduction of authoring by demonstration made GUI tutor authoring take drastically less time than before [5], and more structured content provision editors made it easier for teachers to create new items for language-learning systems [2]. There do not appear to be any studies which have directly evaluated teacher interest in generating intelligent tutors independently.

4. STATEMENT OF THESIS/PROBLEM

My broad research question is: will CS educators use more adaptive practice problems in their classes if they have the ability to create the adaptive content themselves? To address this question, I will also investigate the following two questions in my thesis work:

- What do teachers want their practice problems to look like, and how does this relate to CSED best practices? What kinds of features do teachers want within programming tutors?

- What are the usability concerns that need to be considered when designing a tutor authoring tool for teachers?

5. RESEARCH GOALS & METHODS

For my thesis work, I plan to pursue three primary research phases. The first research phase will address the question of what needs teachers actually have, and what features they require in their own tutored problems. To understand this, I plan to do interviews with CS educators to understand what kinds of educational technology they currently use and whether/how they assign practice work for their students to complete. I also plan to distribute surveys in order to establish a broader understanding of the needs of the population. The result of this phase should be a list of needs and wants, and a description of the current state of the field of practice problems in introductory computer science.

The second phase will involve the implementation of the data-driven tutor authoring tool. In this phase, I intend to take the current ITAP system and embed it in a web interface, and design a system that lets teachers input problem data and modify the resulting tutor's behavior. The system should be designed based on the expressed needs of the teachers (from Phase 1). Throughout the design process, I intend to test prototypes of the system with CS educators, to ensure that the authoring tool is progressing as expected. The result of this phase will be a functional authoring tool.

The third and final phase will involve a usability evaluation of the authoring tool. I will ask CS educators to create their own tutored problems in a lab environment, to study how they create problems, whether they have any difficulties, and which parts of the system are used the most. I will ask the educators to use the resulting problems in their classrooms, and will collect data on how many of the resulting tutored problems are actually accessed by students, and how much time the students spend solving problems in the system. The result of this will be an evaluation of the usability of the system, both in terms of system usability for tutor creation and the usability of the tutored problems that are developed.

6. DISSERTATION STATUS

As was stated before, I have spent most of my research program up until now implementing ITAP, a system which allows data-driven creation of programming tutors. ITAP will form the backend of this project, as it makes it possible for teachers to create tutored problems quickly and efficiently. My recent work has been focused on making ITAP work reliably and well, even when given little data to start with, to reduce the amount of work tutor authors would need to do to create tutored problems. I have also been establishing connections with CS educators across many different universities, and many of these educators have expressed interest in using ITAP; I hope to build a subject pool that extends beyond my own university with the help of these connections.

7. EXPECTED CONTRIBUTIONS

At the conclusion of my thesis work, I plan to have developed an online authoring tool that will have been proven to be both usable and effective, a tool which teachers can easily use to generate tutored problems personalized to their curricula. My hope is that making such a tool open-access and publicized across the CS education community could make more CS teachers aware of the potential intelligent tutoring systems have for improving student learning. It is difficult to say now how effective these tutored problems will be (we hope to determine in the near future whether ITAP improves learning outcomes in a classroom setting), but at least they could potentially reduce student frustration, and maybe make practice a more enjoyable experience for students in introductory programming courses everywhere.

8. ACKNOWLEDGEMENTS

This work was supported in part by Graduate Training Grant awarded to Carnegie Mellon University by the Department of Education (# R305B090023).

9. REFERENCES

[1] Anderson, J. R., Conrad, F. G., & Corbett, A. T. (1989). Skill acquisition and the LISP tutor. *Cognitive Science*, 13(4), 467-505.

[2] Brusilovsky, P., Knapp, J., & Gamper, J. (2006). Supporting teachers as content authors in intelligent educational systems. *International Journal of Knowledge and Learning*, 2(3), 191-215.

[3] Carter, J., Dewan, P., & Pichiliani, M. (2015). Towards Incremental Separation of Surmountable and Insurmountable Programming Difficulties. In *Proceedings of the 46th ACM Technical Symposium on Computer Science Education* (pp. 241-246).

[4] Folsom-Kovarik, J. T., Schatz, S., & Nicholson, D. (2010). Plan ahead: Pricing ITS learner models. In *Proceedings of the 19th Behavior Representation in Modeling & Simulation (BRIMS) Conference* (pp. 47-54).

[5] Koedinger, K. R., Aleven, V., Heffernan. T., McLaren, B. & Hockenberry, M. (2004). Opening the Door to Non-Programmers: Authoring Intelligent Tutor Behavior by Demonstration. In *the Proceedings of 7th Annual Intelligent Tutoring Systems Conference* (pp. 162-174).

[6] Perelman, D., Gulwani, S. & Grossman, D. (2014). Test-Driven Synthesis for Automated Feedback for Introductory Computer Science Assignments. In *Data Mining for Educational Assessment and Feedback (ASSESS 2014)*.

[7] Piech, C., Sahami, M., Huang, J., & Guibas, L. (2015). Autonomously Generating Hints by Inferring Problem Solving Policies. In *Proceedings of the Second (2015) ACM Conference on Learning@Scale* (pp. 195-204).

[8] Rivers, K., and Koedinger, K. (2013). Automatic Generation of Programming Feedback: A Data-Driven Approach. In *Proceedings of the Workshops at the 16th International Conference on Artificial Intelligence in Education AIED 2013* (pp. 4.50-4.59).

Supporting Elementary School Computer Science Learning with Interactive Spoken Dialogue Agents

Jennifer Tsan
Department of Computer Science
North Carolina State University
Raleigh, North Carolina, USA
jtsan@ncsu.edu

ABSTRACT

To meet the demand for young students learning computer science, computer science curricula for students in elementary school (ages 5-11) are emerging. With those curricula comes the question, *how do we gauge young students' computer science knowledge and practices?* This question presents many challenges, in part because no validated assessments exist for computer science in elementary school; written assessments are often not appropriate for this age group; and one-on-one assessment with teachers, a common practice for very young learners, presents challenges with respect to scalability and teacher preparation. To address these challenges, I propose to build an animated spoken dialogue agent that uses embedded assessment techniques to gather information on students' knowledge and practices. The data collected through this agent will help us understand how young children learn computer science, lead us to refine computer science curricula for young learners, and inform the development of adaptive individualized support for these students.

Categories and Subject Descriptors

K.3.2 [**Computers and Education**]: Computers and Information Science Education—*Computer Science Education*.

General Terms

Human Factors

Keywords

K-12, spoken dialogue agent, assessment

1. RESEARCH SITUATION

I am a second year Ph.D. student in Computer Science at North Carolina State University. I plan to complete my written preliminary examination by the end of this upcoming school year, propose my dissertation by the end of my third year, and graduate in May of 2018.

ICER'15, August 09–13, 2015, Omaha, NE, USA.
ACM 978-1-4503-3630-7/15/08.
http://dx.doi.org/10.1145/2787622.2787750

2. CONTEXT AND MOTIVATION

In recent years, the need to educate younger students in computer science has grown. With researchers eagerly working to educate elementary students in computer science [4, 5], we are now faced with a new question: *how do we gauge young students' computer science knowledge and practices?* With challenges related to students' reading and writing skills, limited teacher preparation and time, and the absence of standardized assessments for computer science, gauging students' understanding of computer science calls for a different approach. I propose to build a spoken dialogue agent whose persona is the same age and gender as a student, and interacts with the student using techniques shown to be effective for supporting learning and for gauging understanding. This agent will use embedded assessment techniques to gauge students' understanding of computer science concepts and practices.

3. BACKGROUND & RELATED WORK

There are two highly relevant areas of related work. First, this section presents projects that have focused on assessing students' computer science knowledge at the elementary level. Second, I discuss two projects that have used interactive spoken dialogue agents with elementary school students in domains other than computing.

The Progression of Early Computational Thinking (PECT) model [9] is a framework created to assess and understand how elementary students think computationally. The framework, which is currently undergoing piloting and testing, assesses students' Scratch programs by taking into account the design patterns used and their level of sophistication.

Originally developed for older learners, the SOLO taxonomy is used to classify students' understanding of a given task [2]. It has been used to classify the programs of 4th grade students, finding that students who did not perform well in school often created programs that showed a lesser understanding of computing and the problem structure of the tasks, while more high-performing students were able to complete the tasks presented to them [8].

Relatively little work with interactive dialogue agents has focused on elementary school students. Two systems, Marni [3] and the Reading Tutor [7], focused on reading skill, and Marni was later adapted to tutor science [10]. How to develop agents for computer science, and to leverage embedded assessment, remain open questions.

4. STATEMENT OF THESIS/PROBLEM

The proposed dissertation research addresses the problem of supporting and assessing elementary computer science learning. The proposed project will fall within the intersection of elementary computer science curriculum and assessment and interactive dialogue agents. I will build a spoken dialogue agent that uses embedded assessment techniques to gauge young computer science students' understanding and support their learning.

5. RESEARCH GOALS & METHODS

The project's novel contributions will include embedded assessments about the problem solving process, not only on completed programs. Second, it will generate design principles for spoken dialogue agents that support computer science students in elementary school. Besides measuring students' knowledge and practices, the agent will be designed to gauge self-efficacy and attitude towards computer science throughout the course. The agent will be designed to appear similar in age to the students and converse with them as a peer.

My research question is: *how can elementary students' computer science learning, self-efficacy, and attitudes towards computer science be gauged using spoken dialogue and embedded assessments?* My project will proceed in a design-based fashion. Prototype versions of the dialogue agent will be used to support classroom studies. Data will be collected from these studies, including recordings of children's speech, the automatic speech recognizer's interpretation of the speech, and the system's response to the interpretations. The system will use embedded assessment techniques to prompt students to answer in a meaningful way. Identifying effective embedded assessment techniques will be one focus of the research. I will use the data I collected to evaluate the students' questions and responses as they engage in dialogue with the system.

6. DISSERTATION STATUS

I have just completed my first year as a Ph.D. student. I have worked closely with a partner elementary school to collaboratively design and refine two 4th and 5th grade computer science curricula on computational thinking, robotics, AI, computers in society, and programming. The design of the curricula drew upon CS Principles [1], Exploring CS [6], and the CSTA K-8 guidelines [4].

The 5th grade class has been conducted four times. During each iteration of the class I collected videos of class participation, screen recordings of student programming, and artifacts such as conditional trees and storyboards. I also interviewed students at the beginning and end of the course regarding motivation for taking the class, previous experience, current attitude toward computer science, and attitude towards the class.

In the process of analyzing the data, I faced the challenge that has motivated my proposed dissertation: how to properly gauge students' knowledge, practices, attitudes, and self-efficacy. Additionally, while I believe that interviews are the most promising way to get some of the needed information, some students do not engage readily with a researcher during interviews, and I hypothesize that an animated dialogue agent will address this problem.

This summer, I will begin developing my app using Unity, as it can port to iOS, Android, and Windows devices. In the fall, I will pilot the app and make refinements based on the results. The piloting of the app will be built into the computer science course I designed as a weekly activity for the students to complete. The iterative piloting and refinement cycle will continue for the next year, after which the app will be deployed to collect data that will be analyzed to continue addressing my research questions.

I hope that participating in the doctoral consortium will help me to refine and focus my research question and hypotheses. I also hope to gain insight into the design of my app and studies, as well as gain knowledge that will help me when analyzing my data and validating the results.

7. EXPECTED CONTRIBUTIONS

The findings of my research hold the potential to improve the way young children learn computer science. The data gathered from the app will be used to improve and design elementary computer science courses and to inform future elementary computer science course designers. Finally, the app can become a tool for elementary computer science teachers to use to gauge their students' knowledge and practices, leaving more time for them to teach and guide students in learning the content. With this, I hope to broaden interest and participation in computer science in elementary schools.

ACKNOWLEDGEMENTS This work is supported in part by the Wake County Public School System.

8. REFERENCES

[1] AP Computer Science Principles Draft Curriculum Framework, 2014.

[2] J. B. Biggs and K. F. Collis. *Evaluating the Quality of Learning: The SOLO taxonomy (Structure of the Observed Learning Outcome)*. Academic Press, 1982.

[3] R. Cole, B. Wise, and S. V. Vuuren. How Marni Teaches Children to Read. *Educational Technology*, 47(1):14–18, 2006.

[4] I. Computer Science Teachers Association, Association for Computing Machinery. Computer Science K-8: Building a Strong Foundation, 2012.

[5] D. Franklin, D. Harlow, H. Dwyer, J. Henkens, C. Hill, A. Iveland, A. Killian, and Staff. Kids Enjoying Learning Programming (KELP-CS) -Module 1 Digital Storytelling. A computer science curriculum for elementary school students, 2014.

[6] J. Goode and G. Chapman. Exploring Computer Science: A High-School Curriculum Exploring what Computer Science is and What it Can Do, 2013.

[7] J. Mostow, J. Nelson-Taylor, and J. E. Beck. Computer-Guided Oral Reading versus Independent Practice: Comparison of Sustained Silent Reading to an Automated Reading Tutor That Listens. *Journal of Educational Computing Research*, 49(2):249–276, 2013.

[8] L. Seiter. Using SOLO to Classify the Programming Responses of Primary Grade Students. In *Proceedings of the 46th ACM Technical Symposium on Computer Science Education (SIGCSE)*, pages 540–545, 2015.

[9] L. Seiter and B. Foreman. Modeling the Learning Progressions of Computational Thinking of Primary Grade Students. In *Proceedings of the Ninth Annual International ACM Conference on International Computing Education Research*, pages 59–66, 2013.

[10] W. Ward, R. Cole, D. Bolaños, C. Buchenroth-Martin, E. Svirsky, T. Weston, J. Zheng, and L. Becker. My science tutor: A conversational multimedia virtual tutor for Elementary School Science. *ACM Transactions on Speech and Language Processing*, 7(4):1115–1125, 2011.

Computer Science Meets Social Studies: Embedding CS in the Study of Locally Grounded Civic Issues

Sarah Van Wart
UC Berkeley School of Information
Berkeley, CA
vanwars@berkeley.edu

ABSTRACT

Data science is an emerging 21st century literacy that promises to support learning in a wide variety of disciplines. It also provides an engaging context in which to learn computational thinking skills in existing classroom contexts. For my dissertation research, I will explore whether and how data science can support inquiry-based learning in social studies. I conjecture that data science could provide students with an opportunity to use computing to better understand their social world, while also allowing students to draw from and make sense of their own experiences. I plan to explore this idea by enhancing and evaluating a software tool, *Local Ground,* and creating a curriculum that helps young people identify and describe salient characteristics of their lived realities, moving from unstructured to structured data representations (e.g., photos to tags to databases). This process may generate a rich, motivating data source to explore subsequent ideas in computational thinking and social science.

Categories and Subject Descriptors

K.3.2 [**Computers and Education**]: Computer and Information Science Education – *computer science education.*

Keywords

Data science education, broadening participation, computational thinking, interdisciplinary approaches

1. PROGRAM CONTEXT

I have just finished the third year of my PhD program at the UC Berkeley School of Information (or I School), and am in the process of co-designing and building curriculum and software, with students and teachers, in preparation for my dissertation fieldwork in the fall of 2015. I hope to complete my dissertation in the spring of 2017.

2. CONTEXT AND MOTIVATION

Over the past decade, a new field of *data science* has emerged, promising to deliver fundamentally new understandings of the physical, social, and natural world. This "computational turn" in data-driven sensemaking creates new opportunities for learning and knowledge production, but also raises new questions around ethics, privacy, method, and representation. Given the growing influence of data and computation in contemporary society, learning about the uses of data science while also being critical of it is an important twenty-first century literacy.

Because data science is a blend of statistics and computational thinking (CT), it is also a useful methodology for learning

ICER '15, August 09-13, 2015, Omaha, NE, USA
ACM 978-1-4503-3630-7/15/08.
http://dx.doi.org/10.1145/2787622.2787751

disciplinary concepts in a variety of fields, from science, to social science, to the humanities. Since at least the early 1990s, research in the learning sciences has explored the efficacy of computer-mediated, statistical sensemaking in science and statistics, using readily existing data sets to explore patterns and trends while building conceptual knowledge. Though a promising learning approach, researchers have also warned that in order for data science to be effective, datasets must be interesting to youth, and motivate engaging disciplinary questions and activities [3], which in turn requires that software and curriculum designers do their due diligence in selecting generative datasets. For example, researchers who have done the work of finding motivating "cultural datasets" for particular student communities have seen their power to productively bridge school-world learning [6].

Because culturally relevant datasets can be so powerful, limiting datasets to only those things that (a) already exist the world in spreadsheet format or (b) can be generated from sensors, potentially restricts what might be relevant to learners – particularly those from non-dominant communities whose needs and perspectives are already underrepresented and/or inappropriately characterized in many datasets. Therefore, for my dissertation research, I am interested in exploring how young people can engage computational thinking skills in order to construct their own locally relevant and culturally grounded structured data representations – i.e. databases. This would allow learners to do the work of pulling out salient attributes that are meaningful to them, deciding on variable types, and organizing and visualizing them to make sense of the world. Ideally this process will also help young people to understand the socially constructed nature of many datasets – a critical perspective to foster in a time of pervasive, data-instrumented decision-making.

3. BACKGROUND & RELATED WORK

A growing body of work explores some of the interdisciplinary applications of CT. For example, Bort, Czarnik, & Brylow [1] recently explored how data analysis and visualization techniques could be applied in an English literature class in order to help students better understand contextual information, analyze characters' social networks, and visualize literary techniques. Through this course, researchers saw "analytical and problem-solving abilities develop through these computational approaches...and observed a growing awareness [on the part of students] of the importance and usefulness of analyzing literature as data, as well as data in literature" (p. 137). Plaue & Cook [8] also reported favorable results in their exploration of CT and data science in a graduate journalism course, which incorporated a wider range of data and computing competencies: data acquisition and cleaning, computer programming fundamentals (variables, control structures, functions), web development (HTML/CSS), and data presentation (using a variety of interaction data visualization tools). However, other researchers have found that teaching data science can be tricky, particularly because socially oriented datasets often intersect with racialized discourses and identities, and deficit-oriented notions of communities of color [2, 7]. Therefore – as scholars who study data/computing initiatives highlight [2, 4, 7] – culturally sensitive pedagogies, material and identity resources, critical literacies, and effective tools and curriculum are all important when teaching computing, computational thinking, and data science.

4. STATEMENT OF THESIS/PROBLEM

Few tools or methodologies exist for helping novices construct measures and indicators from underlying real-world phenomena. As a result, some of the key aspects of moving from instance to abstraction can be easily lost on the learner before s/he even begins to analyze and visualize data. In addition, because dominant narratives about people in places get encoded and reified in data structures and representations (e.g., various visualizations of crime maps and "food deserts," education statistics that construct minority youth according to deficit frames, etc.), taking a step back and encouraging historically non-dominant groups to construct their own categories and indicators could provide students with additional ways of connecting their own lived experiences to structured data representations.

5. RESEARCH GOALS & METHODS

For my research, I plan to co-design curriculum and software to help students apply data towards an issue they care about, in a high school social studies classroom, using a design-based research methodology known as a "social design experiment" [5]. I plan to do this by leveraging existing qualitative data collection methods to help students connect their experiences of place with more structured data representations. To support this, I will enhance a visual database tool, *Local Ground,* to allow students to collaboratively tag photos, audio, and videos of interest that have been collected / created by students. The software will guide students to develop a structured database by encouraging them to (a) converge on a set of tags, (b) group like tags into categories, (c) finalize a definitive set of categories, (d) define data types for those categories, and (e) reflect upon the emergent schema. As this happens, data will be automatically classified according to these student-generated categories. The software will also generate a spreadsheet, a mobile data collection form, and some contextualized data visualizations that leverage the typed data schema that students develop. I will ask the following research questions:

1. Does collaborative tagging help students to generate database schemas as well as a larger data collection strategy?
2. Does collaborative tagging help students to better understand patterns and trends surrounding their lived experiences, such as larger social processes around gentrification, the social determinants of health, etc.?
3. Does a social studies context – in which young people apply data and computational techniques to meaningful topics / problems – increase students' appreciation for the applicability and relevance of data skills in research?
4. Does a social studies context encourage students to take a more critical perspective around computer-supported knowledge production, and the role of data and computing in society? Are they more critical of graphs, charts and other forms of information, or less likely to take conventional wisdom for granted? Or are they unmoved?

6. DISSERTATION STATUS

I have already conducted a pilot study in a tenth grade sociology class to explore the use of data science approaches to learn about local social issues of importance. I have also been building a youth-oriented database, *Local Ground* [9], to support many of the data transformation aspects of the proposed workflow above. I will conduct my dissertation research in the fall of 2015.

7. EXPECTED CONTRIBUTIONS

I expect my dissertation research to contribute two perspectives to the existing CSE literature. First, because qualitative accounts of lived experience are generative resources upon which to build more systematic understandings, studying how young people can build abstract schemas to represent social phenomena could provide another way to introduce computational thinking skills in existing classrooms. Second, working with teachers and documenting how a computational thinking module works in an existing social studies class will be a helpful way to understand the tensions and possibilities of an interdisciplinary approach to supporting computational thinking.

8. REFERENCES

[1] Bort, H., Czarnik, M. and Brylow, D. 2015. Introducing Computing Concepts to Non-Majors: A Case Study in Gothic Novels. *Proceedings of the 46th ACM Technical Symposium on Computer Science Education (SIGCSE '15).* (2015), 132–137.

[2] DiSalvo, B. and Guzdail, M. 2009. Glitch game testers: African American men breaking open the console. *Digital Games Research Association Conference.* (2009), 1 – 7.

[3] Edelson, D.C., Gordin, D.N. and Pea, R.D. 1999. Addressing the Challenges of Inquiry-Based Learning Through Technology and Curriculum Design. *Journal of the Learning Sciences.* 8, 3-4 (1999), 391–450.

[4] Goode, J. and Margolis, J. 2011. Exploring Computer Science. *ACM Transactions on Computing Education.* 11, 2 (2011), 1–16.

[5] Gutiérrez, K.D. and Vossoughi, S. 2010. Lifting Off the Ground to Return Anew: Mediated Praxis, Transformative Learning, and Social Design Experiments. *Journal of Teacher Education.* 61, (2010), 100–117.

[6] Lee, C. 2007. *Culture Literacy and Learning.* Teachers' College Press.

[7] Philip, T.M., Way, W., Garcia, A.D., Schuler-Brown, S. and Navarro, O. 2013. When educators attempt to make "community" a part of classroom learning: Thedangers of (mis)appropriating students' communities into schools. *Teaching and Teacher Education.* 34, (2013), 174–183.

[8] Plaue, C. and Cook, L.R. 2015. Data Journalism: Lessons Learned While Designing an Interdisciplinary Service Course. *Proceedings of the 46th ACM Technical Symposium on Computer Science Education (SIGCSE '15).* (2015), 126–131.

[9] Van Wart, S., Tsai, K.J. and Parikh, T. 2010. Local Ground: A Paper-Based Toolkit for Documenting Local Geo-spatial Knowledge. *Proceedings of the First ACM Symposium on Computing for Development.* (2010), 1.

Comparing Text-based, Blocks-based, and Hybrid Blocks/Text Programming Tools

David Weintrop
Northwestern University
2120 Campus Dr. Suite 332
Evanston, IL, USA 60208
dweintrop@u.northwestern.edu

ABSTRACT

This dissertation investigates the comparative affordances and drawbacks of blocks-based, text-based, and hybrid blocks/text introductory programming tools. Blocks-based programming environments are growing in popularity and are increasingly being used in formal introductory programming contexts. To date, much of the work evaluating such tools has focused on their effectiveness in out-of-school contexts and emphasized engagement and attitudinal measures over content mastery. Given their growing presence in classrooms, it is important to understand the benefits and limitations of the use of the blocks-based programming approach in formal learning contexts relative to text-based or hybrid blocks/text alternatives. This dissertation will carry out a quasi-experimental study in high school computer science classrooms to answer questions related to the impact of blocks-based, text-based, and hybrid blocks/text introductory tools, assess the suitability of such tools for preparing students for future computer science learning opportunities, and explore the design space between blocks-based and text-based programming. The goal of this work is to better understand the tools we are using to introduce today's learners to computer science and lay the foundation for creating the tools of tomorrow.

Categories and Subject Descriptors

K.3.2 [**Computers and Education**]: Computer and Information Science Education – *computer science education.*

Keywords

Blocks-based Programming; Introductory Programming Tools; High School Computer Science Education

1. PROGRAM CONTEXT

I am currently a fifth year PhD candidate in the Learning Sciences program at Northwestern University. Northwestern University's Learning Sciences program was the first of its kind and brings together cognition, design, and socio-cultural factors to study how learning happens in the real world. I have defended my dissertation proposal and, this past fall, I conducted a pilot of my dissertation study. I have done some analysis of the pilot data and am in the process of preparing the next iteration of my study, which will take place at the start of the upcoming school year.

ICER '15, August 09-13, 2015, Omaha, NE, USA
ACM 978-1-4503-3630-7/15/08.
http://dx.doi.org/10.1145/2787622.2787752

2. CONTEXT AND MOTIVATION

The ability to express ideas in a computationally meaningful way is becoming a critical skill for students to master in our increasingly digital world. Bringing programming into K-12 education is a critical step for introducing learners to this fundamental skill. A growing number of K-12 computer science classrooms are using blocks-based environments to introduce students to programming. These tools leverage a primitives-as-puzzle-pieces metaphor and support drag-and-drop composition, allowing learners to assemble functioning programs using only a mouse by snapping together instructions. The use of this programming modality has become a prominent feature of many introductory computer science curricula and programming interventions targeted at K-12 students. Notably, national curricular efforts including Exploring Computer Science, the CS Principles project, and Code.org's curricular materials all utilize blocks-based tools to introduce students to programming.

Despite its growing popularity and widespread use, relatively little work to date has focused on the conceptual and affective benefits of using blocks-based tools in formal educational contexts. Open questions remain about the effectiveness of the approach for helping students learn basic programming concepts and whether or not gains made in introductory environments, be they blocks-based or textual, effectively prepare students for future computer science learning opportunities. Further, it is unclear what the strengths and weaknesses of block-based programming tools are compared to isomorphic text-based alternatives. Given the number of initiatives being undertaken to bring programming, and computer science more broadly, into high school classrooms, it is essential that we understand the affordances and drawbacks of the tools we are using to introduce a generation of learners to the field. The goal of this dissertation is to shed light on these questions in order to improve curricular and design efforts that are shaping contemporary high school computer science education and to better inform teachers on how to make the most of the tools they are using.

3. BACKGROUND & RELATED WORK

"The tools we use have a profound (and devious!) influence on our thinking habits, and, therefore, on our thinking abilities." [3]

A growing body of literature is investigating the effects of the blocks-based programming approach. Notable work has been done looking at Scratch with younger learners (e.g., [5]) and Alice with university students (e.g., [8]), with relatively little work focusing on high school aged students. A number of smaller studies have done comparative work looking at textual vs. blocks-based tools side-by-side, such as Lewis' [4] study comparing Scratch and Logo, which found students who worked with text-based Logo were more confident, while students in the Scratch condition performed slightly better on some of the content areas covered. Ben-Ari and colleagues have conducted a number of studies looking at the suitability of Scratch as serving as the primary introductory programming language finding both strengths and drawbacks to the approach [6, 7]. In a recently published paper, they found that students who learned Scratch in middle school more quickly grasped concepts in text-based languages when they reached high school (although they did not perform better on content assessments) [1]. Another thread of work has looked at how learning with introductory blocks-based tools transfers to conventional text-based tools with mixed results [2, 9]. Work on these questions is growing, but large gaps in the literature remain, this study will address some of those gaps.

4. STATEMENT OF THESIS/PROBLEM

This dissertation seeks to answer three sets of interrelated research questions. The first set pertains to the effects of programming modality (blocks-based vs. text-based) on students' learning experience. Specifically, what is the relationship between the programming modality used and learners' understandings of programming concepts? What programming practices do learners develop when working in different modalities? And how does the modality affect students' perceptions of programming with respect to utility, authenticity, and enjoyment? The second set of questions look at the effectiveness of introductory programming tools for preparing students for future computer science learning opportunities. Namely, how do understandings and practices developed while working in introductory programming environments support or hinder the transition to the text-based programming languages used in non-introductory computer science courses? Our final research question investigates the design of introductory learning environments. Can we design hybrid introductory programming environments that blend the strengths of blocks-based and text-based programming to effectively introduce novices to programming and computer science more broadly? All three sets of questions are designed to be comparative as we are interested into how aspects of learning differ across text-based, blocks-based, and hybrid blocks/text introductory environments.

5. RESEARCH GOALS & METHODS

The goal of this research is to understand the affordances and drawbacks of different programming modalities in formal high school computer science contexts. To answer the stated research questions, a quasi-experimental, mixed-method study will be used. The study follows three sections of an introductory programming class for the first 15 weeks of the school year at an urban public high school. For the first five weeks, students will use either a blocks-based, text-based, or hybrid blocks/text introductory programming environments before transitioning to Java for the remainder of the study. Students are randomly assigned to the three sections and will follow the same curriculum regardless of the environment they use. Pre/mid/post content and attitudinal assessments will be administered during the study. We will also carry out one-on-one cognitive interviews with students from all three conditions as well as conduct classroom observations and record all student-authored programs. By gathering this set of data and studying students across the three programming environments, as well as following them as they transition to Java, we will be able to comparatively evaluate the environments and answer the stated research questions.

6. DISSERTATION STATUS

I have completed a pilot study where I followed 90 students in 3 sections of a computer science classroom for the first 10 weeks of the school year. I observed students as they spent five weeks working in three distinct, customized versions of the Snap! environment and then followed them as they transitioned to Java. The customized Snap! environments added features like the ability to see text-based versions of blocks-based scripts, and define new block behaviors in JavaScript. I conducted 27 interviews, administered pre/mid/post attitudinal and content assessments, and collected over 75,000 student-authored programs. As part of the pilot study, I created all necessary curricular and assessment materials and designed interview protocols and automated data collection procedures. To date I have completed a few analyses of these data, including comparative evaluations of student perceptions of the introductory tools and how students performed on the content assessments. I am currently preparing for the second iteration of the study to be carried out this upcoming school year, which includes the development of a hybrid blocks/text tool.

7. EXPECTED CONTRIBUTIONS

I expect that findings of this dissertation will be of great interest to educators, curriculum designers, and the larger computer science education research community. The findings from this dissertation will contribute to our understanding of how the latest generation of block-based programming tools fit into more formal, structured educational spaces, as well as provide insight into the cognitive and affective aspects of such tools. Additionally, this work will provide insight into how blocks-based introductory tools perform relative to text-based programming environments designed for novices and evaluate one potential approach to blending the two modalities. We are at a critical juncture in the history of computer science education. The practices, tools, and curricula that are being developed today will become the standards used for years to come. It is essential that we are confident that the approaches we advocate today are effective at teaching the core concepts, engaging learners from diverse backgrounds, and successful in preparing students for the computational futures that await them.

8. REFERENCES

[1] Armoni, M. et al. 2015. From Scratch to "Real" Programming. *ACM TOCE*. 14, 4 (2015), 25.

[2] Dann, W. et al. 2012. Mediated transfer: Alice 3 to Java. *Proc. of the 43rd ACM SIGCSE*, 141–146.

[3] Dijkstra, E.W. 1982. How do we tell truths that might hurt? *Selected Writings on Computing*. Springer. 129–131.

[4] Lewis, C.M. 2010. How programming environment shapes perception, learning and goals: Logo vs. Scratch. *Proc. of the 41st ACM SIGCSE*, 346–350.

[5] Maloney, J.H. et al. 2008. Programming by choice. *ACM SIGCSE Bulletin*. 40, 1, 367–371.

[6] Meerbaum-Salant, O. et al. 2011. Habits of programming in Scratch. *Proc. of the 16th ITiCSE* (Darmstadt, Gr), 168–172.

[7] Meerbaum-Salant, O. et al. 2010. Learning computer science concepts with Scratch. *Proc. of the 6th ICER*, 69–76.

[8] Moskal, B. et al. 2004. Evaluating the effectiveness of a new instructional approach. *Proc. of the 35th ACM SIGCSE* 75-79.

[9] Powers, K. et al. 2007. Through the looking glass: teaching CS0 with Alice. *ACM SIGCSE Bulletin*. 39, 1, 213–217.

A Competence Graph to Derive Individual Learning Paths

Daniela Zehetmeier
Technische Universität München & Munich University of Applied Sciences
Boltzmannstr. 2
Garching, 85748, Germany
Daniela.Zehetmeier@tum.de

ABSTRACT

A heterogeneous group of students starts to study informatics each year. Observations show that students need individual support, to create well educated computer scientists. Unfortunately, this does not scale to large student numbers. My goal is to offer individual guidance to students in an introductory informatics class in a form that amortizes the expertise of lecturers and tutors. To that purpose I am developing a competency graph and a body of tagged practice materials. The practice materials facilitate assessment of a student's individual state of competence.

Categories and Subject Descriptors: K.3.2 [Computers and Education]: Computers and Information Science Education — *Computer Science Education, Information systems education, Self-assessment.*

Keywords: Software Engineering Education, Competencies, Teaching Methods, Higher Education, Heterogeneity, Learning paths.

1. PROGRAM CONTEXT

Since 2011 our research team at Munich University of Applied Sciences, Faculty of Computer Science and Mathematics has been working on competencies that are relevant to study successfully in the STEM (Science, Technology, Engineering and Mathematics) area. So far, we developed a competence profile for students starting their studies in computer science and related topics. This includes practical as well as self and social competencies, like thinking in an abstract way, accuracy or team-orientation. Additionally, we developed two instruments to assess those competencies: A "self-assessment" [8] and an accompanying knowledge test. Based on the results we now adjust our teaching methods and design new teaching units, which take students' current level of competencies into account. We distinguish between competencies that are not central to the topics of the introductory class and competencies that are essential for their

successful completion. For example, we phased out programming tasks that require elementary algebra as students often struggle with them and introduced more generally accessible domains such as sheep. On the other hand, we explicitly address abstract thinking as well as principles of programming such as structured dissection and separation of concern.

This research is part of the project "Teaching Quality Initiative" which is supported by the German Federal Ministry of Education and Research (BMBF). It provides a framework to give innovative didactic approaches in teaching a try.

In Germany, doctoral programs that correspond to the PhD system in English-speaking countries, are thin on the ground. Therefore, I do my PhD individually as it is common practice in Germany. My PhD supervisors are: Prof. Anne Brüggemann-Klein, Prof. Axel Böttcher and Prof. Veronika Thurner.

2. CONTEXT AND MOTIVATION

Over the last years computer science became more and more important for daily life and business. Hence, industry requires more and better educated software engineers. However, universities denote high drop out rates of over 30% in STEM subjects in Germany. Furthermore, they are faced with highly heterogeneous first-year students, many of whom are ill equipped with the aforementioned competencies.

The dissertation will be a contribution to educate students well under those circumstances. I will develop an approach that addresses the different levels of competencies of a heterogeneous group, but is still effectively applicable for a large number of students in one class. My goal is to individually support the students, thus leading to more graduates, which are even better educated.

3. BACKGROUND & RELATED WORK

Our research on competencies which are necessary to successfully study computer science or related topics, is amongst others based on the findings of Erpenbeck [2] from the pedagogic area and a more software specific selection which can e.g. be found in [4]. To describe and classify educational objectives, we focus on the revised Bloom's taxonomy [1].

Learning paths can be used to support students individually. Foundations on how to classify assignments and to find learning paths can be found in the paper of Santos [3].

The dissertation of Sorva [5] is a good summary of taxonomies of educational objectives, known problems, misconceptions, threshold-concepts and possible solutions, as well as, their interrelations.

4. STATEMENT OF THESIS/PROBLEM

Our previous research supports the assumption that individual support of students is necessary to create well educated computer scientists. This leads to the question, how a heterogeneous group of students can be individually and efficiently educated with respect to the given circumstances like heterogeneity and lecturer/student ratio.

Due to this ratio, the lecturer alone cannot provide the required individual support for all the students by himself/herself. Rather, it should be assisted by automated tools. These should be backed up by well designed learning activities which the students carry out in their self-study phases, corresponding to their individual needs.

To achieve this, among others the following questions have to be tackled: How can we measure student's current level of competencies and how are they related to each other? Which assignment has to be suggested next on the individual learning path and which factors influence this choice? And at last, which teaching format fits which student, and how can this be selected automatically?

5. RESEARCH GOALS & METHODS

The goal is to develop and implement strategies for introductory university courses in informatics and programming that support large and heterogeneous cohorts of students to consistently succeed academically at a high level. The challenge is to devise teaching and learning environments that are individually tailored to a large spectrum of student needs but scale to a large student body. Thus, we hope to be not only able to lower drop-out rates but also to raise skill levels and academic standards.

My vision is a directed graph with a single root node, which represents the classes' learning objective. Additional nodes are competencies (technical or non-technical) which might have different levels according to Bloom and other parameters. The edges between nodes depict assignments. An assignment can contain small or large steps related to the level of knowledge, the complexity or for example focus a specific type of learner. Several nodes will be obligatory, while others can be skipped, depending on the previous knowledge and individual parameters like the maximum delta of complexity an assignment addresses.

After the graph is built, I will investigate a process to position a student at the beginning and to navigate him/her to the final educational goal with respect to the sub-goals in between. Therefore, I need to measure students' competencies at the beginning and during the semester regularly. We already developed a self-assessment test, that focuses on competencies which are necessary to study computer science [8]. To get insight into relevant practical and cognitive competencies we designed an accompanying knowledge test. These instruments are continuously refined. Furthermore, I need to be able to compute the students individual delta to suggest an appropriate learning path, which might skip some nodes. This delta has to be calculated at the beginning and has to be observed and maybe adjusted during the learning process.

6. DISSERTATION STATUS

I started my research in June 2013 in the context of my Master's thesis. Until now, we identified base competencies that are crucial for studying computer science or related topics [6] and got information about the initial competencies and educational qualifications our first-year students have and which students are endangered to drop out due to specific characteristics (*to be published*). Furthermore, we know typical pitfalls and topics students have problems to deal with and we identified the underlying deficits and reasons [7].

These findings are the basis for my PhD thesis, as we now know the problems, but need to find an effective solution to deal with them. Although my PhD started in April 2015, I already achieved relevant research results to build on. For each of the goals named above, there exist thoughts, knowledge and a rough draft as parts of my thesis.

7. EXPECTED CONTRIBUTIONS

The result of my PhD thesis will be a concept how to build a graph representing competencies and assignments. Afterwards, an algorithm will be presented, how individual learning paths, through the emerging graph, can be computed. I will exemplarily put this concept into practice in the context of programming education and evaluate the approach. This will help to effectively provide individual support even for a large and heterogeneous group of students in computer science or related topics.

8. REFERENCES

[1] L. W. Anderson, D. R. Krathwohl, and B. S. Bloom. *A taxonomy for learning, teaching, and assessing: A revision of Bloom's taxonomy of educational objectives.* Allyn & Bacon, 2001.

[2] J. Erpenbeck. Kompetenzdiagnostik und Entwicklung KODE (in German), March 2004.

[3] A. Santos, A. Gomes, and A. Mendes. A taxonomy of exercises to support individual learning paths in initial programming learning. In *Frontiers in Education Conference, 2013 IEEE*, pages 87–93, Oct 2013.

[4] I. C. Society, P. Bourque, and R. E. Fairley. *Guide to the Software Engineering Body of Knowledge (SWEBOK(R)): Version 3.0.* IEEE Computer Society Press, Los Alamitos, CA, USA, 3rd edition, 2014.

[5] J. Sorva. *Visual Program Simulation in Introductory Programming Education.* PhD thesis, Aalto University, 2012.

[6] V. Thurner, A. Böttcher, and A. Kamper. Identifying base competencies as prerequisites for software engineering education. In *Global Engineering Education Conference (EDUCON), 2014 IEEE*, pages 1069–1076, April 2014.

[7] D. Zehetmeier, A. Böttcher, A. Brüggemann-Klein, and V. Thurner. Development of a classification scheme for errors observed in the process of computer programming education (accepted for publication). In *International Conference on Higher Education Advances (HEAd)*, 2015.

[8] D. Zehetmeier, M. Kuhrmann, A. Böttcher, K. Schlierkamp, and V. Thurner. Self-assessment of freshmen students' base competencies. In *Global Engineering Education Conference (EDUCON), 2014 IEEE*, pages 429–438, April 2014.

Author Index